GEORGE III

Jeremy Black is professor of history at the University of Exeter. He is the author of biographies of William Pitt the Elder and of Sir Robert Walpole. Among his many publications are *Maps and History* (1997), *War and the World* (1998), *Italy and the Grand Tour* (2003) and *The British Seaborne Empire* (2004), all published by Yale University Press. He is a Fellow of the Royal Historical Society, Fellow of the Royal Society of Arts, and Member of the Order of the British Empire (MBE).

D0757427

Also in the Yale English Monarchs series

*Available in the U.S. from University of California Press

GEORGE III
AMERICA'S LAST KING

Jeremy Black

YALE UNIVERSITY PRESS
NEW HAVEN AND LONDON

First printed in paperback 2008

For information about this and other Yale University Press publications, please contact:
U.S. Office: sales.press@yale.edu   www.yalebooks.com
Europe Office: sales@yaleup.co.uk   www.yaleup.co.uk

Set in Baskerville by J&L Composition, Filey, North Yorkshire
Printed in Great Britain by TJ International Ltd, Padstow, Cornwall

Library of Congress Cataloging-in-Publication Data

Black, Jeremy.
  George III / Jeremy Black.
    p. cm.—(Yale English monarchs)
  Includes bibliographical references and index.
  ISBN 0–300–11732–9
  1. George III, King of Great Britain, 1738–1820. 2. Great Britain—Politics and government—1760–1820. 3. Great Britain—Kings and rulers—Biography.
4. Monarchy—Great Britain—History. I. Title. II. Series.
DA506.A2B53 2006
941.07'3092—dc22
[B]
                                                                2006014067
A catalogue record for this book is available from the British Library.

ISBN 978-0-300-13621-0 (pbk)

10 9 8 7 6 5 4 3 2 1

Published with assistance from the Annie Burr Lewis Fund.

for Philadelphia friends

CONTENTS

ACKNOWLEDGEMENTS

In the years since 1977, when I first read letters written by George III in a systematic fashion, I have accumulated a number of debts of gratitude that I am happy to acknowledge. Material from the Royal Archives is cited by permission of Her Majesty the Queen. I would also like to thank the Duke of Bedford, the Marquess of Bute, Earl Fitzwilliam and the Wentworth Woodhouse Trustees, the late Earl Harrowby and the Trustees of the Harrowby Manuscripts Trust, the Earl of Elgin, the Earl of Malmesbury, the late Earl Waldegrave, Lady Lucas, Sir Hector Monro and John Weston-Underwood for permission to consult their collections of manuscripts, and the late Earl Waldegrave for his hospitality at Chewton. Lars Struve facilitated access to material on a trip to the Rigsarkivet in Copenhagen, and Steven Blake, Judith Curthoys, Kate Harris, Lorna Haycock, Helen Morse, John Paddock, Ann Smith, Joanne Smith, Jill Tovey and Deborah Watson proved helpful British archivists. I am most grateful to Robert Ingram for help with Secker's papers, to Jim Davies, a true Weymouth expert, and to Earl Bathurst for his advice.

Knowledge of how busy academics can be underlines my gratitude to Nigel Aston, Grayson Ditchfield, Bill Gibson, Matthew Kilburn, Bill Purdue and two anonymous readers for their helpful comments on an earlier version. In addition, Charles Fedorak, Will Hay, Colin Haydon, Nick Henshall, Peter Hoffenberg, William Liddle, Philip Mansel, Jonathan Marsden, Marilyn Morris, Clarissa Campbell Orr, Andrew O'Shaughnessy, Torsten Riotte and David Watkin commented on particular chapters, and I have also benefited from advice from David Aldridge, Peter Barber, Michael Duffy, Piers Mackesy, Frank O'Gorman, Robert Peberdy, Nicholas Rodger, Janet Snowman, Will Tatum, James Thomas and Reg Ward. The University of Exeter and the German Academic Exchange Scheme provided crucial support on archival research trips. I have been helped by the opportunity to present papers to conferences on the personal unions of Saxony–Poland and Hanover–Britain and on the Hanoverian dimension in British policy and politics held at Dresden and Cambridge, respectively, as well as to the University of Virginia's School of Continuing and Professional Studies summer schools on the American War of Independence, to a History Staff Research Day at the University of Exeter, at Mary

Washington and Mississippi State universities and at the University of Plymouth.

Robert Baldock has proved an exemplary editor and a continued encouragement. It is always a pleasure to record my gratitude to Sarah, but particularly so for this book. The ability to discuss matters with a consultant psychiatrist is especially useful when the subject is George III, yet a family holiday in 1989 on the island of Bute that also enabled me to work on the papers at Mount Stuart is a stronger memory.

Dedicating a book is both a joy and the opportunity to record thanks and gratitude, and yet also a problem if one is supposed to match dedicatee with subject. Perversely, given its role in the American Revolution, I do so with this volume in thanking friends I have met through many visits to lecture in Philadelphia, most frequently to the Foreign Policy Research Institute. It is by far my favourite of the big cities on the East Coast, in part because of the fine buildings, many of which make it seem more redolent of an eighteenth-century British city than most in Britain, because of the scale, bustle and variety of the streets, and because of my friends, Jean-Loup Archawski, Annette Bonacquisti, Will Hay, Herb Kaplan, Alan Luxenberg, Harvey Sicherman and the late Russell Weigley. I knew it a nonsense when the guide in Liberty Hall referred to George III as a tyrant, but I could not help but be moved by the quest for liberty that this fine city represents.

PREFACE

'With modern writers everything is either vice or virtue' complained the anonymous author of the *Reflections on Ancient and Modern History* (1746).[1] However moral he sought to be, the life of George III (1738–1820) is not a simple morality tale. It contained strongly etched episodes, and the last years of the king had a pathos in apparently blind, neglected madness that led to unfounded comparisons with King Lear, but much of his life lacked the dramatic darkness of the neo-Gothic, however much contemporaries, particularly Horace Walpole, searched for such a secret history. Yet, if, as biography, there is not what those craving sensation sought – indeed the notorious madness has been explained as the symptoms of the disease porphyria – this is still a life full of importance and interest, necessarily so being that of America's last king.

Here readers should pause. If you like interpretation to arise with the text, and to follow the author through the discussion, please stop, read the book, and return to this Preface at the close. This is not only because to offer interpretation at the outset may unreasonably foreclose your analysis, but also because my preference is for the interpretation to unfold, not to be made clear at the outset.

George III believed in integrity as a moral goal, guide and support. 'I never put pen to paper without wishing to convey in the most explicit manner the sentiments of my heart',[2] wrote the king in 1800. There exists a considerable archive of personal correspondence, as well as numerous memoranda and accounts of conversations with the king. This biography makes full use of these, including much British and foreign material not included in the extensive printed sources, and, as a result, can claim to be the most extensively sourced biography of George. Documents, of course, present problems: they were intended to persuade, and can mislead, particularly if quoted selectively. But these sources enable one to grasp the uncertainties of the past and the roles of chance and perception, and to restore a human perspective to an historical imagination too often dominated by impersonal forces or the search for a quick explanation.

[1] *Reflections*, p. 26.
[2] George to William, Lord Grenville, foreign secretary, 17 July 1800, BL. Add. 58861 fol. 116.

Even for an individual who wrote as commonly as George III much remains unclear, and there are major gaps in the evidence. Relatively little correspondence, certainly compared to what follows, survives for his youth and for his early years as king, perhaps because he sought to have compromising political material destroyed.[3] Furthermore, in common with many of his contemporaries, George kept no diary. In addition, even when royal intentions can be readily established, there are major difficulties in assessing the consequences of George's role. These arise repeatedly, not only in the case of American policy, which is treated more critically in this book than in earlier works, but also in terms of British domestic politics.

There are, and always will be, a range of interpretations of the reign of George III. Indeed, much of George's importance arises from the contrasting roles he played in the perception of contemporaries and subsequent commentators. These are given full rein throughout the text, while, in Chapter 19, George's later reputation is treated as an important aspect of his evaluation; necessarily so as it serves as a reminder that our evaluations are part of the swell of the tide.

The features I intend to be distinctive in this biography include an attempt to shape the discussion and evaluation of George within the comparative context of rulership in the Western world, a context which was indeed changing. Contemporaries compared George with figures as various as George II and George IV of Britain, Louis XV and Louis XVI of France, Gustavus III of Sweden, George Washington, and Napoleon. Second, there is an emphasis on George's strong religious faith, belief in the ever-active role of Divine Providence and powerful sense of moral duty and personal responsibility, all of which are seen as crucial in his life: not only in his policies and practices as king, but also in his character as a man. In 1801, on holiday in Weymouth, George wrote criticizing the lack of 'sufficient firmness of mind' on the part of a fellow-monarch, observing that his strictures were 'equally binding to a man in his political as well as private conduct'.[4] This book addresses both conducts, and the chapters on 'Character and Behaviour' and 'Religion and Morality' are the most crucial to the discussion and evaluation of the king.

Third, there is an attempt to engage with George's range of interests. The major advance in discussion of George since John Brooke's biography appeared in 1972 has been the focus on his cultural and intellectual interests. These are considered substantially in Chapter 9 and also surface in 'The Quest for Empire', the chapter of the book that most reflects the multiple worlds on which George impinged. Fourth, I include a chapter on George as Elector of Hanover. This reflects the important scholarship produced since Brooke's biography. Most earlier biographies overlook this

---

[3] George to Lord Egmont, 7 Feb. 1766, BL. Add. 47012 fol. 114.
[4] George to Lord Hawkesbury, 16 July 1801, BL. Loan 72/1 fol. 80.

role, when in fact George became increasingly committed to Hanover during his reign.

Nevertheless Hanover did not engage him as did the struggle for America in the 1770s and early 1780s, and this plays a central role in the book. George's attitude to American demands before and, even more, during the war reveal much about his personality. Furthermore, as the lengthy quotation from the Declaration of Independence (see pp. 225–6) indicates, George himself, his intentions and his policies, formed a key component of the struggle, and helped mould his subsequent reputation, particularly, but not only, in the United States. An understanding of both George himself, and of the British monarchy, helps explain much about the American Revolution, not least the absence or exhaustion of other constitutional or political remedies.

I have written two earlier biographies, of William Pitt the Elder and of Sir Robert Walpole. Of the three, George was most wide-ranging culturally and intellectually, and also the most considerate as a human being, sensitive to others, and with an endearing shy integrity. The latter speaks powerfully to me throughout the reign, although, as an atheist, I cannot share George's faith. As I hope the biography reveals, my sympathy is not uncritical.

An anonymous article in the *Test*, a London newspaper, on 12 February 1757, declared,

> when the historian gives his narrative of facts, when he rejudges the actions of the great, and, from the ends which they had in view, and the means by which they pursued those ends, ascertains the colour of their characters, then the minds of men are opened, and they perceive honour and conquest, or disappointment and disgrace, naturally following one another, like necessary effects from their apparent respective causes.

Sixteen years later, the cleric William Cooke, in his dedication in *The Way to the Temple of True Honour and Fame by the Paths of Heroic Virtue Exemplified in the Most Entertaining Lives of the Most Eminent Persons of Both Sexes*, stated, 'Real history, which imparts the knowledge of past events, affords the best instructions for the regulation and good conduct of human life'. Such confidence, whether in the historian's capacity to explain or to offer moral guidance, is not part of the modern scholarly world, but there is much in George's life that prompts wider reflection. The role of individuals, the play of contingency, and the impact of unexpected consequences, all matter in the attempt to analyse the reign. At the personal level, we see the gaining of experience,[5] the retention of integrity,

---

[5] George to William Grenville, 22 Nov. 1796, BL. Add. 58859 fol. 98.

sometimes with unfortunate consequences, and a life of duty and conviction. George was a man, exalted by birth, who never lost his sense of public service or his interest in others. Neither grand nor great, but good, and that I hope is a verdict we all can admire.

To foresee evils is the lot of few,
to profit by experience the advantage
of all who have any claim to sense.
George III, 1794

Let not the name of George the third
be a blot in the page of history.
Thomas Jefferson, 1774

ILLUSTRATIONS

Chapter 1

INTRODUCTION

The biography of a king is apt to be that of a reign, the account of ruler and rulership, of policy and politics. This seems particularly appropriate in the case of George III, king from 1760 to 1820, because most of his long life, which stretched from 1738 to 1820, was taken up by his period as ruler. In this he was very different to his first two successors, his sons George IV and William IV, or, indeed, to the present member of the royal family who shows the greatest interest in him, the likely future Charles III. As king, George took a major part in politics. He had clear views on the rights and duties of the ruler, and believed that they had been compromised under his predecessor, his grandfather, George II. To George III, the monarch should and could play a major role in the kingdom, not least by ensuring that politics had a goal: serving not the cause of ministerial interests but that of the nation, which he saw as a moral community with a shared purpose. He emerges from the evidence presented in this study as a man conscious of his duty as king of a country where Divine Providence could be expected to operate in favour of a moral environment, but where the licentious might bring down the rest of the community. George's conception of his task was always led by a commitment to restore and maintain the moral order of society, a position that greatly influenced his attitude towards disaffection in the American colonies. As he acquired experience, he gained greater appreciation of the means he had at his disposal to apply his concept of his responsibilities. This does not mean that, in order to pursue his goals, he wholeheartedly or dramatically adapted to circumstances. Instead, he was able to match the enforcement of his principles to practicalities, but strove not to allow those principles to evolve under pressure from changing political and social fashions.

George not only believed that his role was important, but also actively participated in the politics of the reign. This was notoriously so in his early years, when his determination to bring peace with France and Spain, and to break with his predecessor's ministers, led him to take on a key part in the successive and exhausting ministerial crises of 1761–2. As with other rulers (and statesmen), George found it easier to criticize and overturn the existing situation and to seek to introduce a new order than to develop and sustain the latter. However, the failure in 1763 of the new ministry under his favourite, John, third earl of Bute, owed much to the limitations of Bute, and not to a wider systemic failure in British politics, nor to a failure on George's part to understand political options. There were also successes for the crown. The Bute ministry was able to negotiate peace, and to defend it successfully in parliament. Furthermore, although subsequently embarrassing to the king and ministers, and attracting much interest from modern scholars concerned with the roots of radicalism, John Wilkes and other critics had a limited impact on ministerial and political stability in the 1760s. The decade did witness failures – the repeated difficulties in establishing a stable ministry in Britain, and the serious Stamp Act crisis in some of Britain's North American colonies in 1765–6 being the most prominent, but by no means the only ones. However, these failures can be seen as much as a product of the nature of governmental authority and of politics as of anything specific to George.

Yet the importance of the political issues with which the king was involved ensures that they play a major role in his biography. The War of American Independence (1775–83) helped define the English-speaking world, and was the formative episode in what eventually became the most powerful state on earth. George was also king when Britain confronted, from 1793, Revolutionary and, from 1799, Napoleonic France. Other states succumbed to France or allied with her; Britain resisted for longest, and the defeat of France, first in 1814, and definitively in 1815, set the scene for the nineteenth century, for the subsequent growth of the British empire and, related to this, for a Europe that was not under the hegemony of one power. Within Britain, George's opposition to radicalism and to Catholic emancipation helped define the country in the short and long term, as the legacy of emancipation arguably helped embitter Anglo-Irish relations. In each case, as in his belief in the appropriate role of the monarch in the constitution, George, as he well understood, was a child of the 'Glorious Revolution' of 1688, and he did not have sole responsibility for policy. This was especially true when it came to resisting radicalism and France. Yet, even then, his role was important in helping stiffen ministerial resolve, and it was crucial in the case of opposition to accepting American independence and, later, to Catholic emancipation.

A political focus is therefore understandable, but this is not simply a political life. In order to grasp George's politics, it is necessary to consider his character and, in particular, his faith and his sense of morality; these are central to any account of other aspects of his life. Recent interest in George's cultural and scientific concerns are reflected in this book, and there is also discussion of his relations with his wife and children. I have sought to address the developments in the study of George's place in eighteenth-century politics and culture since the publication of John Brooke's biography in 1972.

An account of George, however interesting, can offer only so much unless accompanied by a considered attempt at evaluation. There have been no shortages of evaluations, and some are discussed in Chapter 19. In reaction to earlier critical accounts – part of what is known as the Whig interpretation of history – the current view on the king is generally favourable, a position indeed described by some critics as neo-Tory. Such a view draws on George's extensive discussion, in his correspondence, of his opinions, and relates the king to the largely conservative nature of much of the political élite and, indeed, of the political nation, a term employed to discuss those who took an interest in politics. In explaining George's views and in refuting earlier criticisms of them as autocratic, if not tyrannical, it is easy to slip into a situation in which the author simply expounds them. The king's ideas and opinions indeed displayed a high level of consistency, while, partly as a result of his diligence and longevity, he had considerable experience of government and politics.

Any evaluation needs to leave room for criticism, and must counter the degree to which the easiest way to mould the appreciation of any period is to leave extensive records. These may result in revelations that prompt an unsympathetic perception by scholars, but they certainly help ensure that issues are defined in terms of whoever or whatever left the records. The material left by George, in particular his correspondence, is so extensive,[1] and the space available in any biography of such a long-lived man is so much under pressure, that it is too easy to allocate insufficient room to a consideration of the criticisms of the king. This would be to adopt the perspective of the king alone, and in a biography that would be a mistake, and is not the position taken here.

For good or ill, George was no spectator of the events of his reign. Active throughout, until illness incarcerated him in the shadows, George had a natural vigour that reflected his sense of purpose and a fit robustness. Lord Eldon, lord chancellor as well as a friend of the king, recorded being told by George that in 1807, after a British joint operation against Copenhagen led to the surrender of the Danish fleet, when the British envoy, Francis Jackson,

> waited on George III on his return, the King abruptly asked him, 'Was the Prince Royal[2] up stairs or down when he received you?' 'He was on the ground-floor, please your Majesty.' 'I am glad of it, I am glad of it, for your sake,' rejoined the King; 'for if he had half the spirit of George III he would infallibly have kicked you down stairs'.[3]

The comparative context is an important one in which to consider George, although he only once met another ruling king: when his brother-in-law and first cousin, Christian VII of Denmark, the father of the Prince

[1] As is the anti-George material.
[2] George's nephew, later Frederick VI.
[3] Twiss, II, 60–1.

Royal just referred to, visited England in 1768.[4] (This trip, which was not an incognito one, unlike some of those elsewhere in Europe by the much-travelled Gustavus III of Sweden and the Emperor Joseph II, was not a success from George's point of view, because he was concerned about the actions and politicking of the mentally unstable Christian.) Unfortunately, far from pursuing the comparative approach, historians have generally approached George largely in British terms, and, indeed, have assessed him in terms of both British high politics and a court life lived only in southern England. This is understandable. His two predecessors never visited Ireland, Scotland, Wales or northern England, but they at least travelled to their German possessions, the Electorate of Hanover, and also saw more of the continent, both as kings and before coming to the throne, whereas George III never left England. George IV, in contrast, though far from fit, while king, visited Ireland, Hanover and Scotland in 1821–2, and William IV, in his period in the navy while a prince, went to the West Indies and New York, although he was far more sedentary as king. Queen Victoria took advantage of the developing technologies of train and steamship to travel during her reign. If George III travelled far less than the other Hanoverian rulers, or than any male ruler of Britain since the short-lived Edward VI in the mid-sixteenth century, his scope was still extensive. Relations with the American colonies were contentious from 1765 to 1783, while it is clear from his correspondence and his scientific collecting that George was interested in British activity around the world. This is a theme of the book.

If the comparative context leads at times to a disconcerting perspective, it is one that is essential, not least if issues of significance and success are to be considered. Despite occasional threats to abdicate, George for example showed a resilient ability to keep his nerve under pressure when compared with Louis XVI's indecision. His handling of the Gordon Riots in 1780 and the serious political crisis of 1783–4 was more successful and more adroit than Louis's actions were to prove in 1788–9.

George's political opportunities and problems can be highlighted by comparison with foreign rulers. He might, like his counterparts, be a limited monarch – powerful except in certain areas delimited by law and custom, rather than a modern constitutional monarch (who lacks the capacity for implementing political policies of their own) – but the histor-ical legacy ensured that assumptions about appropriate royal politics in Britain were different to those in France or Spain. To a British reader, it might appear peculiar to read that in 1784 the country appeared to an informed foreign visitor to be 'une vraye démocratie sous la forme monar-

---

[4] H. Clifford, 'King Christian VII's Visit to England in 1768', in *A King's Feast. The Goldsmith's Art and Royal Banqueting in the 18th Century* (Kensington Palace exhibition, 1991), pp. 11–29.

chique',[5] but to continental commentators contemplating the role of parliament or the absence of the royal use of powers to veto legislation, this was evident. The extent to which the emphasis should be on British exceptionalism or on common themes merits consideration. It is also important to remember that George was Elector of Hanover and that, through his relatives, he was connected with, and concerned about, a number of continental ruling houses.

While not as lengthy as the reign (1837–1901) of his granddaughter Victoria, the reign (1760–1820) of George III was very long. Indeed it was nearly as long as the combined length of the reigns of the other four members of the Hanoverian dynasty in Britain: George I (1714–27), George II (1727–60), and the two of George III's sons who reigned in Britain, George IV (1820–30) and William IV (1830–37); a third son, Ernest, ruled in Hanover from 1837 to 1851. Even if the regency exercised by the future George IV from 1811, while his father was unfit to rule, is excluded, this longevity helped ensure George III a key place in the history of the British monarchy. The king's role in the history of the monarchy and, in particular, in the political history of his reign can crowd out the man himself. Nevertheless, with George, the interest and significance of the personal and family dimension rest in part in his position as monarch. In that, he was similar to Elizabeth I (r. 1558–1603), whose role in cementing the reputation of the Tudors prefigured that of George III for the Hanoverians. Both also faced the ultimate challenges of rebellion and invasion, on more than one occasion.

[5] Lasowski, tutor of François de la Rochefoucauld, to duke of Liancourt, summer 1784, University College, London, MS 138 fol. 177.

Chapter 2

A PRINCE AND HIS EDUCATION

Born in London, at Norfolk House, St James's Square, on 24 May (OS) 1738 (4 June new style),* George was the first son, and second child, of Frederick, prince of Wales, and his wife, Augusta of Saxe-Gotha. His list of names, George William Frederick, proclaimed his position as heir to father and grandfather, as well as, with the reference to William III of Orange, his Whig credentials, but Frederick's relations with his father, George II, were very poor and this provided the background to the early life of Prince George. Indeed the duke of Norfolk's house was being used for Frederick's court, because Frederick had been expelled from St James's Palace by his father. Little is known about George's early years. Born two months premature, there were doubts about whether he would survive, but his wet-nurse, Mary Smith, was effective, earning George's gratitude; she was appointed his laundress after he became king. When she died in 1773, George wrote with characteristic affection and care,

> She suckled me, and to her great attention my having been reared is greatly owing; this ought to make me anxious for the welfare of her children, who by her great imprudence are left destitute of support; I therefore desire you will appoint her youngest daughter Augusta Hicks to succeed as Laundress, who has frequently managed the business during different illnesses with which she has been afflicted.[1]

At the age of four, the future king was described as a lovely child and as fat,[2] at that time seen as a sign of health. Scant trace can be found of the prince in these years. In part, this reflects the growing privacy and domesticity of royal childhoods, with the emphasis on a nursery life removed from the public gaze. There was far more privacy for royal children than there was to be in the newsreel and television age of the twentieth and twenty-first centuries. One of the first mentions of the prince's actions was when he played the role of Marcus Portius Cato in an amateur theatrical (see p. 12), and he was ten at the time. The boy's education can largely be

---

*Unless otherwise stated, all dates are new style. Old style dates are marked (OS).
[1] George to earl of Bristol, 8 July 1773, Fortescue, III, 2.
[2] Aberystwyth, National Library of Wales, Ms. 1352 fols 59–60.

followed only at second hand, through references to the appointment of tutors, and the letters sent him by his father. The first letter from the prince that survives was not written until 23 June 1749[3] when he was eleven, although it is clear from his father's letters that there was earlier correspondence. The letter, sent to his grandfather George II, was an acknowledgement of the honour done him by the investiture the previous day with the Order of the Garter, a public mark of his status.

Three months later, Lord North, one of Frederick's lords of the bedchamber (and the father of the Lord North who was to be George's first minister), was declared governor of the king. George also gained a new tutor, George Lewis Scott, a noted mathematician, who had been recommended by Henry, Viscount Bolingbroke. Scott was expected to oversee the education of George and his brother Edward, later duke of York, and to ensure that they conformed to the demanding timetable for education set by Frederick. This focused on lessons, which took up the morning and the late afternoon, with a play hour and the main meal in the early afternoon. There was little time set aside for outdoor recreations. George travelled with Frederick, visiting Oakley House in Buckinghamshire with him in 1750,[4] but the character and, indeed, extent of their relationship is unclear.

Frederick died unexpectedly, after a brief illness, on 20 March 1751, one of a number of European royal heirs who died before their fathers during the century, including the eldest sons of Philip V of Spain and the three Louis – XIV, XV and XVI – of France. Frederick left his eldest son to succeed him as heir to the elderly George II. This brought Prince George back into the orbit of his grandfather, for George II did not extend to his daughter-in-law or his grandchildren the loathing he had shown for his troublesome eldest son. Augusta sought the king's protection for herself and her children, and he extended it, going to see her, and urging George and Edward to be brave. The entire episode saw the king at his best. Often hot-tempered and clumsy in personal relationships, he had a fundamental integrity and warmth.

The young George succeeded at once to his father's title of duke of Edinburgh, and was created prince of Wales and earl of Chester that April, although he did not receive a separate household until 1756. Frederick's death, however, raised the possibility that, if George II died soon after, there would be a regency and that his second son, Prince George's uncle, William, duke of Cumberland, would play a prominent role in this, to the detriment of Augusta and of the young prince's interests. The sensitivity of regency arrangements was to emerge repeatedly in George III's reign, a product of tensions within the royal family,

[3] Prince George to George II, 23 June 1749, BL. Add. 32684 fol. 78.
[4] W.S. Baddeley, *History of Cirencester* (Cirencester, 1924), p. 274.

ambiguities about the position of specific individuals, and the political importance of the issue. The lack of clear constitutional law on the subject reflected not only the role of parliamentary statute, at once clarifying and destabilizing, but also the need to allow for particular dynastic circumstances and for the health and calibre of individual members of the royal family. This relationship between predictability and responsiveness in regency arrangements can be seen as actually, or potentially, stable, or unstable, depending on both circumstances, in particular the political context, and perception, but the relationship also represented a necessary flexibility. This was more generally true of the constitutional position of the monarchy. In the event, the provisions for the regency that George II recommended to parliament proposed the widowed princess of Wales as regent and guardian, while Cumberland was to be simply a member of the council appointed to advise her. She was to be allowed to exercise certain key royal powers – the creation of peers, the appointment of judges, and the dissolution of parliament – with the advice of the council.

There was also a change in the oversight of the prince's education, one designed to replace the influence of Prince Frederick with that of the government. North was replaced as governor, and Francis Ayscough, a cleric with close opposition links, as the man responsible for religious education: Ayscough had been the tutor from the outset, being supplemented by Scott in 1749. The education of George and his brother Edward was now entrusted to a new team: Simon, first Earl Harcourt, as governor, the head of the household; Thomas Hayter, bishop of Norwich, as preceptor with oversight of the education; George Lewis Scott continuing his crucial educational role as sub-preceptor; and Andrew Stone as sub-governor. Stone was the key political factotum of Thomas Pelham, duke of Newcastle, the leading figure in the ministry. A professional to his fingertips, Stone was the well-educated son of a goldsmith, and a model of conscientiousness. Hayter himself was a demanding guide, keen on exemplary diligence:

> It is proposed, that their Royal Highnesses do rise at seven o'clock, and translate such parts of Caesar's Commentaries as they have before read . . . the utmost attention has been, and will be had to explain and inculcate to their Royal Highnesses, the great duties of Religion and Morality.[5]

[5] J.C.D. Clark (ed.), *The Memoirs and Speeches of James, 2nd Earl Waldegrave, 1742–63* (Cambridge, 1988), p. 14; B.B. Schnorrenberg, 'Who Was George Lewis Scott?', *New Perspectives on the Eighteenth Century*, 2 (2005), pp. 39–53.

These were indeed to be major themes of George's reign, although the political legacy of his period as prince proved more contentious, both at the time and subsequently. In late 1752 there was a clash over George's education, with Hayter determined to exercise control. Stone, backed by Scott, was seen by Harcourt and Hayter as a quasi-Jacobite (supporter of the exiled Stuarts) pushing unwelcome Tory views. This controversy caused both Harcourt and Hayter, who produced no evidence for this claim and were believed by neither George II nor Newcastle, to resign that December. The king reassured Augusta that he did not believe Harcourt, whose relations with her had been poor. The following February and March, Stone was accused of being a Jacobite, but he successfully defended himself before the council, and an attack on the issue in the House of Lords was defeated by the government.

The controversy unfairly affected subsequent perceptions of Prince George, who, indeed, was critical of the political system for reasons other than Jacobitism. And as the education of the future king became controversial, relations between Augusta and George II deteriorated. In large part, this was due to the question of money. George II imagined that he had a strong need for it, which was not correct at this period, while Augusta, with nine young children to support and the debts of her improvident husband an incubus, felt cheated. This was not least because George II had not given his grandson the revenues of the duchy of Cornwall, which were properly only for the monarch's eldest son. Augusta also felt that the ministry was failing to look after the interests of Frederick's former servants. George II, however, was scarcely going to reward former opponents, who included those who had lent money to Frederick in order to fund his opposition to his father's ministers. The prince was clearly affected by his mother's anger, which contributed to the sense of lost rights and misuse of power that affected his response to the political system.

Despite Harcourt's resignation, he was to be sent as envoy to Mecklenburg-Strelitz in 1761 in order formally to demand the hand of Princess Charlotte for the young George; subsequently he served her as master of the horse and, then, lord chamberlain. He also served George as envoy in Paris and as lord-lieutenant of Ireland, while Harcourt's son, George, was a friend of the king. George Harcourt's brother and successor, William, was also close to the king and was made deputy ranger of Windsor Great Park.

Harcourt was succeeded as governor by James, second Earl Waldegrave, a socially adroit courtier who enjoyed considerable favour with George II, while John Thomas, bishop of Peterborough, became preceptor. Thomas did not amount to much, although he passed muster, being preferred to the more prestigious see of Salisbury in 1757, while George III appointed him bishop of Winchester in 1761. Waldegrave, however, was not able to retain the good opinion of Augusta and was to be damned by George III as a 'depraved worthless man'.

These personal issues could not but have contributed to the extent to which, as prince, George developed a sense of antagonism towards a system that he thought oligarchical and factional. The young prince, and his adviser and confidant from 1755, John Stuart, third earl of Bute, favoured the idea of politics without party and of a king above faction. To further his goals, the shy George educated himself by reading about the details of government, including public finance.[6] He thought it necessary that, when once he became king, he personally should take a central political role. George saw this not only as his constitutional part, as one of the three elements in parliament, but also as his moral duty. Particularly as a young man, this moral sense helped characterize George as a prig who regretted the lack of piety and virtue among others.[7] This view owed much to his mother's emphasis on religion and morality, and was an aspect of the North German Protestantism that had a modest impact during the early Hanoverian period.[8] Looked at differently, George was a 'moral zealot', and his self-righteousness gave particular energy to the political views generally associated with the reversionary interest (that of the heir).[9] At the same time, it is necessary to appreciate his cultural interests (discussed in Chapter 9) and what they indicate about his wide-ranging sensitivities. While he was prince, these interests were actively encouraged and greatly developed.

Constitutional duty and moral role fused in the potent idea of George as a 'Patriot King', a notion powerfully formulated by Henry, Viscount Bolingbroke, in his discussion in *The Idea of a Patriot King* (1749).[10] This called for a monarch who was virtuous, impartial and powerful enough to override parties, a traditional view made newly topical by the opposition to George II. These ideas were supported by Frederick, prince of Wales, who, in his youth, had been given a moral course in history by being provided with Clarendon and Burnet to read. Such views were also inculcated in George III as a youth. The pedigree of the ideas was controversial. Bolingbroke, whose critical views of the reign of William III and of the development then of the parliamentary-guaranteed national debt George III found conducive,[11] had also been a prominent Tory politician

---

[6] J. Bullion, '"To know this is the true essential business of a king": The Prince of Wales and the Study of Public Finance, 1755–1760', *Albion*, 18 (1986), pp. 429–54.

[7] George to Bute, 1759, BL. Add. 36796 fol. 46.

[8] J. Bullion, '"George, Be a King!": The Relationship between Princess Augusta and George III', in S. Taylor, R. Connors and C. Jones (eds), *Hanoverian Britain and Empire: Essays in Memory of Philip Lawson* (Woodbridge, 1998), pp. 177–97.

[9] J.L. McKelvey, *George III and Lord Bute: The Leicester House Years* (Durham, North Carolina, 1973), p. xii.

[10] On which recently, see F. Nibelius, *Lord Bolingbroke (1678–1751) and History. A Comparative Study of Bolingbroke's Politico-historical Works and a Selection of Contemporary Texts as to Themes and Vocabulary* (Stockholm, 2003), pp. 147–61.

[11] Bullion, 'Public Finance', p. 432 fn. 9.

under Queen Anne, tainted by the Whigs with accusations of Jacobitism and forced to flee abroad under George I. Bolingbroke had sought his return to British politics in the 1720s, by abandoning Jacobitism, and had played a prominent role in developing a 'Country' ideology, designed to link Tories with opposition Whigs in order to produce a political movement that was at once loyal (i.e. non-Jacobite) and pledged to better government. The latter was understood to mean a virtuous rejection of the financial, political and moral corruption held to characterize the governing 'Old Corps' Whigs, the established politicians who had dominated successive ministries since the accession of George I operating akin to an oligarchy. This 'Country' ideology was the background to the self-styled Patriot politics prominent in Frederick's circle once he moved into opposition in the mid-1730s. The 'Country' critique, however, was rejected by the 'Old Corps', with the argument that the role of Bolingbroke and the attempt to encompass the Tories proved that the 'Country' tendency was in fact a stalking-horse for the Tories, if not the Jacobites, and thus a dangerous threat to Whig cohesion, if not Hanoverian rule. Many Tories in fact found it difficult to fight free of the implications of the belief in the divine origin of political authority, a belief that George III shared but that made the rejection of Stuart rule hard to accept.

For Frederick, and, after him, George, to adopt Patriot ideas appeared a serious challenge to the Whigs and their conception of the constitution. Looked at differently (and the either/or approach is not helpful), however, the adoption of Patriot ideas was also part of the process by which Jacobitism was weakened, as the potent theme of rebirth through the accession of the rightful monarch was taken from the Stuarts and crafted for the Hanoverian heir. The claim that George was secretly educated in Jacobite principles, one that in early 1753 focused on Stone, can be rejected.[12]

George was influenced by the concept of patriarchal government implicit in Bolingbroke's book, as well as in the Book of Kings from the Old Testament which served as the basis for many eighteenth-century sermons. He believed that, in maintaining his right to choose ministers and his ability to block legislation, he was ensuring that he could discharge his functions and – to employ a concept that he understood, that of service – act in an appropriate manner. In this respect, George sought to fulfil the hopes that had centred on his father, and which his father had encouraged. The king was to act as a political redeemer, a notion that reflected a powerful optimistic element in the iconography of kingship, and the 'naïve and nostalgic' aspect of Bolingbroke's thesis.[13] Shortly before he died in

[12] Clark (ed.), *Memoirs and Speeches*, pp. 48–60, 112–45.

[13] S. Varey, 'Hanover, Stuart, and the *Patriot King*', *British Journal for Eighteenth-Century Studies*, 6 (1983), p. 171; I. Kramnick, *Bolingbroke and His Circle: The Politics of Nostalgia in the Age of Walpole* (Cambridge, Massachusetts, 1968).

1762, George Dodington, Lord Melcombe, who had been Prince Frederick's leading political adviser, wondered 'if the times and the temper of the King, should permit him to restore to national justice, the sword, that faction and corruption have long since wrested out of her hand?'[14]

As a result of his political upbringing, George saw himself, and his constitutional role, as acting out of national, rather than sectional, interest, and retained that conviction and goal throughout his reign, while being unwilling to take such a charitable view of others. His attitude was seen across the range of government, and helped link his moral and political conceptions in a common concern with professionalism and public service. For example, in 1784 George both stated his support for forming a government 'on a wide basis', the 'Country' theme of the 1720s–30s, and warned against what he saw as sectional interests in fiscal policy:

> Nothing is more natural than that, such heavy charges requiring many new taxes, those particularly affected by some will from that selfish motive, though conscious of the necessity of new burthens, attempt to place them on others rather than on themselves . . . the coal pits, which are the property of more considerable persons [than the brick-pits], and therefore more clamorous, though not less able to support a new charge on their profits.[15]

One of the first accounts of George is of his acting at the age of ten the role of the virtuous hero in a children's production of Joseph Addison's noted play *Cato* (1711). He was given a new prologue to speak: 'What, tho' a boy! It may with truth be said, A boy in England born, in England bred.' Republican virtue, not imperial monarchy, was a theme of the play, which was an acclaimed Whig text. Another Whig classic, Nicholas Rowe's *Lady Jane Grey* (1715), an account of exemplary Protestant virtue, was also staged by Prince Frederick's children. Rowe was made poet laureate by George I.

A belief in the role of the king, however, did not mean a desire for unlimited royal power. In his writings as prince, George criticized James II and VII, arguing that the Glorious Revolution had rescued Britain 'from the iron rod of arbitrary power', and praised Oliver Cromwell as 'a friend of justice and virtue'. In an essay on the British constitution written at the start of 1760, shortly before he became king, George argued that monarchical authority could itself be a threat. He suggested this, first, because of the risks stemming from the royal powers to create peers, a theme that had been voiced at the time of the unsuccessful Peerage Bill of 1719, and,

---

[14] Melcombe to Bute, 10 July 1762, MS, papers from Cardiff Public Library, 2/93.
[15] George to Pitt, 11 Feb., 1 July 1784, PRO. 30/8/103.

second, because of the existence of the standing army, unless troops were also aware of their role as citizens. Concerned about the threat posed by a large force of regular troops, George also wanted a militia at least twice the size of the army.[16]

Both these views took up earlier Whig themes,[17] and concern about the army had been a staple of 'Country' thought. The militia was seen as a source of independent power not at the disposal of an autocratic ruler, an attitude that was to influence policy in early Republican America. George's concern about the military would have warmed the hearts of many American politicians during the early Republic had they been aware of them,[18] but none of George's essays were for publication. George also wrote in the essay that 'King and people may in some degree be looked upon as contending parties, and the Lords as a mediating power to keep the true balance.' In marked contrast, the future Emperor Joseph II, writing his 'Rêveries' in the spring of 1763, offered an autocratic prospectus, in which he saw necessary radical change as stemming from a powerful monarch, and pressed for the humbling of the greater aristocracy and the suspension of provincial constitutions.[19] British Whig aristocrats were to complain that George treated them in a hostile fashion, but there was certainly no comparison with the headstrong and authoritarian Joseph.

George's interest in good government was encouraged in 1759 when he was provided with copies of the lectures given by William Blackstone who, the previous year, had become Vinerian professor of law at Oxford. These lectures on English law and government reflected Blackstone's emphasis on judicial independence. They had been given to Bute for George by one of Blackstone's Oxford pupils, William Petty, Viscount Fitzmaurice, later second earl of Shelburne and George's leading minister in 1782–3.

Nevertheless, some of George's views, although commonplace in their time, appear less desirable now. In an essay, 'On Industry in Great Britain', written in 1757,[20] he argued that the small size of the population enabled the poor to be idle and to indulge 'in unnecessary things', such as brandy, gin, tea, sugar, foreign fruit, strong beer, printed linens, snuff, and tobacco: 'superfluities' they were able to enjoy because wage rates were too high.

[16] RA. GEO/Add. 32; P.D.G. Thomas, 'Thoughts on the British Constitution by George III in 1760', *Bulletin of the Institute of Historical Research*, 60 (1987), pp. 361–3.

[17] L.D. Cress, 'Radical Whiggery on the Role of the Military: Ideological Roots of the American Revolutionary Militia', *Journal of the History of Ideas*, 40 (1979), pp. 43–60.

[18] L.D. Cress, *Citizens in Arms: The Army and the Militia in American Society to the War of 1812* (Chapel Hill, 1982); T.J. Crackel, *Mr. Jefferson's Army: Political and Social Reform of the Military Establishment, 1801–1809* (New York, 1989).

[19] D. Beales, 'Joseph II's "Rêveries"', *Mitteilungen des Österreichischen Staatsarchivs*, 33 (1980), pp. 142–90.

[20] RA. GEO/Add. 32/259–61.

Similarly, John Wesley, the founder of Methodism, regarded leisure with fierce suspicion. To increase the number of workers, George suggested naturalizing foreign Protestants and using their cheaper labour to drive down wages, which would, he argued, help British employers, farm improvers and exporters. Failing that, workers were to be obliged to 'work moderately six days in the week', while the unemployed poor were to be forced to work. This was a combination of old-established views about labour discipline and recent support for foreign naturalization, not least by the writer and cleric, Josiah Tucker.[21] Furthermore, the naturalization of foreign Protestants was a long-standing Whig view heavily criticized by Tories. They were concerned about increasing the number of inhabitants who were not members of the Church of England.

The approach outlined by George in 1757, however, was discarded as likely to be unpopular. Instead, the following year, he argued in favour of lowering excises on goods consumed by the poor in order to cut wages.[22] A quest for popularity was linked to George's disenchantment with politicians, particularly William Pitt the Elder, and to an improved opinion of the populace whose spirit he saw as important to national strength. This looked toward the presentation of George as a Patriot king when he came to the throne in 1760.[23]

Augusta and Bute were the key influences on George as he grew to manhood in the late 1750s. Augusta's success in keeping him away from louche aristocratic influence and her piety helped mould George's character and give him the taste for a somewhat isolated domesticity which he subsequently reproduced in his own family. Augusta was more influential in the development of George's character than Frederick had been, although she had less success with his nearest brother, Edward.

Taking charge of George's education in 1755, Bute was Augusta's key adviser, rather than, as was widely alleged, her lover.[24] Bute came to play the same role for George: twenty-five years older, he was a surrogate father. The nephew of the second and third dukes of Argyll, the key Scottish politicians for most of the reign of George II, Bute had a formidable political legacy in Scottish terms, but he had also been taught to see

---

[21] G. Shelton, *Dean Tucker: Eighteenth-Century Economic and Political Thought* (London, 1981).

[22] RA. GEO/Add. 32/1220–32.

[23] J. Bullion, 'From "the French and Dutch are more sober, frugal and industrious" to the "nobler" position: Attitudes of the Prince of Wales toward a General Naturalization and a Popular Monarchy, 1757–1760', in P.B. Craddock and C.H. Hay (eds), *Studies in Eighteenth-Century Culture*, 17 (East Lansing, Michigan, 1987), pp. 159–71.

[24] J. Bullion, 'The Prince's Mentor: A New Perspective on the Friendship between George III and Lord Bute during the 1750s', *Albion*, 21 (1989), pp. 34–55, and 'The Origins and Significance of Gossip about Princess Augusta and Lord Bute, 1755–1756', in P.B. Craddock and C.H. Hay (eds), *Studies in Eighteenth-Century Culture* 21 (East Lansing, Michigan, 1991), pp. 245–65.

himself as a Briton and sought to educate George accordingly. Educated at Eton and Utrecht, Bute married Mary Wortley Montagu, a wealthy heiress and daughter of the diarist. He was one of the richest aristocrats in Britain, and a man with considerable artistic, cultural and scientific interests which he tried, with some success, to share with George.[25] Like George, fatherless from an early age, Bute developed the close relationship with his pupil that Earls Harcourt and Waldegrave, the aristocrats successively responsible for his upbringing after the death of Frederick, had lacked, and this helped increase the prince's confidence.

Nevertheless, this greater confidence, or, rather, lesser lack of confidence, was linked to a degree of dependence that provided a basis for the charges of undue favouritism and manipulation by Bute that were to colour George's reputation soon after he came to the throne,[26] and, thereafter, to affect the perception of the king. George's letters to Bute, whom he addressed from 1757 as 'My Dearest Friend', clearly indicate his personal dependence, as well as a sense of frustration that he could not concentrate on business and that his education had been neglected. George's promises of personal reformation in order to make himself suited to his role indicate the degree to which he saw his kingship as a project.[27] Bute, in turn, encouraged George to develop what his adviser saw as his 'quality perhaps unknown to his predecessors; I mean manly firmness, unshaken resolution'.[28]

George II's age (he was born in 1683) ensured that the likely future views of the young prince played a role in the successive political crises of 1754–7. These arose as prospects for a stable ministry were probed in the shadow of an initially unsuccessful war with France, the Seven Years, or French-and-Indian, War. Indeed, in 1757, the prince's uncle, William, duke of Cumberland, suggested, as did some other commentators, that certain politicians were manoeuvring with an eye to the accession of the future George III, 'the proper shop for future bargains'.[29] Politicians sought to win the support of Leicester House, the court of the princess of Wales and of the young Prince George, on the north side of Leicester Square, although in fact he lived, from 1751, with his brother Edward, at next-door Savile House when not in the country with his mother in Kew. Led by Augusta, who had inherited her husband's antipathy to George II, Cumberland and the Pelhams, this court looked to the opponents of the 'Old Corps' Whigs. The key figure among the 'Old Corps' was Thomas

[25] E.g. discussing history, Bute to George, and reply, both undated, BL. Add. 36796 fol. 66.
[26] M. Peters, 'History and Political Propaganda in mid-Eighteenth-Century England: The Case of the Essay Papers', *Studies in the Eighteenth Century*, 6 (1987), pp. 73–4.
[27] George to Bute, 25 Sept., – Dec. 1758, 14 Dec. 1760, BL. Add. 36796 fols 32, 35, 65.
[28] Bute to Andrew Mitchell, envoy in Berlin, 9 Apr. 1762, MS.
[29] Cumberland to Devonshire, 1 July 1757, HP. Chatsworth papers.

Pelham, duke of Newcastle, a secretary of state from 1724 until 1754, and as the first lord of the treasury, the leading minister, in 1754–6 and 1757–62. It was understandable that, with its poor relations with George II, Leicester House should look to opponents of the latter's ministers. This ensured that Newcastle's attempt to win the support of Leicester House in 1756 had little chance of success. His most influential critic, Pitt, whose relations with George II had also been distinctly rocky, was much more to the taste of the young court. At the close of 1756, Henry Fox, an ally of both Cumberland and Newcastle, complained that his rival Pitt 'has Lord Bute and Leicester House absolutely'.[30] This was an article of faith: Henry Digby, Fox's nephew, wrote of Pitt the following June, 'as he has got Leicester House, I think the Duke of Newcastle will be in his power'.[31] As a reminder of the multiple connections of the period, Digby was to be created a lord in the British peerage (1765) and then Earl Digby (1790) by George III, to serve him as a lord of the admiralty from 1763 to 1765 and as lord-lieutenant of Dorset from 1771 until his death in 1793, and to act as George's host at Sherborne castle in 1789.

Augusta feared that the death of George II, which it was expected would be soon, would lead Cumberland to reach for power. She saw Pitt as an ally against Cumberland and his leading supporter in the House of Commons, Fox. There was much talk of Cumberland, the captain-general of the army, as a wicked uncle, and frequent historical references to Richard III, who had removed his nephew, the young Edward V, one of the 'Princes in the Tower', in 1483. In practice, Cumberland, although hostile to his troublesome brother Frederick before the latter's death, was a man of integrity and duty, with a keen sense of appropriate behaviour. He was, in the 1760s, to prove a useful ally to his nephew, and the duke's early death in 1765 robbed George III of a valuable source of advice. The fears of the 1750s, however, helped condition the political atmosphere within which George's response to his family and his sense of his own responsibilities were moulded. For many parliamentarians they were real fears, however extreme, and this is a powerful reminder of the potential nature of dynastic factors in this period.

Sensitivity over the political leanings of the young court helped cause tension between it and the government in 1756 when Prince George came of age on 4 June. Wishing to remove links between Augusta and the prince, the ministers suggested that George II offer him an allowance and invite him to live at court: the prince accepted the first, but not the second. He also asked that Bute be appointed his groom of the stole, a measure uncomfortable to both George II and Newcastle because of Bute's links

---

[30] Fox to Hanbury-Williams, 26 Dec. 1756, Farmington, Connecticut, Lewis Walpole Library, Hanbury Williams papers, vol. 63 fol. 4.
[31] Digby to Hanbury-Williams, 12 June 1757, BL. Add. 69093.

with Pitt. These links helped make Pitt appear a more desirable ally to Newcastle.[32] Bute gained the post that October.

The belief that Pitt could bring the support of both Leicester House and the Tories to any ministry he joined helped strengthen his hand in the complex political manoeuvres of 1757. However, the ministry he played a key role in forming that summer was one that included Newcastle anew as first lord of the treasury, a testimony to the parliamentary importance of the 'Old Corps'. Having looked to Leicester House, Patriots and Tories for his political support, Pitt was now the member of a ministry dominated by the 'Old Corps' Whigs. This was a step that placed his relations with his former supporters under threat and, in particular, undermined his recently improved links with Leicester House, rather as he had earlier broken those with Prince Frederick in the 1740s.

Although Leicester House supported the new ministry, it did so with considerable and growing misgivings. George and Bute were to convince themselves that Pitt had betrayed them in gaining power, although the experience of the government of Pitt and William, fourth duke of Devonshire, in 1756–7 had suggested that any ministry that did not include Newcastle would be unstable. Other issues in the late 1750s also helped to damage relations critically between Leicester House and the ministry. A growing sense that Pitt was failing to consider the views of the young court seriously was a problem,[33] and one that was brought into focus by the harsh treatment of the protégés of the young court responsible for an unsuccessful amphibious attempt on St Malo in September 1757. Furthermore, in 1759, the attack on a Leicester House favourite, Bute's military adviser, Lord George Sackville, who had refused to order the British cavalry to charge during the battle of Minden, aroused resentment in the young court.[34] George's remark that he would receive Sackville at his levee, a public demonstration of approval, however, was not fulfilled: a sensible response to Sackville's unpopularity.[35] Sackville was subsequently, when Lord George Germain, to be responsible, as secretary of state for the colonies from 1775 to 1782, for British military policy in the War of American Independence. Pitt, in turn, was concerned about others developing links with Leicester House, especially his co-secretary of state, Robert, fourth earl of Holdernesse, an accomplished courtier.

The essential problem was the absence of adequate consultation. Pitt certainly kept Bute and, through him, George, informed about developments. Pitt's correspondence among the Bute papers includes letters

---

[32] R. Browning, *The Duke of Newcastle* (New Haven, 1975), p. 239.

[33] Viry, Sardinian envoy in London, to Charles Emmanuel III, 27 Sept., 17 Oct. 1758, AST. LM. Ing. 63; R.R. Sedgwick (ed.), *Letters from George III to Lord Bute, 1756–1766* (London, 1939), p. 18.

[34] George to Bute, – Aug., – Dec. 1759, BL. Add. 36796 fols 45–6.

[35] P. Mackesy, *The Coward of Minden* (London, 1979).

referring to the diplomatic situation. Furthermore, the two men met to discuss events at Pitt's initiative, one undated letter of 1759 reading 'Mr. Pitt would be particularly desirous of half an hour with Lord Bute, on the subject of the intelligence of the French preparations in their ports.'[36] This was a reference to the French invasion attempt wrecked by the victories of the British navy off Lagos and in Quiberon Bay. Robert Wood, one of Pitt's under-secretaries, nevertheless recalled in 1767 that Pitt 'during the late King's reign, had the most intimate connection with Lord Bute . . . the connection between Bute and Pitt had gradually lessened and at length come to perfect dislike'.[37] The key problem was that Bute and Prince George expected to be consulted, as well as informed. In contrast, for reasons both of his own imperious personality and of the exigencies of office, Pitt was not really interested in any consultation that was more than a formality. George, who was quick to take offence, felt more generally snubbed. The young prince visited Drury Lane three times to see *Agis*, a play by John Home, Bute's private secretary and a tutor to George. Dedicated to him, and produced in 1758, *Agis* cast the Prince in a glorious role; he awarded Home £50 and 'expressions of satisfaction with the play'.[38] No such role, however, was available for him in real life, the king fobbing off the prince, by then twenty-one, in July 1759 when Britain was indeed threatened with invasion from France.

By the late 1750s, furthermore, there was a substantial difference over wartime strategy between the minister and the young court. An undated letter of the prince to Bute reveals George's opposition to the dispatch of British troops to Germany, as well as his related hostility to his grandfather: 'I shall soon be going to that hateful Drawing-Room, which I suppose will be fuller than usual, on account of last Monday's news from the foreign dominions. I fear the troops will now with greater ardour be demanded to keep the French from returning'[39] – this comment a reference to the threat that they would invade Hanover anew. George and Bute feared that sending troops to Germany would compromise the popularity of the government and increase the national debt. Indeed, they saw the war as becoming a second version of the debilitating conflict of 1689–97, the Nine Years War or War of the League of Augsburg, which was blamed for corrupting the promise of the Glorious Revolution, and criticized by both opposition Whigs and Tories. George and Bute were also critical of Britain's ally, Frederick the Great of Prussia, whose interests they thought very different to those of Britain.[40]

[36] Sedgwick (ed.), *Letters*, pp. 10–11.
[37] HP. Harris memoranda, 13 May 1767.
[38] George to Bute, 1759, BL. Add. 36796 fol. 48.
[39] MS; Sedgwick (ed.), *Letters*, p. 11.
[40] George to Bute, – Aug. 1759, BL. Add. 36796 fol. 49.

The prince lacked the degree of emotional attachment to, and concern about, Hanover shown by his two predecessors. In 1755 and 1759, in accordance with a strong lead from his mother, this led him to reject the idea of marrying Sophia Caroline, the eldest daughter of the duke of Brunswick, despite George II's strong support for the match.[41] The house of Brunswick (or Brunswick-Wolfenbüttel) was related to that of neighbouring Hanover, and good relations were seen as important to the security of the latter and as paving the way to a possible reunion of the Guelph inheritance, which was never, in fact, to occur. This dynastic politics awaits systematic study, but was to be traced through George III's reign. His sister Augusta married Charles, the heir to the duchy of Brunswick in 1764, and their daughter, Caroline, married his heir, the future George IV, in 1795; their sole child, Charlotte, died in childbirth.

Given the fundamentally opposed views of George II and Prince George over Hanover and over operations in Germany,[42] it was impossible for the ministers to serve both. Pitt's position was particularly sensitive. His testy comments about not being answerable to Bute and the prince for every move before he took it are understandable, but he had used Leicester House as a stepping stone to power, and thus contributed to his future difficulties. Pitt's desertion of the Leicester House line seemed to prove to Prince George and Bute that he was simply another unprincipled politician and that they had to rely on their own efforts.

Ready to oppose the government, George and Bute were also prepared to make threats about what the situation would be when George became king. In 1759, George backed Simeon Stuart when he stood against Henry Legge, the chancellor of the exchequer and a politician closely associated with Pitt, in a by-election in Hampshire. Stuart was supported by James, marquess of Carnarvon, heir to the duke of Chandos, a leading Hampshire magnate, and Carnarvon had secured George's backing. The strength of Legge's position led Stuart to back down, but Legge was then pressed by Bute to promise support in the next general election:

he does out of real friendship to Mr. Legge, beseech him to consider very seriously whether after triumphing over the Prince's inclinations at present, Lord Bute hath any method left of removing prejudices that the late unhappy occurrences have strongly impressed the Prince with, than by being enabled to assure him that Mr Legge will as far as shall be in his power cooperate with his Royal Highness's wishes at the next general election.[43]

---

[41] George to Bute, 1759, BL. Add. 36796 fol. 48.
[42] Sedgwick (ed.), *Letters*, pp. 11, 17–19, 25–8, 45.
[43] Bute to Legge, no date but late 1759, Manchester, John Rylands Library, Eng. Mss. 668.

George did not appreciate the opposition to his wishes. Legge was received gracelessly by George when he came to the throne, was not supported at the subsequent general election (in which he, nevertheless, was elected), and was dismissed from his office the following March as a result of the king's animosity.[44] Backed by the new king, Stuart was also elected for Hampshire in 1761 (most constituencies returned two MPs) and became chamberlain of the exchequer that year, in succession to his father. As a parliamentarian and a politician, Stuart was to be far less distinguished than Legge. He was a reliable supporter of the Bute ministry, and was subsequently listed by Rockingham and Newcastle as a Tory, voting against the repeal of the Stamp Act. His sole reported speech was on a bill to prevent abuses in the packing of hops. A keen fox-hunter, he was regarded as genial. Stuart did not attract the criticism that Legge received on the grounds of his devious personality, but the more ambitious Legge was abler. George's choice was more generally instructive.[45]

There were already clear signs of differences between king and heir in the late 1750s, but the reversionary interest did not develop as it had in the case of Prince George's grandfather and father, or was to do in that of his son, because George II was an old man, and in fact was soon to die. In contrast to George III, George II, born in 1683, did not become king until much later in his life (in 1727), although he also did not oppose the ministers until 1716, later in his life than in the case of the future George III. The same was true of his son, Frederick (1707–51), who became a key opposition figure in 1737. Had Frederick lived as long as his own father, in other words until 1784, and then been succeeded by Prince George, the prince would have had a long period as heir (although it would not have begun until 1760, as Frederick would have been prince of Wales until then). This would have tested George both personally and politically, not least because his personality was very different from that of his father: George III was more conscientious, devout and uxorious. Had Frederick lived, George might have been influenced more by him than by Augusta, in behaviour and mores, as George II was by George I, despite their differences. George III, nevertheless, might also have reacted against Frederick critically, as his own son did to his mores and practice of kingship. Chance, or, as George would have seen it, Divine Providence, however, played the key role, and, as prince, George had enough time to develop his political ideas without becoming bitter, tired or a wastrel, as all too many royal heirs did, including the future George IV.

---

[44] Political Memoir of Lord Holland, 26 Oct. 1760, BL. Add. 51439 fol. 3; Newcastle to Rockingham, 2 Dec. 1760, WW. R1–172; BL. Add. 32919 fol. 42.

[45] L. Namier and J. Brooke (eds), *The House of Commons 1754–1790* (3 vols, London, 1964), III, 503.

The parallels were not, however, all encouraging. Among eighteenth-century monarchs who came to the throne young, Frederick II of Prussia was a success, but the vigour of the Emperor Joseph II was not matched by a prudent understanding of domestic circumstances and governmental limits. For the first fifteen years of his reign, he was co-ruler with his mother, Maria Theresa, but, subsequently, he had a far less successful reign than that of his successor and brother, Leopold II, who came to power in Austria when much older. Peter III, who came to the throne in Russia in 1762, was even more foolish than Joseph. Indeed he was murdered in a coup staged on behalf of his wife and successor, Catherine II, within a year.[46] The nearest parallel to George III was Louis XVI of France (1754–93), who came to the throne in 1774 (at nineteen, a younger age than George), also succeeding his grandfather. Louis, a third son, however, lacked George's ambition, as the latter came to the throne fired up with ideas and with a desire for change. George was the first young man to succeed to the English or British throne since Edward VI (born in 1537), whose brief reign (1547–53) had been dominated by his ministers, while, in 1567, James VI became king of Scotland as an infant. The nearest young monarch not thus dominated was Henry VIII, born in 1491, who came to the throne in 1509. Although Victoria came to the throne in 1837 at a younger age than her grandfather, George III, no subsequent British monarch was to do so. George's youth needs to be recalled when his early years as king are considered. From his period as prince, he brought a potent mix of determination, commitment and sense of self-righteousness, and a difficult mix, for himself and others, of self-confidence and self-doubt.

[46] D. Beales, *Joseph II, I: In the Shadow of Maria Theresa, 1741–1780* (Cambridge, 1987); C.S. Leonard, *Reform and Regicide: The Reign of Peter III of Russia* (Bloomington, Indiana, 1993).

Chapter 3

EIGHTEENTH-CENTURY MONARCHY

we see that every Court and every country has its difficulties and desagrémens, whilst we are idly imagining that we alone are the object of party, faction, and passion.

Joseph Yorke, 1764[1]

When George III came to the throne aged twenty-two, most of the Western world was ruled by hereditary monarchs. There were alternatives, in the shape of elected monarchies and republics, but they were less important both on the international scene and in terms of the image of monarchy. Furthermore, with the exception of the popes, who were also the temporal rulers of the Papal States, but, as unmarried men pledged to celibacy, had no (legitimate) children, the hereditary principle played a role in the prominent elective monarchies. This indicated an important tendency toward the hereditary principle in the practice of monarchy. The experience in 1741 of electing a Holy Roman Emperor who was not a Habsburg, the Elector of Bavaria, Charles Albert, who became the Emperor Charles VII, had proved very divisive. Charles was the son-in-law of a Habsburg emperor, and his election supported the hereditary principle in so far as it was how that principle was to operate that informed the dynastic dispute in the War of the Austrian Succession. After he died in 1745, successive members of the Habsburg family became emperors: Francis I, the husband of Maria Theresa of Austria, in 1745; their son, Joseph II, in 1765; his brother, Leopold II, in 1790; and the latter's son, Francis II, in 1792. He was the last to hold the title, which was abolished in 1806. The hereditary principle also played a role in Poland, where, despite the state being an elective monarchy, the king in 1760, Frederick Augustus II, Elector of Saxony, Augustus III of Poland, was the son of his predecessor. After he died in 1763, however, another Saxon election was thwarted by the choice of a Russian-backed Pole, the last king of Poland, Stanislaus Poniatowski.

In the republics, there was also an important monarchical element alongside the oligarchical one. This was seen with the doge in Venice,

---

[1] Yorke, MP and ambassador in the Hague, to Edward Weston, 10 Aug. 1764, referring to problems in Russia and Austria, BL. Add. 57927 fol. 306.

and, far more in practical terms, and also closer to home, with the *stadholders* of the individual Dutch provinces, a position only held in the eighteenth century by members of the house of Orange. The latter indeed was linked to Britain. William III of Orange had had no children, ensuring that the dynastic union of Britain and the Orange interest (1689–1702) had not survived his death, but William IV of Orange married George II's eldest daughter, Anne, in 1735, so that George III was a cousin once removed of his somewhat unimpressive contemporary William V.[2]

By the time of George III's death in 1820 the situation was very different. Monarchy and hereditary positions had been challenged extensively across the Western world during the previous forty-five years. The first major challenge had been mounted in Britain's North American colonies, with the American Revolution, which began in 1775 and led to the creation of a new state that was also the first republic to be established in the West since the short-lived interregnum experiment in England in 1649–60. By 1820, monarchy, or, at least, rule by established dynasties, had been overthrown across much of Western Europe, most spectacularly with the creation of the first French republic in 1792 and with the execution of the deposed Louis XVI the following year.

In place of hereditary rulers had come monarchs or presidents without any such claim, such as Jean Jacques Dessalines, the first emperor of Haiti (1804–6), Simón Bolívar, president of Gran Colombia (1819–30), both leaders of what became successful national liberation struggles, and, most threatening for Britain, Napoleon Bonaparte, first consul of France (1799–1804), and then its emperor (1804–14), the title an endorsement of monarchy but also a conscious rejection of traditional French kingship. Furthermore, the latter's relatives had been placed on existing thrones (his brother Joseph becoming king of Naples in 1806 and, in its place, king of Spain in 1808, whence he was driven with British assistance in 1813), or had new principalities created for them. Napoleon's stepson, Eugène de Beauharnais, became viceroy for the new king of Italy, who was none other than Napoleon. The Dutch made one of Napoleon's brothers, Louis, king in 1806, in order to avoid annexation to France; not that it prevented annexation in 1810. Another brother, Jérôme, became king of a new German state, Westphalia, in 1807, while Joachim Murat, who succeeded Joseph in Naples, had been made grand duke of Berg, a new German principality created in 1806. Napoleonic allies were also raised to kings, the Electors of Bavaria and Württemberg (George III's son-in-law) in 1805, and the Elector of Saxony in 1806. A Polish state was recreated by Napoleon as the grand duchy of Warsaw,

---

[2] H.H. Rowen, *The Princes of Orange: The Stadholders in the Dutch Republic* (Cambridge, 1988).

with the new king of Saxony becoming grand duke. Legitimate rulers resisting France, in turn, took shelter in Britain, where William V of Orange and Louis XVIII of France were followed, in 1810, by Gustavus IV of Sweden. Other such rulers took refuge in the shadow of British power, as with Ferdinand IV of Naples and III of Sicily, who adopted the style Ferdinand I of the Two Sicilies (Naples and Sicily), and, later, Dom João, the regent of Portugal who, in fleeing to Brazil in 1808, became the first European ruler to visit the Americas.

Alongside new rulers had come the destruction of old states, such as Poland (1795), Genoa (1797) and Venice (1797), and the creation of new ones, such as the Batavian, Helvetic and Ligurian Republics, although some of these were short-lived and, in turn, remoulded into new forms. The Holy Roman Empire and, with it, the established patterns of authority and power in modern Germany had come to an end, and the Habsburgs, in the person of Francis I (formerly the Holy Roman Emperor Francis II), had, instead, become emperors of Austria. The monarchical principle was clearly still important. Having rejected George III as an inadequate monarch and unsatisfactory father figure, the Americans created a new one in the very different form of President Washington. Scottish radicals could turn to an image of Robert the Bruce.[3] Soon after George III died, the popularity of the monarchical model was shown when Augustín de Itúrbide (a general) became emperor of Mexico and Pedro I (son of the king of Portugal) emperor of Brazil, but legitimacy, acceptability and stability proved far harder to secure, as Haiti, France (under both Napoleon and, from 1814, the restored Bourbons) and Mexico all showed.

The house of Hanover owed its royal throne to British exceptionalism, specifically to the overthrow of a native dynasty and the creation of a more limited government. The Glorious Revolution of 1688–9, focused on the expulsion of the Catholic James II (of England) and VII (of Scotland), and his replacement by William III (r. 1689–1702) and his wife Mary II (r. 1689–94), had been underlined by the Act of Settlement of 1701. In excluding Catholics from the succession, and placing it with the Hanoverians – descendants of James I (r. 1603–25) and VI through his daughter Elizabeth, the wife of Frederick V of the Palatinate – the Act designated a family whose dynastic claim was weak (and whose religion, though Protestant, was of the Lutheran variety): numerous Catholics had a better claim to Britain. In particular, the position of the Hanoverians was contested by the descendants of James II and VII through the male line: the 'warming pan baby', 'James III

<hr />

[3] G. Pentland, 'Patriotism, Universalism and the Scottish Conventions, 1792–1794', *History*, 89 (2004), p. 349.

and VIII', the Jacobite claimant from 1701 to 1766, and his two sons, 'Charles III' (Bonnie Prince Charlie), claimant from 1766 to 1788, and 'Henry IX', claimant from 1788 until his death in 1807. Hanoverian control was therefore challenged by the Jacobite supporters of this Stuart line. As a consequence, the legitimacy of Hanoverian rule, particularly as seen in Catholic Europe, was less than secure, and this encouraged rulers otherwise opposed to Britain, such as Louis XV of France in 1744 and 1759, to support the Stuarts.

This was scarcely a distant memory when George III came to the throne in 1760. His uncle, William, duke of Cumberland, who remained a major presence in politics until his early death in 1765, owed his fame to his command of the army that had defeated Charles Edward Stuart, Bonnie Prince Charlie, at Culloden in 1746, and his notoriety to the subsequent treatment of the defeated Jacobites. As recently as 1759 the French had tried to invade Britain, ostensibly on behalf of Charles's father, 'James III and VIII', only for their fleets to be crushed in battles off Lagos (in southern Portugal) and in Quiberon Bay.

Yet the Hanoverians were scarcely alone in having had to fight to secure their inheritance from rival claimants. The Tudors had done so at Bosworth in 1485, the French Bourbons had had to do so in the 1590s in the French Wars of Religion, the Spanish Bourbons in the 1700s in the War of the Spanish Succession, and the Habsburgs in the 1740s. Furthermore, if the struggle for the British succession proved a backdrop to George's reign, it faded out after 1759. The Jacobite claim rapidly became a curiosity, although one that had some arresting echoes, and George's sensitivity to Stuart legitimism and, even more, his successful attempt to reconcile the hitherto excluded Tories to the Hanoverian dynasty and his ardent support for the established Church in England greatly helped in alleviating surviving tensions about the position of the Hanoverians.

In place of British exceptionalism, comparisons with continental monarchies, and not contrasts, are more instructive. In Britain, as elsewhere, the calibre and interests of individual monarchs were unpredictable, while royal courts were the focus of political struggles which affected the aims, conduct and personnel of government. Across Europe, the importance of the attitude of individual rulers made it difficult to ensure continuity in policy between reigns, let alone to institutionalize change, and this represented a powerful element of discontinuity that encouraged those unhappy about patronage and policies to look forward to the accession of the heir to the throne: the reversionary interest. This was greatly to affect George I, George II and George III, and to help mould the politics of their reigns, although not with the drastic consequences seen in the case of Peter the Great of Russia (r. 1689–1725). Opposing Peter's Westernization policies, his son, Alexis, fled Russia; he was brought back, tried and killed in 1718. Seen as a test of Peter's powers of transforming Russia, Alexis's treatment was also a consequence of the failure of Peter's first marriage.[4]

The succession also became a major problem in Savoy–Piedmont, although in a different fashion, as Charles Emmanuel III in 1731 overcame an attempt by his father, Victor Amadeus II (1666–1732), to rescind his abdication of 1730. In August–September 1731, Victor Amadeus sought to regain the throne. Fearing that the situation might be exploited by foreign powers, the council persuaded Charles Emmanuel to order his father's arrest. Victor Amadeus was imprisoned at Rivoli until his death over a year later. An English edition of *History of the Abdication of Victor Amadeus II, late King of Sardinia*, a pamphlet on this episode by Count Alberto Radicati di Passerano, was published in 1732 and the entire episode revealed poor relations between king and heir: Victor Amadeus despised Charles Emmanuel, whom he treated with contempt and bullied. The clash was to be presented on the stage by Robert Browning in his play *King Victor and King Charles* (1842).[5]

The treatment of Alexis and of Victor Amadeus was very different to the position in Britain, but the Hanoverians, far from being distinctive, were in line with the rest of Europe in containing poor family relationships short of violence. Indeed, the treatment of British heirs was closer to the tension seen in the relationship between Maria Theresa and her son, the Emperor Joseph II,[6] than to the treatment of the future Frederick II of Prussia, first cousin of George II, by his father Frederick William I, which included imprisonment in response to Frederick's attempted flight. Like many eighteenth-century continental rulers, George III was driven to paroxysms of rage by the activities of his heir. In George's case, this related to, among other things, the future George IV's willingness to play a prominent role in supporting the parliamentary opposition to his father's ministers and his refusal to contain his expenditure.

Understandable, although, as so often with George III, also somewhat naïve, this rage helped prevent reasonable personal relations between the two men, let alone the development of a working relationship between monarch and heir; and also introduced an important note of instability to government, one that was recurrent from the 1780s. This instability was acute when George III seemed near death, but was also made more serious than other reversionary issues, such as the situation under George I in 1717–20 and under George II in 1736–51, because of the problematic nature of George III's mental health, which became a prominent issue in 1788. Even so, the governmental system in Britain was such that George's

[4] L. Hughes, *Peter the Great. A Biography* (New Haven, Connecticut, 2002).

[5] J.M. Black, '*King Victor and King Charles*: The Historical Background', *Browning Society Notes*, 14 (1984), pp. 39–47.

[6] D. Beales, *Joseph II, I: In the Shadow of Maria Theresa 1741–1780* (Cambridge, 1987).

health created a less serious problem than had that of Philip V of Spain (r. 1700–46). Apparently a manic depressive, whose acute mental instability led to a very peculiar daily routine, Philip shared with George III a commitment to the duties and obligations of his role, but Philip's more central role in government (as well as a court politics that included a very assertive wife) created more acute difficulties.[7] Politically, however, the existence of parliament in Britain ensured that the government could be put under political pressure over arrangements arising from the monarch's health. This was not the case in most states. In Portugal, Maria I (r. 1777–1816) was declared insane in 1792 and her son, Dom João, was appointed prince regent. The Portuguese cortes was in no position to debate the matter: it never met during the century.

Aside from reversionary interests, many European rulers were also inconsistent in their implementation of policies. A tension between the regularization of power, through the establishment and following of agreed administrative procedures, and the personal intervention of the monarch, was characteristic of the states of the period, and was also to arise under George. His position was particularly affected by the role of parliament and the exigencies of parliamentary monarchy, but, aside from that, there was the pressure from the process of government and from bureaucratic interests. For example, Thomas, duke of Newcastle, claimed in 1762 that George Grenville's insistence on limiting borrowing would force an end to British participation in the Seven Years War, 'but the doing of it in this way is the act of the Treasury and not of the King'.[8] In fact, George concurred in wanting to see borrowing limited, but Newcastle was correct to note the potential for disagreement.

The tension between administrative method and royal role also owed something to the extent to which in Britain, as elsewhere, the limited authority of government institutions in a political system where, first, court favour was crucial, second, power was not necessarily based upon tenure of office, and third, only the monarch could arbitrate effectively in disputes, forced rulers to act, and to be seen to act, fulfilling the goal for which they were brought up and educated. Also, a continued display of royal favour was important for the maintenance of the authority of ministers, institutions and edicts, and, if British politics appeared particularly unstable because of the role of parliament, then commentators found those of many other courts similarly, or even more, so due to the vagaries of royal favour.[9]

[7] H. Kamen, *Philip V of Spain* (New Haven, Connecticut, 2001).

[8] Newcastle to Hardwicke, 2 May 1762, BL. Add. 32938 fol. 20.

[9] For example, earl of Buckinghamshire, envoy in St Petersburg, to earl of Halifax, secretary of state, 17 June, 1 July 1763, PRO. SP. 91/72 fols 12, 28.

In Britain (and elsewhere), new ministers sought public shows of approval, such as the conferring of noble status on political allies or the appointment of supporters to posts in royal households, the latter requiring the dismissal of existing holders and therefore especially contentious. Rulers often disliked such pressure, as with George in 1806 when the Ministry of All the Talents insisted on changes. If George was seen as ready to confer honours, such as the Order of the Garter, a markedly conspicuous gesture, in order to support ministers,[10] that depended to a considerable extent on his view of them. In 1762, George's favourite, John, third earl of Bute, was given the Garter and was treated with little warmth by most of his resentful new companions,[11] while in 1786 William Grenville felt it noteworthy that the king had given Cornwallis, the general defeated at Yorktown but a favourite of the king, the Order of the Garter without the knowledge of his ministers.[12] The number of members of the order was fixed, and in 1786 there – crucially – was no Garter for John, third duke of Dorset, who had pressed William Pitt the Younger, the first minister, on the point, not least pointing out his significant political interest in Kent and Sussex.[13] Dorset had to wait until 1787.

Furthermore, whom George spoke to at court, and for how long, was noted carefully, so that only speaking a few words to Charles James Fox in 1785[14] was a good indication that George's opposition to Pitt over parliamentary reform would not extend, as some imagined, to ministerial change. There was marked concern if the king failed to speak to certain individuals. Thomas Conolly, an MP in the Dublin parliament, had to be reassured in 1792 that when George had passed him at the levee just after the regency crisis it was an accident. This was seen by the lord-lieutenant of Ireland as key to his support.[15] Anger with Danish treatment of his sister Caroline Matilda had led George to ignore the Danish envoy in 1772, a conspicuous breach of his practice of talking to everybody when he appeared in public at court.[16] Thomas Jefferson subsequently made much of what he claimed was his poor reception by George in 1786. The nature of chance meetings with the king could also seem of importance.[17]

[10] Marmora, Sardinian envoy, to Sardinian foreign minister, 17 Apr. 1764, AST. LM. Ing. 69; Lord John Cavendish to second marquess of Rockingham, 14 Apr. 1782, WW. R1–2047.

[11] Elizabeth Montagu to Bath, 27 May 1762, HL. MO. 4520.

[12] William Grenville to his brother, George Grenville, 24 June 1786, HL. STG Box 39(20).

[13] Dorset to Pitt, Pitt to Dorset, both 20 Oct., Dorset to Hawkesbury, 21 Oct. 1786, Maidstone KAO. Sackville papers, U269 C183, 182.

[14] Captain Gordon to Robert Murray Keith, 3 May 1785, BL. Add. 35534 fol. 131, cf. earl of Liverpool to earl of Chatham, 6 Apr. 1797, BL. Add. 38310 fol. 192.

[15] Lord-lieutenant to Dundas, 29 Aug. 1792, Aspinall, *George III*, I, 613.

[16] Diede reports, 14, 17 Apr. 1772, Rigs. 1953.

[17] Admiral Keppel to Rockingham, 11 July 1780, WW. R1–1908.

More seriously, across Europe many ministers fell, as Tanucci did in Naples in 1776, and Pombal in Portugal the following year, because they failed at court, losing, or never having, the support of the monarch or his relatives. Britain was not outside this process, as the fall of George Grenville in 1765, Charles, marquess of Rockingham in 1766, the Fox–North coalition in 1783, and the Ministry of All the Talents in 1807, indicated clearly. As another demonstration of their political importance, the role of monarchs created serious problems when they were ill, as George conspicuously was in 1788–9. The role of the king as an individual also attracted attack, literally so in the unsuccessful assassination attempts on Louis XV in 1757,[18] Joseph I of Portugal in 1759 and George himself in 1786 and 1800, and with the killing of Peter III of Russia in 1762, Gustavus III of Sweden in 1792 and Paul I of Russia in 1801.

Rather than Britain being unusual in having a weak monarchy, even when rulers were in control of their courts and ministries, the institutions and personnel of central government frequently proved unresponsive to their demands, particularly if these entailed change. On the continent, royal dissatisfaction with the operation of central government was responsible for a number of fundamental reorganizations, such as those carried out by Peter the Great in Russia and by Frederick William I (r. 1713–40) in Prussia. The process of reform became normative in the second half of the century, during the age of those later termed the 'Enlightened Despots', such as Frederick II, the Great, of Prussia (r. 1740–86), Charles III of Spain (r. 1759–88), Catherine II, the Great, of Russia (r. 1762–96), Gustavus III of Sweden (r. 1771–92), Joseph II of Austria (r. 1780–90), Leopold of Tuscany (r. 1765–90), later Leopold II of Austria (r. 1790–2), and other less prominent rulers. After about 1750, European monarchs were more prepared to risk abandoning traditional norms, a shift due to a different ideology, and also a response to the need to improve governmental capability after the War of the Austrian Succession (1740–8) and the Seven Years War (1756–63).[19]

George, who granted a pension to both Rousseau and Hume and was greatly interested in applied knowledge, can be approached in this context.[20] He shared an interest in good government, but was far less willing than the 'Enlightened Despots' to consider changes that infringed property rights and challenged established practices. George's respect for privilege and precedent was a response to the nature of government, law

---

[18] D.K. Van Kley, *The Damiens Affair and the Unraveling of the 'Ancien Régime' 1750–1770* (Princeton, New Jersey, 1984).

[19] H.M. Scott (ed.), *Enlightened Absolutism: Reform and Reformers in Later Eighteenth-Century Europe* (London, 1990).

[20] D. Watkin, 'George III: Enlightened Monarch?', in J. Marsden (ed.), *The Wisdom of George the Third* (London, 2005), pp. 331–46.

and public culture in Britain, but also a product of his own views on society and the role of the monarch. George was also far less able or willing than his continental counterparts to consider changes. He would scarcely have sent a Press Act to Voltaire, the leading fashionable French intellectual, as Gustavus III did; nor would he have welcomed the latter's praise. In assessing George in this context, we should note the synergy between his understanding of the system and his own views. George did not really try to test greatly the parameters of the position he inherited, which was just as well, because the attempts he did make, and the suggestions that he would do more, created widespread political distrust in Britain and America. George would scarcely have admired Joseph II for greatly increasing the number of governmental decrees issued,[21] and he criticized Gustavus III's reach for power by overthrowing the Swedish constitution in 1772.

It is important, however, not to exaggerate the extent to which all continental monarchs sought to transform government, nor to fall for the fallacy that change equalled reform, and that monarchs, such as George, who failed to introduce major administrative changes were unimpressive, or indeed deserve castigation. There were good political reasons for doubting the feasibility of change, and sound administrative explanations for querying the possibility of improvement. George voiced these in 1791 when told by the French envoy that it was appropriate for the Revolutionary government to abolish feudal rights in Alsace, as 'for the sake of public utility, governments should seek administrative uniformity. The king of England argued that such uniformity could exist only in small states, and that in kingdoms as big as France any attempt to introduce it would create problems.'[22] George's reply was at once a prudent response to idealistic quests for order, a personal distaste for new-modelling systems, and the conviction of a second-rank German ruler operating within the imperial constitution that the rights of his counterparts should not be infringed by more powerful monarchs.

The absence of substantial crown-driven governmental changes under George was not unique; it was matched elsewhere, for example in *ancien régime* France during the 1760s. An important comparison between Britain and France has recently been discerned by Edmond Dziembowski, who sees rivalry between the crown and aristocratic opposition as the key element of convergence in the politics of both states,[23] a contrast, indeed, with the *anglomanie* expressed by many contemporary French progressive

---

[21] P.G.M. Dickson, 'Monarchy and Bureaucracy in Late Eighteenth-Century Austria', *English Historical Review* (1995), pp. 351–4.

[22] AE. CP. Ang. 579 fol. 314.

[23] E. Dziembowski, 'Pitt l'Ancien, la politique britannique et l'espace franco-britannique au XVIIIe siècle' (Dossier d'habilitation, Paris IV, 2005).

commentators.[24] Parallels between Britain and continental states were asserted in the British press, especially by opposition writers keen to argue that national distinctiveness and liberties had been overthrown, as a consequence of corrupting tendencies within British society and/or because of the dangerous, indeed autocratic, tendencies of the government. Looking at British politics through the prism of alleged ministerial corruption made Britain seem similar to continental states. This provided a context for criticism of George. A London item in the *Bristol Gazette and Public Advertiser* of 12 September 1771 claimed that,

> in both [France and Britain] their Parliaments have been essentially suppressed, the one by force, the other by fraud; in both their princes do not rely on the affections of their subjects, but on large standing armies; in both the king's will and pleasure is the only law; in both the just and constitutional rights and liberties of the people have been infringed and trampled upon; in both there have been frequent remonstrances to their kings, which have been totally disregarded; and in both there is such a general ferment and discontent, they may probably bring on a confusion, and end in a change of their present forms of conduct.

Burke indeed argued that the willingness of the government to support the payment of Civil List debts gave the crown 'such an income as is possessed by every absolute monarch in Europe'.[25] Furthermore, despite criticism, and, although the close partnership between crown and landed élite in government service seen in Prussia was not matched in Britain, there was a high degree of widespread consensus within the British élite, as on the continent, on the nature of society.

Alongside comparisons, however, came contrasts, with George being pleased in 1770 that the British government treated its creditors fairly, while, due to a partial bankruptcy, that of France deceived theirs.[26] Returning from France in 1763, the barrister Alexander Forrester compared Britain with France, arguing that monarch and ministers were unpopular in both, and contrasted them with Prussia where, he suggested, 'the reformation of abuses' had made progress.[27] Thus, in some cases, the process of comparison made Britain seem like certain continental states,

---

[24] L.S. Mercier, *Parallèle de Paris et de Londres*, edited by C. Bruneteau and B. Cottret (Paris, 1982). There are interesting contrasts in T.C.W. Blanning, *The Culture of Power and the Power of Culture: Old Regime Europe 1660–1789* (Oxford, 2002).

[25] E. Burke, *Thoughts on the Causes of the Present Discontents* in *The Works of . . . Edmund Burke* (8 vols, London, 1871), I, 364.

[26] George to North, 20 Apr. 1770, Fortescue, II, 141.

[27] Forrester to Andrew Mitchell, 12 Sept. 1763, BL. Add. 30999 fol. 17.

but dissimilar to others. This is certainly true if attention is shifted to the competence and personality of monarchs.

To contemporaries greeting the new king in 1760, the main comparison was with his predecessor, and to this we must turn. George III's reputation rests in part on the perception of that of George II, and an understanding of that, in turn, depends on an appreciation of the nature of the political system. This was a parliamentary monarchy, with annual sessions of parliament, in which contrary interests and opinions had to be reconciled within a system where there was no single source of dominant power. The Revolution Settlement that followed the Glorious Revolution of 1688–9 created the constitutional basis for an effective parliamentary monarchy, with parliamentary control over the finances of the state, while the prohibition of a standing army, unless permitted by parliament, and the insistence on regular elections challenged the ability of the executive to dominate parliament. The division of financial responsibility was particularly important, because, under the Civil List Act of 1698, parliament was responsible for the key expenditure: army, navy and national debt; while the crown was granted for life Civil List revenues designed to cover the costs both of the royal establishments (including those of all the royal family) and of the civil government.

The instability of successive ministries nevertheless suggested that the political environment within which a parliamentary monarchy could be effective had not been created. In the 1760s, this could be attributed in part to the mistakes made by George III, but that underplays both the role of contentious issues during his reign and the extent to which ministries had earlier been unstable: in the 1690s, 1700s, 1710s, and as recently as 1754–7. Looked at differently, the British system worked better than the system of powerful parliamentary government created in Sweden in 1719 and suppressed in 1772.[28] Governmental difficulties in Britain in part reflected the workings of a political system in which there was an absence of autocratic control. Instead there was a division of power and responsibility, as well as a degree of popular participation in politics, and a system in which opposition was permitted. George III was unsympathetic, however, to the view that contention was an inherent characteristic of British politics and government and he had scant sympathy for opposition and limited tolerance of the expression of opposition sentiments.

The Whig myth about George III presented him as an innovator who overthrew the constitutional monarchy established after the Glorious Revolution and the stable world of 'Old Corps' Whig politics. This presentation of George III condemned his policies by a portrayal of those of the reign of George II that left scant role for the views and actions of the

[28] M. Roberts, *The Age of Liberty: Sweden 1719–1772* (Cambridge, 1986).

latter. This view remained influential during the nineteenth century, and was encouraged by the waspish remarks made about George II and his abilities, and the minimizing of his influence, by two contemporaries who were adept at putting the pen in, Horace Walpole and John, Lord Hervey. Walpole's account was first published, as *Memoires of the Last Ten Years of the Reign of George the Second*, in 1822, and Hervey's *Some Materials towards Memoirs of the Reign of King George II* in 1848. These were to be the most influential of contemporary comments, Walpole's being published in new editions in 1846, 1847 (a very slightly revised reprinting) and 1985, Hervey's in 1884 and 1931.

The focus on ministers, not monarch, in the treatment of the reign of George II, a contrast to the coverage of that of George III, continued in the twentieth century. Biographies of the king appeared, but they were based on secondary or printed primary material, with some, but few, additions from manuscript sources. Reginald Lucas's *George II and his Ministers* (1910) was followed by John Davies's *George II. A King in Toils* (1938), and then by Charles Chevenix Trench's *George II* (1973), which presented George as personally vicious – 'abominable temper, parsimony amounting to avarice, vanity and a somewhat unseemly sexual promiscuity', but a good judge of men who 'really understood the limitations on a constitutional monarch'.[29] J.H. Plumb left George II in the shadow of Sir Robert Walpole, not only in his incomplete biography of Walpole, but also in his unsatisfactory portrayal of the king in *The First Four Georges* (1956), and, when the latter was republished in 2000, no effort was made to update it to take note of subsequent work, either for George II or for George III. From this misleading perspective on George II, his grandson appeared as an innovator, and therefore as responsible for the political crises of the period, the Whig view.

At the scholarly level, the major advance after World War II was by J.B. Owen who, in 1973, suggested that George II was far from being an ineffectual monarch. Owen concluded, 'Within the context of eighteenth-century conventions George II managed to get his own way more often than has generally been recognised. Frequently, and often with impunity, he ignored or overrode the advice of his ministers; his was the dominant voice in the conduct of war and diplomacy.'[30] This approach, based essentially on Owen's work on the 1740s, did not, however, lead him to a more major study, and this contrasted with the biography of George III by John Brooke. Owen's argument, nevertheless, was amplified, drawing largely on

[29] C.C. Trench, *George II* (London, 1973), pp. 298–9.
[30] J.B. Owen, 'George II Reconsidered', in A. Whiteman, J.S. Bromley and P.G.M. Dickson (eds), *Statesmen, Scholars and Merchants. Essays in Eighteenth Century History presented to Dame Lucy Sutherland* (Oxford, 1973), pp. 113–34, quote, p. 129. See also J.B. Owen, *The Rise of the Pelhams* (London, 1957).

diplomatic material, in a 1981 article by J.M. Black on the period 1727–35.[31]
Over the last two decades, the coverage of George II has not been extensive, and this despite the favourable response enjoyed by Ragnhild
Hatton's biography of George I, published in 1978. Doctoral theses on
court culture, a fashionable subject in the 1990s and early 2000s, made the
most important contribution.[32] Most important was the publication of
work in German that threw considerable light on George as Elector of
Hanover and added to knowledge of him as king.[33]

In contrast to the situation of George III, there is still very little work on
his predecessor, George II, nor on George III's father, Frederick, prince of
Wales, not least compared to the wealth of publications on George II's
ministers, especially Sir Robert Walpole, Thomas, duke of Newcastle, and
William Pitt the Elder, the last two of whom were to play a significant role
in George III's early years. George II left no major series of correspondence, certainly nothing comparable to the correspondence of his
grandson, George III, but, as Hatton showed in the case of George I, this
is no reason not to produce a scholarly biography. Although the Royal
Archives contain relatively little material, and far less for George II than
for his second son, William, duke of Cumberland, and, ironically, for
George's rival, 'James III and VIII', three types of source stand out for
study. First, there is the type that, of the three, has been most extensively
scrutinized, although never in a systematic fashion and less so than for the
reign of George III: the papers of British politicians. Second, due weight
must be given to material relating to the kings as electors, and third, it is
necessary to understand the extent to which foreign diplomatic archives
provide a mass of information on the royal court.

Diplomats were accredited to the court, not the ministry; they had high-
level access to it, and they took special care to report in detail on the court
as well as on the royal speeches to parliament.[34] Their frequent conversations with the monarch ensure that their reports provide a way to study his

[31] J.M. Black, 'George II Reconsidered. A Consideration of George's Influence in the
Conduct of Foreign Policy, in the First Years of his Reign', *Mitteilungen des Österreichischen
Staatsarchivs*, 35 (1982), pp. 35–56, and '"George II and All That Stuff": On the Value of
the Neglected', *Albion*, 36 (2005), pp. 581–607.

[32] David Flaten, 'King George II and the Politicians: The Struggle for Political Power'
(Ph.D., Fordham, 1999); H. Smith, 'Georgian Monarchical Culture in England, 1714–60'
(Ph.D., Cambridge, 2001); M. Kilburn, 'Royalty and Public in Britain, 1714–1789' (D.Phil.,
Oxford, 1997).

[33] Uriel Dann's *Hannover und England 1740–1760. Diplomatie und Selbstbehauptung* (Hildesheim,
1986) was translated and slightly revised as *Hanover and Great Britain 1740–1760* (Leicester,
1991), but other important work was not translated, particularly Uta Richter-Uhlig's *Hof
und Politik unter den Bedingungen der Personalunion. Die Aufenthalte Georgs II in Hannover zwischen
1729 und 1741* (Hanover, 1992) and Mijndert Bertram's *Georg II. König und Kurfürst* (Göttingen,
2003).

[34] E.g. report of 18 Dec. 1787, AST. LM. Ing. 88.

views. So far, there has been no systematic study of these reports or, in particular, of the information they offer for an assessment of George II and British politics; nor, indeed, for George III, who spoke at length to envoys, sometimes without the presence of his own ministers, and who was ready to raise domestic politics with these diplomats,[35] as well as to press for the recall of those he thought hostile.[36] George Canning was in error in 1825 when he claimed that George III never had private communications with foreign envoys,[37] although there was certainly no equivalent to Louis XV's *secret du roi*, his extensive private foreign policy.

In turn, British diplomats, like many other officials, regarded themselves 'as the immediate servant of the King'. Hugh Elliot, envoy in Copenhagen, glossed this remark in 1784 by adding that he was 'bound to fulfil, to the utmost of my ability, whatever instructions may be conveyed to me through the ministers His Majesty may be pleased to appoint'.[38] This correct interpretation of the processes of government placed the emphasis on the relationship between monarch and ministers, and helps explain why, repeatedly, that was a key issue during George III's reign.

George II's views were controversial as far as contemporaries were concerned, but the source of the controversy was different to the position under his successor. The Whig myth about George III presented him as an innovator whose breach with the conventions of Hanoverian parliamentary monarchy caused a permanent crisis. This account, however, underplays greatly the tensions within government during the reigns of George I and George II stemming from the related issues of foreign policy and the Hanoverian connection. Ironically, these tensions were to be of major importance to the North American colonies, for the opposition critique directed against George I and George II was to be employed by American Patriots against George III. The critique of George I and George II separated them from the office of the crown, a separation based largely on the idea that national (British) interests had been betrayed for the sake of their views as Electors of Hanover, and thus on a treatment of them as alien. The application of the critique to George III, however, was paradoxical, as he never went to Hanover, was not generally associated with its interests, particularly in the 1760s and 1770s, and, at his accession, had consciously presented himself as a Patriot in reaction against the Hanoverian reputation of his grandfather, George II. Nevertheless, once

---

[35] For example, Nivernais to Praslin, 11 May, D'Eon to Praslin, 20 July, Guerchy to Praslin, 21 Oct., 12, 19 Nov. 1763, AE. CP. Ang. 450 fols 337, 497, 451, 452 fols 128–9, 194; Viry to Charles Emmanuel III, 31 May 1763, AST. LM. Ing. 68.

[36] Francis, marquess of Carmarthen, foreign secretary, to Sir James Harris, envoy in The Hague, 1 Feb. 1788, BL. Eg. 3500 fol. 52.

[37] A.G. Stapleton, *George Canning and His Times* (London, 1859), p. 433.

[38] Elliot to Carmarthen, 24 Aug. 1784, PRO. FO. 22/6 fol. 205.

the concept of George III as a Patriot king had fallen victim to differences over policy, American separatism could draw on the anti-Hanoverian critique of the two previous reigns. British critics of George III did not have this recourse, and had to develop a different critique.

That George II, like his successor, sought to foster the interests of the Electorate of Hanover would not have seemed wrong to him. As Electors, they had responsibilities to their subjects, and the greater authority of Elector, compared to king, brought more responsibilities, while a sense of urgency was lent by the vulnerability of Hanover to attack. Unlike George III, George II knew the Electorate well. He had been born and brought up there (as Frederick, prince of Wales, was also to be) and, although he had not been allowed to visit it during the reign of his father, he made frequent visits once he had succeeded him: in 1729, 1732, 1735, 1736, 1740, 1741, 1743, 1745, 1748, 1750, 1752 and 1755; each trip lasting several months. As George II had his heir, Frederick, move to Britain in 1728 (he never returned to Hanover), while George II's uncle, Ernst-August, prince-bishop of neighbouring Osnabrück, the other representative of the Electoral house remaining in Germany when George I left for Britain, died the same year, the presence of the Electoral family depended on George II's visits. The situation was to be different under George III. He did not visit the Electorate, but his second son, Frederick, duke of York, spent part of the reign as prince-bishop in Osnabrück; this recourse to personal representation by a cadet prince was an expedient that was not possible until 1781 when Frederick had attained his majority.

Repeated trips to Hanover, and the severe and repeated criticism they aroused in Britain, did not dull George II's pleasure in these visits, although they clearly influenced Prince George's views in the 1750s. George II would have gone more often had he been able, and this, rather than ministerial relations, provided the context within which George III can be seen as particularly different. Indeed, in 1752, Giovanni Zamboni, a long-standing diplomatic agent in London, reported that it was widely believed that George II would spend the remainder of his life in Hanover.[39] Aside from his sense of duty as Elector, and the obligation that stemmed from it, in Hanover George II was able to pursue his hobbies of hunting and reviewing troops, and did so until his final visit. George III never associated his hobbies, such as hunting, astronomy and farming, with such personal visits to Hanover, although in each there were links with the region.

Similarly, although the reign of William III from 1689 to 1702 had already led to concern about diplomatic relations with the United

[39] Zamboni to Count Kaunitz, 31 Mar. 1752, HHStA., England, Varia 10.

Provinces, the accession of the house of Hanover in 1714 had brought the issue of relations with a foreign dominion to the fore. This issue played a prominent part in politics until, during the Seven Years War, the crisis of Hanoverian neutrality was finessed in 1758 into a British military commitment to Prussia that was generally acceptable because it involved fighting the French in Germany. George III's distancing himself from his grandfather's Hanoverian commitments, a continuation of his attitude as heir during the Seven Years War, however, ensured that, when the alliance with Prussia collapsed in 1762, the relationship with the Electorate did not come to the fore again. The role of Hanoverian commitments was far less under George III, George IV and William IV than it had been under George I and George II; and they were certainly less controversial than under the first two Georges. Useful revisionist work has underlined the interest that these monarchs still showed, especially George III in the 1780s, but the Electorate did not play as large a role as it had under George I and George II. Furthermore, its comparative importance has to be handled with care. For George III, relations with the Thirteen Colonies mattered more than those with Hanover in the first quarter-century of his reign, while, as later for George IV, Ireland and the related issue of Catholic emancipation became more prominent from the late 1790s.

The Hanoverian link was not so dominant that it is inappropriate when studying George III to look for continuities across dynastic divides in order to provide a context within which to study him. The continuities are apparent at both ends of the period. In many respects, George I and George II looked back to William III, an iconic figure, a key statesman in Protestant Europe, and a ruler who had also sought to balance British and continental commitments. The healths drunk during the corporation's entertainment at Penzance town hall in 1735 for the anniversary of George II's accession included the 'Glorious and Immortal Memory of King William'.[40]

If continuity can be seen across the 1714 divide, William IV in many respects should also be seen, alongside Victoria (r. 1837–1901), as a monarch who adapted to new domestic political circumstances while helping the monarchy to recover from the nadir of reputation it had reached under George IV. Such an emphasis on continuity at each end of the period of Hanoverian rule in Britain encourages a search for discontinuity during the course of the dynasty, and there the most apparent occurred in 1760, drawing attention to George III. Speaking with a German accent, George II was both the last of the dynasty to be born in Germany, and the last of the monarchs to be born in the seventeenth century. He ended a cosmopolitan period that, with the exception of the

---

[40] *St. James's Evening Post*, 19 June (OS) 1735.

self-consciously English Anne (r. 1702–14), had begun with Charles II and
James II (of England) and VII (of Scotland), both of whom had spent
many of their formative years in foreign exile, as well as being uncles to
William III and first cousins once removed to George I. Although dynastic
concerns remained important, George III, in contrast, began a period of
English-dominated British monarchy, with Hanover as an appendage, if a
significant one.

Signs of a shift towards the characteristic features of the post-1760
period were already apparent with the conscious espousal of British
Patriotism in opposition to George II, by Frederick, prince of Wales, from
the mid-1730s, and, after his death in 1751, by his son, the future George
III. In 1737, George Lyttelton, an opposition Whig MP, who became secretary to Frederick that year, wrote that the latter would endeavour to
deserve the good opinion of Patriots: 'Indeed his doing so is the last
response of this poor country, and God knows whether all his good intentions may not come too late to save us from destruction: For virtue without
power is as useless as power without virtue is hurtful to us.'[41] As prince of
Wales, the future George III shared these sentiments. George II, in
contrast, continued in his later years to keep earlier commitments and had
little interest in appealing to the constituency that prided itself on British
Patriotism. This gave George III an opportunity to find his own political
niche when he came to the throne.

If continuities are to be sought in the 1660–1760 period, there was a
major political shift in 1688–9, with the removal of James II and VII, and
the real and symbolic limitation of royal power and authority represented
by the Glorious Revolution. All subsequent monarchs had to respond to
this, and it helps explain George III's emphasis, when opposing Catholic
emancipation in the 1800s, on his responsibilities under his coronation
oath. Aside from that, the character and legacy of the Glorious Revolution
were extensively debated during his reign, as it provided a basis for
asserting dynastic, constitutional and political legitimacy (in so far as they
were separable), and for establishing proper governmental practice. The
Glorious Revolution indeed continued as a leading leitmotif of politics in
the reign of George III. It was central to the notion of British uniqueness
and underpinned both the praise of a system encompassing the king and,
conversely, the suggestion that government had subverted the constitution.
The centenary of the Glorious Revolution in 1788 was to see particularly
important discussion,[42] which soon after served as a basis for debate about
the respective merits of French and British political developments. In its
aftermath, the Protestant character of the Glorious Revolution, and of the

[41] Lyttelton to Sarah, duchess of Marlborough, [– Aug. 1737], BL. Add. 61467 fol. 9.
[42] R.B. Sher, '1688 and 1788: William Robertson on Revolution in Britain and France', in
P. Dukes and J. Dunkley (eds), *Culture and Revolution* (London, 1990), pp. 98–109.

subsequent Revolution Settlement under which the house of Hanover had come to the throne, was a valuable guide for George, especially concerning the need to maintain the legal position of the established Protestant churches, in particular in the face of demands for Catholic emancipation.

As far as specific political arrangements were concerned, the process of responding to the Glorious Revolution had largely been completed before 1714, but it was reopened then, both by the accession of a new monarch, and by the need to define, and adjust to, new political issues, particularly the Hanoverian commitment under George I and George II, and imperial issues under George III. Both of these take on significance not only in the history of British foreign policy, but also as a key aspect of the development of British constitutional practice and the politics and perception of the British monarchy. The union of Hanover and Britain was to last five reigns, 123 years, and to be dissolved only because of the lack of direct male descent. There was no reason to believe that it would not be a permanent link, and contemporary views on the implications of multiple states were suffused with a sense of concern about the threat they posed to liberty, an issue that was to be raised, in a different fashion, by the American Patriots under George III. There was also the related danger of neglect, as royal attention was focused on one part of the inheritance. That the kings had responsibilities as Electors of Hanover did not mean that their espousal of Hanoverian interests was free from criticism within the Electorate (and the same was to be fatally true of George III's policies for North America). In particular, the territorial expansionism they pursued as Electors, and the power politics they were involved in as kings, as well as the implications for Hanover of the link to Britain, led to disquiet among the Hanoverian ministers,[43] and were part of a more general tension between Elector and ministers that matched those of crown and ministers, and that was neglected by British commentators. In this context, the abandonment, on George III's accession, of his grandfather's commitment to Hanoverian expansion had an impact on the ruler's political position both in Britain and in Hanover, and helped to define the politics of the reign and the perception of the monarch.

Critics of George III in Britain tended to forget that, far from simply following the lead of his ministers or being manipulated by them, George II had sought to use his position as king to further his interests, as well as his notion of monarchy. He offered an especially bold prospectus after he came to the throne in 1727, prefiguring aspects of the situation after George III became king. For example, the new instructions to John, Lord Carteret, then lord-lieutenant of Ireland, included the following:

[43] Dann, *Hannover und England.*

Whereas we have thought fit to retain to ourselves the power of granting commissions to any officer in our army, or to any governor or other officer of any of our forts and castles in that our kingdom of Ireland, and to reserve the same to our own disposal; and it being also our intention to sign for the future with our own hand, all commissions for such offices or employments when any of them shall become vacant.[44]

As with his successor, George II's actions and attitudes could lead to clashes with ministers, and, under this head, in using his position George both took advantage of the situation and also had to make concessions. The latter tend to be most prominent in the record, with the king parting with favoured ministers – Townshend in 1730, Walpole in 1742 and Carteret in 1744 – as well as being unable to sustain Carteret's return to power in 1746, and failing to thwart Pitt the Elder's rise to high office in 1756 and his retention of it in 1757. These failures appear to prefigure those of George III in the 1760s, with some of the same politicians in attendance, notably Newcastle, Pitt and Carteret, now Granville, but also serve to underline opposition criticisms that George III was acting in a novel fashion in 1762–3 by making an inexperienced favourite, John, third earl of Bute, leading minister, rather than supporting a prominent politician in this role. From this perspective, George II had understood the lessons of parliamentary management, particularly by keeping Walpole in office as first lord of the treasury in 1727 rather than replacing him with his favourite, Spencer Compton, later first earl of Wilmington, as he had initially considered doing. Furthermore, if he tried to create a ministry round Bath (formerly William Pulteney) and Carteret in 1746 at least they were very experienced politicians, unlike Bute. Indeed George III could be presented as failing to follow the model of parliamentary management when he undermined Pitt and Newcastle, the two major ministers at his accession, and gave his confidence to Bute.

This, however, is a less than fair criticism, because neither Pitt nor Newcastle was really determined on the peace and economy that George III justifiably sought, and because the comparison is unjust. In 1744 and 1746, George II had sought to entrust power to Carteret, despite the latter's parliamentary weakness. He failed. Alongside concerns about George II's intentions then, and on other occasions, there were also suggestions, which also influenced the future George III, that the king was too weak and his ministers too strong, although in fact these suggestions have to be seen in terms of *ad hoc* political tensions. Although they did not support Carteret in the mid-1740s, opposition Whigs, both then and

[44] Carteret's instructions, tenth article, PRO. SP. 63/389 fol. 72.

earlier, were apt to argue that George II was the victim of his 'Old Corps' ministers, especially Walpole and the Pelhams (Newcastle and his brother, Henry Pelham). A pessimistic Sarah, duchess of Marlborough, reflected in 1737, 'I don't wonder at anything that the King or Queen does, because they know nothing of the truth', expressing her bleak view of how Walpole was running and ruining Britain.[45] These arguments were to be influential in the political milieu within which the future George III formed his views.

George II's responses to failure – sometimes choleric in the short term, as with the defeat of the Excise Scheme in 1733, and often ruefully accepting in the longer one – define and reflect his status as a constitutional ruler of a limited monarchy, and help explain why foreign commentators stressed the limits of royal authority. For example, there was a major contrast between the position of George II (and later George III), and that of, say, Britain's ally John V of Portugal (r. 1706–50). James, second Lord Tyrawly, the experienced British envoy in Lisbon, reported that 'it is very difficult to penetrate anything here, for one may say, that the King of Portugal is both King and Council, for he advises with nobody, or if he does, he does not regard their advice, and if he should really take any other turn than what we wish, he is capable to resolve to send a minister to France one hour, and send him away the next'.[46] George II and George III could not emulate John, and did not seek to do so, and this was a significant continuity between the reigns. Alongside talk of comparisons, commentators made much of what they claimed were contrasts between British and foreign monarchy.[47]

This made for difficulties for British monarchs. Royal anger and a concern with authority were combined in 1752 when George, then in Hanover, lambasted Newcastle, who had accompanied him, on an espionage matter and about the acquittal in London of a printer, about which the king 'said, he had read, set out in the newspapers: he run into one of the usual, but strongest declamations against our laws, that punished nobody; against our informations from the intercepted letters, which told us nothing, for without *His we* [sic] should know nothing', the 'his' being a reference to interceptions of post going through the Electorate. George III also saw material that came from intercepts,[48] as well as important

[45] Sarah Marlborough to John, second earl of Stair, 6 June (OS) 1737, Beinecke, Osborn Shelves, Stair Letters, no. 6.

[46] Tyrawly to Newcastle, 19 May 1735, PRO. SP. 89/38 fol. 32.

[47] *Old England*, 29 Aug. 1752.

[48] George to Rockingham, [– Apr. 1766], WW. R1–605; Vorontsov, Russian minister, to Vorontsov, Russian envoy in London, 1 Dec. 1787, endorsed 'read by the King', CUL. Add. 6958 no. 433; George to William Grenville, 3 Dec. 1792, BL. Add. 58857 fol. 71.

dispatches from British envoys.[49] Newcastle commented on George II's concern about

> this spirit in the juries and the City [of London] which the King had flattered himself was almost entirely spent, and at an end; and indeed there were great appearances of it. From thence His Majesty fears that quiet which he thought himself sure of, is not so certain, and that he may still be more obliged to follow the advice of his ministers, than he had of late thought himself.

George II, in contrast, was 'extremely well satisfied' with the 'strong direction' of the lord chief justice in the case.[50] George III's attitude to metropolitan independence was not too different.

In considering George III, it would be mistaken to ignore the extent to which, although George II did not initiate domestic policies,[51] he did often get his way in the choice of ministers, and, even more, over army patronage and peerage creations, issues that greatly interested him. Although George II largely left ecclesiastical patronage to his ministers, he expected to play a role, while he also had views on religious topics. One indication was his generosity to foreign Protestants. Comparisons between George III and other monarchs will be considered later in the book, but already it is clear that the simplicities of the Whig myth have to be put to one side. George II was no cipher, and there was tension during his reign over the extent of royal authority. Indeed, in 1761, George Dodington, now Lord Melcombe, an experienced politician who had been close to George's father, Frederick, offered such a perspective on the criticism of George III at the time of Pitt's resignation: 'The insolence of the City [London] is intolerable: they must, and they easily may be taught better manners. I was bred a Monarchy man and will die so, and do not understand, that men of that rank are to demand the reasons of measures while they are under His Majesty's consideration.'[52] The ambiguities of constitutional and political arrangements were to provide a troublesome background to George III's reign and frequently to be an issue during it, interacting with the impact of his political apprenticeship discussed in the previous chapter.

[49] George Grenville to Bute, 29 July 1762, MS, papers from Cardiff Public Library, 3/30.
[50] Newcastle to Henry Pelham, 26 July, Newcastle to Hardwicke, 26 July 1752, BL. Add. 35412 fols 209, 184.
[51] P.D.G. Thomas, *George III. King and Politicians 1760–1770* (Manchester, 2002), p. 2.
[52] Melcombe to Bute, 8 Oct. 1761, MS.

Chapter 4

FIRST YEARS AS KING, 1760–3

Parties are now abolished, and the King is King of his united and unanimous people, and enjoys their confidence and love to such a degree, that were I not as fully convinced as I am of his Majesty's heart, and the moderation of his will, I should tremble for the liberties of my country.
Philip, fourth earl of Chesterfield, April 1761[1]

While straining on his close-stool, George II died suddenly soon after 7 a.m. on 25 October 1760. George III benefited at once from the widespread sense of the bright promise of a new, young and vigorous king. Indeed he was riding when he received the news of his grandfather's death. As he recorded: 'The Prince of Wales was riding at a little after eight between Kew bridge and the Sixth Milestone when a messenger stopped Mr. Breton and told him an accident had happened to the King. On communicating it to the Prince he returned to Kew, ordered his attendants to be silent and pretended his horse was lame.' The messenger brought a note from George II's valet about his accident; as yet, it was not known that George II had died. Once returned to Kew, the prince received a letter from his aunt, Princess Amelia, to report that George II was dead.

It was a good moment to become king. There was little sense of sorrow at George II's passing and, instead, an optimism that owed much to the news of a successful climax of the war in North America. The advance on Montreal had been launched in July 1760 and the greatly outnumbered French surrendered there on 8 September. Three days later, the fort at Trois-Rivières also surrendered. New France had fallen, the harbinger of an eventual peace that would see Britain's sway more extensive than ever before. Bute was subsequently to tell the Lords that 'His Majesty ascended the throne in conquest and in glory.'[2]

From the outset, George accentuated the promise of a new reign by clearly aspiring to put on the mantle of Patriotism, although his personal will was also evident. When Pitt called on George at Kew on 25 October

---

[1] Chesterfield to Bute, 9 Apr. 1761, MS, papers from Cardiff Public Library, 6/82.
[2] House of Lords, 5 Feb. 1762, account of proceedings by Sir James Caldwell, PRO. 30/8/70/5.

and 'told His Majesty that there were some matters of form immediately
necessary on this solemn occasion, the King replied that he would come
and give his own orders'.[3] This was made evident at the Privy Council held
that evening; Henry Fox commented: 'that the ministers knew nothing was
plain from their behaviour which was just that of other standers by. It was
plain too from the Declaration which had not been shown them till they
came to Carlton House, not subjected to their consideration, nor without
difficulty altered the next day.'[4]

Whatever the position for the ministers, there was no doubt of the optimism that surrounded the accession of the new young king, who was
proclaimed in London on 26 October. The duchess of Northumberland
described him as tall, robust, graceful, 'fair and fresh coloured . . . his eyes
. . . blue, his teeth extremely fine. His hair a light auburn'.[5] Loyal addresses
came in from across the British world: from Britain, her colonies, and
merchant communities abroad.[6] The new king, in turn, was also able to
make the right gestures. In his addition to the draft for his first speech from
the throne, George declared,

> Born and educated in this country I glory in the name of Britain; and
> the peculiar happiness of my life will ever consist in promoting the
> welfare of a people whose loyalty and warm affection to me I consider
> as the greatest and most permanent security of my throne.[7]

George's conscious presentation of himself as a Patriot created a
favourable repeating cycle of reports. The *Bath Chronicle* of 25 December
1760 carried an item of London news from the *Monitor*, a paper sympathetic to Pitt but not to George II: 'It is said that His Majesty, in consideration of the war with France, has forbid all French wines of any sort to be
drank in the Palace, not even excepting his own table. It is calculated this
will be a saving of at least £40,000 per annum.' Care for the economy, and
therefore for the people, was also seen in the press report that he would
limit the period for royal mourning, and thus help the textile industry.

Later a critic, Horace Walpole was in no doubt of the propitious
circumstances of George's accession, although, in part, this was a literary
device in order the better to chart a subsequent decline that he attributed

---

[3] Political Memoir of first Lord Holland, BL. Add. 51439 fol. 1.

[4] BL. Add. 51439 fol. 3.

[5] J. Greig (ed.), *The Diaries of a Duchess. Extracts from the Diaries of the First Duchess of
Northumberland* (London, 1926), p. 35.

[6] Frankland to Pitt, 30 Nov. 1760, forwarding loyal address from the British Factory in
Lisbon, PRO. SP. 89/53.

[7] George, draft, BL. Add. 32684 fol. 121.

to Augusta and Bute, 'a passionate domineering woman, and a favourite without talents':

No British monarch had ascended the throne with so many advantages as George the Third. Being the first of his line born in England, the prejudice against his family as foreigners, ceased in his person . . . In the flower and bloom of youth George had a handsome, open, and honest countenance; and with the favour that attends the outward accomplishments of his age, he had none of those vices that fall under the censure of those who are past enjoying them themselves.[8]

Another later critic, Edmund Burke, used a review of a book on Mary, queen of Scots to praise George:

this age, when time, experience, and a succession of good princes, and most of all, the virtues of a king, a native of the country he governs, has united all sects and all parties, religious and civil, in the one wish of continuing the government in him and his family.[9]

The sense of new beginnings entailed the retirement of the baroque state coach made for Queen Anne and the commissioning of a superb state coach, although it was not, in fact, to be ready for the coronation, and was first used only for the state opening of parliament on 25 November 1762. The design and decoration were symbolic of the notes that George was trying to strike. George was to appear as British thanks to the iconography associated with Britannia and Neptune, ruler of the seas, but there was also reference to Apollo, the inspiration of artistic activity, while the depiction of Mercury symbolized peace. The reference to Apollo was to be repeated in Johann Ramberg's painting of the curtain for the theatre of the Electoral palace at Hanover. Painted in 1789, this depicted George, as Apollo, as a fit companion for the Muses. The painter of the state coach, Giovanni Battista Cipriani, was an Italian, and the principal designer, William Chambers, who had taught the new king architectural drawing, was Swedish-born, but the sculptor, Joseph Wilton, who designed the figures and regalia and who was paid the most for the coach, was British, as was the coach-builder, Samuel Butler. The coach is still used for major state occasions, such as the celebration of Queen Elizabeth II's fifty years on the throne.[10]

---

[8] H. Walpole, *Memoirs of the Reign of King George III by Horace Walpole*, ed. D. Jarrett (4 vols, New Haven and London, 1999), I, 6–7.

[9] *Annual Register* (London, 1761), p. 305.

[10] J. Marsden and J. Hardy, '"O Fair Britannia Hail!" The "Most Superb" State Coach', *Apollo*, 153, 468 (Feb. 2001), pp. 3–12; D. Wilson, 'A Bust of Thomas Hollis', *British Art Journal*, 5 (2004), pp. 6–7; J. Marsden, 'George III's State Coach in Context', in Marsden (ed.), *The Wisdom of George the Third* (London, 2005), pp. 43–59.

Anglicization was a popular theme, with the emphasis on a less obviously derivative art and dependent culture linked to national assertiveness.[11] In 1762, with *Artexerxes*, a translation of Metastaso's *Artaserse*, Thomas Arne produced an English equivalent to Italian opera, which enjoyed considerable success. That year, in a less grand fashion, his *Love in a Village* was a successful vernacular pastiche. Also in 1762, Henry Hoare celebrated the accession of George by beginning a monument to King Alfred at the spot on his estate of Stourhead where he believed Alfred had raised the standard against the Danes.[12]

George's British theme was to be criticized, however, in a letter from the pseudonymous opposition newspaper writer 'Junius' to the king on 19 December 1769, which took up the anti-Scottish theme deriving from popular criticism of Bute, and accused him of having 'renounced the name of Englishman'. Concern about Scottish influences centred on Bute was indeed seen from the outset of the reign. Fox recorded of George's speech to parliament on 18 November 1760, 'He was much admired but thought to have too much studied action and it was observed that he laid the accent on the first syllable of Allys and Revenues, which is after the Scotch pronounciation.'[13]

Aside from his striking of patriotic notes, George's personality and youth contributed to his positive reputation, Fox noting of his first week as king that he received 'in the most gracious and pleasing manner crowds of people without number (and by the way the King acts his part in public well)'.[14] George's popularity in his early years was further enhanced by his marriage to Charlotte of Mecklenburg-Strelitz (1744–1818) on 8 September 1761. Given the tendency to focus on George's politics in the 1760s, sometimes apparently to the detriment of much else, it is necessary to note the importance to him and others of his marriage, which was designed to ensure his happiness and to secure the succession. In 1761, the latter looked precarious because George's four brothers, Edward, William, Henry and Frederick, were unmarried, as were his two sisters and his sole paternal uncle, William, duke of Cumberland.

The criteria George employed in looking for a wife centred on disposition and child-bearing ability, although he also responded to what the angry Fox saw as the ridiculous German pride of Cumberland in not looking for a British commoner as a potential spouse.[15] Bute had also

---

[11] L. Colley, 'The English Rococo', in M. Snodin (ed.), *Rococo: Art and Design in Hogarth's England* (London, 1984), p. 17; G. Newman, *The Rise of English Nationalism: A Cultural History* (New York, 1987).

[12] N. Smith, *The Royal Image and the English People* (Aldershot, 2001), p. 149.

[13] BL. Add. 51439 fol. 10.

[14] BL. Add. 51439 fol. 4.

[15] BL. Add. 51439 fol. 23.

pressed for a foreign princess, ruling out Fox's sister-in-law, Lady Sarah Lennox. As prince, George had confessed his passion for her to Bute. Since George's wife would also be Electress of Hanover, and, in response to both law and convention, German princely houses were particularly concerned about issues of rank, the avoidance of *mésalliances* was therefore important, and this influenced George, leading him to reject two princesses on the list originally proposed for him. Two key Hanoverian ministers, the Münchhausen brothers, were instructed to draw up a list, and, among the British ministers, only Bute was consulted, a marked demonstration of trust that reflected George's determination to treat the marriage as a personal matter as much as an act of state.

The initial six women on the list were Protestant princesses, as was necessary, and all were Germans; the two added were the princess of Denmark and the eventual choice, Charlotte, another German. George had never met the last queen, his paternal grandmother, Caroline of Ansbach, who died in 1736, but her reputation for philosophical specula-tion and religious heterodoxy would not have been acceptable to George. Indeed, he excluded his maternal cousin, Frederica of Saxe-Gotha, on the grounds that she was interested in philosophy, in other words possibly inclined to free-thought and secularism, although the fact that she was believed unlikely to have children also mattered. Good health and char-acter were among the necessary criteria. One princess (of Denmark) from the list was believed already promised; two were judged unacceptable because of socially questionable marriages among their ancestors; another was seen as too young; and another two were viewed as bad-tempered by those who reported to George. The last factor ruled out Philippina of Brandenburg-Schwedt, who had been identified by George, Bute and Philipp von Münchhausen as the best candidate when they considered the topic on 2 December 1760. A princess who was opinionated would not be biddable. Whether being a niece of Frederick II helped disqualify Philippina is unclear. Charlotte, on whom an acceptable report was received, was eventually left alone in the field. The difficulty of her being a Lutheran was ended when she expressed her readiness to conform to the Church of England, and George announced his choice to the Privy Council on 8 July.[16]

The marriage was delayed because Charlotte's mother, Elisabeth of Saxe-Hildburghausen, died; as her father, Charles, had died in 1752 (the year after George's father), she was now an orphan. In July 1761, George himself caught chickenpox. Nevertheless, Charlotte set off in August[17]

---

[16] R.R. Sedgwick, 'The Marriage of George III', *History Today*, 10, 6 (June 1960), pp. 371–7.
[17] For reports to Bute from Colonel David Graeme, whom Bute sent to Mecklenburg, 17, 20, 23, 30 June, 15, 20, 24, 27, 31 July, 4 Aug. 1761, BL. Add. 36796 fols 98–108.

and landed at Harwich on 7 September. She arrived in London next day and, after being received by George at St James's, was married that evening at the Chapel Royal there. Such a speedy marriage was conventional in royal circles, and important in order to secure an heir.

On 12 September 1761, Chesterfield wrote from Blackheath, 'The town of London and the city of Westminster are gone quite mad with the wedding and the approaching coronation. People think and talk of nothing else.' The journalist, theatre manager and playwright George Colman the Elder, in the *Genius*, claimed 'The present complexion of the people is such, that I find it absolutely vain and ridiculous to attempt writing to them on any other subject than that of the Royal Wedding and Coronation.'[18] Both were celebrated with special brews of beer. This was certainly a high point of popularity for the king,[19] repeating that of the accession. Coronation celebrations were held around the country, and a large amount of popular participation was permitted, for example crowning Punch in Glasgow.[20]

With a customary contrast between illusion and reality that, in part, in this case reflected a lack of experience, as well as the scale of the occasion, the coronation in Westminster Abbey on 22 September was in fact poorly organized, not least because the mislaying of the Sword of State caused a delay of three hours. Indeed, Francis, tenth earl of Huntingdon, the groom of the stole, ended up carrying the lord mayor's sword. The banquet was also chaotic, with no places for some of the leading aristocrats, while the champion's horse backed into, instead of away from, George, who lost his temper and berated Thomas, Lord Effingham, the acting earl marshal, after the ceremony. This continued a pattern of British coronations that did not live up to the model of uplifting decorum. Nevertheless, George won praise for his conduct during the ceremony: properly serious, benevolent and dignified.[21]

George had taken a close interest in the planning of the coronation. In the letter concerning the anthems that Thomas Secker, archbishop of Canterbury, wrote to William Boyce, master of the king's band of musicians and organist of the Chapel Royal, George's views were revealed:

---

[18] Chesterfield to Richard Chevenix, bishop of Waterford, 12 Sept. 1761, Bloomington, Indiana, Lilly Library, Chesterfield papers, Chesterfield–Chevenix correspondence volume; *Genius*, 1 Sept. 1761.

[19] John de Pontieu to Mark Sykes, 10 Sept. 1761, Hull UL, DD SY 101/48.

[20] Rainey to Viscount Macduff, 27 Sept. 1761, Aberdeen UL, Duff of Braco papers, 2727/1/231.

[21] G.S. Rousseau, '"This Grand and Sacred Solemnity": Of Coronations, Republics, and Poetry', *British Journal for Eighteenth-Century Studies*, 5 (1982), pp. 9–12; B. Connell, *Portrait of A Whig Peer. Compiled from the Papers of the Second Viscount Palmerston 1739–1802* (London, 1957), pp. 28–9.

His Majesty hath signified his pleasure, that the 4th anthem, *Zadok the Priest* etc. should be performed as it was set for the last coronation; and that the other anthems should be as short, and have as little repetition in them, as conveniently may be.[22]

Secker, indeed, helped to compensate for the delay caused by mislaying the sword by preaching a relatively short sermon.

Whatever the shortcomings of the event, the coronation provided an occasion for much celebration. Large-scale provision of food and drink to the poor on coronation day was extensively reported: many were thus able to drink George's health.[23] The royal wedding had an unfortunate consequence, however, for one aristocrat, John, third duke of Roxburgh, who, on his continental tour in 1761, had fallen in love with Charlotte's elder sister, Christiana Sophia Albertina. When Charlotte soon became engaged to the king, it was deemed politically necessary to break off the match, and Roxburgh never married.

Despite his popularity on his accession and at his coronation, George soon became a figure of controversy because of his determination to reign without party. The theme of the king as a dangerous political force, exerting a malevolent role in British affairs, was to be strongly revived in the 1760s. This was after two reigns in which criticism of the monarchs had arisen, instead, largely from their Hanoverian concerns, or from the perspective of a Jacobite loyalism that, in fact, caused most politicians to rally to the Hanoverian dynasty. In part, George's problems can be attributed to his inexperience. He came to the throne young and had little earlier political experience. Helping his mother at the weekly drawing room when George II was away in Hanover, as he was in 1752 and 1755, was not a training in politics. Indeed, one of the most pernicious consequences of the bad relations between the Hanoverians and their heirs was that the latter had little governmental or political experience. What little they did have was as a totem of opposition activity, scarcely the most helpful training for the commitments of the throne.

Yet, far more than inexperience, or indeed the fact that George, while diligent, was not the brightest of monarchs, played a role in George becoming a figure of controversy. It was more important that, unlike his two predecessors, George was, at the outset of his reign, no pragmatist, and was not willing, albeit with grumbles, to conform to the nature of

---

[22] Secker to Boyce, 14 Aug. 1761, Lambeth Palace Library, MSS 1130/I fol. 80, and Secker, memorandum fol. 173. See also A. Ashbee and J. Harley (eds), *The Cheque Books of the Chapel Royal* (2 vols, Aldershot, 2000), II, 104.

[23] G.A. Tresidder, 'Coronation Day Celebrations in English Towns, 1685–1821: Élite Hegemony and Local Relations on a Ceremonial Occasion', *British Journal for Eighteenth-Century Studies*, 15 (1992), p. 6.

politics, at least as defined in terms of the distribution of government posts. He had an agenda for Britain and, as a result, was, politically, the most interesting of the Hanoverians. To many Whigs, the novel practice of rejecting party government and seeking an inclusive political world, including Tory support for the ministry, was a revolutionary political step, and almost an unconstitutional act on the part of the monarch. This aspiration encouraged suspicions about George's intentions, and, in the alarmist, frequently paranoid, political discussion of the period, offered an apparent echo of Stuart autocracy. As such, public concern echoed the controversial charge made in 1752 by Simon, first Earl Harcourt, George's governor, that the young prince and his brother Edward were being educated in Jacobite principles. In 1769 'Junius' attacked George on this head:

> It is not then from the alienated affections of Ireland or America, that you can reasonably look for assistance; still less from the people of England, who are actually contending for their rights, and in this great question, are parties against you. You are not, however, destitute of every appearance of support: You have all the Jacobites, Non-jurors, Roman Catholics, and Tories of this country, and all Scotland without exception.

Throughout the reign, political opponents believed that George was out to increase royal power and that he acted in a manipulative way to do so, allegedly undermining politics by the use of secret advisers, or of ministers who were not committed to fair government. This was a group of villains that began with Bute, a key figure in George's contemporary and subsequent reputation,[24] whose secret influence was asserted in cartoons and newspapers until at least 1780,[25] and that came to include Mansfield, Jenkinson, Shelburne, Thurlow and Auckland. This theme helped inspire, and, in turn, drew heavily on Edmund Burke's *Thoughts on the Cause of the Present Discontents* (1770), which became a key opposition text. What George did was perceived by many from this perspective. The perception of secret influence accorded with a major theme not only in the discussion of politics in both the contemporary world and history, but also in fiction. It was difficult to separate George from the apparent villainy of his advisers and their alleged intentions.

George's opponents argued that he acted in an unconstitutional fashion, and Whig historians naturally believed them. It was, however, the assertion of royal will that was crucial. The real problem in the eyes of the

---

[24] K.W. Schweizer (ed.), *Lord Bute: Essays in Reinterpretation* (Leicester, 1988).
[25] Review of Schweizer (ed.), *Bute* by P.D.G. Thomas, *British Journal for Eighteenth-Century Studies*, 13 (1990), p. 91.

politicians, whatever they alleged, was not George's unconstitutional tendencies, but the opposite. For the first time since William III, whom, in accordance with Whig ideas,[26] George praised in his essays in the 1750s as a liberator, Britain had a monarch who was determined to deploy to the full powers that could be seen as his. In terms of political practice, the novelty entailed by George's attitudes and policies seemed unconstitutional to critics. George was prepared for confrontation, although he complained that it would ruin his health. Prone to see matters in extreme terms and ready later in the reign to threaten abdication, George displayed a cool nerve in confrontations, total conviction of rectitude, and a bloody-minded determination to have his way that flowed from the assumption that he alone was taking a principled stand, and this led others to regard him as peremptory.[27] The clash between such conviction and that of ministers such as George Grenville was serious. Opponents of the king were enraged, spiteful and helpless, which led them to try to constrain him by political pressure on his choice of ministers. The myth of despotism was the public response to anger with George, although discontent over the actions of a young monarch was less politically destabilizing than the now very weak belief that he had no right to rule because of the claims of another dynasty, as had been the case with the Jacobite challenge to George I and George II.

George found that he was expected by many politicians to obey an unwelcome set of unwritten conventions that dictated his selection of ministers. Adding royal relatives to the Privy Council – his uncle, William, duke of Cumberland, and his brother, Edward, duke of York – on 27 October 1760, was not very controversial, but the role of Bute was. The king encountered the argument of William, fourth duke of Devonshire, the lord chamberlain, a former first lord of the treasury (1756–7), and a member of the inner cabinet inherited from George II, that he should retain the latter's ministers:

> The Duke of Newcastle had united with him the principal nobility, the moneyed men and that interest which had brought about the [Glorious] Revolution, had set this Family [the Hanoverian dynasty] on the throne, and supported them in it, and were not only the most considerable party but the true solid strength that might be depended on for the support of government . . . they were infallibly the people that the King must trust to for the effectual support of his government.[28]

---

[26] T. Claydon, *William III and the Godly Reformation* (Cambridge, 1996).

[27] Newcastle to John White, 4 June 1765, BL. Add. 33003 fol. 5.

[28] P.D. Brown and K.W. Schweizer (eds), *The Devonshire Diary: William Cavendish, Fourth Duke of Devonshire. Memoranda on State of Affairs 1759–1762* (London 1982), pp. 54, 60, cf. p. 52.

A critical Henry Fox attributed this view to the fear that many had of losing their posts. George, who did not receive Devonshire graciously (relations between the duke and the court of George as prince of Wales at Leicester House were cool),[29] had other views on the composition of the ministry, which made the king unpopular, although, at the same time, his rejection of 'Old Corps' dominance was far from universally unwelcome. The constitutional ambiguity of the issue captured a tension within the British establishment, as the crown's traditional position, as the pro-active arbiter of aristocratic factions, was reshaped in the new politics of the period. Rather than acting in an unconstitutional fashion, it is more accurate to see George as a naïve idealist who did not appreciate the nuances of politics and government.[30] Equally, those nuances were defined and defended by self-serving politicians, and certainly neither Newcastle nor Pitt was an easy man to deal with. Furthermore, as with the growing opposition to Sir Robert Walpole in the early 1740s, both within and outside government it was necessary, as well as appropriate, to think about a new generation of political leaders. There was no easy system for managing such a transition, and, if George mishandled the situation in 1761–2, Pitt, never an easy colleague, was at odds with most of his ministerial colleagues in 1761, while the ministerial transitions in 1714, 1717, 1721, 1744 and 1756 were even more disruptive. The 'Old Corps' lacked effective leadership: Henry Pelham was dead, Hardwicke and Newcastle old and tired, and Devonshire neither bright nor dynamic.

More than ministerial change was at issue. George's policy in the early 1760s reflected his support for the ideas and ideals of non-party governments, not the Toryism alleged by his critics. He thought that much about the political system was corrupt and, in part, ascribed this to the size of the national debt. As a consequence, George's moral reformism, which drew on his strong personal piety, was specifically aimed against faction and luxury, which were political, social and moral failings in his eyes. George was also influenced by his father's political testament which had urged him to live with economy and to try to cut the national debt.

Aside from his new agenda for the crown, George had to get used to the responsibilities and conventions of kingship. Because the government was the king's, there was, at the least, a formal need for the royal assent that was recorded in the monarch's signature for instructions and appointments. On the third day of his reign, George had to sign such lowly appointments as a cornet in the army.[31] Such signings focused the king's

[29] BL. Add. 51439 fols 4–5.

[30] E. Cruickshanks, 'De l'Accession au trône de Georges III à la Révolution française', in B. Cottret (ed.), *Histoire des Îles Britanniques du XVI* au XVIII* siècles* (Paris, 1994), p. 213.

[31] George signature of appointment of ——— Gregory, 27 Oct. 1760, *Maggs Catalogue*, 1345 (2003), item 85.

power in patronage, but also show the nuances of his relations with ministers. An anonymous memorandum of 1765 noted that 'the method practiced in the nomination of governors in the plantations [colonies] was for the First Lord of Trade to deliver to one of the Secretaries of State a list of three persons to be laid before the King for His Majesty's option, whereupon the Secretary of State made out the warrant accordingly'.[32] George was opposed to the cronyism he associated with the Pelhamite system, and felt it lessened the effectiveness of government. Pluralism and non-residence offended him in state as well as Church, George Grenville noting in 1763, 'I have understood that the King has made it a rule not to give governments [governorships of fortresses or colonies] to such of the general officers as have regiments of horse or dragoons'.[33] Personal feelings also played a role, as in George's reluctance to accept Newcastle's patronage requests.[34]

George's interest in reform and regularity was shown with the Civil List Act of 1760, which transformed the previous position. Instead of the crown benefiting from the voting of revenues by parliament, these revenues were transferred to parliament. In their place, George received a fixed annual Civil List of £800,000. Although nominally the same amount that George II had received, the latter, in addition, had been allowed to keep the surpluses and in the last year of his reign the revenues had yielded £876,988. This surplus reflected the increased wealth and consumption of the country, for the revenues in question derived in part from excise duties. Had George III received the same yield from the Civil List as his grandfather (and neither the ministers nor parliament would have opposed such a request in 1760 on behalf of a popular new monarch), he would have been receiving more than £1 million by 1777 and £1,812,308 by 1798, sums that would have helped him deal with the exigencies and extravagances of his brothers and sons, and possibly led him to encourage them to matrimony and the establishment of independent households capable of supporting spouses and children. Instead, George's fixed income proved inadequate, as Charles Jenkinson explained in response to a parliamentary attack in February 1780, because of inflation and greater burdens, not least his rapidly growing family. In 1791, George lamented 'extremely that the deficiencies of the Civil List should arise from the payments to the younger branches of my family'.[35]

The bad bargain derived from a quest for popularity, a belief in the possibilities of cutting Civil List expenditure if it was economically managed, the exigencies of wartime finances, including the great increase

[32] BL. Add. 33001 fol. 34, undated but in 1765 papers.
[33] George Grenville to earl of Ancram, 13 May 1763, HL. ST. 7 vol. 1.
[34] E. Chalus, *Elite Women in English Political Life c. 1754–1790* (Oxford, 2005), pp. 120, 145.
[35] George to Pitt, 17 May 1791, PRO. 30/8/103 fol. 422.

in state indebtedness, and the example set by Frederick who, in 1747, had committed himself to such a step. George's good intentions were rapidly challenged, however, and in 1761–2 Civil List expenditure averaged £985,231, wiping out the surplus left by George II. From 1763 until 1769 expenditure averaged £908,563, and by 1769 the Civil List was more than £500,000 in arrears. This posed a major problem for George, made him vulnerable to parliamentary comment and ensured that he needed ministerial support, as assistance had to be sought in paying debts in 1769 and 1777. In 1777 the Civil List was increased to £900,000, while, as in 1770, accounts of Civil List expenditure were presented to the Commons, a valuable instance of parliamentary oversight. The limitations of the Civil List provision certainly lessened any possibility that George could, as critics claimed, try to subvert the constitution.[36]

George, like other rulers, found it difficult to forge acceptable relationships with senior politicians on his accession, which contributed greatly to the ministerial and political instability of the 1760s. Pitt's attitude towards Bute was quite unacceptable to George and indeed humiliating to him.[37] Pitt took few pains to soothe Bute's susceptibilities and clearly felt contempt for the man. George, however, made his support for his favourite clear. On 27 October 1760, two days after George's accession, Devonshire recorded in his diary, 'Lord Bute told Mr. Pitt that the King would have no meetings held at which he [Bute] was not present, and that for the future everything should be considered and debated in his presence, and then His Majesty would determine as he thought proper.'[38] Twenty years earlier, Chesterfield had told the Lords that 'Kings are generally for consulting with such as are of their own choosing, and these are often such as have no dignity, privilege or right by their birth.'[39] His comment, which stemmed from George II's backing for Sir Robert Walpole, captures the sense of the king as the powerful factor in the political system, and this was underlined by the vigour of George III's partisanship. George was pressing for more than consultation. He wanted his favourite to be a key player in the ministry, a means that would allow George to play a role in policy formulation and execution.

Aside from favouring Bute, George was also determined to reshape the royal household as he saw fit, and not to see its composition determined by the exigencies of ministerial faction. This even led him to depart from Bute's views. The latter wanted the mastership of the horse to go to Granville, second Earl Gower, who had held that office under George II

[36] E.A. Reitan, 'The Civil List in Eighteenth-Century British Politics: Parliamentary Supremacy versus the Independence of the Crown', *Historical Journal*, 9 (1960), pp. 318–26.
[37] BL. Add. 51439 fol. 9.
[38] Brown and Schweizer (eds), *Devonshire Diary*, p. 43.
[39] Cobbett, XI, col. 732.

and was an ally of the influential John, fourth duke of Bedford, but the young Francis, tenth earl of Huntingdon, who had been Prince George's master of the horse since 1756, intervened: 'Lord Huntingdon flung himself at the King's feet, saying he had nor would seek no other protector to save him from the disgrace of not taking the great but natural step from Master of Horse to the Prince to Master of the Horse for the King . . . this made impression on the King'.[40] The following year, Huntingdon succeeded Bute as groom of the stole, a position he held until 1770 when, no longer enjoying royal favour, he was dismissed.

Huntingdon's appointment was less spectacular than the favour shown to Tories. Although this continued Pitt's policy of trying to win Tory support, it was now far more associated with the crown. Tories, including those who had been Jacobites in their time, such as George, third earl of Lichfield, were received at court. Adding Tories to the lords and grooms of the bedchamber made Newcastle and allies 'stand aghast',[41] although the majority of the holders of both offices under George were not Tories. George's ostentatious displays of favour towards individual Tories, who had been denied access to the benefits of court approval since the Hanoverian accession in 1714, permitted a reshaping of the peerage, as Tories could now be honoured, and this pattern of honour was to extend to royal visits – conspicuously so in 1789 to the earl of Ailesbury, a frequent card-player with George, who came from a family, the Bruces, heavily associated with Jacobitism. Less prominent Tories also received favour, Sir John Philipps, formerly an active Jacobite, being appointed head of the bench of JPs in Haverfordwest in 1761 and to the Privy Council in 1763. In language that would have pleased George, Philipps saw corruption as the threat to 'that confidence which ought always to subsist between the King and his People', and regarded George as particularly deserving of that confidence.[42] John Shebbeare, a prominent Jacobite writer, convicted and imprisoned in 1758 for libel as a result of attacking the influence of Hanover as calamitous, became a supporter of George, who granted him a pension and was reported to have spoken very favourably of him.

George pressed at an open door, as the Stuarts were now weak and discredited and the Tories eager for recognition by the crown, but his willingness to do so assisted in the consolidation of the social élite and its integration with political power. This helped the state weather the serious challenges posed by the American and French Revolutions. By then, Stuart loyalists and their descendants were serving George.[43] In 1775, some

[40] BL. Add. 51439 fol. 10.

[41] BL. Add. 51439 fol. 14.

[42] Philipps to Bute, 23 May 1762, MS. 5/72/1.

[43] G. Glickman, 'The Career of Sir John Hynde Cotton, 1686–1752', *Historical Journal*, 46 (2003), pp. 839–40.

Bostonians apparently offered Charles Edward Stuart the crown of America,[44] but this was a whimsical idea. Jacobitism was exhausted as a cause. Indeed, when 'James III' died in 1766, Charles Edward was not recognised as king by Pope Clement XIII despite conspicuous past papal support for the cause. Charles Edward's fragile personality had already deteriorated under the stress of disappointment and marginality. Increasingly, he became a somewhat disagreeable curiosity, travelling furtively around Europe, drinking heavily and subject to paranoid suspicions.[45] Although he did not die until 1788, four years earlier the British government had felt it safe to restore, to the heirs of their former owners, the estates forfeited as a result of Jacobite activity in the '45.[46] On 22 November 1788, *Felix Farley's Bristol Journal* reported, 'In a town in the North of England, on the Revolution day, a party met to drink health to the *old cause and family* – they were in number thirty, and we suppose comprehend *all* of that opinion in the three kingdoms.' In 1793, George was 'very glad' to see Sir Watkin Williams Wynn, the head of a family once prominent in Jacobite schemes, in 'my uniform' and happy to make him lord-lieutenant of Merioneth.[47]

Tories, such as Samuel Johnson, who were not members of the social élite were also pleased by the new king, and, although his commitment to hereditary right ensured that he never took the oaths of allegiance or abjuration, Johnson was willing, at least by 1773, to recognise a *de facto* title in George III as he never had in George II.[48] The Tory welcome continued a process of political integration that had begun in the mid-1740s; Tory cohesion and identity had been seriously compromised since then, particularly in 1755–7, when Tory support was wooed by Whig politicians, indeed by some Whig ministers. This was brought to fruition by George III, who had a better appreciation than Newcastle of the changes taking place that 'made the admission of the Tories perfectly logical'.[49] As a result of their entry into favour, the Tories atomized in the early 1760s, joining a variety of political groups, including the government establishment in the Commons; just as the 'Old Corps', never anyway a monolith, also split with many remaining in office while others followed Newcastle when he fell from office in 1762. More than patronage was at stake in the Tory support for George and the royal recognition of the Tories. The

---

[44] F.J. McLynn, 'Unpopular Front: Jews, Radicals and Americans in the Jacobite World-View', *Royal Stuart Papers*, 31 (1988), pp. 10–12.

[45] McLynn, *Charles Edward Stuart* (London, 1988).

[46] A.M. Smith, *Jacobite Estates of the Forty-Five* (Edinburgh, 1982).

[47] George to Grenville, 16 Nov. 1793, BL. Add. 58857 fol. 171.

[48] J.C.D. Clark, 'Literature, History and Interpretation', in Clark and H. Erskine-Hill (eds), *Samuel Johnson in Historical Context* (Basingstoke, 2002), p. 299.

[49] R. Middleton, 'The Duke of Newcastle and the Conduct of Patronage during the Seven Years' War', *British Journal for Eighteenth-Century Studies*, 12 (1989), p. 184.

king's Anglican piety was also important, as the Tories associated themselves closely with the interests of the Church of England.[50] This would help ensure that George was perceived by critics, especially Dissenter critics, as a Tory.

The reception of Tories was not the sole issue that caused tension. In the face of very intemperate complaints about patronage made by Charles, third duke of Richmond, George was at first 'firm but very civil' but subsequently 'excessively angry', leading Fox to see him as 'a young King capable of great resentment when his dignity is trenched upon, and if I mistake not, of retaining it'.[51] Lord George Sackville, unfairly in George's eyes court-martialled and dismissed from the army for disobedience and cowardice at the battle of Minden in 1759,[52] was invited to return to court and favourably received, which gave offence to Pitt. As Lord George Germain, he was colonial secretary in 1775–82 and a key figure in the attempt to defeat the American Revolution. In turn, in a symbolic rejection of the ministry's commitment to continental intervention, Sir Henry Erskine, an MP who had been dismissed from the army in 1756 for opposing subsidy treaties, was reinstated, fulfilling a promise George had made as prince.

As he made clear to Bute, however, Pitt was unwilling to accept any change in 'the system of the war'.[53] He was prepared to back Bute as first lord of the treasury, replacing Newcastle, with whom his relations were uneasy, but advised a continuation of the current ministry, and Bute agreed. Hardwicke urged Newcastle to retire, but Bute, Devonshire, Pitt and others persuaded him to continue in office,[54] which ensured that the very experienced Newcastle would manage the 1761 election. Instead of George's determination, both to rely on Bute and to end the war, leading to a rapid change in both ministry and policy, Bute became not first lord, but groom of the stole, a court appointment, and a member of the cabinet council, a position with political possibilities but with no matching responsibilities. Like Walpole in 1727, the ministers appeared to have finessed the views of the new king, with Bute apparently designed to follow the course of honourable inconsequence Spencer Compton had been assigned to in 1727.

Nevertheless, the political world seemed newly volatile and kaleidoscopic. In 1757–60, during the last years of George II's reign, Newcastle and Pitt had become used to a measure of royal support and to a government in

[50] J.C.D. Clark, *English Society 1660–1832* (2nd edn, Cambridge, 2000), p. 121.

[51] BL. Add. 51439 fols 15, 17–18.

[52] P. Mackesy, *The Coward of Minden* (London, 1979).

[53] L. Namier, *England in the Age of American Revolution* (London, 1930), p. 121.

[54] P. Yorke, *Life and Correspondence of Philip Yorke, Earl of Hardwicke* (3 vols, Cambridge, 1913), III, 305–7.

which their policies were followed and in which the principal challenge they faced came from each other. This was vital to Pitt, a man not adept at seeking approval or soliciting support. Now, instead, there was uncertainty, both over the extent to which George would try to implement his own views and over the likely response of leading politicians. The balancing act of a ministry headed by Pitt, who appealed to Patriot and Tory opinion, and Newcastle, who led the Whigs, was threatened by the redefinition of political groups greatly hastened by George. He saw himself as able to appeal to all groups.

The challenge of negotiating peace would have been a problem whoever was monarch. Pitt triumphed over George and Bute in the opening clash of the new reign, insisting that the king's first speech to the Privy Council, delivered on 25 October and drawn up by Bute, should be altered. Instead of referring to 'a bloody and expensive war' and 'obtaining an honourable and lasting peace', the phrases were changed in the printed copy to 'an expensive but just and necessary war', with the insertion, after the words 'honourable peace', of 'in concert with our allies'. The original reflected the indifference, if not suspicion, of George and Bute towards Britain's ally, Frederick II of Prussia, an attitude that was to be transformed to hostility. The changes in the speech were symptomatic of fundamental differences of opinion between George and his leading ministers about the war.

George neither trusted nor felt close to any of the principal ministers he reappointed, and, although Bute was not initially appointed to high office, George obviously intended that his favourite should enjoy predominant influence. He made it clear that anyone who criticized Bute 'speaks against me'.[55] This was a recipe not only for disagreement, but also for distrust of the king, a distrust on the part of a section of the political world that was to dog him for the remainder of his active life, with clear pedigrees from Newcastle to Rockingham, and from Pitt's supporters to metropolitan criticism of the king. George's detailed role, however, is not always easy to disentangle. Sources indeed are far more plentiful for his reign than for those of his two predecessors, which suggests that he was much more 'active' than they were, yet encourages scepticism on that head, as different styles of kingship did not lead to the same documentary trace. Furthermore, despite the availability of archival material, it is difficult to ascertain the source of George's opinions,[56] and there are also problems in assessing the impact of royal views. If George handled the transition to a new reign badly, problems were also created because his grandfather's ministers were unwilling to heed his views. Aside from a conviction of the

[55] Newcastle to Hardwicke, 3 Jan. 1761, BL. Add. 32917 fol. 92; Viry to Ossorio, 9 Jan. 1761, AST. LM. Ing. 66.

[56] J. Bullion, 'George III on Empire', *William and Mary Quarterly*, 51 (1994), pp. 305–10.

value of their own experience, they looked to the example of 1727, when Newcastle was indeed a secretary of state, and Granville (then Carteret) lord-lieutenant in Ireland.

Nevertheless, it was soon to be seen that matters would be different under the new king. One area of activity was that George initialled the cash account books of the first lord of the treasury. In 1766, Newcastle sent Rockingham some account books initialled by George containing 'all the private money which passed through my hands in this reign'. This presumably relates to Newcastle's period as first lord of the treasury under George in 1760–2, and may be part of the account books in Rockingham's papers relating to treasury business, one of which is his original cash account book as first lord in 1765–6, which was signed by George.[57] There were also key ministerial changes. In January 1761, Pitt told the well-connected Sardinian envoy, Count Viry, that George did not have the confidence in him that he should, adding 'my situation is such that I am hindered and impeded in the dispatch of most of my work'.[58] That month, Pitt reacted angrily to the idea that Bute become a secretary of state and thus his equal in ministerial rank; indeed, if he replaced Holdernesse in the northern secretaryship, rather than Pitt swapping posts, Bute would be the secretary of state responsible for relations with Prussia. In March, however, the change, the most important ministerial one in George's early months as king, took place with the approval of Newcastle, who told George that 'Mr. Pitt's ill health was such as rendered it impossible for him to do business with the king for weeks and months at a time', but added 'that his credit and influence were a great service to His Majesty and therefore nothing ought to be done that should give him offence'. Newcastle sought measured change he could manage, but this was not an argument Bute accepted. He also told Newcastle that Pitt's 'popularity was sunk', that 'he never would go into opposition', and 'would never gain the king'. But in the end Bute agreed to leave 'Pitt master of foreign affairs, except where, Newcastle, Hardwicke and Devonshire thought, 'he goes too far.'[59]

A Pittite perspective on George was to prevail widely, both in the short term and in the eyes of posterity. Indeed, Pitt's eventual fall was to be seen as prefiguring the displacement as German chancellor of Otto von Bismarck by the young Kaiser Wilhelm II in 1890: wisdom and success in war discarded to make way for headstrong young folly. It is therefore essential to underline the extent to which Pitt proved a difficult minister in early 1761. Ill with gout, he made little effort to win the confidence of the inexperienced Bute, who complained that he was told nothing about the

---

[57] Newcastle to Rockingham, 25 July 1766, WW. R1–657, account books R15.
[58] Viry to Charles Emmanuel, 13 Jan. 1761, AST. LM. Ing. 66.
[59] Brown and Schweizer (eds), *Devonshire Diary*, pp. 88–90.

affairs of Pitt's department.[60] As a result, the information available to George was limited, and his belief in his own role was affronted. The king clearly played a part when he could. A letter from Pitt to Bute in the latter's papers about sending to Turin (Charles Emmanuel III was playing a role as mediator) both a French memorial and George's answer is endorsed, 'I suppose your Majesty approves this method, if so please let me know it'.[61]

The lack of trust was of growing significance as peace became a pressing subject for consideration. Without relevant experience, George could hardly expect to have a major role in the conduct of the war, but he wanted to ensure peace, although only on reasonable terms. That seemed threatened by Pitt's bellicosity, and, conversely, by the insufficiently robust stand of Newcastle and his allies over peace terms.[62] Pitt's personality also seemed inappropriate: he was to bring to the work of peace the determination and impatience with obstacles that had characterized his war leadership, but this did not make negotiations easy. Relations between Newcastle and Pitt were already poor, and Pitt was isolated in the ministry. In the summer of 1761 Pitt was blamed for his aggressive stance in negotiations with France, although their failure was really due to the latter's ability to win Spanish support, which made the prospect for fighting on much better for France. Forced to confront the possibility of war with Spain, the ministry divided, Pitt and his brother-in-law, Earl Temple, the lord privy seal, pressing for an immediate declaration of war in order to gain the initiative. Unwilling to agree with their colleagues, they declared they would draw up a separate minute for the king, an unconventional step.

Unable to prevail, Pitt resigned on 5 October 1761. He told George that it would only create problems if he remained in office when he disagreed over policy, but also stated that he would neither oppose the king's measures nor attend the Commons except to defend his own policy or support supplies for the armed forces. As an acknowledgement of his services, Pitt was offered the governor-generalship of Canada, a post that would have taken him far from the political centre, or the chancellorship of the duchy of Lancaster, an office of profit not power, but he declined both, accepting a peerage for his wife and an annuity of £3,000, while thanking George for his good will.[63] Had this been all, then George's reputation would have

---

[60] Viry to Charles Emmanuel III, 31 Mar., 7 Apr. 1761, AST. LM. Ing. 61.

[61] Pitt to Bute, 28 Apr. 1761, MS.

[62] K.W. Schweizer, 'William Pitt, Lord Bute and the Peace Negotiations with France', *Albion*, 13 (1981), pp. 262–75, and 'The Cabinet Crisis of August 1761: Unpublished Letters from the Bute and Bedford Manuscripts', *Bulletin of the Institute of Historical Research*, 59 (1986), pp. 225–9.

[63] Pitt to Bute, 8 Oct. 1761, MS.

been safe from controversy related to the ministerial change, but a savage press war was launched by supporters of Pitt eager to suggest that his departure was unfortunate, while Bute's press supporters, in turn, wished to protect George from 'the like audacious treatment' by a future minister.[64]

Pitt stressed that he had not sought his pension, an issue that laid him open to criticism, and the revival of his popularity in London helped compromise that of the king. On 22 October 1761, the common council of the City of London passed unanimously a vote of thanks to Pitt for arousing the 'ancient spirit' of the nation and, on 9 November, when George, with Charlotte, attended the lord mayor's banquet he received less applause than Pitt, a serious blow to his prestige. The king's attendance distinguished him from his grandfather, who had not attended such functions nor sought to cultivate the City of London. The difference in George III's attitude reflected his Patriot self-image. He was also, however, clearly committed to a specific political line. When Pitt defended his conduct and therefore criticized the ministry in the new parliamentary session on 9 December, George took a close interest and 'was in high spirits' about what he saw as Pitt's isolation.[65] Two days later, Pitt was accused in the Commons of a 'want of confidence in the King'.[66] While George's constitutional position as the maker of peace and war was formally at issue, his political opinions were also crucial.

Meanwhile, George was not at a distance from tension within the ministry over policy. Opposed to abandoning 'the German war', support for Hanover and alliance with Prussia, which he saw as the thrust of the views of George and Bute, Newcastle 'talked very plainly to the King'.[67] George, indeed, was believed to be so unsympathetic to Frederick II that it was thought he would be pleased if Austria managed to conquer Silesia from him.[68] Frederick's admonitory tone in correspondence to the younger and inexperienced George was seen as inappropriate, and likened to that of teacher to pupil.[69] George wished to take no lessons from another monarch.

The sense of a breach with the past became stronger the following spring. Having fallen out with Bute over his determination to obtain peace and cut expenditure, and his conduct of the government, Newcastle, to

[64] James Ralph to Bute, 7 Oct. 1761, MS; K.W. Schweizer, 'Lord Bute and William Pitt's Resignation', *Canadian Journal of History*, 7 (1973), pp. 111–25.

[65] Newcastle to Devonshire, 10 Dec. 1761, BL. Add. 32932 fol. 82.

[66] Jenkinson to Bute, 11 Dec. 1761, MS, papers from Cardiff Public Library, 3/124.

[67] Newcastle to Rockingham, 19 Nov. 1761, WW. R1–212.

[68] Viry to Charles Emmanuel, 27 Nov. 1761, AST. LM. Ing. 66.

[69] Frederick to George, 22 Jan. 1762, ST. 6 vol. 1, and Berlin, Geheime Staatsarchiv Preussiche Kulturbesitz, Rep. 96.33F fol. 35; Viry to Charles Emmanuel, 26 Feb. 1762, AST. LM. Ing. 67; Bute to Andrew Mitchell, envoy in Berlin, 9 Apr. 1762, BL. Add. 6820.

George's 'great astonishment', resigned as first lord of the treasury in May 1762, being replaced by Bute.[70] Although frenetic and difficult, Newcastle was instinctually a minister, and more prepared to be accommodating to change, the crown and colleagues than Pitt was. Newcastle's departure from high office, which he had held, with only one brief gap, continually from 1724, reflected the extent to which George and Bute were disrupting established political arrangements. Newcastle felt ignored and that he had lacked George's confidence.[71] Indeed, George had been concerned that Newcastle's continental interventionism risked national bankruptcy and did not ask the duke to reconsider his resignation.[72] George was keen that Bute replace him, countering Bute's claim of 'ignorance in business',[73] a claim which indicated that George was not prepared to accept that Bute was not up to the job.

Having resigned, Newcastle then made a major effort to obtain Pitt's support against Bute, and against the preliminary peace terms with France. In order to shore up the ministry, George intervened in person. On 3 September 1762, he failed, however, in a private meeting to get Newcastle to abandon his opposition to the terms. George told Newcastle that it was impossible to continue the war, but the latter emphasized the need to maintain a continental alliance, while the two men disagreed over the restitution of conquests.[74] In order to associate Devonshire with the peace, the duke was summoned to attend the cabinet, which he refused to do, a step George saw as 'a personal affront'.[75] George was overly ready to personalize issues, and if this proved a way to help him justify his pertinacity, it was also an aspect of his obstinacy. At the same time, he was correct: there was often an element of the personal in politics. George responded in 1762 with a clear display of the consequences of royal disfavour, dismissing Devonshire as lord chamberlain on 28 October and, on 3 November, striking out the duke's name from the Privy Council, a rare act that savoured of revenge and a desire to humiliate. The means of doing it was harsh: 'The King called in the Book and did it himself.' George also refused to see Devonshire in order to receive back in person his badges of office.[76]

[70] George to Bute, 7 May 1762, Sedgwick (ed.), *Letters*, p. 100; Newcastle to Rockingham, 14 May 1762, WW. R1–240(b).

[71] Newcastle to Devonshire, 26 Dec. 1761, Newcastle, 'Substance of what passed with My Lord Lyttelton', 24 Aug. 1762, BL. Add. 32932 fol. 363, 32941 fols 372–4.

[72] K.W. Schweizer and J. Bullion, 'The Vote of Credit Controversy, 1762', *British Journal for Eighteenth-Century Studies*, 15 (1992), pp. 183–5.

[73] George to Bute, 19 May 1762, Sedgwick (ed.), *Letters*, p. 109.

[74] Memorandum, 4 Sept. 1762, BL. Add. 32942 fols 151–2.

[75] Sedgwick (ed.), *Letters*, p. 143.

[76] North to earl of Guildford, 8 Nov. 1762, Bod. MSS North adds c 4/1 fol. 23; Egremont to Bute, – Oct., 11 Oct. 1762, MS, Cardiff papers, 7/169–70; Charles Jenkinson to Sir James Lowther, 30 Oct. 1762, BL. Loan 72 vol. 51 fol. 3.

Devonshire's dismissal was followed by the resignation of his allies; this was seen by government supporters as a way to remove unreliable placemen and to strengthen the ministry by new appointees. Nevertheless, although it was normal to dismiss opponents, George was keen on immediate, and thorough, action to 'frighten others'. Newcastle thought the treatment of Devonshire unprecedented and certain to affect 'all the nobility and all those who ever approach His Majesty'.[77] Thanks to the press, the impact was wider. John Almon dedicated his *Review of Lord Bute's Administration* to Devonshire, because his name 'has long and often stood at the head of those brave and immortal peers who were the staunch supporters of the illustrious house of Hanover'.[78] Newcastle's connection, including minor officials, was removed from local as well as national government, again a harsh step that strengthened hostility to the government. George helped make the political atmosphere vindictive, although the removals had also been called for by experienced ministers. Charles, second earl of Egremont, one of the secretaries of state, reported to Bute the views of Earl Granville, formerly John, Lord Carteret, the experienced lord president of the council, who had been both Newcastle's opponent and colleague, who

> had no doubt of carrying the affairs of Parliament through as well as the King could wish, if the powers of the government (which he lamented not having been sooner exerted) were now put in their full force. But he desired me to say very plainly that the measure once being taken to discipline the Parliament troops, any relaxation afterwards would be decisively fatal: that no rank nor title must protect a man from instant resentment who would not concur with the measures of government, and that upon that tenure only persons must hold the great offices of the state, or aspire to the graces of the Crown. This steadily pursued he answered for success. This departed from, he saw success impossible, and that this might the more easily be held forth by our master, as the common support of the measures was all he wanted; no particular exceptionable jobs either at home or abroad wanted to be swallowed by the Parliament.[79]

Earlier, the king had responded angrily when Bute was opposed by George Grenville in cabinet discussions over the peace terms.[80] In part, this reflected George's commitment not only to Bute but also to the policies he

---

[77] Sedgwick (ed.), *Letters*, pp. 173–4; Newcastle to Rockingham, 28 Oct. 1762, WW. R1–316; Hardwicke to Newcastle, 2 Nov. 1762, BL. Add. 32944 fol. 219.

[78] J. Almon, *A Review of Lord Bute's Administration* (London, 1763), p. iii.

[79] Egremont to Bute, 11 Oct. 1762, MS, Cardiff papers, 7/170.

[80] Sedgwick (ed.), *Letters*, pp. 125–7.

wished to pursue. George's partisanship encouraged him to keep well informed about developments. An indication of the work this involved, and of the potential conflict between the continued nature of the work of the royal bureaucrat and the varied commitments and interests of the king, is suggested by a letter from Egremont to Bute in September 1762: reporting that he had received Bedford's dispatches from Paris, he added, 'which I shall send to meet His Majesty when he comes to St. James's, as they are much too voluminous for him to read in his chaise, had they been sent to meet him'.[81]

Royal supervision was a major theme, but its direction was contentious. Bedford, who had been told by the king, 'the very moment before I left London', to write to Bute in case he wanted George to know anything without it passing via the secretary of state,[82] the basis for a *secret du roi*, was also informed by the secretary of state that 'His Majesty . . . chooses that Your Grace should send over the preliminary articles for his royal inspection, before you proceed to the signature'.[83] Committed to peace, George seemed to the new French envoy, sent in September 1762 to further negotiations, to be embarrassed by his inability to execute his view, specifically by his need to tell parliament when the session began whether there would be peace or war. Indeed, the duke of Nivernais reported that when George spoke of the constitution and of the limitations it imposed on him his embarrassment increased, he went red, and seemed piqued.[84] These limitations were not simply a matter of parliament, for, as Nivernais reported the following month, there were serious divisions within the government. He presented George, Bute and Bedford as being the only ones willing to press through peace in the face of raised expectations about territorial gains following the recent arrival of the news of the capture of Havana from Spain, while the two secretaries of state, Egremont and George Grenville, were depicted as pressing for an alteration in the terms which might make the peace harder to obtain.[85]

In response to this disagreement, the ministry was reshuffled in October 1762, with Henry Fox appointed to manage the Commons, and Grenville replaced as secretary of state by George, second earl of Halifax. Prefiguring later criticism, for example of the failure to bring in opposition politicians in 1778 and 1780 during the War of American Independence (see p. 233), the absence of major ministerial changes was attacked. Newcastle and Pitt were still out of office and William, Lord Mansfield,

[81] Egremont to Bute, – Sept. 1762, MS, Cardiff papers, 7/168.
[82] Bedford to Bute, 20 Sept. 1762, MS, Cardiff papers, 5/160.
[83] Egremont to Bedford, 7 Sept. 1762, PRO. SP. 78/253.
[84] Nivernais to duke of Praslin, foreign minister, 16 Sept. 1762, AE. CP. Ang. 447 fol. 85.
[85] Nivernais to Praslin, 2, 9 Oct. 1762, AE. CP. Ang. 447 fols 197–8, 260, L. Perey, *Un Petit-neveu de Mazarin, le duc de Nivernais* (Paris, 1890), pp. 503–5.

the lord chief justice, wrote to his fellow-Scot Bute, 'This new arrange-ment don't widen your bottom . . . There is no true wisdom but to enlarge the bottom and to acquire national strength to the King.'[86] This argument reflected the potency in political culture of the idea of a ministry above faction and composed of all the talents supporting a benign monarch, but this vision underplayed the extent of real differences, specifically differ-ences over policy, rather than the search for preferment, which could be dismissed as selfish.[87] The counterpointing of 'factious spirits and ambi-tious struggles for power' with 'a good monarch'[88] neglected the extent to which the king was political as well as part of the political process. As far as 1762 was concerned, Fox had a reputation for serious corruption, and his new role scarcely reflected credit on the ministry. It certainly contrasted with the emphasis on probity struck by George as prince of Wales.

George's government and policy, however, had struck a chord. It was not, as was reported, ministerial bribery that carried peace through the House of Commons, but a widespread desire for the end of the war and a willingness to accept the terms, which opposition writers tried to deny.[89] Pro-government publications made much of George's Britishness, now presented in a clearly partisan fashion in order to counterweigh what was presented as the linkage between the opposition and Frederick II, who indeed encouraged hostility to the peace. The *Royal Magazine* of September 1762 asked,

Is it possible to imagine that the people of Great Britain can be deluded to such a degree as to murmur against their Sovereign for having a British heart, and preferring the prosperity of his native country to the interests and passions of a foreign Prince?

Opposition writers argued that the return of conquests as part of the peace was unacceptable, especially the West Indian sugar islands of Martinique and Guadeloupe to France, and also pressed the need for the crown to seek parliament's backing before signing the peace, the crown being understood as both ministry and monarch. 'Britannicus' in the *London Evening Post* of 9 September claimed that 'it would be but a reason-able condescension in the Crown to take the sense of their representatives in Parliament concerning the terms of a peace, before any preliminaries whatsoever shall be signed', and argued that it was in George's honour and interest 'to take and follow the council of his people in Parliament'.

---

[86] Mansfield to Bute, 14 Oct. 1762, MS, Cardiff papers, 4/179.
[87] James Hutton to Mr Phelps, 3 Dec. 1762, Beinecke, Osborn Files, Hutton.
[88] Bath to Elizabeth Montagu, 27 Oct. 1762, HL. MO. 4280.
[89] 'Britannicus', *London Evening Post*, 21 Sept. 1762.

Two days later, the paper pressed the need for 'some proper method . . . to convey the sense of the nation, on this important affair, to the Royal Ear', an argument it returned to on 16 November.[90] In part, as with the *Monitor* on 2 October, this was an aspect of the long-established practice of seeking to differentiate between monarch and ministry. This criticism, however, was seen by governmental writers as a way to restrict the royal prerogative and to control the administration.[91] As a reminder that George was not simply concerned with political developments, his eldest child and heir, the future George IV, was born on 12 August and christened five days later.

The opening of the parliamentary session on 9 December 1762 provided the opportunity for a trial of strength. Pitt attacked the proposed peace terms, but the address of thanks was carried in the Commons by 319 to 65, a decisive majority. 'Such an eminent majority secures administration,' reflected William, Viscount Barrington, the treasurer of the navy. It also appeared to vindicate the king.[92] George acted as a focus for the desire for peace, receiving addresses congratulating him on the Peace of Paris, signed on 10 February 1763, for example that presented by Sir Charles Asgill, on 18 May, on behalf of about 900 London merchants after the lord mayor, William Beckford, an ally of Pitt, had refused to present it. George was also praised in poetic celebrations of the dawning of peace.[93] There is no doubt of his personal belief that peace was necessary. He strongly assured the French ambassador on this head, arguing crucially that it was equally necessary for both kingdoms.[94]

William, earl of Bath (formerly William Pulteney), an experienced politician, reflected in June 1762,

> I fear he will have a very troublesome reign; those who have lately turned out, or resigned as they call it, in my opinion were suffered to stay in too long, and get too great a power in Parliament but if we have a little good fortune abroad, and obtain a good peace, and show that we are determined to pursue steadily right and popular measures at home and above all that the King appears to be resolute and steadfast, I think

[90] Cf. 'Anglicanus Rusticus', *London Evening Post*, 25 Sept. 1762.

[91] *Briton*, 25 Sept. 1762.

[92] Barrington to the earl of Buckinghamshire, 17 Dec. 1762, Norwich, Norfolk Record Office, Buckinghamshire papers 14626.

[93] Grenville to Bedford, 19 May 1763, HL. ST. 7 vol. 1; see also Newcastle to Hardwicke, 7 June 1763, BL. Add. 32949 fol. 52; M.J. Cardwell, *Arts and Arms. Literature, Politics and Patriotism during the Seven Years War* (Manchester, 2004), p. 265.

[94] Nivernais to Praslin, 16 Sept. 1762, 11 May 1763, AE. CP. Ang. 447 fol. 84, 450 fols 337–8; Audience on 20 October 1762, Perey, *Petit-neveu*, pp. 506–7. See also D'Eon to Praslin, 20 July 1763, Guerchy to Praslin, 18 Oct., 12 Nov., 1763, AE. CP. Ang. 450 fols 497–8, 451 fol. 451, 452 fol. 128.

it may still do, and numbers may be persuaded to stick by a young King rather than an old minister. We were very lately, I think, going into an aristocracy or what is worse a King governed by one set of men, and his people by nothing but corruption.[95]

Steadfastness was present on the part of George, and, in October 1762, Bute had called for it 'on supporting the best of Princes'.[96] The following month he wrote of the need to restore 'the lawful rights and liberty of the King'.[97] By February 1763, however, Bute, whose enthusiasm for high office had never been total, was disillusioned with government. As with Lord North in the late 1770s, royal encouragement was important in keeping him in office, but Bute lacked North's persistence, as well as his financial obligations to George. Although the ministry enjoyed solid parliamentary majorities, Bute found the stress of politics, which included reiterated exposure to the expression of rabid anti-Scottish sentiment, unbearable.[98] He also had to defend the proposed cider excise from strong opposition in the Lords in March, and was unwell. Criticism of government extended to George, Fox noting,

A young, civil, virtuous, good natured King might naturally be expected to have such a degree of popularity as should for years defend the most exceptionable favourite. But, which I can't account for, His Majesty from the very beginning was not popular. And now because Lord Talbot has prevented him from being checked to the shameful degree that has been usual in the kitchen, they make prints treating His Majesty as they would a most notorious old miser . . . To this mob are we brought by newspapers and libels and the encouragement given to the mob to think themselves the government.[99]

William Talbot, lord steward as a result of Bute's influence, was appointed partly in order to reform what was seen as a corrupt and costly part of the office,[100] but his position and policies indicated the ambiguity and difficulty of such reform. A womanizer, whose appointment was attributed to the princess of Wales, Talbot held the post until his death in 1782, but public agitation about the human consequences of cost-cutting in his department tarnished the popularity of the royal household. George

[95] Bath to Elizabeth Montagu, 15 June 1762, HL. MO. 4260.
[96] Bute to Shelburne, 11 Oct. 1762, BL. Add. 32797 fols 52-3.
[97] Bute to Major-General Townshend, 2 Nov. 1762, BL. Add. 36797 fol. 16.
[98] J. Brewer, 'The Misfortunes of Lord Bute: A Case Study in 18th Century Political Argument and Public Opinion', *Historical Journal*, 16 (1973), pp. 113-43.
[99] BL. Add. 51439 fol. 59.
[100] Reitan, 'Civil List', pp. 190-1.

played a role, becoming involved, in January 1761, in settling the wages
and privileges of the royal laundresses as part of his cost-cutting drive, an
instance of the king's repeated micro-management that reflected his view
of the obligations and responsibilities of kingship.[101] Talbot's attempt at
reform was part of a wider drive by George and Bute to improve government, not least in order to reduce taxation, a goal that helps explain the
quest for peace, as well as the wish to seek a revenue from the colonies to
pay for the army. The latter, however, was flawed because, in wishing to
give equal priority to the demands of security and economy, George and
Bute committed the government to a contradictory and faulty policy that
flew in the face of the advice of experienced politicians.[102]

The attack on corruption and sinecures was analogous to the wish to
remove what were seen as the political accretions corrupting the
Revolution Settlement, not least reversing Sir Robert Walpole's enslave-
ment of George's grandfather, but was also separate to this wish, and was
to be pushed hard by critics of the crown in the early 1780s, particularly
Edmund Burke. For George and Bute, both processes rested in part on the
appointment of men of integrity committed to good government, and
George consistently valued professional ability, probity and experience, in
both government and politics.[103] While reasonable in its own terms, such
an emphasis cut across the practice of politics, with its stress on appointment for reasons of partisan interest, and on maintenance in office as a
consequence of political reliability, not efficiency.

George's virtues were governmental rather than political, and he saw
others in the same light. The officials who looked to the king, such as
Charles Jenkinson, joint secretary to the treasury, were seen as 'King's
Friends', willing to back the king's government regardless of factional
considerations and praised by George for 'uniform attachment to his
person',[104] but they were also presented by Whig politicians as supporters
of a threat to the constitution, and their intentions were misconstrued.
Indeed, they were seen as a cabal linked to Bute.[105] King's Friends
appeared even more threatening when they held senior posts; for example
John, second earl of Egmont, a former supporter of Frederick, prince of

---

[101] J. Bullion, '"To know this is the true essential business of a king": The Prince of Wales
and the Study of Public Finance 1755–1760', *Albion*, 18 (1986), p. 444, fn. 45.

[102] J. Bullion and K.W. Schweizer, 'The Use of the Private Papers of Politicians in the
Study of Policy Formulation in the Eighteenth Century: The Bute Papers as a Case Study',
Archives, 22 (1995), pp. 39–44; J. Bullion, 'Security and Economy: The Bute Administration's
Plans for the American Army and Revenue, 1762–1763', *William and Mary Quarterly*, 45
(1988), pp. 499–509, esp. 508–9.

[103] R. Pares, *The Historian's Business and Other Essays* (Oxford, 1961), pp. 103–4.

[104] George to Hawkesbury, 4 Nov. 1803, BL. Loan 72/1 fol. 115.

[105] C. Wilkinson, *The British Navy and the State in the Eighteenth Century* (Woodbridge, 2004),
pp. 8–10.

Wales, as first lord of the admiralty from 1763 to 1766. Another King's Friend, William, second Viscount Barrington, treasurer of the navy from 1762 to 1765 and secretary at war from then until 1778, refused at the end of 1762 to follow the advice of his former patron, Newcastle, and resign after the dismissal of Devonshire. Barrington was a minister after George's heart, resisting, in the public interest, pressure over patronage,[106] but concern over the political role of such men is a reminder of the very different ways in which national revival was understood, a situation that created serious problems for George. Describing him as a 'victim of the tensions and contradictions in the Country Interest'[107] is possibly over-dramatic, but the situation was certainly difficult. As early as June 1761 Samuel Johnson had noticed weaknesses in a reign whose outset he had much applauded:

it would be unreasonable to expect much from the immaturity of juvenile years, and the ignorance of princely education. He has been long in the hands of the Scots, and has already favoured them more than the English will contentedly endure. But, perhaps, he scarcely knows whom he has distinguished, or whom he has disgusted.[108]

Baron Haslang, the experienced Bavarian envoy, saw the spirit of party at work in the problems facing a ruler full of virtues who was seeking to do his best.[109] Opposition writers, such as 'An Englishman', in the *St. James's Chronicle* of 18 September 1762, broadened their attack on the peace terms and the pro-government publications, to argue that people's minds were being prepared for the autocratic notions of non-resistance and passive obedience, a charge that made George, at the very least, a means for a fundamental change in the political culture. John Almon, one of the most active political writers of the period, saw George's creation of peers, and the role of the royal household, as key indicators of a drive to subvert the constitution and one that he associated with Toryism. Reference was made to the creation of peers by the Tory government in 1711 when discussing George's creations, and Almon wrote in relation to the latter, 'Those who had the real good of the country, and its constitution, at heart, beheld the increase of the peerage with strong marks of jealousy.' Almon argued that increasing the number of lords of the bedchamber ensured that more peers were dependent on George, and he attacked the impact of crown patronage for MPs, arguing that it threatened the independence of the Commons.[110]

---

[106] T. Hayter (ed.), *An Eighteenth-Century Secretary at War: The Papers of William, Viscount Barrington* (London, 1988).

[107] B. Harris, *Politics and the Nation. Britain in the Mid-Eighteenth Century* (Oxford, 2002), p. 101.

[108] J. Boswell, *Life of Johnson* (Oxford, 1980), p. 257.

[109] Haslang to Wachtendonck, 6 May 1763, Munich, Bayr. Ges. London 241.

[110] Almon, *Lord Bute's Administration*, pp. 51–3. On Almon, D.D. Rogers, *Bookseller as Rogue: John Almon and the Politics of Eighteenth-Century Publishing* (New York, 1980).

Granville was accurate in predicting that, unless 'a plan was formed and steadily pursued', George would be forced, if he was to strengthen the ministry, to employ those he disliked.[111] Bath had been correct to identify the role of chance factors in achieving political stability, as Bute had proved a broken reed, better with abstract ideas than with the realities of political management. George's continued reliance on him was therefore a weakness: the close association of the two men ensured that the unpopularity of the minister cast a shadow over the public reputation of the monarch. Reiterated attacks in the press on the role of favourites affected George's reputation,[112] but this reliance was not to end when an exhausted Bute resigned on 8 April 1763. That month, George wrote to him 'thank God I have a friend . . . that comforts me and makes me look on my ministers as my tools solely in my public capacity'.[113]

[111] Egremont to Bute, 11 Oct. 1762, MS, Cardiff papers, 7/170.
[112] E.g. *Monitor*, 3 July, 28 Aug., 4 Sept. 1762.
[113] Sedgwick (ed.), *Letters*, p. 233.

Chapter 5

MINISTERIAL INSTABILITY, 1763–70

I pity his M—— who sees there is a determination in the great factions
to make him their slave.

Elizabeth Montagu.[1]

Hopes recede. In 1757, George had informed Bute that he would only
accept the throne if he could hope to restore Britain 'to her ancient state
of liberty', free the country 'from her present load of debts', and also
make it 'the residence of true piety and virtue'.[2] In 1763, in contrast, the
focus was more on means when George complained to the duke of
Nivernais, the French ambassador, about

> the spirit of fermentation and the excessive licence which prevails in
> England. It was essential to neglect nothing that could check that spirit
> and to employ firmness as much as moderation. He was very determined
> not to be the toy of factions . . . and his fixed plan was to establish his
> authority without breaking the law.

As George also told Nivernais that he thought peace necessary for both
powers, that he trusted Louis XV, and that he regarded the union of the
two courts as unalterable, he was clearly far removed from the general
thrust of British public life. This was further shown by his choosing the
French envoy as a sympathetic listener.[3]

Alas for George, his wider ambition was to be reduced to the narrower,
but still very troublesome, scope of trying to chart a path between ministerial factions in order to gain his goal of creating a ministry with which
he felt at ease. In the absence of unified parties with clear leadership on
the modern pattern, let alone with a continuous nationwide organization
(or party membership), it should have been possible for George to create
a ministry around the politician most acceptable to him who might be able
to manage parliament, and, conversely, to keep at a distance those whom

---

[1] Montagu to Edward Montagu, 23 Nov. 1762, HL. MO.
[2] R.R. Sedgwick (ed.), *Letters from George III to Lord Bute, 1756–1766* (London, 1939), p. 6.
[3] Nivernais to Praslin, 11 May 1763, AE. CP. Ang. 450 fols 337–8.

he disliked. Even if George had to accept ministers who were not his first
choice, as in 1763, 1765, 1782, 1783, 1804 and 1806, it was possible for him
to try to use a ministry that could manage parliament in order to win
support for royal interests.

George I and George II were reasonably successful in this. Major politicians sought to win the co-operation of the crown, not to limit its power.
If royal wishes were thwarted, this was presented as a bowing to necessity
in which the ministers assisted the monarch to that end. Under the first
two Georges, there was general satisfaction, indeed a considerable
measure of complacency in Whig circles, about the (Glorious) Revolution
Settlement, in so far as the constitution was concerned; and critics of
disturbing features in the political system tended to blame ministerial
corruption, rather than royal activity. Political tension was focused on
ministers. There was a separate Jacobite critique of monarch and ministers, but that had little influence in political circles, especially after the
institution of one-party Whig government following the accession of
George I.

From the reign of George III, the situation changed and George found
that ministers he did not want sought to push through unacceptable policies. There was no longer the binding of Whig ministers to the monarch
that stemmed from a fear of Jacobitism, while George's accession was
followed by a more troubling agenda in domestic and imperial politics.
The Hanoverian issue receded as a source of contention, but George was
associated with domestic issues that were contentious in their own right,
and in which the role of the monarch was particularly sensitive, or
appeared so. In the 1760s, this was true of the choice of ministers and,
from 1765, of policy on the North American colonies. The king
throughout took a close interest in politics, writing in 1766 to Augustus,
third duke of Grafton and first lord of the treasury,

> I am uncertain whether you are apprized that it has ever been the usual
> practice of your predecessors to send me the morning after the meeting of
> the Lords a list of those that attended: I shall therefore expect it to-morrow
> morning, and that evening a note from you with the contents of that day's
> debate.

The meeting in question was that held in Whitehall before the opening of
the parliamentary session to hear the speech George would deliver next
day, and the debate that on the address of thanks. The delivery of the list
was no mere formality, since George commented on it, reflecting his
knowledge of politics,

> I see several names in the list . . . that I did not expect, and remark that
> although the Bedford party speak civily, that none of them appeared on
> this occasion. Lord Egmont's name not being in the list rather surprises

me and makes me fear he is more adverse than I had flattered myself unless he may have stayed away from his disapprobation of the Embargo and thinking it therefore more civil not to attend and object to it.[4]

By 1766, George had had many opportunities to become accustomed to the character of individual politicians. Bute had resigned on 8 April 1763, but, as Granville, second Earl Gower noted,

the King is resolved not to be taken by storm, and be hereafter a prisoner for life, and is therefore forming an administration out of those who have at least not opposed since his accession . . . if something is not formed to stem the present intrusion upon the Court, the King must submit to Mr. Pitt, Lord Temple, Mr. Legge and Lord Hardwicke.[5]

As a result of his determination to keep Pitt from office, George found himself with a ministry under George Grenville as first lord of the treasury; Henry Fox had refused the post. Grenville (1712–70), a member of an extended and influential cousinage, was an experienced MP and minister. He had been an MP since 1741 and had been a lord of the admiralty (1744–7), a lord of the treasury (1747–54), treasurer of the navy (1754–62), a secretary of state (1762), and first lord of the admiralty (1762–3). George had initially seen Grenville as someone of promise. Grenville was addressed by Bute as 'Dear George', and in January 1761 the king saw him as designed for promotion. Later that year, George had successfully pressed Grenville to assume the leadership of the House of Commons. In that position, Grenville helped drive Newcastle from office, before succeeding Bute as secretary of state. However, in 1762 there were clashes over peace terms between Bute and an increasingly assertive Grenville, and the latter was demoted to the admiralty, also losing his leadership of the Commons. Grenville only became first lord when Fox declined the post and reluctantly recommended him.

Relations between George and Grenville were soon poor and mistrustful, not least because George regretted Bute's resignation, while Grenville was an aggressive individual, prone to hector the king and to threaten to resign unless he got his way.[6] This was not an appropriate response to George's character, but Grenville did not manage the clash in their natures well. Furthermore, meetings were uncomfortable as they were held with both men standing. George was unwell in 1762 and, even

---

[4] George to Grafton, 10, 11 Nov. 1766, W. Anson (ed.), *Autobiography and Political Correspondence of Augustus Henry, Third Duke of Grafton* (London, 1898), p. 130.

[5] Gower to Bedford, no date, PRO. 30/29/1/116.

[6] P. Lawson, *George Grenville. A Political Life* (Oxford, 1984), e.g. pp. 165, 214.

more, in 1765 when he did not see his ministers between 25 February and
10 March. His acute irritability then certainly helped sour his relations
with Grenville. The king was also regarded as speaking 'very peremptorily'
to others, including Cumberland.[7] The extent to which Bute remained
influential, especially at first, when George wrote daily, and, even more,
the extent to which he was mistakenly believed still to be very influential,[8]
challenged the working relationship between king and first minister and
led Grenville to distrust George.[9] Nevertheless, although this link with
Bute was a cause of considerable tension, Grenville was also regarded as
difficult by other commentators.[10]

Anger with Grenville encouraged George to press for a strengthening
of the government, with approaches to Hardwicke in July 1763 and to
Bedford in August, the month in which his second son, Frederick, was
born. The Newcastle group and Bedford, however, both made acceptance
conditional on the inclusion of Pitt, but he was unwilling to serve alongside any minister who had negotiated the peace with France, which
excluded Bedford. George can be seen as playing a dubious role in seeking
to destabilize a ministry only recently established, but he was under pressure from Grenville to back the ministry or to form a new one, a challenge
to the royal ability to control the tempo of politics. Having told Grenville
that he would support the ministry, the king changed his mind, informing
Grenville on 26 August that he wanted to include Pitt, which would have
been a major change. The argument that Pitt's inclusion would make the
government more stable enabled Bute to persuade George to take this
course, one of the more kaleidoscopic of the shifts that were to mark the
unsettled politics of the decade. The negotiations, however, were abortive
because George was not prepared to accept Pitt's demands, while, with his
customary focus on his own opinions, Pitt failed to appreciate the king's
views on policy. When George saw Pitt on 27 August, he offered him the
secretaryship of state made vacant by Egremont's death. Grenville
reported,

> The King offered to dispose of the two great offices of Secretary of
> State and President of the Council [Granville had died] in any manner
> that might best contribute to the general satisfaction and to take such
> farther arrangements as could be made agreeable to the parties

---

[7] Diary of Charles Jenkinson, BL. Add. 38335 fol. 126; Newcastle to John White, 4 June
1765, BL. Add. 33003.

[8] Sedgwick (ed.), *Letters*, pp. 212–34; F. O'Gorman, 'The Myth of Lord Bute's Secret
Influence', in K.W. Schweizer (ed.), *Lord Bute: Essays in Re-interpretation* (Leicester, 1988),
pp. 57–81.

[9] Lawson, *Grenville*, pp. 212–13.

[10] D'Eon to Praslin, 24 Apr., 13 June 1763, AE. CP. Ang. 450 fols 311, 398.

concerned in them, but declared that he would upon no account consent to any proposal that was inconsistent with his honour in regard to the measures which he had followed or to the protection of all those whose conduct towards him he had reason to approve. Mr. Pitt on the contrary proposed to exclude all who had any hand in the peace which he represented as dangerous, dishonourable and criminal, although he did not intend to break it but to ameliorate it in the execution. To make an universal change by turning out every civil officer in the King's Service, and by introducing all those who had engaged in the opposition in their stead. He urged that this was a Tory government not founded upon Revolution Principles but adopting the opinions of prerogative and of the power of the Crown and therefore it was necessary to make an alteration of it.[11]

Pitt wanted Temple as first lord of the treasury, and Newcastle and Hardwicke both to take office, in short recreating the Pitt–Newcastle coalition of 1757–61 from which George had earlier freed himself. Pitt perceived himself as the embodiment of the Whig ideal and, in presenting George as a reactionary, justified his position to himself and sought to do so to others. Unacceptable to George, Pitt's demands, however, also appeared to others to be excessive, and his language unwarranted. Edward, fourth earl of Oxford, a Tory and a lord of the bedchamber, argued that,

> The terms insisted upon were not only incompatible with the dignity, and inconsistent with the honour of His Majesty, but of such a nature and extent as must have rendered him dependent upon the power, and left his subjects to the mercy of one set of men, the most dangerous event which could possibly befall this country.[12]

As so often in the relationship between George and Pitt, the response of well-informed 'insiders' was not that of the public. Popular interest, and the sense that the king's negotiations with Pitt were a public matter, were recorded by Elizabeth, Countess Cornwallis:

> Mr. Pitt was alone with the king from twelve o'clock till three yesterday noon at Buckingham House, numbers of people waiting at the gate with anxious countenances the whole time to observe him when he came out ... It is a very remarkable proceeding their choosing this conference should be made so public, as such things are usually kept quite private till they are settled.

---

[11] George Grenville to earl of Oxford, 1 Sept. 1763, HL. ST. 7 vol. 1.
[12] Oxford to George Grenville, 10 Sept. 1763, Bod. MS. Eng. Letters d. 109 fol. 71.

She subsequently noted that, by declining office, Pitt had 'gained great credit'.[13] George, conversely, was seen in an unfavourable light, and Pitt's continued absence from office helped foster reports about Bute's influence on the king.

George was pushed back on Grenville. He felt he had to show contrition on 28 August 1763 when he asked Grenville to continue to head the ministry, and George also responded to Grenville's concern about Bute by assuring him that the former minister would have no influence. Far from being willing to accept the private assurance, Grenville sought to fix it by sending his major supporters a letter outlining the situation, including the promise that Bute would not see George until the suspicion of his influence was ended. George had to listen to this when Grenville read it to him on 3 September, a marked humiliation. Grenville was now the sole key minister, and the secretaries of state assured foreign envoys that Bute was entirely out of politics.

However disagreeable personally, the ministry nevertheless was pursuing policies dear to George, particularly peace and fiscal stability, and Grenville was also a competent minister. Under Grenville, as under Bute, although foreign alliances were pursued, the cautious stance that George encouraged towards continental commitments was maintained.[14] This was a sphere in which George played an important role because instructions to envoys were sent for his approval.[15] Furthermore, the favour shown the Tories continued. This, indeed, spanned the Atlantic. Norbonne Berkeley, a prominent Tory and connection of the Beauforts and a supporter of Bute, who had been made a groom of the bedchamber in 1760, and lord-lieutenant of Gloucestershire in 1762, received a letter from Grenville in 1763 reporting that the conservator of the Forest of Dean had been dismissed in light of Berkeley's complaint about his behaviour towards him, and Berkeley was asked to recommend a successor. In 1764, Berkeley's claim to the Botetourt peerage was confirmed, and in 1768 he was appointed governor of Virginia, a post he held until he died in 1770.[16]

Whatever the difficulties of the ministry from George's perspective, the opposition seemed to be even worse, as they appeared to be trying to make him 'a King in shackles', and, in the words of one informed critic, to be seeking to make the king 'a prisoner for life'.[17] Order and decorum were

[13] Elizabeth, Countess Cornwallis to her son, William, 29 Aug. 1763, G. Cornwallis-West, *The Life and Letters of Admiral Cornwallis* (London, 1927), pp. 30–1.

[14] Halifax to Buckingham, 24 June, 1, 5 July, 16 Aug. 1763, PRO. SP. 91/71 fol. 254, 91/72 fols 2–5, 44.

[15] Sandwich to his under-secretary, Richard Phelps, 1 Aug. 1764, BL. ST. 259 fol. 3.

[16] George Grenville to Berkeley, 30 Apr. 1763, HL. ST. 7 vol. 1.

[17] Philipps to George Grenville, 8 Sept. 1763, in W.T. Smith (ed.), *The Grenville Papers* (4 vols, London, 1852–3), II, 118; Bath to Montagu, 12 Nov. 1763, HL. MO. 4450.

also conspicuously at stake for George when he fully supported the ministry in its clash with John Wilkes. In governmental eyes, this dispute was an attempt to enforce constitutional propriety and royal and ministerial dignity. Wilkes, a libertine MP and an entrepreneur of faction, fell foul of his antithesis, George, as a result of bitter attacks on the government in his newspaper, the *North Briton*, which sought to exploit dissatisfaction in the capital, as well as to express the argument of the *Monitor* that 'the voice of the English nation was never confined within the walls of St. Stephen's Chapel [parliament]'.[18] Wilkes's denunciation of the Peace of Paris in number 45, issued on 23 April 1763, led to a charge of seditious libel. The implication that George had lied in his speech from the throne, as a result of being misled by his ministers, presented the crown as dishonoured:

Every friend of his country must lament that a prince of so many great and amiable qualities, whom England truly reveres, can be brought to give the sanction of his sacred name to the most odious measures, and to the most unjustifiable public declarations, from a throne ever renowned for truth, honour, and unsullied virtue.

In an outraged defence of royal dignity, as well as its own position, the ministry, with the full support of George, who pressed for action, issued a general warrant for the arrest of all those involved in the publication of number 45, sought to arrest Wilkes, despite his parliamentary privilege, and charged him with blasphemy because he attributed his indecent *Essay on Woman* to a cleric. These steps seized 'the attention of the whole nation'[19] and became key issues in parliamentary politics, with the legality of general warrants being a particular point of contention. There had always been criticism of monarchs, but the storm created by the case of the *North Briton* had a powerful impact, as it followed the far more positive response to the new reign. Elizabeth Montagu feared that 'the kingly office has received some wounds'.[20] The king, nevertheless, was pleased by the government's ability to see off parliamentary attacks,[21] not least in February 1764, when the opposition mounted a major, but unsuccessful, parliamentary challenge to the use of general warrants. Grenville pressed for an imitation of 'His Majesty's firmness and temper',[22] and George was willing to back the ministry against Wilkes. Expelled from parliament in

[18] *Monitor*, 23 Apr. 1763.

[19] John Horne Tooke to Madame Hill, 6 May 1763, New York, Public Library, Montague Collection vol. 11.

[20] Montagu to Bath, 28 Oct. 1763, HL. MO. 4594.

[21] Guerchy to Praslin, 19 Nov. 1763, AE. CP. Ang. 452 fol. 194.

[22] George Grenville to earl of Northumberland, 26 Feb. 1764, HL. ST. 7 vol. 1.

January 1764, Wilkes was outlawed that November after he had failed to appear to receive judgment for his conviction on two charges of libel.[23]

The king, however, lacked a harmonious working relationship with Grenville, and he also felt unhappy with aspects of ministerial policy. This included not only concern about the state of the national debt and a feeling that the ministers were governed by self-interest, but also worry about colonial policy, 'North America greatly discontented; and no proper dispositions, or at least, no satisfactory one made, of the new acquisitions.'[24] From the autumn of 1764, his relations with his first lord got worse. Personality was the key issue, George writing to Bute 'When he has wearied me for two hours, he looks at his watch to see if he may not tire me for an hour more.' Grenville, in turn, suspected Bute, with whom his relations had deteriorated, of having continued influence, and blamed the former minister for an opposition to his patronage demands that, in fact, stemmed from the king. Concerned to break with the ethos and practice of the 1750s, George was particularly anxious not to allow the ministers to control patronage and this proved a frequent source of contention with Grenville, who, in September 1763, unsuccessfully pressed George to let him succeed Bute as keeper of the privy purse.[25]

A lack of warmth between the two men contributed to Grenville's suspicion of George's intentions when, in April 1765, as a prudent response to recent illness, the king sought a regency bill to arrange matters in the event of his death. George intended his wife, Charlotte, as the regent, but would not name her, as he did not wish to damage already poor relations with his brother Edward, duke of York. Grenville, in turn, suspected that George wanted his mother, Augusta, to be the regent, a measure that might give Bute influence. The passage of the Act led to embarrassment; for example Grenville pressed George to reveal his choice, which the king did not wish to do. The issue of the definition of the royal family, and whether it should include Augusta, caused contention in parliament.[26]

As a result of his difficulties with Grenville, in whom he had lost confidence as well as losing patience with him, George approached Pitt again in May 1765, although, as Hardwicke had noted in 1763, the king had earlier expressed anger at pressure to turn to the former minister: 'what the king was once reported to have flung out – what do they mean? Do they mean to put a tyrant over me and themselves too'.[27] Cumberland, not Bute, was now George's most influential adviser; as George Sackville reported, 'the king had determined upon a total change of his ministry,

[23] P.D.G. Thomas, *John Wilkes, A Friend to Liberty* (Oxford, 1996).
[24] Newcastle to White, 4 June 1765, BL. Add. 33003 fol. 9.
[25] Lawson, *Grenville*, pp. 165, 212–13.
[26] D. Jarrett, 'The Regency Crisis of 1765', *English Historical Review*, 85 (1970), pp. 282–316.
[27] Hardwicke to Newcastle, 15 Oct. 1763, BL. Add. 32951 fols 429–30.

and . . . the whole power of negotiation was placed in the hands of the Duke of Cumberland', who went to see Pitt at Hayes on 19 May.[28] Pitt, however, refused to take part in the projected ministry because he suspected, correctly, that George had no intention of giving him his confidence. Pitt also wanted the negotiation of a counter-alliance to the Bourbon rulers of France and Spain, in short a return to continental interventionism, and the abandonment of general warrants. Hugh, earl (later duke) of Northumberland, lord-lieutenant of Ireland, who was seen by Pitt and Earl Temple as Bute's man (his eldest son married Bute's daughter Anne in 1764), and who was indeed close to the king, played a prominent role in the negotiations, though George sensibly appreciated that his friend could not be head of the ministry.[29]

George, who did not accept Pitt's policy agenda, thought of an alternative government under George, Lord Lyttelton as first lord and including Egmont and Charles Townshend, an echo of his father's political alliances, but Lyttelton and Townshend refused office. George therefore felt obliged to turn back to the bullying Grenville, as Cumberland and Egmont advised. Far from responding to the king's wish to behave better, Grenville peremptorily laid out humiliating conditions, including the dismissal of Lord Holland, formerly Henry Fox, as paymaster-general, and that George not consult Bute on politics, which the king answered by saying he had not done so since August 1763. George also had to yield to Grenville's demand that James Stuart Mackenzie, Bute's brother, be dismissed as lord privy seal for Scotland and lose his control of government management and policy there, although George had promised him the office for life. Mackenzie and Holland were dismissed on 23 May.[30] George was reported to have told Grenville, 'I will not, by refusing this condition, put my kingdoms into a state of confusion; but remember you forced me . . . You force me to break my word – you must be responsible for the consequences . . . you make me do, *as King*, which I should be *a scoundrel* to do as a *private man*.' Newcastle noted: 'I am told that the daily interviews between His Majesty and his ministers, are very disagreeable to both.'[31] George was so agitated that no drawing room was held on 26 May and he did not take the sacrament that day. He was cold to the ministers in public and, in contrast, conspicuously gracious to Mackenzie. It was not only Grenville who was the issue. George observed to Bute, 'every day I

---

[28] Beinecke, Osborn Files 34.13.

[29] Newcastle to White, 4 June 1765, BL. Add. 33003 fol. 9.

[30] Notes by Egmont on George to Egmont of 23 May 1765, memorandum by George, Fortescue, I, 114–15, 172–3; J.R.G. Tomlinson (ed.), *Additional Grenville Papers 1763–1765* (Manchester, 1962), pp. 269–72.

[31] Jenkinson diary, BL. Add. 38335 fol. 126; Newcastle to John White, 4 June 1765, BL. Add. 33003 fols 15–16.

meet with some insult from these people'.[32] The king, who had played a
key role in the attempted reshuffle,[33] was put under great pressure when
Bedford saw him and remonstrated on his failure to back the ministers and
on Bute's continued influence. An offended George replied that he had
given them 'the confidence necessary for the conduct of the public business',
but that their conduct did not deserve his favour.[34]

George's continued loathing of his ministers, accentuated by his humiliation by their demands and hectoring, led him to authorize Cumberland
to change the government, freeing him from being 'dictated to by low
men',[35] a term that had moral as well as social connotations. This led to a
direct approach to Pitt in June. George followed Cumberland's advice and
saw Pitt in person. In several meetings, the king agreed to the return of
many to office as Pitt requested, and he appears to have accepted Pitt's
view on policy other than on diplomacy, on which they differed, George
not sharing Pitt's desire for a Prussian alliance. For both men, this difference combined prudential considerations with a desire to vindicate themselves by revisiting their differences in 1761–3: each had a tendency to
stubbornness and to self-righteousness. Nevertheless, Pitt was willing to be
accommodating. According to Charles Jenkinson, joint-secretary to the
treasury, he agreed that, if Frederick II refused to accept a treaty without
a subsidy, the same proposition should be made to Austria. Temple was to
gain the treasury under Pitt's plan, but, never an easy man and increasingly
resentful of being expected to follow Pitt's lead, he refused to accept the
office. Without him, Pitt, though declaring 'his entire satisfaction with everything that had passed with the king, both as to measures and persons',[36] was
unwilling to form a ministry in which he might be overborne by Newcastle
and be dependent on Cumberland.

George was disappointed, but unwilling to accept Pitt's advice to keep
Grenville in office. Instead, as George had instructed Cumberland, a
failure to win Pitt led to an approach to the Newcastle connection, and its
members were willing to serve. George, in turn, played an active role in
support of Cumberland, seeking to persuade individuals such as Charles
Townshend (unsuccessfully) and Charles Yorke (successfully) to take office in
the new ministry. The formal change of government took place on 10 July,
George treating the departing Grenville coldly. The new government had

---

[32] Sedgwick (ed.), *Letters*, p. 241; Lawson, *Grenville*, p. 219.

[33] Egmont to Yorke, 7 June, Egmont to George, 7 June 1765, BL. Add. 47012A fols 97–8.

[34] Bedford to duke of Marlborough, 13 June 1765, in Lord John Russell (ed.), *The Bedford
Correspondence* (3 vols, London, 1843–6), III, 286–90; George to Northington, 12 June 1765,
Fortescue, I, 116–17; Jenkinson diary, BL. Add. 38335 fols 128–9.

[35] George to Cumberland, 12 June 1765, Fortescue, I, 118–19.

[36] Newcastle to White, 29 June 1765, BL. Add. 33003 fol. 17; Jenkinson diary, BL. Add.
38335 fol. 130.

the inexperienced Charles, second marquess of Rockingham, at the treasury and the elderly Newcastle as lord privy seal. Born in 1730, Rockingham was a wealthy Yorkshire landowner, with a major political following in this well-represented county. A committed Whig who had joined Cumberland's forces against the Jacobites in 1745, he had resigned as a lord of the bedchamber in 1762 and had opposed Bute. George was to praise Rockingham more as an agricultural improver than as a politician.[37] Cumberland, a key figure in the new government, attended cabinet until his death that October.

Grenville carped that he did not see any prospect of there being the basis for the establishment of a firm and stable administration', and congratulated himself:

> if I should live a hundred years I could never leave the public service more agreeably or honorably to myself than at present when the public measures in Parliament have been attended with the highest success.[38]

The new government, however, faced a crisis stemming from the North American colonies. Grenville had been more worried about 'the exhausted state of the public revenues' than the 'clamour or opposition of any individuals whatsoever',[39] but this led to fiscal legislation that greatly increased 'clamour'. The crisis over the Grenville ministry's Stamp Act of 1765, which imposed a series of duties on the North American colonies, was greater than that within England over the highly unpopular cider tax, because it raised the question of parliamentary authority in America. Indeed, the role of parliament was a significant constraint on George's position with regard to the colonies, as the management of neither was directly handled by the monarch. When, in response to Virginia's rejection in 1765 of parliament's right to levy the stamp duty, George was advised that this was a matter of 'too high a nature for the determination of your Majesty in your Privy Council; and is proper only for the consideration of Parliament', he responded by giving directions that the issue be laid before it.[40] Many American critics of the Stamp Act sought to assert a direct relationship with George which he, constitutionally, could not allow to exist.

[37] R. Hoffman, *The Marquess: A Study of Lord Rockingham 1730–82* (New York, 1973).

[38] George Grenville to Hans Stanley, 12 July 1765, Aylesbury, Buckinghamshire CRO. D56/7/1.

[39] George Grenville to Waller, 29 Sept. 1763, HL. ST. 7 vol. 1; J. Bullion, *A Great and Necessary Measure: George Grenville and the Genesis of the Stamp Act, 1763–1765* (Columbia, Missouri, 1982).

[40] BL. Add. 33001 fol. 34.

The Stamp Act, which was pressed by George,[41] easily passed both houses of parliament, but the response in the colonies was hostile. In America, Nova Scotia and the Leeward Islands, but not the major West Indian colonies,[42] the sense that the levying of taxation for revenue purposes by a parliament that included no colonial representatives was a dangerous innovation, was accompanied by anger about any departure from the traditionally lax enforcement of existing commercial regulations and any restrictions on smuggling with non-British territories. By overthrowing Grenville, George inadvertently helped undermine the Stamp Act, although he did not see the issue in these either/or terms. Concerned about the violent response in America – 'all America is in confusion'[43] – and influenced by pressure from British merchants worried about an American boycott of British goods,[44] the Rockingham ministry favoured the abandonment of the tax, but, at the same time, insisted, by means of a Declaratory Act, on the principle of parliamentary sovereignty.

Characteristically keen on respect for authority, which he saw as prudential as well as moral, George, however, was unenthusiastic about concessions. On 10 January 1766, the king informed Bute that it was acceptable for 'my friends' to oppose them,[45] 'where they think their honour and conscience requires it, that I not only think it right, but am of opinion it is their duty to act so', a course of action that sits ill with George's subsequent willingness from 1767 to dismiss courtiers who took a line of which he disapproved.[46] In 1766, George was not prepared to force his will, in the shape of his opposition to concession, on his ministers, and on 10 January he pressed Bute not to overthrow the government; but he supported a revision of the policy rather than total repeal of the Stamp Act, an approach he made little effort to conceal.

The ministry came under pressure in parliament in early 1766 over its attempt to push through repeal, and was defeated in the Lords on 4 February. This caused Rockingham, three days later, to turn to George and seek his support. As George, third earl of Albemarle, pointed out, a 'public mark of his Majesty's resolution to support his ministers' was required.[47] The

---

[41] P.D.G. Thomas, *George III. King and Politicians 1760–1770* (Manchester, 2002), p. 105.

[42] W.B. Kerr, 'The Stamp Act in Nova Scotia', *New England Quarterly*, 6 (1933), pp. 552–66; A.J. O'Shaughnessy, 'The Stamp Act Crisis in the British Caribbean', *William and Mary Quarterly*, 3rd series, 51 (1994), pp. 203–26.

[43] General Conway to Rockingham, 10 Oct., Governor Thomas Boone of New York to Rockingham, 8 Nov. 1765, WW. R1–502, 522.

[44] Newcastle to Rockingham, 22 Oct. 1765, WW. R1–511.

[45] Sedgwick (ed.), *Letters*, p. 242.

[46] M. McCahill, 'The House of Lords in the 1760s', in C. Jones (ed.), *A Pillar of the Constitution. The House of Lords in British Politics, 1640–1784* (London, 1989), pp. 189–90.

[47] Newcastle to Rockingham, Albemarle to Rockingham, both 31 Jan. 1766, WW. R1–563–4.

role of Bute's friends in the opposition made George's position sensitive,[48] as Bute was still widely believed to be close to the king and his speech in the Lords on 6 February had led many to assume George was opposed to repeal. Indeed, he rejected government approaches to discipline office-holders who opposed repeal.

On 7 February, in a letter which indicated George's awareness that he was undermining the ministers, and which also expressed a concern for secrecy that suggests that other questionable interventions may not have left a trace, George pressed Egmont, whom he regarded as reliable, to contact Bute:

> As the Ministers are so much on the watch, I am cautious of having your chariot [carriage] too often at my door. I therefore send you this that you may not be ignorant of Lord Rockingham's having again this day pressed me to dismiss Mr. Dyson, but I civilly rejected it; I have been revolving over in my mind Lord Bute's speech of yesterday, I think he and his friends are going headlong into a precipice they don't well see; I therefore wish in the course of tomorrow, you could see either Elliot, or Oswald, or Norton, (for perhaps the going to him might awaken the old jealousy of the present set against you) and let them convey to him why you don't go yourself. Show them how friendly you have acted. See whether they won't entrust you to make either some composition with some of the present men, (I don't mean to leave the present wise Treasury) or else to see if the Duke of Bedford cannot be detached; and join you and them. These are my rough thoughts, I wish to learn your ideas; but I own I think something of this kind may make them at least come to their senses and some how or other assist us. This is of so very critical a nature that I beg when you have maturely weighed it, that you will destroy this, I beg to any of them that you will declare you act from yourself and unknown to me, but seeing the danger that is approaching you think every honest man ought to communicate his ideas.[49]

In response to Rockingham's appeal, the king on 7 February told him that he was ready to back repeal of the Stamp Act, and Rockingham was given permission to disclose this view, which he did that day before the debate in the House of Commons. This disclosure helped ensure that, on 7 February, the ministry defeated the opposition's defence of the Stamp Act, a defence in which Grenville was prominent, by 274 votes to 134.

In response to this defeat, the opposition switched tack and pressed for George's policy of modification, rather than the complete repeal backed by

---

[48] Newcastle to Rockingham, 1 Feb. 1766, WW. R1–565.
[49] George to Egmont, 7 Feb. 1766, BL. Add. 47012A fol. 114.

the government or the enforcement called for by Grenville in the
Commons on 7 February. George, however, proved unwilling to co-operate
with the opposition and abandon the ministers and, instead, helped them
get repeal through the Lords in March 1766, especially by accepting
Rockingham's advice that he convince the lord chancellor, Robert, first earl
of Northington, to back the measure. He played a major role in the key
debate on 11 March. George had earlier urged courtiers such as Talbot to
be 'as right as I can desire on the Stamp Act; strong for our declaring our
right but willing to repeal'.[50] The king, who took considerable interest in
the debates,[51] himself benefited from the popularity of repeal: when he
went to parliament to give the royal assent on 18 March he was cheered in
the streets, while he also enjoyed a brief burst in popularity in North
America. When the Stamp Act was repealed, a Declaratory Act was passed
stating that parliament 'had, hath, and of right ought to have full power
and authority to make laws and statutes of sufficient form and validity to
bind the colonies and people of America in all cases whatsoever'.[52]

George's actions during repeal were, at the time and subsequently, a
cause of much controversy. His willingness to authorize James, Lord
Strange, chancellor of the duchy of Lancaster, on 10 February to state his
preference for modification, not repeal, but 'if the different parties were
too wild to come into that', his willingness to accept the latter, caused great
concern to the ministry. Strange reported this extensively, and took this
line in the Commons on 21–22 February. This appeared to contradict
George's assurances to the ministers, as did the refusal to dragoon the
King's Friends, or even to offer them a clear lead. To Horace Walpole, this
was clear villainy,

> a scene ... that exhibited a duplicity, at once so artful and yet so
> impolitic, so narrow minded in its views, and so dangerous in its
> tendency, that the warmest partisans of royalty, of the Princess
> [Augusta] and the favourite [Bute] will never be able to efface the stain.
> What crooked councils, and how insincere the mind, which could infuse
> or imbibe such lessons!

To Walpole, the episode demonstrated George's continued subservience to
Bute.[53] It certainly confused political opinion and helped ensure that the

[50] George to Rockingham, 21 Jan. 1766, Fortescue, I, 244.
[51] George to Rockingham, 17, 26 Mar. 1766, WW. R1–584, 589.
[52] P. Langford, *The First Rockingham Administration, 1765–1766* (Oxford, 1973), pp. 108–98;
P.D.G. Thomas, *British Politics and the Stamp Act Crisis. The First Phase of the American Revolution,
1763–1767* (Oxford, 1975), pp. 154–252.
[53] H. Walpole, *Memoirs of the Reign of King George III*, ed. D. Jarrett (4 vols, New Haven and
London, 1999), III, 22–3.

King's Friends divided on repeal. On 11 March, seven lords of the bed-chamber voted against repeal, as did Bute and George's brother Edward. To George his position was consistent with his moral approach to politics: neither parliamentarians nor he himself should take a stand for political convenience if it was opposed to their conscience, and it would be wrong for him to discipline allies accordingly. The extent to which George felt it necessary to explain himself to Strange did not help the ministry, but, conversely, according to George, Rockingham had exaggerated his support for repeal. The king was aware that he had failed to provide a clear line, writing on 11 February, about 'the late variety of opinions that have been reported to be mine on the Stamp Act'. He claimed to have followed a consistent approach, favouring modification, which 'ascertained the right of the Mother Country to tax its colonies', while showing a desire to redress grievances, but, if British politics did not permit this course, thinking 'repealing infinitely more eligible than enforcing, which could only tend to widen the breach between this country and America'.[54] George had also explained himself to Rockingham, who, on 10 February,

> complained to me as if he was accused of having wrong stated my opinion on the Stamp Act; I told him I had on Friday [7th] given him permission to say I preferred repealing to enforcing the Stamp Act; but that modification I had ever thought both more consistent with the honour of this country, and all the Americans would with any degree of justice hope for.[55]

Yet his letter to Bute of 10 January, leaving it open for King's Friends to oppose repeal, could be seen as undermining the ministry. It certainly contributed to a sense of George as semi-detached from it, and the letter to Egmont underlined this. This aspect of his kingship stemmed from George's position as a limited monarch, who was disinclined to support policies of which he disapproved. His sense of his own integrity and that of the King's Friends did not allow George to offer backing in these circum-stances, but also exposed him to the charge of deceitful, indeed unconsti-tutional, behaviour toward the ministers. George was unhappy about being head of a government he could not influence to follow views he thought acceptable and necessary, and this contributed to an impression of distance that was seen clearly when he complained about his ministers, both during the Rockingham ministry and on other occasions.

[54] Memorandum by George, 11 Feb. 1766, Fortescue, I, 269.
[55] Memorandum by George, 10 Feb. 1766, Fortescue, I, 268–9. On George's position in this crisis, see also Langford, *Rockingham Administration*, p. 168; F. O'Gorman, *The Rise of Party in England: The Rockingham Whigs 1760–82* (London, 1975), pp. 163–7; McCahill, 'Lords', pp. 181–2.

Cumberland's death in October 1765 made the ministry seem weaker, but George assured Rockingham of continued backing and blocked the idea of an approach to Bute. Pitt's opposition to the Stamp Act, instead, had led Rockingham to seek and receive George's permission for another approach to Pitt designed to strengthen the government. At their meeting on 18 January 1766, Pitt, however, had demanded too many ministerial changes, an answer the king thought impracticable.[56] Thereafter, Pitt's attacks on the ministry increased in vigour, and Rockingham told Augustus, third duke of Grafton, secretary of state for the Northern Department, on 21 April that he would never again advise George to send for Pitt. Nevertheless, the king was concerned about the competence of the government and pleased by Pitt's declared willingness to pick a ministry without consideration of faction. In the Commons three days later, Pitt outlined his views on British politics in a way reminiscent of George's attitudes at the start of his reign:

> the government was a free limited monarchy – wishes for such a ministry as the king himself should choose, the people approve, and who should be eminent above others for their ability and integrity – that the people would grow weary of our divisions.[57]

Pitt's apparent dominance of the Commons debates contrasted with Rockingham's weakness as head of a divided ministry, and led George to make a new approach to Pitt, although a concern for stability encouraged him to decide to let the ministry see out the session, while a prudence born of experience made him cautious about Pitt's stance.[58] Grafton's decision to resign because Pitt had not been taken into the ministry precipitated the crisis, not least because it proved difficult to persuade anyone to replace him. Rockingham and Newcastle refused to strengthen the ministry by allying with Bute's group,[59] an instance of the politics of exclusion that was so important to the factionalism of the period; while Rockingham alienated George by failing not only in emollience but also in satisfying his interests, for example not giving the king's brothers the allowance Cumberland had had. George had been pressed on this by his brothers.[60]

George no longer had confidence in Rockingham, but wanted a pretext to dismiss him. This was to be provided by the position of Catholics in

[56] George to Rockingham, 21 Jan. 1766, WW. R1–559.

[57] HP., Harris, 24 Apr. 1766.

[58] Sedgwick (ed.), *Letters*, pp. 247, 250–1.

[59] Egmont to George, [May-June 1766], BL. Add. 47012 fols 124–5.

[60] Sedgwick (ed.), *Letters*, pp. 250–1; George to Egmont, 2 May 1766, Fortescue, I, 301; Edward, duke of York to Rockingham, 27 May, Rockingham to George [27 or 28 May], George to Rockingham, 2 June 1766, WW. R1–620–1, 624.

Quebec and its relation to disputes within the ministry, an issue that looked towards the more prominent role played by Catholic emancipation in the political disputes of the 1790s, 1800s and 1820s. Northington, the lord chancellor, a zealous Protestant, opposed a board of trade recommendation for the use of French civil law in property cases in Quebec. When Rockingham sought his resignation and the appointment, instead, of Charles Yorke, to whom, the previous year, George had promised the job in 1766, the king used the opportunity of Northington's advice, that the government was too weak to continue,[61] in order to act. This was the culmination of a damaging process in which George had repeatedly failed to back his ministers because they did not match his expectations. He supported Bute to the end, but had previously used him to undermine Pitt and Newcastle. In addition, George was hostile to Grenville and destabilized his ministry, and he failed to sustain Rockingham. The king was apt to be aggrieved if his opinions and goodwill were not reciprocated, and reciprocation, in his eyes, tended to entail agreement. This was a matter of his personality and his interpretation of the relationship between Patriot kingship and politicians.

On 7 July 1766 George wrote to Pitt, seeking his views on 'how an able and dignified ministry may be formed' and noting how completely his 'ideas concerning the basis on which a new administration should be erected, are consonant to the opinion' Pitt had given on the subject in parliament on 24 April.[62] Percy, first earl of Thomond, reported 'the day before yesterday the king sent to Mr. Pitt with carte blanche to form a ministry: having given to the present ministers the reason for so doing that they had not formed any plan for acquisition of strength to carry on his government'.[63] Satisfied with Pitt's response, George instructed the ministry, on 9 July, that they would be dismissed. Newcastle later referred to this 'cruel usage'.[64]

Informed that Pitt was ready to form a Ministry of All the Talents,[65] George, hoping 'to extricate the country out of a faction', saw him on 12 July 1766. They agreed to form an administration on as broad a basis as possible, but both were determined to exclude those with whom they felt unable to co-operate. George wanted the objectionable Grenville kept from office, and, indeed, his decision to turn to Pitt had owed much to his being persuaded that the latter had decisively broken with Grenville. Pitt,

[61] Richmond to Rockingham, 8 July, Vere, third earl of Poulett to Rockingham, 14 July 1766, WW. R1–642, 649.

[62] George to Pitt, 7 July 1766, Fortescue, I, 368; W.S. Taylor and J.H. Pringle (eds), *Correspondence of William Pitt, Earl of Chatham* (4 vols, London, 1838–40) II, 436; Thomas, *Stamp Act Crisis*, p. 281.

[63] HL. STG. Box 23 (44).

[64] R. Browning, *The Duke of Newcastle* (New Haven, 1975), p. 316.

[65] Sedgwick (ed.), *Letters*, p. 251.

in turn, had Newcastle and Rockingham dismissed, as he would have no one in the cabinet who had previously served as head of the ministry, and also because he distrusted Newcastle and Rockingham, the duke's chosen heir, partly as exponents of the methods and purposes of connection, or, as it could be termed, faction or party.[66] This matched George's ideas, but Pitt's return to power, like earlier discussions to the same end, seemed to some to be based on the worst kind of secret backstairs deals, so that by 1766 the new generation of Patriots were portraying him as no more than a puppet of Bute, still supposedly influential with George and, inaccurately, held responsible for the change of ministry.[67] Turning to Pitt did not bring George the popular praise lost when he had resigned in 1761.

In fact, the formation of the new ministry was accompanied by the final break between king and his former favourite. George had promised Grenville in May 1765 that he would not consult Bute again. He sent Bute details of the negotiations with Pitt in a letter of January 1766; and that July wrote to him about the formation of the new ministry, explaining that he had not consulted him because of the promise to Grenville. It was the king's last letter to Bute, and, when the earl died in March 1792, George responded with scant interest, and with largely formal courtesy.[68] Breaking with Bute was a key aspect of George's coming to personal and political maturity, and reflected his growing confidence in his judgement of people and circumstances.

Alongside this breach, Pitt accommodated George by making concessions to some of Bute's friends, but, crucially, treated them as the King's Friends, not Bute's faction: Pitt approached them directly, not via Bute, which helped cause the breach between king and former favourite. Bute's brother, Stuart Mackenzie, returned as lord privy seal of Scotland, a step for which George, not Bute, was responsible.[69] Northumberland gained a dukedom, although George had only wanted to advance him to a marquessate. Northumberland, however, backed by Pitt, insisted on the dukedom. In addition, Charles Jenkinson and Hans Stanley gained posts, Jenkinson as a lord of the admiralty, and Stanley first as ambassador to St Petersburg (he never went) and then as cofferer of the household. This strengthened the new ministry. Bedford's group, however, was denied office.

The new ministry was not without talent, but there was no unity of purpose to hold it together, while several of its members were inexperienced. It is known as the Chatham ministry, but this identification of

---

[66] Taylor and Pringle (eds), *Chatham Corresp.* II, 468–9.

[67] Hardwicke to Rockingham, 11 July, Newcastle to Rockingham, 12 July 1766, WW. R1–645–6.

[68] Sedgwick (ed.), *Letters*, pp. 241–54.

[69] *Selections from the Family Papers Preserved at Caldwell* (Glasgow, 1854), II, p. 90.

minister and government was weakened by Pitt's decision not to take one of the leading offices of business, and by his abandonment of the task of leading the Commons when he was created earl of Chatham on 29 July 1766. Because Temple, who objected to being one of Pitt's 'ciphers', refused the post, the inexperienced Grafton became first lord of the treasury, as Pitt requested. Pitt himself became lord privy seal, while Lieutenant-General Henry Conway and William, second earl of Shelburne, were the secretaries of state. Neither was in the leading rank of politicians.

Although the opposition was divided, the chances of Chatham creating a stable and lasting ministry were lessened by his age and, from October 1766, very poor health, and in the spring of 1767 he succumbed to what may have been a severe attack of manic depression. Even before that, the ministry was in serious difficulties. Pitt was certainly unsuited to management, but in 1757–61 he, and also George II, had had Newcastle to do that for him. In 1766–7, however, the duke, who was to die in November 1768, was no longer at his side, there was nobody to take his place, and issues and circumstances were more divisive and less likely to produce countervailing pressures for unity than had been the case during the earlier ministry. Amidst the complexities of peacetime politics, the sense of national unity that Pitt had been able to benefit from, and to foster, during the Seven Years War, and that George III had sought to redefine and redirect, was absent. Furthermore, these complexities helped to place the already poorly united ministry under strain.

King and minister differed on some major policy issues. George lacked Chatham's enthusiasm for the formation of a triple alliance with Prussia and Russia designed to counter the Bourbons. Indeed, George consistently believed that Britain should be 'in a situation to be courted, not to court, foreign powers'.[70] Frederick the Great anyway rejected the British approach, telling Andrew Mitchell, the British envoy in Berlin, that British governmental instability made negotiations with her pointless, an argument increasingly made on the continent in the 1760s. The chances of a Russian alliance were also slight because George was opposed both to granting Russian demands for a peacetime subsidy and to the Russian expectation of a commitment to assist Catherine the Great in any war with Turkey. George's view was a sensible one, as the history of Anglo-Russian relations over the previous half-century had revealed that Russian rulers and ministers would accept British diplomatic initiatives only on their own terms and that alliance with an aggressive power that sought subsidies was not the way to achieve the British goal of stability. George's view on the proposed alliance was also an important example of the manner in which the new departures in policy associated with him after

[70] George to Rockingham, no date, WW. R1–2137.

his accession had been sustained – in this case, opposition to expensive continental intervention.

The ministry's American policies resulted in more serious political problems. The Revenue Act that Charles Townshend, the chancellor of the exchequer, drew up, imposed customs duties in the colonies on a variety of goods, most valuably tea which was imported by the East India Company, and which was to provide half the revenue. The taxation was designed to pay the costs of civil government in the colonies and thus end the dependence of officials and judges on the colonial assemblies. Introduced on 1 June 1767, the legislation passed easily and received the royal assent on 2 July.

This led to a serious deterioration in relations between the British government and its American critics. Unlike the West Indies, the Americans responded with trade boycotts, and on 11 February 1768 the Massachusetts Assembly agreed that the tax infringed the rights of 'American subjects'. To force Massachusetts to back down, the British ministry, in turn, decided to send troops and warships to Boston, an initiative that was to have serious consequences. Chatham had failed to give coherence to Britain's American policy, let alone to devise a new policy that would help to repair recent differences and give a new direction, or even to advance a vision of empire that would win American support. He turned down the idea of a secretary of state for American affairs, a suggestion that would have offered coherence in the implementation of policy, as well as a source of ideas and an agency for links with the colonies. Instead, Chatham showed relatively little interest in America or in American views. In 1767, when the New York Assembly had refused to enforce Grenville's Mutiny Act in full, the cabinet, with Chatham's backing, had decided to insist on obedience and to suspend the Assembly, although, as the latter yielded, the crisis was averted.[71]

The issues that the government confronted were increasingly overshadowed by two related questions: Chatham's health and political rivalries. The latter recalled the situation that George had faced earlier in the decade. Chatham's expectation, in the absence of any 'party' basis around which government business could cohere, that all good men would come forward to further national interests was shown to be naïve, and his lack of persuasive skills reflected the extent to which, like the much younger George, he was, as a politician without connection, weak; though not, like George, inexperienced. It was ironic that George shared Chatham's naïvety, but this helped explain and ease the return of the latter to office. With Newcastle, there was no such similarity.

[71] L.B. Namier and J. Brooke, *Charles Townshend* (London, 1964), pp. 158–72; Thomas, *Stamp Act Crisis*, pp. 287–95, and *The Townshend Duties Crisis. The Second Phase of the American Revolution 1767–1773* (Oxford, 1987), pp. 18–36.

In addition, the power of the crown came into dispute: not because of George's views but as a result of the government's embargo on grain exports. Food riots in 1766 had followed an increase in the price of grain that reflected a poor harvest in both Britain and the continent. Worried about both the state of the people and the disturbances, a characteristic yoking of concerns in George's mind – 'the present risings are only an additional proof to me of the great licentiousness that has infused itself into all orders of men' – he had accepted Chatham's advice for an embargo on grain exports to continental markets, and a royal proclamation issued on 26 September introduced this.[72] It was to take effect until three days after the meeting of the next parliamentary session, by which time it was assumed parliament would have taken the necessary measures. A popular step that helped end the riots, such a prerogative action, however, infringed the Bill of Rights of 1689. Critics argued that, instead of the king relying on prerogative powers, parliament should have been recalled. George's speech opening the session declared that 'necessity' had led him 'to exert my royal authority for the preservation of public safety', but, although parliamentary consent to the extension of the embargo was obtained, there was controversy as to the legality of the proclamation and, therefore, whether an indemnity was required for those who had advised it and acted under it.

In the Lords, Chatham quoted John Locke in arguing that, if there was a clash between the executive power and the people over a right claimed as prerogative, the good of the people must settle the matter, but he implied that the crown must be the sole judge of necessity, a view that clashed with much for which he had stood. Dartmouth wrote of the debate that Charles, Lord Camden, the lord chancellor, and Chatham 'did not assert the legality of an act of the Crown against law, but in the case of inevitable necessity and upon that maxim which is fundamental to all government of every kind, *salus populi suprema lex*. In explaining themselves they did (as men in the eagerness of debate almost always do) drop expressions which taken by themselves, without regard to the scope of the argument, might admit of a construction very foreign to their intentions and sentiments.' Another peer commented that the speakers had 'exposed themselves to very disagreeable and nearly general animadversions. The doctrine of a latent power in the Crown of dispensing with laws justified by necessity of which the Crown was to be judge, could not be brooked ... Lord Chatham, drove to the wall, reasoned for the doctrine, and declared against it.'[73] Bedford's claim that the crown had a suspending power was contradicted by Grenville's emphasis on the Bill of Rights.

[72] George to Conway, 20, 24 Sept. 1766, Fortescue, I, 394, 398.
[73] Dartmouth to earl of Guildford, 13 Nov. 1766, Bod. North Mss. d 10; earl of Buckinghamshire to Colonel Hotham, 13 Dec. 1766, Hull UL, Hotham papers 4/15; P. Lawson, 'Parliament, the Constitution and Corn: The Embargo Crisis of 1766', *Parliamentary History*, 5 (1986), pp. 17-37.

More significantly, the ministry was divided over policy towards America and India, and the ministers were unsuited to their tasks. Chatham found that many politicians would not support the government. Rather, like the Bute ministry for George in 1763, and providing some guidance on how to judge the king's policy, the Chatham administration had failed its creator. Chatham had hoped to demonstrate that government in the national interest and without faction was possible, but instead he had found the first difficult to further, and the second impossible to achieve. Nevertheless, the language of government without faction remained important, helping shape assumptions about both ministers and monarch, and became part of the political language, irrespective of the factional calculation involved. At a time of discussions about strengthening the ministry, Bedford was informed in November 1766 'That the King did not design to proscribe particulars of any denomination . . . but that it was intended to deal the favours of the Crown with an equal hand to those who should have abilities and power to serve it'.[74] In practice, George seems to have had scant wish to bring in Bedford, but the mismatch between ideology and political conduct was a constant, and one that helped confuse the response both to George and to other major political figures.

Probably as a consequence of the combination of stress and depression, Chatham became an invalid and, as minister, did not see George after 12 March 1767. That June, he excused himself from seeing George on the grounds of his nerves. He agreed to see Grafton, the first lord of the treasury, only when pressed by George. Chatham's health prefigured George's position just over two decades later, with Chatham presented as 'disabled by dejection of spirits almost approaching to insane melancholy'.[75] He was seen by Anthony Addington, who had a special reputation for the treatment of mental disease. Addington, the father of the future Prime Minister Henry Addington, also believed that gout was best treated by inducing fits of the condition, and accordingly prescribed alcohol, plenty of meat and little exercise.

Unwilling to have Chatham resign, George was confident that he would recover, a serious misreading both of Chatham and of the political situation. The king, who generally displayed considerable care towards his ministers as individuals if not always sensitivity towards their position and views, provided encouragement and advice on doctors. George also sought to bolster his confidence, assuring Chatham in January 1768 that 'your name has been sufficient to enable my administration to proceed'.[76] In February 1768, however, the office of privy seal held by Chatham was placed into commission and, that October, Chatham asked for permission

[74] Bedford to Marlborough, 29 Nov. 1766, Russell (ed.), *Bedford Correspondence*, III, 355–6.
[75] HP. Harris, July 1767.
[76] Taylor and Pringle (eds), *Chatham Corresp.* III, 318.

to leave office. Faced with political difficulties and personal strain, he could do so. George had no such option short of abdicating.

Meanwhile, with George's permission, Grafton had sought to strengthen the ministry by winning over part of the opposition. George had been very concerned by the pressure the government had been exposed to in the 1767 session,[77] but feared what a reconstitution of the ministry might entail. Grafton declared 'that he had never seen the King so much agitated; that His Majesty was not disinclined to take Lord Rockingham, but protested he had almost rather resign his crown than consent to receive George Grenville again',[78] not the most helpful contribution to reasoned political discussion but an indication of George's willingness to mention abdication when stressed and vexed. This looked forward to the king's anguish over having to accept the Fox–North coalition in 1783. George made an effort to bolster Grafton and to strengthen the ministry, with which he closely identified, writing 'I have 65 votes present and 30 proxies for me in the House of Lords'. George's efforts were concentrated in the Lords, where his personal links and household and episcopal patronage were most effective.[79] Rockingham was offered the treasury by Grafton on 7 July 1767, but disagreements over places led to the failure of Rockingham's attempt to form a new ministry. The government's reputation suffered when Rockingham reported his failure to the king on 22 July, as George said that he had not offered the treasury to him.[80] This caused Rockingham to feel misled by Grafton, but the difficulty of ministerial reconstitution was such that everyone's reputations suffered. George could not escape the process.

Despite their different religious sympathies (Grafton was more liberal), George liked Grafton, but the duke was not really up to the job, either as a minister or as a politician. The Grafton ministry was a continuation of that of Chatham, but its composition was increasingly different. Gower and Weymouth, supporters of Bedford, joined the government in December 1767, although George, who distrusted Bedford, refused to have more than two members of the group in the cabinet. The ministry anyway continued unstable. In response to his independence from his colleagues, Chatham's protégé Shelburne was dismissed in October 1768. George was firmer than Grafton in this crisis. Shelburne's replacement, William, fourth earl of Rochford, an experienced diplomat, met the king's preference for a non-party minister. George's family, at the same time, continued to grow: on 2 November 1767, his fourth son, Edward, was born, his second daughter, Augusta, following on 8 November 1768.

---

[77] George to Grafton, 30 May 1767, Fortescue, I, 477.
[78] Walpole, *Memoirs*, III, 145.
[79] George to Chatham, 31 May 1767, Fortescue, I, 481; McCahill, 'Lords', pp. 191, 197.
[80] Bedford, private journal, 23 July 1767, Russell (ed.), *Bedford Correspondence*, III, 386.

Meanwhile, George was taking an active role in politics. When in the general election of 1768 John Wilkes was elected for Middlesex, George successfully pressed the cabinet to have Wilkes expelled from the Commons, a step that was to expose the government to considerable embarrassment. Three times re-elected by Middlesex in 1769, Wilkes was declared incapable of being re-elected by parliament, and his opponent, Henry Luttrell, was declared elected, a thwarting of the views of the electors that aroused anger. Wilkes was also the focus of more widespread popular opposition to the government, and of a measure of radicalism that led, in 1768, to a series of riots in London, with criticism of George for failing to respond to the Wilkesite petitions. Relations between the king and the City of London became particularly poor, and George's manner when he received City remonstrances was criticized.

The French purchase of the island of Corsica from the republic of Genoa in 1768 brought more immediate problems, with the ministry divided about how best to respond to what was seen as a major increase of French power in the Mediterranean. The Corsican resistance leader, Pasquale Paoli, received secret British help with the support of the king via the Civil List. George subsequently claimed that he was not reimbursed.[81] To French anger, the king received Paoli in London, but George made clear his view that war over the issue should be avoided.[82] Across the Atlantic, opposition to British taxation under the Revenue Act of 1767 led to the dispatch of British reinforcements to Boston in 1768, while in Ireland royal patronage by the lord-lieutenant was used to push through an increase of troops on the Irish establishment.[83]

George himself was faced by a different political agenda to that of his first years as king, and had to adjust to a new generation of politicians. Major figures from the age of George II had died in the 1760s: Dodington in 1762, Granville (Carteret) in 1763, Hardwicke and Bath in 1764, Cumberland in 1765, and Newcastle in 1768. Chatham was still around, but was now very much a fading force. On 7 July 1769, when he returned to court, he saw George for the last time. Characteristically insensitive and self-righteous, Chatham criticized government policy, but also sought to justify himself to the king, who retained a position as the arbiter of political behaviour. He told George that, if he opposed government business in the Lords, he hoped 'His Majesty would be indulgent enough to believe that it

[81] George to Pitt, 26 May 1787, PRO. 30/8/103 fol. 232.
[82] George to Grafton, 16 Sept. 1768, Fortescue, II, 44.
[83] T.W. Bartlett, 'The Augmentation of the Army in Ireland, 1767–1769', *English Historical Review*, 96 (1981), pp. 540–59.

would not arise from any personal consideration'.[84] George, meanwhile, was still supposed to be readier to take in Rockingham than Grenville.[85]

Grafton had survived attack by Rockingham and Grenville, but, in January 1770, Chatham's return to political activity and declaration of opposition led the Chathamites in the ministry, Camden and John, marquess of Granby, to desert Grafton. Chatham inaccurately claimed that Bute had undermined his ministry, sustaining the paranoid tone in politics. In order to put pressure on Grafton, Chatham sought to co-operate with Rockingham, then the most prominent opposition politician. In response, Grafton resigned on 27 January 1770, but his was to be the last of the short-lived ministries, for George turned to Frederick, Lord North, the chancellor of the exchequer, and offered him the treasury. At last, he had found a first minister able to lead the Commons, manage business and maintain a united government, albeit with difficulties, especially under the second head.

[84] W. Anson (ed.), *Autobiography and Political Correspondence of Augustus Henry, Third Duke of Grafton* (London, 1898), p. 237.
[85] Duke of Manchester to Rockingham, 7 Nov. 1769, WW. R1–1247.

Chapter 6

GEORGE AND LORD NORTH, 1770–4

In 1770, Frederick, Lord North was helped by a natural rallying of support to the crown, the focus of most politicians' loyalty, a rallying that took place in response both to the extremism of some of the opposition and to a more general concern about the preservation of order. Furthermore, the reintegration of the Tories into the political mainstream helped heal a long-standing divide dating from the mid-seventeenth century that had posed a challenge to political stability. The disunited character of the opposition, especially the tension between the Chathamites and the Rockinghamites, also contributed to the rallying, while the absence of a reversionary interest, as George, prince of Wales, was only born in 1762, removed the alternative of a loyal opposition centred on another member of the royal family. Cumberland's death in 1765 had contributed to the same situation. The collapse of Bute's influence was also important to the king's recovery in popularity, while George was more adroit than he had been in the early 1760s.

Although the absence of a dynastic rival (or alternative dynasty) was valuable, it forced some opponents to seek more radical methods of attack, helping to make republicanism attractive and viable again in the age of the American Revolution, both in America and in Britain, but this also lessened the appeal of opposition in Britain. For most contemporaries, concern, even paranoia, about the position and objectives of the king did not extend to republicanism, although the establishment of a republic in North America indicated the potential for change. Furthermore, within Britain the political atmosphere was affected by the willingness and ability of some politicians to create a coherent connection or party that focused much of its ideology and energy on hostility towards what were seen as royal attitudes and views.

North himself was an experienced and astute politician, and an effective minister. Six years older than George III, he had been an MP since 1754. Unlike the king, North benefited from his father's longevity. Indeed, he did not succeed him as earl of Guilford until 1790. This helped give North personal stability, while staying in the Commons ensured that he was politically crucial, as the leadership of this House was correctly seen as more difficult than that of the Lords, and therefore as more important. Like Robert Walpole and Henry Pelham, North combined leadership of the Commons, from January 1768, with a valuable knowledge of the public finances. A lord of the treasury from 1759 to 1765, he had been joint paymaster-general from 1766 to 1767, and chancellor of the exchequer from 1767: George had instructed Grafton to offer North the post when Charles Townshend unexpectedly died.

North was regarded as exceptionally talented: efficient, reliable, honest, and everything the British mean by sound. Even as joint paymaster-general, a junior post, he had occasionally been invited to attend cabinet. Grafton had even given North treasury business that was the responsibility of the first lord, and this gave George a greater opportunity to get to know him as a minister, as North took the warrants to the king for his signature. As a good-tempered and courteous individual with whom George felt relaxed, North was the opposite of Grenville and very different to Pitt. His ability to solve the Middlesex election question in 1769 commended North further to the king. An effective debater, he was a good leader of the Commons.

George was happy to offer North the treasury in 1770 when he could not persuade Grafton to remain in office; indeed he gave North no real choice in the matter.[1] George successfully exercised his claim to appoint ministers in whom he had confidence, irrespective of the parliamentary situation. The latter could be managed. There was no difficult transition comparable to those of the 1760s, and, from the king's perspective, this represented a welcome reduction in tension. In political terms the situation was far less propitious, as the junction of the Chathamites and the Rockinghamites made opposition threatening and challenged the morale of government supporters, while North did not yet seem a major politician. On 25 January 1770, the ministry's majority in the Commons fell to forty-four. George, however, was encouraging,[2] and characteristically emphasized the role of willpower: 'Believe me a little spirit will soon restore a degree of order in my service.'[3]

George was also keen to be firm, in part in order to avoid undermining ministerial supporters. In responding to remonstrations from the livery of London, George felt 'that the sober party cannot be hurt with it when they find the answer is firm'.[4] He believed it necessary to be 'dry and short'[5] in reply to inappropriate remonstrances.

Helped by a widespread belief that the crown should be supported against factions, North saw off predictions that the government would fall. Instead, he consolidated his position in the 1770 session, while opposition cohesion did not survive the year. North benefited from the death of

[1] George to North, 23 Jan. 1770, Fortescue, II, 126.
[2] George to North, 12 Feb. 1770, Fortescue, II, 129.
[3] George to North, 1 Feb. 1770, Fortescue, II, 128.
[4] George to North, 20 Mar. 1770, Fortescue, II, 137.
[5] George to North, 15 Nov. 1770, Fortescue, II, 171.

George Grenville in November 1770, after which most of his followers joined the ministry, and from the successful handling of the confrontation with Spain and its ally France over the Falkland Islands, to which Britain and Spain had competing claims. In the crisis, Spain was seen to back down in the face of a British naval mobilization, reversing the impression created by the failure to stop France gaining Corsica. Like North, George had wanted to avoid conflict, 'for every feeling of humanity as well as the knowledge of the distress war must occasion makes me desirous of preventing it if it can be accomplished provided the honour of this country is preserved'.[6] The king also commented on the diplomatic tactics.[7] He was in favour of 'firm though temperate language', and this indeed characterized the government position.[8]

Rumours that Grafton would return to play a role in the ministry, balancing North, proved unwarranted. The strengthening of the ministry in turn enabled North to push through policies in Ireland and America that temporarily shelved problems in the rule of both, while the Wilkes issue receded.

'Though I never incline to dejection',[9] George himself benefited from a revival in popularity. In London, there were still signs of unpopularity. George was hissed when he drove to parliament in 1771 to give his assent to a number of bills; an apple was thrown at his carriage. The king, characteristically, called for resolution in the face of such popular action, arguing that this would discourage its repetition.[10] There were also, however, much-reported indications of popularity. In 1773, the painter Sir Joshua Reynolds wrote after George's return from the review of the fleet.

> The King is exceeding delighted with his reception at Portsmouth. He said to a person about that he was convinced he was not so unpopular as the newspapers would represent him to be. The acclamations of the people were indeed prodigious. On his return all the country assembled in the towns where he changed horses. At Godalming every man had a branch of a tree in his hand and every woman a nosegay which they presented to the King (the horses moving as slow as possible) till he was up to the knees in flowers, and they all singing in a tumultuous manner, God Save the King. The King was so affected that he could not refrain shedding abundance of tears, and even joined in the chorus.[11]

[6] George to North, 28 Nov. 1770, Fortescue, II, 174.
[7] George to Rochford, 6 Dec. 1776, Fortescue, II, 176.
[8] George to Sir Joseph Yorke, 9 Jan. 1771, Fortescue, II, 204.
[9] George to North, 18 Dec. 1770, Fortescue, II, 189.
[10] George to North, 28 May 1771, Fortescue, II, 245.
[11] Reynolds to Grantham, 20 July 1773, Bedford, Bedfordshire CRO., Lucas papers 30/14/326/2.

Hans Stanley, who combined the governorship of the Isle of Wight with the cofferership of the household and being MP for Southampton, reported after spending three days in Portsmouth,

> I am no courtier in saying that one of the parts which I was the most pleased with was the King's address and behaviour. I knew him sufficiently before, to be persuaded that he did not want either politeness, or a certain degree of play and imagination in conversation, but as he has lived so much in retirement, I thought he would have been embarrassed and reserved in so large a company . . . but Charles II could not have been more affable, more easy, or more engaging at his table, and would not have had so much discretion and propriety; I did not attend him in his survey of the docks, where none but those of the marine department assisted, but I am told his questions were all manly, sensible, and pertinent, and that he made every note and observation, from whence this expedition might be a real instruction to him, and not a mere amusement.[12]

He was recorded in four paintings by Dominic Serres, marine painter to George, who presumably commissioned them. In one, the king is clearly shown standing in the stern of the royal yacht *Augusta*. George Stevens cashed in on the popularity of the royal visit with his play *The Trip to Portsmouth*. Portsmouth was a special case, with huge numbers of its inhabitants directly dependent on the crown. Any association with the navy was popular, and this was to be shown anew when George visited the base in 1778, but the account of the response on the journey back is instructive and suggests that the usual chronology for shifts in George's popularity – a decline following Pitt's resignation in 1761 and a revival from 1784 – requires revision, a point supported by the degree to which the image of the king as a model of domestic virtue predates 1784 by several years. In particular, the extent of royal unpopularity outside London needs to be qualified. In 1778, George noted his 'thorough satisfaction at the manner in which I have been received by all ranks of people on my late tour', which had taken him also to Essex.[13]

[12] Stanley to Lady Spencer, 29 June 1773, BL. Add. 75688; *Annual Register* (1773), pp. 202–7; G. Marsh, 'An Account of the Preparation made for and the Entertainment of the King at Portsmouth in June 1773', *Colburn's United Service Magazine* (1887), pp. 433–49, 517–30; C. Fox, 'George III and the Royal Navy', in J. Marsden (ed.), *The Wisdom of George the Third* (London, 2005), pp. 281–8.

[13] George to North, 5 Oct. 1778, RA. GEO/3089. I agree here more with P. Langford, *Public Life and the Propertied Englishman, 1689–1798* (Oxford 1991), p. 509, than L.J. Colley, *Britons. Forging the Nation, 1707–1837* (New Haven and London, 1992), pp. 208–9.

By then, in combining his diligence as a royal bureaucrat with his growing willingness to tour, George had successfully blended 'two approaches to the public face of kingship', that of 'his grandfather with his father's English gentleman Prince. These were quite different ideas. George II was a businesslike king, doing his duty as he saw fit. Frederick, in searching for a meaningful role in Britain, effectively took the personal presence . . . to the "people".'[14] George III, in contrast, was both conscientious and publicly approachable, and was perceived as such.

Signs of a more widespread popularity for the government were seen in the elections, although most constituencies did not vote on national political grounds. Incumbent governments generally won elections, 1741 proving an unusual exception, and then in part because of Frederick, prince of Wales's refusal to accept Walpole's continuation in office, but it was still important that North had little difficulty in winning the general elections of 1774 and 1780, or in keeping the Rockinghamite opposition at bay. The latter was convinced that there was a royal conspiracy against liberty, and brought a paranoid tone to discussion about George, one echoed across the Atlantic, but the number within, or outside, the British political nation who believed they were suffering under executive tyranny was smaller than the noise they made. This belief could not serve as the basis for an effective politics. The nature of parties in this period was that they were essentially connections, held together by shared objectives, but not large enough on their own to dominate the Commons. To do so, it was necessary for several connections to combine and/or for one connection to impress the independent country gentlemen who composed a fair percentage of the MPs. Paranoia did not provide this cement.

George thought party factious, but Charles, third duke of Richmond, a prominent Rockinghamite Whig, wrote of North in 1771,

> I had a great objection to him, and that is that he is a single man . . . That as such I thought he ought not to be the minister of this country, for that as such a man did not depend upon the opinion of the world for his consequence but merely upon the King's pleasure, he could not follow his own opinions or those of the nation, and must be in too literal a sense the *servant* of the crown.[15]

Because North lacked a strong political connection independent of the king, he was dependent on him. The ministry was not reliant on a sizeable party majority in parliament, as the 'Old Corps' Whig governments had been. Instead, in a system of administration and opposition, not political

---

[14] M. Kilburn, 'Royalty and Public in Britain, 1714–1789' (unpublished D.Phil. thesis, Oxford, 1997), p. 132.
[15] Richmond to Rockingham, 22 Jan. 1771, WW. R1–1352.

parties,[16] it relied on royal backing, the support of a number of political groupings, and the assent of the bulk of the independent peers and MPs, although each had also played a role in the 'Old Corps' system. Royal backing was crucial against ministerial rivals.[17] Such a system, however, was inherently unstable if the bulk of the independent MPs withdrew their support, as they did after news of the defeat at Yorktown.

George was personally friendly with North, and felt at ease with him. His father had been George's governor from 1749 until 1751, and the two men shared a devout Anglicanism. The king bestowed the Order of the Garter on North in 1772, a conspicuous mark of honour,[18] not least for a commoner (North was not a peer; his title reflected his position as eldest son of a peer), and one that associated North with Walpole who had been similarly honoured. George also paid North's debts of nearly £20,000 in 1777, and far more willingly than he helped members of his own family. Paying the debts gave North obligations to George, and the minister accepted this.[19] These obligations were strengthened in 1778 when George gave him the wardenship of the Cinque Ports, a worthwhile sinecure, but only, in North's case, to be held at the king's pleasure, and also promised him the first tellership of the exchequer, another worthwhile post.[20] George's affection for North was not lastingly destroyed by the serious political breach of 1783 when he allied with Charles James Fox, nor by their disagreement in 1784 over money for election expenses North owed. In 1788, during George's severe attack of porphyria, North was in the king's mind:

> he has frequently named you with particular regard . . . A few days ago he wrote you a letter perfectly coherent and dictated by a heart full of affectionate friendship . . . In his conversations he has said he loved you, that you was his friend, that though you once deserted . . . he never could forget how you had first stood by him in the line of trouble.[21]

Furthermore, in 1801 he praised his ministerial skill and personality, returning to this theme the following year.[22]

North was an active minister, but George kept a close eye on politics and his correspondence was a testimony to his activity. Like William Pitt

[16] P.D.G. Thomas, 'Party Politics in Eighteenth-Century Britain', *British Journal for Eighteenth-Century Studies*, 10 (1987), p. 207.

[17] Diede report, 20 Mar. 1772, Rigs. 1953.

[18] Diede report, 3 Apr. 1772, Rigs. 1953.

[19] W.P. Pemberton, *Lord North* (London, 1938), pp. 249–51.

[20] George to North, 19 May 1778, Fortescue, IV, 145–6.

[21] —— to North, [Dec. 1788], BL. Add. 61860 fol. 8.

[22] F. Bickley (ed.), *The Diaries of Sylvester Douglas, Lord Glenbervie* (2 vols, London, 1928), I, 148–50, 326.

the Younger later, North wrote regular parliamentary reports for George; in the 1760s, Rockingham[23] and Grafton had already done so, but, typically, intermittently. North was pressed by the king to take steps to win over or inspire particular parliamentarians,[24] and expected to provide information on topics such as the attendance at pre-sessional meetings.[25] This reflected the extent to which the king was aware of, and concerned about, the role of individuals. In part, this was a matter of George's sense of duty and responsibility, which led him to be angry when ministers failed to speak on behalf of government measures.[26] But this was part of a wider determination to see the ministry succeed. George also took a close interest in division figures and the general situation in parliament,[27] being pleased when the government majority rose in the spring of 1770.[28] Successes in 1771 were also applauded.[29]

George, however, was characteristically against change in the shape of newspaper reporting of parliament. In 1762, the Commons had reaffirmed its right to control the publication of its proceedings, and printers were accordingly punished in 1764, 1765, 1767 and 1768. The prominence of the Commons in expelling John Wilkes and subsequently denying him election for Middlesex made reports of its activities ever more interesting and important, and the leading London papers sought to satisfy the demand, but, in doing so, they pressed against not only the privilege of parliament, but also the monopolization of politics by the privileged. In 1771, reports about the reaffirmation by the Commons of their prohibition of publication, on the motion of Wilkes's opponent George Onslow, resulted in action against eight newspapers. The City of London, where Wilkes was now an alderman, gave shelter to the printers who refused to answer charges at the Commons, and a clash between the two jurisdictions vindicated the Commons but made the political dangers of suppressing debates all too clear. As a result, from 1771, little attempt was made to limit reports, and they swiftly became a major feature of the press.[30] George was against this, but also concerned to contain the crisis. His advice to rely on the Lords, however, reflected not only his social politics, but also an

[23] George to Rockingham, 17, 26 Mar. 1766, WW. R1–584, 589.

[24] George to North, 7, 29 Jan. 1770, RA. GEO/934, 939.

[25] George to North, 13 Nov. 1770, RA. GEO/1024.

[26] George to North, no date [1771], Fortescue, II, 216.

[27] I.R. Christie (ed.), 'John Robinson's "State" of the House of Commons, July 1780', *Camden Miscellany*, 30 (London, 1990), p. 442.

[28] George to North, 20, 28 Feb., 16 Mar., 5 Apr. 1770, RA. GEO/946, 948, Fortescue, II, 134, 139.

[29] George to North, 4, 14, 26 Feb., 5 Mar. 1771, Fortescue, II, 215, 218, 221, 223.

[30] P.D.G. Thomas, 'The Beginnings of Parliamentary Reporting in Newspapers, 1768–74', *English Historical Review*, 74 (1959), pp. 623–36.

unwillingness to grasp the central role of the Commons, both in the political process and in ensuring public consent:

> I have very much considered the affair of the Printers that is now coming before the House. I do in the strongest manner recommend that every caution may be used to prevent its becoming a serious affair; and if you are of opinion that any Alderman will take the unjustifiable part you hinted at yesterday, why may not the messenger be made to understand that on summoning them he could not fine them; it is highly necessary that this strange and lawless method of publishing debates in the papers should be put a stop to; but is not the House of Lords as a Court of Record the best Court to bring such miscreants before, as it can fine as well as imprison; and as the Lords have broader shoulders to support any schism that this salutary measure may occasion in the minds of the vulgar.[31]

Responding to the role of the Commons's opposition over this issue, George comforted himself that it 'must offend every moderate man'.[32] In practice, the presentation of his position as moderate entailed a stubborn firmness that prefigured a similar policy towards the American Patriots. George was inclined to see matters in an extreme light:

> the authority of the House of Commons is totally annihilated if it is not in an exemplary manner supported tomorrow, by instantly committing the Lord Mayor and Alderman Oliver to the Tower [of London] ... You know very well I was averse to meddling with the printers, but now there is no retracting. The honour of the Commons must be supported.[33]

Far from this being a passing view, George reiterated the theme of danger when he urged 'resolution' two days later.[34] His assumptions were clear. To George, opposition politics threatened 'a contempt of the laws and of that subordination that alone can preserve liberty of which they pretend to be the guardians'.[35] As a reminder of the extent to which the personal was interspersed with the political, George's tenth child, Adolphus, was born on 24 February and christened on 24 March, George standing by the archbishop, Frederick Cornwallis, during the latter ceremony. In October 1774,

---

[31] George to North, 21 Feb. 1771, Fortescue, II, 220.
[32] George to North, 13 Mar. 1771, Fortescue, II, 229.
[33] George to North, 17 Mar. 1771, Fortescue, II, 233.
[34] George to North, 19 Mar. 1771, Fortescue, II, 233-4, cf. 20, 26 Mar., 235, 242-3.
[35] George to North, 26 Apr. 1771, Fortescue, II, 247.

when George expressed concern about the electoral situation in London and Westminster, insubordination was again an issue:

> Had the City affairs been managed with as much activity prior to Mr Robinson's being in office as he does, the Court of Aldermen would not have been composed of a majority favourable to so disgraceful a member as Mr Wilkes; Mr Robinson having fully stated the state of the mayoralty and the meeting at Guildhall for proposing candidates for the county is very agreeable.[36]
>
> . . . by the conduct of the mob towards Lord Thomas Clinton this day it may be seen that riots will be attempted; Mr Robinson will therefore keep the Peace Officers in the way during the Westminster Election.[37]

Clinton was successful, a major blow to the Wilkesites, and one eagerly sought by George and North for that reason. George was impressed by North who he knew played a key role in both Westminster and Whitehall. Nevertheless, like George, although for different reasons, North was to be found wanting in the crisis caused by the breakdown of relations with the Thirteen Colonies. In part, this was to be a crisis of governmental system. The fissiparous consequences of a departmental method of government[38] required firm co-ordination by a well-conducted cabinet, but North was unable to ensure that, and George did not enforce it. If this crisis was partly institutional, as exacerbated by the problems of fighting a major transatlantic war, there were also faults stemming from North's personality and position, and, again, George bears a portion of the responsibility. Working hard at treasury business, in particular, North found it difficult to confront the full range of his commitments and seems to have been especially at fault in the co-ordination of government, at least in so far as his cabinet colleagues were concerned. In 1778, North himself informed George that he was without the 'authority of character' a prime minister should possess.[39] Decisiveness might have partly compensated for these problems, but the affable North was the very opposite, being instead (as George complained)[40] indecisive and, therefore, self-doubting and unable to impose himself on government. As such, he did not compare with Walpole.

---

[36] George to Robinson, 7 Oct. 1774, BL. Add. 70990.

[37] George to Robinson, 8 Oct. 1774, BL. Add. 37833, fol. 4. For interest in Westminster, George to North, 20 Apr. 1770, Fortescue, II, 141.

[38] Diede report, 19 Jan. 1773, Rigs. 1954.

[39] North to George, 16 Nov. 1778, Fortescue, IV, 221.

[40] George to Robinson, 25 May, 6 June, 13 Aug., 17 Oct. 1779, BL. Add. 37834 fols 88, 93, 133, 157.

Probably overly influenced by comparisons with other first ministers who had served him, George, however, found North a key support, referring to him in 1775 as his sheet anchor, and three years later adding,

> From the hour of Lord North's so handsomely devoting himself on the retreat of the Duke of Grafton, I have never had a political thought which I have not communicated unto him, have accepted of persons highly disagreeable to me because he thought they would be of advantage to his conducting public affairs, and have yielded to measures my opinion did not quite approve.

Friendship clearly played a role, and, allowing for the difference in circumstances, there were echoes of the relationship with Bute. Like Bute, North was older than George, and had an agreeable personality. Paying his debts, George wrote:

> I want no other return but your being convinced that I love you as well as a man of worth as I esteem you as a minister. Your conduct at a critical moment I never can forget, and am glad that . . . I am enabled to give you this mark of my affection.

In 1778 George added, 'Where can you repose your undigested thoughts more safely than in the breast of one who has ever treated you more as his friend than minister.'[41]

In the early 1770s, the difficult stage of their relationship lay ahead. King and minister were still enjoying a successful and easy partnership. Foreign policy was a field in which George took a particular interest, and in this relations with France remained the key issue. In November 1763, he had told the French envoy Guerchy of his desire for good relations, adding that they would be advantageous for the two nations, that other powers benefited from Anglo-French disunion, and that this was a reason not to heed their insinuations.[42] A desire for better relations with France readily accorded with the wish to end the Seven Years War and was an obvious rejoinder to Pittite pressure for action against the Bourbons. Co-operation over Poland, the French goal, however, had not been viable in 1763.[43] Neither power was in a position to exercise much influence in eastern Europe, the British domestic situation was not conducive to the political risks, and there was an important agenda of Anglo-Bourbon colonial disputes. This had become increasingly prominent in the 1760s. Indeed, in

[41] George to North, 2 June, 14 Nov. 1778, 19 Sept. 1777, Fortescue, III, 46, IV, 220, III, 479, IV, 163.

[42] AE. CP. Ang. 452 fol. 128.

[43] PRO. SP. 91/72 fols 155–6; AE. CP. Ang. 452 fol. 41.

1771, when George outlined his views on foreign policy they were directed against France. The king also offered his pedigree, looking back to the Whig lodestar of William III's interventionism:

> my political creed is formed on the system of King William. England in conjunction with the House of Austria and the Republic seems the most secure barrier against the Family Compact [the alliance of the Bourbon monarchies of France and Spain], and if Russia could be added to this, I think the Court of Versailles would not be in a hurry to commence hostilities; but this plan may be difficult to be effected, though I am sure it is the real interest of the four states.[44]

Yet, with George's customary concern about expenditure, and looking back to his attitudes as prince of Wales, such interventionism did not extend to a willingness to gain the alliance of Sweden by a peacetime subsidy.[45]

Talk of co-operation with France revived in 1772. Choiseul's replacement as foreign minister, D'Aiguillon, believed that Britain and France must co-operate to limit Russia's rising power in eastern Europe, and, in order to woo Britain, adopted a conciliatory attitude towards Anglo-French relations. The first partition of Poland by Austria, Prussia and Russia made the situation urgent and lent point to the proposals for co-operation. The initial French approaches in February and March 1772 were unsuccessful, but in July George suggested that he would be glad to facilitate an alliance, and this view was shared by William, fourth earl of Rochford, the secretary of state for the Southern Department, a King's Friend.[46] George, however, appears to have abandoned the idea in late October 1772. There were prudential international and domestic reasons for such a decision, while Gustavus III's restoration of royal authority in Sweden from 19 August, a step that George followed with great interest,[47] made him wary of Gustavus's ally, France. In the short term, an Anglo-French alliance would be unlikely to prevail against the partitioning powers, while, in the longer term, it was reasonable to hope that they would divide, a point made by George to the Sardinian envoy.[48] It was also appropriate to fear that French policy would change, not least because Louis XV was elderly: he was to die in 1774. George's commitment to

---

[44] George to Sir Joseph Yorke, 9 Jan. 1771, Fortescue, II, 204.

[45] George to North, 28 Feb. 1771, Fortescue, II, 222.

[46] G.W. Rice, 'Archival Sources for the Life and Career of the Fourth Earl of Rochford, 1717–81, British Diplomat and Statesman', *Archives*, 20 (1992), p. 257.

[47] Diede report, 1 Sept. 1772, Rigs. 1953.

[48] AST. LM. Ing. 78, 2 Oct. 1772; M. Roberts, 'Great Britain and the Swedish Revolution, 1772–3', *Historical Journal*, 7 (1964), pp. 1–46.

good relations nevertheless emerges through the conventional phrases of diplomatic actions. In January 1774, Rochford wrote that there could be no close connection with France, as such a policy would be unpopular and probably unsuccessful, but he noted that 'any measures that tend to the preservation of the public peace tally so exactly with the king's views, that they cannot but meet with His Majesty's entire approbation'.[49]

North's ministry is overshadowed by the war in North America that broke out in 1775, but, however important, this risks the distorting perspective of hindsight. Policy towards the American colonies was a key aspect of government activity in the early 1770s, but by no means the sole one. Given George's relations with North and the success of the ministry in parliament, these years can be seen as indicative of what he really wanted from government. If so, the dominant note was one of continuity, not least in the key area of foreign policy, and also in response to pressure on behalf of Dissenters (see p. 195). Peace abroad provided a benign environment for politics at home. This was to cease dramatically and with serious consequences as reports of war crossed the Atlantic.

[49] PRO. SP. 78/291 fol. 19.

Chapter 7

CHARACTER AND BEHAVIOUR

My mind is not of a nature to be guided by the object of obtaining a
little applause . . . rectitude of conduct is my sole aim.

George, 1796[1]

In many respects, George was middle-aged when young and stayed thus
throughout his life. He always wished to project an image as respectable,
and the older he became the more scope he had to do so. The older man
for the most part fulfilled the aspirations of the younger. Shortly after
George's accession, a retired senior official wrote to a former colleague,

> The character given me of our present sovereign by an authentic hand
> not to be suspected of flattery is that he has naturally a most deep and
> lively sense of true religion and every social virtue; is master of his
> passions and appetites, and can without pain sacrifice any private incli-
> nation of his own to the public good; is perfectly instructed in our consti-
> tution, and resolved to act conformably to it, and as far as in him lies to
> preserve the union he found subsisting among his subjects . . . Several
> particulars I have heard that indicate much affability and good nature.[2]

Conscientiousness might seem the obvious definition of George's character, but commitment is more appropriate. He regarded himself, and was
seen, as indolent in his early years, probably due to the difficulty of his
personal circumstances after the death of his father in 1751, but under
Bute's careful tutelage he came to work much harder and to have a
stronger sense of responsibility, which led him to lament misspent time
and to promise improvement,[3] and, also, to have more wide-ranging interests. Working hard at the business of majesty, not least reading 'voluminous reports',[4] and 'ready to take any burden on my shoulder',[5] George,

---

[1] George to William Grenville, 31 Jan. 1796, BL. Add. 58859 fol. 47.
[2] Charles Delafaye to Edward Weston, 28 Jan. 1761, Iden Green, Weston–Underwood
papers.
[3] George to Bute, 14 Dec. 1760, BL. Add. 36796 fol. 65.
[4] George to Sydney, 13 Aug. 1785, Aspinall, *George III*, I, 182.
[5] George to North, 21 Nov. 1779, BL. Add. 37835 fol. 36.

however, was no royal drudge. Instead, he saw royal office as a welcome duty that provided him with an opportunity to exercise the responsibility placed upon him. Knowing that he had done his duty was important to George, particularly in crises.[6] Although his context was very different, not least because of the royal emphasis on the religious dimension of duty, George would have understood the claim by the radical London Corresponding Society, published in the *Moral and Political Magazine* of January 1797, that 'The king is no less the servant of his people than the dock-yard man.' Indeed, duty as a theme brought together George's commitment to good kingship with the interest in republican virtue seen, for example, in his commissioning Benjamin West to paint *The Departure of Regulus from Rome*.

George's approach reflected his personal piety but was also the product of a sense of Christian kingship that drew both on British examples and on the sense of duty and moral resolution associated with German pietism.[7] Agostino Carlini, a founder member of the Royal Academy, captured this resolution in his 1773 marble bust of the king, while duty also stands out from George's copious correspondence. It is not simply that there is so much of it, or its stunning contrast with that left by George I and George II, but rather that George's habit of dating his letters to the minute makes clear the long hours he worked, a point supported by other evidence including a comment by Charlotte in 1778 during the American War of Independence.[8] Aside from writing the letters himself, George sometimes copied them as well. The precision shown in his dating to the minute, as well as in his related interest in clocks, astronomy and scientific observation, was also seen in George's knowledge of ceremonial. Thomas Secker, the archbishop of Canterbury, recorded of the coronation in 1761 that he stood at Westminster Hall 'on the right hand of the King, who was very attentive to the delivery of the regalia, and rectified several mistakes of the Heralds with much good humour'. During the service, 'In reading the Declaration to the King, I omitted in one place the word *profess*; but he spoke it, giving me a smiling look. He also, with the same look, said *can*, when I read, *may*', in the latter case correcting a mistake in the printed office.[9]

Duty, diligence and precision ensured that George acquired much knowledge. Indeed, by the 1770s he had as much experience of politics as his ministers. After the ministerial revolution of December 1783 that

[6] George to Pitt, 13 Jan. 1784, PRO. 30/8/103 fol. 31.

[7] R.L. Gawthrop, *Pietism and the Making of Eighteenth-Century Prussia* (Cambridge, 1993).

[8] Charlotte to her brother Duke Charles of Mecklenburg-Strelitz, 27 Mar. 1778, cited in C.C. Orr, 'Dynastic Perspectives 1714–1837', in B. Simms and T. Riotte (eds), *The Hanoverian Dimension in British History* (Cambridge, 2006).

[9] Secker, notes, Lambeth Palace Library, MS 1130/I fols 177, 174.

brought William Pitt the Younger to power, George had far more knowledge. Earlier, in 1771, George told Sir Stanier Porten, an under-secretary, of his view that Rochford 'was more active and had more spirit than the others', as well as his conviction that government offices must ensure 'regularity and secrecy . . . Clearness essentially necessary. System and secrecy the fundamentals of offices. Disliked circulation, believed few read papers themselves, at least few could enter into discourse with him on any matter.' Having had a ninety-minute audience on his return in 1787 from northern Europe, Sir John Sinclair 'was astonished with the extent of information which the King displayed upon a variety of subjects'.[10] George's knowledge of foreign parts was considerably augmented by his topographical collection of maps and plans. Five years earlier, William, second earl of Shelburne, the secretary of state for home affairs, had informed Charles, second marquess of Rockingham, the first lord of the treasury, about George's view on a matter of parliamentary protocol, with the gloss about the king 'whose accuracy you know'.[11] In 1793, reading 'with great attention' a draft declaration to the French nation by William Grenville, the experienced foreign secretary, George 'made a few verbal corrections (in pencil) for your consideration, some were certainly mistakes of the copyist, and the others are such as I thought more clearly carried the meaning you proposed'.[12]

Conscientiousness guided George in his attitude to others, not least his conviction that personal merit was crucial to appointment and conduct in church and state. His correspondence provides many insights on his views on this point. The king spent much time in meetings discussing individuals.[13] His knowledge, for example about the character of judges[14] or military commanders,[15] enabled him to make points about candidates that were not in the ministerial correspondence he received about them, as when he approved the appointment, as lieutenant-general of Quebec, of Alured Clarke, 'who certainly has shown much temper and prudence whilst at Jamaica' in that role.[16] George was credited with insisting that

[10] Porten, 'Notes of interview with the King', 23 June 1771, G.W. Rice, 'Archival Sources for the Life and Career of the Fourth Earl of Rochford, 1717–81, British Diplomat and Statesman', *Archives*, 20 (1992), pp. 265–6; Sinclair to Hawkesbury, 2 July, 22 Sept. 1787, BL. Add. 38222 fols 90, 130.

[11] Shelburne to Rockingham, [7 Apr. 1782], WW. R1–2034a.

[12] George to William Grenville, 27 Sept. 1793, BL. Add. 58857 fol. 162.

[13] F. Bickley (ed.), *The Diaries of Sylvester Douglas, Lord Glenbervie* (2 vols, London, 1928), I, 147–8.

[14] Twiss, I, 327; Bickley (ed.), *Diaries of . . . Glenbervie*, I, 322.

[15] George to Jenkinson, 10 Apr. 1779, BL. Loan 72/1 fol. 7.

[16] George to William Grenville, 23 July 1789, BL. Add. 58855 fol. 9; cf. George to Hawkesbury, 8 June 1805, BL. Loan 72/1 fol. 142.

William Blackstone, long unsuccessful in his pursuit of judicial office, should finally become a judge in 1770.[17]

Propriety and the maintenance of rank and status[18] were also aspects of merit as far as George was concerned, and this was seen both in official positions and in social status. The king saw prudential considerations at stake in both. In 1790, William Grenville's promotion to the House of Lords was applauded by George because 'the uniform conduct he has held is a very strong earnest to me that the public service will be materially benefited by his showing that zeal and ability' he had already displayed in the Commons.[19] At a far more mundane level, but one that reflected George's interest in people and posts of very varied ranks, and his concern for the application of general principles, in 1789 the king wrote from Weymouth, 'I cannot have the smallest doubt of the present vacancy in the 13th of Foot that it is but just to let Captain Black, the eldest captain succeed, he being an old officer, and if no attention is had to length of service all emulation and indeed zeal for the service will soon be destroyed'.[20]

Merit was not simply a matter of individual qualities. To George, the maintenance of rank and privilege involved the preservation of rights, and it is no surprise that several of the ministers in whom he had the most trust were lawyers, most obviously Thurlow, Eldon and Perceval. Discussing the distribution of honorary services at his coronation with the archbishop of Canterbury, George was told that the lameness afflicting the bishop of Bath and Wells ensured that he could not support the king on his left hand, which was the prerogative of that see. Secker noted, 'His Majesty directed me to get some entry made to prevent his non-attendance from being a prejudice to his successor.'[21] Precedence was a matter of great importance throughout society, and at the royal wedding and coronation the Irish peers were also concerned about their position. In 1789, George intervened in a proposed promotion to an Irish earldom, 'Mr. Grenville will order the proper warrants for advancements in the peerage of Ireland agreeable to the recommendations of the Lord Lieutenant of Ireland except in the case of Lord Earlsfort whose quick promotion and passing by the rank of Viscount would be subject to future as well as present inconvenience.'[22] Eight years later, George intervened against a promotion

---

[17] P.C. Yorke (ed.), *The Diary of John Baker* (London, 1931), p. 320; W. Prest, 'Blackstone on Judges; Blackstone as Judge', *Murdoch University Electronic Journal of Law*, 22 (2004).

[18] George to Robinson, 26 Sept. 1776, BL. Add. 37833 fol. 48.

[19] George to William Grenville, 23 Nov. 1790, BL. Add. 58855 fol. 155.

[20] George to William Grenville, 28 July 1789, BL. Add. 58855 fol. 10, cf. George to Robinson, 20 Oct. 1776 and 16 Mar. 1779, and to Dundas, 4 Aug. 1792, BL. Add. 37833 fol. 93, 37834 fol. 53, 40100 fol. 47.

[21] Secker, notes, Lambeth Palace Library, MS 1130/I fol. 175.

[22] George to William Grenville, 14 July 1789, BL. Add. 58855 fol. 6.

to baronet on the grounds that it would make judges reluctant to accept simple knighthoods.[23]

The awarding of benefits was George's most closely followed activity, and one that registered along the tendrils of society, especially polite society. Far from being a monolith, the latter had many gradations, and George's ability to master their nuances, and to plan and act accordingly, ensured that the patronage system operated in accordance with his views, and avoided or lessened the anger that, otherwise, would focus on him.[24] George's sensitivity to the views of others came into play repeatedly. In proposing the Order of the Bath for General Clinton in order to send him 'back to General Howe in good humour', George drew attention to the fact that Clinton came from 'so honorable a family'. Joseph Yorke, an MP and a long-standing envoy in the Hague, of whom George thought highly, was extremely grateful that the king gave him 'one of the best and most lucrative regiments in his service':[25] he had been transferred from being colonel of the 8th Dragoons to that of the 5th Dragoons, and George would be expected to appreciate the difference. He was always being asked for something.

George took his responsibilities in appointments seriously, and was opposed to 'personal jobs'[26] and unmerited 'favour',[27] and to promising what was not yet vacant;[28] although he was put under a lot of pressure from his ministers and had often to yield to it. In 1787, this resulted in George Pretyman Tomline adding the deanery of St Paul's to his bishopric of Lincoln, George writing to Pitt, 'I cannot let my reason guide me against my inclination to oblige you . . . fear will serve as a precedent to the like applications'. In 1789, the king instructed William Grenville to write a private letter to the lord-lieutenant of Ireland granting permission for Lieutenant-Colonel St George to retire

> from the service as so deserving an officer as Major Wilford is recommended to succeed him; but it would be very irregular that after quitting the service Mr. St. George should be Inspector of the Recruits in the room of Major Hobart, the Lord Lieutenant of Ireland should therefore point out some person either on full or half pay for this military office.[29]

[23] George to Dundas, 25 July 1797, BL. Add. 40100 fol. 194.

[24] Cornwallis to Lieutenant-Colonel Ross, 3 Nov. 1784, C. Ross (ed.), *Correspondence of Charles, First Marquis Cornwallis* (3 vols, London, 1859), I, 175–7.

[25] George to Robinson, 11 Mar. 1777, Yorke to Weston, 3 Apr. 1764, BL. Add. 37833 fol. 155, 57927 fol. 181.

[26] George to William Grenville, 27 Jan. 1791, BL. Add. 58856 fol. 3.

[27] George to Pitt, 30 Sept. 1792, PRO. 30/8/103 fol. 460.

[28] George to Pelham, 27 Oct. 1801, BL. Add. 33115 fol. 28.

[29] George to Pitt, 22 Jan. 1787, PRO. 30/8/103 fol. 208, George to Grenville, 12 Aug. 1789, BL. Add. 58855 fol. 13.

Still on holiday, but now at Saltram, George continued eight days later, linking his defence of principle to his concern with the deserving:

> The permitting an officer to continue in the service after he has sold his commission is so contrary to every principle of the military profession as well as known custom of the service that the case of Major Hobart with reason gave surprise and perhaps dissatisfaction to many deserving distressed officers; the making that a precedent for a second arrangement must therefore be big with mischief; the Lord Lieutenant of Ireland cannot fail of occasions of conferring some civil mark of favour on Lieutenant Colonel St. George which is the natural recompense for civil merits, and may not be incompatible with his remaining in his present military situation.[30]

The issue of the inspectorship of recruits in Ireland recurred later that year, and again the king expressed his concern about a job, as well as his anxiety about bad precedent:

> perhaps no subject could be stated wherein I feel more difficulty to comply for I feel that every arrangement of propriety lies against the proposed arrangement it being diametrically in the teeth of every military rule practiced in this or any other service, and the late Lord Lieutenant ought not to have engaged himself in what he must by every dispassionate person be thought much to blame. But as he is now out of office I will consent to this unfortunate measure but trust it will be remembered that it must never be brought forward as a precedent for continuing this irregular practice and Lt. Col. St. George must feel that having sold his regimental commission he can never have any claim to farther advancement in the army. I am aware how unpleasant it must be to Mr. Grenville to have renewed the subject, and he may rest assured that I have no reason to blame any part of his conduct.[31]

These letters were all written by hand: George had no secretary until he started to go blind in 1804.

In 1800, appropriate patronage was again the issue when George noted, 'In consequence of Earl Spencer and Mr. Pitt's opinions, I consent to confer the vacant General of Marines on Lord Bridport and the Lieutenant General on the Earl of St. Vincent though I cannot deny but my own inclination would have been more gratified in advancing the Generals of Marines and conferring the Major General on Lord Hugh

---

[30] George to William Grenville, 20 Aug. 1789, BL. Add. 58855 fol. 14.
[31] George to William Grenville, 17 Oct. 1789, BL. Add. 58855 fol. 44.

Seymour.'[32] In this, George, in part, reflected his concern about the use of the Marines in order to reward admirals with what would be sinecures (although Seymour, the stepson-in-law of George's brother William, duke of Gloucester, was a vice-admiral), but also his willingness to yield to the views of the relevant ministers, Spencer being the first lord of the admiralty. More generally, George was anxious not to delegate his powers of patronage.[33] The Marines reflected George's concern with appropriate hierarchies. He did not want Marine officers promoted in the army.[34]

George's reluctance to award unmerited patronage extended to his family. Urging his son William, later William IV, to behave at sea as 'the Prince, the gentleman and the officer', he claimed 'that by the propriety of your conduct I can alone with justice to my country advance you in your profession'.[35] Indeed, William was to gain rank in the navy, but not to be allowed to use it, which removed the value of the promotion as far as William was concerned.

Until he became ill, George continued the diligence seen under his predecessors since the accession of James II and VII in 1685, although he displayed more of it than any of them had done. As prince of Wales, George's father, Frederick, had given few such signs. In his artistic interests, political opportunism, blundering, irresponsibility and self-indulgence, he had prefigured George IV. As Frederick, however, did not become king, he left to his grandsons, George III's numerous progeny, the task of recreating the monarchical habits associated with Charles II (r. 1660–85). If George III was scarcely unique among British monarchs in being industrious, his energies were directed differently from those of his predecessors and his industry was more conspicuous. In addition, he came to play a role in a political world that had grown accustomed during the last fourteen years of the reign of his elderly grandfather to a monarch of lesser energy who, although far from being a cipher, accepted the direction of most domestic affairs by his leading ministers.

The political world was to see George as industrious, committed and pertinacious. These characteristics owed much to an inner conviction that drew on a strong personal piety and a clear sense of morality; a conviction inclined to rectitude, not subtlety. George believed in finding and following the right policy, writing in early 1784, 'I am perfectly composed as I have the self-satisfaction of feeling I have done my Duty'.[36] Duty and resolution played a major role in his self-image, and crises revealed his sense of both, as well as a feeling of being under great pressure: 'indeci-

[32] George to Spencer, 23 Aug. 1800, BL. Add. 75839.
[33] Cornwallis to Sydney, 10 Apr. 1786, Ross (ed.), *Cornwallis*, I, 208.
[34] George to Robinson, 15 Nov. 1779, BL. Add. 37835 fol. 22.
[35] George to Prince William, [? Aug. 1784], Aspinall, *George III*, I, 77.
[36] George to Pitt, 13 Jan. 1784, PRO. 30/8/103 fol. 31.

sion is the most painful of all situations to a firm mind . . . we must be men, and if we mean to save the country we must cut those threads that cannot be unraveled. Half-measures are ever puerile and often destructive.'[37] In response to crises, George felt it necessary to display 'the cool firmness' which he believed should be 'the natural attendant of Englishmen'.[38] Having been shot at by James Hadfield in 1800, George said, 'A man on such an occasion should immediately feel what is his duty.'[39] Resolution was seen by George as important not only in his own life, but also more generally. During the French Revolutionary War, he was concerned about how to preserve 'that ardour which alone can give success' to the troops.[40]

One of George's strengths was that he instinctually knew what his duty was, and displayed far more determination and fortitude in the face of adversity than Louis XVI of France; a major weakness was that this conviction was not always illuminated by careful reflection, and could therefore seem both obtuse and stubborn. He was critical of those who tried to temper what he thought appropriate; as far as he was concerned, they were dangerous waverers. In 1794 he claimed that the war was likely to be successful 'provided we act on a fixed plan, and do not depart from it by drawing our meanings to fresh objects'.[41] This was an unrealistic assessment of the situation.

George associated moral failings with personal and collective disorder. This was an assessment convenient to his shy and proper personality. In 1763 it was claimed that George was timid, as well as ill at ease in one-to-one meetings, and that he was a hundred times more embarrassed than those to whom he gave audience.[42] Such shyness made meetings with overbearing personalities who lacked affability, such as George Grenville, first minister from 1763 to 1765, particularly difficult, and at this stage in his life George was younger than most of those whom he met, his wife being a conspicuous exception.

Shyness was related to the king's seriousness. As Henry Fox noted of the new king, 'His Majesty is not given to joke',[43] although, when relaxed, he was later to show a willingness to do so. George, in turn, emphasized the value of discretion, 'the first requisite in treating with foreign ministers', especially from France,[44] who might be expected to exploit

[37] George to Pitt, 25 Jan. 1784, PRO. 30/8/103 fol. 41.
[38] George to Pitt, 26 Feb. 1797, PRO. 30/8/104 fol. 137.
[39] *Morning Chronicle*, 23 May 1800.
[40] George to William Grenville, 25 May 1794, BL. Add. 58858 fol. 35.
[41] George to William Grenville, 18 Feb. 1794, BL. Add. 58858 fol. 19.
[42] D'Eon to Praslin, 20 July 1763, AE. CP. Ang. 450 fol. 498.
[43] BL. Add. 51439 fol. 21.
[44] George to Carmarthen, 28 Dec. 1783, BL. Add. 27914 fol. 1.

unguarded remarks, and an aspect of the decorum that he stressed as crucial to majesty. The *gloire* sought by the 'Sun King', Louis XIV of France (r. 1643–1715), was very distant from his goal. Instead, George sought a true politeness, not the superficial gentility castigated by satirists of social manners, but a gentlemanly integrity and measured purposefulness.

Seriousness, a clear sense of morality and an awareness of duty all came across clearly in George's attitude to his role in confirming death sentences. The king was willing to be merciful, responding favourably to a recommendation that a sentence be changed to transportation for life because the culprit's 'crime was the effect of liquor not of any premeditated intention of burglary',[45] but he could also reject recommendations for mercy. George's belief in the exemplary nature of punishment,[46] and his concern for due process in the shape of maintaining the authority of the judiciary,[47] were apparent when one such recommendation from Frederick, duke of York, a son to whom he felt close, was dismissed in 1791:

> though ever inclined to mercy when I can indulge that sentiment without doing harm by not letting the law take its course, I must think that on the present occasion an example may act very forcibly on the regiment now serving at Windsor and prevent robberies which might be more frequent if the convict escaped the sentence to which he has been condemned and which the judge has certainly had no doubt of the propriety or he would have respited him till he could make a report.[48]

Conscientiousness and the sense of responsibility that the king strove to inculcate in his children[49] can be related not only to George's piety and sense of morality, but also to his mental health. This is sometimes discussed in clear-cut terms. In the mid-twentieth century, at a time when personality traits were linked to psychiatric conditions, not least repressed sexuality, there was a widespread failure to consider the relationship between mental illness and physical causes. In accordance with this, the relevant book-length account, by Manfred S. Guttmacher, an American psychiatrist, *America's Last King. An Interpretation of the Madness of George III* (1941), claimed that the king was 'a victim of neuropathic tainting . . . and manic-depressive insanity', and linked his bouts to frustration with himself. His personality 'became unbalanced when he found himself impotent and unable to act . . . [George] could not tolerate his own timorous uncer-

---

[45] George to William Grenville, 28 Feb. 1791, BL. Add. 58856 fol. 16.
[46] George to Prince Augustus, 19 Dec. 1786, Aspinall, *George III*, I, 260.
[47] George to William Grenville, 22 Mar. 1791, BL. Add. 58856 fol. 23.
[48] George to William Grenville, 12 Mar. 1791, BL. Add. 58856 fol. 19.
[49] George to Sydney, 4 Jan. 1785, Aspinall, *George III*, I, 119.

tainty'. Guttmacher also found psychiatric causes for what appeared to be physical conditions, suggesting that, in George's last years, it was probably a complete psychological inaccessibility to those around him that was interpreted as deafness.[50]

Subsequently, there was a shift in psychiatry towards looking more closely at the relationship between mental disorder and physical health. In the case of George, research indicated that he suffered from the disease porphyria, which had consequences in terms of his mental health.[51] This work has been extremely helpful, but it may be that too much is explained away as the symptoms of porphyria. In particular, more attention could be devoted to George's mental state during the bulk of his reign, when he was not ill, for example 'his natural hurried manner'.[52] The interaction of conditions needs probing, and it is possible that George suffered from a cyclothymic personality disorder, rather than manic depression. This would account for his compulsive characteristics, although much should also be attributed to the functional issue of his interpretation of the *métier* of kingship, and the pressures this put him under. The volume of paperwork he had to confront was considerable and, in some respects, reminiscent of the situation of Philip II of Spain, also the head of a world-spanning empire;[53] although, unlike Philip, George had a head of the ministry who was responsible for co-ordinating at least some of the functions of government. To assume a single explanation of George's condition is problematic. George's desire for order may have owed something to his personality, or even to his concern about his own anxiety when faced by disorder, but it is also important to note the role of his political beliefs.

For George, the *métier* of kingship did not provide release, resolution or glory in war. His male predecessors back to Charles I had led troops into battle, but in this George represented a major break in the practice of British kingship. In contrast, the political battleground was not one on which George drew blood or risked his life. Circumstances, rather than character, played the key role in keeping George from direct participation in war, with George II's refusal to let him serve being crucial. As a young man, George followed his father in neither being trained for war nor being given opportunities to serve, despite his firmly pressed request to do so in 1759,[54] which was rejected by George II. This was very different to the experience, as heirs, of George I and George II, and to that of his paternal uncle, Cumberland. In the case of his father, Frederick, military service

[50] M.S. Guttmacher, *America's Last King* (New York, 1941), pp. xii–xiv, 390.

[51] J.C.G. Röhl, M. Warren and D. Warren, *Purple Secret. Genes, 'Madness' and the Royal Houses of Europe* (2nd edn, London, 1999), pp. 75–90.

[52] Bickley (ed.), *Diaries of . . . Glenbervie*, I, 322.

[53] G. Parker, *The Grand Strategy of Philip II* (New Haven, Connecticut, 1998).

[54] Prince George to George II, 20 July 1759, BL. Add. 32893 fols 154–5.

had moved to the second son, Cumberland, and this pattern was sustained
with the sons of both Frederick and George III, although, had Frederick
become king, he planned that George would be lord high admiral. Of
George's brothers, Edward, duke of York (1739–67), began a military
apprenticeship during the Seven Years War, William, duke of Gloucester
(1743–1805), was considered for (although not appointed to) the post of
commander-in-chief of the army during the War of American
Independence, and Henry, duke of Cumberland (1745–90), had a nominal
position in the navy. George's second son, Frederick, duke of York,
became a very active commander-in-chief of the army in 1795, the third,
William, duke of Clarence, served in the navy, the fourth, Edward, duke
of Kent, with the British army, and the fifth, Ernest, duke of Cumberland,
and the youngest, Adolphus, duke of Cambridge, with the Hanoverian
forces. The eldest, George, prince of Wales, later George IV, however,
followed George III and his father, Frederick, in not pursuing a military
career, although, like his father, he unsuccessfully sought a role,[55] irritating
the king by doing so. No warrior, except at second hand, George was very
much a family man and enjoyed a close and stable marriage that was
different from that of many eighteenth-century monarchs.

If these circumstances helped mould his character, George nevertheless
took an interest in military matters as well as fulfilling his responsibilities.
He was particularly active in controlling promotions, about the permuta-
tions of which he displayed considerable knowledge,[56] and was described
by Bute in 1763 as looking 'upon the army to be his own department'. A
quarter-century later, George could still be described as extremely jealous
of his authority in the army, and this remained the case in the 1800s.[57]
Fortifications were a key element of George's interest in topography,[58] he
was far from averse to militaria, and, from the early 1770s, chose to have
himself painted wearing uniform. In 1780, the opening exhibition of the
Royal Academy displayed Benjamin West's *Portrait of His Majesty* (1779),
showing George in military uniform and holding a relevant document.
George's creation of the Windsor uniform in 1777 as a new court costume
reflected his eagerness to accept the idea of discipline and duty in dress,
and, while it derived from the hunt coat created by his father, Frederick,
prince of Wales,[59] it was also to some degree a manifestation of his interest
in the army.

[55] J. Mollo, *The Prince's Dolls* (London, 1997).
[56] George to Lord Herbert, 18 Apr. 1789, Trowbridge, Wiltshire CRO. 2057/F4/42.
[57] Bute to Henry Fox, 2 Mar. 1763, BL. Add. 51359 fol. 141; Barthélemy, French envoy, to
Montmorin, French foreign minister, 1 Apr. 1788, AE. CP. Ang. 565 fol. 7; George to
William Grenville, 3 Feb. 1806, BL. Add. 58863 fol. 19.
[58] I. Cobbin, *Georgiana: or Anecdotes of George the Third* (London, 1820), p. 16.
[59] S. Llewellyn, 'George III and the Windsor Uniform', *Court Historian* (1996); P. Mansel,
Dressed to Rule. Royal and Court Costume from Louis XIV to Elizabeth II (New Haven, 2005),
pp. 57–8.

In June 1771 Frederik Hannecken, the Danish secretary of legation, reported that it was almost superfluous to note that George reviewed troops twice or thrice weekly, as this was his normal occupation each June. The Guards were particularly subject to review by the king and this continued throughout the reign.[60] George was not simply concerned with the opportunities for display presented by reviews, but also sought to increase the army's effectiveness. This involved the oversight of promotions – and to George individual character was always the key – and also responding to disputes over the system of command[61] and considering weaponry. In 1786 Sir William Fawcett, the adjutant-general, returned to George two guns the king had sent him, 'the bayonet of that which is intended for the use of the Light Infantry having been made to fix, agreeably to your Majesty's directions'.[62] On his travels, George frequently reviewed troops, and they formed part of the backdrop of his life. For example, visiting Nuneham Courtenay in 1785, 'The band belonging to the Oxfordshire militia reached Nuneham in time to perform several pieces of martial music during dinner, and, at the departure of their Majesties, struck up "God Save the King".'[63]

George visited the fleet in 1773, 1778, 1781, 1789 and 1794, and, during his visits to Weymouth, spent many happy hours on board the warships that guarded him while he was there. This became a more important issue after war broke out with France in 1793. In 1774, the addition of a Marine Gallery to Queen's House (later known as Buckingham Palace) helped associate George with the country's naval glory. George paid minute attention to the naval review of 1778, and followed the court-martial of Admiral Augustus Keppel after he failed to defeat the French off Ushant that year.[64] On his visit to Plymouth in 1789 George visited the dockyard twice, going on board the *Royal Sovereign*, and inspecting the victualling office and the gun house; he also 'went on board the Southampton to see the sham fight'. These commitments took four days, and in 1804 George noted that 'viewing the business of dockyards is ever a most pleasing entertainment to him'. In 1798, George attended a breakfast off Portsmouth on the *St Fiorenzo* in honour of Nelson's victory at the battle of the Nile.[65] More generally, victories led to celebration that reflected glory

---

[60] Hannecken reports, 11, 18, 25 June 1771, Rigs. 1952; George to Hawkesbury, 8 June 1805, BL. Loan 72/1 fol. 142.

[61] George to Jenkinson, 18 Mar. 1779, BL. Loan 72/1 fol. 1.

[62] Fawcett to George, 22 Feb. 1786, Aspinall, *George III*, I, 211.

[63] *Gentleman's Magazine*, 55 (1785), II, 830.

[64] C. Fox, 'George III and the Navy', in J. Marsden (ed.), *The Wisdom of George the Third* (London, 2005), pp. 291–312.

[65] Diary of Sarah White, 17–20 Aug. 1789, Plymouth, Acc. 3102, Saltram Archival Documents, Box 2; George to Melville, 10 July 1804, PRO. 30/8/104 fol. 374; S. Burrard, *The Annals of Walhampton* (London, 1874), p. 129.

on the crown, as with Thomas Newcomb's *On the Success of the British Arms: A Congratulatory Ode Addressed to His Majesty* (1763).

George's close marriage contributed to an impression of domesticity which was underlined by Charlotte's habit of accompanying him on most of his travels from 1778. George's response to Weymouth, which he visited most summers from 1789 to 1805, was totally different to that of John, second earl of Buckinghamshire, who had written thence in 1783,

> There is a peculiar gentility in Weymouth which softens even the Eastern and Northern Blasts. It is to this warmth we own the semblance of living in a state of primeval innocence. Wherever you turn your eyes nakedness greets them without fig leaves or blushes. It seems indeed . . .

> > That e'en as you list you may stick in your T
> > To a Jolly Brown C or a Lilly White A.[66]

Far from being in a political or social world separate to George, Buckinghamshire was ·a lord of the bedchamber from 1756 until 1767, ambassador to Russia from 1762 to 1765, and lord-lieutenant of Ireland from 1776 to 1780. George's views coexisted with other moralities, helping both to distinguish the king's assumptions and to ensure that they struck others as a challenge.

Just as earlier George's life had been removed from that of the libertine elements of the Society of Dilettanti, so the king's life in Weymouth was very different to that of his eldest son at Brighton. Like Weymouth, Brighton was a newly fashionable resort based on the belief that sea bathing was healthy. From 1783, the prince spent summers there and, needing a residence, had a house transformed into a villa by 1787. Subsequently, the Brighton Pavilion became an oriental pleasure palace, to contemporary taste a luridly exotic setting for a louche lifestyle. George III left no such legacy at Weymouth. Expenditure was another key difference. George disapproved of the extravagance of his sons. Although he was willing to spend substantial sums, especially in purchasing paintings and books and, eventually, in building, he was cautious with money. Writing to his son William, George linked financial caution with his own position, and with both sensibility and integrity:

> with thirteen children I can but with the greatest care make both ends meet and am not in a situation to be paying their debts if they contract any, and to anyone that has either the sentiments of common honesty or delicacy, without the nicer feelings which every gentleman ought to

[66] Hull UL, DDHO/4/22.

possess, the situation of not paying what is due is a very unpleasant situation.[67]

Indeed, heavy expenditure was held up in 1801 as evidence that George was not well, 'the manner in which he is now expending money in various ways, which is so unlike him when well, all evince that he is not so right as he should be'.[68] George's constant awareness of the public accountability of the monarch's Civil List helps explain his cautious expenditure.

The king's domesticity owed much to his character and interests, and the shock of George's madness was in part because his behaviour now rejected that domesticity. The fluidity of unconstrained public socializing clearly worried the king and separated him from his sons. Unlike George II, who was very fond of them, George was opposed to masquerades, and part of his dislike of the visit of Christian VII was that the latter held a masquerade when in Britain, which George felt obliged to attend. This hostility to masquerades was indicative of his sustained preference for integrity over artificiality and performance. In 1795, George was impressed by Wilhelmina, princess of Orange, his second cousin, who, with her husband, William V, his first cousin, had taken refuge in Britain from the French invaders: 'She has a dignity that seems to make her situation still more interesting'.[69] In contemporary British social observation, the widespread sense of flux and uncertainty challenged notions of identity and behaviour, leading to an emphasis on performance as the condition of mankind, as in comedies of manners. In opposition to this, and to the related pressure for artificiality, George, in his behaviour and attitude, offered a critique of affectation and a preference for honesty as an aesthetic and, even more, moral choice. His increased dislike of London and favour for the country was at one with this preference.

The king also disliked gambling, and tried to stop his sons from engaging in it,[70] although he played cards as a matter of course, and they were a major evening activity at court, although not on Sundays, Good Friday, Christmas Day or on the anniversary of Charles I's execution.[71] George was an active player of backgammon as well. Significantly, however, he did not play cards with a group of hard-drinking men, as, for example, his grandfather, George II, and his grand-uncle, Frederick William I of Prussia (r. 1713–40), had done. Queen Charlotte, for example, recorded in her diary that George played backgammon with Lady Mary

[67] George to Prince William, [? Aug. 1784], Aspinall, *George III*, I, 77.

[68] Thomas Willis to Eldon, 16 June 1801, Twiss, I, 381.

[69] George to William Grenville, 31 Jan. 1795, BL. Add. 58858 fol. 144.

[70] Re. Frederick, duke of York, George to Richard Grenville, 17 May, 16 July 1782, BL. Add. 70956.

[71] Richard Grenville to Cornwallis, 19 Jan. 1791, Ross (ed.), *Cornwallis*, II, 110.

Howe, the wife of the recently ennobled admiral, on 5 and 12 October
1794. He never visited Newmarket, as George II had done in 1728,
although the king's horses continued to race there. In contrast, his
antithesis, Charles James Fox, a liberal in politics and religion, was also a
libertine, pursuing pleasure, and, in George's eyes, politically irresponsible.[72] When Fox became bankrupt, this compounded his faults in
George's eyes and made the opposition contemptible.[73] Aside from financial stability, the king thought early nights a good idea.[74] He rose early:
when at Cheltenham for the waters in 1788, he reached the well most
mornings at six.

A dislike of show and a concern to avoid the consequences of
overeating and drunkenness contributed, alongside his shyness and parsimony, to a simple lifestyle, especially in contrast to the Roman emperors
made known to his contemporaries by Edward Gibbon's popular *Decline
and Fall of the Roman Empire* (1776–88). When George and Charlotte stayed
at Saltram in 1789, they used 'nothing but the set of Gilt Staffordshire
ware ... The King's Plate was not unpacked'. Furthermore, the house
servants 'were all perfectly satisfied' with their treatment by the royal
guests.[75] This way of life, which accorded with the strengthening of the
ideals of privacy and family life in the Habsburg and French courts,[76] was
to lead to the king being known as 'Farmer George', although that suggestion of ordinariness was an inappropriate description of the punctilious-
ness of his life. By modern standards, the court appears formal and
George overly concerned with form and propriety, and there were
certainly critics of court life, not least his eldest son and Frances Burney,[77]
but it struck other observers as pleasantly domestic and the opposite of
grand.[78]

George wore simple clothes, including on his own birthday, but wore
new clothes for that of Charlotte. In the midst of frequently splendid, and
certainly ample entertainment, he was cautious in what he ate and drank,
trying, for example, not to eat sugar. This was a matter of health, not a

[72] L.G. Mitchell, *Charles James Fox* (Oxford, 1992).

[73] George to Pitt, 7 June 1793, PRO. 30/8/103 fol. 496.

[74] George to Jenkinson, 7 Mar. 1783, BL. Add. 38564 fol. 25.

[75] Anne to Frederick Robinson, 17 Oct. 1789, Plymouth 1259/1/37.

[76] J. Duindam, *Vienna and Versailles. The Courts of Europe's Dynastic Rivals, 1550–1780*
(Cambridge, 2003). pp. 189–90.

[77] C. Barrett and A. Dobson (eds), *Diary and Letters of Madame d'Arblay, 1778–1840* (6 vols,
London, 1904–5).

[78] C. Papendiek, *Court and Private Life in the Time of Queen Charlotte*, edited by V.D.
Broughton (2 vols, London, 1887); *Mary Hamilton afterwards Mrs John Dickinson at Court and at
Home*, edited by E. and F. Anson (London, 1925); Elizabeth, duchess of Northumberland,
in J. Greig (ed.), *The Diaries of a Duchess. Extracts from the Diaries of the First Duchess of
Northumberland* (London, 1926). Re. Weymouth in 1805, A. Henstock, 'The Diary of Abigail
Gawthorn, 1751–1810', *Thoroton Society* 33 (1980), p. 118.

rejection of the British Atlantic world of plantations worked by slaves. Declaring that he preferred 'eating plain and little to growing diseased and infirm',[79] the king was a model of slimness compared with his eldest son and with Louis XVIII. Indeed, George's poor health in 1788 initially led to the suggestion that the 'abstemious system which His Majesty has invariably pursued' had led to a dropsy as he had insufficient wine.[80] He was certainly careful in what he drank, taking lemonade rather than wine,[81] and Richard Cooksey was sufficiently surprised when George took two glasses of port with dinner (the afternoon meal) on his visit to Croome in 1788 that he underlined the two.[82] George liked plain food and preferred family meals to banquets, and in his ordinary meals, which he ate rapidly, he avoided grandness both in what he ate and in how he was served. This was particularly, but not only, so when George was in rural retreats or on holiday. Visiting George at Kew in August 1804, the dowager countess of Elgin saw him 'eat his dinner heartily of pudding and dumpling' and noted that George 'made even the coffee himself'.[83] George cut down what he ate in the 1790s in response to the domestic crisis caused by poor harvests.[84]

Although lampooned for frugality by John Wolcot, who wrote under the pseudonym of Peter Pindar, particularly in the *Louisiad* (1785–95), the extent to which George 'kept no state' was to be praised,[85] and passed on to influence future views of the king, by, for example, Melesina Trench (1768–1827), whose journal and correspondence formed the basis of a work published in 1862. Trench, a serious daughter of the Church, who disliked frivolity and modishness and found the relationship between Nelson and Emma Hamilton deplorable, clearly approved of George. A sense of calm and decorous informality was also expressed in paintings by Johann Zoffany. The king's preference for life outside London, where he could more readily assume a gentlemanly lifestyle, contributed to his ease and reputation.[86] So also did an informality that led him to walk among

[79] Barrett and Dobson (eds), *Diary and Letters of Madame d'Arblay*, II, 318.

[80] London report in *Berrow's Worcester Journal*, 30 Oct. 1788.

[81] Bickley (ed.), *Diaries of . . . Glenbervie*, I, 407, re. 6 Dec. 1804; Greig (ed.), *Diaries of a Duchess*, p. 199.

[82] Cooksey to Lord Deerhurst, 29 July 1788, Croome Estate Trust, Coventry papers, CEA. F66/3.

[83] Dowager countess of Elgin to Queen Charlotte, 4 Sept. 1804, Aspinall, *Prince of Wales*, V, p. 96; M. Winterbottom, 'Dining with George III and Queen Charlotte', in Marsden (ed.), *The Wisdom of George the Third*, pp. 231–42.

[84] George to Pitt, 17 July 1795, PRO. 30/8/104 fol. 44; O. Hedley, *Queen Charlotte*, p. 207.

[85] R.C. Trench (ed.), *Remains of the Late Mrs Richard Trench* (London, 1862), p. 470.

[86] B.B. Schnorrenberg, 'The Castle of Ennui or Sweet Retreat: The Court of George III', *Consortium on Revolutionary Europe: Selected Papers, 1997* (Tallahassee, Florida, 1997), pp. 45–52, esp. pp. 51–2.

his subjects without guards or servants, as at Cheltenham in 1788, or with very few, a practice praised by the French radical Louis-Sébastien Mercier in 1787.[87] More generally, George was believed to have a good nature.[88]

In cultural terms, the nature of the grand projects, the Royal Academy, the royal library and the chapel for revealed religion, accompanied by the continued established routine of court festivals and the embellishment of palaces, which ensured that portraits were painted and furniture and porcelain purchased, were crucial in the shift from 'grand' culture to a 'domestic' culture that was more acceptable to the middling orders. Rather fancifully, a critical French observer reported in 1763 that the court resembled an affluent bourgeois household with pleasures constrained by matrimony. A king allegedly captivated by his wife, his mother and his favourite, Bute, who also worked hard at his job, might seem dull and out of keeping with the pleasure-seeking of the social élite,[89] but it matched widely held assumptions about decorum, propriety and true gentility. There was a benign and ordered, if to its critics somewhat boring, character to George's court. In 1783, the king wrote about his son William that 'polishing and composure are the ingredients wanting to make him a charming character'.[90] This was not a world of dangerous liaisons, certainly not of public ones, although several of George's daughters found them the only route to happiness.

The values of the court were very different to a world of sexual intrigue. George, furthermore, was a kindly host, writing in January 1793,

> As I find Lord and Lady Grenville are invited to a ball here on Thursday evening, I am desirous at this season of the year that Lady Grenville should not run any risk of catching cold; I have therefore directed a well aired apartment to be prepared for them in Windsor Castle.[91]

If George was a considerate host to those who attended major state considerations, he also received with kindness the large numbers who attended the levees and drawing rooms he regularly held while in London: generally twice weekly each, the levees attended only by men and the drawing rooms by men and women. The pattern under which those who

---

[87] Mercier, *Tableau de Paris*, X (1787), pp. 122–5, cited in T.C.W. Blanning, 'Louis XVI and the Public Sphere', in M. Crook, W. Doyle and A. Forrest (eds), *Enlightenment and Revolution: Essays in Honour of Norman Hampson* (Aldershot, 2004).

[88] Theresa Villiers to Catherine Robinson, 9 July, – Sept. 1805, Plymouth 1259/2/734, 745.

[89] D'Eon to Praslin, 1 July 1763, AE. CP. Ang. 450 fol. 430.

[90] George to Richard Grenville, 15 July 1783, BL. Add. 70956.

[91] George to William Grenville, 8 Jan. 1793, BL. Add. 58857 fol. 79.

had been introduced at court were subsequently permitted ready access was replicated when George was on his travels. As Abigail Gawthorn noted in Weymouth in 1805, at the Assembly Rooms,

> in part of the room enclosed by a silk cord where the royal family enter, and every body who has been introduced stand within the cord and have an opportunity of hearing the conversation; the band keeps playing during the royal family's stay in the room, which in general is an hour.[92]

Well aware that 'little attentions often do good',[93] George made a practice of speaking to all who attended his levees, which necessarily brought him in touch with most of the social elite (and many others), and indeed with many individuals whom he did not know or did not know well. Aside from the pressure on his voice,[94] this was a strain for George, and for those he met, and led to a platitudinous quality in many of his comments.[95] Under court etiquette, George had to speak first, and courtesy required him to press on if those he met were too nervous to say anything, or if they responded with only a few words. A shy child, George learned to speak in public and to put others at their ease. Although mocked, his 'What what?' at the end of comments was designed to bring others out, or to displace his shyness.

Those who met the king frequently commented on how agreeable he was and how much knowledge he showed of individuals and their connections;[96] he compared very favourably on the former head with his two predecessors on the British throne and with most of his European counterparts. George was not rude like George II and was far less waspish than Frederick the Great. A critical Richard Cooksey was unimpressed by George's jokes in 1788 but noted his good humour:

> The King was in remarkable high spirits and to use the expression of one who followed him in his ride 'You can't conceive, Sir, how he laughed and joked with Lord Coventry. A King's joke will always be received with a smile – what kind of smile His Majesty's would excite I leave to those who are within the sphere of his jests. I was at

[92] Henstock, 'Gawthorn', p. 117.
[93] George to Robinson, 27 Oct. 1779, BL. Add. 37834 fol. 170, cf. George to North, 21 Nov. 1779, BL. Add. 37335 fol. 36.
[94] George to Jenkinson, 17 Jan. 1782, BL. Add. 38564.
[95] Theresa Villiers to Catherine Robinson, – Dec. 1802, Plymouth 1259/2/670.
[96] Anne Robinson to Frederick Robinson, 5 Nov. 1784, Bedford CRO. L30/15/50/56; Anne Robinson to Catherine Robinson, 8 Oct. 1789, Theresa Villiers to Catherine Robinson, 13 Nov. 1799, Plymouth 1259/2/71, 1259/2/478.

Cheltenham for two or three days where I heard some of his bon mots not of the best.'[97]

One that was recorded was addressed to the pumper at the spa, Hannah Forty: 'Mrs Forty, you and your husband together make eighty.'[98]

The court's values were not vicious or macho, and George was of course a supporter of matrimony, as in 1795 when he pressed for that of Robert Banks Jenkinson, the future second earl of Liverpool, to Lady Theodosia Louisa Hervey, a match about which Jenkinson's father, Lord Hawkesbury, a favourite of George, was unhappy.[99] Linked to this backing of matrimony and large families[100] was George's hostility to divorce. He was held partly responsible for the Bill that passed the Lords in 1771 prohibiting the remarriage of adulterous wives, a measure designed to make divorce less attractive, but one lost in the Commons.[101] George could also show his moral disapproval of individuals at levees, as when he 'rumped' Nelson and spent time instead talking to an undistinguished general. To George, vices were the cause of ruin.[102] The 'paternal views' of George 'for this his own country',[103] however, faced the problem that paternalism was an ambience, according with the German ideas of the ruler as *Hausvater*, rather than a practice of politics, and one that was ill suited to the adversarial, populist and legalistic aspects of the British system.

Tone and accessibility did not mean that George's lifestyle was that of the middling orders. The monarch was head of society, in what was very much an aristocratic monarchy, and, as such, court routines were very important. There was public magnificence where necessary, and private modesty, which was in accord with 'middle-class' mores (and cultural aspirations, given that the public could now buy items marketed as used by royals, such as Wedgwood's Queensware or Boulton's vases) and also with that part of the aristocracy adhering to Christian and modest standards, either from tradition (like the Portlands) or from new appreciation of evangelical sentiment.[104] Josiah Wedgwood became Potter to Her Majesty.

[97] Cooksey to Deerhurst, 29 July 1788, Croome Estate Trust, Coventry papers, CEA. F66/3.

[98] E. Humphris and E.C. Willoughby, *At Cheltenham Spa* (London, 1928), p. 65.

[99] P. Jupp (ed.), *The Letter-Journal of George Canning, 1793–1795* (London, 1991), p. 210.

[100] George to earl of Dartmouth, 14 May 1804, HMC, *Manuscripts of the Earl of Dartmouth* (London, 1887), p. 443.

[101] J.A. Home (ed.), *Letters and Journals of Lady Mary Coke* (4 vols, Edinburgh, 1889–96), III, 52–3.

[102] George to Robinson, 3 Oct. 1776, BL. Add. 37833 fol. 71.

[103] Bute to Sir John Philipps, no date but reply to letter of 23 May 1762, MS, 5/72/3.

[104] For conflicting expectations of the royal family, M. Morris, 'Princely Debt, Public Credit, and Commercial Values in Late Georgian Britain', *Journal of British Studies*, 43 (2004), pp. 339–65.

The splendour of the court, its settings and activities, and yet also George's willingness to be a working ruler, in this case spending time with key ministers, was shown at the celebration of the queen's birthday held in the ballroom at St James's Palace on 19 January 1801:

At a quarter past ten, the King rose, which was the signal for the dancing to conclude . . . Mr. Pitt, the Duke of Portland, and the Earl of Chatham, to whom he addressed himself all the evening . . . The King was dressed in scarlet and gold, and wore a great quantity of the richest diamonds, different orders, his star, sword-hilt, button and loop, rings, etc; but above all a Turkish aigrette fastened in his hat, which he held on his arm, exposing the aigrette to full view. In the shape of a hand, it was composed of a vast number of the finest diamonds ever beheld, which attracted and fixed the attention of the whole room. Behind it was a heron's feather, worth at least 500£. The King was in excellent spirits, laughed much, and chatted all the time with his ministers.[105]

Alongside reports of George, particularly outside London, as an accessible individual, walking, riding and travelling without pomp and state, often travelling almost entirely without protection, came the reporting of court life, which presented a very different resonance. The *Morning Post* of 17 March 1786 noted that

Yesterday morning at two o'clock their Majesties, accompanied by the Princess Royal and Princess Augusta, came from the Queen's Palace, St. James's, where there was a drawing-room, at which were present, His Royal Highness the Prince of Wales, Mr. Pitt, the Dukes of Richmond, Grafton, Queensbury, Ancaster, Montagu, and Chandos; Marquis of Carmarthen; Lords Salisbury, Chesterfield, Herbert, Harcourt, Melbourne, Beauleu, Scarsdale, Rivers, Courtown, Amherst, Sydney, Howe, Hinchinbroke, Gray, Parker, and Ailesford; all the Foreign Ministers; Sir G. Yonge, Sir P. Hales, General Hyde, Mr. Stanhope, Mr. Grenville, Mr. Adams, Mr. Eden, Mr. Grenville, etc,

followed by a long list of distinguished and noble women. The article presented a social circle that was very much that of the aristocracy, and to which entry was gained accordingly. It closed: 'Yesterday Mrs Dawkins was presented to their Majesties, on her marriage, by Lady Catherine Tylney Long.' At such gatherings, as well as at his levees, George learned the gossip of high society and evaluated the personalities of those who pressed him for favour. Aside from the routine splendour of court life,

---

[105] *Courier*, 20 Jan. 1801. See also e.g. *Gentleman's Magazine*, 60 (1790), p. 80.

there were periodic highpoints. Many under George revolved around the Order of the Garter, a chivalric body that greatly attracted the king. It linked the royal family, leading aristocrats and foreign notables; and George was keen that the royal family should play a prominent role in it. For example, on 19 June 1771 the king held a chapter (meeting) of the Order at St James's. The late earl of Halifax was replaced as a member by George's young second son, Frederick, duke of York, who was given the Garter by his uncle, William, duke of Gloucester, while the king himself gave him the ribbon with the St George.

At times, the king's concern with social rank caused difficulties. In 1792, Henry Dundas came close to resigning as a minister when, on the grounds that he was a commoner, George was reluctant to nominate him to the vacant governorship of the Charterhouse, a post of considerable and long-standing prestige that, he noted, had usually been held by 'men of rank'. The formality of the court focused in large part on respect for rank, and the king's friendships were generally defined accordingly, although with exceptions such as Henry Addington.[106] Wary of people who had 'been stimulated by motives alone of private interest', and claiming that 'low men when they have been fortunate seem more easily to forget themselves than their betters',[107] George associated rank, in contrast, with a sense of duty. Proposing George, fourth earl of Macclesfield, a lord of the bedchamber, for promotion in the household in 1804, the king referred to the services of the family, 'both those of his great grandfather, the expense of the Oxfordshire election [of 1754] to his father, and his own merit and services'. Macclesfield became captain of the Yeomen of the Guard, a post he held until 1830.[108]

George, nevertheless, showed an ease in his contact with people of all ranks that reflected a certainty of position and purpose and a belief that dignity did not lie in social distinction. For George, Christian notions of benevolence and human sympathy cut across social notions of hierarchy and even politeness. He can be fairly described as gentlemanly. Indeed, his serious illness in 1788–9 led him to a stress on common humanity, as with the newspaper report that, when already troubled, and shortly before being taken seriously ill, George had remarked, 'Lord bless us. The best of us are poor creatures.'[109] This was underlined for the king when he was

[106] George to Pitt, 30 Sept. 1792, PRO. 30/8/103 fol. 460; C.J. Fedorak, *Henry Addington, Prime Minister, 1801–1804* (Akron, Ohio, 2002), p. 30; P. Ziegler, *A Life of Henry Addington, First Viscount Sidmouth* (London, 1965), pp. 222–3.

[107] George to Robinson, 29 Mar. 1777, 16 Mar. 1779, BL. Add. 37833 fol. 189, 37834 fol. 53.

[108] George to Pitt, 22 June 1804, PRO. 30/8/104 fol. 358. Cf. re. Earl Poulett and lord-lieutenancy of Somerset, 6 Aug. 1792, 103 fol. 450.

[109] *Berrow's Worcester Journal*, 27 Nov. 1788.

subsequently informed of the comments he had made when ill. This emphasis on humanity remained an important part of the king's image and resonance, seen not only in his illness and family problems, but also in accounts of George's travels, especially round Windsor. On 17 November 1820, the date of his funeral, *The Times* claimed that most of George's qualities 'were imitable and attainable by all classes of mankind'.

From the outset, George had been concerned to strike the appropriate note, a clear legacy of his upbringing in terms of royal duty and the politics of Patriotism. This was seen in 1764 when, in an episode that echoes Richard II's initial response to popular discontent during the Peasants' Revolt in 1381, George was reported as displaying purposeful clemency towards subjects far from his social ambit suffering hardship:

> Yesterday morning several thousand journeymen silk weavers went in procession from Spitalfields, and waited on his Majesty at the Queen's palace . . . with a petition, representing the miserable condition themselves and families are reduced to by the clandestine importation of French silks.

Two gentlemen presented the petition to George who answered,

> That he would send immediate orders to put an entire stop to the importation of French silks; that an affair of such consequence to the kingdom should be properly laid before his Parliament, and that they might depend on his care and protection.[110]

'Publicly approachable' has to be seen within its social context. For reasons of hierarchy, familiarity and practicality, George visited the aristocracy on his travels. On 20 October 1794 George, Charlotte, Prince Ernest and six of the princesses went from Windsor to visit George, second Earl Harcourt, a friend of the king, at Nuneham Courtenay, returning that day. The social politics of Nuneham Courtenay, which George and Charlotte had earlier visited in 1785, 1786 and 1788,[111] reflected the power relationships of the period. The medieval village and its church had been destroyed to make way for Simon, first Earl Harcourt's new Palladian villa and park in 1759, although Harcourt, George's governor in 1751–2, did provide the displaced villagers with well-built, spacious houses a mile away. In October 1804, the royal family travelled from Weymouth to stay with George, second earl of Dorchester, at Milton Abbey. The tenants there had also been rehoused in improved cottages.

---

[110] *London Evening Post*, 10 Apr. 1764.
[111] On the Harcourts and the royal family, C.C. Orr, 'Queen Charlotte, "Scientific Queen"', in Orr (ed.), *Queenship in Britain 1660–1837* (Manchester, 2002), pp. 253–8.

Milton Abbey was a convenient distance for a trip from Weymouth, and the royal family visited it again in 1805, staying three nights. While staying at Milton Abbey in 1804, the royal family visited Stalbridge, a seat of Henry, earl of Uxbridge.[112]

The role of the king as the head of the nobility was largely social and ceremonial, but nevertheless took much of George's time, and indeed endorsed his constitutional views on the relationship between the parts of parliament. The king was head of society, as his activities on court days testified, with the presentation of the young when they came of age, and of brides and bridegrooms to be. This overlapped with more official aspects of the recognition of merit, particularly investitures, and the kissing of the king's hand by those newly appointed to posts or honours, such as bishops and diplomats. The role of the crown in the granting of honours was extended with the foundation of the Order of St Patrick in 1783, the enlarging of that of the Bath in 1772, and the enlarging of that of the Garter in 1786 and 1804: George responded to the size of his family by making those of his sons whom he wished to install as knights of the Garter, members in addition to the existing number of knights.[113] Under pressure in 1786 from James, third duke of Chandos, the lord steward, and John, third duke of Dorset, ambassador in Paris, for whom there were no vacancies, George was at great pains to make sure that Pitt 'thoroughly' understood the situation, just as in 1793 he wanted Pitt to help ensure a good attendance for the next chapter of the Garter.[114] The acceptance of foreign orders also depended on George's consent.[115]

George also took an interest in issues of etiquette that arose in high society. These were very important in affirming status and also involved practical questions, such as permission to drive through the royal parks (a privilege overly sought, in George's view), and to have the automatic right of entrance to the palaces.[116] In 1791, George gave Hugh, second duke of Northumberland, 'a dispensation for wearing the Star whilst out of the Kingdom';[117] he had received the Garter in 1788. In 1803, George decided that those elected knights of the Bath could not wear the star of the order until they had been installed, adding a characteristic explanation: 'it is by no means wise to lessen the dignity of any order, and more especially in the present days'.[118] An emphasis on the ceremony focused attention on

[112] J. Hutchins, *The History and Antiquities of the County of Dorset* (4 vols, 3rd edn, Westminster, 1861–74), IV, 395–6.

[113] George to Pitt, 30 Dec. 1804, PRO. 30/8/104 fol. 404.

[114] George to Pitt, 28 May 1786, 7 June 1793, Aspinall, *George III*, I, 225, PRO. 30/8/103 fol. 496. Re. sensitivity about vacancies, George to Pitt, 16 Jan. 1805, PRO. 30/8/104 fol. 415.

[115] George to Dundas, 27 Aug., 8 Sept. 1799, BL. Add. 40100 fols 229, 233.

[116] George to Pelham, 18 July 1802, 7 Aug. 1803, BL. Add. 33115 fols 89, 158.

[117] George to Dundas, 24 Sept. 1791, BL. Add. 40100 fol. 23.

[118] George to Pelham, 14 Jan. 1803, BL. Add. 33115 fol. 113.

the role of the crown. The king was also believed to be particularly suited to settle disputes between aristocratic officers.[119] Of necessity, these concerns were very much a closed world, but flashes of awareness of the rest of society are seen in the king's correspondence, as when considering how to record the naval victory over the Dutch at Camperdown in 1797. This hard-won victory had affirmed the troubled loyalty of the sailors and lessened the danger of invasion by France,

> As by Mr. Secretary Dundas's note Lord Duncan seems desirous of adding the representation of the medal to his arms surmounted by a naval crown and the word Camperdown, I do not in the smallest degree disapprove of it; but hope the supporters of his arms are to be two sailors, the one holding a blue flag, the other a reversed Dutch one.[120]

George's role as head of the nobility ensured that men and women of rank could expect a private audience if they sought one. This provided them with the opportunity to press for patronage in a way that those who could only attend levees were unable to do. George's power as social arbiter and recipient of patronage demands, however, was limited, as was testified by the many who complained that petitions had not been heeded. Furthermore, George's role was restricted in the face of demands from unwelcome foreigners, most obviously French *émigrés*. Status was set by the crown, and it was important not to erode it, George deciding

> there can be but one line adopted as to the multitude of French that are now arrived here to present none at Court but such whose characters are known or are brought by some person who can answer for them.[121]

Earlier, the cause of kings, or at least propriety, had been at stake when George had been ready to receive the former French first minister, Charles-Alexandre de Calonne, as he did 'not see any expressions in his book that reflect either on the French King or the French Royal family'.[122]

Any emphasis on the role of the aristocracy in the politics of the period, particularly in sustaining opposition to the ministers, necessarily draws attention to George's part in responding to their views and sensitivities. Although the king's intentions were suspected by some leading aristocrats, especially those who led the Rockinghamite Whigs, he could draw on the support of the majority. This was most apparent in wartime. During the

[119] Field-Marshal Conway to Rockingham, 11 June, Rockingham to Shelburne, 12 June 1782, WW. R1–2109–10.

[120] George to Dundas, 4 Dec. 1797, BL. Add. 40100 fol. 200.

[121] George to William Grenville, 5 Oct. 1792, BL. Add. 58857 fol. 50.

[122] George to Carmarthen, 31 Dec. 1787, BL. Add. 27914 fol. 19.

War of American Independence, the domestic correspondence of Jeffrey, first Lord Amherst, who was acting commander-in-chief of the army from 1772 to 1782, gives the impression of a society in which aristocratic lord-lieutenants had a significant military function.[123] The upsurge of domestic radicalism from 1792 gave a similar prominence to lord-lieutenants, with the appointment of whom George took considerable care,[124] while the aristocracy also played a key role in commanding volunteer and militia forces. George kept himself well informed, and believed that his praise was appropriate and useful. In 1803, he recalled that George, earl of Euston, lord-lieutenant of Suffolk and later fourth duke of Grafton, had brought his West Suffolk regiment the previous year 'to such perfection' that it seemed to call 'for a few lines in addition to the formal approbation of the Kings seeing with particular pleasure his coming forward on the present occasion'.[125] This reduced the impact of the move of Augustus, the third duke, the former first minister, towards opposition positions. Euston also held the prestigious posts of ranger of Hyde Park and St James's Park.

Responding to their quest for patronage, George also called on the support of the social élite in the Church. The percentage of bishops who were the sons or close relatives of peers rose in George's reign, becoming more pronounced in its second half.[126] The end of Tory exclusion ensured that the number of Tory gentry appointed as JPs also increased, while more of the landed gentry entered the Inns of Court, enhancing the position of the élite in law.[127] George made more critical remarks about the handling of business in the Commons rather than the Lords, but this reflected his irritation with its conduct, not an obsession with rank, although the king tended to know the peers far better than the MPs and was more sympathetic to, and interested in, them. Factiousness, over-long debates and speeches, and a failure to restrict comment to business before the House angered the king, as in 1786 when he criticized David, Viscount

---

[123] PRO. War Office corresp. vol. 34; George, warrant to Richard Rigby, paymaster-general, 30 Apr. 1779, to reimburse John, third duke of Dorset, for his expenses as colonel of the West Kent militia, Maggs to author, 7 Mar. 2005.

[124] George, Marquess Townshend to John Blofield, 11 Nov. 1792, Bod. MS. Eng. Lett. c. 144 fol. 274; re. Townshend's appointment, George to Pitt, 15 Feb. 1792, PRO. 30/8/103 fol. 434.

[125] George to Pelham, 28 May 1803, BL. Add. 33115 fol. 144.

[126] N. Ravitch, 'The Social Origins of French and English Bishops in the Eighteenth Century', *Historical Journal*, 8 (1965), pp. 319–20.

[127] P. Lucas, 'A Collective Biography of Students and Barristers of Lincoln's Inn, 1680–1804: A Study in the "Aristocratic Resurgence" in the Eighteenth Century', *Journal of Modern History*, 46 (1974), pp. 227–61; L. Colley, 'Eighteenth-Century English Radicalism before Wilkes', *Transactions of the Royal Historical Society* (1981), pp. 17–18.

Stormont, a prominent opposition speaker in the Lords, for the last, while noting that such behaviour occurred often in the Commons.[128]

Similarly, the reply to a letter from Pitt asking if the proposal from the East India Company to give General Archibald Campbell command over its forces was at one level a bald and inappropriate statement of social snobbery: 'Whilst the army in India remains in such unfit hands as those of a Company of merchants I cannot expect any good can be done.'[129] Yet George was also reflecting the view that the Company was a poor employer, and that the army there needed reform, for otherwise there would be a major burden on British regular forces.[130]

George also made himself more generally approachable. Staying with Thomas, first earl of Ailesbury – a friend and also lord chamberlain to Charlotte – at Tottenham Park in 1789 on the way back from Weymouth, George not only played cribbage, drove in an open chaise round Savernake Forest (George himself driving), and looked at the earl's collection of prints, but also, more publicly, although in a very controlled fashion, received an address from the mayor and corporation of Marlborough.[131] The reception of such addresses, for example from Worcester in 1788 and from Devizes, Exeter and Plympton in 1789,[132] was an important aspect of George's public politics, with loyalty and graciousness displayed in an interactive pageant, as they were in Southampton in 1801 and 1804. On their visit to Oxford in 1786, the royal party – George, Charlotte and three of their daughters – received an address from the university at the Sheldonian Theatre, returned 'a most gracious answer', then went to the council chamber, where an address was presented by the city 'and most graciously received by his majesty'. George then conferred a knighthood on Richard Tawney, the senior alderman of the city. At Lymington in 1787, George was received at the town hall (since demolished), and the mayor and corporation, having been presented by John, Earl Delawarr, lord warden of the New Forest, kissed the hands of George and Charlotte.[133] To underline the pattern of social links created by royal service, Delawarr's father, John, second earl, had been vice-chamberlain to Charlotte (1761–6), her master of the horse (1766–8), and then lord chamberlain.

[128] George to Pitt, 24 Jan. 1786, Aspinall, *George III*, I, 208; cf. George to Pelham, 7 June 1803, BL. Add. 33115 fol. 146.

[129] George to Pitt, 23 Sept. 1784, Aspinall, *George III*, I, 95.

[130] R. Callahan, *The East India Company and Army Reform, 1783–1798* (Cambridge, Massachusetts, 1972).

[131] Queen Charlotte's diary, 16, 17 Sept. 1789, RA. GEO/Add. 43/1; Earl of Cardigan, *The Wardens of Savernake Forest* (London, 1949), pp. 286–7.

[132] Address from Plympton, Plymouth 1676/176.

[133] *Devizes Gazette*, 28 June 1849; E. King, *Old Times Revisited in the Borough and Parish of Lymington, Hants* (2nd edn, London, 1900), pp. 129–31.

To give a further flavour of how George spent his leisure, or rather of the public nature of his role, in which duty and leisure were as one, this visit to Oxford, on 13 August 1786, began when George left George, second Earl Harcourt's seat at Nuneham Courtenay after divine service. The party reached the great gate of the Bodleian soon after one o'clock and visited the chapel at New College, Wadham, Trinity, Lincoln and Brasenose Colleges, and Christ Church, of which George was visitor, and where he was entertained to a banquet, before returning to Nuneham the same evening, at about 6.30 p.m., ending a characteristically crowded day. Next day, George went to Blenheim.[134] On his other visit to Oxford, in 1785, George, Charlotte and six of their children arrived at 10 a.m., attended divine service in Christ Church, and then toured the college, visiting the library and hall before calling at Corpus Christi, Merton, New, All Souls, St John's, Queen's and Magdalen. They were received at the Sheldonian by the senior academics and knighted the mayor at the town hall. After a visit against the background of bells 'incessantly ringing', the royal party left at 5.30 p.m.[135]

In contrast, George did not spend time walking round London, as his nephew, the future Frederick VI of Denmark did in Copenhagen, having pushed through a governmental change in April 1784, 'receiving, everywhere, the strongest demonstration of affection from all ranks'.[136] Instead, George repeated the standard line voiced by Tories and opposition Whigs that London was over-large, and therefore a source of problems. He referred to 'the overgrown metropolis'.[137]

En route to Walhampton to dine with his friend Captain Sir Harry Neale in 1801, George passed through Lymington, where he spoke in the town hall to the mayor and 'several gentlemen'. In Southampton, he 'spoke most graciously to all the members of the corporation' and examined the list of burgesses in which his own name appeared, as he had been made an honorary burgess while prince of Wales.[138] In 1789, aside from Tottenham Park, where his visit was commemorated with a column, and Longleat, George also visited Lord Digby's seat of Sherborne castle on 4 August and was applauded by 'vast crowds' in the Park. Neale, who played a role in dealing with the naval mutiny at the Nore in 1797, was a baronet who became a groom of the bedchamber. George visited him again in 1804. Henry, seventh Lord Digby was lord-lieutenant of Dorset and was

---

[134] *Annual Register* (1786), p. 208; H. Thompson, *Christ Church* (London, 1900), p. 178. The kitchen accounts do not survive for this period.

[135] *London Gazette*, 17 Sept. 1785, describing visit on 13 Sept; *Gentleman's Magazine*, 55 (1785), II, 829–30.

[136] Elliot to Dorset, 17 Apr. 1784, KAO. U269 C188/4.

[137] George to Hawkesbury, 3 Feb. 1805, BL. Loan 72/1 fol. 135.

[138] Rose to Eldon, 1 July 1801, Twiss, I, 386; *Hampshire Chronicle*, 6 July 1801.

attendant on the king at Weymouth during his stay. His brother was vice-chamberlain to Charlotte and had attended George during his illness. The game book, housekeeper's accounts and wine stock book all provide evidence of the visit, while the estate accounts record expenses for new china and silver.[139] George stayed to dinner. Echoing the work at Windsor, the extension to the house built in 1787 had been given three pointed Gothic arches. Digby was created Earl Digby the following January.

Like many of his subjects, George was interested in seeing fine houses.[140] These included old ones such as, in 1789, Cotehele, the seat of George, first Viscount Mount Edgcumbe, who was raised to an earl during George's visit. Cotehele contrasted greatly with the contemporary splendours of Saltram, the seat of John, first earl of Morley, where the royal family stayed that year. On the same trip, George also visited Mount Edgcumbe. The number of houses visited was considerable and the pace vigorous. In 1789, George also visited the King's House at Lyndhurst, the seat of the lord warden of the New Forest, and Cuffnells, the seat of George Rose, the secretary to the treasury. He visited Carne House near Dorchester on 7 July, went to Lulworth on 3 August (this date is in the parish register), and visited Milton Abbey on 6 September (Lord Milton borrowed the cook from Sherborne Castle), stopping again at Sherborne Castle for lunch on 14 September on his way to see Redlynch, the seat of the earl of Ilchester, and Stourhead, whither the Digbys accompanied him. After an overnight stop at Longleat, he then returned to Windsor. Milton was created earl of Dorchester in 1792.

In 1788, George had stayed near Cheltenham at the recently built house of Henry, second earl of Fauconberg, a lord of the bedchamber. On that trip, George also visited the seats of Henry, second Earl Bathurst, a former lord chancellor whom he regarded as a loyal supporter,[141] George, sixth earl of Coventry, a former lord of the bedchamber, Francis, third Lord Ducie, Sir George Paul and George Augustus Selwyn.[142] Opportunities were provided for him to be seen. *Berrow's Worcester Journal* of 31 July recorded,

> On Saturday last their Majesties accompanied by the Princesses, passed and repassed through Tewkesbury on their way to and from the seat of the Earl of Coventry. Upon which occasion the inhabitants gave every

---

[139] Sherborne Castle, Archives. I am most grateful for the assistance of the curator and archivist, Ann Smith.

[140] A. Tinniswood, *The Polite Tourist: A History of Country House Visiting* (London, 1998); C.H. Mayo, 'George III's Visit to Sherborne', *Somerset and Dorset Notes and Queries*, 4 (1894), pp. 156–7; George to Ailesbury, 3 Oct. 1784, Aspinall, *George III*, I, 96.

[141] George to Sydney, 1 May 1786, Aspinall, *George III*, I, 220. For George's interest in the family, George to Grenville, 6 Oct. 1796, BL. Add. 58857 fol. 87.

[142] B. Little, 'The Gloucestershire Spas: An Eighteenth-Century Parallel', in P. McGrath and J. Cannon (eds), *Essays in Bristol and Gloucestershire History* (Bristol, 1976), p. 194.

proof of their loyalty and attachment to their sovereign. A grand triumphant arch was erected across the street at the post office, adorned and decorated with flowers and garlands, and with flags streaming, on the top of the arch their Majesties arms were placed and beneath an inscription with these words 'King George I before his accession to the throne was Baron of Tewkesbury'. 'May the illustrious house of Hanover flourish to the latest posterity'. A band of music was placed on an eminence near the arch, who as their Majesties passed played, 'God Save the King'. The 29th Regiment of Foot was drawn up in form by the Earl of Harrington, and every other method used to testify the pleasure they received from a view of so many branches of the Royal Family.

The same issue described the visit to the earl of Coventry's seat at Croome, which was far from private. Arriving, George was received 'amidst the acclamations of some thousands of all ranks', and walked for over two hours in the grounds 'gratifying their own and the curiosity of the numerous spectators, whose plaudits they received with pleasure, and returned by repeated salutes', while,

> After dinner, the royal guests, desirous of satisfying as much as in their power, that wish they had excited, appeared at the windows, where they continued for some time, expressing by their looks and gestures the happiness they experienced in the evident and almost incessant marks of loyalty and affection shown them, by thousands of their surrounding subjects; in fact, the joy of the sovereign, his family, and his people, seemed totally reciprocal.

Richard Cooksey, a not conspicuously enthusiastic observer, estimated that George and his suite were followed when he rode over the park and Lady Coventry's farm 'by at least 500 horsemen, women on horseback and the most motley group conceivable . . . the lawn . . . covered with about 4,000 people'.[143] The relatively modest number of attendants who accompanied the royal family helped give such calls an aura in keeping with their status as private visits.[144] At the same time, visits might involve lavish hospitality and much state, as with that in 1789 to Longleat, the seat of the groom of the stole and former secretary of state, Thomas, first marquess of Bath.[145] In 1801, the seats George visited included George Rose's of Cuffnells, Lord Mendip's of Paultons, and Captain Michel's of Northerwood Lodge,

---

[143] Cooksey to Deerhurst, 29 July 1788, Croome Estate Trust, Coventry papers, CEA. F66/3.
[144] M. Kilburn, 'Royalty and Public in Britain 1714–1789' (unpublished D.Phil., Oxford, 1997), p. 151.
[145] D. Burnett, *Longleat. The Story of an English Country House* (London, 1978), pp. 122–4.

but in Southampton on 1 July he also appeared on the balcony of the Audit-house and, as the *Hampshire Chronicle* of 6 July noted, was 'greeted with the huzzas of the surrounding multitude'. In 1804, George returned to Cuffnells and Milton Abbey.

In both Britain and America, rural pursuits were in part a matter of social expression: a proclamation of virtuous activity and appropriate status in face of the dissolving prospects of the social fluidity represented by new wealth.[146] This factor may have played a role for George, but personal preferences were key to his increased favour for Windsor from the 1770s. On his estate there, George's much-reported personal supervision of his tenants was seen as displaying both public and private functions, and helped in the presentation of the human side of the monarch, as with James Gillray's engraving *Affability* (1795), which depicted George talking to a surprised rustic. He became popularly known as Farmer George and this became a recognizable peg in cartoons such as 'Summer Amusement at Farmer G——'s near Windsor' (1791), probably by Richard Newton.

Especially from the 1780s, George was interested in farming, and, in order to permit his pursuit of agricultural interests in the Home Park at Windsor, the deer stocked there were moved to the Great Park. In 1804, the 'objects and scenes of the King's favourite amusements and habitual occupations', were described as 'his parks, farming, plantings and building'.[147] George read the *Annals of Agriculture*, toured farms on his estate, and was interested in the farming when he visited country houses. At Croome he also saw the dairy and walked round the plantations. He expected his sons to cultivate a strip on a model farm he had devised, an activity they did not relish. George became well known for his agricultural concerns, which bridged patriotism and philanthropy. This was not an unusual pastime. Both Castlereagh and Liverpool were also interested in amateur farms. Farm animals were one of George's particular enthusiams, and in 1798, pleased to receive an Irish ram and ten ewes from the marquess of Buckingham, he asked that they be sent to the Home Park in Windsor.[148] The king's import of merino sheep played a role in improving the British wool stock, and in this George was more successful than Rockingham, who had pursued the same goal.[149] It contrasted with George I's focus on improving the stock of game in the royal forests.

George III was also an active hunter, like other monarchs including both Louis XV and Louis XVI, and keen to protect his interest. When, in

[146] T.P. Thornton, *Cultivating Gentlemen: The Meaning of Country Life among the Boston Elite, 1785–1860* (New Haven, Connecticut, 1989).

[147] Bickley (ed.), *Diaries of . . . Glenbervie*, I, 358; J. Roberts, *Royal Landscapes. The Gardens and Parks of Windsor* (New Haven, 1997).

[148] George to William Grenville, 18 Nov. 1798, BL. Add. 58860 fol. 126.

[149] Thomas Lodge to Rockingham, 9 May 1767, WW. R1–783.

1782, the ministry moved to abolish a whole tranche of household offices, George preserved that of master of the buckhounds, using the argument that 'every private person keeps hounds'.[150] The royal buckhounds were transferred to new buildings close to Ascot Heath in about 1790. References to his hunting occur in his correspondence,[151] while Queen Charlotte, who disliked hunting and did not hunt, recorded in her diary for 29 September 1794, 'After breakfast the Prince and Ernest went out coursing with the King' and, for 11 October, that George went hunting with Ernest. Three days later, George and Ernest went stag hunting after breakfast; on 17 October he went hunting after breakfast, and again on 18 October, this time with the prince of Wales. George went hunting again on 21 October, and on the 25 October with the prince of Wales after breakfast; again after breakfast on 28 October, 1, 4, 8, 11, 18, 22 and 29 November, and 2, 6 and 9 December.[152]

Training his sons to hunt was an essential prerequisite to their success as cavalry officers and gentlemen and offered the King a way to socialize with them. Thus, he hunted with the duke of York on 16 December 1794. Hunting also involved much exercise, as, during a day, the hunt would cover substantial areas. On 7 February 1801, 'His Majesty, with His Royal Highness the Duke of Cumberland [Ernest], and other attendants, took the diversion of hunting; the deer, after a long chase, was taken near Maidenhead Thicket. The King was on horseback from half-past nine in the morning, till four in the afternoon.'[153] This hunt, and George's attendance at St George's Chapel the next day, were the central episodes on a brief visit to Windsor: George had left London on 6 February, returning on the 9th. George not only went hunting at Windsor, but also visited Windsor in order to go hunting. Windsor was close enough to the capital to serve as a hunting seat, and its ready access to good hunting country helped explain its popularity as a residence. The king was depicted in hunting scenes, including those by John Bewick, who illustrated William Somerville's poem *The Chase*. Although written in 1735, meaning that the references to the prince of Wales would be to Frederick, the illustrations were drawn in 1795, so the hunting scene at Windsor is likely to have been a contemporary one.[154] The social politics of hunting, however, were harsh: the game laws restricted hunting to wealthy landed gentry and laid down harsh penalties for poaching. Supplementary legislation in 1771 and 1773 was directed at night-time poaching.[155]

[150] Memorandum by George enclosed with George to Rockingham, 28 Apr. 1782, Fortescue, V, 501.

[151] George to Pitt, 2 Feb. 1793, PRO. 30/8/103 fol. 476.

[152] RA. GEO/Add. 43/3.

[153] *Courier*, 9 Feb. 1801.

[154] W. Somerville, *The Chase* (London, 1802), p. 78.

[155] P.B. Munsche, *Gentlemen and Poachers: The English Game Laws, 1671–1830* (Cambridge, 1981).

Like much of the social élite, the king rode frequently, an exercise encouraged by Bute, and was interested in horses. For example, the queen recorded in her diary that George went riding after breakfast on 31 October, 13, 17, 20 and 21 November. His correspondence occasionally noted his rides, usually characteristically in explaining why he did not handle government business at once. In Windsor, on 10 April 1795, 'I was just getting on horseback when Sylvester arrived with Lord Grenville's note and box, and being more inclined to ride than to write, I delayed redispatching him till now.' On 23 May 1797, he 'was out on horseback' at Windsor when a box of admiralty papers arrived, on 9 May 1798 he returned 'from my ride' to Queen's House to find a box of Foreign Office papers, and on 16 June 1803 he promised to return home in time for a Privy Council.[156] George went riding both as part of his ordinary routine and while on his holidays. In 1788, he rode in Earl Bathurst's park, in 1789, in the park at Sherborne Castle, and in 1791 he covered 32 miles, from Weymouth to Lulworth, in one day. On the day of his Jubilee in 1809, the king's usual morning ride in Windsor Great Park became a public event with military bands and rosetted spectators. He is commemorated in Windsor Great Park with a large equestrian statue, commissioned by George IV and finished in 1831.

The amount of time that George devoted to riding and hunting does not adequately emerge from his correspondence, much of which was on governmental business. This record also creates a somewhat misleading account of the people with whom George spent his time. Newspaper reports provide a useful corrective, as they frequently note royal activity. On 6 January 1801 the *Courier* reported,

Yesterday morning, His Majesty, accompanied by Lord Chesterfield, General Gwynne, and his usual attendants, rode up in the Great Park [at Windsor], and after inspecting the different improvements, took the diversion of hunting with the harriers, in company with a number of gentlemen sportsmen.

On the 9th, the paper added,

The King yesterday morning, accompanied by His Royal Highness the Duke of Kent, Lords Cathcart and Walsingham, and Colonel Cartwright, Equerry in Waiting, rode up in Windsor Great Park to inspect the different improvements, and at twelve o'clock His Majesty

---

[156] George to William Grenville, 10 Apr. 1795, George to Spencer, 23 May 1797, George to William Grenville, 9 May 1798, George to Pelham, 16 June 1803, BL. Add. 58859, 75805, 58860, 33115.

hunted with the harriers attended by a number of gentlemen sportsmen.

Again on the 13th,

> His Majesty yesterday morning, after breakfast, attended by Lords Walsingham and Cathcart, General Harcourt, Colonel Cartwright and Mr. Wyatt, viewed the different improvements and plans laid out for the decorations of the Castle; after which His Majesty hunted with the harriers.

The paper added on 14 January,

> His Majesty yesterday morning, attended by Lords Cathcart and Walsingham, and Colonel Cartwright, rode to Ascot-heath, where a deer was turned out for the day's diversion. The King was met by Earl Sandwich, Sir Henry Gott and son, Sir John Lade, Mr. Freemantle, and a number of gentlemen sportsmen.

George made hunting at Windsor easier by appointing friends and those he could trust to positions there. His uncle Cumberland and then his brother Cumberland were rangers of Windsor Park and Caroline of Brunswick was ranger of Blackheath. This underlines the role of the royal household as a large family in the eighteenth-century sense, a role which explains why they took economic reform in the 1780s rather badly. William Harcourt, later third Earl Harcourt, was deputy-ranger of Windsor Great Park. He also served for many years as a groom of the bedchamber and as deputy-lieutenant of Windsor castle. Francis, second marquess of Hertford, who was master of the horse from 1804 to 1806, had been cofferer of the household in 1780–2, and royal favour was shown when he received the Order of the Garter in 1807. James, Lord Brudenell, from 1790 fifth earl of Cardigan, who had been master of the robes to George as prince and then king from 1758, instead became constable of Windsor Castle in 1791, holding the position until he died in 1811.

As a reminder of the myriad interconnectedness of the élite and their multiple links with the royal family, Cardigan was related to the Ailesburys, friends of the king, through his mother, while his first wife, Anne, was North's stepsister and his second wife, Lady Elizabeth Waldegrave, was a daughter of Maria, dowager countess Waldegrave, who secretly married George's brother William, duke of Gloucester, in 1766. Elizabeth's first husband, her cousin, George, fourth Earl Waldegrave, had been vice-chamberlain of the household from 1782 to 1784 and master of the horse to Charlotte from 1784 until his death in 1789, succeeding his father, the third earl, who held the post from 1770 until his death in 1784. This was an aspect of the role of duty and dynastic thinking in society, with generations of courtiers and office-holders serving the crown. George's longevity meant that generations from the same family served him, creating powerful mutual obligations.

George continued to ride in his later years, and his ability to do so was seen as a testimony to his recovery from poor health.[157] On 16 June 1801 he rode out at 10 a.m., returning at 4 p.m.[158] Despite his poor eyesight, *The Times* of 7 November 1805 noted, after breakfast the previous day he had ridden in Windsor Great Park, accompanied by the dukes of York and Cambridge and Princesses Augusta, Sophia and Amelia. George also went riding when on his summer trips, for example at Weymouth. *En route* there in 1801, he stayed with George Rose, secretary of the treasury from 1784 to 1801, at his seat of Cuffnells. The day after arriving, the king rode to Walhampton and, the following day, ten miles to Southampton.[159] In 1804, he rode back from Milton Abbey to Weymouth, the following year riding while there in the pleasure grounds. *The Times* of 7 September 1805 noted that George took his 'usual ride' at 7 a.m.

George's interest extended to the horses that pulled his carriage. On 23 August 1804, George visited Cumberland Lodge on the Windsor estate to inspect the cream-coloured horses already brought from the Royal Mews in London in preparation for the royal family's journey to Weymouth. On 1 September 1805, he inspected his stables at Weymouth. George's correspondence showed considerable knowledge of the administration of the royal stables, and he was finally able in 1807 to bring back James, third duke of Montrose 'the best Master of the Horse ever in my service'.[160] Montrose, who held the post in 1790–5, was to hold it again from 1807 to 1821. Unlike Charles III of Spain,[161] however, George was not keen on fishing.

George's interest in riding did not preclude walking, and he particularly enjoyed visiting gardens on foot. George frequently walked round Kew and Richmond gardens. As natural sights, such as trees in spring bloom, provided the king with evidence of the 'goodness of Divine Providence', it is not surprising that he relished being outdoors.[162] Staying in the deanery in Exeter in 1789, the king 'enjoyed his usual practice of very early and salutary walking'.[163] Mentioned in a work originally published in 1806, this account provided during his lifetime an appropriate description

---

[157] Theresa Villiers to Mrs Robinson, 19 Apr. 1801, Plymouth, 1259/2/574.

[158] Twiss, I, 381.

[159] Twiss, I, 386.

[160] George to Pitt, 16 May 1805, PRO. 30/8/104 fol. 342.

[161] Frederick Robinson to Anne Robinson, 8 Aug. 1774, 7 Aug. 1775, Bedford CRO. L30/17/2.

[162] George to Prince Augustus, 29 Mar. 1787, Aspinall, *George III*, I, 274.

[163] *Jenkins's Civil and Ecclesiastical History of the City of Exeter* (2nd edn, Exeter, 1841), p. 309.

of exemplary activity. At Weymouth, on 1 September 1805, George walked upon the esplanade soon after 7 a.m. George was a walker, not a stroller, still less a *boulevardier*. Striding forth, he pushed himself forward, his walking in part reflecting the nervous intensity seen in much of his conversation. Walking a lot helped keep the king fit, although, ironically, his active exercise was seen as a threat to his health,[164] and in 1788 his illness was blamed on standing and walking 'five hours in the wet'.[165] Walking was one of the many activities that left very little impact on George's correspondence, but there are occasional mentions, as on a summer evening in 1793 when, 'on returning from walking I have found Lord Grenville's box', or in June 1804 when, 'on returning from his walk in the garden', the king found a note from Eldon.[166] Ministers could also expect a walk. On 1 May 1804, Addington and George walked in the garden, probably of Queen's House, for ninety minutes as they discussed the tense political situation. Such a walk provided privacy and a release from tension. Ministers could expect meetings to be timed so that George could 'prolong his airing'.[167]

As far as his family was concerned, walking offered an activity he could share, in particular with the royal women, although Charlotte did not much like muddy walks. Visiting Exeter in 1789, George took advantage of the extensive gardens of the bishop's palace, especially the view of the nearby country: 'On this terrace his present Majesty, with his royal consort and daughters walked for some time, and greatly admired the beauties of the surrounding scene.'[168] On 10 February 1801, George, Queen Charlotte, and their children Augusta, Edward, Elizabeth and Mary took an airing to Kew where they walked in the garden. In March 1789, Sir William Fawcett had found the king in the garden when he visited Kew.[169] Walking, however, was not only a matter of visiting gardens. The *Courier* of 26 January 1801 reported that 'His Majesty on Saturday [24th] intended taking the diversion of hunting; but was prevented by the frost ... The King, attended by General Garth and his equerries in waiting, walked in Windsor Little Park, and afterwards to Frogmore.' Arriving at Cuffnells that June at about 3 p.m., the king forthwith 'walked about a little'.[170]

George's personality as a mature man was already clear in some respects when he came to the throne. His sense of propriety, diligence and

[164] Sydney to Cornwallis, 27 Jan. 1790, Ross (ed.), *Cornwallis*, II, 29.

[165] Anne to Frederick Robinson, 9 Nov. 1788, Bedford CRO. L30/15/50/163.

[166] George to William Grenville, 13 June 1793, BL. Add. 58857 fol. 124; George to Eldon, 8 June 1804, Twiss, I, 454.

[167] George to Pitt, 9 May 1804, PRO. 30/8/104 fol. 336.

[168] *Jenkins's ... History*, p. 309.

[169] Ross (ed.), *Cornwallis*, I, 412.

[170] Twiss, I, 386.

commitment had been honed by his upbringing. It was to be put under brutal pressure in the maelstrom of politics, and yet the personality that matured was an attractive one. King George was generally good-humoured,[171] and a kindly, gentlemanly, often (but not always) generous, charitable,[172] worrying person. Even Henry Brougham, one of his most bitter critics, referred to him as 'a man of amiable disposition, and few princes have been more exemplary in their domestic habits, or in the offices of private friendship'.[173] George could turn against those to whom he had once been close, conspicuously so in the case of Bute and North, while his relationship with his heir was bitter; but he was also capable of loyalty and valued 'integrity and fidelity'.[174] He was ready to apologize, as when he called on Dundas after the 1801 Egyptian expedition to admit that he had been wrong to oppose his plan to send a force to contest French control of Egypt. The assessment of his character seen in recent work contributes powerfully to the more generally positive treatment of the king, linking with interest in the contributions he made to the country's cultural and scientific life. Whether this interpretation should extend equally to his political role is less clear.

[171] Hannecken report, 4 Feb. 1772, Rigs. 1953.
[172] George to Dundas, 8 Sept. 1799, BL. Add. 40100 fol. 233.
[173] H. Brougham, *Historical Sketches of Statesmen Who Flourished in the Time of George III* (2 vols, Philadelphia, Pennsylvania, 1842), I, 14.
[174] George to Hawkesbury, 18 Dec. 1808, BL. Loan 72/1 fol. 151.

Chapter 8

FAMILY

the anxiety I have for the success of my endeavours to fit my children for the various stations they may fill, and that they may be useful and a credit to their family.

George, 1781[1]

Family played a central part in George's life. His roles as son, husband and father were important to him, but each posed problems. In November 1759, George fell in love with Lady Sarah Lennox, a beautiful fifteen-year-old, who was sister of Charles, third duke of Richmond, and sister-in-law of Henry Fox. George, however, realized that this was unlikely to be an acceptable match, both because she was a commoner and because Fox was a controversial politician. He accepted Bute's advice not to pursue the matter, but, despite his belief that only marriage would end the struggle between prudence and his desire for women, was unwilling, while still a prince, to seek a German princess. This reflected his view that any such negotiation would give too much opportunity to the hated George II to meddle in his affairs. According to Fox, at his first birthday ball as king, George only had eyes for Lady Sarah, 'He stopped very remarkably as he was going and turned and spoke again and again as if he could not force himself from her.'[2] In 1788, during his attack of porphyria, George raved about Lady Sarah. This contributes to the depiction of George as a highly sexed puritan suffering from repressed sexuality, a depiction that may have had some truth in 1759,[3] but that is based on an inaccurately negative portrayal of his marriage.[4] The first unmarried monarch to ascend the throne since Charles II in 1660, George married Charlotte, second daughter of Duke Charles Louis Frederick of Mecklenburg-Strelitz, on 8 September 1761 (see pp. 46–8). The celebrant, Archbishop Secker, noted George's piety and also his commanding role, not least his determination that English (which Charlotte did not know) be used in the service,

---

[1] George to Richard Grenville, 6 Feb. 1781, BL. Add. 70956.
[2] BL. Add. 51439 fols 37–8.
[3] George to Bute, 1759, BL. Add. 36796 fol. 46.
[4] For such a depiction, J.H. Plumb, *The First Four Georges* (London, 1956), pp. 95–6.

The words of espousal and contract, as well as the rest of the service, were in English, by the King's order: and by the same order I called both him and the Queen only by their Christian names. When I asked them the proper question, the King answered very solemnly laying his hand on his breast, and suggested to her to answer, Ich will, which she did: but spoke audibly in no other part of the service . . . When I desired the King . . . to acquaint the Queen that she, as well as he, was to receive the Sacrament at their coronation, he said she knew it; and was no less in respect of religion, than in every other, just what he could wish; her Instructor in Germany . . . having always told her, that he thought the Church of England the best in the world.[5]

Charlotte was an attractive woman with light brown hair and blue-grey eyes. An arranged marriage, theirs was far happier than those of most monarchs of the period, not least because George loved his wife greatly and did not pursue other women. The marriage made George happy and he was uxorious. Indeed, somewhat improbably, his devotion to his wife was mentioned by the villain in an episode of the British detective series *Taggart*.[6] Like Louis XVI, but unlike many other monarchs, for example Louis XV, as well as Charles Edward Stuart, George did not have any mistresses. In contrast, Charles, duke of Brunswick, was unfaithful to George's sister Augusta, and Christian VII to his other married sister, Caroline Matilda. It was alleged that George had already in 1759 secretly married the 'very engaging' Hannah Lightfoot, a Quaker by whom he had a son and who was married off in return for a large sum.[7] There is no evidence for this rumour, which was depicted in the caricature *The Fair Quaker of Cheltenham*.

George and Charlotte had fifteen children, nine boys and six girls. George I had two children by his wife and three by Melusine, duchess of Kendal. George II had three sons and five daughters, and Frederick, prince of Wales, had five sons and four daughters. Charlotte, unlike Queen Anne, had no miscarriages or stillborn infants. The births were frequent and lasted for over two decades: 1762, 1763, 1765, 1766, 1767, 1768, 1770, 1771, 1773, 1774, 1776, 1777, 1779, 1780 and 1783. In contrast, Louis XVI had difficulties, either medical or of sexual technique, and did not consummate his marriage for seven years.[8] George was a keen family man, and could write, without irony, 'Heaven having blessed me with a numerous progeny'.[9] His purchase in 1765 of Van Dyck's *The Five Eldest*

[5] Secker, notes, Lambeth Palace Library, MS 1130/I fols 96–7.
[6] Broadcast on 8 August 2005.
[7] A. Hamilton, *Secret History of the Court of England* (London, 1832), pp. 2–4.
[8] D. Beales, *Joseph II, I: In the Shadow of Maria Theresa, 1741–1780* (Cambridge, 1987), pp. 371–5.
[9] George to Pitt, 28 Mar. 1786, PRO. 30/8/103 fol. 187.

Children of Charles I reflected his commitment to family. Being head of the royal family, however, proved a heavy burden. Sir Joshua Reynolds noted of George's return from reviewing the warships at Portsmouth in 1773,

> When he came to Kew he was so impatient to see the Queen that he opened the chaise himself and jumped out before any of his attendants could come to his assistance. He seized the Queen, whom he met at the door, round the waist, and carried her in his arms into the room; I trouble with these particulars as everything relating to Kings is worth hearing.

George was very strongly committed to domestic life, and, in contrast, does not seem to have had close friends or favourites after Bute. Charlotte shared George's commitment to duty, propriety, piety and philanthropy, his seriousness, and his dislike of ceremonial and expense.[10] James Harris, who became comptroller and secretary to Charlotte in 1774, an interesting choice as he was known as a philosopher and a keen lover of music, recorded that in his first audience, Charlotte, after discussing music and Harris's works 'fell into an encomium upon the King's worth and goodness'. Unlike George II's wife, Caroline, Charlotte was a critic of freethinking, which was one of the reasons why George III married her and a reason why she disliked Frederick II of Prussia. Elizabeth, duchess of Northumberland, a lady of the bedchamber to the queen, noted that their table 'was neither sumptuous nor elegant and they always dined Tete a Tete'.[11] They usually dined together at four o'clock. The couple shared many interests, including music (both music-making and attending performances), reading, theatre, botany and walking. Frederik Hannecken, the Danish secretary of legation, noted in 1771 that when George and Charlotte were in town they profited from every good morning, on days that were not court days or when there was no council, to go to Richmond and walk for a couple of hours in the garden there.[12] In the painting of the marriage of his eldest son in 1795, George is depicted as almost doting on matrimony.

Charlotte's activities were an appropriate model for the monarchy, and one that was fully reported in the press. Thus, *Berrow's Worcester Journal* of

---

[10] Reynolds to Lord Grantham, 20 July 1773, Bedford, Bedfordshire CRO. Lucas papers 30/14/326/2; L. Namier and J. Brooke (eds), *The House of Commons 1754–1790* (3 vols, London, 1964), II, 589; O. Hedley, *Queen Charlotte* (London, 1975); C.C. Orr, 'Queen Charlotte, "Scientific Queen"', in Orr (ed.), *Queenship in Britain 1660–1837* (Manchester, 2002), pp. 236–66.

[11] J. Greig (ed.), *The Diaries of a Duchess. Extracts from the Diaries of the First Duchess of Northumberland* (London, 1926), p. 79.

[12] Hannecken report, 29 Nov. 1771, Rigs. 1952.

23 October 1788 noted that Charlotte had established a school in Datchet for poor girls to learn spinning: 'a laudable endeavour . . . to promote habits of industry . . . she is a constant visitor'. Her careful economy was praised, although also caricatured as avarice.[13] The need to support her daughters from her income was a particular problem. At the same time, Charlotte did not seek a political role in Britain, although she served to strengthen George's knowledge of, and commitment to, German dynastic politics and interests. Theirs was an unusually long union: Charlotte died in 1818, matching the pattern of royal spouses between the wives of William III and William IV in not surviving the monarch. George and Charlotte had children until the early 1780s. They were generally together, more so than most monarchs, and wrote frequently while apart.

When George was ill, however, his feelings towards Elizabeth, countess of Pembroke (1737–1831), one of his wife's ladies of the bedchamber, confused contemporaries: while ill in 1788–9, George had imagined that he had married her, and in 1804, Elizabeth, by then a widow, complained that she was pestered with love letters from the king. Lady Georgiana Buckley was also represented as the subject of George's interest. By then, relations between George and Charlotte were poor, certainly in comparison to the 1760s and 1770s, although there seems no basis for the report that the king had been intimate with a housemaid called Sally.[14] Charlotte found George's bouts of ill health a great strain, and, indeed, they caused her hair to go white. His blasphemy and violent outbursts while ill were a particular difficulty. The nervous tension wrought in Charlotte had an effect on the whole family. George and Charlotte continued to live together and Charlotte accompanied George on his travels, but the relationship had changed, and this must have hurt George as he had invested so much passion in uxoriousness. In 1804, Addington was informed

> that there is one great source of uneasiness to the King which, if not done away, will . . . stand in the way of recovery. The Queen will not admit the King to her apartments – in revenge he will not dine with her, and he lives in a part of the Lodge [at Weymouth] to himself. The Queen is either afraid or affects to be afraid of him – never allows him to be alone with her – and it is visible . . . that she does not treat him with any but exterior kindness.[15]

---

[13] F. Prochaska, *Royal Bounty: The Making of a Welfare Monarchy* (New Haven, Connecticut, 1995), pp. 17–20; M. Pointon, 'Intrigue, Jewellery and Economics: Court Culture and Display in England and France in the 1780s', in M. North and D. Ormrod (eds), *Art Markets in Europe, 1400–1800* (Aldershot, 1998), pp. 201–19.

[14] Colonel McMahon to duke of Northumberland, 25 Aug. 1804, Aspinall, *Prince of Wales*, V, 91.

[15] Mr Bond to Addington, 17 Sept. 1804, Exeter, 152M/C1804/OR44.

Subsequent concern with the royal image led to the letter being endorsed 'so private as not to be published'. Whatever his thoughts, George did not embarrass his family, inconvenience his ministers or compromise the image of monarchy by having a mistress, let alone the female favourite attacked by the *Monitor* of 12 June 1762 in the person of Louis XV's Madame de Pompadour. George's conduct in this matter was also politically valuable, because the French Revolutionary crisis was to show that pornography could serve the cause of radicals,[16] while, in France, Louis XV's lifestyle helped sap respect for the monarchy.[17] Similarly, the separation between George I and his adulterous wife as well as his long-standing relationship with the duchess of Kendal, and George II's record, had provided critics of the Hanoverian connection with many opportunities for comment, while Frederick, prince of Wales's active love life had been the subject of James Miller's *Vanelia: or The Amours of the Great* (1732), the text of an unperformed opera that went through at least six editions.

Although his simple life gave rise to satire at his expense, especially on the themes of parsimony and of 'Farmer George', George's domestication of the monarchy and his lack of ostentatious grandeur made a valuable contribution to a revival in the popularity of the monarchy. This served it well in the political crisis stemming from the French Revolution, acting as a powerful counter to the lifestyle associated with the eldest son. George indeed was the originator of the emphasis on domesticity in the British royal family.[18] George I was scarcely in a position to do so, while George II had been noted for his interest in women other than his wife, who, anyway, died in 1737, less than halfway through the reign. The behaviour of the royal family had become increasingly important, in part because it was now played out under a more observant public gaze, one that was far from confined to the contained public sphere of the court. Noting the scrutiny of the press on all those in public employment, Joseph Yorke commented, 'one must be master of the most unblemished character or the most hardened indifference to withstand all that is said'.[19] As a consequence of this public gaze, the conspicuous contrast between George's behaviour and that of his sons redounded to his credit. With George, family life and political attitudes were closely intertwined. His concern for the proper conduct of government and society illuminated his committed

---

[16] I. McCalman, *Radical Underworld: Prophets, Revolutionaries and Pornographers in London, 1795–1840* (Oxford, 1993).

[17] V. Cameron, 'Political Exposures, Sexuality and Caricature in the French Revolution', in L. Hunt (ed.), *Eroticism and the Body Politic* (Baltimore, Maryland, 1991), pp. 90–107.

[18] M. Morris, 'The Royal Family and Family Values in Late Eighteenth-Century Britain', *Journal of Family History*, 21 (1996), pp. 519–32, and *The British Monarchy and the French Revolution* (New Haven, Connecticut, 1998).

[19] Yorke to Edward Weston, 13 Sept. 1763, BL. Add. 58213 fol. 292.

Anglicanism, his determination to ensure the appropriate government of the Church of England, his interest in public morality, and, not least, his desire that the royal family should set an example of laudatory behaviour. He forbade dice at court and shunned masquerades. The report of George's visit to the Theatre Royal, Cheltenham, on 15 August 1788, in *Berrow's Worcester Journal* six days later, noted that, when George and Queen Charlotte entered they expressed 'much satisfaction at Mr Watson's good management, the most perfect order and regularity being observed throughout'. George disapproved of duelling. In April 1790 he remarked that John Curran, an opposition MP in the Irish parliament, who had challenged Major Hobart, the Irish chief secretary, to a duel, would not benefit from having brought on the dispute.[20]

It is customary to emphasize George's differences with his children, but the problems in the royal family were more than just a matter of different generations. Aside from Frederick, who died young in 1765, his brothers each gave cause for concern and, from George's perspective, displayed neither princely responsibility or behaviour nor the necessary family solidarity. None had received the attention Augusta lavished on George. Thus, Edward, duke of York (1739–67), closest to George in age, did not share his brother's religious beliefs (he was a latitudinarian) or his moral conduct. Freed from the burden, but not the privileges, of royal status, York was able to follow his own wishes. He visited Italy in 1763–4, the first member of the British royal family to go there as a tourist (although prior to 1714 several members of the house of Brunswick had done so), showing particular interest in Venice. York sailed from Plymouth to Genoa where he spent ten weeks, in part because he was attracted by Angela Serra (Madame Durazzo), an amateur painter with whom he appeared hand in hand at a reception at the Palazzo Ducale.[21] York pressed on via Florence to Rome, where Pope Clement XIII held a reception in his honour and gave him gifts. Cardinal Henry, the Jacobite duke of York, left Rome in protest at this sign of papal determination to work towards reconciliation with Britain and the Hanoverians, a policy that owed much to Cardinal Alessandro Albani, who, in his role as protector of Germans, took an interest in the Hanoverian dynasty. After Rome, where he also sat for his portrait by Pompeo Batoni, York pressed on to Bologna, Parma, Venice, Padua and Milan, where he was interested in the copy he was given of Beccaria's *Dei delitti e delle pene*, a call for the end of capital punishment, not a cause close to George's heart. York then returned to Genoa, and sailed back to Dover. On his trip he had been keen on the company of attractive women, but also took part in a round of activities befitting his status,

---

[20] George to William Grenville, 9 Apr. 1790, BL. Add. 58855 fol. 83.
[21] BL. Add. MS 34887 fol. 155.

including hunts and receptions. York heard the castrato Giovanni
Manzuoli sing, played the violin and attended scientific experiments, all of
these activities in which George would have been interested. He died in
Monaco in 1767, *en route* to Italy for a second visit.

In many respects, York was more similar to their father, Frederick,
prince of Wales, than to his royal brother George, while George's eldest
son, later George IV, had much in common with his uncle. The contrast
between the royal brothers serves as a reminder of the play of personality
and contingency and highlights the interests the king did not have. Henry
Fox noted 'How very different are persons of this family . . . I believe and
I hope in God that his present Majesty is as much the reverse of that
express image of his worthless father, the Duke of York.' Henry, duke of
Cumberland (1745–90) was also very different from his brother George,[22]
another warning against placing too great an emphasis on clashes between
generations.

The other royal brother, William, duke of Gloucester (1743–1805), to
whom the king was close, visited Italy in 1770–2, in large part to find relief
for his asthma, although also in order to meet by arrangement Madame
Grovestein. He travelled to Italy again in 1775–7, this time with his wife,
Maria, and daughter, Sophia. He went to the continent again in 1784–7,
on this occasion with his family and his mistress, the beautiful Lady
Almeria Carpenter, who was officially his wife's lady-in-waiting.
Gloucester's royal status made him a field marshal, but did not lead him
to military fame: George refused to let him serve during the War of
American Independence. George was upset when Gloucester, his last
surviving brother, died in 1805.[23]

Cumberland, who had been promoted to admiral in 1778, was also not
allowed to serve. George's brothers, like his father and his eldest son,
suffered from the lack of a role. Nor did the brothers make dynastically
advantageous matches. Cumberland's personal life caused a public furore
that embarrassed and inconvenienced George. Cumberland had got into
trouble in 1769 over an affair with Harriet, Lady Grosvenor. Found guilty
in 1770 of adultery, he was ordered to pay damages of £10,000, which
obliged him to borrow £12,000 from the unenthusiastic George.
Cumberland's clandestine marriage to a commoner (Anne Luttrell,
daughter of the first earl of Carhampton, and widow of Christopher
Horton), on 2 October 1771, infuriated George because it was an unequal
marriage in imperial law that not only prevented any children from inher-
iting Hanover, but also brought discredit on the royal family. George
pressed Cumberland to disavow the marriage, and, when he would not do

[22] BL. Add. 51439 fol. 8.
[23] Theresa Villiers to Catherine Robinson, 30 Aug., – Sept. 1805, Plymouth 1259/2/743,
745. But also see Anne Robinson to Catherine, 3 Sept. 1805, 1259/2/746.

so, barred him from his presence, while he would not receive his wife. The duke's failure to request George's permission led to the king's sponsoring of the Royal Marriages Act of 1772, which the minority of peers who opposed it presented as an infringement of constitutional values. George in turn pressed for the legislation to be passed 'with a becoming firmness . . . I have a right to expect a hearty support from everyone in my service and shall remember defaulters'.[24] The future George IV was himself influenced by his uncle, Cumberland, who introduced the prince to gambling and encouraged him in drinking and womanizing.[25]

Of his sisters, Caroline Matilda (1751–75) caused George most problems. Married in 1766 at the age of fifteen to her cousin Christian VII of Denmark (1749–1808) in order to assist British and Hanoverian diplomatic interests, she led a life very different from that of her sister-in-law, George's wife, Charlotte. Her youth and isolation, and the mental instability and unfaithfulness of her schizophrenic husband, help excuse her affair with the court doctor and leading favourite, Johann Friedrich Struensee, but, when he was overthrown in a court coup on 17 January 1772 she was left in a very exposed position. Struensee's execution caused concern about her fate: Caroline Matilda's adultery was a very serious offence. It was indeed intended that she be imprisoned, although there was also anxiety in London that she might be tried, thus exposing the British royal family to embarrassment. The unsympathetic Danish envoy thought George too keen to insist that his views be followed and his concern for his sister ensured that he certainly directed British foreign policy to an unprecedented extent during his reign. The threat of naval action against the much weaker Denmark was used in order to ensure her release into exile in the Electorate of Hanover.[26] George then treated his sister with kindness as well as care, ensuring she had books and musicians, but there was no doubt that the scandal affected the reputation of the family. He made it clear that she was not welcome in Britain, and she was obliged to remain at Göhrde, where she did not have the opportunity to act as a public figure. George's concern to act in an appropriate fashion was shown when he responded cautiously to suggestions that a coup be launched to return Caroline Matilda to power, a somewhat quixotic scheme. The king insisted that, if the coup was successful, there be no killing of the ministers. Before matters could proceed, Caroline Matilda

---

[24] George to North, 26 Feb. 1772, Fortescue, II, 325.

[25] C.N. Gattey, *Farmer George's Black Sheep* (Bourne End, 1985).

[26] H.M. Scott, *British Foreign Policy in the Age of the French Revolution* (Oxford, 1990), pp. 171–7; M. Bregnsbo, 'Danish Absolutism and Queenship: Louisa, Caroline Matilda, and Juliana Maria', in Orr (ed.), *Queenship in Europe*, pp. 350–4; S. Tillyard, *A Royal Affair. George III and his Troublesome Siblings* (London, 2006).

died in 1775.[27] As an interesting indication of the difficulty of establishing the character of illness in the royal family, her death has been variously attributed to porphyria, scarlet fever and smallpox.

The difficulties he encountered with his siblings made George more acutely concerned about his children, but the outcome was no happier. As their numerous children grew to adulthood a conflict arose between George and Charlotte's sense of propriety and the dissolute life adopted by most of their brood of boys. The members of the younger generation were especially loath to accept the king and queen's views on marriage and choice of marriage partners, and entered into liaisons which, while often stable and personally fulfilling, hardly lived up to the increasingly respectable, almost prudish, image that George wished to promote. The alienation between the generations was represented most strikingly in the endless disputes between the king and the prince of Wales, and in the very public sense of glee that 'Prinny' demonstrated when his father became too ill to rule; but George had reason to complain of all his sons' 'want of economy'.[28] Irrespective of this, the need for establishments for his sons was a financial strain for George.[29] Gambling, which was a fashionable activity in the aristocratic salons of London, was a pastime that captured the difference between parents and sons. George and Charlotte disliked both gambling and what it led to, but to the princes it both provided and symbolized excitement and style. George's rigid views clearly alienated his sons, just as they brought his daughters scant happiness.

George's keenness on court etiquette, not least precedence among the royal family, meant he was concerned in 1791 about whether his eldest daughter or his daughter-in-law, the new duchess of York, should have precedence: he decided in favour of the former, much to the anger of the latter. George was aware his concern might seem 'punctilious in the extreme',[30] but order in all matters was of concern to him. Indeed, etiquette to George helped contain, or at least organize, the self-importance of individual members of the royal family and of courtiers. Religion and religious observance was another area of contention between parents and sons, and a focus of the rebelliousness of the elder sons.

As adults, the princes did not suffer the constraints their sisters encountered, but in earlier days the king's love for them was expressed in a carefully planned emphasis on dutiful conduct and exemplary education. The response was similar to that of many American colonists: royal good inten-

[27] Hannecken reports, 4, 7–8 Feb., Diede reports, 13, 20, 27 Mar., 43, 10, 14, 17, 21, 25, 28 Apr. 1772, Rigs. 1953; H. Jørgensen, *The Unfortunate Queen. Caroline Mathilda's Last Years 1772–75* (Copenhagen, 1989).

[28] George to Dundas, 14 Aug. 1798, BL. Add. 40100 fol. 210 re. Augustus.

[29] George to Robinson, 21 Aug. 1780, BL. Add. 37835 fol. 147.

[30] George to William Grenville, 20, 21 Nov. 1791, BL. Add. 58856 fols 114, 117.

tions did not suffice. The king sought to reduce passion to order, but was frequently defeated. Thus, Frederick, duke of York, was a favourite of the king, who tried to ensure not only an exemplary upbringing but also a continuing supervision that included a marriage ceremony in England after the one in Prussia;[31] but George had to face his son's ability to lose large sums in gambling and racing.

George, prince of Wales, was also financially irresponsible and repeatedly incurred debts that he could not meet, leading to demands for assistance that worried his father.[32] In 1781, George III had to pay £5,000 to buy back the love letters that the prince had written his mistress, Mary Robinson, a prominent actress whom he had seen playing Perdita. She was also given a life annuity of £600 and £200 for her daughter (who predeceased Prince George), in return for surrendering the prince's promise of £20,000 when she came of age. Three years later, debts made the prince threaten to leave the country, which the king, who found the size of the debts inconceivable, had to forbid. The prince's secret marriage on 15 December 1785 to Maria Fitzherbert was in defiance of the Royal Marriages Act of 1772, under which descendants of George II (with the exception of the descendants of princesses who married abroad) could only marry before the age of twenty-five with royal permission; thereafter, they had to give a year's notice to the Privy Council, and parliament had not expressly to disapprove of the marriage. Under the Act of Settlement of 1701, Maria's Catholicism also made the marriage invalid. As the prince of Wales made no official marriage until he married his cousin Caroline in 1795, the likely line of succession appeared to go via Frederick, who married in 1791, but he was childless. Occasionally unfaithful and more constantly difficult, the prince stayed with Maria until 1794, when he left her for his new mistress, Frances, countess of Jersey. Maria was given a settlement of £3,000 a year.

George III's energy contrasted with the lethargy of his heir. Having arrived at Worcester on the evening of 5 August 1788, on the following morning 'his Majesty, being a very early riser, had surveyed the cathedral and its precincts, and walked to almost every part of the town before seven o'clock'.[33] This was not an hour the prince of Wales often saw. George repeated his early morning perambulation the next day, unsurprisingly so as he had early habits, rising regularly in the 1760s at 5 a.m.[34] The heir to the throne also posed a key political problem, and it was not one that George ever resolved. The prince associated with opponents to the

---

[31] George to Thurlow, 23 Nov. 1791, *Maggs Catalogue* 1173 (1994), p. 34, item no. 76.

[32] George to Pitt, 6 June 1791, PRO. 30/8/103 fol. 424.

[33] V. Green, *The History and Antiquities of the City and Suburbs of Worcester* (2 vols, London, 1796), I, 297.

[34] Greig (ed.), *Diaries of a Duchess*, p. 78.

government, as his governor, Robert, fourth earl of Holdernesse, complained in 1776. This became a more pressing issue in the 1780s and was politically crucial during the regency crisis. George did not trust his son with positions of responsibility, and indeed, in 1798 and 1801,[35] rejected his request to go on active service. This was one of the few ways in which princes could fulfil a role and gain a reputation, and George's sons all showed an interest in such service. This was encouraged by the success of Frederick, duke of York, in this role, but the prince of Wales's desire to serve potentially challenged his brother's position. The king had to be mindful not only of his responsibility – his eldest son would have been a hindrance – but also of the likely ministerial and political response if he made representations on behalf of his son.

At the same time, George was unwilling to accept the consequences of his eldest son's independence. He seems to have learned little from his own sense of political frustration while heir to the throne, and simply wishing that his son would behave appropriately and relying on admonition was not enough. The prince was eventually to turn against the Whigs who so offended his father, but this owed nothing to the latter. At the same time, the prince's role in supporting parliamentary opposition echoed those of his father, grandfather and great-grandfather. Furthermore, however unpleasant for George, the prince proved less disruptive than the duke of Orléans, the head of the cadet Bourbon line, did for Louis XVI.

Distance did not encourage George to relax his oversight of his sons. The flavour of George's attitudes can be gained from his instructions to Colonel Richard Grenville, who had been appointed governor to Frederick, duke of York, on his going to Germany to reside as prince bishop of Osnabrück. For example,

> Though in this country I highly disapprove of masquerades, I do not put any injunction to his not frequenting them at Hanover, where the Officer of the Guard has power to prevent all irregularities, and in reality it is necessary from the established custom in Germany of not permitting the Bourgeoisie to mix with the Nobility but in Mask at Balls and Assemblies ... [Frederick] must attend Divine Worship in the chapel of my palace every Sunday morning.[36]

Frederick himself was urged to read the Bible every morning and evening, not least because it provided the opportunity for self-examination.[37]

George's visit to Portsmouth in 1773 increased his interest in the navy, leading him to decide that his third son, William, born in 1765, should

[35] Addington to prince of Wales, 11 Sept. 1801, Exeter, 152M/C1801/OR71.
[36] George to Richard Grenville, 29 Dec. 1780, BL. Add. 70956.
[37] George to Frederick, duke of York, 29 Dec. 1780, RA. GEO/16222.

enter naval service. George having made plans to that end in 1778, William did so in 1779, beginning as an able seaman and, in 1780, becoming a midshipman, seeing active service that year. Keen that naval life should not mean inappropriate habits, a goal shared by evangelical naval commanders, in 1779 George arranged that Henry Majendie (whose father, John, had instructed Queen Charlotte in English and been tutor to William's elder brothers) should teach William on board the *Prince George*; Majendie was listed as a midshipman. In 1781, he was to be appointed William's preceptor. He clearly commended himself to George, becoming a canon of Windsor in 1785, vicar of Windsor and a canon of St Paul's in 1798, and bishop of Chester in 1800. In 1780, however, when William caused concern by disorderly behaviour in London, George had him returned to his ship.[38] Repeated worries made George write to Richard Grenville in 1783,

I hope speedily to send William to Germany not thinking this a safe place on many accounts for one of his age and not less so who by having been two years abroad must expect more liberty than I can approve on this side of the water . . . Frederick has succeeded so well that his example cannot be too closely followed . . . William is rather giddy and has rather too much the manners of his profession [the navy], polishing and composure are the ingredients wanting to make him a charming character.

The following year, George wrote to William,

I am glad you propose being more regular in your correspondence; it is impossible you cannot want for topics if you take pains to improve your mind; the natural attendance whilst at sea certainly was no advantage to your manners nor could your education be so closely followed as could be wished either in your station as a prince or as an officer for seamanship is but a very small part of the requisites necessary in superior commands and for want of which the service has on many opportunities most fatally suffered. The knowledge of the springs that actuate men is necessary to know how to turn them to the pursuits that are honorable to themselves or of utility to the state; that you may by diligence become what it might be your own desire as well as that of those who wish you well will ever be my objective.[39]

George's moral concerns found few echoes among his sons, and the same was true of his cultural preferences which, particularly his interest in

[38] George to Sir Samuel Hood, 13 June 1779, BL. RP. 2283.
[39] George to Richard Grenville, 1, 15 July 1783, George to William, 13 Feb. 1784, BL. Add. 70956.

the work of Handel, were related to his moral concerns. Handel said of George, 'While that boy lives, my music will never want a protector',[40] and, in this, as in much else, the boy was father to the man. In contrast, his brother Cumberland, who was also very fond of music, lacked these moral concerns.

In the royal family, George's legacy was unhappy; parental love and care did not have the desired effect. In general, the king had a firm, not to say authoritarian or Teutonic, attitude to parenthood. George seems to have liked his children less once they grew up and could answer back. He was greatly saddened by the early deaths of Princes Octavius and Alfred, especially the former, and, when unwell in 1812, had long imaginary conversations with both. George and Charlotte, neither of whom really had any youth free from responsibilities, could not understand why the boys did not buckle down to duty as they had both done from a very young age, although George had a high opinion of Frederick, duke of York.

The six princesses had pleasant early years,[41] with Lady Charlotte Finch proving a warm governess. The girls did not experience the firm discipline meted out to their brothers, with whom they spent a fair amount of time. This warm family background lasted until George's illness, although, as the princes grew older and lived away, the contrast between the life of the girls and the independence of their brothers became more apparent, and more trying to the girls. Their brothers were often sympathetic. A sense of restraint is captured by a description of life at Windsor in the 1800s:

> When the King rises, which is generally about half-past seven o'clock, he proceeds immediately to the queen's saloon, where his majesty is met by one of the princesses; generally either Augusta, Sophia or Amelia; for each, in turn, attend their revered parent . . . breakfast . . . The king and queen sit at the head of the table, and the princesses according to seniority. Etiquette in every other respect is strictly adhered to.[42]

The princesses complained about living, under their mother's unwelcome dominance, in a 'Nunnery', where they were kept under supervision and constantly chaperoned. Queen Charlotte regularly read sermons to them. She wanted the girls to stay close to her, and also feared that any discussion of their marriage would threaten George's mental stability, as he was known to be unsettled about the idea.

The daughters had a particularly difficult life, not in terms of material circumstances, but because they felt constrained. Court life, however

---

[40] J. Simon (ed.), *Handel: A Celebration of his Life and Times, 1685–1759* (London, 1985), p. 251.
[41] F. Fraser, *Princesses. The Six Daughters of George III* (London, 2004).
[42] R. Huish, *The Public and Private Life of His Late Excellent and Most Gracious Majesty George the Third* (London, 1821), p. 660.

enlivened by holidays in Weymouth and by excursions, was not preferable to the relative freedom of presiding over their own households. The conventional limitations of the upbringing of princesses were accentuated by their parents', particularly the king's, subsequent opposition to their marrying. The marital economy of princely houses was not encouraging, because six was a large number of marriageable daughters, but, as they were born between 1766 and 1783, the princesses would not have all been released on to the marriage market at once. An emphasis on German spouses characterized George's children, both sons and daughters. These German marriages helped differentiate the monarchy from the aristocracy. Just before he was ill in 1788, George said he would take the girls to Hanover and hold court so that they would find suitable husbands. Later, the conquest of states by France, or their co-operation with her, reduced the number of opportunities, but neither was a serious factor as far as Protestant Europe was concerned until the 1800s, not least because most North German Protestant princes were, like Hanover, part of the Prussian-directed neutrality zone from 1795.

Nevertheless, the rank of spouse available for earlier princesses was difficult to find. George I's only sister, Sophia Charlotte (1668–1705), had, in 1684, married the electoral prince of Brandenburg, who eventually became king in Prussia. Their heir, Frederick William, later king in Prussia, in 1706 married George II's sole sister, Sophia Dorothea (1687–1757). George II had five daughters, of whom three married: Anne (1709–59), in 1734, to William IV of Orange, Mary (1723–72), in 1740, to Frederick, later Frederick II of Hesse-Cassel, and Louisa (1724–51), in 1743, to Frederick, later Frederick V of Denmark, helping to make George father-in-law to Protestant Europe. Of George III's sisters, two married, the other two, Elizabeth (1741–57) and Louisa (1749–68), dying before marriage became an issue. In 1764, Augusta (1737–1813) married Charles (1753–1806), heir to the duchy of Brunswick. Their daughter, Caroline, was to marry George, prince of Wales, in 1795. In 1766, Caroline Matilda (1751–75) married her cousin, Christian VII of Denmark (1749–1808). The emphasis on a Protestant monarchy stemming from the Glorious Revolution and the stress of the house of Hanover on German marriages, ensured that these were rulers of states very different to Britain. Denmark was a composite monarchy including Norway and Iceland, but Brunswick, Hesse-Cassel, Saxe-Gotha and Mecklenburg-Strelitz were all German principalities junior to Hanover in rank (none was an electorate) and importance. They also benefited from the prospect of British assistance, as in 1762 when Mecklenburg pressed George on the danger posed by the outbreak of war between Denmark and Russia.[43]

[43] George Grenville to Walter Titley, envoy in Copenhagen, 16 July 1762, PRO. SP. 75/114 fol. 256.

The only one of George's daughters to marry at this rank was the eldest, Charlotte (1766–1828), the sole daughter to marry before the regency. In 1797 she married the hereditary prince of Württemberg, Frederick William Charles (1754–1816), who became duke in 1797, Elector in 1803 and king in 1806. An extremely fat forty-two-year-old widower, first married to George's niece Augusta (elder daughter of Augusta and Charles of Brunswick), who had died in 1788, he was not prepossessing, but he had rank and was determined to gain dynastic status. With a characteristic emphasis on paternal care and authority, George had tried to block the marriage: 'knowing the brutal and other unpleasant qualities of this prince I could not give any encouragement to such a proposal . . . after the very unhappy life my unfortunate niece led with him, I cannot as a father bequeath any daughter of mine on him'. George made enquiries about the prince's character and resolved that his view on the matter should prevail.[44] The marriage, which was delayed by his caution, was, in the event, to be reasonably happy. As was to be expected in an age when members of ruling families travelled little, George never again saw his daughter, who, like his sister Elizabeth, shared his agricultural and architectural interests; her husband's support for Napoleon and French conquests made George's correspondence with Charlotte difficult.[45] Furthermore, the house of Württemberg became linked to the Bonapartes, Charlotte's stepdaughter Catherine marrying Napoleon's brother Jérôme, whose kingdom of Westphalia included some of Hanover, which Napoleon had conquered. Charlotte had earlier been interested in the prince royal of Prussia, later Frederick William III, but she was older than him. Instead – a catch that evaded George's daughters – in 1793 he married her cousin, Louise of Mecklenburg-Strelitz (1776–1810).

George and Charlotte were unreceptive to the foreign princes who did make approaches,[46] rejecting, for example, the exiled duke of Orléans, the future king Louis-Philippe of France, when he sought the hand of Elizabeth in 1808. Elizabeth (1770–1840), was finally, in 1818 at the age of forty-eight, able to marry Frederick, hereditary prince of Hesse-Homburg (1769–1829). Meanwhile, Mary (1776–1857), in 1816 at the age of forty, had married William, duke of Gloucester, her first cousin, but both had had a long wait for marriage, and the couple had no children.

The other sisters did not marry. Two fell in love, but found their mother unaccommodating. Amelia (1783–1810), the youngest daughter and the king's favourite, fell in love with the much older Colonel Charles Fitzroy

[44] George to William Grenville, 14 Nov. 1795, 3 Apr., 25 Dec. 1796, 8, 11 Mar. 1797, BL. Add. 58859 fols 41, 59, 110, 116, 120.

[45] Miss Planta to Stephen Rolleston of the Foreign Office, 23 Feb., Rolleston to Planta, 29 Dec. 1807, BL. Add. 47012A fols 146–7, 156.

[46] George to William Grenville, 6, 7 July, 5 Aug. 1797, BL. Add. 58860 fols 7, 10, 17.

(1762–1831), a royal equerry, whom she planned to marry after George's death. There were rumours that she had secretly married him and had a child, but, in the event, she died on 2 November 1810 after long years of tuberculosis and erysipelas. There were also reports of a secret marriage between Princess Augusta (1768–1840) and Sir Brent Spencer, another of George's equerries; the queen's opposition left them no alternative. Yet another equerry, Major-General Thomas Garth (1744–1828), probably entered into a secret marriage with Princess Sophia (1777–1848), and in 1800 she secretly bore him a child, named after his father. These links reflect the restricted circle within which the girls were allowed to socialize, as well as the problems of rank and the widespread concern from the 1780s for emphasizing female purity as an aspect of national stability.[47]

George was more indulgent to his daughter-in-law, Caroline of Brunswick (1768–1821), second daughter of George's elder sister Augusta, and her daughter, his granddaughter, Charlotte. The latter's governess, the dowager countess of Elgin, reported on a visit to Kew in August 1804 at which George was 'most kind', while in 'Grandpappa in his Glory!!!', a caricature of 1796, James Gillray depicted him as a doting figure, happily feeding Charlotte as she sat on his knee. George was keen to maintain close relations with his granddaughter, then his sole grandchild, and, due to the estrangement of her parents, his likely successor.[48] He felt sorry for her, and was unimpressed by her father, the prince of Wales. George had been delighted by the latter's marriage to Caroline in 1795, but each was disappointed by the other and the marriage was a failure.

If George's legacy was an uncomfortable one as far as his heir was concerned, that was principally due to his encouragement of his son's unhappy marriage. Unfortunately for George, one aspect of this was that this most family-conscious of monarchs had only one legitimate grand-child before his final loss of sanity. This loss at least spared him the knowledge that this grandchild, the prince's daughter Charlotte, died in childbirth in November 1817, and the child, who would have been George's first great-grandchild, was not saved. George never saw the granddaughter who was eventually to succeed him, Victoria.

George's sense of royal dignity, and a certain lack of charitableness towards those who did not meet his standards, was shown by his treatment of his brothers and sons who married secretly against his wishes.

---

[47] D. Wahrman, '*Percy*'s Prologue: From Gender Play to Gender Panic in Eighteenth-Century England', *Past and Present*, 159 (1998), pp. 113–60; K. Binhammer, 'The Sex Panic of the 1790s', *Journal of the History of Sexuality*, 6 (1996), pp. 409–34; M. Morris, 'Marital Litigation and English Tabloid Journalism: Crim. Con. in *The Bon Ton*, 1791–1796', *British Journal for Eighteenth-Century Studies*, 28 (2005), pp. 50–1.
[48] Dowager countess of Elgin to Princess Elizabeth, 21 Aug., and to prince of Wales, 22 Aug. 1804, Aspinall, *Prince of Wales*, V, 77, 83.

The Royal Marriages Act led Gloucester to reveal that he had married Maria, the widow of the second Earl Waldegrave, George's former governor, in 1766. He was banned from court, and there was consideration of a second marriage service.[49] Neither Gloucester nor Cumberland was received again by George until 1780, when the offer of help in the crisis created by the Gordon Riots changed the king's attitude, but their wives were never received.[50] When he was informed that his favourite son, Prince Augustus, had married the pregnant Lady Augusta Murray in 1793, George ordered the government to proceed in accordance with the Royal Marriages Act, and the marriage was declared void in 1794. Augustus paid no attention for many years, having a second child by Augusta in 1801, but, influenced by inaccurate reports about Augusta's conduct, and by his own convenience, he eventually accepted the verdict. In the meanwhile, under the threat that the correspondence on the marriage would be published, George had paid Augustus's debts, but had insisted that he remain outside his dominions. The king had also been outraged when Augusta and her son went to join him in Berlin.[51]

Another of George's sons, Adolphus, wished to marry his widowed cousin, Frederica of Mecklenburg-Strelitz (1778–1841), and, in 1798, she accepted him, but, despite Charlotte's support for this union with her niece, George refused to give him permission to marry until the end of the war, leading Frederica to turn to Frederick William of Solms-Braunfels. Authority and morality combined to harm relations within the royal family, and this difficulty was possibly accentuated as the king's health became more of an issue in the 1800s.

Queen Charlotte was also a firm pursuer of restraint, however. In 1815 she expressed her concern about the marriage of Ernest, duke of Cumberland, to his now twice-widowed cousin Frederica because of imputations about the latter's character: she had been pregnant at the time of her second marriage, to Frederick William of Solms-Braunfels, and was widowed while divorcing him. There was reference to Charlotte's 'anxious desire to preserve society upon the respectable footing which it had ever been the King's and her own study to maintain', and Charlotte refused, until the end of her life, to receive Frederica.[52] Had she done so, Charlotte would have made it easier for the estranged princess of Wales to claim that she was being unfairly treated in being excluded from court.

[49] George to Gloucester, 28 May 1773, BL. Add. 70990.
[50] George to Fox, 22 June 1782, Fortescue, VI, 65.
[51] Queen Charlotte's diary, 25 Jan. 1794, RA. GEO/Add. 43/3; George to William Grenville, 11 July 1798, George to Dundas, 21 June, 14 Aug. 1798, 29 Aug. 1799, BL. Add. 58860, fol. 96, PRO. 30/8/104 fol. 241, BL. Add. 40100 fols 210, 231; George to Pitt, 13 May 1800, PRO. 30/8/104 fols 281–2.
[52] Exeter, 152M/C 1815/OR 111–114.

George at least was spared the knowledge of this tension by his loss of sanity, but it left an awareness or sense of failure in the family sphere. The royal family was conspicuously short of the dutiful love George had sought to ensure. He bears some of the responsibility because of his failure to understand, and help create appropriate roles for, his siblings and children.

Chapter 9

CULTURE

A philistine whose cultural activity was best summed up by his teaching his dogs to dance.

Peter Pindar, 1795[1]

The description of George as a philistine by John Wolcot, a satirist who wrote as Peter Pindar, was inaccurate. *The Arts Protected by George III*, the subject of a 1760 medal by Thomas Pingo, more accurately predicted an aspect of the reign that has received insufficient attention in biographies of the king. George grew up into a rich cultural heritage. Aside from the influence from his father, Frederick, a noted patron of the arts,[2] George's mother, Augusta, was a patron of the architect William Chambers (1726–96). Chambers had a significant artistic influence on George, teaching the young prince architectural drawings three mornings a week and also providing him with guidance to the new archaeological discoveries, not least Robert Wood's work on Baalbek and Palmyra. He offered George both practice and theory, the latter represented by the manuscript essay 'The Origins of Buildings and Orders' which he wrote for George. This work was the basis for Chambers's successful *Treatise on Civil Architecture* (1759). George permitted its publication, headed the list of subscribers, and may have borne much of the cost of publication. The book was dedicated to Bute, a major art collector[3] and also a significant cultural influence on George. Chambers was employed by Augusta to adorn the gardens of her house at Kew, and in 1757–62 erected a number of buildings there in oriental or Classical styles that had a great impact. George funded Chambers's *Plans, Elevations, Sections and Perspective Views of the Gardens and Buildings at Kew* (1763).

The new reign brought promotion to Chambers, who in 1761 was appointed one of the two joint architects of the Office of Works, the government body responsible for royal buildings; the other was Robert

[1] *The Complete Works of Peter Pindar* (3 vols, London, 1794), II, 35.

[2] K. Rorschach, 'Frederick, Prince of Wales (1707–51) as Collector and Patron', *Walpole Society*, 55 (1989–90); J. Harris, 'George III's Parents: Frederick and Augusta', in J. Marsden (ed.), *The Wisdom of George the Third* (London, 2005), pp. 15–27.

[3] F. Russell, *John, 3rd Earl of Bute, Patron and Collector* (London, 2004).

Adam. In 1769, he became comptroller of the works, and in 1782 the first holder of the new office of surveyor-general and comptroller. Chambers was also prominent in the foundation of the Royal Academy, drafting the foundation document, serving as the first treasurer, a post chosen by the king, and representing George's views.[4] The dedication to George of the third edition of Chambers's treatise, published in 1791, testified to the king's interest: 'The present publication treats of an Art, often the amusement of Your Majesty's leisure moments, and which, in all ages, great princes have delighted to encourage.' George certainly produced a large number of architectural drawings. In these, he followed Chambers's style. These drawings include at least one for a modest building, a farm labourer's cottage on the Windsor estate in the 1790s. Aside from buildings, George designed decorative features, including the doorcases added to the Queen's House (Buckingham House) in the early 1760s. When he was ill in 1788–9, and detained in the White House at Kew, George took solace in architectural drawings; finding an order and harmony from within himself, he 'resorted to an occupation not uninteresting to him in settled days. He drew plans of the house, and contrived and sketched alterations to it – and this he did with tolerable accuracy . . . in his more sedate moments he amused himself with drawing plans'.[5] His interest in architecture was one that was widespread in the British (and American) élites of the period. It joined George to some of his bitterest critics, most obviously Jefferson.

As a young man, George was given a varied artistic education. This included perspectival drawing under Joshua Kirby, who was appointed drawing master in 1756, and forty-five loose drawings survive in a volume entitled 'Landscapes drawings drawn by H.M.' Classical buildings play a key role, understandably, as this was a culture in thrall to the classics. One, of about 1758, of a ruined Corinthian temple in a landscape, reflected contemporary interest in ruins, as well as a clearly English riverscape that may contain elements of George's observation of the Thames. George had Kirby write *The Perspective of Architecture* (1761), which was dedicated to the king, who funded it, and he made Kirby and his son joint clerks of the works at Richmond and Kew.

George had varied cultural interests, especially in art and music. He was a major collector of books, art, maps, music and scientific equipment. In 1762, he acquired for the substantial sum of £20,805 the important large art and book collection of Joseph Smith, who had been consul in Venice and a major cultural intermediary between Italy and Britain. George's largest single purchase, this included 500 paintings and drawings by Canaletto, Visentini, Sebastiano and Marco Ricci, and Zuccarelli.

[4] J. Roberts, 'Sir William Chambers and George III', in J. Harris and M. Snodin (eds), *Sir William Chambers: Architect to George III* (New Haven, Connecticut, 1996), pp. 41–54.
[5] R.F. Grenville, *Diaries*, edited by F. Bladon (London, 1930), pp. 119, 152.

The paintings were displayed in the Queen's House.[6] Bute's brother, James Stuart Mackenzie, was responsible for the purchase, which also included coins and engraved gems. This was part of an active process of acquisition by George in the 1760s, not least the cabinet of drawings of Cardinal Alessandro Albani, purchased for £3,600 in 1762, which included the earlier collections of Carlo Maratti and Cassiano del Pozzo.[7] In addition, Richard Dalton, who had been appointed George's librarian by Bute in 1755, was sent to Italy to purchase drawings and other works of art. His acquisitions included, in 1763, a large collection of drawings by Guercino.

These Italianate purchases, and the fact that Italian paintings were hung in the king's closet in the Queen's House, might appear at variance with George's British patriotism and zealous Protestantism, but this was not a contrast that was pushed in the cultural world of the British social and artistic élite. Instead, appropriate taste was largely focused on a Classical inheritance mediated through Catholic Europe. Italy was crucial to this, although George also greatly admired the work of the seventeenth-century French painter Poussin. Aspects of seventeenth-century art clearly appealed to George, for he also liked Van Dyck. This was an important part of his admiration of the aesthetic of Charles I's patronage; in contrast, there was no such favour for Dutch masters. This again was far from unusual.

George's admiration for Poussin and the Classical inheritance led him, in accordance with the stylistic conventions of the age, to commission 'history works', moral accounts of Classical episodes, including *Timon of Athens* from Nathaniel Dance in 1765 and *The Departure of Regulus from Rome* from Benjamin West in 1768. This was a widespread artistic preference of the period, reflecting the notion that culture should be exemplary. Timon rejected luxury and Regulus was a self-sacrificing hero of Republican Rome. History painting was a public, demonstrative and declamatory art, proclaiming noble and elevated ideals and depicting the actions of heroes at moments of moral or historical significance. Such painting remained at

---

[6] F. Vivian, *The Consul Smith Collection. Masterpieces of Italian Drawings from the Royal Library Windsor. Raphael to Canaletto* (Munich, 1989); A. Griffiths, 'The Prints and Engravings in the Library of Consul Joseph Smith', *Print Quarterly*, 8, 2 (June 1991), pp. 127–39; J. Roberts, *A King's Purchase: King George III and the Collection of Consul Smith* (Queen's Gallery exhibition catalogue, London, 1993).

[7] A. Griffiths, 'The Print Collection of Cassiano dal Pozzo', *Print Quarterly*, 6, 2 (Mar. 1989), pp. 2–10; J. Fleming, 'Cardinal Albani's Drawings at Windsor. Their Purchase by James Adam for George III', *Connoisseur*, 142 (1958), pp. 164–9; D. Mahon and N. Turner, *The Drawings of Guercino in the Collection of Her Majesty the Queen at Windsor Castle* (Cambridge, 1989); Roberts, 'George III's Acquisitions on the Continent', in Marsden (ed.), *The Wisdom of George the Third*, pp. 102–10.

the top of the French academic hierarchy of subjects,[8] and, if British aristocrats tended to prefer portraits, this did not preclude interest in heroic
art, for example the genre of naval battle scenes. In the case of George,
the problematic nature of making a clear contrast between British/
Protestant and Italian/Catholic art can also be illustrated by the case of
the Florentine, Francesco Zuccarelli (1702–88), a master of the poetic
landscape. George acquired many of his paintings as part of the Smith
collection, and in 1771 spent £428 8s commissioning two more from
Zuccarelli, but the painter, who spent much of 1752–62 and 1764–71 in
England, was himself fairly anglicized and was indeed one of the founding
members of the Royal Academy.[9] Far from being interested only in
Italianate work, George was a keen supporter of the contemporary British
artistic world, being a key patron of Chambers and of Thomas
Gainsborough (1727–88), from whom he commissioned a series of
portraits of the royal family. This support was politically astute, and, in the
public perception of the royal role, there was a contrast between that of
George and that of George IV, who was seen as a supporter of foreign
works, although George IV was also a most generous patron of living
British artists such as Sir Thomas Lawrence. George III was also a more
important patron than Louis XVI, whose artistic taste was limited.[10]

Culture was linked to patriotism in the foundation of the Royal
Academy in 1768, the constitution of which the king signed on 10
December. George's support – not least £5,116 from the privy purse from
1769 to 1780 in order to balance the Academy's financing, and his
knighting in 1769 of the Academy's president, Joshua Reynolds – was a
central part of the sponsoring of British culture. In turn, the Academy
enhanced monarchy and represented a link with the king's father, who had
been seen as a supporter of the creation of an academy for the arts.
Making available the royal apartments in Somerset House for the
Academy from 1771 (the Royal Society and the Society of Antiquaries
followed), George continued his interest in the Royal Academy into the
1800s.[11]

This was part of a more general pattern in eighteenth-century
European monarchy, although George had less control than his royal
counterparts and was not keen on the selection of Reynolds, whom he

[8] P. Conisbee, *Painting in Eighteenth-Century France* (Oxford, 1981), p. 8; R. Mortier, *Diderot
and the 'Grand Goût': The Prestige of History Painting in the Eighteenth Century* (Oxford, 1982).

[9] M. Levey, 'Francesco Zuccarelli in England', *Italian Studies*, 14 (1959), pp. 1–19.

[10] W.G. Kalnein and M. Levy, *Art and Architecture of the Eighteenth Century in France*
(London, 1972), p. 176.

[11] H. Hoock, *The King's Artists: The Royal Academy of Arts and the Politics of British Culture,
1760–1840* (Oxford, 2003), and 'George III and the Royal Academy of Arts: The Politics of
Culture', in Marsden (ed.), *The Wisdom of George the Third*, pp. 245–61.

disliked, as first president. In 1754 the Danish Royal Academy of Art had been founded by Frederick V, an uncle by marriage of George. In 1786, Gustavus III of Sweden both reorganized the Academy of Letters, established in 1753, and founded a Swedish academy devoted to Swedish language and literature, himself selecting the first members. George's patronage of such organizations in Britain associated the monarchy with national quality and achievement. It was also related to his hostility to cosmopolitanism in the shape of French influences: George commented on the 'bad qualities' acquired 'from too much intercourse with that immoral nation'.[12]

The commission for the state portrait of the new king was given to Allan Ramsay, a conspicuous display of patronage to a Scot who held the post of king's principal painter from George's accession until his own death in 1784, when he was succeeded by Reynolds. Ramsay, who had already produced a successful portrait of George as prince of Wales, painted, in the state portrait of 1761, an impressive and very much reproduced work (at least 179 versions); the subject is splendidly clothed and set, and also calmly thoughtful, the whole effect being one of dignified majesty. The depiction of the king illustrates current themes in portraiture rather than the theme of imperial pomp seen in baroque descriptions of monarchy with their conscious emulation of Classical Rome. George, instead, was captured as at once both royal and a gentleman of poise and distinction.

A very different portrait of the king had been commissioned from George Stubbs by the marquess of Rockingham. It was to show George on Whistlejacket, one of the marquess's favoured horses, but Rockingham resigned when the duke of Devonshire was dismissed in November 1762 and the painting was left unfinished, with the horse lacking its rider.[13] George's image is best known through the Ramsay portrait. A more vivid, later portrayal was by John Bacon in 1789: a bronze statue of the king in the courtyard of Somerset House in a Roman costume holding the rudder of a ship, attended by a majestic lion and above a colossal figure of Father Thames presented as a reborn Neptune.

The king's patronage had artistic, political and personal factors. His support for Gainsborough in the 1780s was in part possibly related to Reynolds's links with the opposition round the prince of Wales or, at least, that he did not get on with Reynolds. Gainsborough was easier, less pompous and more sympathetic company. George's patronage has been criticized for lacking consistency, as has his taste for preferring the exact topography of Canaletto to true connoisseurship,[14] but this is overly harsh, and in the case

[12] George to Jenkinson, 30 May 1779, BL. Loan 72/1 fol. 11.
[13] B. Taylor, *Stubbs* (London, 1971), pp. 205–6.
[14] J.H. Plumb, *New Light on the Tyrant George III* (Washington, D.C., 1978), p. 10.

of Gainsborough George was artistically bold, as Gainsborough's sparing use of paint was less fashionable than Reynolds's habit of slapping it on. Gainsborough was to call George 'a good connoisseur'.[15]

Other painters George favoured included Paul Sandby and Benjamin West. Sandby (1725–1809), a master of the watercolour, who made numerous drawings of Windsor where he lived, was, like his brother Thomas (1721–98), one of the twenty-eight original members of the Royal Academy nominated by George. He taught Queen Charlotte and became drawing master to the prince of Wales. Thomas Sandby, deputy ranger of Windsor Great Park, was, with George's backing,[16] made joint architect of His Majesty's Works in 1777, following with the master carpentership in 1780.

Born in Springfield, Pennsylvania, Benjamin West (1738–1820) came to England in 1763, acquired a reputation as a history painter and in 1768 was commissioned by George, who admired his neo-Classical *Agrippina Landing at Brundisium with the Ashes of Germanicus* (1768), to paint *The Departure of Regulus from Rome*. George read to West Livy's account of the episode in which Regulus, a Roman consul, returns to his captivity in Carthage and certain death, the story a demonstration of dedication, honour and self-sacrifice. George then became an active patron, nominating West to the Royal Academy, appointing him historical painter to the king in 1772 and surveyor of the king's pictures in 1791, and paying him an annual stipend of £1,000 from 1780 until relations deteriorated in 1801. West painted six history paintings to join *The Departure of Regulus* on the walls of the Queen's House. *The Death of Epaminondas* and *The Oath of Hannibal* shared in the theme of republican virtue, and *The Death of the Chevalier Bayard* and *The Death of Wolfe* that of heroic self-sacrifice, while *The Family of the King of Armenia before Cyrus* and *Segestes and his Daughter before Germanicus* emphasized magnanimity. With studios there and in Windsor Castle, West was close to George and benefited from his friendship. Renting a house in Windsor from about 1780 to 1809, he represents the increasing Windsor focus of the reign, which was important to the changing character of George's kingship, not least the growing emphasis on rural pursuits. The topographical depiction of the crowded townscape seen in the Canalettos George had bought in 1762 was not the style of the painters he favoured in his later years.

As an historical painter, West responded to the serious crises of the late 1770s – not only the American War of Independence but also rising discontent in Ireland and the Franco-Spanish invasion attempt of 1779 – by depicting crucial victories from the past: *The Battle of the Boyne* and the

---

[15] H. Angelo, *Reminiscences of Henry Angelo with Memoirs of his Late Father and Friends* (2 vols, London, 1828–30), I, 354.
[16] George to Robinson, 15, 19 Mar. 1777, BL. Add. 37833 fols 170, 172.

Destruction of the French Fleet at La Hogue, events that had occurred in 1690 and 1692, the first a victory for William III in person. Exhibited at the Royal Academy in 1780, these paintings greatly increased West's popularity. Subsequently George employed West from 1786 to 1789 to decorate the audience room in Windsor Castle with eight pictures from the life of Edward III. These were designed to provide an appropriate historical background to George's commitment to the Order of the Garter, which had been founded by Edward in 1348. Paintings such as *Edward III Crossing the Somme* (1788) and *The Burghers of Calais* (1789) showed that successful past monarchs could be portrayed in a dramatic (and colourful) fashion that reflected glory on their current successor.[17] George also commissioned West to produce thirty-six pictures (eighteen were executed) on the progress of revealed religion (in this case Christianity) for a new royal private chapel at Windsor, called the Chapel of Revealed Religion, that was never in fact built. Richard Hurd, bishop of Worcester and clerk of the closet, a favourite with George, helped in drawing up the programme. West was commissioned to provide an altarpiece and paint a design for a large stained-glass window of the Resurrection of Christ for St George's Chapel, the latter completed at the start of 1787. By 1801 West, who in 1792 succeeded Reynolds as president of the Royal Academy, had produced sixty-four pictures and other designs for George, who had paid him £34,187.[18] George proved the key patron for history painting, a subject that, like painting on religious subjects, appealed to relatively few contemporary British patrons.

West's career, and the reputation of history and religious painting, illustrates the extent to which the English élite were not guided by crown and court and throws much light on George's particular type of neo-classicism: it was always the style of duty, but for George this became religious duty, with a sense of the continuity of kingship. The emphasis on Edward III and the Garter was not so much a recently established dynasty claiming lineage, although that became important in response to Napoleon, not least with the installation of knights of the Garter in 1805,[19] but an instance of a king seeking an exemplary model. The reflected heroism of the past was useful in an age in which monarchs could not match contemporary notions of heroism as their baroque-era predecessors had sought

---

[17] R. Strong, *And when did you last see your father? The Victorian Painter and British History* (London, 1978), pp. 78–85.

[18] R.C. Alberts, *Benjamin West: A Biography* (Boston, Massachusetts, 1978); N.L. Pressly, *Revealed Religion: Benjamin West's Commissions for Windsor Castle and Fonthill Abbey* (San Antonio, Texas, 1983); H. von Erffa and A. Staley, *The Paintings of Benjamin West* (New Haven, Connecticut, 1986); C. Lloyd, 'George III and his Painters', in Marsden (ed.), *The Wisdom of George the Third*, pp. 85–92.

[19] L. Colley, *Britons. Forging the Nation 1707–1837* (New Haven, Connecticut, 1992), pp. 216–17.

to do.[20] It was a measure of the degree to which George was anglicized that he did not search for figures with a Germanic dimension. The stress on the Garter, accompanied by the neo-Gothic seen at Windsor, also represented a shift in emphasis from the Italianate culture of George's early years. In part, this reveals developments in George's preferences, but there was also a response to a more general cultural move away from cosmopolitan influences and themes.

Popular interest in Edward III was seen in George Colman the Younger's successful play *The Surrender of Calais* (1791), in which the king declares, 'And still may ever successes crown an English enterprise'. Ironically, Edward III had been held up alongside Henry V by the *Monitor* of 16 October 1762 when it wished to use their alliance with the dukes of Burgundy to criticize George's abandonment of Frederick II of Prussia, who, like the medieval dukes of Burgundy, had been an ally against France. References to Edward or, as in the *London Evening Post* of 13 November 1762, to Henry were intended as criticisms of George for failing to stand up to France. In the *Monitor* of 9 October 1762, the comparison was more pointed, as the theme was bad favourites: Mortimer, the lover of Edward III's mother, and Bute. By 1791, however, the historical frame of reference and international context were both very different and George was widely seen as a defender of national interests.

George's patronage was not restricted to painting. His own book collection, which later became the kernel of the national library housed in the British Museum, was assembled for private use but also open to scholars.[21] Spending considerable sums, £1,500 annually from 1770,[22] he built up a large library, housed next to his bedchamber in the Queen's House. By his death in 1820, this library consisted of 65,250 books (in contrast to about 10,000 in 1769), as well as 19,000 tracts and pamphlets, and the first substantial British collection of maps and charts, for which large map presses and map stands were constructed. George built the collection entirely from funds supplied from his privy purse, and derived pleasure from the acquisitions, being friendly with the senior library staff.[23] At Windsor, he dropped into bookshops to scan the latest publications. It is, nevertheless, clear that he regarded the collection as a national resource, indeed as a library intended to help him govern. George also had smaller libraries at Kew, Richmond, Weymouth (his summer retreat from the 1780s) and Windsor. He did not intend that his collection should go to the British Museum; he meant it to be retained for his successors, but

---

[20] F. Folkenflik (ed.), *The English Hero, 1660–1800* (Newark, Delaware, 1982).

[21] E.M. Paintin, *The King's Library* (London, 1989).

[22] J. Brooke, 'The Library of King George III', *Yale University Library Gazette*, 52 (1978), pp. 38–9.

[23] Haslang to Beckers, 17 July 1772, Munich, Bayr. Ges. London 250.

George IV prefered to dispose of the books.[24] The collection was offered to the country by George IV (but, typically, after he had failed to sell it), and became the King's Library within the British Museum (which had been founded by George II). This was in accordance with a pattern of royal gifts. The old royal library had been presented to the British Museum in 1757, and, five years later, George III had purchased and presented to the Museum a large collection of Civil War pamphlets.

A critic of what he saw as the tendency of 'the present age . . . to have the matter entirely digested [rather] than any part left for the diligence of the reader',[25] George was particularly interested in works on theology, history,[26] jurisprudence, science, the arts and the Classical inheritance, and less so in fiction, even though the period saw the development of the novel, in which British writers played a key role. Indeed, George did not really take to novels until he became blind, when one of his daughters read them to him nightly.[27] His reading affected his views on literature, and George was able to comment on literary style, praising seventeenth-century writers such as Hooker, Bacon, Sanderson and Hakewill.[28] The choice of writers cited is indicative: three were clerics. George Hakewill (1578–1649), rector of Exeter College, Oxford from 1642 to 1649, was author of works such as *King David's Vow for Reformation, delivered in twelve Sermons, before the Prince his Highness* (1621). Robert Sanderson (1587–1663), a chaplain to, and favourite preacher before, Charles I, lost his living and the divinity chair at Oxford because he refused to subscribe to the Parliamentarians' Solemn League and Covenant. His writing includes numerous sermons, as well as *Nine Cases of Conscience occasionally determined* (1678). George found reading enjoyable as well as instructive, but accepted that his sons had other interests, writing of Frederick, 'I cannot expect to put an old head on young shoulders. Therefore though I wish his love for reading was greater . . .'[29]

Among contemporaries, Samuel Johnson, who advised on the purchases for the royal library, was a beneficiary of George's largesse, and this served to permit James Boswell to offer an encomium:

> The accession of George the Third to the throne of these kingdoms, opened a brighter prospect to men of literary merit, who had been honoured with no mark of royal favour in the preceding reign. His

[24] Report on lecture by Robert Lacey, *Court Historian*, 9, 2 (Dec. 2004), p. 189.

[25] George to Pitt, 29 Jan. 1792, PRO. 30/8/103 fol. 430.

[26] George to Pitt, 10 Feb. 1800, PRO. 30/8/104 fol. 263 re. the defence of British policy in the 1790s by Rev. Herbert Marsh, fellow of St John's, Cambridge.

[27] F. Bickley (ed.), *The Diaries of Sylvester Douglas, Lord Glenbervie*, (2 vols, London, 1928), II, 76.

[28] J. Boswell, *Life of Johnson* (Oxford, 1980), p. 157.

[29] George to Richard Grenville, 29 Nov. 1782, BL. Add. 70956.

present Majesty's education in this country, as well as his taste and beneficence, prompted him to be the patron of science and the arts.[30]

Johnson recorded that his *Journey to the Western Islands of Scotland* (1775) was eagerly read by George, and also provided an account of the sociable way in which the king read it: 'the King fell to reading the book as soon as he got it, when any thing struck him, he read aloud to the Queen, and the Queen would not stay to get the King's book, but borrowed Dr. Hunter's'.[31] Charlotte herself was a bibliophile with a large private library.[32] Reading aloud in this fashion was an aspect of George's somewhat excitable nature, as was his repetition of reflections he found arresting.

During his reign, scholars were permitted to use the library in the Queen's House. Johnson was a frequent visitor, and George met him there in February 1767. Unlike many who met the king, the noted writer was not tongue-tied. Having discussed Oxford and libraries before praising Johnson's works, George asked Johnson's opinion of a number of writers and periodicals and urged him to undertake the literary biography of the country. Johnson, very pleased with the king's courtesy, described him as 'the finest-gentleman I have ever seen'.[33] The two men shared an interest in Latinity, the king being very concerned that, if his judges spoke Latin, it should be good Latin.[34] Not only did he make an impact on Johnson: George's conversations with James Beattie and Charles Burney left good impressions. Approbation of a different sort is suggested by a sampling of book dedications during the century which reveal that George III was by far the leading dedicatee, with the second-ranking royal (and third-ranking individual) being his father, Frederick.[35]

George was interested in the appearance as well as the content of books. He founded a royal bindery at Queen's House in about 1770, showing his engagement with typography and book design; and visited it on many occasions. George liked his books unbound for his first reading and afterwards bound to match his other books.[36]

George also took a keen interest in music: he played the flute, harpsichord (frequently) and pianoforte, collected music, including works by Lully, Palestrina and Scarlatti, and was a great enthusiast for Handel's oratorios. Indeed, in his last years he played snatches of music from

---

[30] Boswell, *Life of Johnson*, p. 264.

[31] R.W. Chapman (ed.), *The Letters of Samuel Johnson* (3 vols, Oxford, 1952), I, 423.

[32] O. Everett, *A Royal Miscellany from the Royal Library Windsor Castle* (Queen's Gallery exhibition catalogue, London 1990), p. 7.

[33] Boswell, *Life of Johnson*, pp. 379–84.

[34] Twiss, I, 403.

[35] P. Rogers, 'Book Dedications in Britain 1700–1799: A Preliminary Survey', *British Journal for Eighteenth-Century Studies*, 16 (1993), pp. 222–3.

[36] Viscount Howe to George, 31 May 1784, Aspinall, *George III*, I, 66.

Handel, including the lamentation of Jephthah at the loss of his daughter, and Delilah's mad love song from *Samson*, as well as arranging imaginary concerts.[37] Earlier, the accounts of both king and queen frequently record the purchase of musical instruments – three harpsichords by George in 1764 – and the appreciation and performance of music helped bind them together. Charlotte's interests accentuated the cosmopolitan dimension of court culture, although this remained less pronounced than under George II. Johann Christian Bach and Charlotte's singing teacher, Carl Friedrich Abel, a member of the Queen's Band, staged public concerts under her patronage, while visiting musicians included the eight-year-old Mozart, who played three times before George and Charlotte in 1764. Although invited on several occasions, Beethoven did not visit London. George attended the opera frequently, on Saturdays in the season in the 1760s, and was shot at by James Hadfield on one occasion in 1800. He went to the opera with Charlotte and with other members of the royal family. On 1 January 1782, the New Year saw a major attendance at court, with the circle lasting until 5 p.m., after which George, Charlotte, the prince of Wales and three princesses went to the opera.

George was not particularly interested in modern music, such as that of Haydn, although he was courteous to him on his visits; he preferred composers of the baroque, especially Handel. He actively collected copies and arrangements of Handel's oratorios in the 1760s, and in the early 1770s was presented by Handel's amanuensis, John Smith, a favourite of Bute, with the composer's manuscript scores and harpsichord, and with his bust by Roubiliac. The king had a learned appreciation of Handel's musicality, and in 1804 he annotated the *Life of Handel*.[38] Although Handel's works were not frequently performed in the Chapel Royal in the 1760s and 1770s, George played a conspicuous role in the concerts held at Westminster Abbey in 1784 to celebrate the centenary of Handel's birth, a significant move on the part of the king towards public commemoration. The subject and theme of Handel's oratorios – the king as leader of the people of Israel and the travails of virtue – were of concern to George. His patronage was politically appropriate, and not in the specifically partisan fashion of works attributed to Catherine the Great: for example she had a comic opera satirizing Gustavus III of Sweden performed in her private theatre in 1788, and an operatic ballet staged in 1791 that implied that she was the heir to a Russian prince who had led a successful attack on the Byzantine empire in 900.

---

[37] M.S. Guttmacher, *America's Last King* (New York, 1941), p. 392; P. Scholes, 'George the Third as Music Lover', *Musical Quarterly*, 28 (1942), pp. 78–92; S. Roe, 'Music at the Court of George III and Queen Charlotte', in Marsden (ed.), *The Wisdom of George the Third*, pp. 141–59.
[38] Aspinall, *Prince of Wales*, V, 115.

Aside from attending the Handel concerts, George supported the 'king's concerts' held in London by the Academy of Ancient Music of which he became a patron in 1784. From 1785, he chose the programmes.[39] Further afield, George visited Worcester in 1788 for the Three Choirs Festival in the cathedral, and, for the festival, added his own private band to the orchestra. The festival brought together many of George's concerns, as it was intended for the relief of the widows and orphans of the clergy, and included a cathedral service. On 6 August, George heard the *Coronation Anthem*, the overture from *Esther*, and the *Dettingen Te Deum*, the last a reference to his grandfather's brave service to the nation in 1743, and all by Handel. The previous month, George had also heard the *Coronation Anthem* when attending Sunday service in Gloucester Cathedral. On 7 August, in Worcester, there was more sacred music by Handel, and on 8 August the *Messiah* and later a 'miscellaneous concert', a typical festival programme. William Boyce, a Handelian, who was master of the king's music from 1755 (though only appointed in 1757) until his death in 1779, published a three-volume collection of *Cathedral Music* (1760–73), the first ever anthology.

Royal concert-going continued and was noted in the press, the *Courier* of 5 February 1801 reporting that 'Their Majesties and the Princesses last night honoured the Antient Music Concert with their presence.' At a less exalted level, George enjoyed sailing off Weymouth with his band playing, although some of the musicians found shipboard performing a strain.

George was a frequent visitor to the theatre, both in London (weekly in the season in the 1760s) and on his tours, including three times in less than a month in Cheltenham in 1788,[40] and attended often on his summer stays in Weymouth. At Cheltenham he saw Dorothy Jordan, who was subsequently to live with his son William, in *She Would and She Would Not*, *The Sultan* and *The Merry Wives of Windsor*. In 1804, when George gave a fête on his yacht in Weymouth, he had the actor Robert Elliston, a favourite of his, summoned from London, and Camp also acted in the theatre at Weymouth. The following year, Princess Amelia recorded four visits a week to this theatre.[41] These visits included seeing the noted comedian John Bannister in *Marplot* and *The Busy Body*.[42] London visits provided a way for people to see the king on his way to the theatre, entering the

---

[39] W. Weber, 'The 1784 Handel Commemoration as Political Ritual', *Journal of British Studies*, 28 (1989), pp. 61–7, and *The Rise of Musical Classics in Eighteenth-Century England: A Study in Canon, Ritual and Ideology* (Oxford, 1992).

[40] Cheltenham Art Gallery and Museum has an extensive collection of playbills, some of which cover the time of the royal visit.

[41] Aspinall, *Prince of Wales*, V, 241; W.B. Barrett, 'George III and the Weymouth Theatre', *Somerset and Dorset Notes and Queries*, 9 (1904), pp. 155–6.

[42] *The Times*, 13 Sept. 1805.

house, and during the performance.[43] The press reported such visits, such as that to see 'the new comedy of *The School for Prejudice*' in Covent Garden on 21 January 1801.[44] There are also references to visits in George's correspondence.[45] Theatre was an interest that George shared with Charlotte: they went to see David Garrick in *The Rehearsal* at Drury Lane two days after their wedding. Fine arts, music and reading were other interests they had in common.

Although not a builder on the scale of his son George IV, or of such contemporaries as Catherine the Great, in large part because he believed in restraining expenditure, George was very interested in architecture and a leading patron.[46] Once he had purchased the Queen's House in 1762, George had it considerably altered by Chambers, mainly in order to house his growing library, and also furnished. The focus on the new palace represented a rejection of St James's Palace, although the latter remained the setting for royal ceremonial, including twice-weekly drawing rooms and thrice-weekly levees. As the setting for formal occasions, St James's Palace housed much of the staged royal culture. For example, on 1 January 1772 the New Year led to a very numerous court for the king's levee and the Queen's circle, with the door to the council chamber left open; from there came the sounds of the New Year ode composed by the poet laureate and set to music by William Boyce. St James's, however, was regarded as uncomfortable and there was also the question of how best to respond to George's rapidly growing family. In the 1790s, it was St James's state rooms that were refurbished, not the living quarters.

Kensington Palace, which had been in royal hands since the reign of William III and Mary II, was largely neglected under George, although it proved convenient for lesser members of the royal family, being the home of the duke of Kent from 1804, and of Caroline of Brunswick, the prince of Wales's estranged wife, from 1808 to 1813. Many of the artistic treasures in Kensington were moved to the Queen's House soon after George bought it. Hampton Court Palace, which had been in royal hands since the reign of Henry VIII, was neglected, becoming grace and favour apartments rather than a royal residence. George rarely visited the palace. In 1795, a large suite there was granted to William V of Orange who had fled the advancing French.

The changes at the Queen's House, which George bought for £28,000, reflected the taste both of George and of the times. Built in 1702–5 for

[43] E.g. Anne Robinson to her brother Frederick, 5 Nov. 1784, Bedford CRO. L30/15/50/56.

[44] *Courier*, 22 Jan. 1801; George to Hawkesbury, 21 Nov. 1804, BL. Add. 38564 fol. 78.

[45] George to Robinson, 18 Dec. 1779, BL. Add. 37835 fol. 79.

[46] J. Roberts (ed.), *George III and Queen Charlotte: Patronage, Collecting and Court Taste* (London, 2004), pp. 90–151; D. Watkin, *The Architect King: George III and the Culture of the Enlightenment* (London, 2004).

John, duke of Buckingham, it included many baroque features that George found unwelcome, such as a row of statues on the skyline and angle pilasters. These were removed, and the neo-Classical style was accentuated, with the addition of a pediment over the front door. By 1774, £73,000 had been spent on building and redecoration. George's interests were prominent in the additions, not only in the four library rooms built in 1762–73, but also in the riding house. From the king's bedroom, a door led directly into the great library. Function was not incompatible with grandeur, as the entrance hall and saloon at the Queen's House demonstrated. The latter provided an appropriate setting for the large Raphael cartoons moved from Hampton Court in 1763. The king's apartments were far less lavish, instead being characterized by a relative plainness, certainly in comparison with those of his successor.

Outside London, George's first country residence was Richmond Lodge. Rebuilt in 1704, this had been a residence of George II as prince of Wales, and then of his wife, Queen Caroline. Part of George III's honeymoon was spent there, and from 1764 it became the principal country retreat of the royal family, who stayed there each year from June to late October. The lodge, however, was fairly small, particularly for a growing family, so it was visited for the last time in 1771. In 1772, Richmond Lodge was demolished and the summer residence was spent at the White House in Kew, which had been the country home of George's parents. The death of the dowager princess of Wales in February 1772 created this new opportunity. George continued the lease until he was able to acquire the freehold in 1788. The White House was too small for George's growing family, but it offered a privacy removed from the pressures of court, which is why George was taken there in 1788 and 1801 when he became ill.

In 1804, however, he was taken to the neighbouring Dutch House, as the White House had been demolished in 1803 to make way for the Castellated Palace. This was the product of George's wish for a new palace in the Richmond/Kew area, of which he was very fond. Personal experience and happy memories were accentuated by the presence in the area of friends, including the duke of Northumberland at Sion House and the earl of Holdernesse at the since-demolished Sion Hill. Bute was the ranger of Richmond Park.

George's desire for a new palace had initially resulted in a series of plans for a Richmond palace close to the site of Richmond Lodge. In 1765, Chambers produced a design for a major neo-Classical work in accordance with the tradition of British country-house (i.e. rural palace) building associated with Colen Campbell, and with William Kent, the architect of Holkham Hall. The main façade was to be 328 feet long. This scheme fell victim, however, to the cost, estimated at close to £90,000, which the overly small size of the Civil List made unacceptable, and also to a feature that reflected the limited power of British monarchs: George was unable to purchase some land adjacent to his property which he saw as necessary for the palace, and certainly could not expropriate it. He was best placed when he could resume his ownership of hitherto rented-out land.[47] George's sense of himself as under the law was also shown in his concern about rents on land purchased with the Queen's House,[48] and also about the consequences for parish revenues if he purchased land, as the crown was exempted from taxes.[49] These were not problems that affected his continental counterparts, and may eventually have become a factor in the move to Windsor. Instead, in 1770, construction started on a more modest palace, but it had only reached ground-floor level when it was abandoned in 1775, meaning that there would be less need for purchasing paintings than had been anticipated. Even less came of George's interest in reviving Charles II's plan for a Winchester palace.[50]

In 1776, George decided to use the Queen's Lodge at Windsor as a personal residence. Aside from the fact that the existing residences in Richmond and Kew were too small for his growing family, Windsor's parkland provided good opportunities for riding and hunting. The royal apartments, however, were deemed unsatisfactory, in part because they were occupied by grace and favour tenants. Chambers therefore set out to enlarge and upgrade the accommodation so that the entire family could live at Windsor. This began a series of works on the Windsor site that, from the late 1790s, were entrusted to James Wyatt, from 1796 surveyor-general and comptroller of the office of works. He was George's favourite architect after Chambers, and in the 1790s designed a more magnificent staircase for the Queen's House. The fashionable character of the decoration at the Queen's House was matched by the work at Windsor. The castle saw much building and decoration in the then fashionable Gothic style, with George spending over £133,000 from his privy purse: his patronage helped make Gothic the national style and one conspicuously proper for major buildings, and he played a major role in the works, supervising them on his frequent visits. Gothic tracery, vaulting and plasterwork were applied in the rebuilding and redecoration of the castle. The work done for George at Windsor by Henry Emlyn and Wyatt was intended to be, and very largely was, quite accurate, i.e. Gothic, not Gothick, the half rococo, half frivolous taste of the 1750s with its pretty ogees.[51] In 1804, George declared that 'he intended to fit up Windsor like a Palace, and to live from henceforward like a king'.[52] To him, monarchical state could project moral virtue in a complementary fashion to a religious building.

[47] George to John Robinson, 29 Mar. 1779, BL. Add. 37834 fol. 58.
[48] George to John Robinson, 10 July 1779, BL Add. 37834 fol. 113.
[49] George to Pitt, 9 July 1800, PRO. 30/8/104 fol. 289.
[50] H.M. Colvin (ed.), *The History of the King's Works* (6 vols, London, 1963–73), V, 224–7; F. Russell, 'Lord Bute and King George III', in Marsden (ed.), *The Wisdom of George the Third*, p. 38.
[51] J. Roberts, *Views of Windsor. Watercolours by Thomas and Paul Sandby* (London, 1995).
[52] Bickley (ed.), *Diaries of . . . Glenbervie*, I, 407.

George's use of the castle combined public and private functions, and enabled him to avoid London, which was regarded as 'dreadful' in hot weather.[53] Windsor, which had been neglected under George II, was the setting for royal ceremonials. St George's Chapel was restored and remodelled as part of George's revival of the cult of the Garter, an important aspect of Windsor's role as a setting for exemplary kingship. George II had moved Garter installations to Kensington Palace, and when George III held his first at Windsor in 1762, it was the first to be held at the castle since 1730. David Garrick's play, *The Institution of the Garter* (1771) was a compliment to George's interest in the Order. The grand Garter ceremony of 1805 was a riposte to Napoleon's self-proclamation as emperor the previous year.

The chapel, the religious seat of the Order of the Garter, was George's preferred place of worship in Windsor, not the chapel in the state apartments. The Chapel of Revealed Religion that George planned, which would have filled in an open court that was in fact filled twenty years later by George IV's Waterloo Chamber, was never built. In St George's Chapel, George paid for a series of changes made between 1785 and 1792 under the supervision of the carver Henry Emlyn, including the almost complete rebuilding of the altar wall and additional choir stalls.[54] Scenes from the lives of St George and Edward III were carved into the chapel panelling, and when the chapel, which united George's major interests of religion, art and architecture, was formally opened in 1787 the service included an offering of gold and silver by the king in accordance with the original institution. George III, George IV and William IV were all buried in the chapel, whereas Charles II, William III, Mary II, Anne and George II had been buried in Westminster Abbey; James II and VII was buried in Paris and George I in Hanover.

Garter celebration also played a role in the state apartments, particularly in the audience chamber where the decorative scheme focused on the order. Another aspect of national heritage honoured in Windsor was the patron saint of England: between 1807 and 1811, Matthew Cotes Wyatt painted a scene from St George's life on the ceiling of the King's dressing room. This must have seemed appropriate at a time when George III was the nation's leader in a bitter battle with Napoleon. Indeed, in 1805 James Gillray had depicted the king saving a fallen Britannia from a dragon with the head of Napoleon, in his caricature 'St George and the Dragon – a Design for an Equestrian Statue from the Original in Windsor Castle'. Gillray depicted Napoleon wearing two crowns, while George, the true monarch, had none, and instead wore uniform.

---

[53] Anne to Frederick Robinson, 16 Sept. 1791, Plymouth 1259/1/81.
[54] J. Roberts, 'Henry Emlyn's Restoration of St. George's Chapel', *Report of the Society of the Friends of St. George's and the Descendants of the Knights of the Garter*, 5 (1976–7), pp. 331–8.

The Castellated Palace, begun at Kew in 1801, represented a revival of George's plans for a major new palace, but in a different style to the planned Richmond Palace. As he wrote in 1803, 'I never thought I should have adopted Gothic instead of Grecian architecture, but the bad taste of the last forty years has so entirely corrupted the professors of the latter, I have taken to the former from thinking Wyatt perfect in that style'.[55] George's frequent demands for changes in the plans for the new palace, however, delayed matters, while the rising cost also became a factor: £40,000 had been allocated in 1800, but expenditure was £100,000 by 1806 and may have been £500,000 by 1811, when, soon after he gained the power to do so, the prince regent stopped work on the largely complete building. His father had last visited Kew in January 1806, and after that the project lacked relevance. The castle was demolished in 1827–8. The Gothic was also favoured when George provided £1,000 towards rebuilding the tower of Salisbury Cathedral, a product of his commitment to the established Church and the national heritage. George did not favour symbolic gestures; instead, his help was generally practical.

George also played a role in landscaping, although less so than in architecture. In Richmond Park he replaced the ornamental landscaping, carried out under George II and Queen Caroline, with the contemporary natural look popularized by 'Capability' Brown, who was responsible for the new design as he was for the grounds of the seats of much of the élite. The formal gardens of Mary II and Anne at Kensington Palace were similarly replaced by lawn. In Hanover, in 1779, the grounds of Montbrillant, the summer residence, were landscaped.

George's visits to aristocratic seats were also memorialized in their grounds. For example at Croome Park, the seat of George, sixth earl of Coventry, which George visited in 1788, a spirally fluted stone urn on a square pedestal base, commemorating the visit, was designed for, and remains in, the home shrubbery. A similar urn was erected for George's Jubilee (and the death of the sixth earl), and is located in the shrubbery to the east of the walled garden.

Unlike his son, the patron of John Nash, George showed little interest in urban design, but in 1804 he approved a parliamentary bill to lay open Westminster Abbey to Palace Yard. Characteristically, there was an emphasis on the morally uplifting consequences of this project, not on an aesthetic of urban improvement:

whatever makes the people more accustomed to view cathedrals must raise their veneration for the Established Church. The King will with equal pleasure consent, when it is proposed, to the purchasing and

---

[55] Aspinall, *George III*, IV, 135.

pulling down the west side of Bridge Street and the houses fronting Westminster Hall; as it will be opening to the traveler that ancient pile, which is the seat of administration of the best laws, and the most uprightly administered; and if the people really valued the religion and laws of this blessed country, we should stand on a rock that no time could destroy.[56]

The comment on the people reflects George's concern for moral revival, while the last image is typically religious.

Although the landed élite played a greater aggregate role in artistic patronage than the monarchy, George was important as an individual patron. Only in architectural drawing was he reasonably well trained, but his interest in science, music and painting was valuable. Nevertheless, aside from architecture and gardens, the history of theatre and music during this period also reveal the declining significance of royal patronage. Handel's livelihood came to depend on the commercial success of his works on the London stage. Mozart, in 1764, and Haydn, in 1791 and 1794, came to London in search of the same success. 'Taste' came from outside the royal court, although George IV would have liked to spend enough to challenge this, while, earlier, Frederick, prince of wales's sponsorship of the rococo was significant. Court ceremonies did, however, provide important occasions for patronage and performance.

This did not ensure that the crown played a central role in patronage, as was conspicuously shown by the calibre of the poet laureates. William Whitehead, laureate from 1757 until 1785, gained the position because Thomas Gray had rejected it, and was criticized for his poetry, especially by Charles Churchill. The lacklustre quality of Whitehead's poetry was amply illustrated by his New Year ode for 1785, which predicted that the newly independent American colonies would return to their loyalty, and that Britain

> Shall stretch protecting branches round,
> Extend the shelter, and forget the wound,
> Two Britons thro' the admiring world,
> Shall wing their way with sails unfurl'd;

The work of Whitehead's successor, Thomas Warton, helped to revive interest in the sonnet, but his own poetry was less influential than his *History of English Poetry* (1774–81). Plumbing the depths, Henry Pye held the laureateship from 1790 until 1813, but his undistinguished poetic writings made less of an impact than his *Summary of the Duties of a Justice of the Peace*

---

[56] George to Eldon, 8 June 1804, Twiss, I, 454.

out of Sessions (1808), and he probably owed his position to his loyal voting record as an MP. Pye certainly did his job as a laureate, and dedicated to George his *Naucratia; or Naval Dominion* (1798), but he also attracted the scorn of other poets. In contrast, Pye's successors, Robert Southey (1813–43), William Wordsworth (1843–50) and Alfred Tennyson (1850–92), transformed the credibility of the post.

Despite the scale and style of the royal court, and the grandeur sought by George IV, the Hanoverians presided over an embourgeoisement of British culture. If morality was increasingly prescribed and indulgence proscribed in many works – Richardson's first novel, *Pamela* (1740), being a very popular work on the prudence of virtue and the virtue of prudence – this, however, represented not so much a bourgeois reaction against royal and aristocratic culture as a shift in sensibility that was common to both, and one certainly seen to be in accord with the views and wishes of George III. Furthermore, there was no cultural critique of the established order. For every decadent aristocrat depicted on the stage in the second half of the eighteenth century, there were several royal or aristocratic heroes.

Nevertheless, the cultural and artistic role of monarchy and the monarch had changed. Both were still important, but they were less central to national identity. In part, this was due to political changes. The failure of the Jacobite challenge, which was clear after the defeat of Charles Edward Stuart at Culloden in 1746, meant there was less of a need to emphasize the links of dynasty and government, while George's lack of the martial propensities and achievements of his predecessors was related to a situation in which national glory, and the glorification of achievement, did not focus on the monarch. Had George matched the military commitments of his relative, Frederick II (the Great) of Prussia, then the situation might have been different, not least because there would have been political pressure to celebrate (or criticize) royal achievements, although George might have sought to fight in the War of American Independence, with disastrous consequences for his reputation.

But more than the character of the monarch was at stake. There was also a broad pattern of socio-political development that affected cultural interests and artistic activity. However much it may have been supported by a monarch, militarism had limited appeal to the landed order in England, which was one reason why, numerically, the Scottish and Anglo-Irish élites were over-represented in the senior ranks of the army. More generally, the English élite was not necessarily going to be guided in cultural and artistic matters by the crown and the royal court, and, just as the development of architectural and landscape styles clearly reflected this, so it is difficult to see a different pattern of royal patronage determining the cultural views and artistic interests of the élite. The image of the crown was also affected by the long-term demystification of monarchy. Indeed, George was the target of vigorous, and often vicious, satire, not least in caricature prints.[57] This criticism, which was greater in scale than that directed at his two predecessors, in part due to advances in printing, was not simply a comment on George, but also on the politics of his reign. There was a comparable process in France, and one that was more politically significant and damaging because of the more central role of the monarch in the French political system.[58]

The limited role of the crown was even more apparent in face of the expanding wealth and influence of urban society, especially its mercantile and professional elements. Demographic and economic expansion from mid-century greatly underwrote this, accentuating social fluidity and creating new challenges as to how best monarch and monarchy could respond to expectations about appropriate leadership. The cultural patronage with which George was associated, particularly the foundation of the Royal Academy, was a successful response to a changing political culture, being patriotic, public and institutional, and it was a different response from what his predecessors had felt necessary.[59] An informed paternalism seemed appropriate and necessary; the ruler as patriarch was no longer feasible, as was readily apparent in the 1780s in the public drama of tension between George and his sons. George III's reputation also benefited from the equivocal response to George, prince of Wales's patronage and leadership of taste: the aristocracy and the middling orders did not look for aestheticism in their monarch, especially when it was combined with loose morals and extravagance.[60] Stylistically, George III's preferences were appropriate, with the exception of the major expense of the Gothic architecture of his later years. Just as the king did not like sumptuous dinners, so his apartments were decorated in a more modest fashion than Charlotte's. His aesthetic sympathies were also shown in his choice of watches for personal use, with the emphasis on functionality, not ornamentation.

Like his father, who had shared the fashionable concern with astronomy, George was interested in science. He had been taught physics and chemistry as a boy, benefiting in 1755 from demonstrations by the successful lecturer Stephen Demainbray. Naturally inquisitive, and displaying an erratic intelligence which had the insight to appreciate the

---

[57] V. Carretta, *George III and the Satirists from Hogarth to Byron* (Athens, Georgia, 1990).

[58] J.W. Merrick, *The Desacralization of the French Monarchy in the Eighteenth Century* (Baton Rouge, Louisiana, 1990).

[59] Hoock, *The King's Artists*; T.C.W. Blanning, 'Personal Union and Cultural Contact? The Role of Courts in the Unions of Hanover/England and Saxony/Poland', in R. Rexheuser (ed.), *Die Personalunionen von Sachsen–Polen 1690–1763 und Hannover–England 1714–1837. Ein Vergliech* (Wiesbaden, 2005), p. 480.

[60] S. Parissien, *George IV. The Grand Entertainment* (London, 2001).

ideas of those he recognized as more learned than himself, George shared
Bute's enthusiasm for science; the earl had supervised the prince's scientific education. As king, George revived links with the Royal Society,
collected scientific instruments, which were used in experiments, particularly in the 1760s, maintained his own astronomical observatory, and was
a prominent supporter of the astronomer William Herschel. Princess
Augusta showed how well she knew her son when she had Chambers
design the King's Observatory as a gift to enable him to watch the transit
of Venus in 1769. Demainbray became the first keeper. Far from being a
matter of idle curiosity, the transit of Venus provided an opportunity to
ascertain the scale of the solar system. When he visited Oxford in 1785,
George was reported as seeing the observatory at St John's College,
probably the Radcliffe Observatory over the road.

Born in Hanover and settling in England in 1757, Herschel (1738–1822)
had moved from music to astronomy. On 13 March 1781 he discovered
Uranus, the first planet to be found since antiquity and the first that could
not be seen by the naked eye, although Herschel initially thought it was a
comet. In honour of the king, Herschel named it the 'Georgium Sidus', a
reference to Virgil's *Georgics* that claimed immortality for George. The
following year George met Herschel, who subsequently exhibited his telescope before him and became the king's principal astronomical adviser
and a pensioner of the crown. Herschel moved to live near Windsor, and
George continued to take considerable interest in Herschel's work,
funding his construction of a larger telescope, with a grant of £2,000 in
1785 and a further £2,000 in 1787, as well as an annual payment of £200
for repairs. This support enabled Herschel, now with the largest telescope
of his day, to discover two of the satellites of Uranus in 1787 and two of
those of Saturn two years later, as well as to begin the classification of
nebulae. George walked through the 39-foot-long telescope tube before
the mirror was inserted, reportedly encouraging the archbishop of
Canterbury, John Moore, to follow him: 'Come, my lord bishop, I will
show you the way to heaven.'[61] George was not only interested in mapping
the heavens. He also gave £3,000 to the Society of Arts in 1784 in order
to finance a triangulation intended to establish the difference in longitude between Greenwich and Paris, and thus to permit the standardi-
zation of longitude. This was one of the major scientific endeavours of
the age.

[61] Herschel to Sir Joseph Banks, 9 Aug. 1785, no date, Aspinall, *George III*, I, 178–81,
297–9; J.B. Sidgwick, *William Herschel: Explorer of the Heavens* (London, 1953); M.A. Hoskin,
William Herschel and the Construction of the Heavens (London, 1963); K. Beuermann, 'Die
Herschels – eine hannoveranische Astronomenfamilie in England', in E. Mittler (ed.), *'Eine
Welt allein ist nicht genug'. Grossbritannien, Hannover und Göttingen 1714–1837* (Göttingen, 2005),
pp. 246–52.

George's scientific interests included a fascination with all kinds of measurement and the instruments for this, and specifically with timekeeping. He supported the search for longitude and had a collection of clocks and barometers, and he paid the Scottish clockmaker Alexander Cumming £1,178, a large sum, for a barograph, a mechanical device that recorded changes in atmospheric pressure, completed in 1765. George Adams the Elder, mathematical instrument maker to George, was a famous maker of globes and his *Treatise on the Globes* (1766) describing how to do so, had a dedication to George written by Samuel Johnson that was appropriate for a monarch 'distinguished for his love of the sciences'.[62] From Adams, George ordered a large collection of scientific apparatus including two silver microscopes.[63] Adams was succeeded on his death in 1773 by his son, who held suitable values from the king's perspective, being a religious Tory, and he, in turn, was succeeded, on his death in 1795, by his brother Dudley. Family traditions of service meant much to George. John Elliott, clockmaker to the king, shared George's interest in astronomy. He was succeeded as clockmaker to the king by his son Edward. Like Louis XVI, George was very interested in clock and watch mechanisms, and he devoted much time to perfecting his skill, which extended to writing out the correct sequence of watchmaker actions.[64] He was always interested in how things were made, and in making them himself. George learned to make buttons in his youth, and after touring Portsmouth dockyard in 1773 he pressed for details on how ropes were made for the navy, the topic that had interested him most on his visit.[65]

At Kew, George was a patron of botanical science. A botanic garden was developed in the grounds of Frederick, prince of Wales's residence, with Bute, a great enthusiast for the subject, playing a key role until 1772, when Joseph Banks replaced him. George authorized the dispatch of seeds and plants to Catherine the Great.[66] His interest was not restricted to Kew. In 1776, George and Charlotte visited William, third duke of Portland's seat at Bulstrode to see the *Hortus siccus* (dry garden), in which flowers were carefully imitated in painted paper by Mary Delany. He also greatly liked the flower garden at Nuneham Courtenay. The king was also fascinated by historical sites. In 1788, he spent an hour visiting the remains of a Roman camp near Cheltenham.[67]

[62] Boswell, *Life of Johnson*, p. 386.

[63] A.Q. Morton and J.A. Wess, *Public and Private Science: The King George III Collection* (Oxford, 1993); J. Millburn, *Adams of Fleet Street, Instrument Maker to George III* (Aldershot, 2000); J.A. Wess, 'George III, Scientific Societies, and the Changing Nature of Scientific Collecting', in Marsden (ed.), *The Wisdom of George the Third*, pp. 313–30.

[64] RA. GEO/15794–7.

[65] George to John, fourth earl of Sandwich, first lord of the admiralty, 13 Aug. 1773, London, National Maritime Museum, Sandwich papers SAN F/45c/16.

[66] George to William Grenville, 16 Nov. 1793, BL. Add. 58857 fol. 171.

[67] G. Hart, *A History of Cheltenham* (Stroud, 1965), p. 141.

George's engagement with scientific developments was shown in 1766 when, in place of the royal midwife, Mrs Draper, it was decided to entrust Charlotte's fourth pregnancy to a male midwife, a choice made more controversial by the fact that he was a Scotsman, William Hunter.[68]

George's engagement with watches, clocks, astronomy, botany and the music of Handel has been attributed to a striving to take refuge from the pressures of his personality in obsessive intellectual activities centring on the clear demonstration of order and regularity.[69] This, by its nature, is argument by assertion, and is anyway somewhat reductive, ignoring in particular the role of individual interest and general fashion. Astronomy, botany and the measurement of time were all beneficiaries of the latter, and many who shared in this interest presumably did not match the pop psychology just cited. It is all too easy to offer such alleged insights. Was George's zest for hunting a desire to escape the travails of his life, a preference for open air pursuits, the product of a frustrated desire to command, a substitute for military activity, or something else? The same goes for his frequent walking, or for his interest in farming. At least with George it is not necessary to bring in the Freemasons; and, unlike a number of Protestant rulers and princes of the 1780s, such as Frederick William II of Prussia and George's cousin, Prince Charles of Hesse-Cassel, he was not a Rosicrucian. Gustavus III of Sweden and the future Frederick VI of Denmark were also interested in mystical religion and freemasonry.[70] As far as the arts and sciences are concerned, it is best to note George's role as an informed and committed patron, with wide-ranging cultural and intellectual interests and a desire to become engaged, as he showed in his performance of music. George was no mere spectator, a verdict that is more generally appropriate.

[68] L.F. Cody, *Birthing the Nation. Sex, Science, and the Conception of Eighteenth-Century Britons* (Oxford, 2005), pp. 196–226.

[69] Plumb, *New Light*, pp. 16–17.

[70] Hugh Elliott to Carmarthen, 29 Nov. 1788, PRO. FO. 22/10 fols 450–2.

Chapter 10

RELIGION AND MORALITY

It is with great satisfaction I perceive by your letters that your mind is impressed with those sentiments of duty to our Great Creator which alone can preserve you from the snares of this world or make you with comfort either look forward to a future state or pass your life with satisfaction; besides, no real confidence can be placed in any one whose intentions are not known to be guided by a due observance of the Laws of God, for any other tie is so weak that it must break when evil advice or any inclinations pull against it . . . Moral Philosophy, till a proper foundation has been made in the principles of Religion, cannot be with utility pursued.

George III to Prince Augustus, 1787[1]

On 2 November 1760, Thomas Secker, the archbishop of Canterbury, saw the new king alone in his closet. Though not friends, the two men had a closeness stemming from George's piety and Secker's role as a religious guide: he had been present at the birth of George and had baptized him, and was to go on to preside over his marriage and coronation. They discussed a letter from Thomas Sherlock, bishop of London, and Secker then recorded,

> When I was going from the King, he called me back, and said he hoped the proclamation against Vice and Profaneness would be regarded and have a good effect. I answered that such proclamations had been apt to be considered as matters of course, but that his example, I was persuaded, would give life and vigour to this. He replied, that he thought it was his principal duty to encourage and support religion and virtue. I applauded this sentiment in a few words highly: and mentioned it afterwards in conversation as his.[2]

The king's gravity and piety were shown the following month when George readily agreed to Secker's proposal for a general fast, adding that 'he would have it during the session of parliament: both because the

---

[1] George to Augustus, 5 Mar. 1787, Aspinall, *George III*, I, 273.
[2] Secker, memorandum, 2 Nov. 1760, Lambeth Palace Library, MS 1130/I fol. 30.

attendance of the two Houses added a solemnity to it, and because he feared the people would be in a less proper disposition for it after the Dissolution [of Parliament], while steps were taking towards a new election'.[3] As in the political sphere, this emphasis on revival stemmed from the ideas he had developed while prince,[4] and there was a similar interest early in his reign in signs of a new royal tone.[5]

George was an active supporter of the Church of England, with a strong faith, unlike his father, grandfather and great-grandfather. This faith extended to his personal safety. From the outset, George relied on divine protection against assassination. The report, in December 1778, of a plan to kill him *en route* to the theatre led the king to respond by expressing scepticism, urging investigation, before adding:

> As to my own feelings, they always incline me to put trust where it alone can avail – in the Almighty Ruler of the Universe who knows what best suits his allwise purposes, this being the week I go to Holy Communion, I had no thoughts of going unto the play.[6]

After the attempt by Margaret Nicholson to assassinate him by stabbing him in the street outside St James's Palace in 1786, George wrote about 'the interposition of Providence in the late attempt on my life by a poor insane woman'.[7] His response in 1795 to danger was no different. Lord Chancellor Eldon recorded George as saying to a startled attendant of rank when his coach was apparently shot at, on the way to the opening of parliament, 'Sit still, sir, let us not betray any fear of what may happen.' George also responded calmly to James Hadfield's attempt to shoot him when he visited Drury Lane theatre for a performance of *The Marriage of Figaro* in May 1800. Eldon was convinced of the king's bravery and fortitude, noting that, at the time of the Gordon Riots in 1780, he was more determined than the ministry: 'he said, he should act without their advice, and would order his horse to the door, that he might go at the head of the troops in person, and give them orders to disperse the rioters by force'. During the French Revolutionary Wars, however, the king set a bleaker note, saying 'in those times . . . that he might perhaps be the last King of England'.[8]

---

[3] Secker, memorandum, 24 Dec. 1760, Lambeth Palace Library, MS 1130/I fol. 34.

[4] R.R. Sedgwick (ed.), *Letters from George III to Lord Bute, 1756–1776* (London, 1939), pp. 12–13.

[5] W. Warburton, *Letters from a Late Eminent Prelate* (2 vols, London, 1809), I, 317.

[6] George to Bute, 14 Dec. 1760, BL. Add. 36796 fol. 65; North to George and reply, both 21 Dec. 1778, RA. GEO/3160–1.

[7] George to Richard Grenville, 29 Aug. 1786, BL. Add. 70956; cf. to earl of Hertford, 7 Aug. 1786, Aspinall, *George III*, I, 242.

[8] Twiss, I, 293–4.

George was a devout Anglican. He was personally pious, and noted as such, not least for his signs of devotion and his fervent responses in divine service. The promise of 'endless bliss' after death was real to the king, as was gratitude to the 'Great Preserver'. These were mainstream, not unusual, views, and they were shared by many whose moral conduct did not match biblical or royal injunctions. Horatio Nelson's prayers indicate the widely held view of an ever-present and watchful God. The absence of such beliefs in others shocked George. When Edward Despard was hanged in 1803 for his role in organizing an unsuccessful plot to kill George, the latter reflected 'It is melancholy that a man should appear so void of religion at so awful a moment.'[9] Despard had refused to attend chapel or receive the sacrament after he was condemned. George's dependence for salvation on divine mercy, not on human merit, was accompanied by a belief in the need to show thanks for the divine gift of life by means of appropriate conduct. These beliefs guided George's conduct and helped structure his time.[10] Sundays were special to the king and he tried not to handle government business on them,[11] while court life deferred to religious duty. Drawing room on Sunday was held after morning service and no presentations were made. No levees or drawing rooms were held during Passion or Whit weeks. George was an appropriate figure to issue royal proclamations for a general fast, such as that held on 13 February 1801. Fast days were punctiliously observed by the king, just as, on Christmas Day, the sacrament was received by the royal family.

The early influences on George contributed to guiding his sense of seriousness in an explicitly religious direction, and to ensuring that his Christian convictions were very much framed in terms of duty. Lutheran by upbringing, his mother became a devout Anglican, particularly critical of latitudinarianism, and she had a strong influence on George. Clerics, successively Francis Ayscough, Thomas Hayter and John Thomas, were prominent in his upbringing; and Hayter, a firm opponent of popery and licentiousness, placed a very strong emphasis on Divine Providence in his sermons. Bute was a Scottish Episcopalian, convinced of the importance of Christian teaching in royal education.[12]

The model of George's behaviour was held out by Secker when drawing attention to complaints that the queen had not kneeled 'at any part of the service at the chapel . . . what stress people sometimes lay on such things . . . there is a plain rule for her: to be in the same posture with

[9] George to Pelham, 21 Feb. 1803, BL. Add. 33115 fol. 120.
[10] George to Prince Augustus, 29 Mar. 1787, Aspinall, *George III*, I, 274.
[11] G. Pellew, *The Life and Correspondence of the Right Honble. Henry Addington, First Viscount Sidmouth* (London, 3 vols, 1847), I, 307.
[12] RA. GEO/Add. 32/1731 fol. 8.

the King . . .'[13] George soon after displayed his piety during the coronation service, a public affirmation of faith and one in which he was keen to take appropriate advice:

> At the Communion the King asked me if he should not take off his crown. I said the Office did not mention it. He asked, if it would not be more suitable to such an Act of Religion. I said, Yes, but the Queen's crown could not be taken off easily. He asked what must be done. I said, as Ladies heads are used to be covered, it would not be regarded. He put off his crown immediately; and all the peers, that saw it, took off their coronets.[14]

George saw divine intervention at work in the affairs of man, and awareness of God and divine injunctions as being a particular guide to monarchs. As Frederick the Great, a noted sceptic, neared death, George commented,

> To any one who in the least reflects, it cannot but occasion much surprise, that when Divine Providence gave him such warning of his approaching disposition it should not have given rise to thoughts more fitting his situation.[15]

It was not formulaic when George thanked God for favourable events, thanks that were given privately as well as publicly. Such events encouraged George in his sense of mission and duty and provided a welcome boost:

> I trust with the protection of Divine Providence I shall extricate this country by becoming spirit and activity out of its present difficulties. The strong instance of that protection is very visible in the safe arrival of the Leeward Island Fleet . . . a great encouragement.[16]

As did so many of his contemporaries, George trusted in Divine Providence whenever things were difficult, relying on it in 1777 to save North's life when he had a fever and in 1779 when Britain was confronted with the threat of Bourbon invasion; seeing its workings in French defeats in 1793 and 1796, as well as thanking it for restoring the health of his daughter Charlotte after a miscarriage in 1798, and for arranging the

[13] Secker to William, fourth duke of Devonshire, 19 Sept. 1761, Lambeth Palace Library, MS 1130/I fol. 123.
[14] Secker, memorandum, Lambeth Palace Library, MS 1130/I fols 178–9.
[15] George to Carmarthen, 26 Aug. 1786, BL. Add. 27914 fol. 17.
[16] George to Robinson, 2 Aug. 1772, BL. Add. 37833 fol. 1.

rescue of Grenville's diplomat brother from shipwreck in 1799.[17] Providence was more widely seen as framing the king's life, and clerics had no hesitation in sending forth the message. God, for example, was seen by Andrew Kippis, a prominent Presbyterian pastor, as answering George's wish for a spouse: 'Such was the blessing our sovereign sought for, and providence has graciously answered his petition. Providence has sent him a princess . . .'[18]

George himself was convinced that 'the protection of the Almighty' had preserved his 'political existence' in the political crisis of 1783–4, while the apparent end of the crisis with Spain in 1790 led the king to express his 'thanks to the Almighty for having prevented a catastrophe', war.[19] Seeing divine intervention was easier for the king because he was an eclectic, not a systematic, thinker. George's mental health, however, was a testing aspect of divine judgement. This was true for the king himself, and also for his critics. Henry Hunt saw insanity as a judgement on an unsatisfactory 'bloody reign'.[20]

George's sense of personal responsibility gave rise to a measure of rectitude and self-righteousness which irritated some critics. They saw the king's piety as self-serving, when it would be more correct to argue that it contributed to his obstinacy. Personal piety was also linked to acceptable cultural preferences in George's favour for Handel's oratorios. Furthermore, the explicit morality that George displayed helped make him an attractive model for the devout. His Anglican piety added another moral dimension to good government. He showed many of the virtues applauded by evangelicals, and in 1787 issued a Proclamation against Vice. This coincided with the beginning of work by William Wilberforce (and other evangelicals) to revive the country through a reformation of manners, and not least to encourage the upper classes to behave better. George supported Wilberforce's effort. He was probably prompted by concerns for the prince of Wales and his efforts caused much amusement in Whig circles.

George was not restricted in his Anglicanism: although he had his own preferences among clerics and ecclesiastical views, his Anglican orthodoxy was inclusive in practice, a useful response to the diversity and irenicism of

---

[17] George to Robinson, 1, 2 Mar. 1777, 28 June, 31 Oct. 1779, George to William Grenville, 29 Sept. 1796, 9 May 1798, 3, 7 Mar. 1799, BL. Add. 37833 fols 114, 116, 37834 fols 99, 175, 58859 fol. 85, 58860 fol. 88, 58861 fols 18, 21; George to Pitt, 9 Apr. 1793, PRO. 30/8/103 fol. 490.

[18] A. Kippis, *Observations upon the Coronation. A Sermon Preached at the Chapel in Long-Ditch . . .* (London, 1761), p. 9.

[19] George to Hertford, 7 Aug. 1786, Aspinall, *George III*, I, 242; George to William Grenville, 5 Aug. 1790, BL. Add. 58855 fol. 135.

[20] S. Poole, *The Politics of Regicide in England, 1760–1850. Troublesome Subjects* (Manchester, 2000), p. 15.

the Church of England.[21] The theological works he kept at hand imply a broad view of Anglicanism.[22] Again, the fact that he was not a theorist helped enormously, and also played a role in explaining his preference for plain sermons. If George was committed to Trinitarian orthodoxy, this was the norm for Anglicans, while his commitment to Christian piety led George to be impressed by the Wesleys and the evangelical William, second earl of Dartmouth, as well as by more conventional Trinitarians. George was not enthusiastic about latitudinarianism, and his response was a combination of both inclination and theology.

Furthermore, George awarded James Beattie a pension for his *Essay on the Nature and Immutability of Truth* (1770), a commonplace work that attracted notice because of its criticism of the philosophical basis of deism, and specifically the work of David Hume. Visiting London in 1773, Beattie was presented by Dartmouth to the king and soon after awarded £200 a year. When received at Kew, he was told by George that he had given his book to Lord Hertford to read. Beattie and George shook their heads over what they saw as the advance of atheism, George repeating several times his observation that no thinking man could be an atheist unless he thought he had made himself.

George took his role and God-given responsibilities as Supreme Governor of the Church very seriously, far more so than his two predecessors had done. Under considerable pressure for preferments,[23] George fulfilled his responsibilities in large part by taking great care with his appointment of clerics: all senior appointments were in his gift, and bishops paid him homage when appointed. A 'conscientious promoter of merit',[24] he was concerned, alongside, and as part of respectability,[25] about the pastoral qualities and doctrinal orthodoxy of candidates, including their temper, discretion and willingness to be resident. This was an abrupt shift from George I and George II, who had shared their ministers' determination to use the Church to maintain Whig strength, a position eased by the fact that they were Lutherans and only nominal members of the Church of England. George III, instead, sought to promote clerics whom he thought orthodox, such as Thomas Balguy,

---

[21] G.M. Ditchfield, 'Ecclesiastical Policy under Lord North', in J. Walsh, C. Haydon and S. Taylor (eds), *The Church of England c. 1698–c. 1833: From Toleration to Tractarianism* (Cambridge, 1993), pp. 228–46; B. Young, *Religion and Enlightenment in Eighteenth-Century England: Theological Debate from Locke to Burke* (Oxford, 1998); W. Prest, 'The Religion of a Lawyer? William Blackstone's Anglicanism', *Parergon*, 21 (2004), pp. 155–66.

[22] G.M. Ditchfield, *George III. An Essay in Monarchy* (Basingstoke, 2002), p. 186, fn. 10.

[23] Bishop Hurd of Worcester to George, 27 Aug. 1785, Aspinall, *George III*, I, 183.

[24] P. Langford, *A Polite and Commercial People. England 1727–1783* (Oxford, 1989), p. 595. For George's interest, see e.g. George to Pitt, 22 Aug. 1792, PRO. 30/8/103 fol. 456.

[25] George to Pitt, 20 Aug. 1792, PRO. 30/8/103 fol. 454. See also e.g. 2 Oct. 1804 30/8/104 fol. 386.

Richard Hurd, Beilby Porteous and Samuel Horsley. A protégé of Thurlow who was trusted by George, Horsley was appointed to St David's (1788) and translated to Rochester (1793) and St Asaph (1802). His strong opposition to Dissenters, apocalyptic conviction that the French Revolution was the work of Antichrist, and powerful belief in the Incarnation of Christ present a picture of the late Georgian Church far removed from liberal rationalism.[26] George was clear in his emphasis on clerical merit. When Lord Pelham, the home secretary, responded in 1802 to his brother George being appointed bishop of Bristol by thanking the king for the mark of favour to his family, the latter replied,

> though the King is truly sensible of the attachment shown to his family ever since they mounted this throne by the House of Pelham yet had he not heard the most favourable accounts of the piety and good conduct of Mr. Pelham he should not have thought himself justified from regard alone to his relations to have placed him in so conspicuous a station in the church.[27]

'Character as well as birth' was the reiterated theme.[28]

George indeed was occasionally willing to thwart his ministers' wishes over appointments, turning down Pitt's friend and tutor, George Pretyman Tomline, the bishop of Lincoln, for Canterbury in January 1805, much to Pitt's anger. Instead, George fulfilled his earlier promise of the post to Charles Manners-Sutton, bishop of Norwich. A personal friend of George and a grandson of John, third duke of Rutland, Manners-Sutton was part of the Windsor connection, as he had been dean of Windsor since 1794. Like George, he had a large family and was an opponent of Catholic emancipation (as was Tomline), while his personal qualities were more apparent than his intellect. By getting his way in this appointment, George showed that he remained the key patron and demonstrated his concern for the Church. Catholic emancipation had made the leadership of the Church a particularly sensitive matter, and George was convinced that if he could not appoint the archbishop of Canterbury he could not be king. This was partly because he feared who would be chosen and partly because of the principle involved. The latter was the major factor, hence George's earlier resistance to Pretyman as bishop of Lincoln in 1787 because Pretyman was Pitt's man.

---

[26] F.C. Mather, *High Church Prophet: Bishop Samuel Horsley, 1733–1806, and the Caroline Tradition in the Later Georgian Church* (Oxford, 1992); A. Robinson, 'Identifying the Beast: Samuel Horsley and the Problem of Papal AntiChrist', *Journal of Ecclesiastical History*, 43 (1992), p. 607.

[27] Pelham to George, 17 Dec., reply 18 Dec. 1802, BL. Add. 33115 fols 109–11.

[28] George to Pitt, 31 Jan. 1805, PRO. 30/8/104 fol. 417.

The Windsor connection extended to Eton College. Many of its senior teachers became canons of St George's Windsor, while the king was interested in the college, which propagated views dear to him. This interest extended to the pupils. Visiting Windsor in 1794, George Canning met the king and queen on the terrace:

> their Majesties were graciously pleased to recognize me, not having seen me since I left Eton – and to honour me with many kind and sensible observations – such as 'that I was much grown' – 'that I must be very happy in revisiting Eton now and then' – 'that they hoped I had not forgotten our old friend the Microcosm [a school magazine Canning co-edited in 1786–7] – for they had not'.

This conversation testified to George's interest in the school. He had certainly not taken the opportunity to discuss politics with the newly elected Pittite MP. A subsequent meeting on the terrace, in 1795, witnessed the same conversation, but Canning was introduced then by the provost of Eton. It is clear from his account that the king knew the names of old Etonians.[29]

While clerics deemed orthodox were favoured, George was less ready than his two predecessors to promote those with a questionable reputation. Benjamin Hoadly, who died in 1761, had received much preferment under George I and George II, but would have been less fortunate under George III, although Balguy, one of his former protégés, was preferred. William Paley did not receive preferment, possibly because his *Principles of Moral and Political Philosophy* (1785) seemed insufficiently prudent. Although Thomas Filewood was reported to have got the living of Dunsford on the strength of selling George a horse the king liked and then asking him for the living, George's correspondence indicates that he took care to check on Filewood's suitability.[30]

Nevertheless, political factors other than George's preferences did play a role in some appointments. At an early age, George had been exposed to what he regarded as an unacceptable bishop when, following the death of his father, Thomas Hayter, bishop of Norwich, a then supporter of the duke of Newcastle, was appointed as preceptor. George was later to describe him as unworthy, although Hayter successfully paid court to Bute and, against Newcastle's wishes, was translated to succeed Sherlock in London in 1761. In 1769, the free-thinking Augustus, third duke of Grafton, then first minister, was responsible for the appointment of Edmund Law, John Hinchliffe and Jonathan Shipley as bishops, but they

[29] P. Jupp (ed.), *The Letter-Journal of George Canning, 1793–1795* (London, 1991), pp. 137, 288.
[30] Hurd to George, 17, 22 Nov., Thomas Drake to Hurd, 21 Nov. 1785, Aspinall, *George III*, I, 193–6.

clearly did not satisfy George as none was translated after 1769. Hinchliffe was critical of the government's American policy and Shipley voted against the Quebec Act. Similarly, the latitudinarian Richard Watson was appointed under Shelburne. He was fairly respectable then, having published a critique of Gibbon, but was never translated from Llandaff, not the most prominent of sees. Other factors also played a role in church appointments. George was very careful to balance Oxford and Cambridge graduates, while his attempt to follow an inclusive policy by reaching out to individual Tories has to be seen as a matter of religious policy and ecclesiastical politics as much as one of secular politics. Indeed, the secular policy owed something to its religious counterpart and made it far easier to put the stress on personal calibre when assessing clerics.

George's interest did not cease when clerics were appointed. He corresponded with and saw them. This was true not only in London but also on his travels. George made private visits to the bishops of Gloucester and Worcester in 1788, staying at the palace in Worcester from 5 to 9 August; visiting Exeter the following year, George held a levee at the bishop's palace and stayed at the deanery. He also attended service at the cathedral and that afternoon returned to tour the building. The royal party 'minutely observed every thing worthy of notice, and seemed highly gratified in observing the beauty of the building, the organ, Bishop's throne, painted windows, and other ornaments'.[31]

Familiarity with clerics through their role with the royal family helped George support them for promotion. John Thomas (1712–93), a royal chaplain, became dean of Westminster in 1768 and bishop of Rochester in 1774, and Frederick Keppel (1729–77), the son of William, second earl of Albemarle, became bishop of Exeter in 1762, having been a canon of Windsor (1754–62). In 1765, Keppel added the deanery of Windsor and the registrarship of the Order of the Garter. John Fisher (1748–1825), who had been preceptor to Prince Edward from 1780 to 1785, became a canon of Windsor in 1786 and bishop of Exeter in 1803, and was translated to the more prestigious see of Salisbury in 1807.[32] The links between clerics and the king were closer and warmer than under his two predecessors, and there were clerics to whom George felt close. Richard Hurd (1720–1808), who was appointed, with George's strong approval, bishop of Lichfield in 1775 and translated to Worcester in 1781, was appointed preceptor to the prince of Wales and Prince Frederick in 1776. Hurd also confirmed Prince Edward and Princess Augusta and preached before the king, who offered him the archbishopric of Canterbury in May 1783, which the bishop declined. George visited Hurd at his seat of Hartlebury Castle in 1788 and

[31] *Gloucester Journal*, 18 Aug. 1788; *Jenkins's Civil and Ecclesiastical History of the City of Exeter* (2nd edn, Exeter, 1841), p. 219.

[32] George to Sydney, 13 Aug. 1785, Aspinall, *George III*, I, 182.

in 1805 gave him a collection of books.[33] A critic of Hume and Gibbon, Hurd backed North's ministry, was very critical of the American Revolution, opposed the Dissenters Relief Bill of 1779, voted against the Fox–North ministry's India Bill, backed the government over the Regency Bill, and was opposed to the French Revolution, the Foxite Whigs and Catholic emancipation. This was very much a churchmanship close to George's heart.

Clerics were seen by the king as the prime educators of the young. When George in 1804 drew up his plans for the education of his granddaughter Charlotte, he wrote,

> His Majesty proposes that a Bishop shall under his peculiar inspection have the superintendance of the education of the young Princess, and shall form a plan for that purpose; that he shall recommend a clergyman to instruct her in religion and Latin; that she shall have an instructor in history, geography, belle letter and French and a writing, drawing and music master.[34]

George's attitude was not simply a matter of clerical appointments, but made religious issues even more central in politics than they might otherwise have been, and helped ensure that those of the Anglican devout who had been uneasy about the Glorious Revolution and the Hanoverian succession rallied to the crown, strengthening the identity both of the Church of England and of the nation.[35] This matched the political reconciliation with the Tories and thus redrew the contours of the politico-religious world, ending the rift that had been continual since 1714 and episodic since 1689. In turn, however, new divisions were created, and indeed the ending of the earlier rift was interpreted in these terms, with the rallying of Anglican clergy to the crown seen by the Whigs as evidence of the authoritarian tendency of the king. In 1792, Charles James Fox claimed that 'the Church party' was 'the most determined enemy of the Whig'.[36] Whereas Nonconformity had been associated with the 'Old Corps' Whigs, and thus with loyalty to the Hanoverians under George I and George II, it was now seen as conducive to political opposition, a tendency accentuated by the alliance of Low Church Anglicans and Dissenters in the American Revolution.

[33] S. Brewer (ed.), *The Early Letters of Bishop Richard Hurd 1739–1762* (Woodbridge, 1995), p. xix.

[34] George to Pitt, 18 Nov. 1804, Aspinall, *Prince of Wales*, V, 131.

[35] J.C.D. Clark, 'Protestantism, Nationalism, and National Identity, 1660–1832', *Historical Journal*, 43 (2000), pp. 249–76.

[36] Fox to Robert Adair, 29 Nov. 1792, Lord John Russell (ed.), *Memorials and Correspondence of Charles James Fox* (4 vols, London, 1853–7), III, 261.

George's attitude ensured opposition to heterodox tendencies within the Church of England, as well as to attempts to compromise its position and pretensions. The former led him in 1772 to oppose the Feathers Tavern petition. This was an attempt to end Anglican clerical subscription to the Thirty-Nine Articles as a necessary precondition for becoming graduates or clerics (at Oxford students subscribed to the Articles at matriculation). The attempt was rejected by the Commons on 6 February, and again on 5 May 1774. Seen as a threat to civil and ecclesiastical peace,[37] this was a litmus test for attitudes that were to play a more sustained role in differences over, first, the American and, then, the French Revolution. George congratulated Balguy on his sermons in favour of reducing support for the petition. Also in 1772, George opposed a Dissenter petition for relief from the necessity for subscribing to the doctrinal Articles of the Church for those who wished to register as schoolteachers and ministers. To the king, this provision entailed a clear distinction between Socinians and Christians: like many of his contemporaries, he was unwilling to accept denial of the Trinity and the Atonement.[38] The problems raised by Arianism and Socinianism for orthodox Church of England clergy helped explain George's outlook.

The more contentious nature of ecclesiastical debates of the 1770s helped in the development of George's views, not least in thinking of politics, as well as religion, in terms of a Dissenter challenge, a view that was readily extendable to the American colonies. It is all too easy to underrate the fear that the Church of England was in danger in 1772, but it was never far from George's mind; Lord North's unwillingness to give ground on this issue further confirmed George's confidence in him. Not only the king was affected. In the fourth edition of his *Dictionary of the English Language* (1773), Samuel Johnson replaced quotations from James Thomson's *The Seasons*, and turned, instead, increasingly to religious references. The American War of Independence was to strengthen concerns about heterodoxy, and this linked George to an important segment of opinion.[39] Subsequently, George showed a firmness, not to say rigidity, in his opposition in 1787–90 to the repeal of the Test and Corporation Acts,

[37] G.M. Ditchfield, 'The Subscription Issue in British Parliamentary Politics, 1772–79', *Parliamentary History*, 7 (1988), pp. 35–80, and '"How Narrow will the Limits of this Toleration Appear?" Dissenting Petitions to Parliament, 1772–1773', in S. Taylor and D.L. Wykes (eds), *Parliament and Dissent* (Edinburgh, 2005), pp. 90–106; B. Young, 'A History of Variations: The Identity of the Eighteenth-Century Church of England', in T. Claydon and I. McBride (eds), *Protestantism and National Identity. Britain and Ireland c. 1650–c. 1850* (Cambridge, 1998), pp. 105–28.

[38] W.B. Donne (ed.), *The Correspondence of King George the Third with Lord North from 1768 to 1783* (2 vols, London, 1867), I, 89.

[39] J.E. Bradley, 'The Anglican Pulpit, the Social Order and the Resurgence of Toryism during the American Revolution', *Albion*, 21 (1989), pp. 361–88.

an opposition supported by parliament: moves to repeal the Acts were defeated in 1787, 1789 and 1790.[40] George also took pains to retain the distinction whereby addresses from Dissenters were received in his closet, in other words privately, and not from the throne.[41]

The issue of Catholic rights proved more explosive, both politically and literally on the streets of London in 1780. The Anglican ascendancy in England, Wales and Ireland, and its Presbyterian counterpart in Scotland, discriminated against other Protestants, but the threat posed by Catholicism defined its core logic and certainly its relationship with a monarchy whose dynastic and ecclesiastical position rested on the denial of Catholic claims. By inclination, George was certainly no persecutor. Indeed he was personally friendly with several prominent Catholics. The linkage of anti-Catholicism and monarchy seen in the violently anti-Catholic *The Patriot King: Displayed in the Life of Henry VIII, King of England, from the Time of his Quarrel with the Pope till his Death* (1769) by Edward Lewis, an Oxfordshire rector, did not act as a model for George. Indeed, in 1772 the papal nuncio at Cologne was received at court. Furthermore, the Quebec Act of 1774 was seen as a pro-Catholic move and was criticized in Convocation the following year for failing to maintain the royal supremacy, while in 1776 George was dubious about the report of a Catholic plot in Ireland.[42] In 1780, George was presented as overly sympathetic to Catholicism: the agitation against the relaxation of legal disabilities on Catholics, particularly the Catholic Relief Act of 1778, which culminated in the Gordon Riots of 1780, grouped George with his ministry as a focus for criticism. His good personal relations with Catholics included visiting them. In 1778 George stayed at Thorndon Hall, the seat of Robert, ninth Lord Petre, a prominent Catholic peer, and in 1789 he visited Lulworth castle, the home of Thomas Weld, a prominent patron of Catholic religious orders, including the Jesuits. In 1787, the prince of Wales stayed the night at Henby Hall, the seat of Sir Carnaby Haggerston.

Later in the reign, however, the issue of Catholic emancipation was to lead to George being seen as a conservative figure. He was actively opposed to emancipation, and particularly what he saw as the fundamental question at issue, his coronation oath to protect the Church. The

[40] George to Pitt, 29 Mar. 1787, *Maggs Catalogue* 1390 (2006), no. 69; G.M. Ditchfield, 'The Parliamentary Struggle over the Repeal of the Test and Corporation Acts, 1787–1790', *English Historical Review*, 89 (1974), 'Debates on the Test and Corporation Acts, 1787–90: The Evidence of the Division Lists', *Bulletin of the Institute of Historical Research*, 50 (1977), pp. 69–81, and 'Ecclesiastical Policy during the Ministry of the Younger Pitt, 1783–1801', *Parliamentary History*, 19 (2000), pp. 64–80.

[41] George to Pelham, 21 May 1802, 21 Feb. 1803, BL. Add. 33115 fols 77, 120.

[42] George to Robinson, 28 Sept. 1776, BL. Add. 37833 fol. 53.

Protestant creation of the ascendancy in Ireland had been an understandable response to the exigencies of security in a world made threatening by confessional conflict and confrontation, and subsequently also by
dynastic rivalry in the shape of the Jacobite challenge. Ireland's capability
of serving as a Stuart stronghold had been demonstrated in the 1640s and
in 1689–91. In Ireland, however, this ascendancy resulted in the creation
of a narrow, confessional state, in which the success of the Church of
Ireland minority in entrenching itself was by the late eighteenth century
no longer useful to Britain, because of the difficulties posed by the exclusion of so large a proportion of its inhabitants from citizenship. As
Catholics and Protestant Dissenters had no real political outlets they
criticized the prevailing system, creating pressures for change.[43]

In the 1780s, 1790s and 1800s, George generally opposed the removal of
all legal disabilities from Catholics in Ireland and Britain, and he showed
favour to politicians, such as Eldon, who shared his views, although in 1791
he accepted the Second Catholic Relief Act. This gave Catholics freedom
of worship. Chapels and priests were registered at the quarter sessions.
Furthermore, in 1793, there is no sign that George opposed Hobart's Act
– the grant of the vote for the Dublin parliament to Catholics – nor relief
for Scottish Catholics. There was no real reason why George should
oppose Hobart's Act. He had not opposed previous concessions to Irish
Catholics, especially if they were propertied, and, in light of relations with
Revolutionary France, 1793 could be seen as an emergency in which it was
necessary to gain support. In 1784, however, the willingness of Frederick,
bishop of Derry and fourth earl of Bristol, to support the extension of the
franchise to Catholics had aroused George's ire.[44] Catholics still suffered
disadvantages, for example the liability to the double land tax, while
Hardwicke's Marriage Act continued to be an inconvenience to them.
Catholic emancipation still remained a goal.

George's attitude helped to focus the defence of order, hierarchy and
continuity much more on religion than would otherwise have been the
case in a period of revolutionary threats. He was motivated not only by his
religious convictions (in the shape of defence of the Church of England,
rather than anti-Catholicism), but also by the argument that the position
of the Church of England rested on fundamental parliamentary legislation. By making his case on the basis of 'religious and political duty'
George proposed a clear superiority over supporters of emancipation
who, he suggested, could only plead expediency.[45] He also rejected what
he saw as intellectual sophistry when he dismissed Henry Dundas's suggestion that the coronation oath bound the king in his executive, not his

---

[43] T. Barnard, *The Kingdom of Ireland, 1641–1760* (Basingstoke, 2004).
[44] George to Sydney, 26 July 1784, Aspinall, *George III*, I, 75.
[45] George to Addington, 7 Feb. 1801, Exeter, 152M/C1801/OR 61.

legislative, capacity, declaring 'None of your damned Scotch meta-physics.'[46] In France, the royal position as defender of the Church also proved controversial, both during the Revolution and at the outset of the reign of Louis XVI, who rejected a ministerial suggestion for a modern-ized coronation as well as a new coronation oath that focused more on the nation and left out the promise to destroy heresy in France.[47]

In practice, the challenge posed by Catholicism in Britain had been greatly lessened by the demise of Jacobitism as an issue, and by the care taken by Catholic clerics to win George's backing. In 1791 Cardinal Antonelli, the prefect of the Congregation for the Propagation of the Faith, who had authority over the Irish Catholic Church, instructed the four archbishops there on the religious duty of obedience to the govern-ment of George, and in 1792 Pope Pius VI sought British assistance in deterring the threat of French attack on Rome. English Catholics also showed loyalty to George. Catholic priests fleeing France were given refuge with George's approval in 1792, although the king wanted 'some attentive persons . . . kept there that government may be apprised of the conduct of those who have that shelter'.[48] Furthermore, in 1799 George opposed Castlereagh's idea that the government should provide financial support for the Irish Catholic clergy.[49] Nevertheless, George was more concerned about the revolutionaries, 'the enemies of mankind',[50] than about Catholics.

George was still seen as anti-Catholic, although, in many cases, this represented an extrapolation from his opposition to Catholic emancipa-tion, rather than accurate report. For example, in 1797, the fear that the prince of Württemberg might follow his father into the Catholic fold was held responsible for George's reluctance about the marriage of the prince with his eldest daughter, although that was not the reason George gave.[51] As an indication of the reports that circulated, and the way in which George's supposed religious views were related to signs of instability and also to cultural preferences, a dubious account by a hostile observer, possibly Sir Robert Wilson, of a visit to George's yacht off Weymouth in 1804 presented the king as motivated by an instinctive anti-Catholicism: 'he desired the Band to play some music from Handel to which were the words "We will never bow down", I presume to images, for the King immediately on their commencing cried out "Now let the Roman

[46] M. Fry, *The Dundas Despotism* (Edinburgh, 1992), p. 238.

[47] J. McManners, *Church and Society in Eighteenth-Century France, I: The Clerical Establishment and its Social Ramification* (Oxford, 1998), p. 15.

[48] George to Dundas, 23 Sept. 1792, BL. Add. 40100 fol. 65.

[49] George to Pitt, 24 Jan. 1799, PRO. 30/8/104 fol. 253.

[50] George to William Grenville, 18 Jan. 1795, BL. Add. 58858 fol. 129.

[51] E. Sheppard, *Memorials of St. James's Palace* (2 vols, London, 1894), II, 96; George to William Grenville, 14 Nov. 1795, BL. Add. 58859 fol. 41.

Catholics come on, I wish they were all here". He then lapsed into a devotional reverie.'[52] Despite criticism, George's opposition to Catholic emancipation helped to establish him as a Protestant standard-bearer and to strengthen his popularity.[53] As he suggested in 1805, his stance reflected 'the opinions of the people without doors'.[54]

In opposing any Catholic advance, George was maintaining the position of his predecessors, although the demise of Jacobitism ensured that there was no need for him to consider having to do so on the battlefield. The opposition to Dissent, however, contrasted with the position under George I and George II. Indeed, under George I there had been a drive by the Whig ministers to repeal laws aimed against Dissenters. The Occasional Conformity (1711) and Schism (1714) Acts were repealed in 1719, while the Corporation Act was diluted. George I, and his leading ministers, James, Earl Stanhope and Charles, third earl of Sunderland had also envisaged the repeal of the Test Act. This was not the position of George III, and this helped to define both his own politics and the response to him. To George, those who sought repeal were not only enemies of the constitution and opponents of good government but also politicians whose dangerous intentions could be gauged from their inappropriate ecclesiastical views. Charles James Fox indeed introduced the motion to repeal the Acts in 1790. Because the Test and Corporation Acts had survived the 1710s, Anglican prerogatives and privileges had become an apparently permanent feature of the Whig state (they were not repealed until 1828), and pressure for repeal came to denote opposition to the dominant system. George's attitude therefore helped to focus Dissenter criticism. Animosity between Anglicanism and Dissent was an important political axis, and it became stronger during the reign, in part in the shadow of a more prominent Unitarianism which increased Anglican concerns.[55] This animosity extended to Ireland, of which George wrote in 1776, 'I can easily believe the Presbyterians ready for any mischief'.[56]

George's interest in the Church reached overseas, where the spread of an Anglican presence was encouraged. An Anglican bishopric for Nova Scotia was created in 1787, while, four years later, an Act provided large endowments to support the Church in Upper Canada. George also supported the Naval and Military Bible Society, as well as the Society for the Propagation of the Gospel, and his religious and Hanoverian interests

---

[52] Memorandum by ?Sir Robert Wilson, Aspinall, *Prince of Wales*, V, 113.

[53] G.M. Ditchfield, 'Church, Parliament and National Identity, *c.* 1770–*c.* 1830', in J. Hoppit (ed.), *Parliaments, Nations and Identities in Britain and Ireland, 1660–1850* (Manchester, 2003), p. 66.

[54] George to Pitt, 15 May 1805, PRO. 30/8/104 fol. 447.

[55] K. Haakonssen (ed.), *Enlightenment and Religion: Rational Dissent in Eighteenth-Century Britain* (Cambridge, 1996).

[56] George to Robinson, 3 Oct. 1776, BL. Add. 37833 fol. 71.

coincided in his support for the German Protestant Mission to the East Indies. This concern was very much in line with a powerful current in British religiosity. The Baptist Missionary Society was founded in 1792, the London Missionary Society in 1795 and the Church Missionary Society in 1799.

George also maintained the concern of his two predecessors with the position of Protestants in Europe, although less so than they had done, in part because the confessional situation was less bitter. Secker recorded in 1760 that he

> took the same opportunity of being with the King in his Closet to recommend to him the continuance of his predecessors' bounty to the French Protestants and Vaudois [in Savoy–Piedmont] . . . and to recommend also, that he would endeavour to procure at making a peace the release of the French Protestants committed to the gallies for their religion; which I said I had mentioned to the late King, who answered that I might name it to him again when a peace was nearer. The present King made the same answer as to that point: and said as to the others, that he was very desirous to support the Protestant cause and very willing to give money to the charity, because that was doing good with it.[57]

The combination of religious, dynastic and Hanoverian concerns led George to display concern about the situation in Hesse-Cassel, where his uncle by marriage, Frederick II (r. 1760–85), had converted to Catholicism. George's aunt, Mary, and her sons relied on the protection of first George II and then George III, also receiving an annuity from parliament.[58]

George's notion of a Christian kingdom was ably captured at Weymouth on Sunday, 4 August 1805, when the recently born eldest son of the fifth earl of Chesterfield (with whom George often hunted) was, after Sunday service at Weymouth church, christened George by the bishop of Bristol, George Pelham, being named after his sponsor, the king.

Personal piety and a conviction about appropriate behaviour for the head of the Church contributed to George's serious and persistent clash with his heir. More generally, religion and religious observance were a major difference between George and Charlotte on the one hand and their sons on the other, and also a focus of the rebelliousness of the elder sons. George's desire that the royal family should be committed Christians, who set an example of correct behaviour, was both fruitless and the cause of political problems. George's sons did not appreciate sermons and soda

[57] Secker, memorandum, 24 Dec. 1760, Lambeth Palace Library, MS 1130/I fol. 35.
[58] Mary of Hesse-Cassel to Bute, 7 Aug. 1761, BL. Add. 36796 fol. 108.

water, nor indeed the banning of dice at court. Their actions, for example the prince of Wales, in 1784, threatening to economize by leaving the country, and, in 1796, pressing the king to keep the bailiffs away, seemed totally inappropriate to George. When criticizing the prince's conduct in 1785, George first mentioned 'his neglect of every religious duty'.[59]

George was religious, but the sacral nature of monarchy associated with the Stuarts – not least the touching for the 'king's evil' originally begun in 1058 but ended by George I, as well as the Stuart belief in the divine right of kings – was not revived. In particular, George was wary of the High Church tendencies associated with the memorialization of Charles I. He had criticized the royal martyr in an essay written as prince, and, as king, did not attend the sermons given on 30 January, the anniversary of the execution in 1649, although in 1772 George played a key role in blocking the proposal that the relevant state services be removed from the Prayer Book. This followed a contentious sermon by Thomas Nowell before the Commons defending the royal prerogative. He received no subsequent preferment. In 1795, lack of attendance led to the suspension of the 30 January parliamentary ceremony, but George had it revived in 1807 and, three years later, rejected the request of the prime minister, Spencer Perceval, an evangelical, for its abandonment.

High Churchmen found George's defence of continuity and orthodoxy an inspiration, and royal preferment was open to them on a scale not seen under his two predecessors, although few were promoted to high office, and George did not promote a 'party' of them. The University of Oxford was treated far better than under George I and George II, with North becoming its chancellor in 1772, and George the first Hanoverian monarch to visit the university in 1785,[60] a conspicuous sign of favour that was underlined when George returned in 1786. The higher reaches of the Church were not uninhibitedly thrown open to High Church Oxonians, but some, such as Lewis Bagot and George Horne, were preferred to sees. Although he never visited Cambridge, George was careful to be fair to both universities throughout his reign. George was visitor of Christ Church, and, characteristically, thought the education there preferable to that provided in Scotland, which at that time enjoyed a reputation for advanced and liberal ideas. When he visited Oxford in 1785, Christ Church was 'distinguished by marks of particular favour'.[61] The period of George's visitorship was one of remarkable calm when, in spite of the decline in achievement through the rest of the university, Christ Church reached possibly its greatest academic heights.

[59] George to Colonel Hotham, 21 June 1785, Aspinall, *George III*, I, 168.
[60] *Gentleman's Magazine*, 55 (1785), II, 827–8; *London Gazette*, 17 Sept. 1785.
[61] John Randolph to Thomas Lambard, 22 Sept. 1785, Bod., MSS Top. Oxon. D. 353/1 fol. 34.

As far as the limitation of sacral monarchy was concerned, George III consolidated the shift seen under George I. This was a major change in the symbolization of British monarchy, away from the sacred and magical. Thereafter, royal philanthropy was to be different in its character. Support for institutional provision and patronage would be the basis of the modern position of the monarchy, which established multiple contacts between the royal family and the public.[62] George, nevertheless, emphasized religious needs and goals in philanthropy alongside the more conventional secular ends. He succeeded his grandfather as patron of the Foundling Hospital, and added the Smallpox Hospital and the Jennerian Society. Alongside this institutionalization of care, George continued older practices, for example funding the annual Maundy ceremony.

George regarded piety as conducive to morality, and the latter as essential to appropriate conduct. This combination was important to him not only within the royal family but also as far as other spheres of public service were concerned. Officials and others were judged accordingly, and, if found acceptable, this was regarded as assisting in their advancement. In 1800, George wrote from Weymouth to George, second Earl Spencer, the first lord of the admiralty,

> I have received with infinite satisfaction Earl Spencer's information on the subject of Sir Allan Gardner, as I am certain there are few admirals that have more merit in the profession, and as private men none exceed him in the goodness of his heart, the manner in which he has received the offer of the appointment to the command of the Irish station is a strong proof of the latter.

There was also praise for Sir Henry Harvey, 'whose good temper and correct manner of doing his duty cannot fail of succeeding with the Earl of St. Vincent'.[63] Seeking Henry Addington's support against Catholic emancipation the following year, George wrote 'of the high regard I have for the uprightness of his private character'.[64]

George's moral tone and intentions were publicly criticized by those who doubted his intentions. A royal proclamation against vice, profaneness and immorality was issued in 1787.[65] However, in the *British Mercury* of

[62] F. Prochaska, *Royal Bounty: The Making of a Welfare Monarchy* (New Haven, 1995).

[63] George to Spencer, 12, 24 Aug. 1800, BL. Add. 75839.

[64] George to Addington, 29 Jan. 1801, Exeter 152M/C1801OR 39.

[65] J. Innes, 'Politics and Morals: The Reformation of Manners Movement in Later Eighteenth-Century England', in E. Hellmuth (ed.), *The Transformation of Political Culture: England and Germany in the Late Eighteenth Century* (Oxford, 1990), pp. 57–118; M.J.D. Roberts, *Making English Morals. Voluntary Association and Moral Reform in England, 1787–1886* (Cambridge, 2004).

23 June 1787, the radical John Oswald, in the persona of a Chinese philosopher, attacked the proclamation on the grounds that its goals included 'to check, and perhaps entirely overturn, under the specious pretence of suppressing licentious publications, the liberty of the press'.[66] Oswald, however, was an atypical figure compared to James, second earl of Fife, who, in 1783, sought personal reform, 'the Reformation within doors', rather than that of the constitution, specifically complaining about gambling and dissipation, and how they encouraged corruption.[67] The extent to which such views arose from religious considerations varied, but the king's concerns drew on a widespread (although far from universal) constituency of support.[68] It was one that focused on William Pitt the Younger after North's apostasy in allying with the 'reprobate' Charles James Fox in 1783.[69] George saw public conduct as at once collective and individual, and he was concerned about both. His awareness of public conduct stemmed from a variety of sources, including the newspapers he was anxious to keep reading in 1777.[70]

Concern about individual conduct underlay an interest in relieving debtors in order to provide them with an opportunity for a new start, but the king was concerned that the debtors, like those whose death sentences he commuted, should be deserving. He did not have an indiscriminate attitude towards charity. Debtors were relieved when he visited Portsmouth in 1773 and Worcester in 1788, and at Dorset County Jail in Dorchester in 1792 he discharged the debt owed by a poor cottager, William Pitfield, the inmate pointed out to him when he asked if there was any case of peculiar hardship. The action was brought to general attention when recorded in a 'Royal Beneficience' painting by Thomas Stothard, which was then engraved by Charles Hodges.[71] On the occasion of his Jubilee on 25 October 1809, George gave £2,000 from his privy purse to the Society for the Relief of Persons confined for small debts. Others were also the recipients of royal charity. Touring the infirmary on a visit to Gloucester in 1788, George left a donation of £50.

Propriety was a key term of praise from the king.[72] Decorum was expected by George in both public and private life, and attracted his

---

[66] D.V. Erdman, 'Grub Street behind the Skirts of Margaret Nicholson', *Factotum*, 12 (July 1981), p. 27.

[67] Fife to William Rose, 12 Apr. 1783, A. and H. Taylor (eds), *Lord Fife and his Factor* (London, 1925), p. 158.

[68] *Leeds Mercury*, 13 Nov. 1787.

[69] Robert Wharton to Brand, 5 May 1783, Durham UL. Wharton papers, no. 223.

[70] Donne (ed.), *Correspondence of King George the Third with Lord North*, II, 85.

[71] R.G. Bartelot, 'King George III's Visit to Dorchester Gaol', *Somerset and Dorset Notes and Queries*, 17 (1921), pp. 29–30.

[72] E.g. George to Sydney, 27 Apr. 1785, Aspinall, *George III*, I, 157.

approbation: 'The respect due to the memory of so reputable a character as that of the late Countess of Holdernesse makes the intention of Lord Pelham [her son-in-law] of not appearing in public till after the funeral highly proper.'[73] In 1793, Henry Dundas was congratulated on his recent marriage, his wife, Lady Jean Hope, being praised on the grounds of 'the good character' she had always borne[74] (his first marriage had ended in divorce). George's correspondence makes it clear that he favoured those whose demeanour suggested seriousness and whose behaviour was appropriate. This extended to those who were not political supporters, such as Frederick Montagu, a Rockinghamite lawyer who advocated the relief of Protestant Dissenters and was active against the war in America. Yet George described him as 'the calm honest man I have ever taken him to be' and wrote of him as showing 'the same temper of mind that has made me respect him'.[75] George also saw personal merit as important to royal charity and his interest survives in his correspondence:

> The King approves of Lord Pelham's recommendation of Mr. William Denman . . . to be a Poor Knight of St. George's Chapel in Windsor Castle, as distressed gentlemen and of good morals are the persons for whom this endowment was originally intended.[76]

A determination for decorum, however, led to a lack of tolerance for others, most obviously John Wilkes, Charles James Fox, and George, prince of Wales, all of whom were seen as irresponsible rakes with dangerous political views. In 1791, George refused to receive Elizabeth, Lady Craven (1750–1828). Separated because her husband had found her involved with the French envoy, Elizabeth, a noted traveller, found it convenient to spend much time out of Britain; although she was the daughter of an earl, George was not willing to receive her at court. She had met Christian, margrave of Ansbach (1736–1806), a relative of the king, both through his grandmother, Caroline of Ansbach, the wife of George II, who was the sister of Christian's grandfather, William Frederick of Ansbach, as well as through Christian's Prussian mother. Christian and Elizabeth lived together until her husband's death in 1791 allowed her to marry him. The margrave abdicated and sold his principality to Frederick William II of Prussia in 1792 and they moved to England. George was unsympathetic, typically adding the issue of precedence:

[73] George to Pelham, 19 Oct. 1801, BL. Add. 33115 fol. 22.
[74] George to Dundas, 7 Apr. 1793, BL. Add. 40100 fol. 75.
[75] George to Robinson, 6 Sept. 1780, BL. Add. 70990; George to North, 25 Oct. 1780, Fortescue, V, 143.
[76] George to Pelham, 25 Sept. 1801, BL. Add. 33115 fol. 15.

The strange step the Margrave of Ansbach has taken of marrying Lady Craven makes it necessary for me to be explicit on that business previous to my receiving him; I therefore desire Lord Grenville will see Count Redern and express my willingness of seeing the Margrave . . . not . . . receiving that Lady, which he must feel that the misfortunes in my own family and my declining receiving Countess Hohenheim when brought here three years since by the Duke of Wirtemberg who had married her renders impossible.[77]

George's prohibition did not stop British society as a whole from recognizing Elizabeth as margravine. After the margrave died in 1806, Elizabeth left the country, eventually dying in Naples in 1828. Countess Hohenheim was Franziske Theresia von Bernerdin, who became lover to Duke Carl Eugen of Württemberg in 1770. At this point both were still married: Carl Eugen to his estranged wife, Elisabeth of Bayreuth (who, in turn, was related to the Ansbach branch of the Hohenzollerns), and Franziske to Freiherr Friedrich Wilhelm Reinhard von Leutrum. She divorced Leutrum in 1772, but was named as the guilty party. The Emperor Joseph II raised her to Reichsgräfin von Hohenheim in 1773, but refused Carl Eugen's request to make her a princess. She married the duke in 1785. He was the uncle of the Frederick William of Württemberg who married George's eldest daughter in 1797.

A concern with decorum also affected George's treatment of diplomats. In 1792 he expressed his preference for the continued presence of the long-serving Swedish envoy, Gustav Adolf, Baron Nolken, as 'the person intended to succeed the Baron is a gentleman of very indifferent character and not one that could be agreeable here'.[78] Uprightness and decorum were also seen by George as important in foreign policy, not least in relations with those, such as Napoleon, who he felt lacked them.[79] Decorum was at issue in George's response to parliament. In May 1784, he praised a speech by William Pitt the Younger because it did not 'run into that rudeness which though common in that House certainly never becomes a gentleman; if he proceeds in this mode of oratory he will bring debates into a shape more creditable and correct.'[80] The note of improvability was a characteristic one.

A bleaker side of his concern with uprightness and decorum was shown in George's support for the moral strictures and penalties of society, although, in providing this, the king, as with his other views, was very

[77] George to William Grenville, 19 Dec. 1791, BL. Add. 58856 fol. 125.
[78] George to William Grenville, 29 Sept. 1792, BL. Add. 58857 fol. 41.
[79] George to William Grenville, 30 July 1796, BL. Add. 58859 fol. 69; George to Hawkesbury, 1 Oct. 1801, 29 Aug. 1802, BL. Loan 72/1.
[80] George to Pitt, 26 May 1784, PRO. 30/8/103 fol. 105.

much a figure of his time. Homosexual acts in the navy earned his condemnation:

> There cannot be a doubt of the propriety of the sentence of the court martial on the two seamen of the *St. George* for the commission of a most detestable and unnatural crime. Earl Spencer is therefore to give the proper order for its being enforced.[81]

Not a great believer in mercy, unless there was a particular reason, George could also be fairly firm with offences against property. William Dodd, a former royal chaplain, was denied a pardon in 1777 and was executed for fraud. In June 1790, the king decided that the law should take its course in the case of three men convicted of a burglary: 'White not having been known to have been guilty of any offense is not sufficient reason when his guilt in this instance has been so clearly proved'.[82] A proportion of George's surviving correspondence deals with his role in supporting execution for, or pardoning, convicted felons.[83] The correspondence reveals George as conscientious and firm.[84] George was also critical of suicides. He saw suicide, which was understood as a rejection of divine grace, as 'so unnatural a crime', and 'a strong symptom of insanity', and expressed his horror at 'the dreadful step'.[85]

In these, as in other attitudes, George was not out of line with a dominant ethos that treated religion, conduct and morality not as private activities outside the ken of public supervision, but as matters of concern and control. Again, the king was expressing the commonplace view that for conduct to be moral it had to be motivated by religious faith, and that crime therefore represented a defiance of divine guidance that required admonition. Unless he took this view, George would be failing in his duty. This was a heavy duty, and one that George found increasingly difficult to undertake optimistically. Referring in 1802 to those who were to be transported to Australia, George reflected: 'as to the reforming the morals of those who have deserved that punishment the King from now a long experience is not sanguine in expectations on that head'.[86] As in other matters, experience confirmed George's existing dispositions. Two years later, he argued that 'undue lenity' in the treatment of prisoners of war 'degenerates easily into a gross neglect of duty'.[87]

---

[81] George to Spencer, 17 Dec. 1800, BL. Add. 75839.
[82] George to William Grenville, 29 June 1790, BL. Add. 58855 fol. 127.
[83] E.g. Joseph Harrison to Richard Farrer, 3 Apr., George to Rockingham, – Apr. 1766, WW. R1–593, 605.
[84] Twiss, I, 399.
[85] George to William Grenville, 1 June 1793, BL. Add. 58857 fol. 121.
[86] George to Pelham, 7 Mar. 1802, BL. Add. 33115 fol. 56.
[87] George to Hawkesbury, 18 May 1804, BL. Loan 72/1 fol. 120.

The wayward behaviour of his brothers and sons similarly was, for George, a matter of far more than inappropriate conduct and royal embarrassment. This very behaviour showed that George's views were not shared by all in the élite, but others also sought the assistance of 'the Hand of God'[88] in order to save the country. Morality was linked to political conduct and goals, as when George, seeing opposition in 1780 in terms of idleness, expressed his preference for North letting business

> come forward as soon as possible, and keep Parliament constantly employed whilst assembled, instead of frequently from a wish of putting off the evil of deciding, leaving the House idle which always encourages Opposition to run into speculative matters that ever tend to sap the constitution.[89]

George's emphasis on the desirability of moral behaviour was not the imposition of piety on an amoral, secular culture, but the bringing together of two powerful currents: the ideal of a Christian people led by a Christian king, and the need to ensure that society and the common good was preserved from the inroads of corruption. Indeed the centrality of corruption to much of the political language of George's early years is important to an understanding of his views. Rather than adopting the twentieth-century notion of an obsessive personality requiring order,[90] it is more helpful to see George as emphasizing duty for himself and others in the face of sin and corruption. The ability to heed the call of duty was necessary not only for the king but also for his subjects if they were to avoid a fall into savagery, a view that brought together Christian notions of sinfulness, Patriot anxieties about corruptibility, and anthropological assessments of a hierarchical differentiation of peoples. At a time of disturbances about grain prices in 1766, George fulminated, 'if a due obedience to law and the submitting to that as the only just method of having grievances removed does not once more become the characteristic of this nation, we shall soon be no better than the savages in America. Then we shall be as much despised by all civilized nations as we are as yet revered for our excellent constitution.'[91] In 1780 he referred to 'the strange, wild and wicked conduct of Opposition'.[92]

George's concern with morality appeared particularly appropriate in the 1780s, as the political crisis stemming from the American war was widely regarded as encapsulating a more profound failure of public

---

[88] Morton Eden to his brother William, 31 Oct. 1784, BL. Add. 34419 fol. 425.
[89] George to Robinson, 22 Sept. 1780, BL. Add. 70990.
[90] J.H. Plumb, *New Light on the Tyrant George III* (Washington, D.C., 1978).
[91] George to Conway, 20 Sept. 1766, Fortescue, I, 394.
[92] George to Jenkinson, 14 Apr. 1780, BL. Loan 72/1 fol. 39.

culture that, in turn, led to discussion of Britain in terms of the rise, and now fall, of empires. The popularity of Edward Gibbon's *History of the Decline and Fall of the Roman Empire* (1776–88) contributed to this. The person best placed to stem 'depravity'[93] was the king, but even he felt challenged by the workings of Providence. The French Revolution and the 'wicked principles'[94] it propagated brought this challenge into renewed focus. Clear in his own mind about the need to defend religion, society and the rights of independent states,[95] George rarely expressed doubts, but, in 1793, he wrote to William Grenville,

> I am sorry though not surprised that the cruel wretches who have possessed themselves of power in France have ordered the unhappy Queen Mother to be tried, the result of which can be most easily conceived. To a man who looks on the conduct of those savages with the rational eye Lord Grenville does, it must be equal surprise as with me what lengths Divine Providence will permit them to go, and I am certain he has been equally choaked with me at their blasphemous comparison in the National Assembly on Marat.[96]

Five years later, George greeted misleading news of French defeat more characteristically, by reflecting that the defeat

> must in the opinion of every religious mind appear the interposition of Divine Providence against that wicked nation, and ought to rouse every European power to step forth in defence of everything that is dear to them.[97]

---

[93] *Daily Universal Register*, 4 Jan. 1785.

[94] George to William Grenville, 28 Dec. 1796, BL. Add. 58859 fol. 112. Cf. e.g. 15 Jan., 12 May 1798, 26 May 1799, 58860 fols 50, 91, 58861 fol. 38.

[95] George to William Grenville, 1 Dec. 1797, BL. Add. 58860 fol. 33.

[96] George to William Grenville, 11 Aug. 1793, BL. Add. 58857 fol. 141. The Revolutionary leader Marat had been assassinated.

[97] George to William Grenville, 14 Dec. 1798, BL. Add. 58860 fol. 138.

1 *George III* by Allan Ramsay (1761–2). The state portrait of the King in coronation robes. This was a much-reproduced painting, over 150 copies are known.

2 *George, Prince of Wales (later George III)* by Jean-Etienne Liotard (1754). Commissioned by his mother, Augusta, this pastel portrait of the sixteen-year-old George captures his looks at this period and also the rich clothes a prince could wear.

3 *George III, Queen Charlotte and their six eldest children* by Johan Zoffany (1770). Deliberately looking back to Van Dyck's work, this painting links the dynasty to its Stuart predecessors. George III himself was keen on Van Dyck and bought his *Five Eldest Children of Charles I* in 1765.

4 *George III* by Johan Zoffany (1771). Exhibited at the Royal Academy, this portrait was seen as a very good likeness. The king, wearing the general officer's coat and the Garter, is presented as ready for action.

5 *Windsor Castle: The King's Audience Chamber* by Charles Wild (1818). George began to refurbish his Windsor apartments from the 1770s, his architect William Chambers playing a key role. George's concern with the Garter was seen in the paintings for this room produced by Benjamin West which depicted scenes from the life of Edward III, the founder of the Order.

6 *Buckingham House: The Staircase* by James Stephanoff (1818). In 1795 the staircase was transformed so that the initial central flight divided at a half landing and then returned in two final flights – a dramatic approach.

7 *Buckingham House: The Saloon* by James Stephanoff (1818). The largest room in Buckingham House, the saloon was decorated in this fashion from 1787, while the furnishings were supplied in 1799. Formal receptions could be held here rather than in St James's Palace.

8 *Queen Charlotte* by Allan Ramsay (*c*.1762–4). Charlotte wearing her coronation robes.

9 *Princess Amelia in 1807* by Andrew Robertson (1811). Appointed miniature painter to the Duke of Sussex in 1805, Robertson was commissioned to paint portraits of the duke's sisters. George III commissioned a replica when Amelia was dying of tuberculosis in 1810.

10 *The Prince of Wales* by Richard Cosway (*c.*1793). The Prince's patronage of Cosway, his principal painter, reflected the extent to which the Prince created an alternative source of cultural activity to that of his father.

11 *George III returning from Hunting* by Matthew Dubourg, after James Polland (1820). Depicting a scene earlier in George's life, this print captures one of George's preferred leisure activities and also suggests the (limited) accessibility hunting gave rise to. Windsor Castle is in the background.

12 *John Bull Ground Down* by James Gillray (1795). George III's rise in popularity in the 1790s was scarcely challenged by that of his son. This caricature was a response to the marriage of the prince to Caroline of Brunswick. The British public is shown being ground into money to pay off the prince's debts with William Pitt the Younger turning the handle.

13 *Affability* by James Gillray (1795). George III presented as 'Farmer George' visiting one of the farms on his Windsor estate. George was a keen and knowledgeable visitor of farms, and was better able than most contemporary monarchs to make contact with his subjects. He is shown with Queen Charlotte.

14 Shortly before it became common knowledge that George III was seriously ill, William Dent produced this caricature of the opposition Whigs seeking to overthrow the Constitution. George was thus presented in favourable terms, in marked contrast to James II who had been overthrown in 1688.

15 *The Surrender of Amsterdam, or The Duke of Brunswick in a Bustle* by James Gillray (1787). George III's brother-in-law routing republican opponents, in a classic display of princely activity.

16 *Taming of the Shrew* by James Gillray (1791). Gillray's caricature was a response to the confrontation with Catherine the Great over the Ochakov Crisis. In the event, Britain backed away from war, although George continued to be a marked critic of Russia.

17 *George III* by Joseph Nollekens (1773). George supported the appointment of Nollekens as a Fellow of the Royal Academy in 1772 by commissioning a bust. Nollekens made more money from his busts of Pitt and Fox.

Chapter 11

WAR WITH AMERICA

Good kings have sometimes been made tyrants by finding their mild
government insulted. Confidence between King and people, as between
man and wife, is the strongest bond of fidelity.

Elizabeth Montagu, 1762[1]

George never crossed the Atlantic, an omission regretted by his descendant
Prince Charles in 1972 and again in 2004,[2] although at the bicentenary of
Yorktown in 1981 the prince gave a modest speech along the lines of 'if we
had to lose, we are glad it was to you'. It would have been a lengthy
journey for George, and no other European monarch, including Louis
XVI and Charles III of Spain, visited overseas colonies; although, had he
had any, Joseph II of Austria would probably have done: he travelled over
30,000 miles, spending a quarter of his life travelling and using his journeys to gather detailed knowledge. Furthermore, in the length of time
George II spent in Hanover in 1736, George III could easily have got to
Boston, New York or Philadelphia, and back; due to the introduction of
the helm wheel soon after 1700, journey times across the Atlantic had
become shorter and more predictable.[3]

A visit, however, might not have greatly helped matters. Instead, it could
have inflamed feelings, especially in New England where there was considerable opposition to the prospect of a resident Anglican bishop. George's
determination to maintain royal authority certainly played a major role in
the crisis in relations with the American colonies that led to revolution
there in 1775. Already, in the Stamp Act crisis of 1765–6 (see pp. 81–5),
George had been 'more and more grieved at the accounts from America.
Where this spirit will end is not to be said; it is undoubtedly the most
serious matter that ever came before Parliament. It requires more deliber-
ation, candour and temper than I fear it will meet with.'[4] George had also

---

[1] Elizabeth Montagu to earl of Bath, 4 Sept. 1762, HL. MO. 4539.
[2] Foreword to J. Brooke, *King George III* (London, 1972), p. ix.
[3] I.K. Steele, *The English Atlantic 1675–1740. An Exploration of Communication and Community*
(Oxford, 1986).
[4] BL. E.g. 982, fol. 12.

been unenthusiastic about the Rockingham ministry's compromise that defused the crisis in 1766: an abandonment of the tax, albeit with the contentious insistence, by a Declaratory Act, on the principle of parliamentary sovereignty. Furthermore, George's moves within Britain had already helped to spawn a critical political literature that condemned his alleged despotic attitudes and policies, a literature that influenced the American response to successive ministerial plans to increase American revenues or to maintain control in the colonies. Nevertheless, the enthusiasm in the American colonies that had greeted George's accession had not collapsed rapidly. The dissemination of Bolingbroke's ideas, which included colonial editions of his *Letters on the Spirit of Patriotism* in 1749 and 1756, had had a powerful impact in North America from the 1750s, and George's accession focused and stimulated it. John Adams thought that George's declarations contained 'sentiments worthy of a King – a Patriot King'.[5]

At the same time, there was widespread colonial concern with the attempts of the British government after the Seven Years War to reform the workings of empire and, at least partly, to seek an imperial solution for the accumulated debts of war. Already, in November 1762, the duke of Bedford had linked agreement on the peace terms with France to the opportunity, and need, to focus on American affairs:

> I most heartily wish that this event may so far strengthen the hands of administration, as to enable the King to carry most effectually into execution such plans of government, as the great increase of territory in America, and the present circumstances of the rest of his dominions may require for the good of his people harassed by a long, bloody and expensive war.[6]

George had been more concerned with the security of the new acquisitions (Canada from France and Florida from Spain), arguing, in February 1763, that 10,000 troops should be stationed in North America to protect it in the event of a new war with France. He made no reference to the use of troops to overawe the older colonies, but he came to support his ministers' views that the colonists should pay for their security, a measure seen as necessary in order to respond to the concerns of British Tory politicians about the allocation of such a force, not least due to the cost. Yet George and Bute failed to appreciate the likely risks of this legislation in North America, and also ignored the views of experienced British ministers:

---

[5] W.D. Liddle, '"A Patriot King, or None": Lord Bolingbroke and the American Renunciation of George III', *Journal of American History*, 65 (1979), pp. 951–70; L.M. Butterfield, L.C. Faber and W.D. Garrett (eds), *Diary and Autobiography of John Adams* (4 vols, Cambridge, 1961), I, 200–1.

[6] Bedford to Bute, 16 Nov. 1762, MS, papers from Cardiff Public Library, 5/162.

Newcastle felt that the planned force was too large and therefore overly expensive, while Legge was concerned about the extension of ministerial power.[7]

This specific measure and, more generally, the increased interest that British politicians took in the country's imperial position were unwelcome to many colonists. Yet George's reputation was initially unaffected. Instead, unpopular measures, whether those of colonial governors or of the ministry in London, were blamed on evil ministers, an approach that readily interacted with the cult of the Patriot King. Here, apparently, was another iteration of the pernicious overawing of George II by Sir Robert Walpole. The Stamp Act crisis was seen in this light and the dismissal of George Grenville in 1765 interpreted as a welcome release by, and of, the king, one, indeed, that showed him as more successful than George II. This was underlined when the new Rockingham ministry appointed by the king repealed the Stamp Act. The subsequent celebrations were characterized by praise of George.

Indeed, this was an instance in which transatlantic distance helped the king, for it ensured that little was known in North America about his views and role. Furthermore, the ministry–crown duality apparently provided a context within which further controversies could, and would, be viewed. Unwelcome legislation, such as the Townshend duties of 1767, could be blamed on a parliament corrupted by the ministry, and a notion of the, in effect, contrast between the branches of government – ministry in parliament versus crown – was linked to a sense of the division of sovereignty. Limited criticism of George appeared before 1774, and the king was not blamed for the failings of the ministry. This again was a view that proximity rendered difficult in Britain.

Support for the Wilkesite cause existed in America,[8] but it did not translate there into a full-scale assault on George. Wilkes's blasphemy and the violence associated with his supporters did not recommend the cause to many Americans. News about Wilkes in the comparatively well-developed American press,[9] however, was extensive, and certainly fostered the sense that the British political system was unsuccessful, if not pernicious. General Thomas Gage, the commander-in-chief in North America, observed to the secretary at war in 1772, 'Your papers are stuffed

[7] J. Bullion, '"The Ten Thousand in America": More Light on the Decision on the American Army, 1762–1763', *William and Mary Quarterly*, 3rd ser. 43 (1986), pp. 646–57, esp. pp. 651–2, and 'Security and Economy: The Bute Administration's Plans for the American Army and Revenue, 1762–1763', 45 (1988), pp. 499–509, esp. 507.

[8] S.F. Duff, 'The Case against the King: The *Virginia Gazettes* Indict George III', *William and Mary Quarterly*, 6 (1949), pp. 383–97; P. Maier, 'John Wilkes and American Disillusionment with Britain', *William and Mary Quarterly*, 20 (1963), pp. 373–95.

[9] C.E. Clark, *The Public Prints. The Newspaper in Anglo-American Culture* (Oxford, 1994).

with infamous paragraphs which the American printers, especially those of Boston, seldom fail to copy with American additions.' Two years later, he added from Boston, 'The seditious here have raised a flame in every colony which your speeches, writings, and protests in England have greatly encouraged.'[10]

By 1774, George's reputation in North America was indeed under great pressure; this was due not so much to the impact in America of the domestic British critique of his supposed autocratic policies as to the actual measures being followed in America in order to sustain the furthering of the integrated imperial policy. Specifically, the British government had found its authority at issue because of the measures it took to strengthen the empire by influencing relations between its parts. These measures focused on trade, more particularly tea. Far from proving a cash cow, the viability of the conquests in India, and indeed of the entire position of the East India Company, was challenged by the combination of dividend demands by the company's shareholders, the costs of defence, the difficulties of revenue collection in India, and weakness in the market for tea, a major source of company finances. This hit governmental fiscal expectations, particularly when the company sought both the rescheduling of customs payments and a loan.[11] Tea imports into North America apparently offered a way to tackle company finances, as well as to provide, through import duties, a means of paying the salaries of colonial officials, thus ending their dependence on the colonial assemblies, a measure seen as particularly threatening by many colonists. The tea duty had been retained in 1769 (on a cabinet vote of five to four)[12] when the other duties introduced by Charles Townshend in 1767 were repealed, a conciliatory measure George approved. The tea duty symbolized parliament's right to tax, and public finances benefited from this duty, a key point, not least because the American boycott of British imports, introduced in 1768, failed in 1770.[13]

Smuggled Dutch tea, however, challenged company sales, and in 1773 the government passed a Tea Act that abolished British duties on the tea re-exported to America and allowed the company to sell its tea directly to consignees to the American colonies, a measure designed to cut the cost of tea there and thus boost sales. The Americans would still have to pay duty on the imported tea. This was condemned by Patriot activists, who were unwilling to accept parliament's right to impose direct taxes on the

[10] Gage to Viscount Barrington, 2 Sept. 1772, 18 July 1774, BL. Add. 73550.

[11] H.V. Bowen, *Revenue and Reform. The Indian Problem in British Politics 1757–1773* (Cambridge, 1991).

[12] P.D.G. Thomas, *George III. King and Politicians 1760–1770* (Manchester, 2002), p. 206.

[13] P.D.G. Thomas, *The Townshend Duties: Crisis: The Second Phase of the American Revolution, 1767–1773* (Oxford, 1987).

colonies and concerned about the political implications of a greater governmental revenue in America. Opposition culminated in the Boston Tea Party on 16 December 1773, when the Sons of Liberty, led by Samuel Adams, seized 340 chests of tea from three ships in Boston harbour and threw it into the water. Colonial protesters had fashioned a powerful symbol of resistance. A fresh non-importation movement directed against Britain followed in 1774–6.

The Boston Tea Party dramatized the breakdown of imperial authority for at least some of the colonists, a breakdown that was the first stage of a more general collapse in European control in the New World. Rather, however, than seeing this as suggesting an inevitable clash, it is necessary to underline the continued similarities between the societies of Britain and British North America, and also the colonists' sense of themselves as British. It is also important to explain why the process of reaching, and endlessly redefining, a consensus that underlay and often constituted government in this period, broke down; and also to consider why this process did not break down for the large numbers of colonists who remained loyal.

The origins of the American Revolution looked back to seventeenth-century British traditions of resistance to unreasonable royal demands, and, in some respects, it was a second version of the Civil War of the 1640s, and a war of religion. In this, non-Anglicans played the key role in resistance, while the principal source of support within the colonies for royal authority came from Anglicans; and George's support for authority and order was seen in large part, by both him and others, as influenced by religious considerations. Many colonists resisted parliament's efforts to project its sovereign authority across the Atlantic; these efforts, however, were seen as natural in Britain in order to secure the coherence of the empire. The debate over the terms of the empire that grew out of the Seven Years War had become, in North America, an effort to limit the exercise of state power by defining and asserting the natural and constitutional rights of individuals and groups within the body politic. These disagreements over the colonial bond cut to the core of the nature of the empire, which was that of a reciprocal benefit controlled by the state, as expressed through the sovereignty of parliament. This understanding of empire was challenged by autonomous tendencies in the colonies, that, in turn, led to uneasiness in the metropole. Joseph Yorke, a well-connected diplomat and MP, remarked in 1763, 'I cannot bear the thought of the North Americans selling powder to the savages to murder the King's troops whilst they look on', a reference to Pontiac's War.[14]

Tension also arose from other developments within the colonies, including the disruptive consequences of rapid population growth, as well

---

[14] Yorke to Edward Weston, 25 Oct. 1763, BL. Add. 58213 fol. 308.

as the Great Awakening in Protestant religious consciousness. One result of the former was that the relative share of the colonial population in the British empire increased, but without any comparable increase in the fiscal support provided by the colonists. The Great Awakening, a powerful revival movement, ensured that rumours about the possible establishment of an Anglican episcopacy in North America, in contrast to the previous position in which George II had denied a bishop to America, were greeted with strong hostility by the large number of non-Anglicans. Protestant concerns made the granting of rights to French-speaking Catholics under the Quebec Act of 1774 a matter of particular sensitivity, as it compromised notions of Protestant nationhood and threatened American opportunities to expand west of the Appalachians. More generally, there were challenges to established patterns and practices of authority and social influence, and these necessarily involved the prestige and authority of the crown. This was certainly true of opposition in Massachusetts to Thomas Hutchinson, the governor, in the early 1770s.[15]

Nevertheless, the American Revolution occurred not because of a general desire to fight for liberty, but rather as a hesitant, if not unwilling, response on the part of many to the confused tergiversations of British policy. These policy changes, which arose as remedies for the fiscal burden of imperial defence, were sought by the British government in the context of heavy national indebtedness, the policy changes apparently pointing the way to new forms of imperial governance. This led in the colonies to a pervasiveness and depth of alienation that was underrated in Britain, at least by the government, or that was misleadingly seen as restricted to a few troublemakers.

Meeting George on 1 July 1774, Hutchinson recorded that the king had 'so perfect a knowledge of the state of his dominions'.[16] This, however, was not the same as an appreciation of their dynamics. More generally, a lack of understanding of American colonial society and aspirations on the part of the imperial government, not least George and North, played a major role in the developing crisis. America was less well understood than Ireland. George did not grasp the degree to which the individual colonies were joining together in response to successive crises, making joint action on their part increasingly an option. This failure of appreciation was exacerbated in 1774 by the view that concessions would be seen as weakness, and lead only to fresh demands. The legislation of that year, the Coercive or Intolerable Acts, terms used to describe what were unpopular laws, was

---

[15] D.C. Lord and R.M. Calhoon, 'The Removal of the Massachusetts General Court from Boston, 1769–1772', *Journal of American History*, 55 (1969), pp. 735–55.

[16] P.O. Hutchinson (ed.), *The Diary and Letters of His Excellency Thomas Hutchinson* (2 vols, New York, 1971), I, 159. On Hutchinson, B. Bailyn, *The Ordeal of Thomas Hutchinson* (Cambridge, Massachusetts, 1974).

designed to provide exemplary punishment and a remedy for disorder, and stemmed from a belief that the latter arose from the actions of a small number, rather than from widespread disaffection; in short that conspiracy and agitation were at issue, not revolution. Of the Coercive Acts, the Boston Port Act – closing the port and moving the customs house for overseas trade until the East India Company was reimbursed for the tea – was designed to protect trade and customs officials from harassment; the Massachusetts Charter Act to strengthen the executive, particularly by reducing the elective character of the legislature; and the Administration of Justice and Quartering Acts to make it easier to enforce order.

These measures struck colonists across the Thirteen Colonies as an infringement of charter rights that threatened the liberties of all colonies,[17] and were criticized by the opposition in Britain as excessive, but they were passed in parliament by overwhelming majorities. The Boston Port Bill was unopposed in parliament, and the opposition motion to repeal the tea duty was defeated in the House of Commons by 182 votes to 49. George, who was pleased by the Coercive Acts, was delighted by parliament's backing for the legislation. Furthermore, parliament was dissolved a year earlier than was made necessary by the Septennial Act, partly to capitalize in the general election on the popularity of the Coercive Acts in Britain. American issues played only a modest role in the general election, which sustained the position of the North ministry.[18]

Nevertheless, the situation was deteriorating, with increasing hostility in the colonies to British authority. More troops were sent to Massachusetts, while General Thomas Gage, was appointed governor of the colony and ordered to use force to restore royal authority, a significant militarization of policy. Shocked by the Boston Tea Party, the king supported the firm line, as he saw the status quo as no longer an option, matters as beyond compromise, and leniency as destructive of order and good government. The collapse of authority seemed to threaten Britain's position as a great power. In September 1774, George wrote to North, 'the die is now cast, the colonies must either submit or triumph', adding, two months later, 'The New England governments are in a state of rebellion ... blows must decide whether they are to be subject to this country or independent'.[19] New England was seen as the centre of opposition and the focus for government action; and the extent of opposition elsewhere was minimized,

[17] D. Ammerman, *In the Common Cause: American Response to the Coercive Acts of 1774* (Charlottesville, 1974).

[18] P.D.G. Thomas, 'George III and the American Revolution', *History*, 70 (1985), pp. 16–31, and *Tea Party to Independence: The Third Phase of the American Revolution, 1773–1776* (Oxford, 1991).

[19] George to North, 11 Sept., 18 Nov. 1774, Fortescue, III, 131, 153; R.L. Bushman, *King and People in Provincial Massachusetts* (Chapel Hill, North Carolina, 1985).

a view criticized in parliament in February 1775 by Edmund Burke, a vocal Rockinghamite Whig.[20] George was against any suspension of the Coercive Acts, a course pressed by Gage,[21] and thought that concessions would be seen as weakness. This conviction was strengthened by George's belief that the repeal of the Stamp Act in 1766 had caused many of the problems in North America,[22] and by the extent to which parliament supported firmness and the maintenance of its authority and the rule of law. There was no chance of the king following the advice of Thomas Jefferson, in his critical pamphlet *A Summary View of the Rights of British America* (1774), and vetoing parliamentary legislation that affected American rights and interests. Jefferson called on George to accept a theory of kingship that was actually in accordance with many of his assumptions, but to an end he could not accept:

> That these are our grievances which we have thus laid before his majesty, with that freedom of language and sentiment which becomes a free people claiming their rights, as derived from the laws of nature, and not as the gift of their chief magistrate. Let those flatter who fear; it is not an American art . . . kings are the servants, not the proprietors of the people. Open your breast, sire, to liberal and expanded thought. Let not the name of George the third be a blot in the page of history. You are surrounded by British counsellors, but remember that they are parties . . . It behoves you, therefore to think and to act for yourself and your people.[23]

Jefferson offered a view of the empire as a series of parts, each with rights, under the care of the crown. This was an approach that was also advocated by Irish patriots and by British radicals, such as John Cartwright.[24] It was to be taken up for the 'white' colonies in the nineteenth century, when the growth of 'responsible government' meant that colonial governors were henceforth to become politically 'responsible' to locally elected legislatures, rather than to London. Then, although the Colonial Laws Validity Act of 1865 declared colonial legislation that clashed with that from Westminster invalid, the Act was rarely invoked. Alongside signs of unity in action, such as, from 1887, the colonial and

---

[20] J. Flavell, 'British Perceptions of New England and the Decision for a Coercive Colonial Policy, 1774–1775', in Flavell and S. Conway (eds), *Britain and America Go to War. The Impact of War and Warfare in Anglo-America, 1754–1815* (Gainesville, Florida, 2005), pp. 108–9, 99.

[21] George to North, 18 Nov. 1774, Fortescue, III, 154.

[22] George to North, 4 Feb. 1774, Fortescue, III, 59.

[23] M. Jensen (ed.), *Tracts of the American Revolution* (2nd edn, Indianapolis, 2003), pp. 274–5.

[24] R.E. Tookey, *Liberty and Empire: British Radical Solutions to the American Problem 1774–1776* (Lexington, Kentucky, 1978).

imperial conferences, which helped give the Dominions a voice in imperial policy, there was also a recognition of self-government under the crown. An imperial conference in 1926 defined the Commonwealth as 'the group of self-governing communities composed of Great Britain and the Dominions', and this formed the basis for the Statute of Westminister (1931), which determined that Commonwealth countries could now amend or repeal 'any existing or future act of the United Kingdom Parliament . . . in so far as the same is part of the law of this Dominion'. A 'common allegiance to the Crown' was seen as characteristic of the 'freely associated members of the British Commonwealth of Nations'.

In a way this was what Jefferson meant when he urged George to 'deal out to all equal and impartial right', but such a system, let alone the republican monarchy proposed by John Adams in March 1775,[25] was scarcely politically practical in the 1770s. The Westminster parliament, and, indeed, many British ministers, would not have accepted an increase in royal power that would have stemmed from the king 'holding the balance' of the empire, as he arbitrated between its parts. To them, royal authority was a matter of the crown-in-parliament, and this could not be separated without loss to both, as a more powerful crown risked becoming a tyranny, and thus losing support and becoming weaker.[26] More generally, mutual suspicion, a product of a loss of the sense of political community between Britain and the American colonies, was a key problem.[27]

The Jeffersonian prospectus was also inappropriate, in that it implied that the same policies would not have been adopted had George been conscious of his duties to all his subjects. Instead, the king's view of the necessary interdependence of the empire was not one that was opposed to the government's fiscal policies. Furthermore, George's stress on the need for order and, in particular, on the importance of defending it when challenged, would have ensured problems in responding as the American Patriots wanted, whatever the role of parliament, and even if it was only a question of supporting existing authorities within the colonies. This was also to be true of Ireland in the 1790s, where the willingness of the United Irishmen to seek a federal relationship with Britain[28] flew in the face of the political realities of the Anglo-Irish relationship.

[25] R.A. Ryerson, 'John Adams, Republican Monarchist', in E.H. Gould and P.S. Onuf (eds), *Empire and Nation. The American Revolution in the Atlantic World* (Baltimore, 2005), pp. 76–7.

[26] J.G.A. Pocock, 'Empire, State and Confederation: The War of American Independence as a Crisis in Multiple Monarchy', in J. Robertson (eds), *A Union for Empire: Political Thought and the Union of 1707* (Cambridge, 1995), pp. 318–48.

[27] N. York, 'Federalism and the Failure of Imperial Reform, 1774–1775', *History*, 86 (2001), pp. 155–79.

[28] M. Elliott, *Partners in Revolution: The United Irishmen and France* (New Haven, Connecticut, 1982).

Eventually, the British government was to adopt the path of imperial conciliation. It did so unsuccessfully in America in 1778, when the Carlisle Commission was sent to try to negotiate a settlement, but successfully, at least in terms of defusing an immediate problem, in 1782–3, when British legislative authority was renounced in favour of the Dublin parliament. Similarly, in England in 1779, the legal position of Dissenters, which had not been eased in 1772–3, changed, when they were allowed to assent to the scriptures in order to become undergraduates or clerics, rather than having to subscribe to the Articles of the Church of England.[29] Although earlier compromises in the case of the American colonies were floated, it would have been difficult to win widespread support in America, and there was no consensus in Britain in favour of a compromise. In February 1775 North proposed that, in return for a colony being willing to provide for its defence and civil government, it would be exempt from parliamentary taxation. This, however, was an offer too late, as it was incompatible with the position of the Continental Congress, which had met in Philadelphia since the previous September. Though presenting itself as a loyal body, the congress claimed that the colonies should raise revenues as they thought appropriate, a rejection of parliament's right to legislate. Congress formally rejected North's proposal in July 1775.

The emptiness of the imperial ethos for many Americans had been revealed in paranoia and in symbolic and practical acts of defiance. In 1775, the spiral of violence ended in full-scale conflict, with the militarization of authority by the British government clashing with attempts by the Patriots to defy the latter. Fighting began on 19 April 1775, when the British tried to seize a cache of arms reported to be at Concord, a town 16 miles from Boston, past the village of Lexington. At the village, the troops found about seventy militia drawn up in two lines. Heavily outnumbered, the militia began to disperse, but a shot was fired – it is not clear by whom – and the British opened fire, scattering the militia. The shedding of blood outraged much of New England, and a substantial force, largely dependent on their own muskets, soon encircled Boston. Elsewhere in the Thirteen Colonies, British authority collapsed: due to the concentration of troops in Massachusetts, governors elsewhere were defenceless.

Although only a minority of colonists wished for independence at the outbreak of fighting, the strength of separatist feeling within this minority was such that compromise on terms acceptable to the British government appeared increasingly unlikely. Anything else was unacceptable to the bulk of the British political nation, although there was a significant tranche of support for conciliation.[30] With his emphasis on duty and a vigorous

[29] G.M. Ditchfield, 'The Subscription Issue in British Parliamentary Politics, 1772–1779', *Parliamentary History*, 7 (1988), pp. 62–5.

[30] J.E. Bradley, *Popular Politics and the American Revolution in England. Petitions, the Crown and Public Opinion* (Macon, 1986).

response, George did not offer a lead capable of challenging, let alone overturning, this inability to appreciate colonial viewpoints. He was scarcely going to heed the call in Burke's speech on conciliation, delivered on 22 March 1775, for 'magnanimity in politics', and, instead, interpreted 'the greatness of that trust to which the order of Providence has called us' very differently. The following month, George was unwilling to hear a pro-American petition from the Livery of London while sitting on the throne.[31] In response to the Olive Branch Petition, in which congress declared a wish to remain in the empire, but also underlined their conviction of the justness of their cause in protection of their constitutional liberties, George adopted the legalistic position of rejecting the petition because congress had no legal status and indeed was composed of rebels. This greatly helped undermine American moderates, who did not wish to move from resistance to independence, leaving them no alternative but war.

For George, it was a war not only for the authority of a sovereign parliament, 'the Battle of the Legislature' in his terms,[32] but also against the political and moral challenges of disorder. As discussed in Chapter 10, George was very concerned with what he saw as right and fair before God, and duty, legality and order were crucial to his politico-moral assumptions. They led him to oppose what he saw as a rebellion very different to that which had ended in the overthrow of James II and VII in 1688. In August 1775, a royal proclamation, which the king had pressed for, declared that George's American subjects were 'engaged in open and avowed rebellion'.[33] Not only American iniquity was involved. Richard Hurd, a favoured cleric, preaching a fast sermon before the House of Lords in December 1776, presented this rebellion as divine punishment for the sins of the British.

During the American War of Independence (1775–83), George sought to stiffen opposition to what he saw as rebellion. Whereas, prior to 1775, the colonists had tended to focus their hostility on ministers and parliament, correctly believing them largely responsible for unwelcome legislation, there was now a major shift, so that George was seen by the Americans as the cause of their problems. In a line-cut for Freebetter's *New England Almanack*, Nathan Daboll depicted America spewing back into George's face the tea he is pouring down her throat while she is held down, a powerful image of violated womanhood, as one of George's assistants lifts her skirt. Britannia, askance, turns away, a vivid rejection of George's earlier association with Patriotism. Furthermore, the sense that British

---

[31] George to North, 7 Apr. 1775, Fortescue, III, 201.

[32] George to North, 10 Sept. 1775, Fortescue, III, 256.

[33] George to North, 18 Aug. 1775, Fortescue, III, 248; J. Bullion, 'The *Ancien Regime* and the Modernising State: George III and the American Revolution', *Anglican and Episcopal History*, 68 (1999), pp. 67–84.

officials and troops were, in the words of Colonel Webb of Connecticut, George's 'servants and slaves'[34] fortified the negative portrayal of the king. He was believed by many Americans to have played a key role in the policies they blamed for imperial breakdown.[35]

There was also a breakdown of paternalism: George was seen as a bad father, 'with the pretended title of FATHER OF HIS PEOPLE', in the words of Tom Paine's *Common Sense* (1776); while, in turn, George saw the colonists as 'rebellious children',[36] at once an instructive reiteration of Jacobite views about the Glorious Revolution, but also the standard response to disaffection and rebellion in monarchies in which the personal role of the ruler remained central. The extent to which American attitudes were affected by altering concepts of parenthood, emphasizing filial autonomy rather than paternal control, and a changing, less Calvinistic understanding of God,[37] is unclear.

In judging George's views on America, it is necessary to avoid the traps of hindsight and the prejudices of eighteenth- and nineteenth-century Whigs. That said, the American fiscal policies of George and his ministers were arguably not only inappropriate in functional terms, resting as they did on a failure to understand American circumstances, but also challenged the assumptions of politics, not so much on a British scale as on its imperial equivalent. By the Western standards of his own time, George's policies required some sort of consent. The colonial empires of the period were overseas extensions of composite states created by the addition of yet more pieces of territory, and this was particularly the case with British colonies that were dominated by settlers. Imperialism was continuous with composite monarchy, not distinct from it and probably incompatible with it. A misunderstanding on the latter head has been compounded by the fact that state formation and colonialism, composite monarchies and imperialism tend to be studied by different types of historian. Yet similar strategies, conventions, obligations and rights prevailed in both processes.

Unless there was a States-General covering all the territories of a monarch, the monarchs of composite states usually observed the right of estates (or parliaments) in component territories to assemble and legislate only within their own territory. French colonists were not granted representation in French legislative bodies until after the French Revolution when the colonies were admitted to a national assembly. Crucially, the

---

[34] Webb quoted in S. Conway, *The War of American Independence 1775–1783* (London, 1995), p. 32.

[35] W.D. Jordan, 'Thomas Paine and the Killing of the King, 1776', *Journal of American History*, 60 (1973), pp. 294–308.

[36] George to Lord Dartmouth, 10 June 1775, HMC. *Dartmouth, Supplementary*, p. 502.

[37] J. Fliegelman, *Prodigals and Pilgrims: The American Revolution against Patriarchal Authority, 1750–1800* (Cambridge, 1982).

unifying institution in composite states was the crown, not a representative body. The monarch ruled with the advice of separate estates in each of his component territories. An assembly in one territory of a composite state claimed no authority over an assembly in another. The British parliament was the first to do so when, with the Declaratory Act, it declared its sovereignty over the Irish parliament in 1720. This claim was not pressed at the time, but, by the mid-eighteenth century, the British parliament was working out a complicated theory of the unified sovereignty over the empire of the king-in-parliament, the Westminster parliament. The Americans, in contrast, had no initial problem with *royal* sovereignty, but were clear that the king should tax them through their own assemblies, rather than through the Westminster parliament. It seems insufficiently stressed that it was the latter that had everything to lose from this American formulation, and not the king. Rebutting Charles James Fox's claim that the ministry was Tory, North declared in the Commons, on 26 October 1775, that 'the aim of toryism was to increase the prerogative. That in the present case, the administration contended for the right of Parliament, while the Americans talked of their belonging to the Crown.'[38] Despite charges that his intentions were despotic, George was not interested in the radical option of rejecting the pretensions of the Westminster parliament.

Once rebellion had erupted, George strongly advocated the normal eighteenth-century procedure of crushing it by force, although he failed to appreciate how many troops would be required. Indeed, George foolishly rejected advice from William, Viscount Barrington, the secretary at war, on this head, in part because he disapproved of Barrington's alternative of a naval blockade of the colonies.[39] Before simply castigating George for inappropriate firmness, it is worth pointing out that it is by no means clear that the sort of retreat in the face of disaffection seen with Leopold II (r. 1790–2) in Hungary, a retreat that reversed the disruptive consequences of Joseph II's maladroit policies, would have made the outcome any different. This would have been particularly the case if weakness on the part of George had been sensed by the determined revolutionary minority he confronted. After his political mistakes in the 1760s, George had clearly become aware of the calamitous dangers of failing to back his freely chosen ministers through thick and thin (although he offered no such support to those he disliked). As in the continental European monarchies, anything else was open incitement to a factional free-for-all. The baleful examples of Louis XV and XVI were available for inspection. It rightly became a top priority not to be seen to wobble. Yet, wobbling in the case

---

[38] *Parliamentary Register*, III, 42–3.
[39] S. Barrington, *The Political Life of William Wildman, Viscount Barrington* (London, 1814), pp. 158–9; George to North, 26 Aug. 1775, Fortescue, III, 250; S. Conway, *The British Isles and the War of American Independence* (Oxford, 2000), pp. 14–15.

of America might have accentuated the serious differences between the colonists, creating the basis for a popular loyalism.

In assessing George's policy towards America, it is important to note first that there had been previous clashes between royal authority and colonists, and also that George was not out of line with his royal contemporaries. The history of England's North American colonies in the seventeenth century had reflected the instability of the homeland. Rather than thinking primarily in terms of a tension between colonial autonomy and English authority, differing political positions spanned the Atlantic, with the overthrow of James II and VII accomplished not only in Britain in 1688–9, but also in the colonies. Furthermore, prior to George's reign, governors had clashed with assemblies. There was a strong sense of local rights and privileges that were seen as the necessary encapsulation of British liberties. Opposition to the power and pretensions of governors was widespread and frequent. If, therefore, British government was more intrusive and demanding after the Seven Years War, this was not a case of totally new issues.

There were not only tensions in British colonies. Louisiana, which was transferred from France to Spain after the Seven Years War, found the restrictions of an imperial trading system as unacceptable as Boston did. In October 1768, New Orleans rebelled against Spanish rule, after trade outside the Spanish imperial system or in non-Spanish ships was banned. Having expelled the governor and his men, the Louisiana Superior Council appealed to Louis XV to restore French rule. Faced with Spanish determination to restore authority, the French, however, did not act, and in August 1769 a Spanish force occupied New Orleans and executed the revolt's leaders.

More generally, Charles III of Spain followed policies similar to those of George, and policies with which, like George, he also was closely identified. There was a long-standing tension in Spanish America between *peninsulares* (natives of Spain) and *criollos* (creoles, American-born descendants of Spanish settlers), and this was exacerbated by reforms. These can be seen as pragmatic devices by officials concerned to maximize governmental revenues, but, as with Britain, this pragmatism was an aspect of the search for economic benefit from empire in the context of serious competition in the Atlantic world. Just as the British ministry was anxious to protect empire, a goal George affirmed when he visited the fleet at Portsmouth in 1773 and 1778, so Spain sought to strengthen it, not least in the aftermath of the shocking fall of Havana to the British in 1762.[40] It was returned as part of the Peace of Paris, but at the cost of yielding Florida to Britain.

---

[40] A. Ortiz, *Eighteenth-Century Reforms in the Caribbean. Miguel de Muesas, Governor of Puerto Rico, 1769–76* (Toronto, 1983).

Charles's reforms generally ignored creole aspirations, both in economic regulation and in political matters. The former policy was motivated by a desire to help Spain, rather than its colonies, and also to exclude other colonial powers; a goal in which the British government followed established practice. Measures were taken to restrict foreign ships trading with Spanish colonies, a process explicitly seen as likely to strengthen Spain's control over its colonies. The role of creoles in government was also restricted, and administrative reorganization was designed to strengthen governmental control, with the establishment in 1787 of a viceroyalty of the Rio de la Plata and of a captaincy-general of Caracas. The new capital of Caracas had a central treasury, a high court of justice, and a regiment of troops.[41] The deficiencies highlighted in the Seven Years War led Charles III to send regular regiments for garrison duty in leading colonial centres and to set in train the raising of large forces of militia. Combined, these forces provided government with security to introduce changes, including new taxes, although there was resistance.[42] A similar militarization of political authority was not to work for the British in Massachusetts, although the background in the 1770s was more charged than the situation across most of Spanish America, and there was also a more socially cohesive reaction against imperial authority.

Similarly, Sebastião, marquess of Pombal, the chief minister of Portugal in 1750–77, sought to alter the relationship between the mother country and its principal colony, Brazil. Aiming to derive more economic benefit for the state, Pombal founded chartered companies to monopolize the trade of the Amazon region and north-east Brazil.

To note that others matched elements of George's policies without precipitating revolution invites the response that the Iberian empires in the New World were to collapse by 1825. At the same time, it lessens the charge that George was exceptionally foolish or wicked. It becomes more interesting to ask why the British New World empire was the first to experience a major rebellion. There, as later in the Spanish and Portuguese colonies, the attitude of the social élite was crucial. Across the American colonies, élite families sought to exploit the resources of settled lands and 'wilderness', to control the institutions of local government, and to become representatives of the kingdom and the metropole, an always shifting combination.[43] The breakdown of this process in the Thirteen Colonies in the 1770s reflected a serious alienation, to which

[41] M.P. McKinley, *Pre-revolutionary Caracas: Politics, Economy and Society 1777–1811* (Cambridge, 1985).

[42] J.R. Fisher, A.J. Kuethe and A. McFarlane (eds), *Reform and Insurrection in Bourbon New Granada and Peru* (Baton Rouge, Louisiana, 1990).

[43] A.C. Metcalf, *Family and Frontier in Colonial Brazil. Santa de Parnaiba 1580–1822* (Berkeley, California, 1992).

suspicion of royal and ministerial intentions contributed powerfully. This was symbolic as well as constitutional. On 9 July 1776, after the colonial assembly of New York gave its assent to the Declaration of Independence, the inhabitants of New York City pulled down a gilded equestrian statue of the king erected on Bowling Green in 1770 (its metal was to be used for cartridges),[44] while, more generally, the royal arms were taken down, and usually treated with contempt. The king's name was removed from governmental and legal documents, royal portraits were reversed or destroyed, and there were mock trials, executions and funerals of the king, each a potent rejection of his authority. The Revolution was also to lead to the renaming of streets and buildings. Two famous instances were the changing of King Street in Boston to State Street, and the alteration of King's College in New York to Columbia. Fewer changes occurred in the South, not least because names and titles related generally to earlier monarchs and to others. Georgetown went unchanged, as did Georgia. Prince and Duke Streets remained in Alexandria, Virginia. The name George also had a resonance of Washington, and could be associated with him.

The outbreak of fighting transformed the colonial relationship with the king, as he could now be presented as using British forces to kill Americans, in short as a monarch of evil intent and action. Many refused to travel this road and for others it was a hesitant process, but, alongside the habit of referring to the British troops as ministerial or parliamentary rather than royal, there were steadily stronger calls for a new order. To Paine in *Common Sense*, George was a 'hardened, sullen-tempered Pharoah' and a 'royal brute', who composedly slept with American 'blood upon his soul'. This condemnation had an impact on American thought.

In March 1776, however, Congress was still unwilling to accept a motion by George Wythe and Richard Henry Lee that George, not the ministry, nor parliament, be seen as 'the author of our miseries'. This became possible only because George in effect disowned the Americans as rebels and treated them accordingly.[45] British policies, including the ban on trade with the rebellious colonies, were designed to hurt, while the government's attempt to recruit subsidy forces ('foreign mercenaries') was associated directly with George, not least because these troops were Germans.

Much of the Declaration of Independence adopted by the Continental Congress on 4 July 1776 consisted of a lengthy criticism of George, and of him personally, rather than of the position of monarch or the role of ministers. This was in part because the Americans had already in their

[44] A.S. Marks, 'The Statue of King George III in New York and the Iconology of Regicide', *American Art Journal*, 13 (1981), pp. 61–82.

[45] N.L. York, *Turning the World Upside Down. The War of American Independence and the Problem of Empire* (Westport, Connecticut, 2003), p. 89.

ideas broken with parliament. Now they were keen on breaking with George, as part of the transfer of political legitimacy.[46] It was easier to personalize misgovernment as the acts of a tyrant and thus to justify rejection, rather than pressure for reform, and the Declaration is worth quoting at length because it both reflected anger with George and has framed his subsequent reputation in the USA:

The history of the present King of Great Britain is a history of unremitting injuries and usurpations, all having in direct object the establishment of an absolute tyranny over these States ... He has refused his assent to laws the most wholesome and necessary for the public good.

He has forbidden his Governors to pass laws of immediate and pressing importance, unless suspended in their operation till his assent should be obtained; and when so suspended, he has utterly neglected to attend to them.

He has refused to pass other laws for the accommodation of large districts of people, unless those people would relinquish the right of representation in the legislature, a right inestimable to them, and formidable to tyrants only.

He has called together legislative bodies at places unusual, uncomfortable, and distant from the depository of their public records, for the sole purpose of fatiguing them into compliance with his measures.

He has dissolved representative houses repeatedly, for opposing with manly firmness his invasions on the rights of the people.

He has refused for a long time after such dissolutions to cause others to be elected, whereby the legislative powers, incapable of annihilation, have returned to the people at large for their exercise, the State remaining in the meantime exposed to all the dangers of invasion from without and convulsions within.

He has endeavoured to prevent the population of these states; for that purpose obstructing the laws for naturalization of foreigners; refusing to pass others to encourage their migrations hither, and raising the conditions of new appropriations of lands.

He has obstructed the administration of justice, by refusing his assent to laws for establishing judiciary powers.

He has made judges dependent on his will alone, for the tenure of their offices, and the amount and payment of their salaries.

He has erected a multitude of new offices, and sent hither swarms of officers to harass our people and eat out their substance.

---

[46] J.G. Marston, *King and Congress. The Transfer of Political Legitimacy, 1774–1776* (Princeton, New Jersey, 1987).

He has kept among us, in times of peace, standing armies without the consent of our legislatures.

He has affected to render the military independent of and superior to the civil power.

He has combined with others to subject us to a jurisdiction foreign to our constitution and unacknowledged by our laws; giving his assent to their acts of pretended legislation: for quartering large bodies of armed troops among us; for protecting them by a mock-trial, from punishment for any murders which they should commit on the inhabitants of these states; for cutting off our trade with all parts of the world; for imposing taxes on us without our consent; for depriving us in many cases of the benefits of trial by jury; for transporting us beyond seas to be tried for pretended offences; for abolishing the free system of English laws in a neighboring province [Quebec], establishing therein an arbitrary government, and enlarging its boundaries, so as to render it at once an example and fit instrument for introducing the same absolute role into these colonies, for taking away our charters, abolishing our most valuable laws, and altering fundamentally the forms of our governments; for suspending our own legislatures, and declaring themselves invested with power to legislate for us in all cases whatsoever.

He has abdicated government here by declaring us out of his protection and waging war against us.

He has plundered our seas, ravaged our coasts, burnt our towns, and destroyed the lives of our people.

He is at this time transporting large armies of foreign mercenaries to compleat the works of death, desolation and tyranny, already begun with circumstances of cruelty and perfidy scarcely paralleled in the most barbarous ages, and totally unworthy the head of a civilized nation.

He has constrained our fellow citizens taken captive on the high seas to bear arms against their country, to become the executioners of their friends and brethren, or to fall themselves by their hands.

He has excited domestic insurrections amongst us, and has endeavoured to bring on the inhabitants of our frontiers the merciless Indian savages, whose known rule of warfare, is an undistinguished destruction of all ages, sexes, and conditions.

In every stage of these oppressions we have petitioned for redress in the most humble terms: our repeated petitions have been answered only by repeated injury. A prince whose character is thus marked by every act which may define a tyrant is unfit to be the ruler of a free people.

A draft had added,

Future ages will scarcely believe that the hardiness of one man adventured, within the short compass of twelve years only, to lay a foundation so broad and so undisguised for tyranny over a people fostered and fixed in principles of freedom.

The extended criticism of George in the Declaration, attributing to him measures that had often in fact been taken by provincial governors, helped personalize the war, but also reflected the strong role of loyalty to the sovereign in the political culture of the age, and the powerful disillusionment with George that affected so many Patriots in 1774–6. The listing of what Samuel Adams termed George's 'catalogue of crimes' was the indictment of a conspirator, who had misused his executive powers as well as combining with parliament to attack American liberties. The list also accused him of waging war in a cruel fashion, producing, by reiteration, at once a black portrayal and a harsh indictment. Some of the language was biblical, making George akin to an Old Testament plague.[47] The Loyalist Thomas Hutchinson commented that the clauses were 'most wickedly presented to cast reproach upon the King'.[48] Indeed, the attack on the king's reputation was later to leave some Patriots uncomfortable, John Adams claiming that it contained 'expressions which I would not have inserted, if I had drawn it up, particularly that which called the King tyrant'.[49] Nevertheless, the damage had been done.

Once fighting had broken out in America in 1775, George kept a close eye on the details of activities linked to the war, as was clearly shown in his correspondence with John Robinson, the secretary to the treasury and a key assistant to North:

Mr Robinson has the honour to transmit herewith pursuant to His Majesty's orders a précis of the several proceedings at the Treasury relative to America since the first of January last with the correspondence thereon, and also a state of all the provisions furnished by the contractors drawn into one view, together with an account from Mr Adair of the medicines sent for the use of the army.[50]

Mr Robinson has the honour to send, by Lord North's directions, for H.M.'s inspection, two casks of sour grout [sic], put up with valves in

[47] S.G. Fisher, 'The Twenty-Eight Charges against the King in the Declaration of Independence', *Pennsylvania Magazine of History and Biography*, 31 (1907), pp. 257–303; W.L. Hedges, 'Telling Off the King: Jefferson's Summary View as American Fantasy', *Early American Literature*, 22 (1987), pp. 166–74; S.E. Lucas, 'The Stylistic Artistry of the Declaration of Independence', *US National Archives and Records Administration*, 30 Jan. 2005, www.archives. gov.

[48] T. Hutchinson, *Strictures upon the Declaration of the Congress at Philadelphia* (London, 1776), p. 16.

[49] A.J. O'Shaughnessy, '"If Others Will Not Be Active, I Must Drive". George III and the American Revolution', *Early American Studies*, 2, 1 (spring 2004), p. 1.

[50] Robinson to George, 11 Oct. 1775, BL. Add. 37833, fol. 17.

the same manner as the casks shipped for America; and also one of the valves. The cask marked No. 1 has been sometime made and may be nearly fit for use, that marked No. 2 is at present in a state of strong fermentation.[51]

A detailed concern with supplies reflected George's engagement with practicalities.[52] The weight of correspondence led to particular arrangements:

Mr Robinson has the honour by Lord North's directions to send to H.M. drafts of dispatches to Generals Carleton, Howe, and Burgoyne, and to the Paymaster General and Mr Gordon Commissary at Cork; Mr Robinson finding that the Treasury has occasion to trouble H.M. often on the American business, and East India affairs, has presumed, to have some boxes made in order to save H.M. the trouble of making up packets, and to send inclosed a key in which he humbly hopes he shall not offend.[53]

Although no Frederick the Great, George's close supervision can be readily illustrated:

the dispatch to General Carleton is drawn up with the clearness that always is to be found in papers drawn up by Mr Robinson, the proposal to Lord North in the margin that more money should be sent under the head of Extraordinaries seems highly necessary, otherwise the General will during the winter be under the greatest difficulty to issue subsistence to his army, as the pay cannot be issued farther than until the 24th of December. I have signed the warrants. The digesting the several matters of dispute and inquiry under different heads that relate to the affairs of Bengal undoubtedly will be most useful, and I hope with a little management that when Lord North fairly sets his shoulders to that arduous task that he will find it less difficult than he seems to apprehend; if he would fix his own ideas on the subjects and not give ear to such various counselors, he would be less perplexed, and the right path would certainly be followed.[54]

On 26 October 1775, opening a new session of parliament, George rejected conciliation, a measure advocated by a large section of British

[51] Robinson to George, 2 Nov. 1775, BL. Add. 37833 fol. 18.
[52] E.g. George to Robinson, 11 Jan., 5 Sept. 1778, 20 Aug., 2 Sept. 1779, BL. Add. 37833 fol. 214, 37834 fols 1, 136, 139.
[53] Robinson to George, 25 June 1776, BL. Add. 37833 fol. 20.
[54] George to Robinson, 14 Sept. 1776, BL. Add. 37833 fol. 28.

opinion.[55] Instead, coercion was to come first. His step undermined American moderates. Indeed, George declared that it was necessary 'to put a speedy end to these disorders by the most decisive exertions'. This led him to favour campaigns on land, rather than simply the blockade proposed by Barrington, the secretary at war, who in 1774 had opposed persisting with unpopular taxation. Grafton, the lord privy seal, used the debate on the address to express his doubts about coercion, only to lose his post.[56]

George, however, was not interested in parliamentary debates on the rights of the conflict,[57] but, rather, in winning it. Not a war minister, and faced with Lord George Germain's determination to control strategy,[58] the king still took a part in planning, arguing, for example, that the expedition North planned for the Carolinas in early 1776 should aim first for North Carolina, where the Scottish settlers were believed to be favourably inclined.[59] He also pressed for vigour, responding to Carleton's retreat towards Canada from Lake Champlain in late 1776 by suggesting that the general was possibly 'too cold and not so active as might be wished'.[60] This was a reasonable response to Carleton's failure to maintain the initiative, but a little surprising given George's lack of military experience. Indeed, Burgoyne's greater boldness in advancing south from Canada the following year was to end in surrender at Saratoga. In 1777, George wanted Howe to show more vigour in order to bring the war to the quickest end by finding the 'mode of war . . . most distressing to the Americans'.[61] The demand for action led George to underrate reports that France was planning war. He denigrated the sources of such reports,[62] although, in fact, they were accurate.

Domestic criticism did not encourage George to desist. More attractively, his personal commitment to the struggle was shown by his generosity to loyalists: George felt a sense of responsibility and of obligation to them. George had also convinced himself that leniency was a mistake. His commitment to empire and lack of empathy with the Americans was shown in 1776 when he suggested that American prisoners might beneficially be sent to India.[63] The British possessions there were

[55] J. Bradley, *Popular Politics and the American Revolution in England: Petitions, the Crown and Public Opinion* (Macon, Georgia, 1986).
[56] George to North, 26 Aug. 1775, Fortescue, III, 250.
[57] George to North, 9 Nov. 1775, Fortescue, III, 282.
[58] George to Robinson, 3 Mar. 1777, BL. Add. 37833 fol. 124.
[59] George to North, 16 Oct. 1775, Fortescue, III, 270.
[60] George to North, 13 Dec. 1776, Fortescue, III, 406.
[61] W.B. Donne (ed.), *The Correspondence of King George the Third with Lord North from 1768 to 1783* (2 vols, London, 1867), II, 84.
[62] George to North, 27 Sept., 22 Nov. 1777, Fortescue, III, 481–2, 498.
[63] George Robinson, 3 Oct. 1776, BL. Add. 37833 fol. 71.

short of white settlers, but they were unhealthy destinations. Furthermore, American privateers were seen by George as pirates.[64] Firmness, not animosity, was George's attitude, and commenting on a draft of the royal speech to parliament, he wrote, 'Notes of triumph would not have been proper when the successes are against subjects not a foreign foe.'[65]

Responding to Chatham's attack in the Lords on government policy in May 1777, an attack from a politician, like Grafton, he had formerly called to head the ministry, George underlined his firmness, representing the Americans in terms of the sin of pride, and linking the maintenance of authority in America to that in Britain:

> like most of the other productions of that extraordinary brain it contains nothing but specious words and malevolence, for no one that reads it, if unacquainted with the conduct of the Mother Country and its colonies, must but suppose the Americans poor mild persons who after unheard of and repeated grievances had no choice but slavery or the sword, whilst the truth is that the too great leniency of this country increased their pride and encouraged them to rebel; but thank God the nation does not see the unhappy contest through his mirror; if his senti-ments were adopted, I should not esteem my situation in this country as a very dignified one.[66]

Experience of the war doubtless lay behind George's reflection in 1799 that

> it is impossible without being on the spot and seeing the face of the country that any well grounded directions can be given, farther than pointing out what is the general object wished, but how to be effected or when must be left to those who are on the spot.[67]

Following the American war created particular problems due to the length of time it took to receive news,[68] and the difficulty of checking its veracity speedily. This put pressure on the king and his ministers. Eager for news of campaigning,[69] George's personal familiarity with commanders and officers added to his involvement and he also wanted news of the German contingents.[70]

---

[64] George to Robinson, 26 Oct. 1776, BL. Add. 37833 fol. 99.
[65] Ibid.
[66] George to North, 31 May 1777, Fortescue, III, 449.
[67] George to Dundas, 9 Oct. 1799, BL. Add. 40100 fol. 235.
[68] Hannecken report, 13 Sept. 1776, Rigs. 1957.
[69] George to Robinson, 27 Sept. 1776, BL. Add. 37833 fol. 51.
[70] Hannecken report, 27 Sept. 1776, Rigs. 1957.

The war broadened out when first France (1778) and then Spain (1779) joined in against Britain. George had earlier shown an unwillingness to go to war with these powers. During the Falkland Islands crisis of 1770, he wrote to North that 'every feeling of humanity as well as the knowledge of the distress war must occasion makes me desirous of preventing it if it can be accomplished provided the honour of this country is preserved', and on that occasion he had tried to suggest a way to keep negotiations going.[71] In 1777 he was confident that, if Britain acted 'an open firm part', peace with France could be maintained.[72]

In 1778, however, George's views on the integrity of the empire gave him no options in the face of French determination to recognize the rebels. He argued that to give way in America would lead to the loss of other colonies, not least because Ireland and the British West Indies would find it useful to follow suit, in particular due to their commercial links with America. The impact of his strong convictions and his sense of the need for fortitude was shown clearly.

Outraged by 'the faithless and insolent conduct of France',[73] George nevertheless refused to be dismayed by French entry into the war:

Lord North must feel as I do the noble conduct of the three fifty gun ships that with so much bravery have driven off separately ships of far superior strength; I doubt not whenever it shall please the Almighty to permit an English fleet fairly to engage any other a most comfortable issue will arise.

The following month, the king added,

If Lord North can see with the same degree of enthusiasm I do, the beauty, excellence, and perfection of the British constitution as by law established, and consider that if any one branch of the empire is allowed to cast off its dependency then the others will infallibly follow the example, that consequently though an arduous struggle that it is worth going through any difficulty to preserve to latest posterity what the wisdom of our ancestors have carefully transmitted to us; he will not allow despondency to find a place in his breast, but resolve not merely out of duty to fill his post, but will resolve with vigour to meet every obstacle that may arise he should meet with most cordial support from me.[74]

---

[71] George to North, 28 Nov., 6 Dec. 1770, RA. GEO/1037, 1040.
[72] George to Robinson, 7 Sept. 1777, BL. Add. 37834 fol. 3.
[73] George to North, 26 Mar. 1778, Fortescue, IV, 80.
[74] George to North, 13 Oct., 14 Nov. 1778, RA. GEO/3094, 3116; George to Robinson, 12 Sept. 1778, BL. Add. 37834 fol. 11.

George also displayed his habitual firmness, which contrasted with his father's habitual irresolution but could seem petulant. It was only grudgingly that he accepted the concessions offered the American revolutionaries by the Carlisle Commission of 1778. This represented an acceptance that the war would be ended by compromise, and that the imperial relationship would have to be substantially altered. The commission, however, was unsuccessful and George was clearly thinking of America when he wrote of Ireland, 'experience has thoroughly convinced me that this country gains nothing by granting to her dependencys indulgences, for opening the door encourages a desire for more which if not complied with causes discontent and the former benefit is obliterated'.[75] He hoped that favourable war news would influence opinion there.[76] In Ireland, economic disruption stemming from the war led to pressure for more favourable commercial regulations, pressure resisted by competing British interests. In 1779, when a boycott of British goods began in Ireland, it became apparent that the breakdown of control seen in North America might be repeated.

Eventual defeat in America did not make George readier to accept colonial viewpoints or reduce his concern for constitutional proprieties. This was seen in 1789 when he responded to complaints about Captain Thomas Orde, governor of the West Indian colony of Dominica since 1783. George replied to William Grenville,

> The letter from the three gentlemen who have taken on themselves to transmit a supposed petition from the Assembly of Dominica against Governor Orde could not with any kind of propriety authorize Mr. Grenville to receive them with that paper, his letter therefore to Mr. Gregg [one of the three] was on the most constitutional ground, that gentleman having since privately transmitted the above petition Mr. Grenville is as regular in having communicated it to me and in the answer he proposes to send to Mr. Gregg, as well as in his dispatch to Lieutenant Governor Bruce on the whole proceedings, which if the Assembly are serious in their complaints on their Governor will make them send it in an authentic manner through the channel of the Lieutenant Governor.[77]

Orde was vindicated with a baronetcy in 1792 and remained governor until he returned to active naval service following the outbreak of war in 1793.

[75] George to North, 12 Nov. 1778, RA. GEO/3114; cf. George to Robinson, 20 Oct. 1779, BL. Add. 37834 fol. 162.

[76] George to Robinson, 3 Oct. 1776, BL. Add. 37833 fol. 71.

[77] George to William Grenville, 9 Dec. 1789, BL. Add. 58855 fol. 54.

During the War of American Independence, George also showed himself unaccommodating in domestic matters, repeatedly rejecting North's attempts either to strengthen the ministry with fresh supporters or to retire. When, in March 1778, North recommended an approach to Chatham in order to weaken the opposition, George replied that

> no advantage to this country nor personal danger can ever make me address myself for assistance either to Lord Chatham or any other branch of the Opposition . . . I would rather lose the Crown I now wear than bear the ignominy of possessing it under their shackles.

Chatham's demands helped wreck the negotiations, but so also did George's attitude[78] to a man he had described in 1775 as 'a trumpet of sedition'.[79] George's views were seen as crucial in any negotiations about ministerial change,[80] and in 1780 Rockingham was advised that he should only listen to approaches if they came from the king in person.[81] Indeed George was determined to thwart negotiations unless opposition leaders agreed to keep the empire complete, and he expected an explicit commitment: humiliating in its lack of trust, this also reflects the king's legalistic confidence in documents. This requirement looked toward George's insistence in 1807 that his ministers provide a written assurance that they would not raise anew the issue of Catholic emancipation. In a letter reflecting George's conviction that his integrity took precedence, he wrote to North in June 1779,

> What I said yesterday was the dictates of frequent and severe self-examination. I never can depart from it. Before I will ever hear of any man's readiness to come into office I will expect to see it signed under his hand that he is resolved to keep the Empire entire and that no troops shall be consequently withdrawn from thence [North America], nor independence ever allowed.

Having made this clear in 1779, he would not budge in 1780.[82]

George's reaction to opposition was unforgiving. Chatham's death in May 1778 was followed by a response that made George's attitude to his

---

[78] Fortescue, IV, 54–88.

[79] George to North, 9 Aug. 1775, Fortescue, III, 242.

[80] Keppel to Rockingham, 13 July 1780, WW. R1–1913.

[81] Keppel to Rockingham, 9 July 1780, WW. R1–1903.

[82] George to Jenkinson, 30 May 1799, BL. Loan 72/1 fol. 11; George to North, 22 June 1779, 3 July 1780, George to Thurlow, lord chancellor, 16 Oct. 1779, George to Jenkinson, 16 Oct. 1779, Fortescue, IV, 370, V, 96–7, IV, 458, 477; I.R. Christie, 'The Marquess of Rockingham and Lord North's Offer of a Coalition, June–July 1780', in Christie, *Myth and Reality in Late-Eighteenth-Century British Politics and Other Papers* (London, 1970), pp. 109–32.

commemoration seem pedantic and grudging, as well as seriously out of tune with the public mood. On the day of Chatham's death, the Commons voted unanimously an address for a public funeral and a monument in Westminster Abbey. This measure surprised George, who informed North that he would find it offensive if intended as a compliment to Chatham's 'general conduct'.[83] George's low view of parliamentarians was seen later that year when he pressed North on the need to tackle inadequate attendance in the Commons.[84]

In 1778, George associated himself with the war effort by visiting the naval dockyards at Chatham and a crowded Portsmouth, where the fleet was fitting out,[85] and he pressed the need for vigour in the new war with France. He also visited military encampments at Windsor and near Salisbury that had been set up in response to the fear of French invasion. George wished to encourage both the army and popular support for the war effort. As a result of these visits, George was seen by a large number of his subjects and was very pleased with the popular response to his appearances, writing to North about his 'thorough satisfaction at the manner in which I have been received by all ranks of people on my late tour'.[86] Sympathy for the Americans declined, in part because of their alliance with France.[87]

Visiting an encampment on Warley Common south of Brentwood in Essex, on 20 October 1778, George took part in a review and, from a stand, saw a mock attack. He stayed from 10 a.m. to 4 p.m. and returned to the camp after dinner. George also visited the camp at Cox Heath, near Maidstone in Kent. There were about 10,000 troops at Warley, including eight battalions of militia: the royal visit brought the king into contact with men who were not part of the regular army but part of a different voluntary stream on which the security of the country also appeared to depend. George's impact was personal, in that he was introduced to several officers who had taken part and was seen by many more participants, and his impact also spread by report. Aside from printed accounts, for example in the *Annual Chronicle*, two paintings of the visit to Warley were commissioned from Philippe Jacques de Loutherbourg by Lieutenant-General Pierson. They were presented to George and exhibited at the Royal Academy in 1779. The camps were also celebrated on the stage and in fiction.[88] Visiting Warley, George and Charlotte (who also accompanied

[83] George to North, 12 May 1778, Fortescue, IV, 139–40.

[84] George to North, 25 Oct., 2 Nov. 1778, RA. GEO/3099, 3106.

[85] Admiral Keppel to Rockingham, 26 Apr. 1778, WW. R1–1776.

[86] George to North, 5 Oct. 1778, RA. GEO/3089.

[87] J. Sainsbury, *Disaffected Patriots: London Supporters of Revolutionary America, 1769–1782* (Kingston, Ontario, 1987).

[88] G. Russell, *The Theatre of War: Performance, Politics and Society, 1793–1815* (Oxford, 1995), pp. 33–46; Conway, *British Isles*, pp. 120–2.

him to Portsmouth) stayed at Thorndon Hall on 19 and 20 October 1778, the seat of Robert, ninth Lord Petre, and this was an important stage in the reintegration of the Catholic élite and the crown.[89]

Giving rise to more concern than opposition moves, George was confronted by his first minister's pessimism about Britain's prospects, and by his repeated talk of resignation. This in part stemmed from a long-standing hesitation on North's part about aspects of politics,[90] but it was disruptive of government cohesion and affected the wider political world.[91] More optimistic than North,[92] George frequently urged him to vigour, writing in November 1778:

> engaged in many difficulties, and an opposition to government formed of men that if they could succeed would restrain no one of the absurd ideas they have sported, I think the duty nay personal honour of those in public stations must prompt them with zeal to make every effort to assist me, who have unreservedly supported them.[93]

As the war dragged on, success seemed remote (although not to George), while the injunction in Prince Frederick's political testament of 1749 to reduce the national debt was made steadily more implausible by its rise to hitherto unprecedented heights. As the war became more difficult, George drew on the resources of monarchical prestige and on the social resonances of the established order. For example, at the close of 1777 the government resolved to raise twelve more regiments for the army at the expense of city councils and leading aristocrats who, with George's permission, were to appoint most of the officers. George had initially been hesitant about raising new regiments, as he was worried about the professionalism of such units, concerned to ensure that the old regiments were not under strength, and mindful of the views of officers in the latter. He preferred to take the accustomed path of hiring German auxiliaries, but changed his opinion under the pressure of circumstances. Political preferences also played a part, as George was worried about the consequences of giving more power to hostile aristocrats. In 1779, the invasion scare led the élite to take on an important role in organizing volunteer support, but proposals to raise volunteer forces in Sussex led George to worry that this would provide an opportunity for the lord-lieutenant, the duke of Richmond, to strengthen his patronage system.[94] Characteristically,

---

[89] M.D. Petre, *The Ninth Lord Petre* (London, 1928), pp. 39–48.

[90] North to earl of Guildford, 8 Nov. 1763, Bod. MS. North adds. C 4/1.

[91] Diede report, 7 Feb. 1776, Rigs. 1957.

[92] George to Robinson, 16 Sept. 1776, BL. Add. 37833 fol. 32.

[93] George to North, 10 Nov. 1778, RA. GEO/3112; George to Robinson, 6 Nov. 1778, 11, 12 May 1779, BL. Add. 37834 fols 39, 72, 77.

[94] George to North, 1 Sept. 1779, Fortescue, IV, 418.

George also wanted enthusiasm directed in a prudent direction. In response to the duke of Northumberland's proposals to raise men for the navy and the militia, and for a volunteer force to defend Middlesex, George complained that he had neglected what was 'most necessary at this hour, the assisting in raising recruits for the old corps',[95] the established regiments in the army. Insistent on approving the commandants of any new units, George was happy to approve the raising of a regiment by the duke of Ancaster, but insisted that he only hold the rank of major, as 'a steady man' was necessary for the command.[96]

George continued to take a major interest in the planning of military operations. Indeed, his role increased as the conflict became more complex with the greater number of opponents and spheres of operation and the consequent need to make choices about force allocations that involved possible clashes between ministers. At times, his role was simply that of approval, as with the attack on the slaving base of Goree in 1778 – George urging the need to maintain secrecy.[97] He readily moved from suggestions and comments on specific military issues – 'might not some attempt be made to intercept the [French] convoy from Lorient to North America'[98] – to general remarks about the rightness and necessity of the struggle, the two potently interacting in his mind:

> I have no doubt next spring, Spain will join France but if we can keep her quiet till then I trust the British navy will be in a state to cope with both nations; Lord North must feel as I do the noble conduct of the three fifty gun ships that with so much bravery have driven off separately ships of far superior strength; I doubt not whenever it shall please the Almighty to permit an English fleet fairly to engage any other a most comfortable issue will arise; armed as France and Spain now are no peace could either be durable or much less expensive than a state of war . . . I trust in the justness of my cause and the bravery of the nation, and you may depend on my readiness to sheath the sword whenever a permanent tranquillity can be obtained which certainly the present moment is not the one for accomplishing.[99]

Justice and will, however, were not enough, and George pressed for still more resources:

> the misfortune is we have more to defend than we have ships ready to employ; if Parliament can adopt some mode of raising a sufficient

[95] George to North, 12 July 1779, Fortescue, IV, 394.
[96] George to Jenkinson, 29 June 1779, BL. Loan 72/1 fol. 13.
[97] George to North, 5 Oct. 1778, RA. GEO/3089.
[98] George to North, 5 July 1779, Fortescue, IV, 388.
[99] George to North, 13 Oct. 1778, RA. GEO/3094.

number of men for the navy and army; I doubt not that our number-less difficulties with spirit, assiduity and attention would soon vanish.[100]

Professionalism as well as dedication seemed necessary. In 1777, George had been annoyed by the time it took to get information from abroad, while in 1778, concerned about factionalism in the navy, he pressed for a new head of the Admiralty Board in place of John, fourth earl of Sandwich, with ability placed ahead of political weight when considering merit:

> In time of peace I am not convinced whether men of more general education may not fill that station as well; but in a war and more so in the present which is a naval one it is highly advantageous to have in the Cabinet a person able to plan the most effectual manner of conducting it.[101]

Three years later, he was concerned about the absence of officers from the garrison at Jersey, which was vulnerable to French attack.[102]

Policies supported by ministers in whom the king had the greatest confidence, such as David, Viscount Stormont, in 1781, were believed to be particularly likely to succeed,[103] and George lobbied ministers to remain loyal,[104] but he could not compensate for the fundamental lack of cabinet cohesion. George insisted that North consult him before making promises about ministerial vacancies,[105] and ministers were individually responsible to him and to parliament, ensuring that George was effectively head of the cabinet. The king might indeed be his own prime minister,[106] and did not see North in this role,[107] but however much George might encourage ministers to support the recommendations of colleagues,[108] he did not preside at cabinet. Instead, George left the business of government to ministers, such that an attack on one posed issues of collective responsibility, and thus of the stability of the ministry. This made it very difficult to part with individual ministers, however much their competence had been criticized, as in 1778–9 with Sandwich, the first lord of the admiralty.[109]

---

[100] George to North, 12 Nov. 1778, RA. GEO/3114.

[101] George to Sir Stanier Porten, under-secretary of state, 11 Oct. 1777, I.R. Christie (ed.), 'George and the Southern Department: Some Unprinted Royal Correspondence', *Camden Miscellany* XXX (London, 1990), p. 422; George to North, 28 Dec. 1778, RA. GEO/3167.

[102] George to Porten, 9 Jan. 1781, Christie (ed.), 'Southern Department', p. 427.

[103] Dreyer reports, 27 Apr., 8 June 1781, Rigs. 1964.

[104] George to Robinson, 7 Nov. 1779, BL. Add. 37835 fol. 9.

[105] George to Robinson, 28 June 1778, BL. Add. 37833 fol. 234.

[106] L. Namier, *Monarchy and the Party System* (London, 1952).

[107] George to Robinson, 13 Aug. 1779, BL. Add. 37834 fol. 133.

[108] George to Robinson, 13 Mar. 1777, BL. Add. 37833 fol. 161.

[109] C. Wilkinson, *The British Navy and the State in the Eighteenth Century* (Woodbridge, 2004), pp. 203–4.

North found it hard to manage the situation: he was no Walpole; instead, he was closer to Henry Pelham, with the crucial difference that Pelham had died in 1754 before he could be tested by the strains of the Seven Years War. North's repeated requests to retire echoed Bute's lack of nerve in 1763, and made George, who, in general, did not like the idea of changing office-holders,[110] seem the steadier of government. Prefiguring later advice that he himself should not be exposed to 'hurry', George urged calm on North: 'I hope will enable you to spend the next week quietly at Bushy, that you may recruit your mind'.[111]

George felt that he had to take an active personal role in 1779 when Britain was threatened by Franco-Spanish co-operation after Spain joined in the war. He pressed the Admiralty hard to ensure that they took a vigorous stance, and argued that it was important to engage the Combined Fleet even though it was far larger than the available British fleet,[112] as a failure to engage would endanger national morale. George was confident that the British fleet was equal to the task, possibly a mistaken confidence, but one that was saved by the failings of the Bourbon expedition, including disease on board the ships and poor command.[113] A sense of national emergency caused George to consider distributing pikes to 'the Country People'.[114] It also made him agreeable to Rockingham, who had taken a prominent role in ensuring that Hull was able to resist any attack by John Paul Jones.[115] The king's determination anticipated that which he was to display when French invasion threatened in 1803. The martial theme in 1779 can be seen in the portrait by the American loyalist Benjamin West of the king as commander-in-chief, his royal robes discarded in favour of activity; George is wearing a uniform and holding the plan of a military camp. This theme was underlined when Prince William joined the navy.

The failure of the Bourbon invasion plan offered encouragement. George, anyway, was optimistic about the strategic situation, believing that Bourbon entry into the war did not block prospects for an acceptable end to the rebellion. In June 1779, he wrote to North:

The different papers from America show very clearly that had not Spain now thrown off the mask that we should have soon found the

[110] George to North, 27 June 1779, Fortescue, IV, 380.

[111] George to North, 18 Apr. 1778, Fortescue, IV, 118.

[112] Keppel to Rockingham, 19, 20 Aug. 1779, WW. R1–1845–6.

[113] George to North, 27 June 1779, Fortescue, IV, 380; N.A.M. Rodger, *The Insatiable Earl. A Life of John Montagu, 4ᵗʰ Earl of Sandwich* (London, 1993), pp. 259–60; A.T. Patterson, *The Other Armada: The Franco-Spanish Attempt to Invade Britain in 1779* (Manchester, 1960).

[114] Conway, *British Isles*, pp. 158–9.

[115] Weymouth to Rockingham, 1 Oct., Amherst to Rockingham, 2 Oct. 1779, WW. R1–1852–3.

colonies sue for pardon to the mother country; I do not yet despair that with the activity [General Sir Henry] Clinton is inclined to adopt, and the Indians in the rear, that the provinces will even now submit.[116]

Signs of providential support were welcome.[117]

Confidence in success enabled George to avoid the difficult issue of reasonable terms. Later that month, in a letter which suggests that he had not got far beyond a view of his relationship with America as based on paternalism, George wrote again to North:

The enclosed papers . . . confirm me in an opinion long entertained that America unless this summer supported by a Bourbon fleet must sue for peace, and that it would ever have been unwise to have done more than what is now adopted, the enabling the Commander in Chief to put provinces at peace, but that propositions must come from them to us, no farther ones be sent from hence; they ever tend only to increase the demands. I can never agree to healing over an uncured wound, it must be probed to the bottom, if it then proves sound, no one will be more ready to forget offences, but no one sees more forcibly the necessity of preventing the like mischief by America's feeling, she has not been a gainer by the contest; yet after that I would show that the parent's heart is still affectionate to the penitent child.[118]

At the close of 1779, George argued that the Americans were coming close to being willing to negotiate.[119] This belief, which took political shape in his cajoling North into staying in office and in refusing to heed opposition views, helped keep the war going, as a resignation on North's part would have undermined governmental cohesion and entailed a new ministry that would probably have had to incorporate opposition elements. George was prepared to accept that, but not yielding to opposition and a change of measures.[120] Against the depressing background of a 'damp, cold and dark London,'[121] the king was aware of North's lack of leadership, indeed irresolution, but felt that letting him go would encourage his opponents at home and abroad.[122] As a result, George

---

[116] George to North, 22 June 1779, Fortescue, IV, 369.
[117] George to Jenkinson, 2 Aug. 1779, BL. Loan 72/1 fol. 15.
[118] George to North, 27 June 1779, Fortescue, IV, 379.
[119] George to North, 20 Dec. 1779, Fortescue, IV, 526.
[120] George to Jenkinson, 7, 12 Nov. 1779, BL. Loan 72/1 fols 17–19.
[121] Thomas, second Lord Grantham to Anne Robinson, 26 Nov. 1779, Bedford CRO. L30/17/2.
[122] George to Jenkinson, 20 Nov., 9 Dec. 1779, BL. Loan 72/1 fols 23, 31; W.B. Pemberton, *Lord North* (London, 1938), pp. 252–3.

treated North's pressure to resign as a threat of desertion.[123] Indeed, there was a lack of alternatives to North, and his position in the Commons was a valuable one for the conduct of government business. Conscious of the importance of the Commons, George argued that MPs who sought his approbation must speak there as well as vote.[124]

Unlike North, whom he pressed hard to do his job effectively, George saw the war in terms that scarcely permitted compromise, writing in 1779, 'The present contest with America I cannot help seeing as the most serious in which any country was ever engaged.'[125] If God was appealed to fervently by some of his American opponents, George's emphasis on will-power gave him a similar conviction:

> I begin to see that I shall soon have enfused some of that spirit which I thank Heaven ever attends me when under difficulties. I know very well the various hazards we are open to; but I trust in the protection of the Almighty, in the justness of the cause, the uprightness of my own intentions, and my determination to show my people that my life is always ready to be risked for their safety or prosperity.[126]

The emphasis on personal readiness for self-sacrifice in this letter was both a reflection of George's sense of duty and also somewhat typical of the often overblown rhetoric of the period. The theme of the royal body under threat was an aspect of the king as neo-Classical hero that needs to be set beside the more accessible post-war image of 'Farmer George'. As neo-Classical hero, however, George was distinctive in being a self-consciously and self-proclaimed Christian one. Certain in his own fortitude, George expected the same of others: 'no man has a right to talk of leaving me at this hour.'[127] He played a crucial role in keeping the ministry focused on the war. Indeed, on 21 June 1779 he met the cabinet, defended the American policy and pressed for the ministers' support.[128] George thought it necessary to face challenges and not to procrastinate:

> my mind always inclines to meet difficulties as they arise, and I would much rather have them soon fall on my head if not to be avoided than to know that in future that must inevitably happen. Public men ought always to act on system.[129]

---

[123] George to North, 27 Mar., 2 June 1778, 12 Feb. 1779, Fortescue, IV, 84–8, 163, 275–6.
[124] George to Jenkinson, 20 Nov. 1779, BL. Loan 72/1 fol. 21.
[125] George to North, 11 June 1779, Fortescue, IV, 351.
[126] George to North, 24 June 1779, Fortescue, IV, 374.
[127] George to Robinson, 2 July 1779, BL. Add. 37834 fol. 101.
[128] George to North, 21 June 1779, Fortescue, IV, 367.
[129] George to Robinson, 6 June 1779, BL. Add. 37834 fol. 93.

George's attitude might seem an impressive display of pertinacity and resolve,[130] indeed an anticipation of Churchillian determination, were it not based on a flawed assessment of the military and political situation in North America. George understood the distinction between battle and war, and appreciated that victory in the former would not ensure success in the latter, but he underestimated the difficulty of getting the Americans to accept that they might have sufficiently lost to ensure negotiations. George also, as yet, failed to appreciate the depths of the strategic dilemma posed by Bourbon entry. His politics ensured that the war could not be reconceptualized as a struggle with the Bourbons, the course urged by the opposition, and one that would have freed the British from the strategic incubus of conflict in North America. George was still determined to defeat the Americans.

[130] George to Robinson, 29, 30 Aug., 8 Sept. 1778, 28 June 1779, BL. Add. 37833 fols 236, 240, 37834 fols 5, 99.

Chapter 12

REPEATED CRISES, 1780–4

In 1783, riding to London from his nearby house, John Robinson was over-taken in Kensington by George. Recognizing his former joint-secretary to the treasury, George pulled up and engaged him in conversation. Having been reassured about Robinson's health, George responded, 'I am heartily glad of it for you are always the same, you do not change with the times. You are always steady . . . These are bad, bad times indeed.'[1]

By late 1779, the war over America had become part of a more general crisis affecting George's policies and position. This crisis was to test George to a far greater extent than the unpopularity and ministerial insta-bility of the 1760s. While closely linked to the war, the crisis was far more wide-ranging. Within Britain, attacks on the ministry became more pronounced at the close of the decade as the war continued, apparently without prospect of end or success. These attacks were linked to an upsurge in reform demands focusing on the nature of the political system, with particularly strong demands for change coming from Yorkshire and Ireland. It has been claimed that it was in 1779–80 that George's system was most in jeopardy.[2] A county petitioning movement for reform devel-oped. Electoral reform was designed to lessen court influence,[3] and the Society for Constitutional Information, established in London in April 1780 by a group of Rational Dissenters, pressed for parliamentary reform. The nature of elections was the key issue, with calls for changes that were to influence reforming aspirations into the next century, extending in some cases to include universal manhood suffrage, annual elections, and the secret ballot. The role of the monarchy was also an issue.

George was not free from more specific criticism. The substitution of North for the more contentious Bute in opposition demonology had left the king more exposed, while the emphasis on corruption led to a concern about the Civil List that exposed George to comment and appeared to justify claims of a pernicious royal prospectus. The increase of the Civil List in 1777, to an unprecedented annual sum of £900,000, had led the

---

[1] Minute by Robinson, 13 Nov. 1783, BL. Add. 37835 fol. 203.

[2] H. Butterfield, *George III, Lord North and the People, 1779–1780* (London, 1949), p. vi.

[3] Revd Christopher Wyvill to Pemberton Milnes, 5 Dec., John Lee to Wyvill, 14 Dec. 1779, Rockingham to Henry Zouch, 23 Mar. 1780, WW. R1–1868, 1870, 1883; E. Royle and J. Walvin, *British Radicals and Reformers 1760–1848* (Brighton, 1982).

Speaker to remark, when he presented the Bill to George, on the need for royal economy. There was criticism of the Speaker but he was vindicated from parliamentary complaint in a significant moment of triumph for the opposition.[4] In 1779, the issue was taken up in a circular letter sent by the Reverend Christopher Wyvill, inviting the gentry of Yorkshire to attend a meeting designed to prepare a petition to the Commons. Wyvill wanted this to include an inquiry into the Civil List, which was to be linked to an assault on sinecures and pensions, in short 'economical reform'. Ironically, George had supported such reform in the early 1760s: it clearly reflected a widely held aspiration.

By the late 1770s, however, as a consequence of the intervening politics, including the perception of George's policies, such a policy had the crown, its power and reputation as target, not means. In December 1779, Richmond and Rockingham in the Lords attacked the Civil List as corrupt. Rockingham saw its reform as a way to ensure appropriate limits on the influence of the crown, presenting this as less disruptive than parliamentary reform. Leonard Smelt, a tutor of the prince of Wales, told a reform meeting in York that George was 'unable now to curb that licentiousness with which he was every day talked of in every company, and in every street. He was unable to put to silence the numerous libels with which he was daily insulted.'[5] Concerned about this meeting and showing a sensitivity to the impact of public politics, George had pressed for the attendance in York of 'friends of the constitution'.[6]

The war he was playing a key role in helping to sustain ensured that George was to be exposed to the pressure for reform. Furthermore, the crisis in America had affected George's international reputation, as liberal circles on the continent took up the cause of the Americans, seeing it in the light of their claims to liberty and freedom. This contributed greatly to anglophobia.[7] The war brought serious criticism of British policy, and, if it was directed at the ministry, there was also criticism involving George. As Britain was also at war, or had poor relations, with much of Europe from 1778, this affected George's reputation. At the same time, there was some surprising praise for the king. The *Courrier d'Avignon*, one of the major newspapers published in French, although not in France (Avignon was a papal enclave), applauded George in 1779 as ruler, not least for his paternal relationship with parliament and people.[8]

---

[4] Cobbett, XIX, cols 213, 224–34.

[5] C. Wyvill, *Political Papers, Chiefly Representing the Attempt . . . to Effect a Reformation of the Parliament of Great Britain* (5 vols, York, 1794–1802); I.R. Christie, *Wilkes, Wyvill and Reform* (London, 1962).

[6] George to Robinson, 23 Dec. 1779, BL. Add. 37835 fol. 81.

[7] F. Acomb, *Anglophobia in France, 1763–1789* (Durham, North Carolina, 1950), pp. 51–68.

[8] J. Censer, 'France, 1750–89', in H. Barker and S. Burrows (eds), *Press, Politics and the Public Sphere in Europe and North America, 1760–1820* (Cambridge, 2002), pp. 166–9.

On 6 April 1780, against ministerial wishes, the Commons, on a division of 233 to 215 votes, had passed a resolution proposed by John Dunning: 'The influence of the Crown has increased, is increasing and ought to be diminished.'[9] This was followed by a successful motion to investigate Civil List expenditure. George felt personally attacked, but chose to blame 'factious leaders' rather than 'the majority',[10] a classic refrain in his treatment of opposition. Although the mechanics of royal power in the shape of placemen and government pocket boroughs had in fact declined since 1761,[11] the attack on the royal position was a reasonable response to George's key role in keeping the ministry behind the American war, but ensured that the king was even more resolved to doubt the opposition's motives and to keep them from office.

War and criticism strengthened George's determination, and in September 1780 he wrote, 'I never have seen any part of Opposition inclined to make the smallest concessions, and no power on Earth shall ever reduce me to deliver myself into the hands of any of them'.[12] That year, the situation eventually became more favourable to George as the result of a dramatic series of events, especially the anti-Catholic Gordon Riots in London and victories in the war at Charleston and Camden. The general election was also a success for the ministry.

The Gordon Riots, which broke out on 2 June 1780, arose from a pattern of legislative relief for Catholics that matched moves across much of Europe in favour of those hitherto at a disadvantage as a result of not being members of the established Church. George was willing to back these measures: Catholic Relief Acts were passed for Ireland in 1772, 1774 and 1778, and for England in 1778. These did not confer equality, or anything like it, but increased property rights and eased the position on education in the Catholic faith. The prospect of similar measures proved unacceptable, however, in Scotland, and was met with riots which reflected the popularity of anti-Catholicism and resulted in the shelving of the legislation.[13]

Furthermore, the leader of the Protestant Association, Lord George Gordon, sought to reverse the legislation already passed in England. An attempt to present the Association's petition for repeal to parliament on 2 June 1780 led first to violent scenes and then to disturbances that spread

[9] Cobbett, XXI, col. 90.

[10] George to North, 7, 11 Apr. 1780, Fortescue, V, 40, 42.

[11] I.R. Christie, 'Economical Reform and "The Influence of the Crown", 1780', in Christie, *Myth and Reality in Late-Eighteenth-Century British Politics and Other Papers* (London, 1970), pp. 309–10.

[12] George to John Robinson, 6 Sept. 1780, BL. Add. 70990 fol. 8.

[13] R.K. Donovan, *No Popery and Radicalism: Opposition to Roman Catholic Relief in Scotland, 1778–1782* (New York, 1987).

across London. George was unimpressed by Gordon. He took a close interest in the suppression of the riots and pressed for firm action, 'for I am convinced till the magistrates have ordered some military execution on the rioters this town will not be restored to order'. As on other occasions, George displayed considerable resolution. What could be seen as stubbornness was also pertinacity in the face of crisis. George's emphasis on doing his duty emerged clearly in the public presentation of the crisis. 'The King said in Council, "That the magistrates had not done their duty, but that he would do his own" . . . There has, indeed, been an universal panic, from which the King was the first that recovered.'[14]

After the suppression of the riots, George was unprepared to assuage the strength of popular anti-Catholicism by making concessions. He did not favour a bill to that end and, instead, wrote of the need to protect 'the lives and properties of all my subjects'.[15] His attitudes and policies in the 1770s and early 1780s did not clash with his subsequent opposition to Catholic emancipation, because, to George, an emphasis on amelioration did not extend to compromising his rights and responsibilities as head of the established Church. Furthermore, with his sense of duty, George did not see himself as a populist: he was ready to oppose bigotry in 1780 and to sustain discrimination in the 1790s and 1800s, and did not see these as contradictory.

A reaction against the Gordon Riots helped the government recover the initiative against popular politics, now associated with disorder, and this was exploited by calling a general election, a year earlier than was necessary under the Septennial Act, a step pressed by George.[16] During the campaign George was attentive to electoral matters, although he was affected by the birth of his last son, Alfred. George's varied activities included personally canvassing tradesmen in Windsor who were dependent on the castle, successfully so, on behalf of the ministerial candidate and against Admiral Keppel,[17] as well as writing to Robinson about another seat:

There cannot be the smallest doubt that driving Sir Lawrence Dundas out of the Orkneys is a very desirable object. I am clear Mr. Robinson ought to encourage the Lord Advocate of Scotland to manage this business; I trust he has some proper candidate in view.

[14] George to Jenkinson, 8 June 1780, BL. Add. 38564 fol. 17; J. Boswell, *Life of Johnson* (Oxford, 1980), pp. 1054–5; C. Hibbert, *King Mob: The Story of Lord George Gordon and the London Riots of 1780* (London, 1958).

[15] George to North, 5 June 1780, Fortescue, V, 71.

[16] George to Robinson, 29 June, 1 Aug. 1780, BL. Add. 37835 fols 129, 139.

[17] S. Conway, *The British Isles and the War of American Independence* (Oxford, 2000), pp. 305–6. For George's concern about the seat in 1797, PRO. 30/8/104 fols 131–3.

Secret Service funds were indeed provided for the election in the Orkneys, which the government candidate, Robert Baikie, won in October 1780, having secured control of the head count; although in February 1781 he was unseated for his misconduct of the election. This letter also made clear, through the comment on the unsuccessful attempt to negotiate, via Frederick Montagu, a coalition with the opposition, that George's close interest in the mechanics of politics, an interest that he had somewhat shunned at the idealistic outset of his reign, was related to his firm determination to maintain his political position:

> The letter from Mr. Montagu shows the negotiation is quite over. Indeed I never expected it could come to anything, for I have never seen any part of opposition inclined to make the smallest concessions, and no power on Earth shall ever reduce me to deliver myself up into the hands of any of them.[18]

This firmness towards the opposition reflects the extent to which the war remained central to George's thoughts.

Aside from seeking to imprint his determination on his ministers, George continued to associate himself publicly with the war effort. He resumed his touring reviews, visiting the fleet at the Nore in August 1781. George was still optimistic about the prospects for success, although, in March 1781, he had noted that no troops or ships could be spared for southern India where Haidar Ali of Mysore was proving a serious challenge.[19] News crossed the Atlantic slowly, and on 23 November 1781 George could still write about Cornwallis's force besieged by Washington and the French at Yorktown in Virginia:

> the moment is very critical but his good sense, valour and the bravery of the troops under his command make me hope that he will extricate himself well, and if Sir Henry Clinton [the commander in New York] can arrive in time perhaps this moment may put an end to the rebellion.[20]

Failure in America, however, was to plunge the political system into crisis. George was greatly affected, not only because he was a key figure in the conduct of government and politics, but also because he was the pillar of last resort, the grounding of stability if the politicians could not cohere satis-

---

[18] George to Robinson, 6 Sept. 1780, BL. Add. 70990. For George's interest, see also George to Robinson, 5, 8, 14 Sept. 1780, BL. Add. 37835 fols 156, 162, 164.

[19] George to Porten, 27 Mar. 1781, I.R. Christie (ed.), 'George and the Southern Department: Some Unprinted Royal Correspondence', *Camden Miscellany* XXX (London, 1990), p. 431.

[20] George to Richard Grenville, 23 Nov. 1781, BL. Add. 70956.

factorily. This situation ensured that he had responsibilities and functions that were far from simply ceremonial.

Cornwallis's surrender at Yorktown on 19 October 1781, news of which reached London on 25 November, brought down the North ministry in March 1782, beginning a period of instability that lasted until 1784. The king was initially determined to fight on in order to save the empire, leading to criticism that George was ready to see Britain become a much weaker power rather than yield American independence.[21] He, however, still saw conceding independence as the end of empire. George accepted the cabinet minute of 8 December 1781 arguing that there was no point in sending more troops to North America, but was not prepared to acknowledge that victory against the Americans was therefore not feasible and that peace could be obtained only by accepting independence. To George, the issue was linked with his position in Britain. In January 1782, he wrote to North,

> I shall never lose an opportunity of declaring that no consideration shall ever make me in the smallest degree an instrument in a measure that would annihilate the rank in which this British Empire stands among the European states, and would render my situation in this country unsustainable.[22]

Parliamentary defeats forced George to change tack, but, by waiting to be forced, he had lost the opportunity to have North manage a change of policy, including a reconstitution of the ministry that was more favourable to royal views than the one that ultimately occurred. The ministers, instead, were forced by George's refusal to accept political realities to defend a policy they no longer believed in. They could not display a willingness to negotiate peace, a position that weakened them greatly. It was to be the House of Commons (the Lords gave the government no such problems), not the ministry, before whom George had to give way;[23] a course he had in fact anticipated in 1779.[24]

Pressed by North to respond to the views of the Commons,[25] where the independents were no longer prepared to back the war, George sought to create a new ministry, authorizing his leading confidant, Lord Chancellor Thurlow, to sound out two experienced former ministers, Earl Gower and Viscount Weymouth, both of whom had already held senior office during the War of American Independence. The king wanted to retain the positions the British still held in the Thirteen Colonies – Charleston, New York and Savannah. He also wished to attempt, by agreements with the

---

[21] Dreyer report, 31 Dec. 1781, Rigs. 1965.
[22] George to North, 21 Jan. 1782, Fortescue, V, 334-5.
[23] I.R. Christie, *The End of North's Ministry 1780-1782* (London, 1958), pp. 325-6.
[24] George to Jenkinson, 7 Nov. 1779, BL. Loan 72/1 fol. 17.
[25] North to George, 18 Mar. 1782, Fortescue, V, 395.

individual American states, to detach the Americans from France, but only provided the American states remained separate from each other.[26]

This policy was not viable in terms of British or American politics, so George had to turn to the Rockinghamites and accept that peace would entail the abandonment of the colonies. The king's position had been compromised by his close association with the cause of war. Distrust of George also affected the initial discussions with Rockingham, which were handled by Thurlow. Rockingham, who had experience of George's way with ministers he distrusted or came to distrust, was insistent that he be assured of George's confidence before a new ministry was formed, and also wanted to see the king's opinions in writing,[27] while, for his part, George was unwilling to 'treat *personally*' with Rockingham.[28] George had not wanted North to resign, but his minister insisted on the need to respond to the fall in Commons support.

Faced by the collapse of his expectations and hopes, the king even drafted an abdication speech in which he announced he would move to Hanover, but it was never delivered.[29] Thurlow pressed the king not to go there.[30] He did not do so, but despair at the political situation in the early 1780s played a role in George sending his sons Frederick and William to Hanover, although educational and perhaps dynastic considerations were probably the primary factors.

Succeeding North, Rockingham obliged George to agree to unwelcome terms, including accepting all of the new ministry's legislation and nominations for office, and the reform of the Civil List by parliamentary legislation rather than the 'interior regulation' George proposed.[31] Changes in the royal household included George, fourth duke of Manchester, a Rockinghamite supporter of the Americans, becoming Lord Chamberlain. There was to be no coalition with the former ministry,[32] although George succeeded in having Thurlow retain office as lord chancellor and in placing William, second earl of Shelburne, in the government, as secretary of state for home affairs, as a counterweight to Rockingham.[33] There was also a shift in the conduct of business: in place of ministers presenting business for cabinet consideration after first

---

[26] George to Thurlow, 28 Feb. 1782, R. Gore-Browne, *Chancellor Thurlow* (London, 1953), p. 173.

[27] Rockingham to Thurlow, 16, 18 Mar. 1782, WW. R1–1996, 1998.

[28] George to Jenkinson, 24 Mar. 1782, BL. Add. 38564 fol. 33.

[29] Draft message from George, Mar. 1782, Fortescue, V, 425.

[30] Gore-Browne, *Thurlow*, p. 179.

[31] George to Thurlow, 18 Mar., George to Shelburne, 12 Apr., George to Rockingham, 28 Apr. 1782, Fortescue, V, 392, 452–5, 496–502.

[32] Memoranda on Rockingham's terms, WW. R1–2019.

[33] F. O'Gorman, *The Rise of Party in England. The Rockingham Whigs, 1760–1782* (London, 1975), pp. 446–56.

submitting it to the king, business was laid before the cabinet without such approval.[34] However, like other aspects of the politics of 1782–3, the decline in royal power was more clearly a feature of the 1790s.[35]

George had scant confidence in the new ministry, and, in expressing his views to Shelburne, helped undermine it. There was an element of paranoia when, in May 1782, George wrote:

> I own I begin to think that there is a plan of bringing things if possible into confusion; the ill success all their hasty negotiations have as yet met with; the inutility of so openly avowing American independency which is an article in all Mr. Fox's letters to the ministers abroad and his adoption of all the wild ideas of Russia concerning the Neutral League give but too much reason to authorize such an idea.[36]

The news of Rodney's victory at the Iles des Saintes south of Guadeloupe over the French fleet in the West Indies on 12 April, which was greeted in Britain with great enthusiasm, encouraged George to feel that the war might have to continue. Cutting across government policy, he argued that France had no intention 'of making peace upon such terms as this country can accept'.[37] George, himself, sought peace but only 'if it can be obtained without forfeiting the honour and essential rights of my kingdom'.[38]

Meanwhile, the government was pressing forward its policies for change. The nature of empire was being transformed in Ireland. Under pressure from the Volunteer movement, which demanded legislative independence for Ireland, the Rockingham ministry felt it important to make concessions. The Declaratory Act of 1720 that had proclaimed the right of the Westminster parliament to legislate for Ireland was repealed, and the Dublin parliament then ended the right of the British Privy Council to oversee Irish legislation. Ireland was now in effect independent under the crown, a position the American colonies had been denied.[39]

In Britain, to George's anger, the court was affected by the process of reform, with the attack on places, pensions and royal influence leading to the abolition of many sinecures and the wholesale restructuring of the smaller royal household, as well as unwelcome changes in personnel. The plan for economical reform introduced by Burke on 11 February 1780 had

---

[34] Shelburne to George and reply, both 29 Apr. 1782, Fortescue, V, 503–5.

[35] R.E. Willis, 'Cabinet Politics and Executive Policy-making Procedures', *Albion*, 7 (1975), pp. 9–23.

[36] George to Shelburne, 7 May 1782, Fortescue, VI, 10.

[37] George to Fox, 18 May 1782, Fortescue, VI, 34.

[38] George to Fox, 22 May 1782, Fortescue, VI, 41.

[39] G. O'Brien, *Anglo-Irish Politics in the Age of Grattan and Pitt* (Blackrock, 1987).

included the ending of many household offices, such as treasurer, cofferer and comptroller. His subsequent motions to this end were defeated in the Commons in 1780 and 1781. As part of the creation of the Rockingham ministry, George, however, had had to accept change, although the marquess was careful not to drive George too far, and was also aware that many independent MPs did not want the household itself to be affected. He promised the king that the offices to be abolished served the interests of the ministers, not the person of the monarch or 'the splendour of your Court'. Burke's bold prospectus of 1780 was retrenched. Nevertheless, a major reform programme brought the Civil List under parliamentary examination and regulation, and also hit royal influence by reducing the number of royal placemen, as it was intended to do.[40] This was constitutional reform and revenge politics, although, helped by Shelburne, the king was able to lessen the intended blow.[41] The issue raised the subject of royal rights and the extent to which they could properly be qualified. Specifically, there was the issue of how far the position established at the outset of the reign had to be continued, a question that was also to be an issue in the debate over Catholic emancipation. Richard Rigby, the paymaster-general, emphasized that the Civil List had been settled on George for life. In 1782, there were extensive changes in the household: long-standing departments, such as the office of the great wardrobe and the jewel office, the treasurership of the chamber and the cofferership of the household, were abolished, as were the sinecure posts of the master of the stag hounds and the master of the harriers. In place of a series of autonomous offices, the household was, from 1782, organized under the authority of the lord steward, the lord chamberlain and the master of the horse. In the absence of a detailed study of George III's court, the impact of such moves is unclear, but they certainly drove home to George the consequences of having critical ministers. Similarly, in the spring of 1782 he was obliged to give four vacant Orders of the Garter to friends of the new government, rather than Northite courtiers. George was also concerned about the human cost of the reforms on his servants, an aspect of his more generally considerate nature.

Anticipating the death in 1806 of William Pitt the Younger before his time, Rockingham's death, on 1 July 1782, led to another new ministry. George, who felt that he had been kept in the dark about Rockingham's health, wanted 'a broad bottom' ministry, not another Rockinghamite one.[42] He chose as first minister not the new leader of the

---

[40] WW. R1–2063–4; E.A. Reitan, 'Politics, Finance, and the People: Economical Reform in England, 1763–1792'. I would like to thank Professor Reitan for letting me have a copy of his unpublished book.

[41] J. Norris, *Shelburne and Reform* (London, 1963), pp. 155–8.

[42] George to Shelburne, 1 July 1782, Fortescue, VI, 70.

Rockinghamites, William, third duke of Portland, but William, second earl of Shelburne, a former protégé of Pitt the Elder, who had had experience of government as first lord of trade and secretary of state for the Southern Department. Shelburne had also been secretary of state for home affairs in the recent Rockingham ministry, being correctly seen then as enjoying royal favour, unlike Rockingham. Careful to note rifts in the political world, George had been confident that Shelburne would not join with Rockingham in putting pressure on him. As a young man, Shelburne had been a King's Friend, close to Bute and Henry Fox, and an aide-de-camp to George. From Pitt the Elder, Shelburne took an opposition to party, a theme that linked him to George. This helped ensure that, although his interest in reform and his somewhat radical views, illuminated by French Enlightenment ideas, were unwelcome to George, and were later to become far more so, nevertheless he was acceptable as a first minister in 1782, certainly more so than any Rockinghamite.

George's determination to defend his prerogative of choosing his own ministers was generally accepted, although prominent Rockinghamites, especially Charles James Fox, resigned. Shelburne defended the king's right to choose his ministers and his rejection of Foxite ideas regarding the choice of prime ministers and collective responsibility within the cabinet. Declaring that Shelburne had his fullest support, George foresaw 'a struggle whether I am to be dictated to by Mr. Fox'.[43] Shelburne, however, was widely unpopular, which compromised his value for the king. He had a justified reputation for arrogance, could be aloof and cunning, which led to his description as Jesuitical, and failed to consult with colleagues.

Peace on good terms was Shelburne's major task. He presented himself to the French envoy as having to bring round a king who had been misled by his predecessors into believing that he was the greatest monarch on earth, and one who would subjugate the Americans and defeat the French navy. This was an inaccurate impression of George: while it was true that he was reluctant to abandon the struggle,[44] he acted a conscientious part in supporting his ministers in negotiating peace. Nevertheless, he only wanted to accept American independence if the terms were right, arguing, with a reference to a public opinion that was not generally his leading theme, that this was necessary to 'make this Kingdom consent to it. Besides, he must see that the great success of Lord Rodney's engagement [the battle of the Saints] has again so far roused the nation, that the peace which would have been acquiesced in three months ago would now be matter of complaint.'[45] George backed Shelburne, supported him in

[43] George to Jenkinson, 13 July 1782, BL. Loan 72/1 fol. 67.
[44] Gérard de Rayneval, French envoy, to Vergennes, foreign minister, 18 Sept. 1782, AE. CP. Ang. 538 fol. 203.
[45] George to Shelburne, 1 July 1782, Fortescue, VI, 70.

seeking co-operation with France, and was ready, in the face of cabinet opposition, to abandon his and Shelburne's policy of relinquishing Gibraltar to Spain in return for better terms in the West Indies.[46]

Shelburne fell not because of the king, but because of his political opponents. His attempt to strengthen the ministry by bringing in North, and that of his young colleague William Pitt the Younger, the chancellor of the exchequer, to do the same by bringing in Fox, both failed: Pitt would not accept North and Fox would not accept Shelburne. Instead, Fox and North came to terms, a process aided by North's anger at the failure in the peace preliminaries to protect the American loyalists. As a result, on 17 and 21 February 1783, the peace preliminaries signed in Paris in January were rejected by the Commons, and on 24 February Shelburne announced that he would resign. The crisis showed that the largest groups in the House, those led by Fox and North, were aiming to secure office and were prepared to do so regardless of any claim by George to choose his ministers. George eagerly took up Shelburne's suggestion that Pitt, an effective Commons speaker who could resist Fox, succeed him, but Pitt turned him down as he would have lacked a Commons majority and therefore would have been dependent on North. George then approached North, but he refused to serve without Fox, and George was obliged to turn to the Fox–North coalition's leader, William, third duke of Portland, the leader of the Rockinghamites. A disagreement among its principals over places gave George an opportunity to approach Pitt anew, ending his talks with Portland, but Pitt's position in the Commons was too weak. The king was disappointed, not least because to him the stakes were of the highest. He wrote to Pitt,

> I am much hurt to find you are determined to decline at an hour when those who have any regard for the constitution as established by law ought to stand forth against the most daring and unprincipled faction that the annals of this kingdom ever produced.[47]

Indeed, after 26 March George did not write to him until 23 December. Shelburne resigned on 26 March, and Pitt five days later.

In April 1783 George finally had to accept a coalition ministry headed by Portland, and in which the most prominent members were North and Fox. He also had to part with Thurlow, the minister he most trusted.[48] The alliance of these formerly bitter enemies was presented by North as the best way to bring the harmony and strength likely to produce a firm and

[46] A. Stockley, *Britain and France at the Birth of America. The European Powers and the Peace Negotiations of 1782–1783* (Exeter, 2001), pp. 144–6.
[47] George to Pitt, 23, 25 Mar. 1783, PRO. 30/8/103 fols 5, 11 (quote).
[48] George to Robinson, 25 May 1779, BL. Add. 37834 fol. 88.

stable ministry, and the coalition was backed by many independent parliamentarians. To George, however, the coalition seemed a hypocritical device. He personally disliked Fox, the libertine friend of his eldest son, blaming him for leading the prince astray. George also saw Fox as a threat to the role of the crown. Nevertheless, there was considerable force in North's argument for the need to respond to circumstances. In March 1783, North reminded George that

> Your Majesty's gracious orders to me were certainly to form a plan of an administration for your Majesty's inspection upon the most extensive basis possible. It was not in my power to attempt to form any such arrangement without the concurrence of the Duke of Portland and his friends . . . I humbly stated to your Majesty on a former occasion, not only as my opinion, but as the opinion of such of my friends as were the best able to judge of the question, that the present state of parties and of the House of Commons rendered it impossible for the public business to be conducted in that House by a junction of my friends with the remainder of the administration; From hence your Majesty will judge to what little purpose I could attempt, by myself, to prepare an arrangement fit for your Majesty's inspection. Nothing can result from such an attempt useful, respectable, permanent, or capable of answering, in any respect, your Majesty's expectations.[49]

The formation of the ministry demoralized George, and his habitual self-righteousness brought him no solace. The king indeed revised his abdication declaration. His unsuccessful resistance to taking Fox into office had led only to mortification, and it was believed that George's health was affected, with agitation and chagrin resulting in an abundance of bile. Fox was not the sole issue. On 24 March, George had written to Pitt, 'After the manner I have been personally treated by both the Duke of Portland and Lord North, it is impossible I can ever admit either of them into my service.'[50] In 1782, George's anger at having to yield to Rockingham had also visibly affected him. Now, the king claimed that his health would suffer if the coalition continued.[51]

Having probed possibilities as he sought in the spring of 1783 to resist the formation of the new ministry,[52] George now conspicuously failed to show it support. He made no real attempt to ease differences or to

---

[49] North to George, 18 Mar. 1783, BL. Add. 61860 fols 1–3.

[50] PRO. 30/8/103 fol. 9.

[51] Dreyer report 29 Mar. 1782, 11 Mar., 4 Apr. 1783, Rigs. 1965–6; George to Earl Temple, 1 Apr. 1783, Fortescue, VI, 330.

[52] Grantham, account of meeting with George, 3 Mar. 1783, Bedford, Bedfordshire CRO. L 29/596; George to Temple, 1 Apr. 1783, Fortescue, VI, 329; A. and H. Tayler (eds), *Lord Fife and his Factor* (London, 1925), p. 156.

surmount them with personal graciousness. In particular, he refused to grant any British peerages in accordance with its wishes, a potent mani-festation of a lack of favour that was politically important in the House of Lords and was to be reversed when Pitt was appointed to office in order to help him.[53] Irish peerages were still granted but they did not bring the right to vote in the Westminster House of Lords. George's grudging tone and sense of acting out of necessity, were readily apparent:

> my finding on the coolest reflection that at an hour when the supplies are not yet found for the navy, army, and unfunded debt, that a bank-ruptcy must ensure if I did not sacrifice myself to the necessities of my people, I have therefore taken the bitter portion of appointing the seven ministers named by the Duke of Portland and Lord North to kiss hands, who are after that to form their plan of arrangements. I do not mean to grant a single peerage or other mark of favour, those cannot be called matters that regard the conduct of public affairs and if they fly out at that . . . I cannot fail in such a case to meet with support.[54]

George's attitude to the coalition was obvious. Elizabeth, duchess of Manchester, wife of a supporter of the new ministry, reported from court that the king's 'looks and manner strongly mark his dislike to all his present Court – he certainly is endeavouring to work a change as soon as he can', and the evidence for that, as so often was given in terms of access to the king: 'Lord S——ne [Shelburne] and the late Ministry are constantly with him'.[55] George was particularly opposed to the financial settlement pro-posed for the prince of Wales, which was seen as a way to increase the prince's political power, and which George presented as a support for his indulgences; and was angry that the prince publicly backed Fox. The king, however, backed down over this issue, as he did not think the moment appropriate for a new political crisis.

The establishment of yet another ministry also contributed to a more general sense of political failure, which suggests that contemporary expec-tations of the political system were not, as occurred in 1782–4, of frequent changes of government in response to shifts in parliamentary and electoral opinion, but, rather, of a stable ministry responsive to (and thus, if neces-sary, limited by) responsible parliamentary and popular opinion. The sense of Britain as weak, and of George as a failure, was furthered by the unsympathetic attitude of foreign rulers, such as Catherine II (the Great)

[53] W.C. Lowe, 'George III, Peerage Creations and Politics, 1760–1784', *Historical Journal*, 35 (1992), pp. 606–8.
[54] George to ———, 2 Apr. 1783, Bod. MS. Eng. Lett. c.144 fol. 77.
[55] Duchess to duke of Manchester, 27 May 1783, Huntingdon, Huntingdonshire CRO. DDM 21B/6.

of Russia, Frederick II (the Great) of Prussia, and the Emperor Joseph II.[56] Catherine said of George's loss of the Thirteen Colonies, 'Rather than sign the separation of thirteen provinces, like my brother George, I would have shot myself', a theme she returned to less vividly in 1787.[57]

The defeats in the Commons in February 1783 had been blows against specific clauses in the preliminaries and against Shelburne, rather than a rejection of the peace. The coalition, indeed, accepted the preliminaries, and on 3 September 1783 peace with France, Spain and America was signed at Versailles. The British kept Canada, but American independence was acknowledged and the British accepted a frontier that gave the new state the 'Old North West': the area between the Great Lakes and the Ohio. The native population, typically, was not consulted. France won minor gains, particularly Tobago and Senegal, while Spain regained Florida and Minorca from Britain.

Opening parliament on 5 December 1782, George said that he hoped for 'reconciliation' and 'union' with independent America,[58] but, despite strains in Franco-American relations, this was unrealistic. Instead, the peace settlement appeared to be a fundamental weakening of the empire, and this was linked to a widespread sense of Britain as a decayed power. A memorandum for the French foreign minister argued that only the ghost of kingship remained in St James's, and that liberty had degenerated into licence in Britain, a claim with which George would have concurred.[59] There was also the question of the impact of ministerial changes on the effectiveness of government. In part, this was a matter of the challenge to confidence – the views, in particular, of foreign powers and of domestic and foreign investors; but the workings of administration were also at issue.[60] In January 1784, Vergennes, the experienced French foreign minister, remarked that while George's views on Turkish–Russian affairs, as expressed to the French envoy, were satisfactory, his intentions were not always those of his ministers and he was obliged to follow the latter.[61]

British commentators also made unfavourable comparisons with foreign states, and some focused on the qualities of their monarchs, an implicit criticism of George. Robert Murray Keith, the long-serving envoy in Vienna, presented Austria as a more effective monarchy:

---

[56] Frederick to duke of Brunswick, 14 Jan. 1782, *Politische Correspondenz Friedrichs des Grossen* (46 vols, Berlin, 1879–1939), 46 (1939), p. 427.

[57] P. Mansel, *Prince of Europe: The Life of Charles-Joseph de Ligne* (London, 2003), p. 105; Louis Philippe, count of Ségur, French envoy in St Petersburg, Armand, to count of Montmorin, foreign secretary, 24 Sept. 1787, AE. CP. Russie 122 fol. 100.

[58] Cobbett, XXIII, col. 204.

[59] Memorandum by comte d'Albon, [1781], AE. MD. Ang. 2 fols 35–6.

[60] B. Lavery, *The Ship of the Line: The Development of the Battlefleet 1650–1850* (2 vols, London, 1983), I, 109.

[61] Vergennes to Jean-Balthazar, count of Adhémar, French envoy, 3 Jan. 1784, AE. CP. Ang. 547 fol. 14; George to North, 7 Sept. 1783, Fortescue, VI, 443.

The Emperor [Joseph II] attacks and overthrows a great many destructive prejudices, and knows not, neither has the smallest reason to know, a grain of fear. The people of this country, though not the most enlightened or brilliant of Europe, have many essential good qualities, and amongst others that of loving and respecting their sovereign, whose paternal care is demonstrated every week, by some new ordinance for the good of his people. This monarchy will soon be the best regulated of any in Europe, whilst our once happy island is daily shaking off every remnant of good order and subordination.[62]

These were also difficult personal years for George. He had had no personal experience of miscarriages or stillborn infants to prepare him for the grief when the first of his children died. Born in 1780, Alfred died in 1782, followed in 1783 by Octavius, who had been born in 1779: the latter was particularly mourned by George. Furthermore, no royal children were born in 1781–2, the longest period hitherto in which George and Charlotte had not had a child since they had been married. Their last child, Amelia, was born on 7 August 1783. At the same time, their older children, particularly the prince of Wales, were becoming more distant and difficult.

The resolution of the political crisis created by George's unwillingness to accept the coalition, in the shape of a stable ministry under Pitt, was far from inevitable. It was not certain that Pitt would secure a Commons majority simply because George appointed him to office on 19 December 1783, after the king helped secure the defeat in the Lords of the East India Bill, a crucial item of government business. The Bill aimed to lessen the power of the East India Company and give power to seven commissioners nominated by parliament and, in effect, chosen by the current ministry. This offered a marvellous field for patronage in the apparent cornucopia of Indian influence and power. George's actions, both against the East India Bill and in appointing a first minister who lacked a Commons majority, brought out the lack of agreement on the constitution and were regarded by some as unconstitutional. George does not seem to have given Portland the possibility of compromise by providing him with a warning of his opposition to the Bill, but he felt in a weak position. The Bill had already passed the Commons: on its third reading, on 8 December, with a substantial majority of 208 votes to 102. George also regarded the coalition as an aberration that he had been forced into accepting.

In a memorandum of 1 December, the king was asked to act against the Bill by George, second Earl Temple, a cousin and ally of Pitt, and his own

---

[62] Keith to his cousin, Frances Murray, 8 Feb. 1782, HL. HM. 18940, pp. 215–16.

adviser Thurlow, and it is probable that Pitt was party to this approach.[63] The royal veto had not been used since 1708 and to employ it after the Bill passed the Lords seemed too grave a step. Instead, the two peers suggested that George secure the measure's defeat there by making his opposition known, as it had not been when it was debated in the Commons. George himself sought confirmation of Pitt's support against the Bill, before acting by authorizing Temple on 11 December to state that any peer voting for the Bill would be considered a personal enemy, a view revealed on 17 December. Pitt had agreed to serve on condition that the king's opposition to the Bill was made clear, and on that day, when Portland asked George for permission to deny reports that he was hostile to the Bill, the king gave the bleak reply that he had never approved the Bill, and could not therefore give the duke the reassurance he sought. There was none of the equivocation displayed over the repeal of the Stamp Act in 1766 (see pp. 82–5). George's stance clearly had an impact. Some of the peers who adjourned the Bill on 15 December by 87 to 79, and defeated it two days later, did so as a result of self-interested concern about George's views: this was true of the majority of the bishops and of most of the peers with posts in the royal household. There was also concern about the measure itself, specifically that giving parliament, not the crown, the power to appoint commissioners to oversee the East India Company would give the ministry too great a field for patronage. This was the view not only of Pitt and Thurlow but also of reformers such as Wyvill. The role of the crown as a bulwark against over-mighty ministers seemed a reality. Defeating the measure in the Lords was less contentious than simply dismissing the ministry, and also avoided the potential clash of crown and parliament.

Though defeated in the Lords, the coalition did not resign, so that, on 18 December, George had to dismiss them. He then asked Pitt to form a new government. Pitt became first lord of the treasury, Temple both foreign and home secretary, and Gower lord president of the council, Thurlow being appointed lord chancellor on 23 December. Faced, however, by the unity of the coalition and the collective resignation of many office-holders angry at the treatment of North and Fox and unwilling to serve under Pitt, George saw himself as 'on the edge of a precipice' and hinted at abdication.[64] It seemed that his grandfather's failure to sustain Carteret in office in 1746 was about to be repeated. On 17 December, by a vote of 153 to 80, the Commons had already deplored the use of the king's name in securing the defeat of the India Bill, voting that 'to report any opinion, or pretended opinion, of his Majesty, upon any Bill or other proceedings, depending in either House of Parliament, with a view to

[63] M. Duffy, *The Younger Pitt* (Harlow, 2000), p. 17.
[64] George to Pitt, 23 Dec. 1783, PRO. 30/8/103 fol. 15.

influence the votes of the members, is a high crime and misdemeanour, derogatory to the honour of the Crown, a breach of the fundamental privileges of Parliament, and subversive of the Constitution of this country'.

In the face of considerable hostility and fearing impeachment, Temple, on 22 December, resigned from the new government; this was seen as a serious blow to it. There is evidence that Pitt, once appointed, intended to dissolve parliament and call a general election immediately in order to use government patronage to help secure a more pliant Commons, but a Land Tax Act had to be passed and the necessary parliamentary timetable did not allow time for a new parliament to meet and pass a Mutiny Act before 25 March when the current one expired. This was crucial to the position of the army. Pitt had to hang on and fight it out, despite his weak position in the Commons.[65] Many prominent individuals rejected office, including Grafton, Camden and Cornwallis, and some of the appointments that were made brought little political experience or support, including Francis, marquess of Carmarthen as foreign secretary, a former lord of the bedchamber (1776–7) and lord chamberlain to the queen (1777–80), and as home secretary Thomas, Lord Sydney, who had earlier held the post under Shelburne. The ministry was particularly weak in the Commons, and it was there that the opposition concentrated its attempt to overthrow the government before it could arrange a general election to its liking.

Changes in the household made George's views clear. He had more room for manoeuvre with court posts than he had had in the spring of 1782, and he exploited this freer hand to help the government. Those who had backed the coalition lost their posts. William, second earl of Dartmouth, North's half-brother, the lord steward, was replaced by James, third duke of Chandos, while James, seventh earl of Salisbury, became lord chamberlain, in place of Francis, earl of Hertford; George, Lord de Ferrers, became captain of the band of gentlemen pensioners, in place of George, fourth earl of Jersey. The earl of Orford succeeded Sandwich as ranger of St James's and Hyde Parks.[66] George also worked hard to try to win backing for the new government, not least by offering honours. Henry Carteret became Lord Carteret, Sir Thomas Egerton was created Lord Grey de Wilton, the duke of Northumberland was also made Lord Lovaine, with a remainder for this peerage to his second son, and Edward Eliot became Lord Eliot. The latter two were important borough patrons.

Commons defeats in January 1784, particularly of the new ministry's Bill for the government of India on the 23 January (an opposition majority

---

[65] P. Kelly, 'The Pitt–Temple Administration: 19–22 December 1783', *Historical Journal*, 17 (1974), pp. 157–61; J. Ehrman, *The Younger Pitt. The Years of Acclaim* (London, 1969), p. 125.

[66] George to Pitt, 24 Dec. 1783, PRO. 30/8/103 fol. 17.

of eight), however, led Pitt to think of resigning and George to reiterate his willingness to abdicate, although declaring his determination to fight on. He had been distressed to find the Commons 'much more willing to enter into any intemperate resolutions of desperate men than I could have imagined', and emphasized his hostility to 'this faction'.[67] On 26 January George sought to stiffen cabinet resolve, and declared that he 'would quit the kingdom for ever' sooner than let Fox beat him.[68] The perseverance, stubbornness and inflexibility seen in his handling of America was again evident, but, from George's perspective, to yield would be an unacceptable compromise of the royal position and an invitation to further disorder,[69] in a struggle between decorum and anarchy.[70] The ministry's position in the Commons continued vulnerable, and the coalition, which still had a majority there, maintained its pressure for the king to dismiss his ministers, but the resolve of George and Pitt was fortified by signs of increasing public support. George's confidence, by February, in this support led him to write of

the present strange phenomenon, a majority not exceeding 30 in the House of Commons thinking that justifies the stopping the necessary supplies when the House of Lords by a majority of near two to one and at least that of the People at large approve of my conduct and see as I do that not less is meant than to render the Crown and the Lords perfect ciphers; but it will be seen that I will never submit.[71]

The crisis indeed crystallized the ambiguities of the political system. Parliamentary monarchy is the usual formula used to describe the system, but its neatness is deceptive. If rulers were constrained, or at least affected, by the need to find ministers who could manage parliament, the nuances of that relationship still contained plentiful material for dispute. The crucial issue was the appointment of ministers. In normal times, and for most of the political nation, it was only necessary for the monarch to find ministers acceptable to himself. Acceptance by parliament would then follow, as, by a mixture of patronage and moral support from the monarch, and loyalty from most MPs, the king's choice commanded a majority. The alternative advocated by Fox – parliamentary majorities rather than royal choice, as the basis for ministries – was a minority view in the 1780s, although the overthrow of the coalition had

---

[67] George to Pitt, 13 Jan. 1784, PRO. 30/8/103 fol. 31.

[68] O. Browning (ed.), *The Political Memoranda of the Duke of Leeds* (London, 1884), p. 95.

[69] George to Pitt, 26 Jan. 1784, PRO. 30/8/103 fol. 42.

[70] George to Pitt, 17 Jan. 1784, PRO. 30/8/103 fol. 35.

[71] George to Richard Grenville, 13 Feb. 1784, BL. Add. 70957.

sapped confidence in royal choice. On 16 January 1784, the Commons, on a majority of 205 to 184, carried a motion

> that, in the present situation of his Majesty's dominions, it is peculiarly necessary there should be an administration which has the confidence of this House and of the public; and that the appointments of his Majesty's present ministers were accompanied by circumstances new and extraordinary, and such as do not conciliate or engage the confidence of this House; the continuance of the present ministers in trusts of the highest importance and responsibility is contrary to constitutional principles and injurious to the interests of His Majesty and his people.

As was his wont, George looked on the bright side, seeing the measure as an extreme one that would alienate moderates.[72] The opposition case continued, however, to be supported by the Commons. On 2 February, a motion 'that it is the opinion of this House that the continuance of the present ministers in their offices is an obstacle to the formation of such an administration as may enjoy the confidence of this House, and tend to put an end to the unfortunate divisions and distractions of the country' was passed 223 to 204, and, the following day, it was agreed by 211 to 187 'that the said resolutions be humbly laid before his Majesty by such members of this House as are of his Majesty's most honourable Privy Council'. George responded to Commons majorities by arguing that 'any man must indeed be totally ignorant of this Constitution or much blinded by party that does not see that a faction is now in the most shameless manner openly avowing that to get the executive power into its hands is the only cause of the violent steps now pursuing'. To George, this power was clearly vested in the crown, a situation that could not be changed as each branch of the legislature had its fixed bounds, a belief in continuity and limits that underlined his general approach to politics.[73] Feeling that the position of the crown was being compromised by the Commons, George again threatened to abdicate and leave for Hanover.[74] If the Commons, on 1 March 1784, on a vote of 201 to 189, passed an address to George to remove Pitt, and with Fox arguing that it had a right to advise the king on the use of his prerogative, this step, nevertheless, helped lessen support for Fox, and the majority was a slight one. George, moreover, was firm, replying to the Commons on 4 March

---

[72] George to Marlborough, 17 Jan. 1784, Aspinall, *George III*, I, 23.
[73] George to Sydney, George to Pitt, both 3 Feb. 1784, Aspinall, *George III*, I, 29, PRO. 30/8/103 fol. 46.
[74] George to Pitt, 4 Feb. 1784, PRO. 30/8/103 fol. 48.

that he knew of no additional step he could take to meet the Commons' expectations.[75]

Fox was a maverick who wanted to change the constitution and whose ideas were widely rejected; hence the erosion of Fox and North's majority in the Commons against Pitt in early 1784, and the verdict of the subsequent general election in favour of Pitt and George. There was a whiff of republicanism about Fox and his friends that put them well outside the general run of politicians angling for power, for republicanism had scant support among the political élite. Johnson told Boswell that Fox had 'divided the Kingdom with Caesar; so that it was a doubt whether the nation should be ruled by the sceptre of George the Third, or the tongue of Fox'.[76] Already, in April 1783, Thomas Brand, a cleric, had reflected on 'the history of Party for so I think the history of modern Great Britain should be called. It is really a dreadful thing. If the King had any sinister views, what an opportunity to increase his prerogative for surely the nation must be sick of Patriots.'[77] The alternative, in early 1784, was a government comprehending ministry and opposition, the goal of many of the independents. Pitt was willing to explore the option, and a very unenthusiastic George[78] allowed him to do so, but the opposition said that Pitt must first resign, and that was not an acceptable basis for discussion as far as George was concerned.

The lengthy crisis in Britain was a severe trial for George. Alongside desperate, but somewhat histrionic, threats to abdicate, this crisis helped confirm his belief that persistence was the appropriate policy and would reap its rewards. Ironically, the opposite lesson was suggested by his earlier management of American politics. Yet, pertinacity was in George's eyes a legitimist creed designed to protect rights, not an aggressive one born of an interest in extending power. He made his views clear as he sought to rally support, speaking to the bishops at court on New Year's Day and writing three days earlier to a near-contemporary, George, fourth duke of Marlborough (1739–1817), seeking the support of his electoral interest in Oxfordshire:

The times are of the most serious nature; the political struggle is not as formerly between two factions for power, but it is no less than whether a desperate faction shall not reduce the Sovereign to a mere tool in its hands. Though I have too much principle ever to infringe the rights of

[75] P. Kelly, 'British Politics, 1783–4: The Emergence and Triumph of the Younger Pitt's Administration', *Bulletin of the Institute of Historical Research*, 54 (1981), pp. 62–78.

[76] Boswell, *Life of Johnson*, p. 1292.

[77] Brand to Robert Wharton, 16 Apr. 1783, Durham UL, Archives and Special Collections, Wharton papers, no. 578.

[78] George to Pitt, 30 Jan. 1784, PRO. 30/8/103 fol. 44.

others, yet that must ever equally prevent my submitting to the executive power being in any other hands than where the Constitution has placed it. I therefore must call on the assistance of every honest man, and trust the Duke of Marlborough will zealously engage his friends to support Government on the present most critical occasion ... my cause, which indeed is that of the Constitution as fixed at the [Glorious] Revolution, and to the support of which my family was invited to mount the throne.

Marlborough hastened to offer his zealous support, but also indicated the unfixed nature of issues and the difficulty of deciding whether to distinguish crown from minister, by explaining that he had given his proxy vote for Fox's Bill as 'he thought it calculated rather to increase than to diminish the power of the Crown'.[79] In such a context, the clarity offered by George's vigorous partisanship was important.

George's role in the overthrow of the Fox–North ministry can be seen as rash, but he was concerned that they threatened a major change with their India Bill, and he was confident that the coalition would collapse in opposition. In tactical terms, an error was made with the assumption that office-holders would continue serving the crown: the hold of the coalition over its supporters was underestimated. Nevertheless, alongside charges of rashness, a note of caution could be heard, not least in the king's response to international opportunities during this period, in this case the prospect of negotiations between Sweden and France leading to an Anglo-Russian counterpart. George wrote, 'till I see this country in a situation more respectable as to army, navy and finances I cannot think anything that may draw us into troubled waters either safe or rational'.[80]

Pertinacity, an appropriate support of the constitution, and due caution. The case for the defence is clear, but, aside from the general issue of the need to respond to changing problems, in this case the government of India (also an issue in Churchill's politics of the mid-1930s), there was also the question of George's methods. The use of influence in the Lords appeared to confirm earlier suspicions of illicit and questionable political practices on the part of the king. At a ball in Vienna for the visiting Frederick, duke of York, Joseph II told the French envoy that the divided situation of her politics and other difficulties in Britain were such that George more than ever needed to be firm.[81] Firmness, however, had to be married to good judgement. If the crisis in 1783–4 is seen as a conse-

---

[79] George to Marlborough, and reply, both 29 Dec. 1783, Aspinall, *George III*, I, 15; George to Pitt, 30 Dec. 1783, PRO. 30/8/103 fol. 21.

[80] George to Francis, marquess of Carmarthen, foreign secretary, 6 July 1784, BL. Add. 27914 fol. 3.

[81] Marquis de Noailles to Vergennes, 4 Aug. 1784, AE. CP. Autriche 348 fol. 3.

quence of that over the American colonies, then judgement is less favourable to George than if it is depicted as another clash between the king and political groups seeking unwarranted power. George, nevertheless, was to be vindicated politically in the elections held in 1784. In a monarchy, there was no real question of any choice between the king and Charles James Fox if the choice was presented in those terms, as indeed it was.

Chapter 13

GEORGE AND WILLIAM PITT THE YOUNGER, 1784–90

Beware of Prerogative . . . I charge you sully not the name of Pitt, by sacrificing the privileges of the people and the happiness of your expiring country to the desires of an obstinate – whose prejudices have ever been accompanied with public ruin.

Pitt the Elder to Pitt the Younger in *The Vision*,
caricature published 12 March 1785

Hanging on in the political crisis of the winter of 1783–4 helped George and the new government benefit from a swelling tide in popular opinion, shown in a large number of addresses from counties and boroughs, with over 50,000 signatures in total, in favour of the free exercise of the royal prerogative in choosing ministers. These addresses were also a testimony to the potential popularity of the monarchy. In 1784, however, this was clearly presented in a political fashion – against the factionalism represented by Fox – while, at George's accession, his popularity had been far more inclusive. The loss of America had been cathartic as well as divisive, and if the circumstances of 1783–4 made it harder to present Fox and North as a 'Patriot' opposition they ensured that George's popularity was more compromised than it had been in 1760. Pitt was further aided by the active support of many peers, not least their influence with dependants in the Commons; and by the uncertainty of his opponents as to whether they should use their majority in the Commons and that House's power to refuse supplies in order to force a change of government.

George's role owed much to his influence in the House of Lords, which still played a major role in the political system, albeit a lesser one than a century earlier. It posed fewer problems of management than the Commons. The 'Party of the Crown', composed of archbishops, bishops, royal household officers, Scottish representative peers, and newly created or promoted peers, provided a consistent basis for the ministerial majority.[1] George's influence with the peerage reflected the natural

---

[1] D. Large, 'The Decline of the "Party of the Crown" and the Rise of Parties in the House of Lords, 1783–1837', *English Historical Review*, 78 (1963), pp. 669–95; J. Cannon, *The Fox-North Coalition. Crisis of the Constitution* (Cambridge, 1969), p. 225; M.W. McCahill, *Order and Equipoise. The Peerage and the House of Lords, 1783–1806* (London, 1978), pp. 31–6.

concern of the aristocracy with stability and hierarchy, which was accentuated by the king's success in personal relations. This was seen not only in his relationship with the senior clergy, but also in his socializing with the aristocracy, which became more obvious in the late 1780s as he travelled more extensively. The backing of the Lords lessened the severity of the political crisis in 1783-4 and obliged Fox to concentrate his efforts on the Commons. There, Fox's bluff was called over the voting of supplies and he suffered from a leakage of Northites both before and during the 1784 election, which revealed the unstable nature of the Fox–North alignment. There were significant tensions within it, and it was also weakened by failure and the loss of office and patronage, the last especially serious for the Northites.

North himself had a large debt on his election account dating from the 1780 general election – £30,000 borrowed from George's banker, Henry Drummond, on the king's authority, and £2,754 owed to George personally – but in 1782 George had accepted responsibility for only £13,000 and stated that North would have to pay the balance, a harsh decision that the former minister accepted. The money was still owing in 1784. George then ordered Drummond to obtain the money from North, only for North to tell the banker he could not pay it, a move that provoked outrage from the king, who referred to 'the most barefaced fraud' on the part of North.[2]

By 8 March 1784 Fox's majority in the Commons was down to one, much to George's satisfaction,[3] while Pitt's success in gaining the initiative in parliament helped bring about a turnaround of public opinion in his favour. Parliament was dissolved on 25 March when Pitt felt able to face a general election. The subsequent elections, with many constituencies contested on national political grounds by an electorate much of which could not be taken for granted by patrons,[4] were very favourable for the ministry, amounting to a 'national verdict'.[5] The government had a majority of about 150 seats and won many constituencies with large electorates, including Yorkshire, an important victory because of the county's leading recent role in reform agitation. At a meeting of the Yorkshire freeholders on 25 March, Henry, second Earl Fauconberg, who was to be George's host in Cheltenham in 1788, had asked, 'Is George III or Charles

[2] P.D.G. Thomas, *Lord North* (London, 1976), pp. 134–5, 144–5; I.R. Christie, 'George III and the Debt on Lord North's Election Account, 1780–84', *English Historical Review*, 78 (1963), pp. 715–24; George to Drummond, 24 Oct. 1784, Aspinall, *George III*, I, 105; George to Robinson, 1 Nov. 1784, BL. Add. 70990.

[3] George to Pitt, 9 Mar. 1784, PRO. 30/8/103 fol. 71.

[4] R.M. Sunter, *Patronage and Politics in Scotland 1707–1832* (Edinburgh, 1986).

[5] F. O'Gorman, 'The Unreformed Electorate of Hanoverian England: The Mid-Eighteenth Century to the Reform Act of 1832', *Social History*, 11 (1986), p. 51.

James Fox to reign?'[6] This meeting accepted an address justifying the dismissal of the Fox–North ministry as a 'just exertion' of the royal prerogative, and the coalition candidates for Yorkshire did not risk a poll. Opposition politicians could only explain developments in terms of a disease. Henry, second Viscount Palmerston, wrote of 'the epidemical kind of spirit that has gone about the country in favour of the King's prerogative against the House of Commons' and, although he was elected, William Eden referred to a 'frenzy of the people'.[7]

George took an interest in the elections, including the choice of Scottish representative peers.[8] He helped finance the government's election fund and obtained daily reports on the course of the election. His interest extended to individual constituencies and candidates, although he found that his advice was not necessarily taken, even by Pitt. Westminster, where he wanted Fox defeated, was a seat that particularly interested George and he urged Pitt to seek Quaker support there. With characteristic regret about the prevalence of hypocrisy, George also wrote of a member of the key Grenville connection,

> Mr. James Grenville has in the handsomest manner consented to be nominated of the Committee of Council on the Affairs of Trade which shows that his actions ever agree with his declarations. It would be well if this was less singular. I think if the gentlemen of Somerset look out for a respectable representative in the room of Mr. Coxe they ought to fix on him; but I believe their intentions are not known, some say they mean to offer Mr. Pitt this honourable testimony of approbation which he will certainly decline; Bath has offered to elect him which I strongly advised, but he has so strong a predilection to the University of Cambridge that he cannot be prevailed upon to give up that doubtful pursuit, and which if he succeeds all his friends agree with me in opinion will be inconvenient to him from the solicitations he must be subject to from the clergy.[9]

[6] P. Kelly, 'British Politics, 1783–4: The Emergence and Triumph of the Younger Pitt's Administration', *Bulletin of the Institute of Historical Research*, 54 (1981), pp. 62–78; F. O'Gorman, *Voters, Patrons and Parties. The Unreformed Electorate of Hanoverian England, 1734–1832* (Oxford, 1989), pp. 295–6. For other factors at work, T.R. Knox, '"Peace for Ages to Come": The Newcastle Elections of 1780 and 1784', *Durham University Journal*, 84 (1994), pp. 13–15 and P.D.G. Thomas, 'The Rise of Plas Newydd: Sir Nicholas Bayly and County Elections in Anglesey, 1734–84', *Welsh History Review*, 16 (1992), pp. 174–6.

[7] B. Connell (ed.), *Portrait of A Whig Peer Compiled from the Papers of The Second Viscount Palmerston, 1739–1802* (London, 1957), p. 152; Eden to Lord Sheffield, 10 Apr. 1784, BL. Add. 45782.

[8] Leeds memoranda, undated, BL. Add. 27918 fol. 119.

[9] George to Richard Grenville, 30 Mar. 1784, BL. Add. 70956.

In fact James Grenville was re-elected on the family interest in Buckingham. He was an instance of the strengthening of the government interest. An independent in the 1770s who had been a bitter opponent of the American war, Grenville had opposed Fox's East India Bill and was to be created Lord Glastonbury in 1797 when his Commons career came to an end. Richard Hippisley Coxe was declared a lunatic in 1784.

The overall results greatly cheered the king, and encouraged him to feel that his resolve had not only been vindicated but had helped save the country. He wrote of 'the lists of members returned which seems on the whole more favourable than even the most zealous expected',[10] and was pleased with the government's majority in the new session.[11] The 'popular' aspect of the elections was clear to contemporaries. The election results reflected the unpopularity of the Fox–North coalition, and especially considerable distrust of Fox, both for backing the Americans and because of his alliance with North. The results were also the result of widespread support for George as the symbol, and indeed reality, of stability and continuity, a position very different from two decades, or even one year, earlier. The prerogative had become popular. A caricature, *The Royal Hercules Destroying the Dragon Python*, published on 24 April 1784, showed George wrestling against a dragon with the heads of the major opposition leaders. The notion of a Patriot King above faction seemed fulfilled. It is necessary to note the contentious nature of George's actions, the extent of opposition, and the way in which the dismissal of the Fox–North ministry lent new force to its concerns, but there was no equivalent to the unpopularity focused on the French royal court seen with the scandal of the Diamond Necklace Affair of 1785.

In Britain, there was a renewed burst of popularity when George survived an attempt to kill him on 2 August 1786: Margaret Nicholson, the culprit, was mentally ill and convinced that she had a claim to the throne, rather than motivated by political ends, as was James Frith, who threw a large stone into George's carriage as he went to open parliament in 1790.[12] George was not injured by Nicholson's dessert knife, and, instead, was solicitous about his assailant, declaring 'The poor creature is mad; do not hurt her, she has not hurt me.' Examined by the Privy Council and declared insane, she was committed to Bethlem for life, remaining there until she died in 1828.

Despite an irritability that, in part, was possibly a result of poor health, George had matured in office, becoming a practised politician. His conscientious nature shines through his copious correspondence, while in 1788,

---

[10] George note, 4 Apr. 1784, New York Public Library, Montague collection, vol. 4.
[11] George to Pitt, 26 May 1784, PRO. 30/8/103 fol. 105.
[12] William Grenville to George, 21 Jan. 1790, BL. Add. 58855 fol. 63; *Gentleman's Magazine*, 60 (1790), p. 81.

in his answer to the speech of welcome by the recorder of Worcester he is reported to have said: 'The loyalty and affection which I have experienced amongst my subjects in this part of the Kingdom, and especially on this occasion, are an ample recompense to me for the public service of twenty-eight years'.[13]

This conscientiousness was related not only to George's idea of service but also to his sense of his position as the pivot of an inclusive civil politics. Although very aggrieved if his goodwill was not reciprocated, George felt that the monarch could reach out, beyond the antipathy and factional self-interest of politicians, to a wider, responsible and responsive public opinion. The fundamental feature of the Pitt ministry was that it was very much a royal creation. In the mid-1780s, George had therefore played a major role in ensuring the recreation of a political world that accorded with his aspirations at his accession. He used royal proclamations to galvanize public opinion on a range of issues. Once crown-élite consensus had been restored – at least in so far as was measured by the crucial criterion, the ability of George to co-operate with a ministry enjoying the support of parliament – Britain was essentially politically stable. This stability was a reflection of that ability, and it required a willingness to adjust, or even to compromise, on the part of the king. The distinction is not a particularly helpful one, but the situation can be seen as at once conservative and modern. George's conservative conviction of his crucial constitutional role was, thanks to the signs of widespread support for the royal position in 1784, married to an awareness of the possible popular resonance of the crown.

A broader basis for political stability was reflected in, and strengthened by, the increase in the granting of aristocratic status. Whereas there had been 66 peerage creations under George I, and 74 under George II, George III created 197 between 1760 and 1800, the number granted per year increasing notably after 1784, for in his early years George kept to his original intention to limit creations and to avoid political influences in his choices.[14] The peerage had risen to 267 by 1800. In part, this higher rate of creation reveals a shift from a more Germanic attitude under the first two Georges, with their relatively restrictive concern with the lineage of candidates for the peerage, to an emphasis on service under George III, although few of the new peerages ennobled new blood,[15] and the cadet branches of the aristocracy were more likely to be favoured. The end of Tory proscription expanded the number of families the king was willing to

[13] V. Green, *The History and Antiquities of the City and Suburbs of Worcester* (2 vols, London, 1796), I, 297.

[14] J.C. Sainty, *Peerage Creations, 1649–1800* (London, 1998); J. Cannon, *Aristocratic Century: The Peerage of Eighteenth-Century England* (Cambridge, 1984); W.C. Lowe, 'George III, Peerage Creations and Politics, 1760–1784', *Historical Journal*, 35 (1992), pp. 587–609.

[15] Cannon, *Aristocratic Century*, pp. 21–2.

reward with peerages or promotions in the peerage, creations led to competition for matching gains in status,[16] and George's knowledge of and personal good relations with many of the landed élite was also important. Keen to encourage 'obligations to the Crown', and to reward 'character as well as situation' in the localities and support for the government, George took a close interest in the expansion of the peerage.[17] The needs of the government, in the shape of inexpensive rewards in return for political support, were also to the fore under George from 1784. Newcastle, of all people, referred in 1762 to 'the shameful number of new Lords',[18] but George had limits.[19] He did not wish to make non-royal dukes,[20] and did not make any after, in a position of weakness in 1766, being forced to create two. George was also averse to specific promotions.[21] Nevertheless, there were criticisms of his use of the royal prerogative in this respect. In the caricature *English Coronet Auction, By K. P. and Co. or Comfort for the late French Noblesse*, published on 8 July 1790, George and Pitt are shown selling peerages to French nobles fleeing the Revolution, the king declaring

'This is a lot, gentlemen, a lot gentlemen, of superior brilliancy to the last, this, this raises you above your fellows in a very high degree indeed – I pity your distresses from my soul – what, what, what was that you were saying about jewels, Madame, throw 'em in, throw 'em in, you cannot bid too high – you may ride over the necks of half the nation with this upon your coach, you may get in debt as fast as you please and never pay. Mind that. Gentlemen never pay.'

The note of social criticism of the king and his role as a mouthpiece for false values was clear. In Ireland, where, of the 240 peerages in existence in 1801, 135 had been created since George's accession, the rise in landed income was crucial in justifying creations.[22]

From 1784, Pitt dominated politics for over two decades, serving as first lord of the treasury from December 1783 until 1801, and then again from 1804 until his death in 1806. His prudent fiscal management helped stabilize government. Pitt understood the crucial importance of sound finance. George, however, was unhappy with some aspects of Pitt's policies,

---

[16] Viscount Townshend to Charles Townshend, 9 Oct. 1766, Bury St Edmunds, West Suffolk CRO., Grafton papers 423/461.

[17] George to Robinson, 21 Aug., 2, 5 Sept., 3 Oct. 1780, BL. Add. 37835 fols 147, 151, 154, 175; George to Pitt, 24 Sept. 1804, 22 Apr. 1805, PRO. 30/8/104 fols 384, 433.

[18] Newcastle to Hardwicke, 2 May 1762, BL. Add. 32938 fol. 20.

[19] E.g. George to Rockingham, 5 June 1766, WW. R1–632.

[20] Aspinall, *George III*, I, 172, 171 fn. 6.

[21] Keppel to Rockingham, 29 May 1782, WW. R1–2103.

[22] A.P.W. Malcolmson, 'The Irish Peerage and the Union, 1800–1971', *Transactions of the Royal Historical Society*, 6th ser., 10 (2000), p. 300.

especially his support for parliamentary reform in 1785. This was symptomatic of more serious differences. Pitt's background was not that of a
'King's Friend', and indeed he sought to limit their political power.
Instead, he had a background, as his father's son, as a politician suspicious
of the court and, not least as a protégé of Shelburne, as a reformer.
George's principles were far from identical to Pitt's. In March 1784, he
thanked Pitt for having helped him to save the constitution (an important
indication of George's views of his ministers), adding that it was 'the most
perfect of human formations'.[23]

Pitt, however, was responsive to the reform aspirations of the early
1780s, which had helped him win support in the 1784 election, and ready
to change the constitution. His willingness to talk to Wyvill on this subject
alarmed George, who described Wyvill as 'a known demagogue'.[24] In
1785, Pitt proposed to extinguish thirty-six borough seats with small electorates. As voting was often a matter of property rights, the electors were
to be compensated financially and the seats transferred to London and the
English counties. Pitt also suggested the enfranchisement of copyholders
and certain categories of leaseholder, as well as a system of local polling
centres. Such steps would not have meant a major increase in the size of
the electorate, but a majority of the Commons shared George's antipathy
to change, and the proposals were defeated by 248 to 174 on 18 April 1785.
Pitt had threatened to resign if George instructed household members
who were MPs to vote against the Bill.[25] Out of regard for him, George
did not do so but, characteristically, he raised the issue of integrity,
informing Pitt that it would be wrong if any MP allowed 'his civility to any
one to make him vote contrary to his own opinion'.[26]

In turn, Pitt, who knew that the government interest was divided, was
careful not to push this divisive issue after it had been defeated. This
caution helped to align his ministry with conservative opinion and to
create a gulf between Pitt and political and religious reformers that looked
toward future division in response to pressure for the repeal of the Test
and Corporation Acts and to the French Revolution. Whatever their
differences, Pitt was very much George's own minister, and both men
were crucial, the earl of Morton writing in July 1784 that, 'the existence of
the Ministry depends on his and one other life, either of which failing, the
whole would fall to the ground'.[27] The two men agreed on the need for
national revival after the crisis of the early 1780s, and they could accom-

[23] George to Pitt, 9 Mar. 1784, PRO. 30/8/103 fol. 71.
[24] George to Sydney, 4 Jan. 1785, Aspinall, *George III*, I, 119.
[25] Pitt to George, 19 Mar. 1785, Aspinall, *George III*, I, 139; Lord George Germain to John,
third duke of Dorset, envoy in Paris, 11 May 1785, KAO. U269 C192.
[26] George to Pitt, 20 Mar. 1785, PRO. 30/8/103 fol. 149.
[27] Morton to Sir Robert Murray Keith, 13 July 1784, BL. Add. 35532 fol. 142.

modate their different understandings of such a revival; indeed, increasingly so as Pitt became less enthusiastic about reform and Dissent. George supported Pitt's fiscal reforms and benefited from his minister's support in 1786 over Civil List debts. Both issues brought out George's characteristic emphases on probity, reform and economy, themes that had been his since he was prince of Wales. He praised Pitt's plan to pay off at least £1 million of the national debt each year: this, at the same time, sought to control the temptations of the short term, 'putting it out of the power of a minister by an hasty vote to turn such a sum to defraying the expences of the year'. George assured Pitt that the Civil List debt arose from inflation and the size of his family, and not from extravagance.[28]

George was scarcely likely to turn to the Fox–North opposition, whose factiousness in being willing to leave the British possessions in the West Indies defenceless he found 'extraordinary'[29] and, during the Pitt ministry, there was an essential stability at the centre of established politics. Relations between George and Pitt were also smoothed by their ability to agree on most issues of patronage, although this was not always an easy matter.[30] Reports that George wanted to humiliate Pitt[31] were devoid of substance. Instead, he was pleased with the ministry's success in parliament.[32] The king needed Pitt to keep Fox out, and his animus was strengthened by Fox's links with the prince of Wales.[33] George was clearly partisan: successfully seeking to ensure that Richard Wellesley became MP for Windsor in 1787, George was motivated in part by the hostile principles of a rival candidate.[34]

Similarly, the importance of the independent MPs[35] underlined the significance of royal backing for the ministry, as most independents tended to look to the crown. MPs and peers still conformed to a political world of office-holders, faction members and independents rather than clear-cut parties, but the 1784 election had given an apparent cohesion, in which there was an apparent king's party underlying government. In practice, this was not an approximation to later concepts of party identity, organization and unity. Nevertheless, Pitt benefited greatly from signs of royal support, particularly because the general impression of political stability was matched by specific difficulties, especially as the ministry established itself. In 1785 the ministry was defeated over the Westminster scrutiny, a

---

[28] George to Pitt, 30, 28 Mar. 1786, PRO. 30/8/103 fols 188, 187.

[29] George to Pitt, 11 Dec. 1787, PRO. 30/8/103 fol. 268.

[30] M.J. Turner, *Pitt the Younger. A Life* (London, 2003), pp. 100–3.

[31] La Luzerne to Montmorin, 22 Apr. 1788, AE. CP. Ang. 565 fol. 95.

[32] George to Pitt, 6 May 1785, PRO. 30/8/103, fol. 165, Manchester, John Rylands Library, Eng. Mss. 912 no. 28.

[33] George to Thurlow, 31 Aug. 1784, Aspinall, *George III*, I, 85.

[34] George to Pitt, 24 June 1787, PRO. 30/8/103 fol. 238.

[35] *Daily Universal Register*, 15 Jan. 1785.

division that ensured that Fox was returned for a seat whose representation always concerned the king. That year, the ministry withdrew its
proposals for a new commercial relationship between Britain and Ireland
in the face of serious opposition from the Irish House of Commons, while,
in 1786, the British House of Commons rejected a plan for fortifying the
country's leading naval dockyards.

Pitt, however, was largely successful, the session that began in
December 1787 being particularly favourable.[36] As a result of the general
stability, the king tended to be more in the political background than hitherto, although he retained a special interest in foreign policy, on which he
made perceptive remarks.[37] Indeed, international relations led George to
adopt a position appropriate to his sense that he should exercise oversight
over policy:

> The dispatches from Sir James Harris are very material and well worthy
> of *speedy* and *mature* deliberation, I wish Lord Carmarthen [foreign
> secretary] would without loss of time consult Mr. Pitt on them and then
> collect those ministers in town, but not send for any that are many miles
> distant, lay them before them and send me the result of this opinion.[38]

The king took a cautious view of negotiations that might lead to alliances
as the latter might take Britain into war, a view that worried Carmarthen,[39]
although he was also against other powers gaining territory.[40] George's
views sometimes caused difficulties and unease for his ministers, not only
over the *Fürstenbund* of 1785 (see pp. 317–19), but also in 1787 when he
expressed reluctance about the ministry's desire to oppose the pro-French
Patriots in the United Provinces,[41] although he came round.[42] The
following year, the Danish envoy was convinced that Britain's hostile policy
towards Catherine the Great of Russia stemmed directly from the king
(who had indeed been angry with her commanding response to the
Fürstenbund), and that, but for that, Pitt would have taken a different line.[43]

[36] William Fraser to Liston, 6 Dec. 1787, National Library of Scotland MS. 5549 fol. 109;
marquess of Carmarthen, foreign secretary, to Dorset, 7 Dec. 1787, KAO. U269 C168A;
North to earl of Sheffield, 29 Jan. 1788, BL. Add. 61980 fols 26–7.

[37] George to Carmarthen, 5 Dec. 1784, Aspinall, *George III*, I, 114.

[38] George to Carmarthen, 12 Nov. 1785, BL. Add. 27914 fol. 11.

[39] George to Carmarthen, 6 July 1784, 4 Oct. 1785, BL. Add. 27914 fols 3, 9; George to
Pitt, 30 Mar. 1786, PRO. 30/8/103 fol. 188.

[40] George to Carmarthen, 30 Jan. 1786, BL. Add. 27914 fol. 15.

[41] Carmarthen to Pitt, 8 Jan. 1787, PRO. 30/8/151 fol. 38; George to Pitt, 8 Jan. 1787,
PRO. 30/8/103 fol. 206.

[42] George to Pitt, 26 May 1787, PRO. 30/8/103 fol. 232.

[43] Schönborn report, 2 Dec. 1788, Rigs. 1971; George to Pitt, 7, 10 Aug. 1785, PRO.
30/8/103 fols 172, 178; Hugh Elliot to Carmarthen, 29 Nov. 1788, PRO. FO. 22/10 fol. 424.
See also La Luzerne to Montmorin, 23 Dec. 1788, AE. CP. Ang. 567 fol. 313.

There were 'King's Friends' in both ministry and parliament, particularly Lord Chancellor Thurlow and also Charles Jenkinson, who was created Lord Hawkesbury in August 1786 and first earl of Liverpool in 1796, but others who might have been seen in this light did not receive office; Viscount Sackville, the former Lord George Germain, for example, did not become foreign secretary in 1785. Jenkinson was mentioned for the same post the following year, but instead became president of the Board of Trade and a peer. There seems scant basis for the report that George pressed for Jenkinson coming into the cabinet and that a hostile Pitt thought of resigning, as Pitt, in fact, supported his promotion to his new post; but it is instructive that Jenkinson was not promoted to the cabinet until 1791, and that tension over his position between George and Pitt was still being reported in 1788.[44]

Such reports show the currency of suspicion about George that dated back to Bute and the early 1760s and that had been revived by the overthrow of the coalition. These views were not only of importance for domestic politics. They also affected foreign perceptions of British policy, giving it an apparent edge of insincerity and weakness. In place of the situation sought by George, of a minister chosen by the king ensuring parliamentary management and providing coherence and stability to government, came the view that George wished to undermine his ministers. In 1786, the French *chargé d'affaires* reported that Jenkinson was a protégé of Bute and that the latter's principles were still those of George, who was unwilling to abandon them for the sake of Pitt. Instead, Barthélemy claimed that, while happy to see Pitt in difficulties, George wanted a young first minister as it gave him more power, and that anyway he did not know whom to replace him with.[45] The impact of past example was shown the following year when Gilbert Elliot, an opposition supporter, suggested that George would like to overthrow Pitt as he had done the coalition in 1783.[46] In 1786, Charles, fourth duke of Rutland, the lord-lieutenant of Ireland and an ally of Pitt, wrote, 'I have always supposed that the King's predilection is to Lord Thurlow', and that if he could

---

[44] Sir Gilbert Elliot to his wife, 21 June 1786, Countess of Minto (ed.), *Life and Letters of Sir Gilbert Elliot* (3 vols, London, 1874), I, 106; Stanhope, I, 306; marquess of Lansdowne (formerly earl of Shelburne) to Francis Baring, 5 Aug. 1786, E. Fitzmaurice, *Life of William, Earl of Shelburne* (2nd edn, 2 vols, London, 1912), II, 294; Thomas Orde, chief secretary in Ireland, to duke of Rutland, 13 May, 1, 29 July 1786, HMC. *Rutland* III (London, 1894), pp. 299, 319, 327; François de Barthélemy to Montmorin, 1 Apr. 1788, AE. CP. Ang. 565 fol. 8; George to Pitt, 29 Jan., 30 Apr. 1791, PRO. 30/8/103 fols 413, 420.

[45] Barthélemy to Vergennes, 18 July, 22 Aug., 5 Sept., 5, 26 Dec. 1786, Barthélemy to Montmorin, 19 Aug. 1788, AE. CP. Ang. 557 fols 45-7, 197-8, 262, 558 fols 232, 321, 566 fol. 192; Pollon, Sardinian envoy, to Victor Amadeus III, 30 Jan. 1787, AST. LM. Ing. 88.

[46] Elliot to his wife, 27 Mar. 1787, *Life and Letters*, I, 140.

manage without Pitt, 'perhaps he would not scruple to sacrifice him'.[47] Thurlow was both a talented manager of the Lords and regarded as a favourite of the king,[48] who indeed thought highly of him.

Whatever the intention, the impression was of royal power. This was not simply a matter of the gossip that made up much of the currency of political and diplomatic discussion and speculation. Instead, all those who could read newspapers were given an account of politics in which the king played a major role, albeit one in which the interaction with ministerial factionalism was close but obscure. The *Daily Universal Register* of 2 September 1786 reported that the ministry was divided over whether Jenkinson should have the sinecure of chancellor of the duchy of Lancaster for life, as Jenkinson sought, or only 'during pleasure', on which Pitt was insistent, 'the members waited till the arrival of his Majesty from Windsor, to take his pleasure on the point, which, if it had been in favour of an appointment for life, would have determined Mr. Pitt and his friends to relinquish office. The King healed the division, by giving his consent to an appointment only during pleasure.'

The press underlined the royal role when it reported, during the Dutch crisis of 1787, that Pitt and Carmarthen had audiences with the king and that he had had a long conference with William Eden, who had recently served as an envoy in France.[49] The crisis, in which a British-sponsored Prussian invasion overthrew the pro-French Patriots, while a British naval mobilization helped discourage the French from intervening, indicated the range of reporting about George, with one letter sent to the French ministry of marine (which used its consular system to provide a secondary source of reports to supplement those of the diplomats) claiming that no British monarch had dominated his ministry to the extent that George then did, and that he was motivated by hatred of France and revenge for the loss of America.[50] The perception of George as manipulator and conspirator, using, for example, ministerial differences to ensure his power,[51] was thus not only well established but also spanned foreign policy, foreshadowing the rumours about hostility to France that circulated during the French Revolution. Within Britain, the crisis led to a more positive portrayal of the king, who was linked with resolve and success in Gillray's caricature *Amsterdam in a Dam'D Predicament – or – The last Scene of*

[47] Rutland to Orde, – July 1786, HMC. *Rutland*, III, 321. For reports of tension between Thurlow and Pitt, Germain to Dorset, 14 July 1784, KAO. U269 C192.

[48] La Luzerne to Montmorin, 1 July 1788, AE. CP. Ang. 566 fols 5–6.

[49] E.g. *London Chronicle*, 12, 14 July 1787.

[50] Letter from London, 19 July 1787, Paris, Archives Nationales, Archives de la Marine, B⁷453.

[51] Barthélemy to Montmorin, 9 Aug. 1788, La Luzerne to Montmorin, 17 Mar. 1789, AE. CP. Ang. 566 fol. 134, 568 fols 338–9.

the Republican Pantomime. While presenting the republican Dutch as frogs, this juxtaposed two monarchs, showing Louis XVI in consternation while George shakes a club inscribed Oak, says 'I'm ready for you', and stands as if about to attack Louis. George himself told the French envoy that he wanted good relations with France,[52] although his protestations were not believed.[53]

Politically, he found himself opposed by his heir, George, prince of Wales. The latter was against the frugality, virtue and duty of his father, and opposed to Pitt. He preferred Fox, who, unlike the prince, had talent, but, like him, lacked self-control. This was to prove a key cause of tension during the regency crisis.

George remained politically influential during the long Pitt ministry, and the extent to which his serious illness in 1788–9 contributed to a major political crisis is strong evidence of his continued importance. The public view was expressed in *Felix Farley's Bristol Journal*, which claimed on 22 November,

> Among other serious inconveniences arising from the Sovereign's indisposition, is that of a considerable interruption in the foreign correspondence; for, abstracted from the mere signatures of official papers, it is a fact that his Majesty was peculiarly assiduous in carrying on a very extensive communication with all the foreign courts in his own hand, and actually took upon himself the conduct of a great part of that business.

The surviving correspondence suggests that, although George aroused the comment of foreign envoys by seeing British diplomats without ministers present,[54] this statement is an exaggeration, but it indicates the significance attached to George's personal links and initiatives.

George's symptoms of insanity caused the regency crisis of 1788–9. They were probably an indication of the metabolic disorder porphyria, although it has also been suggested that George suffered from the effects of the arsenic used in his wig. If so, there would be a parallel with Napoleon, whose death in 1821 may have been a result of arsenic in the wallpaper in his accommodation in St Helena. Porphyria had probably been transmitted to the Hanoverians from the Stuarts via Elizabeth of Bohemia and George I's mother Sophia,[55] and it has sparked the strongest

---

[52] Barthélemy to Montmorin, 5 Oct. 1787, AE. CP. Ang. 563 fol. 75, cf. La Luzerne to Montmorin, 15 July 1788, AE. CP. Ang. 566 fol. 49.

[53] La Luzerne to Montmorin, 22 July, Barthélemy to Montmorin, 19 Aug., 30 Sept., La Luzerne to Montmorin, 16 Dec. 1788, AE. CP. Ang. 566 fols 90, 193, 320, 567 fol. 276.

[54] La Luzerne to Montmorin, 3 June 1788, AE. CP. Ang. 565 fols 233–4.

[55] I. Macalpine and R. Hunter, *George III and the Mad Business* (London, 1969) and, more recently, J.C.G. Röhl, M. Warren and D. Hunt, *Purple Secret: Genes, 'Madness' and the Royal Houses of Europe* (2nd edn, London, 1999), pp. 75–90.

modern interest in the king, most prominently expressed in Alan Bennett's successful play *The Madness of George III* (1991), which was subsequently adapted for the screen as *The Madness of King George* (1994). Royal madness dramatized changing notions of self and personal identity,[56] and posed practical issues of rulership, as also happened elsewhere. George's first cousin and former brother-in-law, Christian VII of Denmark, had had symptoms of mental illness since the late 1760s, interspersed with moments of lucidity, and did not recover; he died in 1806. His stepmother until 1785, and thereafter his heir, the future Frederick VI, wielded power, although, because the Danes did not have regency provisions, Christian still discharged the ceremonial functions of monarchy, presiding at council meetings and state banquets, and receiving foreign envoys.

Since his attack in 1765, George's health had generally been good, although in 1770 a 'severe cold in my breast' prevented him from speaking, in 1778 he had 'a little feverish complaint', in 1782 a cold that made it difficult to talk, and in 1786 a 'nettle rash' that delayed his return to London from Windsor.[57] In June 1788 George had had a bout of ill health, a strong bilious attack leading to colic, but he had then had a holiday cure, going, as Sir George Baker, one of his doctors suggested, to Cheltenham to drink the waters, which were recommended for bilious attacks. George was careful with his health on this trip, declining dinner when he visited Earl Bathurst as his 'then regimen would not permit him to partake'.[58]

Apparently recovered, George returned to Windsor on 16 August. Although concern about his health continued to arouse speculation,[59] it was subdued. But on 17 October George was taken ill with a savage bilious attack. Made tired by his medicines,[60] and reported to be suffering from gout, he recovered to take a levee on 24 October,[61] and Pitt wrote to him about Baltic developments on 25 October and 5 November.[62] George, however, was, from 26 October, talking rapidly and uncontrollably, and suffering from physical problems including rheumatic pain and lameness. Problems with sight, hearing and memory followed. George became

[56] D. Wahrman, *The Making of the Modern Self. Identity and Culture in Eighteenth-Century England* (New Haven, 2004).

[57] George to North, 15 Dec. 1770, 30 Nov., 2 Dec. 1778, Fortescue, II, 185, RA, GEO/ 3129–30; George to Jenkinson, 8 June 1780, BL. Add. 38564 fol. 17, George to Sydney, 23 June 1786, Aspinall, *George III*, I, 230 fn. 2.

[58] W.S. Baddeley, *History of Cirencester* (Cirencester, 1924), p. 274.

[59] Barthélemy to Montmorin, 19 Aug. 1788, AE. CP. Ang. 566 fols 191–2.

[60] George to Pitt, 19 Oct. 1788, PRO. 30/8/103 fol. 310; Barthélemy to Montmorin, 21 Oct. 1788, AE. CP. Ang. 567 fol. 44.

[61] Hawkesbury to Dorset, 23 Oct. 1788, KAO. U269 C182.

[62] Pitt to George, 25 Oct., 5 Nov. 1788, PRO. 30/8/101 fols 5, 7.

delirious while at Windsor on 5 November, and on 7 November it became common knowledge that he was seriously ill.[63]

At the time of the attack, George was fifty, and the auguries for a long life were not good. His father had died at the age of forty-four, while, of George's eight siblings, six died before the age of fifty – Edward, duke of York (1739–67), Elizabeth (1741–59), Henry, duke of Cumberland (1745–90), Louisa (1749–68), Frederick (1750–65), and Caroline Matilda, queen of Denmark (1751–75), Elizabeth and Louisa of tuberculosis – although Augusta, duchess of Brunswick (1737–1813), and William, duke of Gloucester (1743–1805), lived to over sixty.

The illness, particularly the symptoms of mental confusion, caused personal anguish, family crisis and political difficulties. It soon became apparent in 1788 that it would be necessary to make provisions for a regency, and also that this arrangement might have to last until George's death, as his recovery seemed problematic. On 15 November 1788, Hiley Addington reflected the general view when he wrote to his brother Henry:

> Immediate danger perhaps is not to be apprehended; – but as all accounts agree in declaring His Majesty's disorder to be seated in the brain; which continues notwithstanding the abatement of the fever, surely his case must be hopeless.[64]

The alternation of apparent madness with intervals of lucidity, of paroxysms of rage with hours of calm, proved particularly disconcerting. When lucid, George was aware of his situation.

Although Queen Charlotte was mentioned, it was clear that, if there was to be a regency, the prince of Wales, now of age, would be regent. The ministry would therefore change, as the prince was close, politically and personally, to Fox. The extent of his likely powers as regent was unclear, however, and that would have to be determined by parliament, which met on 20 November, only to be adjourned to await developments in George's health. As with other monarchs supposed mad,[65] the perception of George's mental health in part mirrored political interests.

The political interest and inherent drama of the occasion attracted intense public interest. The conduct of the prince and the Whigs, who were eager for power and hopeful of George's death or continued madness, aroused much criticism, as in Thomas Rowlandson's caricature *Filial Piety*

---

[63] Hawkesbury to Dorset, 28, 31 Oct., 7 Nov. 1788, KAO U269 C182; Pitt to Pretyman, 10 Nov. 1788, Ipswich CRO. HA119 T108/42 no. 263.

[64] Hiley to Henry Addington, 15 Nov. 1788, Exeter, 152M/C 1788/F36.

[65] V.H.H. Green, *The Madness of Kings: Personal Trauma and the Fate of Nations* (Stroud, 1995); B. Aram, *Juana the Mad. Sovereignty and Dynasty in Renaissance Europe* (Baltimore, 2005), p. 167.

published on 25 November.[66] This encouraged sympathy for George. The criticism of the Whigs also flowed directly from government themes prior to the crisis, with *Revolutionists*, a caricature published on 30 October, depicting the followers of the prince trying to storm a hill marked 'Constitution' on which George sat. As an interesting comment on perceptions of the appropriate relationship between monarch and ministerial choice, there was a widespread conviction that, if regent, the prince would dismiss Pitt and call on Fox, and, also, considerable disquiet on this head, Dorset writing, 'I see nothing but confusion if he is dismissed, a measure the nation will never long submit to'.[67]

When, on 3 December, the king's five doctors were examined before the Privy Council, they disagreed as to whether he was likely to recover. Two days later, a new doctor, Francis Willis, under whose attention George was to improve, first saw his new patient. Willis had considerable experience with mental illness, having run a private lunatic asylum at Greatford near Stamford for over a decade. He was called in because the physicians-in-ordinary, such as Sir George Baker, had been unable to produce a cure. George's illness created serious strains at court because he turned against his wife, whom he unfairly accused of adultery. The king professed himself in love with one of Charlotte's ladies of the bedchamber, Elizabeth, countess of Pembroke, a theme that was to recur in later breakdowns. The crisis proved a dangerous strain on Charlotte, whose hair turned grey. Willis was recommended by the Harcourts, who were close to the royal family: he had treated the countess's mother, and was ready to distinguish between delirium and insanity. Willis, who declared that George would recover,[68] proved a controversial figure, first because he insisted on exclusive medical control and, second, because of his methods, which rested on enforced calm, including the use of a gag, a strait-jacket and a restraining chair. This restraint was designed to end the over-excitement that he believed caused madness. The majesty of monarchy was ignored as George was bullied and coerced, although, in order to help his recovery, Willis allowed George to read Shakespeare and to shave himself.[69]

Meanwhile politics did not stand still, and there were serious parliamentary clashes on the Regency Bill. On 15 December, George's second

[66] See also, John, second Lord Boringdon to Catherine Robinson, 22 Dec. 1788, and to Frederick Robinson, 19 Feb. 1789, Plymouth 1259/2/63, 1259/1/91.

[67] Dorset to Nathaniel Wraxall, 27 Nov. 1788, Beinecke, Osborn Files, Dorset.

[68] Hawkesbury to Dorset, 9 Dec. 1788, KAO. U269 C182.

[69] For the background, K. Jones, *Lunacy, Law and Conscience, 1744–1845: The Social History of the Care of the Insane* (London, 1955), R. Porter, *Mind-Forged Manacles: A History of Madness in England from the Restoration to the Regency* (London, 1987); A. Ingram, *The Madhouse of Language: Writing and Reading Madness in the Eighteenth Century* (London, 1991); and J. Andrews and A. Scull, *Customers and Patrons of the Mad-Trade. The Management of Lunacy in Eighteenth-Century London* (Berkeley, 2003).

son, Frederick, duke of York, spoke against the ministry in the House of Lords, providing a clear view not only of his attitudes but also of those of his elder brother.[70] Next day, James, second earl of Fife, a supporter of the ministry, asked 'Can anything describe the violence of the present times?'[71] The Commons debates on 10 and 16 December were unusually bitter, and a majority of 64 in a house of 472 on the 16 December was not a good result. In the absence of firm party groupings, the votes of many MPs were unpredictable, as indeed was indicated by the development of the 'Armed Neutrality' group led by the duke of Northumberland. This group of about twenty peers and thirty MPs wanted Pitt to continue in office, but they opposed his policy of restrictions on the power of the prince as regent.[72]

The Armed Neutrality group reflected what had already been apparent in early 1784, that, at moments of constitutional tension, there was a powerful tendency in favour of conciliation, compromise and coalition, and one that could look to support among the independents. During the great crisis that began in late 1792, under the double threat of French success and domestic radicalism, this tendency was to benefit the government, but in the winter of 1788–9 the situation was worrying for Pitt.[73] He could appear to be delaying the establishment of a regency, and thus sustaining instability, while the focus of loyalty and order for many was now the regent-to-be. The longer the crisis lasted, the more obviously independents would adapt to the new situation, while ministerial cohesion would collapse as some ministers and place-holders sought favour in the emerging political order, as Thurlow was widely believed to be doing. On 2 January 1789, a political tug-of-war was depicted in the caricature, *The Tories and the Whigs Pulling for a Crown*.

Recovery took time and led to much discussion of medical options, as did the consideration of causes, Lord Sydney, the home secretary, blaming 'the imprudent and immoderate use of Cheltenham waters'. The cricket-loving and womanizing Dorset, then ambassador in Paris and much concerned about the political consequences of a change of government, suggested that Willis try 'the blood of a jack-ass which after passing a clear napkin through it two or three times is given afterwards to the patient to drink'.[74] This was unnecessary, as, from early February, George began to improve, in time to prevent the creation of a regency and to thwart the Emperor Joseph II's attempt to dictate arrangements for Hanover.

[70] J.W. Derry, *The Regency Crisis and the Whigs, 1788–9* (Cambridge, 1963).

[71] Fife to William Rose, 16 Dec. 1788, Aberdeen UL, Mss. 2226/131.

[72] Pitt to prince of Wales, 15 Dec. 1788, Ipswich CRO. HA119 T108/42.

[73] On parliament and the care of George by the queen, Pitt to the latter, 31 Dec. 1788, PRO. 30/8/101 fol. 98.

[74] C. Ross (ed.), *The Correspondence of Charles, First Marquis Cornwallis* (3 vols, London, 1859), I, 407; Dorset to Wraxall, 5 Feb. 1789, Beinecke, Osborn Files, Dorset.

There had also been problems over the position of the ruler in Ireland, since the Dublin parliament adopted a different position from that of Westminster, in overcoming the opposition of the marquess of Buckingham, the unpopular lord-lieutenant, and inviting Prince George to assume the royal functions without conditions. In ceding to the Dublin parliament, in 1782–3, the sort of rights of independent initiative and legislation demanded by the American colonists before their rebellion, the Westminster parliament appeared to have created an unstable relationship affecting the position of the crown.

George's restoration to health pre-empted the Whigs, who had been allocating ministerial portfolios,[75] and ended the matter, although it is unclear whether this recovery was due to Willis, who was granted an annual pension of £1,000 by parliament and celebrated with a token bearing his likeness and on the reverse 'Britons Rejoice. Your King's Restored. 1789', or to a spontaneous recovery from the attack of porphyria. On 8 February 1789 Henry Addington wrote to his father, the doctor who had treated Chatham, and who had predicted the king's early return to health,

> He has indicated no disposition to violence for several days, and is in general composed and easy. Dr Warren said yesterday that he had not seen him *so near himself* since his illness; and I understand, that the other physicians are of the same opinion: Dr Willis, whose hopes and fears have not been much affected by the fluctuations in the disorder, now declares, that the probability of recovery is greatly strengthened, and that everything is going on to his utmost wishes. Most people, I am sorry that I cannot say all, begin to look cheerful again, and to flatter them-selves with the hopes that the interests of the nation may yet be preserved, and that the only consequences of His Majesty's malady may be a knowledge of the faithful attachment of the people at large, and a discovery of those who have proved or forfeited their pretensions to his confidence and favour.[76]

On 19 February, the House of Lords was told that George was in a state of convalescence, a situation already announced in the medical bulletin of 17 February. The following day, Thurlow for the first time resumed talking to the king about business,[77] while, on 23 February, George recommenced his correspondence with Pitt. 'Aprized of what has passed and of the conduct of everyone',[78] he was able to review the political situation in

[75] Fox to Portland, 20, 21 Jan., 6, 11, 12 Feb. 1789, BL. Add. 47561 fols 92–109.
[76] Henry to Anthony Addington, 8 Feb. 1789, Exeter, 152M/C 1789/F 9.
[77] Sydney to Cornwallis, 21 Feb. 1789, *Cornwallis*, I, 405.
[78] Hawkesbury to Dorset, 26 Feb. 1789, KAO. U269 C182.

light of the recent crisis. It confirmed his strong antipathy to his son and the Whigs, and left George angry with Joseph II. When the emperor's compliments on his recovery were presented, the king was unimpressed: 'the Emperor's conduct in my late unfortunate indisposition has been contrary to the very Law of Empire and he does not therefore deserve more than bald civility'.[79]

George's recovery from the attack may only have been partial,[80] and the French foreign minister was sceptical about his ability to direct the government.[81] However, there are also indications of a complete recovery and of subsequent good health,[82] and George's signature by late March was strong and even. As far as the public was concerned, there was a complete recovery, necessarily so, as assumptions about the structure and practice of royal authority required the king's mental and physical health.[83] This recovery provided the opportunity for a renewed burst of royal popularity, one that was far more focused on George personally than had been the case in 1784. Already, during the crisis, there had been strong signs of George's popularity. Fife, a keen royalist, wrote from London about 'the gratitude of the public to the amiable King. In both Playhouses they every night oblige them to play and sing "God save Great George our King." The Gallery would pull the house down if they did not do it.' Newspaper reports and addresses from around the country ensured that the public was well informed of the issues.[84] The widespread unpopularity of the opposition's conduct strengthened support for the king.[85]

KING PERFECTLY RECOVERED, announced a London report in the *Leeds Intelligencer* of 24 February 1789. The celebrations for the recovery provided an opportunity for a focus on the links between crown and God, and George stated that his motive for the service of thanksgiving at St Paul's Cathedral on 23 April 1789 was 'purely one of piety'.[86] 'God Save the King' had been the prayer of the nation, underlining the importance of religious themes of monarchy. The service at St Paul's provided a dramatic display of the nation's thanks, and one that was more vivid because it was held in London, earlier the centre of Wilkesite opposition

[79] La Luzerne to Montmorin, 16 Feb. 1789, AE. CP. Ang. 568 fols 201–2; George to ———, 5 Apr. 1789, *McDowell and Stern Catalogue*, no. 27, p. 5; Reviczky to Leeds, 4 Apr., reply 5 Apr. 1789, PRO. FO. 7/17 fols 126, 128.

[80] Ralph Payne to Malmesbury, 1, 9 Oct. 1789, Winchester, Hampshire RO, Malmesbury papers, vol. 162.

[81] Montmorin to Vauguyon, 27 Feb. 1789, AE. CP. Espagne 626 fol. 158.

[82] Henry to Anthony Addington, 7 Dec. 1789, Exeter, 152M/C 1789/F7.

[83] H.C.E. Midelfort, *Mad Princes of Renaissance Germany* (Charlottesville, 1994), p. 16.

[84] Fife to William Rose, 4 Jan. 1789, Aberdeen UL, Mss. 2226/131; *Leeds Intelligencer*, 17, 24 Feb. 1789.

[85] Hawkesbury to Dorset, 20 Feb., 13 Mar. 1789, KAO. U269 C182.

[86] Catherine Robinson to Frederick Robinson, 7 Apr. 1789, Plymouth 1259/1/199.

and of the Gordon Riots. The crowds that lined the streets in 1789 served George, Lord Macartney as the touchstone for assessing the numbers that turned out to watch him enter and leave Beijing in 1793: he thought the numbers in London larger. Palmerston recorded: 'the King . . . looking much as usual did not seem particularly affected nor should I have known from his appearance or behaviour that anything particular had happened to him . . . the entering into the church was very magnificent, an avenue all through it being formed by Guards and Beefeaters in a double row and in the centre under the dome the astonishing mass of charity children piled up quite round. Their singing as the King came in and went out had a great effect.'[87] Reports and engravings spread accounts of the service. A sense of majesty emerges clearly from illustrations such as Edward Dayes's two views of the interior of the cathedral and Robert Pollard's mezzotint of the same.

Thanksgiving services were held across the country, as were public celebrations in which sponsorship enabled the poor to participate. The king's recovery was much celebrated in verse and applauded by loyal addresses; although the latter were criticized as servile by Richard Price.[88] More private, but still very much reported celebrations were held with the very crowded 'Grand Restoration Drawing-room' in London on 26 March 1789, and balls took place at Windsor castle on 3 April and 1 May. The lavish ball and supper held by Charlotte and the princesses on 1 May was the occasion for the first use of the new dining service commissioned to mark George's recovery. The supper was described as exceeding 'any thing of the kind ever given in this kingdom'.[89] As a counterpoint to the celebrations, James Gillray on 29 April published *The Funeral Procession of Miss Regency*, a caricature mocking opposition hopes in which Burke, carrying an 'Ode upon his Majesty's Recovery', preceded the coffin on which rested a crown with the prince's feathers and two symbols of a style very different to that of George III: dice and an empty purse.

George's summer travels that year drew crowds, including allegedly 17,000 people in Longleat Park. Queen Charlotte recorded: 'His Majesty, the three Princesses and myself went in an open chaise down the avenue and back again to satisfy the populace who were extremely desirous to see the King.' George Huntingford, master of the school at Warminster, reported of the same occasion, 'at least twenty thousand persons were assembled to see them. With much condescension the King, Queen, and Princesses moved slowly on in an open carriage, so that every one present

[87] J.L. Cranmer-Byng (ed.), *An Embassy to China. Being the Journal Kept by Lord Macartney* (London, 2004), p. 104; Connell (ed.), *Portrait of A Whig Peer*, p. 197.

[88] R. Price, *A Discourse on the Love of our Country* (London, 1789).

[89] *Annual Register* (1789), pp. 252–3; E. Chalus, *Elite Women in English Political Life c. 1754–1790* (Oxford, 2005), pp. 102–5.

beheld them, and I believe nineteen out of the twenty were most highly gratified.'[90] There was 'an amazing number of spectators' when George arrived in Exeter on 13 August 1789, and, that evening, in stark contrast to the situation facing Louis XVI in Paris, 'there were bonfires, fireworks, and illuminations, with many emblematic transparencies'.[91] The press widely reported the king's travels.

Alongside growing signs of division in France, this burst of royal popularity created a considerable degree of confidence in the British system, which represented a major change in attitude from the early 1780s. George himself noted the contrast, writing of 'the present confused state of Europe, which places this kingdom in almost the only favourite situation'.[92] Indeed, there was a rallying of the social élite and of much opinion around country, crown and Church that prefigured the loyalism of the 1790s. George was featured in resulting comments, *Berrow's Worcester Journal* of 14 August 1788 claiming,

> While anarchy and confusion pervade the French dominions; and the irritated subjects of Louis seem ripe for rebellion, the King of Great Britain and his family are enjoying a pleasing relaxation amongst their subjects, all of whom, from the peasant to the peer, give the most ample testimony of their fidelity and attachment.

The year 1789 saw George's first visit to Weymouth. United by Act of Parliament with neighbouring Melcombe Regis in 1571, Weymouth was on the sea and George was therefore able to take the benefit of sea air and bathing, which he found 'certainly agrees'.[93] The orientalist Sir William Jones, who had stayed at Weymouth in 1771, described pleasant rides in the nearby country and the sheltered bathing which was just right for the convalescent king: 'One may bathe here at all hours, and in all weathers, the tide making no difference; and the descent from the shore is so gradual, that the middle of the bay would not come over my shoulders.'[94]

---

[90] Queen Charlotte's diary, 15 Sept. 1789, RA. GEO/Add 43/1; Huntingford to Henry Addington, 17 Sept. 1789, Exeter, 152 M/C 1789/F 12; RA. GEO/Add 9/79; Anon., *A Summary Account of the King's visit to Longleat, the seat of the Marquis of Bath, in September, 1789* (Bath, 1789); account by Mr Cruse, probably Jeremiah Cruse, a surveyor then employed by the estate, printed by B. Botfield in *Stemmata Botevilliana* (Westminster, 1858), pp. cccxcix–ccciii; D. Burnett, *Longleat, the History of an English Country House* (London, 1978), pp. 122–4. I am most grateful for the advice of Kate Harris.

[91] *Jenkins's Civil and Ecclesiastical History of the City of Exeter* (2nd edn., Exeter, 1841), pp. 218–19.

[92] George to William Grenville, 6 Aug. 1789, BL. Add. 58855 fol. 12.

[93] George to William Grenville, 4 Aug. 1789, BL. Add. 58855 fol. 11; J. Hutchins, *The History and Antiquities of the County of Dorset* (3rd edn, Westminster, 1861–74), II, 469–71.

[94] Jones to George Spencer, 1771, BL. Add. Althorp G1; C.B. Andrews (ed.), *The Torrington Diaries, containing the tours through England and Wales of the Hon. John Byng* (4 vols, London, 1934–8), I, 87.

Willis advised against George's plan to visit Hanover, and, instead, proposed a trip to the coast. The resort was recommended to the king by his brother William, duke of Gloucester, who had wintered there for the first time in December 1780: he suffered from physical symptoms similar to George, with major attacks in 1771 and 1777.

The king's trip there helped give a new direction to his travels but also confirmed his tendency to visit southern England. George travelled more widely in England than any of his eighteenth-century predecessors, although never outside it. In addition to Weymouth, which he visited every year bar three from 1789 to 1805, providing satirical copy for John Wolcott/Peter Pindar,[95] helping to lead to his featuring subsequently in a Thomas Hardy novel, George visited Oxford in 1785 and 1786, Cheltenham[96] and Worcester in 1788, and the Plymouth area (staying at Saltram) in 1789.[97] The below-average number of prevailing westerlies that decade made the weather more clement than usual in the West Country.[98]

George, however, did not see most of the country, nor did he repeat his tours of 1788–9, so that hopes, in 1791 and 1801,[99] of a visit to Saltram proved abortive, as did plans in 1805 to visit Richard Hurd, bishop of Worcester, 'a very rational amusement'.[100] Lengthy journeys away from the seat of government business would have been difficult without uprooting large numbers of government personnel. Given the fact that he had more time available to travel in Britain, both because he never went abroad and because of his longevity, it is striking, nevertheless, how close he stayed to home. In that respect, he was far more like Louis XVI, who, as king, only visited Rheims (1775) and Cherbourg (1786), and fled as far as Varennes (1791), or George Washington, who never visited Europe, than the much-travelled Joseph II of Austria or Gustavus III of Sweden. He did not visit Liverpool, Manchester, Leeds, York, Newcastle or Norwich. Had the French invaded in the 1800s, then a strongpoint at Weedon in Northamptonshire was designed as George's refuge and constructed to that end, but it never proved necessary to flee there. George also thought of taking refuge in the bishop of Worcester's rural seat at Hartlebury Castle.

[95] 'Pindar', *The Royal Visit to Exeter* (London, 1795) and *The Royal Tour and Weymouth Amusements* (London, 1795).

[96] Cheltenham Library, 63G828GEO, 63G394; G. Powell, 'King George III at Cheltenham in 1788', *Cheltenham Local History Society Journal*, 3 (1985).

[97] Diary of Sarah White, 15–27 Aug. 1789, Plymouth, Acc. 3102, Saltram Archival Documents, Box 2.

[98] J. Kington, *The Weather of the 1780s over Europe* (Cambridge, 1988).

[99] Anne to Frederick Robinson, 16 Sept. 1791, Theresa Villiers to Catherine Robinson, 29 June, 22 July, 15 Aug. 1801, Plymouth 1259/1/81, 1259/2/581, 590, 594.

[100] Theresa Villiers to Catherine Robinson, 9 July 1805, Plymouth 1259/2/734.

George's pattern of visits contrasted with his brother-in-law, Christian VII of Denmark, who visited northern England in 1768, travelling along the Bridgewater canal and seeing industrial sites in Leeds. Christian also visited Paris. George was very different to his heir, who, once he became George IV, visited Edinburgh, Dublin and Hanover. Among George's brothers, Edward, duke of York, visited Yorkshire in 1761 and 1766, and Henry, duke of Cumberland, Berwick in 1771. In this period, George travelled little, not, for example, visiting Plymouth in 1774 as had been hoped.[101] Instead, he stayed close to his wife, who, frequently pregnant or with babies, did not travel much. Indeed, the scope of his travels increased only when he was in his fifties and at a time when his fitness for the 'exertion' of travelling was limited.[102] Possibly, there was a degree of rivalry within the royal family, for the prince of Wales and the duke of York visited Yorkshire and Lincolnshire in 1787. Charlotte, significantly, accompanied the king, helping strengthen his reputation for domesticity. After 1804, George again travelled little, though his nephew William of Gloucester visited Edinburgh (1795), Glasgow (1795), Liverpool (1804) and Birmingham (1805).

Whereas George I had taken the waters at Pyrmont in Germany, George III took those at Cheltenham. He also visited industrial sites, although only in the south. In 1788, George toured a pin manufactory at Gloucester and a carpet works and a china factory at Worcester and, on an outing from Cheltenham, the area round Stroud, which was 'deservedly distinguished for industry and manufactures'. There, he was shown 'in regular gradation, the whole process of making cloth'. At Cheltenham that year, George had already seen Carey's mechanical representation of cloth manufacture. At Gloucester, he visited the jail and the hospital. In his visit to Earl Bathurst in 1788 George inspected the new Thames–Severn Canal and the Sapperton Tunnel through which it runs on the Bathurst estate, and the next day, *en route* to Stroud, he stopped to watch barges passing through canal locks. The following year, George visited the carpet works at Axminster, 'attended to the workers and asked many questions concerning the principle and processes of the manufacture'.[103]

Despite his fascination with instruments and new technology, such as steam engines, part of his view that science should be used to benefit man and society, George's interest in economic development was neither well informed nor pronounced, and his knowledge of industry did not match

---

[101] Thomas, second Lord Grantham to Anne Robinson, 25 Apr. 1774, Bedford CRO. L30/17/4.

[102] George to William Grenville, 4 Aug. 1789, BL. Add. 58855 fol. 11.

[103] *Berrow's Weekly Journal*, 21 Aug. 1788; Baddeley, *Cirencester*, p. 274; T. Gray (ed.), *East Devon. The Travellers' Tales* (Exeter, 2000), pp. xiii–xvi, quote from the factory owner p. xv.

that of agriculture. Nevertheless, on his travels he benefited from the marked improvement in the roads stemming from the expansion of the turnpike system, while there were indications of his concern for commerce. In 1787 he sought copies of the laws of the Holy Roman Empire about coin-clipping and in 1789 he demonstrated his awareness of the relationship between credit and confidence, writing from Weymouth,

> In a country where paper currency is so considerable a vehicle of trade it cannot but be highly necessary to let the law take its course in cases of forgery but where very particular favourable circumstances occur; the present case of Thomas Phipps the Younger is certainly not of that nature, for two other indictments were found for similar offences, though not brought forward he having been found capital guilty of the former. I cannot therefore see any reason for my preventing that example being made which it is to be hoped will prevent others from committing a crime so detrimental to society.[104]

Two years later, George commented on another aspect of the financial revolution in paper currency and credit, when he voiced his suspicion that the non-arrival of dispatches from the British forces in India was the result of deliberate action on the part of stockjobbers, not necessary delay: 'among the advantages of commerce, these evils must at times arise'.[105] That George was prepared to accept this practice as an unavoidable consequence of the financial world, but was ready to press for the execution of forgers, was in part an aspect of the social politics of the period. It reflected the state of the law, and George was not outside that. In private, he did not draw attention to the contradictions of this politics, still less reject their harsh nature, and in 1777 refused to pardon William Dodd, a royal chaplain convicted of forgery, despite much public interest on his behalf.

George's visits to Weymouth were designed to assist his recovery. At the same time, the king became more conscious of the health of others, writing that

> The feeling in my own case how much relaxation from business nay from any exertion even of an amusing kind is necessary to remove the remains of lassitude which I am told is the common attendant of severe illness, makes me easily comprehend that it may be also essential in Lord Buckingham's present situation.[106]

---

[104] Carmarthen to Sir Robert Murray Keith, envoy in Vienna, 25 Dec. 1787, George to William Grenville, 1 Sept. 1789, BL. Add. 35539, 58855 fol. 17.

[105] George to Dundas, 31 Jan. 1792, BL. Add. 40100 fol. 29.

[106] George to William Grenville, 18 June 1789, BL. Add. 58855 fol. 1.

By the end of the decade, George was the beneficiary of a popularity that stemmed from the specific events of 1783–4 and his recent illness, but also from a more general attention, in the developing moral climate of the period, to the royal family. A concern with probity and honourable conduct could not but highlight the contrast between George and his eldest son, as well as the supporting contrast between Pitt and Fox. George did not change his attitudes, but benefited from a rise in a social and political sensibility that was widely grounded.[107] As a young man, in contrast, George had received his political education in a context in which patriotism, integrity and honour were linked, but the social resonance of order was less focused on the personality of the monarch, while the moralizing religious dimension that was to be present towards the end of the century was less pronounced, especially in terms of evangelicalism. George gained from the shift, symbolizing a much desired stability at a time of rapid, and to many disconcerting, social change and in the aftermath of a major and humiliating national crisis.

[107] M. Morris, 'Representations of Royalty in the London Daily Press in the Decade of the French Revolution', *Journal of Newspaper and Periodical History*, 4, 2 (1988), pp. 2–15 and 'The Royal Family and Family Values in Late Eighteenth-Century England', *Journal of Family History*, 21 (1996), pp. 519–32.

Chapter 14

THE REVOLUTIONARY CRISIS, 1790–3

George's recovery in 1789 led to renewed confidence in the constitution. In an image that the king, with his interest in the astronomical researches of William Herschel, would have understood, the 'Address to the Public' in the first volume of *The Senator: or, Parliamentary Chronicle* (1791) referred to

> that firmness, beauty, and magnificence of our excellent constitution, founded on the mutual consent of Prince and People; both moving, as it were, in one orb, reciprocally influencing, attracting, and directing each other; whose united power may be compared to a machine for determining the equality of weights.

George had again become a factor to reckon with in the political world, although, as before the regency crisis, his general agreement with government policy meant that his position was uncontentious. Furthermore, as he convalesced, and before he recouped his strength with his summer trip of 1789, George had written on 23 February, 'I must decline entering into a pressure of business, and indeed for the rest of my life shall expect others to fulfil the duties of their employments, and only keep that superintending eye which can be effected without labour or fatigue.'[1] The following spring, Henry, second Viscount Palmerston, reported

> The King's health is perfectly re-established and I believe he is free from any symptoms whatever of mental or bodily disorder. His spirits however are affected by the perfect consciousness which he possesses of what has passed, and the apprehension which he must feel of a return ... His mind has lost much of its activity and fondness for business; and ever since the affair of the proposed Regency the Queen has taken a much greater part ... Pitt possesses her confidence, while the Chancellor [Thurlow] is thought to have a larger share of the King's.[2]

George certainly continued to hold strong views on political developments. He was cautious in 1790 when, in the Nootka Sound crisis, war

[1] PRO. 30/8/103.
[2] B. Connell (ed.), *Portrait of A Whig Peer Compiled from the Papers of The Second Viscount Palmerston, 1739–1802* (London, 1957), p. 207.

with Spain appeared a likely outcome of competing claims to what eventually became the west coast of Canada. Although approving the government's use of the navy to intimidate Spain,[3] he reflected a hesitation about
conflict not generally associated with British attitudes during a great age
of imperial expansion, but, nevertheless, one that was widely shared and
can be seen as reflecting a Tory attitude to foreign policy:

> I cannot conclude without expressing that thanks to the Allmighty for
> having prevented a catastrophe that however honorable it might have
> been, must when fresh taxes had been laid must [sic] have shown how
> little the country is in a state to carry on war, and might have occasioned
> that discontent which would have been encouraged by too many ill
> disposed persons.[4]

Drawing a link between war and domestic stability reflected the experience
of the War of American Independence, and encouraged a caution that
George shared with Pitt. The crisis also brought out his characteristic
emphasis on duty. In refusing a request from the lord-lieutenant of Ireland
that an officer be allowed to remain in Ireland when his regiment was
ordered to the West Indies, George wrote, 'any indulgence at present must
be highly detrimental to the public service as well as to military discipline'.[5]
In the event, war was avoided as Spain backed down when its ally France
proved unwilling to provide support. A satisfied George offered Pitt the
Garter and when the latter declined and, instead, asked for the honour for
his brother, John, second earl of Chatham, the first lord of the admiralty,
George agreed as a public sign of approbation for the entire family.[6]
Chatham and Leeds were created knights of the Garter on 15 December.

   In 1791, George took a keen interest in the government's parliamentary
majorities during the Ochakov crisis with Russia, as he hoped they would
give energy to government policy and have an impact abroad.[7] Alliance
with Prussia against Russia accorded with the tendency discerned in
George's policy by hostile commentators. The ultimatum to Russia was
drawn up by Pitt on 25 March after he, Leeds and Chatham had seen
George two days earlier. The king believed it necessary to take a stand
against Catherine the Great, whose expansionism at the expense of the
Ottoman (Turkish) empire appeared, to him, to threaten European order.
The British climb-down in the face of domestic opposition, inspired the

---

[3] George to William Grenville, 24 June 1790, BL. Add. 58855 fol. 121.
[4] George to William Grenville, 5 Aug. 1790, BL. Add. 58855 fol. 135
[5] George to Pitt, 11 Oct. 1790, PRO. 30/8/103 fol. 399.
[6] George to Pitt, 12, 13, 14 Dec. 1790, PRO. 30/8/103 fols 405, 407, 411.
[7] George to William Grenville, 30 Mar., George to Pitt, 30 Mar. 1791, BL. Add. 58856 fol.
26, PRO. 30/8/103 fol. 416.

caricature *Saint Catherine and St. George*, published on 15 April, which showed Catherine sitting on a prostrate George. Five days later Gillray published *Taming of the Shrew*, with Pitt riding George against Catherine, the 'G.R.' on the horse replaced by 'P.R.' and George saying 'Heigho! to have myself thus rid to death, by a Boy and his playmates, merely to frighten an Old Woman. I wish I was back in Hanover to get myself a belly full.' Disappointed by the climb-down, Leeds resigned.

British policy had been motivated by a desire to limit Russian expansionism, and there is no doubt of George's support for peace and the status quo in Europe. Indeed, that had been a major strand in his thought since his accession, and he considered himself the victim of American rebellion and Bourbon aggression during the War of American Independence. A commitment to peace also affected George's perception of ministerial choices. When William Grenville succeeded Leeds in 1791, George wrote: 'in addition to his ability and diligence, the knowledge of his decided opinion how essential peace is to the welfare of this kingdom makes me think it most advantageous that he should hold the seals of the Foreign Department'. Later that year, Grenville was appointed to the rangerships of St James's and Hyde Park, a marked sign of royal favour.[8]

In the Ochakov crisis, George supported the ministry when, in response to parliamentary criticism, it eventually backed away from confrontation with Russia, even though this strained relations with Prussia. Again he referred to the general value of peace – 'whatever can tend to secure a continuation of peace to my dominions must meet with my fullest approbation' – but also to the need to respond to the marked opposition in parliament to war with Russia, noting 'how impossible it would be at present to incline this country to take a cordial part in any measures that might involve it in a war'.[9] At the same time, because George was convinced that Anglo-Prussian support had enabled the Ottoman empire to gain better terms from Russia than would otherwise have been the case, he hoped that the British 'nation' would view government policy in a favourable light.[10]

Subsequently, George's opposition to the French Revolution and to domestic radicalism matched that not only of the ministers but also of the bulk of the British political élite, and it is difficult to distinguish the royal role from that of the ministers. The Revolution and the response to it in Britain posed central questions about the nature of civil society and the legitimacy of the British system, with new directions and urgency in ideological divisions and a more extensive public engagement in politics. The

[8] George to William Grenville, 30 Apr. 1791, BL. Add. 58856 fol. 39; George to Pitt, 23, 30 Apr., 10 Dec. 1791, PRO. 30/8/103 fols 418, 420, 428.
[9] George to William Grenville, 19 Apr. 1791, BL. Add. 58856 fol. 34.
[10] George to William Grenville, 14 Aug. 1791, BL. Add. 58856 fol. 67.

sense that crown, Church and élite must join together, in response, was captured by William, Lord Auckland, British envoy in the Hague, who, in November 1792, urged 'every possible form of Proclamations to the People, orders for Fast Days, Speeches from the Throne, Discourses from the Pulpit, Discussions in Parliament etc.'[11] George, indeed, had a long-standing view that the élite must stand together to support order. In response to disturbances in Dublin in 1784, he had written: 'as usual there seems to be much timidity in the magistrates. I hope the men of property will feel the necessity of standing forth in aid of the Lord Lieutenant.'[12]

In the early 1790s, the king was more concerned about domestic support for the French Revolution, and the resulting threats of radicalism and instability, than about developments in France. The outbreak of the Revolution had led to pointed comparisons with the situation in Britain, many favourable to the British political system, but some critical. Initially, this criticism generally did not extend to the person or position of George, but in some cases it did. Having passed through Paris in July 1789, being there when the Bastille was stormed, Samuel Boddington (1766–1843) wrote to his father Benjamin, a prominent London West India merchant and one of the senior Dissenters who had conveyed to George the congratulatory address on his recovery, linking social oppression to the perception of the crown:

The eyes of the kingdom are now opened and they have those ideas of their own consequence and the rights and privileges they are entitled to that I trust will effectually humble that superiority which the nobles have so unjustly arrogated to themselves. When the King [Louis XVI] came to Paris it was not as formerly Vive le Roi but Vive la Nation. I hope Englishmen will have the good sense to take a hint and not let their late loyalty carry them too far.[13]

The following March, the radical John Hurford Stone used the French example to predict the overthrow of a British political system presided over by 'an idiot King'.[14] In response to signs of radical activity in Britain, George urged vigilance, writing in July 1791,

That the meeting at the Crown and Anchor yesterday produced no disturbance of consequence is more to be attributed to the proper steps

---

[11] Auckland to William Grenville, 26 Nov. 1792, BL. Add. 58920, fol. 178.

[12] George to Lord Sydney, 5 July 1784, PRO. 30/8/103.

[13] Samuel to Benjamin Boddington, 24 July 1789, London, Guildhall Library, MS. 10823/5b.

[14] J. Graham, *The Nation, the Law and the King, Reform Politics in England, 1789–1999* (Lanham, Maryland, 2000), p. 156.

taken to meet any outrage that might have been attempted than to the conduct of the promoters of that assembly. By Mr. Dundas's account the names of those most conspicuous are of but little note, the papers published on the occasion are evidence sufficient that the object of the meeting was not the avowed cause and therefore deserves attention, though no public steps seem to be called for.[15]

The anti-Priestley riots later that month in Birmingham[16] made George affirm his commitment to order, even if he sympathized with the anti-radical views of the rioters. The government's duty to uphold the rule of law emerges clearly from his correspondence on the issue, which also reveals George's detailed knowledge of military matters. On 16 July 1791 he wrote to Dundas, the newly appointed home secretary,

> The orders for three troops of the 15th Regiment of Dragoons to march towards Birmingham to restore order if the civil magistrates have not been able is incumbent on government; though I cannot but feel better pleased that Priestley is the sufferer for the doctrines he and his party have instilled and that the people see them in their true light; yet cannot approve of their having employed such atrocious means of showing their discontent.[17]

The following day, he returned to the charge:

> There is not a more indispensable duty in the executive power than to support the civil magistrates in suppressing riots, where it cannot otherwise be effected. As such I approve of the measures proposed of reinforcing the military corps already ordered to Birmingham.[18]

Later that day, news that disturbances continued led George to conclude that only troops could restore order, but he noted that most of the horses of the 15th Dragoons were at grass, which would delay matters.[19] In response to government concerns, George agreed to the additional dispatch of two infantry regiments, although he was less alarmist than Pitt and Dundas.[20] On 20 July, he indicated his concern with practicalities and cost, the former in particular a reiterated theme in George's correspondence:

[15] George to Dundas, 15 July 1791, BL. Add. 40100 fol. 2.
[16] R.B. Rose, 'The Priestley Riots of 1791', *Past and Present*, 18 (1960), pp. 68–88; G.M. Ditchfield, 'The Priestley Riots in Historical Perspective', *Transactions of the Unitarian Historical Society*, 20 (1991), pp. 3–16.
[17] George to Dundas, 16 July 1791, BL. Add. 40100 fol. 3.
[18] George to Dundas, 17 July 1791, BL. Add. 40100 fol. 4.
[19] George to Dundas, 17 July 1791, BL. Add. 40100 fol. 6.
[20] George to Dundas, 18 July 1791, BL. Add. 40100 fol. 9.

The accounts seem to be so confident that the riot at Birmingham has subsided that I trust the mischief in the neighbouring places will also cease. This is a sufficient reason to prevent the taking up the horses of the cavalry except the Royal Regiment of Horse Guards which should continue to go to Coventry from whence it may detach one squadron to Birmingham to relieve the three troops of the 15th which ought to return to Nottingham, and another troops of the Blues may be sent from Coventry to Wolverhampton. Those regiments that have taken up their horses should not turn them again to grass as the expense of the grass money will not be equal to the loss that will attend turning out the horses again, particularly if they have begun this month.[21]

Later that year, the king applauded criticism of the French Revolution from the opposition Whigs:

The letter of Mr Burke and its enclosure [a letter of support to Edmund Burke from William, second Earl Fitzwilliam] both deserve commendation so far as they convey the genuine sentiments of the writers of the bad example set in France to all established governments; yet I am sorry to see Lord Fitzwilliam's resolution of only whispering opinions that ought to do him credit if he publikly avowed them and consequently adopting a conduct that must make the uniformed suppose him indifferent on so material a question.[22]

Like many commentators, especially High Churchmen, George drew on an already strong sense that order and religion were under threat from conspirators and the heterodox, and applied it in the new context.[23] An emphasis on order was linked to the revival of Toryism as a coherent political position, which was associated in particular with the defence of the Church of England. Indeed, in March 1790 George had greeted the defeat in the House of Commons of Fox's motion for the repeal of the Test and Corporation Acts: this was 'most welcome news', and George hoped that it would end the matter. His view of responding to reform initiatives was that of lancing boils:

That the debate should have proved long, having so favourable a conclusion seems advantageous, as it shows the question has been

---

[21] George to Dundas, 20 July 1791, BL. Add. 40100 fol. 11.

[22] George to ———, 8 Oct. 1791, *Maggs Catalogue* 1292, p. 49, item no. 79.

[23] N. Aston, 'Burke and the Conspiratorial Origins of the French Revolution: Some Anglo-French Resemblances', in B. Coward and J. Swann (eds), *Conspiracies and Conspiracy Theory in Early Modern Europe. From the Waldensians to the French Revolution* (Aldershot, 2004), pp. 213–33.

thoroughly discussed, and consequently I should hope Parliament will
not be again troubled with this most improper business.[24]

Although George's views helped focus the defence of order, hierarchy
and continuity on religious issues, a confessional dimension to politics was
already pronounced. The long-standing rift between Anglican and
Dissenter had a strong influence both on the continuation of local political
divisions and on the configuration of the national division between the Pitt
ministry and the Whig opposition. It was important in the general election
of 1790, which was a major success for the government, despite the relative
sophistication of opposition organization.[25] Religion also played a central
role in political motivation in Ireland and Scotland. There was always some
Nonconformist praise for George, but the most bitter criticism of the king
came from this direction.

The response to radicalism at home was matched by growing concern
about the situation in France. At first, George had not been sorry to see
France in difficulties. Indeed, in September 1788, François de Barthélemy,
the French minister plenipotentiary, had reported that George shared the
widespread hopes that the forthcoming Estates-General would end in
chaos. The following September, George's expression of goodwill towards
Louis XVI was met with suspicion.[26] The government, however, soon had
to define its attitude to the French domestic situation in response to
requests for assistance from the French *émigrés* and from foreign supporters
of their cause. In March 1790, George gave a cautious response to an
approach from Spain. Pitt was allowed to be explicit about no money
having been used to sustain disorder in France, a claim made by those
adept at finding British conspiracy behind the Revolution, but the king
continued:

In the present posture of affairs with Spain, I do not see we can take
any step towards that Court; but, should that storm blow over, there
cannot be any objection to assure her of our resolution not to prevent

[24] George to Pitt, 3 Mar. 1790, PRO. 30/8/103 fol. 381.
[25] G. Ditchfield, 'The Campaign in Lancashire and Cheshire for the Repeal of the Test
and Corporation Acts, 1787–1790', *Transactions of the Historic Society of Lancashire and Cheshire*,
126 (1977), p. 132; J. Fiske (ed.), *The Oakes Diaries, I. Business, Politics and the Family in Bury St.
Edmunds, 1778–1800* (Woodbridge, 1990), pp. 262–3; Pitt to Edward Eliot, 9 July 1790,
Ipswich CRO. HA 119 T108/39 no. 293; R.G. Thorne (ed.), *The House of Commons
1790–1820* (5 vols, London, 1986), I, 115–26; D.E. Ginter, *Whig Organization in the General
Election of 1790* (Berkeley, 1967). F. O'Gorman, *Voters, Patrons and Parties: The Unreformed
Electorate of Hanoverian England, 1734–1832* (Oxford, 1989). pp. 350–2, 359–68; R. Hole,
Pulpits, Politics and Public Order in England, 1760–1832 (Cambridge, 1989).
[26] La Luzerne to Montmorin, 22 Sept. 1789, AE. CP. Ang. 571 fols 10–11.

the French constitution from being re-established on terms conformable to the sentiments of the Comte d'Artois[27]

– the counter-revolutionary brother of Louis XVI. Louis's cousin, Philip, duke of Orléans, an opportunist populist who opposed him, helped discredit the radical cause with George. He had visited London frequently, but he had close links with the prince of Wales, and was blamed by George in 1784 for encouraging the latter's plan to settle in France. George was displeased by Orléans's mission to London in October 1789.[28]

Tacit support for the cause of counter-revolution, however, was equivalent to offering none. In his cautious response, George sketched out what would become, under the pressure of foreign requests, an increasingly clear British response. No assistance would be provided unless vital British interests were affected. George told foreign diplomats, including Barthélemy, that he did not think that the new French political system could last, but he was not proposing to act to that end.[29]

George was understanding of Louis XVI's difficult position and sympathetic to the royal family's attempt to escape from France in June 1791. He observed that 'should they providentially get out of France, it will bring to the test whether the nobility, clergy and law will join the regal cause'.[30] Stopped at Varennes, which 'much affected' George,[31] Louis's attempted flight caused a major increase in international tension. His brother-in-law, the Emperor Leopold II, responded, on 6 July 1791, to Louis's failure by issuing the Padua Circular, an appeal to Europe's rulers for concerted action to restore the liberty of the French royal family. On 27 August, this was followed by the Austro-Prussian Declaration of Pillnitz. Leopold and Frederick William II of Prussia sought the backing of Britain, as did the *émigré* princes. The response, however, was unfavourable. George wrote to Leopold to state that he would not take a role in French internal affairs, and to Louis XVI's brother, the comte de Provence, later Louis XVIII, that Britain would maintain an exact neutrality.[32] The additional reference in diplomatic instructions to Vienna to George's hope to establishing with Austria a system of good understanding designed to help promote European peace[33] was all too vague for those pressing for action.

[27] George to Pitt, 28 Mar. 1790, PRO. 30/8/103 fol. 387.
[28] George to Thurlow, 31 Aug. 1784, Aspinall, *George III*, I, 85; A. Britsch, 'L'Anglomanie de Philippe-Egalité d'après sa correspondance autographe, 1778–1785', *Le Correspondant*, 33 (1926), pp. 280–95; George to Leeds, 19 Oct. 1789, BL. Add. 27914 fol. 23.
[29] Barthélemy to Montmorin, 4 Mar. 1791, AE. CP. Ang. 576 fols 267–8.
[30] George to William Grenville, 23, 25 27 June 1791, BL. Add. 58855 fols 48, 53, Bod., Bland Burges papers, vol. 52 fol. 117.
[31] George to William Grenville, 27 June 1791, BL. Add. 58856 fol. 52.
[32] George to Leopold II, 23 July 1791, Broomhall, Fife, Elgin papers 60/1/93; George to Provence, 19 Sept. 1791, PRO. FO. 90/17.
[33] William Grenville to Sir Robert Murray Keith, 19 Aug. 1791, PRO. FO. 7/27 fols 182–3.

Hanoverian conduct was also criticized in Vienna.[34] At the same time, George was keen that the government should not appear to approve developments in France.[35]

Britain remained neutral as war approached. In April 1792, conflict broke out between Austria and France, Prussia coming to the aid of Austria the following month. Prior to this, a French mission, whose most prominent member was Charles Maurice de Talleyrand, had sounded the British government on the possibility of an alliance, although George was not in favour of seeing them.[36] Talleyrand discerned an essential division in British policy between Pitt, Grenville and Dundas, allegedly favourable to reconciliation with France, and Camden, Thurlow and, in particular, George, who were totally against such a policy.[37] This accorded with a tradition of seeing George as a malign force, but there is no evidence for such a division in the spring of 1792. A comprehensive formal under-standing with France was not on the agenda. Fox was to tell the Commons on 15 December 1792 that British diplomatic action might have prevented the outbreak of hostilities, but this was wishful thinking, and George certainly did not thwart any ministerial drive for negotiations.

Neutrality was combined with a determination to maintain domestic order, and in this the royal family played a symbolic and practical role, helping focus rising concern within the social and political élite about signs of increasing domestic radicalism and leading them to join in support for what George termed 'good order and our excellent Constitution'.[38] On 21 May 1792 a royal proclamation against seditious meetings and publications was issued. Ten days later, the prince of Wales, giving his first speech in the Lords, spoke in favour of the proclamation. This was an aspect of a move towards a fundamental political realignment that would unite the ministry, its independent supporters and conservative Whigs, and also help the prince of Wales to be more sympathetic to government policy. The realignment, which saw George pleased with support in the debate on 25 May from hitherto 'warm opposers',[39] and which also even-tually divided the Whig party down the middle, was not necessary for parliamentary reasons: there was no doubt of Pitt's control of both houses, and Whig divisions ensured this without any need for political shifts. Instead, these discussions reflected a potent sense of unease within the social élite about public tranquillity. Political calculation, however, was

---

[34] Keith to William Grenville, 31 Dec. 1791, PRO. FO. 7/28.

[35] George to William Grenville, 6 Oct. 1791, BL. Add. 58856 fol. 100.

[36] George to William Grenville, 28 Apr. 1792, BL. Add. 58856 fol. 153.

[37] Talleyrand to Lessart, French foreign minister, 2 Mar. 1792, AE. CP. Ang. supp. 29 fol. 240.

[38] George to Pitt, 1 May 1792, PRO. 30/8/103 fol. 440.

[39] George to Pitt, 26 May 1792, PRO. 30/8/103 fol. 444.

also involved, and, with George's permission, Pitt sought Portland's support in checking any attempt that might threaten public order.[40]

The Whig crisis was one of division, loss of direction and uncertainty, causing those unhappy with either Fox's determination to maintain opposition to the government during the international crisis, or his reluctance to condemn the direction of the Revolution, to look increasingly to Pitt. Some were willing to join the government, more were ready to support it or, at least, not to oppose it, but, whatever the decisions of individuals, they helped to weaken and fragment the Whigs. Long-standing causes of the crisis included the failure of the Fox–North ministry, defeat in two successive general elections in 1784 and 1790, the prevailing success of the Pitt government, and the obvious absence of royal backing for the Whigs. They had all caused disappointment and lowered morale in Whig ranks from 1784, and the deflation of hopes raised by George III's illness in 1788–9 was especially serious.[41]

In 1792, there was also a crisis within the government created by Pitt's successful demand that he or Lord Chancellor Thurlow, who was opposing Pitt in both the Lords and the cabinet, go; Thurlow's relations with Grenville were extremely bad.[42] The crisis, however, was short-lived and also important in helping to ensure ministerial unity. Thurlow was the most prominent King's Friend, whose 'value and faults' George knew.[43] In response to Pitt's pressure, George decided on 16 May that Thurlow must go, 'a decision . . . revolting to my feelings', though, in order to cause the minimum disruption to legal business, he remained chancellor until 15 June.[44] François, marquis de Chauvelin, the French envoy, depicted a royal 'parti' headed by Thurlow and Hawkesbury, a rival group headed by Pitt, who was supported by Chatham, Grenville and Dundas, and a middle group of Camden, Richmond and Stafford, that moved first one way and then the other. Far from being dangerous for France, Chauvelin argued, Thurlow's departure had helped to cement the triumph of Pitt and Grenville who were determined to stop Britain entering the war.[45] In practice, although Thurlow and Pitt had long been rivals, their quarrels in

---

[40] Pitt to Portland, 9 May, Portland to Pitt, 9 May 1792, PRO. 30/8/102 fol. 222, 30/8/168 fol. 72.

[41] L.G. Mitchell, *Charles James Fox and the Disintegration of the Whig Party 1782–1794* (Oxford, 1971), pp. 153–93.

[42] Pitt to George, 16 May 1792, PRO. 30/8/102 fol. 178; *Bonham Books* (Catalogue), 15 Apr. 1991, lots 169–70; G.M. Ditchfield, 'Lord Thurlow', in R.W. Davis (ed.), *Lords of Parliament. Studies 1714–1914* (Paolo Alto, California, 1995), pp. 75–6.

[43] George to William Grenville, 29 Sept. 1791, BL. Add. 58856 fol. 96.

[44] George to Dundas, 16 May 1792, PRO. 30/8/103; George to Thurlow, 17 May 1792, BL. Eg. 2232 fol. 85; Richard Duke of Buckingham, *Memoirs of the Court and Cabinets of George the Third* (4 vols, London, 1853–5), III, 207.

[45] Chauvelin to Dumouriez, foreign minister, 23 May 1792, AE. CP. Ang. 581 fols 44–6.

early 1792 had apparently been over the slave trade and financial measures,[46] not over foreign policy. The clear occasion of the final crisis was
Thurlow's public opposition to the Sinking Fund Bill in the Lords on 14 May,
which nearly led to the defeat of the Bill. George felt that Thurlow had let
him down as 'it is unbecoming to the highest degree to be wasting the
present hour in personal disputes'.[47]

That summer, a major military review was staged on Sydenham
Common, George reviewing the troops under the duke of York. At that
stage, war still seemed far distant, but neutrality became less abstract in
August 1792 when the advance towards Paris of Prussian forces under
George's brother-in-law, Charles, duke of Brunswick, a Prussian field
marshal, led to a sense of the revolution as both threatened and betrayed,
and, on 10 August, to the storming of the Tuileries palace. The monarchy
was suspended by the legislative assembly, and on 13 August Louis XVI
was in effect imprisoned in the Temple keep. The theory, and, to a limited
extent, practice of popular sovereignty was thrust to the fore as public
virtue was enforced on those seen as reprobate. On 17 August, a special
tribunal was established in Paris to try those accused of political crimes,
and between 2 and 7 September over a thousand were killed as the prisons
were purged. Already, in May, George had claimed that 'from the
commencement of the revolution more acts of barbarity have been
committed than by the most savage people'.[48] His commitment to public
virtue was more accommodating and less sanguinary than that of the
French enforcers of moral regeneration.[49]

Foreign diplomats had been accredited to Louis XVI, and the collapse of
his government meant a break in formal diplomatic relations, not least
because it was unclear who was now wielding authority in Paris. The
cabinet on 17 August decided to recall the British envoy, George, Earl
Gower, in part because of the danger to his life.[50] George approved the
instructions,[51] and criticized Chauvelin, who had initially condemned the
events of 10 August, for pressing for the return of the note he had delivered:
'It is remarkable that he chooses to retract the only proper step he has taken
since the commencement of his mission.'[52]

The September massacres were unacceptable even to Fox, and the
response of less sympathetic commentators was more hostile. Horrified

[46] J. Ehrman, *The Younger Pitt* (3 vols, London, 1969–96), II, 174–5; M.W. McCahill, *Order
and Equipoise: The Peerage and the House of Lords 1783–1806* (London, 1978), p. 135.

[47] George to Pitt, 15 May 1792, PRO. 30/8/103 fol. 442.

[48] George to William Grenville, 4 May 1792, BL. Add. 58856 fol. 156.

[49] N. Hampson, *Prelude to Terror: The Constituent Assembly and the Failure of Consensus,
1789–1791* (Oxford, 1988).

[50] Dundas to George, 17 Aug. 1792, BL. Add. 58968 fol. 29.

[51] George to Dundas, 18 Aug. 1792, BL. Add. 40100 fol. 51.

[52] George to Dundas, 19 Aug. 1792, BL. Add. 40100 fol. 53.

anyway by developments in Paris, including the report that Marie
Antoinette was to be put on trial, George pointed out that there was no
solid government in France.[53] With the king's approval, the government
departed to a certain extent from its path of neutrality by warning that if
Louis XVI was treated with violence, those responsible would not receive
asylum in Britain. Amnesty was, however, offered if they avoided harming
the French royal family.[54]

The king followed the campaign in France on a map,[55] but the situation
was transformed 108 miles from Paris at Valmy on 20 September when the
advancing Prussians under Brunswick turned back in the face of more
numerous French defenders without a full-scale engagement. Their subsequent retreat was followed by rapid French advances into neighbouring
territories. Frankfurt fell on 22 October, and an invasion of the Austrian
Netherlands (Belgium) on 3 November led to its fall within a month: the
Austrians were defeated at Jemappes on 6 November and the French
entered Brussels on 13 November, Ostend on the 16th, Antwerp on the 29th
and Namur on 2 December. In response, the British government promised
their Dutch ally support if the French attacked. At the same time, concern
over domestic radicalism grew. Valmy and its consequences helped create
a sense of unease and unpredictability, increasing interest among some of
the Whigs in a coalition designed to produce unity against radicalism.
Faced with reports of agitation around the country, the government
responded by a reliance on the landed élite, alongside an attempt to
encourage a mass movement of loyalism.

As the ministry prepared to face war or revolution, it also had to decide
how far it was possible to negotiate a settlement with the French government, which was becoming increasingly radical. On 19 November, the
National Convention passed a decree declaring that the French people
would extend fraternity and assistance to all peoples seeking to regain
their liberty. In late November, Grenville and Pitt were keen on responding
to a French approach for negotiations in The Hague, but George was
more sceptical, though for prudential, rather than legitimist, reasons:

> I feel the advantage of a general peace if it can be effected to the *real*
> satisfaction of the various parties concerned, but at the same time not
> less forcibly a disinclination to France gaining this point and perhaps
> laying a foundation to encourage other countries to attempt the same
> game; for it is peace alone that can place the French Revolution on a
> permanent ground as then all the European states must acknowledge

[53] George to William Grenville, 3, 4 Sept. 1792, BL. Add. 58857 fols 30–1.
[54] William Grenville to George, 21 Sept., reply 22 Sept. 1792, BL. Add. 58857 fols 34–6.
[55] William Grenville to George, 25 Sept., George to William Grenville, 26 Sept. 1792, BL.
Add. 58857 fols 37–9.

this new republic ... I am far from sanguine either that the French
general [Dumouriez] will venture to speak out or that if he would we
can manage the business in a manner to satisfy the various courts
concerned, or even escape blame from an appearance of being the first
to acknowledge the French Revolution.[56]

George was properly sceptical about the likely success of negotiations;
but the alternative, as he recognized in his letter, was bleak, and the British
envoy was authorized to take part. At the same time, the prospect of an
imminent war with France made domestic signs of radicalism especially
alarming. Concerned about the position in Britain, George refused to send
any troops thence to Ireland.[57]

A loyalist upsurge proved the best counter to radicalism in Britain. On
20 November 1792, the Association for Preserving Liberty and Property
against Republicans and Levellers was launched at a meeting at the
Crown and Anchor Tavern in London. The association was encouraged
by the government, although far from dependent on its support.[58] It
proved difficult to sustain the level of engagement, and the relationship
between government and loyalism could be ambiguous; nevertheless, in
much of the country, a network of loyalist associations was established and
this provided a crucial prop to the government. The crown played a major
role as a focus for loyalism, George approving the calling out of the
militia,[59] but this did not lead the king to seek any more political power.
Furthermore, he and his household played no direct role in organizing
loyalism. Instead, government officials were prominent, such as James
Bland Burges, under-secretary in the Foreign Office, who took an active
part in the foundation of the *True Briton* and the *Sun*. George, however, did
take a continuing interest in the negotiations with France, usually pressing
for caution. In early December, as Pitt's desire for negotiations continued
to lead to a favourable response to French approaches for talks, George
agreed with Grenville that it was best to handle discussions in London, not
Paris. The king felt that it would be easier to control discussions in
London, but added that any negotiation would probably fail and that, in
light of this, it was necessary not to allow the French to embarrass the

[56] George to William Grenville, 25 Nov. 1792, BL. Add. 58857 fol. 59.
[57] George to William Grenville, 26 Nov. 1792, BL. Add. 58857 fol. 62.
[58] R. Dozier, *For King, Constitution, and Country. The English Loyalists and the French Revolution*
(Lexington, Kentucky, 1983); H.T. Dickinson, 'Popular Loyalism in Britain in the 1790s', in
E. Hellmuth (ed.), *The Transformation of Political Culture: Germany and England in the Late
Eighteenth Century* (Oxford, 1990), pp. 503–34; D. Eastwood, 'Patriotism and the English
State in the 1790s', in M. Philp (ed.), *The French Revolution and British Popular Politics*
(Cambridge, 1991), pp. 146–68.
[59] George to William Grenville, 1 Dec. 1792, BL. Add. 58857 fol. 66.

British government by revealing how far they had been willing to go to make concessions.[60]

The growing radicalism of the French government was a major problem, as the trial of Louis XVI made the French demand for diplomatic recognition an extremely sensitive issue. The direction of British politics was also against concessions. When the parliamentary session began on 13 December, Fox attacked the ministry for failing to negotiate with France, but this amendment was heavily defeated because, on 11 and 12 December, meetings of prominent Whigs at Burlington House had agreed not to oppose the address, a position George had failed to anticipate the previous month.[61] Portland, indeed, had already approved the draft of the royal speech he had been shown. Fox, in contrast, was convinced that the Revolution had taken an unfortunate path because it had not been allowed to develop without external threats. He saw France's enemies as united in a crusade of despots seeking to suppress liberty, and viewed George in this light, but this approach enjoyed little support within the political élite. George and the latter had a better sense of the extent to which the Revolution threatened to be at once an attempt for social transformation and a reality of anarchy.

Anglo-French discussions were vitiated by a general mutual distrust, and by the commitment by both governments to positions from which they were not willing to recede. Far from detracting from negotiations, the dispute over recognition encapsulated the points at issue. On 6 January 1793 George argued that, in light of signs that the French government intended to go to war with Britain, 'in the actual state of things it seems the most desirable conclusion of the present crisis'.[62] The following day, Chauvelin again compromised the attempt to discuss issues by insisting on recognition. Grenville informed George that the ministry had decided that his note was inadmissible because presented in the character of minister of the French Republic, and George supported the step.[63]

The news of the sentence of death on Louis XVI, pronounced by the National Convention on 17 January, reached London on the 21st. George, who was greatly encouraged by the size of the government's majority in the Commons,[64] told Pitt that when news of the execution arrived he would call a Privy Council to order Chauvelin's expulsion. When it came on the 23rd, the royal audience in the drawing room was cancelled, as was a planned visit by George to the theatre. Next day, the Privy Council met

[60] George to William Grenville, 3 Dec. 1792, BL. Add. 58857 fol. 71.
[61] George to Pitt, 26 Nov. 1792, PRO. 30/8/103 fol. 462.
[62] George to Chatham, 6 Jan. 1793, Aspinall, *George III*, I, 642.
[63] William Grenville to George, 7 Jan. 1793, Aspinall, *George III*, I, 642; George to William Grenville, 8 Jan. 1793, BL. Add. 58857 fol. 79.
[64] George to Pitt, 22 Jan. 1793, PRO. 30/8/103 fol. 464.

with George present, and Chauvelin was ordered to leave by 1 February. George also ordered the assembly of a force of 13,000 Hanoverians to serve in the Low Countries.[65] The French were convinced that George was pro-war, but their overall perspective predisposed them to that view. Hugues-Bernard Maret, a senior official from the French Foreign Ministry who took part in informal talks in London that winter, discerned a government divided into two parties, one 'purely royalist', which sought a war of counter-revolution and did not think of anything else, and a group led by Pitt that feared the financial consequences. Indeed *The Times* of the previous 19 November had printed the rumour that Pitt would resign because his views on relations with France were irreconcilable with those of George, while, in 1808, William Miles, a self-appointed intermediary with France in 1792–3, was to claim that Pitt was ordered by George to fight or to resign.[66] Guided by practicality, prudence and a distaste for the French regime and its British supporters, George was certainly unwilling to make a commitment to preserving peace, but there is little sign of any serious difference between him and Pitt.

On 1 February 1793, the National Convention decided to declare war on Britain. George was accused of supporting the Austro-Prussian alliance in its enmity towards France, and, making use of the idea that war was declared on sovereigns, the convention also agreed to a motion that the British people were to be asked to rebel. Convinced that 'duty as well as interest' called for action by Britain,[67] George found the news of the French declaration of war 'highly agreeable ... as the means adopted seems well calculated to rouze such a spirit in this country that I trust will curb the insolence of those despots and be a means of restoring some degree of order to that unprincipled country, whose aim at present is to destroy the foundations of every civilized state'.[68] British radicals, in turn, were rejecting the symbolic power of the crown. Daniel Eaton, a radical London bookseller, wrote later in the year, 'Away with stars and garters: the trappings of monarchy are the patents of slavery.'[69] The following year, he was acquitted for a story about a gamecock that was directed at George. The pressure of prosecutions, however, led Eaton to flee to America in 1796.

George's social conservatism, which he would have associated with an emphasis on the importance of duty and merit, was not only seen in his

[65] William Grenville to George, 23 Jan. 1793, C.R. Middleton, 'Some Additional Correspondence of King George III', *Notes and Queries*, new series, 26 (1979), p. 221; Grenville–George corresp. on 24 Jan. 1793, BL. Add. 58857 fols 80–5; George to Pitt, 24 Jan. 1793, PRO. 30/8/103.

[66] Maret to Pierre Lebrun, foreign minister, 31 Jan. 1793, AE. CP. Ang. 586 fols 344–7; W.A. Miles, *A Letter to His Royal Highness the Prince of Wales* (London, 1808), p. 84.

[67] George to Pitt, 2 Feb. 1793, PRO. 30/8/103 fol. 476.

[68] George to William Grenville, 9 Feb. 1793, BL, Add. 58857, fol. 87.

[69] Eaton, *Politics for the People, or Hog's Wash*, 16 Nov. 1793.

response to the Revolution. The king's correspondence on military promotions was also indicative of his attitudes. After the capture of a French frigate in 1795, George applauded the promotion of the captain and the first lieutenant, adding,

> as the Second Lieutenant Mr. Maitland conducted himself very well, I trust he will soon meet with the same favour, being a man of good family will I hope also be of advantage in the consideration, as it is certainly wise as much as possible to give encouragement if they personally deserve it to gentlemen.[70]

Frederick Maitland was indeed a brave officer and was to have a distinguished naval career. His father, Frederick, the godson of George's father, was son of Charles, sixth earl of Lauderdale and had been commander of the royal yacht.

The growing crisis in France had provided an opportunity for George to reveal his interest in the Stuarts, prompted by the fate of the archives of the Scots College in Paris. In 1789, the National Assembly had passed a resolution for the expropriation of foreign colleges, leading the principal of the Scots College, Alexander Gordon, to approach Pitt, seeking protection, affirming loyalty and proposing to convey to Britain the archives, which contained much material relating to James II and VII and to subsequent Jacobite activity.[71] The matter of a possible sale was discussed for over two years. John Douglas, bishop of Salisbury and dean of Windsor, a cleric with literary interests who in 1787 had been appointed a trustee of the British Museum, co-operated with James Bland Burges in trying to win the support of George. Douglas's report throws light on George's wishes, but also on the degree to which their execution was dependent on ministerial support. The king's sensitivity to the views of formerly Jacobite families, such as the Ailesburys, with whom he had recently stayed, an aspect of his more generally considerate nature, also emerged:

> I put your letter into his hands; and he read it with great attention . . . though His Majesty did not seem inclined to place these singularly important papers in his private library (not having made it his object to collect historical manuscripts) he expressed, without the least reserve, his wishes that a method might be devised for lodging them in some public repository . . . I ventured to suggest the great propriety of an application to the House of Commons to purchase them for the British Museum. His Majesty was pleased to express his approbation . . . If this proposal should be adopted, the Trustees may be directed to lay down

[70] George to Spencer, 17 Mar. 1795, BL. Add. 75779.
[71] Gordon to Pitt, 14 Oct. 1789, BL. Add. 28068 fols. 310–12.

proper restrictions, as to the mode of consulting the manuscripts that the private correspondence between James, and his friends in England after the Revolution may not be indiscreetly made public.[72]

Ministerial opposition to the scheme's cost appears to have killed it,[73] but a belief that George would purchase the archive and donate it to the museum led to a report in the *Public Advertiser* of 7 May 1792 that threw light on the notion of kingship as trust: 'When sovereigns employ thus usefully and thus honourably the revenue with which their country has entrusted them, how properly do they consider their own character and duty, as well as the welfare of that country over which they preside.' The papers themselves, however, remained in France until an attempt made to smuggle them out ended in their being burnt in order to prevent the holder from being compromised.[74] A decade later, *The History of the Rebellion of 1745* by John Home was dedicated by permission to George. As another instance of reconciliation, this account by a Scottish Presbyterian left out Cumberland's contentious actions after Culloden. Furthermore, after the home at Frascati of 'Henry IX', the Jacobite claimant to the British throne, was sacked by the French and his property seized in 1799, George III sent him £2,000. When Henry died in 1807, he left the crown jewels that James II and VII had taken out of the country to the prince of Wales.

The fate of the papers of the Scots College indicated a concern with heritage that was appropriate in a crisis in which the royal position rested on continuity and the authority that stemmed from this. At the same time, in responding to the criticism of the role of the crown and the aristocracy, the loyalist response did not simply rest on such a defence, but, instead, presented monarchy and aristocracy as aspects of a modern, progressive society.[75] More generally, the 1790s saw a stronger emphasis than hitherto on a monarchical, as opposed to a 'balanced', constitution, and this was closely associated with a positive portrayal of George.

---

[72] Douglas to Burges, 10 Nov. 1791, Bod., Bland Burges papers, vol. 19 fol. 30.

[73] Douglas to Burges, 13 Nov. 1791, Bod., Bland Burges papers, vol. 19 fol. 31. See also D. McRoberts, 'The Scottish Catholic Archives, 1560–1978', *Innes Review*, 28, 2 (1977), pp. 59–128.

[74] *Edinburgh Review*, July 1808.

[75] A. Goodrich, *Debating England's Aristocracy in the 1790s. Pamphlets, Polemics and Political Ideas* (Woodbridge, 2005).

Chapter 15

ELECTOR OF HANOVER

I certainly feel myself as warmly and zealously attached to my Electoral Dominions as any sovereign can be and never will part with them but with my life.

George, 1798[1]

'You must take care of the Hanoverian Horse' (the heraldic symbol of the Electors of Hanover), declared George to Pitt in William Dent's caricature of 30 April 1792 *Gallic Declaration of War or Bumbardment of all Europe*. In this, the French National Assembly appears as a battery of bums bombarding rulers with liberty, while George is placed among the mass of German rulers now at war with France. In contrast, on 10 February 1786, Hedges, the printsellers on Cornhill, had published a caricature that affirmed the value of Hanover. *Sketch of Politicks in Europe 24th January 1786, Birth day of the King of Prussia* showed George and Frederick the Great as allies defying Universal Monarchy in the shape of Austria. The toasts offered included 'The Wooden Walls of Old England' and 'May the United Strength of the British Lion and the Prussian Eagle preserve the Ancient Constitution of the German Empire and the Protestant Interest'. Continental interventionism was thus defended, but, in fact, George had entered the League of Princes with Frederick, as Elector of Hanover, and this was a contentious step.

Yet, compared to the disputes over 'Hanoverianizing' under George I and George II, this criticism was unusual. Indeed, current interest in George III's support for Hanover[2] should not overshadow the fact that in practice this support did not amount to what had been seen under his two predecessors. George had a clearer sense of Britain as a separate entity with its own political interests, but he also sought to affirm his rights as both Elector and king. His concern to defend his position as Elector, for example in response to the Emperor Joseph II's attempt to take control of the government of Hanover when George became seriously ill in the

---

[1] George to William Grenville, 24 July 1798, BL. Add. 58860 fol. 97.
[2] See, in particular, T. Riotte, *Hannover in der britischen Politik, 1792–1815. Dynastische Verbindung als Element aussenpolitischer Entscheidungsprozesse* (Münster, 2005) and B. Simms and T. Riotte (eds), *The Hanoverian Dimension in British History* (Cambridge, 2006).

winter of 1788–9, matched his determination, as king, to protect his position in North America and over Catholic emancipation.

More significantly, however, the character of the dynastic union changed under George and he did not share his predecessors' zeal for the expansion of the Electorate.[3] Prior to his accession, there had been a conviction that the relationship with Hanover would alter under George, although the provision for the separation of Britain and Hanover in his father Frederick's political testament (of 1749) addressed to George was not known. In 1751, the diplomat Sir Charles Hanbury-Williams had written,

> The grief at Hanover for the death of the late Prince of Wales [Frederick] is very great. They look upon themselves (and I hope with reason) as likely to become in reality a province subservient to the interests of Great Britain, and it is high time they should be so for during my stay at Hanover last summer I saw so much of the insolence of those ministers that it made me sick. But now I think the scene must change for 'tis impossible that a Prince [George III] not born there can possibly like such a poor scrubby town and such barren and melancholic country.[4]

Indeed, the prince wrote to Bute in August 1759, 'as to the affairs on the Weser they look worse and worse; I fear this is entirely owing to the partiality the King [George II] has for that horrid Electorate which has always lived upon the very vitals of this poor country; I should say more and perhaps with more anger did not my clock show it is time to dress for Court.' As king, George III showed his determination to end Britain's involvement in the German part of the Seven Years War:

> though I have subjects who will suffer immensely whenever this kingdom withdraws its protection from thence, yet so superior is my love to this my native country over any private interest of my own that I cannot help wishing that an end was put to that enormous expence by ordering our troops home . . . I think if the Duke of Newcastle will not hear reason concerning the German war that it would be better to let him quit than to go on with that and to have myself and those who differ from him made unpopular.

Conscious of the importance of popularity, George informed Bute in 1762 that he would 'never wish to load this country with' subsidies to foreign

[3] J. Black, 'Hanover and British Foreign Policy 1714–60', *English Historical Review*, 120 (2005), pp. 303–39, and *Continental Commitment. Britain, Hanover and Interventionism 1714–1793* (London, 2005).

[4] Hanbury Williams to Henry Fox, 17 June 1751, BL. Add. 5193 fol. 52.

rulers, which were seen as the concomitant of any continental commitment.[5] In the 1760s, indeed, George was not conspicuous as an advocate of Hanoverian interests nor of British commitments to aid the Electorate. As a consequence, the king's views on foreign policy were not as politically contentious as those of his two predecessors. This owed much also to the dominance of colonial, commercial and maritime issues both in foreign policy in the 1760s and in the political and public discussion of it. In addition, after the end of the war in 1763, foreign policy ceased to be such a consistently contentious sphere for, and source of, political debate. Domestic and American constitutional, fiscal and political issues helped to divert attention from foreign policy, with which it was difficult to link them. Those who challenged George or his ministers therefore did not need to refer to foreign policy. The collapse of Jacobitism and the political shifts of the 1750s helped further to create a new agenda in which Hanover and the royal role in foreign policy played little part. This argument must not be pushed too far – foreign policy was not forgotten and reference was made to George's views, but a substantial change followed his accession.

The break with his grandfather's ministers was intertwined with the break with the policies of the 1750s. It was not only that the alliance with Prussia was abandoned as a prelude to the end of the war, but also that the gap was not filled by an alliance with another major continental power. The motives for such an alliance – royal anxiety about Hanover, ministerial concern about this anxiety, and the sense that defensive arrangements for Hanover could, and should, serve as the basis for a British alliance system – had been largely lost. So also had the interventionist habit of mind and the concomitant diplomatic assumptions. Newcastle had written of the response of the elderly George II to a Prussian victory,

> The King, who gives the tone to the nation, and is the foremost to extol and admire the great actions of this great prince, talks of this victory with the affection of a friend and near relation; the satisfaction of an ally, highly interested in the same cause; and with the praise, and admiration, of a general, who knows the real merit of it, and the extent of the genius which must, under God, have brought it about.[6]

The views of George III were very different. George might be very gracious to Carteret, now Earl Granville, soon after his accession, but he had limited interest in the interventionist views that that minister had once stood for. In March 1761, Baron Haslang, the long-serving Bavarian and Palatine envoy in London, pointed out that the prince-bishopric of

---

[5] R.R. Sedgwick (ed.), *Letters from George III to Lord Bute 1756–1766* (London, 1939), pp. 28–9, 78–9, 177.
[6] Newcastle to Mitchell, 8 Sept. 1760, BL. Add. 6832 fol. 51.

Hildesheim, which George II had long sought to acquire, was both vacant and actually occupied by George III's forces. George, however, did not share his grandfather's views on Hildesheim, while the Hanoverian ministers who wanted an end to the expensive war were not particularly keen on territorial gains either. Three weeks after reporting that Hildesheim was vacant, Haslang observed that the predilection for Hanover was no longer so strong, and also suggested that there would be no returns of British conquests from France in order to make gains for the Electorate.[7] This was at a time when another German ruler, Frederick Augustus II, Elector of Saxony, Augustus III of Poland, was seeking territorial gains from the Archbishopric-Electorate of Mainz.

When, in June 1761, the French envoy, François de Bussy, began peace negotiations with the British ministry, he was told by Granville that the British had little interest in Hanoverian affairs. When Bussy told Pitt that France would expect compensation for returning her conquests in the Electorate, on the grounds that, in order to pursue her operations on the continent France had diverted resources from the defence of her colonies, Pitt replied that the argument would have had a great effect during the reign of George II, but that the situation had changed. This was a position that Choiseul, the French foreign minister, found difficult to accept, though, prior to George III's accession, he had already commented in February 1760 that it would not matter to Pitt if France devastated Hanover.[8]

Bussy returned to the subject when he saw Pitt on 23 June 1761. He claimed that the Electorate should be regarded as a province of England, because George II, as king, had broken the 1757 Convention of Klostezeven for the disbandment of the Hanoverian army, and because the army subsequently commanded by Prince Ferdinand of Brunswick for the defence of Hanover acted in accordance with George III's orders and for 'the cause of England', but this was an argument George III would not have accepted. Bussy reiterated the charge that French losses in the colonies were due partly to their operations on the continent.[9] Pitt was willing to moderate his attitude, and offered the return of Guadeloupe as compensation for the French evacuation of her gains in Hanover and the territories of the latter's allies. In the end, however, the negotiations

[7] Haslang to Baron Wachtendonck, Palatine foreign minister, 10, 31 Mar. 1761, Munich, Bayr. Ges. London, 238.

[8] Bussy to Choiseul, 11 June, Choiseul to Bussy, 19 June 1761, AE. CP. Ang. 443 fols 176, 180, 445 fol. 10; Choiseul to Ossun, envoy in Madrid, 19 Feb. 1760, AE. CP. Espagne 527 fol. 235.

[9] Bussy to Choiseul, 26 June, 9 July, Choiseul to Bussy, 27 June 1761, AE. CP. Ang. 443 fols 277, 339, 445 fol. 17; Choiseul to Ossun, 30 July 1761, AE. CP. Espagne 533 fol. 173; Viry to Charles Emmanuel III, 30 June 1761, AST. LM. Ing. 66.

failed as a result of the Third Franco-Spanish Family Compact signed on 15 August, the deterioration of Anglo-Spanish relations, and the British delay in offering acceptable terms to France. Although Pitt had shifted his ground on Hanover, it was clear that George and his leading ministers were not willing to allow Hanoverian concerns to play a major role in the negotiations. Haslang had noted in July 1761 that whatever happened in the empire (the Holy Roman Empire, essentially Germany) would have little effect on British government policy, adding that it was no longer the time of George II. Three months later, Bute told Viry, the Sardinian envoy, that France would not gain better terms if she took Hanover.[10] In January 1762, as war with Spain meant new British military commitments, Newcastle opposed the wish of Bute and George to recall the troops from Germany 'with great force and warmth'.[11] Newcastle feared isolation:

> abandoning the Continent entirely would now render the House of Bourbon absolute master of all Europe, and enable them to oblige every neutral power to submit to such conditions as they should think proper to impose upon them. The other maritime powers would be obliged to shut up all their ports against us.[12]

Having served to distract attention from Hanover and to limit antagonism towards continental engagements, the disintegration of the Prussian alliance was linked to both. In contrast to earlier periods of marked hostility to such engagements, however, in 1762 Hanover played a minor role and the king was not criticized on its account. This was because the move to restrict commitments, and to limit policy to recognizably British goals, came from the monarch. The *Briton*, a weekly newspaper established by Bute, admitted in July 1762 that there was a danger of Hanover being invaded if Britain refused to assist Prussia, but added,

> it is the duty, the interest of the Germanic body to see justice done to any of its constituent members that shall be oppressed: but should they neglect their duty and interest on such an occasion, I hope the Elector of H—r will never again have influence enough with the k——g of G——t B——n, to engage him in a war for retrieving it, that shall cost his kingdom annually, for a series of years, more than double the value of the country in dispute.

---

[10] Bussy to Choiseul, 26 July 1761, AE. CP. Ang. 444 fols 67–8; Haslang to Wachtendonck, 28 July 1761, Munich, Bayr. Ges. London 238; Viry to Charles Emmanuel III, 23 Oct. 1761, AST. LM. Ing. 66.

[11] Cabinet minute, 6 Jan. 1762, PRO. 30/47/21.

[12] Newcastle to Joseph Yorke, 8 Jan. 1762, BL. Add. 32933 fols 113–14.

The paper calculated the annual cost of the 'herculean task' of the defence of Hanover as £6 million.[13] The continental commitment had become far more unpopular, and the king was in accord with this trend. Israel Mauduit's pamphlet, *Considerations on the Present German War* (1760), with its call for isolationism and for the end of a military commitment to the continent and, specifically, to Hanover, had caught a developing mood.[14]

At the same time as the king, and the British government he helped reconstitute, disentangled themselves from the 'German war',[15] there was an instructive sign that George was not without concern for the position of the Electorate, albeit a concern in which territorial aggrandizement did not play a role. In September 1762 the Hanoverian minister, Baron Behr, suggested to Haslang that, once a general peace had been made, a German league, of at least the leading Electors, should be formed so that the participants were not always at risk of being invaded on the slightest pretext. He added that George would seek agreement first with Maximilian III Joseph, Elector of Bavaria.[16] The same month, Nivernais, the French envoy, was reporting that George and his British ministers wished to make the fewest links possible in the empire and to spend no money there, and that peace was likely to be followed on the part of Britain by 'un système d'indifférence' to the empire.[17] There was no real contradiction between Behr's approach and Nivernais's report, given that George both seemed determined to retain the distinction between Britain and Hanover and revealed little interest in territorial acquisitions for the latter. Furthermore, Newcastle's charge that the British government was intent on 'abandoning the Continent'[18] was true only in so far as the war in the empire was concerned. The personal, indeed emotional, attachments to Hanover of George II and to continental interventionism of Newcastle were not matched by their successors. Once freed of the incubus of the war, however, George and his British ministers were willing, and, in some cases, eager, to revive the search for allies.

The attempt to revive negotiations with Austria and Russia, nevertheless, was not matched by any comparable attempt to use British diplomatic assistance to support Hanoverian interests in north-western Germany. The death, on 7 February 1761, of the Wittelsbach episcopal pluralist

---

[13] *Briton*, 10, 24 July, 22 Oct., 4 Dec. 1762. On costs, C. Eldon, *England's Subsidy Policy towards the Continent during the Seven Years War* (Philadelphia, Pennsylvania, 1938).

[14] See, for example, *Royal Magazine*, Dec. 1762.

[15] K.W. Schweizer and J. Bullion, 'The Vote of Credit Controversy, 1762', *British Journal for Eighteenth-Century Studies*, 15 (1992), pp. 175–88.

[16] Haslang to Wachtendonck and to Count Preysing, Bavarian foreign minister, 7 Sept. 1762, Munich, Bayr. Ges. London 239.

[17] Nivernais to Choiseul, 24 Sept. 1762, AE. CP. Ang. 447 fols 146–8.

[18] Newcastle to Hardwicke, 31 July 1762, BL. Add. 32941 fol. 126.

Clement-Auguste, Archbishop-Elector of Cologne and prince-bishop of Hildesheim, Münster, Osnabrück and Paderborn, produced a tremendous opportunity not only for ecclesiastical place-seekers and advocates of secularization, but also for those who wished to enhance their influence in this region. George, however, made little attempt to intervene in the elections, in marked contrast to the position in the 1720s when they had last occurred. His second son, Frederick, became prince-bishop of Osnabrück in 1764 (shortly after his birth in 1763) under the system for the alternate filling of the see by a member of the house of Hanover, but although in 1763 the Hanoverian attitude to the position in Osnabrück gave rise to some concern, secularization was not pursued.[19] Indeed, the French government thought it possible to press George and his British ministry for support for the episcopal claims of Clement of Saxony, the brother-in-law of the dauphin, Louis.[20]

Haslang was told that George would go to Hanover in the summer of 1763, and he suggested that this would be not only a great consolation for his subjects but also an opportunity to arrange many things for the general good of the empire.[21] George himself argued that an heir to the throne should visit 'the different parts of the dominions',[22] but he never travelled to Hanover, just as he did not visit Scotland, Ireland, Wales or northern England. Brief visits by George's brothers Edward (1765) and William (1769 and 1770) were no substitute. George's failure to visit Hanover ensured that it was more difficult in the course of British foreign policy to further Electoral interests. Because George did not visit, his British ministers did not go there, and thus Hanover ceased to be the episodic focus of British foreign policy. The possible importance of royal visits was indicated by the role of Frederick, who went to Hanover in 1781, staying there until 1787. From 1783, his presence and actions helped to improve relations between George and Frederick II of Prussia. A visit by George might have served for earlier negotiations. Imminent visits to Hanover by George were

[19] Nivernais to Praslin, French foreign minister, 11, 17 Dec. 1762, 5, 8 Jan., 13 Feb., 21 Apr. 1763, Chatelet, French envoy in Vienna, to Praslin, 3, 25, 31 Aug., 11, 21 Sept., Praslin to Chatelet, 16 Sept. 1763, AE. CP. Ang. 448 fols 268, 325, 449 fols 40, 67, 306, 309–10, 450 fol. 287, AE. CP. Autriche 295 fols 135, 240–6, 266–8, 303–4, 330–1, 310–11; C. van den Heuvel, 'Justus Möser und die englischen-hannoversche Reichspolitik zwischen Siebenjährigem Krieg und Fürstenbund', *Zeitschrift für Historische Forschung*, 29 (2002), pp. 383–423.

[20] Nivernais to George, second earl of Halifax, secretary of state for the Northern Department, 12 Feb. 1763, MS, papers from Cardiff Public Library, 10/129; Nivernais to Praslin, 13, 17 Feb. 1763, AE. CP. Ang. 449 fols 306–10, 353–4; Haslang to Preysing, 11 Mar., Preysing to Haslang, 17 Mar. 1763, Munich, Bayr. Ges. London 241.

[21] Haslang to Preysing, and to Wachtendonck, 11 Mar. 1763, Munich, Bayr. Ges. London 241.

[22] G.M. Ditchfield, *George III. An Essay in Monarchy* (Basingstoke, 2002), p. 24.

reported several times, for example after the end of the parliamentary session, by *Owen's Weekly Chronicle* on 17 and 31 March 1764, and he talked of such a visit in 1789 after he recovered from his illness,[23] but none occurred. The impact of this was commented on by British travellers. In *A Tour from London to Petersburg* (1780), John Richard noted,

> The absence of the Elector renders the court of Hanover exceeding gloomy . . . Party matters formerly carried some Englishmen so far as to treat Hanover with the greatest contempt, and the Hanoverians do not mention England with any marks of cordial friendship. They seem to consider the absence of their Elector as a disadvantage to them, and this is probably true.[24]

Alexander Thomson added, in his *Letters of a Traveller* (1798),

> The towns in these dominions are not without trade and manufactures; but the whole of the Electorate has suffered much by the accession of the house of Hanover to the crown of Great Britain; notwithstanding a respectable civil and military establishment is constantly maintained, out of the revenues of the country.[25]

In a powerful commitment, nevertheless, George himself abandoned the idea, considered by his predecessors, of separating Hanover from Britain, for his Testament of 1765 established the succession of George, his firstborn, the future George IV, as heir to both. Furthermore, the king's marriage to a German maintained the family practice and increased the number of German princely visitors to London. In June 1771, these included no fewer than two of the queen's brothers, one of whom, Charles, received an Irish pension and was governor of Hanover in 1776–83 (the other, Ernest, became governor of Celle), as well as the prince of Anhalt-Bernbourg. That June, the court went into mourning for the death of William of Saxe-Gotha, one of George's maternal uncles. Charlotte remained close to her German relatives and very interested in their concerns, and George showed his customary sensitivity in being thoughtful about when best to pass on the news of the death of one of her brothers, George.[26] There was also a German component in the royal

---

[23] George to Prince Augustus, 24 Mar. 1789, Aspinall, *George III*, I, 403.

[24] J. Richard, *A Tour from London to Petersburg* (London, 1780), pp. 185–7.

[25] A. Thomson, *Letters of a Traveller* (London, 1798), p. 163.

[26] C.C. Orr, 'Charlotte of Mecklenburg-Strelitz, Queen of Great Britain and Electress of Hanover: Northern Dynasties and the Northern Republic of Letters', in Orr (ed.), *Queenship in Europe, 1660–1815. The Role of the Consort* (Cambridge, 2004), pp. 368–402; M. Köhler, 'The Courts of Hanover and Strelitz', in J. Marsden (ed.), *The Wisdom of George the Third* (London, 2005), pp. 60–81; George to Carmarthen, 26 Nov. 1785, BL. Add. 27914 fol. 13.

household. In 1772, Wilhelm Christof Diede zum Fürstenstein, Danish envoy since 1767, noted that in the past he had avoided the slow, and sometimes indiscreet, channel of the British ministry, by communicating with the royal family through their German servants.[27] George spoke German with envoys who knew the language,[28] while he continued his predecessor's close links with the Hanoverian chancery in London.[29]

Hanover did not play a major role in foreign policy in the 1760s, earning George praise in the British press.[30] As Elector, he did not take the forceful part of his two predecessors, although he was interested in the Electorate and communicated regularly with his Hanoverian ministers, writing in German, at which he was adept.[31] Visiting London in 1763, the Hanoverian diplomat Friedrich Karl von Hardenberg swiftly realized that there would be little support for Electoral goals,[32] but Hanoverian issues and those relating to nearby territories continued to crop up in diplomatic correspondence, and British ministers were approached, sometimes unwillingly, by foreign envoys accordingly.[33] In 1763, George ordered John, fourth earl of Sandwich, a secretary of state, to sound the Austrian envoy on the prospect of help if Prussia attacked Hanover in pursuit of its claims for compensation for wartime assistance.[34] Hanover, nevertheless, became a less contentious public issue as part of a long-term process of disassociation,[35] and Newcastle worried about Bute, not about the king's Hanoverian advisers. Haslang indeed reported that the British ministers were not informed about German affairs.[36] In 1766, George, third earl of Albemarle, blamed the replacement of the Rockingham ministry by that of Pitt on George's concern for Hanover:

> You will stare and perhaps shake your head when I tell you it was by the advice of his German ministers. The King of Prussia, tired of soliciting England for the arrears due to him, informed the Hanoverian ministers

[27] Diede report, 13 Mar. 1772, Rigs. 1953.

[28] Diede report, 17 Apr. 1772, Hannecken report, 13 Sept. 1776, Rigs. 1953 1957.

[29] T. Riotte, 'The Hanoverian Dimension in British Foreign Policy and Domestic Politics', *Bulletin of the German Historical Institute, London* 27 (2005), p. 125.

[30] *St. James's Chronicle*, 10 Apr. 1764.

[31] S. Conrady, 'Die Wirksamkeit Königs Georgs III für die Hannoverschen Kurlande', *Niedersächsisches Jahrbuch für Landesgeschichte*, 39 (1967), pp. 150–91.

[32] A. Klausa, *Friedrich Karl von Hardenberg, 1696–1763* (Hildesheim, 1990), pp. 122–45.

[33] E.g. re. Bentheim and Osnabrück, Nivernais to Praslin, 14 Mar., 5 Apr. 1763, AE. CP. Ang. 450 fols 89, 194.

[34] Sandwich to Stormont, 27 Dec. 1763, PRO. SP. 80/199.

[35] F. Frensdorff, 'Die englischen Prinzen in Göttingen', *Zeitschrift des Historischen Vereins für Niedersachsen* (1905), pp. 421–81; H. Wellenreuther, 'Von der Interessenharmonie zur Dissoziation. Kurhannover und England in der Zeit der Personalunion', *Niedersächsische Jahrbücher für Landesgeschichte*, 67 (1995), pp. 23–42.

[36] Haslang to Baron Baumgarten, 7 May 1765, Munich, Bayr. Ges. London 243.

that unless he was paid (or indemnified . . .), that he would seize upon the Duchy of Lauenburg and immediately. This so alarmed Munchhausen that he sent an express to the King with his alarms, and saying at the same time that no man could deal with the King of Prussia . . . but Mr. Pitt . . . This determined the King so suddenly, and so unexpectedly to send for Mr. Pitt.

The more experienced Newcastle was more sceptical.[37] Similarly, the report in the *St. James's Chronicle* of 23 January 1766 that 'the treaty lately concluded with Russia, is said to be for the mutual defence of the German dominions of both powers' was wrong.

Angered by George's lack of interest in backing the Elector Palatine against the decision of the Imperial Aulic Council in the Elector's dispute with the city of Aachen, the Palatine foreign minister complained that George was overly pro-Austrian and insufficiently forceful.[38] The Hanoverian government was scarcely in a position to be the latter. Participation in the Seven Years War had led to an increase in the size of the army, to 37,146 in 1763, but peace brought a reduction, as financial exigencies hit home, and the peacetime strength was an average of just 14,218 men. Just as for Prussia[39] and Saxony, the aftermath of the war saw reconstruction at home and caution abroad. Hanover, moreover, was not near the centre of international contention as far as Britain was concerned. Indeed, in the decade after the Seven Years War, British foreign policy focused on opposition to the Bourbons, and that centred on colonial and naval rivalry.

Hanover played a more prominent role in British foreign policy in the 1770s than the Electorate had done in the late 1760s, although it was still very much a secondary one. The Electorate first featured in 1772, when the possibility that Britain would take a firm line, in response to the seizure by Austria, Prussia and Russia of much of Poland in the First Partition of Poland, was regarded as reduced by the threat of an attack on Hanover. A report from London in the *Bristol Gazette and Public Advertiser* of 30 April noted,

It is generally imagined by those who seem best acquainted with the secret springs of government, that the dread of a Prussian army in the Electorate of Hanover has altered the intentions of our court relative to the propriety of sending a squadron up the Baltic.

[37] WW. R1–692, 694; Newcastle to Rockingham, 17 Sept. 1766, BL. Add. 32977 fol. 92; *St. James's Chronicle*, 27 Sept. 1766.
[38] Zeedhuitz to Haslang, 11 June, 22 July, Haslang to Zeedhuitz, 30 June, 7 July, Munich, Bayr. Ges. London 247.
[39] H.M. Scott, 'Aping the Great Powers: Frederick the Great and the Defence of Prussia's International Position, 1763–86', *German History*, 12 (1994), p. 290.

Nevertheless, there is little sign that this was a key element in policy. D'Aiguillon, the French foreign minister, had set out deliberately to make concessions in colonial disputes with Britain in order to improve relations, and in March 1772 he proposed concerted pressure on Austria and Russia in order to dissuade them from partitioning Poland. Interventionism by Britain on the continent was thus to be encouraged by making 'Blue Water' opposition to France unnecessary. George, however, responded coolly to the approach, and, when the French-backed Gustavus III staged a coup to strengthen monarchical authority in Sweden in August 1772, seizing power from a ministry inclined to Britain and Russia, suspicion of France increased in Britain.

Hanoverian concerns meanwhile increased with relations between Hanover and Austria deteriorating in the 1770s, as the Electoral government opposed what it saw as the Emperor Joseph II's dictatorial attitude in the empire, while, in turn, Joseph was angered by Hanoverian independence in the Imperial Diet. In 1774, the Austrian envoy in London threatened to suspend all relations with Hanover, while in Vienna they were regarded as broken. Repeating a theme from the 1720s, the Hanoverian minister attached to George in London from 1771 until 1795, Behr's successor, Johann Friedrich Carl von Alvensleben, declared that Joseph was the chief, but not the master, of the empire. Tension was reflected in the British press, with a report that the Austrian envoy had declared that 'If the King of Great Britain avowed the language lately held by his Electoral minister, he must expect the Emperor to oppose him in every step he took in the Empire.'[40]

Fortunately for Hanover, the War of American Independence did not result in any attack on the Electorate. Had such an invasion occurred, in the absence of gains during the American war, there would have been a need to consider handing over pre-war British territories in order to obtain the return of Hanover. The legality of such a course was far from clear, while, politically, it would have been disastrous for the British ministry. The loss of the Thirteen Colonies itself led to the raising of the question of whether the crown had the right to part with territories without parliamentary authority.

George was very opposed to Austrian policy in the empire and, combined with concern over the security of Hanover in the developing crisis with France and advice from Queen Charlotte, he, as king, offered Prussia in early 1778 an alliance and, in return for Prussian protection of Hanover, a subsidy. Reassured about Russian and French attitudes,

---

[40] Haslang to Beckers, Palatine foreign minister, 14 June, 19 Aug. 1774, Beckers to Haslang, 10 Dec. 1774, Ritter, envoy in Vienna, to Beckers, 27 Apr., 3, 24, 31 Aug., 7 Sept., 5, 26 Oct. 1774, Munich, Bayr. Ges. London 252, Wien 702; *Westminster Journal*, 3, 17 Sept., 1 Oct. 1774.

Frederick II did not respond positively, while his expectation of
Hanoverian support against Austria was unacceptable to George.
Antagonism between Joseph II and George as Elector led the latter,
however, towards Frederick, and it is not surprising that, during the War
of the Bavarian Succession between Austria and Prussia (1778–9), the
Elector adopted a pro-Prussian position, to the anger of British diplomats
such as Robert Murray Keith, envoy in Vienna, who feared that this
policy was needlessly irritating to Joseph II.[41] This was at a time
when France's refusal to support her ally was a serious blow to Austria,
leading British diplomats to see an opening for better relations, although
unrealistically so.

George's growing interest in German politics reflected in part his frustration with the political situation in Britain, but also, to a considerable
extent, his opposition to change in the empire, a sentiment that most
German rulers shared. This helped to perpetuate the decentralized imperial political system at a time when, in most of Europe, attempts were
being made to strengthen central government. Just as George I had
opposed the efforts of the Emperor Charles VI to stress the authority of
imperial courts in disputes between German rulers, and George II had
sought to stop Frederick II's invasion of Silesia and the development of
two-power Austro-Prussian preponderance in the empire, so George III
was concerned about Joseph II's attempt to increase Austrian power
within the empire. There was a genuine problem in combining
Hanoverian policy and, in particular, the need to respond to specific issues
and initiatives by other German states, with the British aspiration for
better relations with Austria. It was too easy for British diplomats and
ministers who sought the latter, and who believed that it was in Austria's
interests, to blame their failure on Hanover, underestimating the impact of
other factors that lessened the chance of better relations.

In the aftermath of the War of American Independence there was an
opportunity for the ministry of Pitt the Younger to make a new start in
foreign policy. Alliance with Austria and her ally Russia was one of the
major options, but this was complicated by the policy of George as
Elector. Although suspicious about Prussian intentions, George and his
Hanoverian ministers moved closer to Prussia in 1784,[42] and news of the
Austrian plan to exchange the Austrian Netherlands (modern Belgium) for
Bavaria, a measure seen as likely to increase greatly Austrian power within
the empire, lent urgency to this attempted alignment. Frederick, George's

[41] Hugh Elliot, envoy in Copenhagen, to Keith, 11 Aug. 1778, Joseph Yorke to Keith, 9
Oct. 1778, Keith to Stormont, 4 Dec. 1779, BL. Add. 35514 fol. 242, 35515 fol. 154, 35517
fol. 311; H.M. Scott, *British Foreign Policy in the Age of the American Revolution* (Oxford, 1990),
pp. 37, 269–70.
[42] Kaunitz to Kageneck, 9 Mar., 13 Nov. 1784, HHStA., EK. 129.

favourite son, who was resident as prince-bishop of Osnabrück, was tangible proof of George's growing personal commitment to Hanover and played a major role in the negotiations. He warned George that Joseph II's brother, Max Franz, who in 1784 became Archbishop-Elector of Cologne and prince-bishop of Münster on Hanover's borders, was also seeking the coadjutorship (succession) of the prince-bishoprics of Paderborn and Hildesheim.[43] The latter extended to within a few miles of the city of Hanover and helped separate it from the southern portion of the Electorate. Habsburg power so close was very unwelcome.

George responded rapidly to Prussian approaches in early 1785,[44] more so than his Hanoverian ministers, who had to be pushed on by George and York, a contrast that was hardly new. Indeed, the tendency in British public debate to treat Hanover as a unit motivated by clear Hanoverian concerns was generally inaccurate. At Berlin, on 23 July 1785, representatives of Prussia, Hanover and Saxony signed a treaty agreeing to the preservation of the imperial system as currently constituted, to co-operation at the Imperial Diet, and to opposition to the Bavarian exchange and any similar further projects.[45] The resulting *Fürstenbund*, or League of Princes, which grew rapidly in the following months as other German princes acceded, met with serious Austrian and Russian complaints which were held to harm British diplomatic interests, particularly the hope of improved relations with the two powers.[46] It also led to parliamentary attacks on the government which stood, as a result of George's role, on 'ticklish ground'.[47] In the Commons, Fox declared,

As it was obvious that the Regency of Hanover ought neither to form laws nor enter into any treaties which might prove injurious to Great Britain, consequently it behoved the ministers of this country to have prevented their entering into any alliances which might involve serious consequences to the interests of England.[48]

Although there was no equivalent to the criticisms in France of Marie-Antoinette for supposedly representing Austrian interests,[49] Hanoverian participation in the *Fürstenbund* caused an upsurge of criticism in the

---

[43] York to George, 28 Feb. 1785, Aspinall, *George III*, I, 178.

[44] Draft in George's hand, RA 6071.

[45] T.C.W. Blanning, '"That horrid Electorate" or "ma patrie germanique"? George III, Hanover and the *Fürstenbund*', *Historical Journal*, 20 (1977), pp. 321–26.

[46] Fitzherbert to Keith, 2 Aug. 1785, BL. Add. 35535 fol. 31; Carmarthen to Pitt, 4 Jan., Carmarthen to Keith, 17 Jan. 1786, PRO. 30/8/151 fol. 35, FO. 7/12.

[47] Reginald Pole Carew, MP to Sir James Harris, 30 Jan., Harris, Winchester, Hampshire CRO. Malmesbury papers, vol. 146.

[48] Cobbett, XX, cols. 1019–20.

[49] T.E. Kaiser, 'Who's Afraid of Marie-Antoinette', *French History*, 14 (2000), pp. 241–71.

British press of specific aspects of the Hanoverian connection, such as the patronage of German plays, music and army officers by the royal family, and the 'Germanic' habit of excluding the public from royal gardens. This was extended to the education of royal princes in Hanover: William was there from 1783 to 1785, Edward was sent there in 1785, staying until 1787, and, in 1786, Ernest, Augustus and Adolphus were dispatched to the university at Göttingen,[50] a step that reduced the burden on the Civil List.[51] Augustus stayed until 1790, his brothers until 1791. George was interested in the development of the university with which his predecessor had been closely involved. Indeed it served as an important intermediary between British and German intellectual life, not least as a result of the activities of one of the professors, Georg Christoph Lichtenberg, who became a fellow of the Royal Society.[52] George's varied engagement with Germany included frequent use of the large number of German tradesmen in London. He encouraged tourism to German lands, telling James, second earl of Courtown and his wife Mary in 1783, 'You cannot do better than send your son to Vienna.' The son, James George, the third earl, was a godson of the king and, like his father, was to be treasurer of the royal household, an instance of the hereditary nature of royal service.[53] Three years later, George told the visiting Sophie von La Roche, 'my heart will never forget that it pulses with German blood'.[54]

The *Fürstenbund* gave rise to a widely held view that George was controlling British policy for the benefit of Hanover and Prussia, while moves against British trade in both Austria and Russia were blamed on the *Fürstenbund*.[55] George defended his role, arguing, reasonably, that 'if no one has such dangerous views, this Association cannot give umbrage' and that he had been motivated by 'what I owe in my Electoral capacity to the future stability of the Empire'.[56] He certainly took an active part in seeking the support of German princes for the league. Personally dubious

---

[50] F. Frensdorff, 'Die englischen Prinzen in Göttingen', *Zeitschrift des Historischen Vereins für Niedersachsen* (1905), pp. 421–81; W.R. Röhrbein and A. von Rohr (eds), *Hannover im Glanz und Schatten des britischen Weltreichs* (Hanover, 1977), pp. 53–7.

[51] George to Pitt, 17 May 1791, PRO. 30/8/103 fol. 422.

[52] H. Wellenreuther, 'Göttingen und England im achtzehnten Jahrhundert', in N. Kamp, H. Wellenreuther and F. Hund, *250 Jahre Vorlesungen an der Georgia Augusta 1734–1984* (Göttingen, 1985), pp. 30–63, and 'Lichtenberg und England', *Niedersächsisches Jahrbuch für Landesgeschichte*, 66 (1994), pp. 215–32; H.L. Gumbert, *Lichtenberg in England* (2 vols, Wiesbaden, 1977).

[53] Duke of Montagu to Robert Murray Keith, 6 Sept. 1783, BL. Add. 35529; George to Pitt, 21 June 1793, PRO. 30/8/103 fol. 500.

[54] C. Williams (ed.), *Sophie in London 1786* (London, 1936), p. 200.

[55] For example, *Daily Universal Register*, 2, 3, 5 Jan., 4, 15, 22, 26 July, 14 Aug., 1 Sept. 1786.

[56] George to Pitt, 7 Aug. 1785, PRO. 30/8/103 fol. 172, Manchester, John Rylands Library, Eng. Mss. 912 no. 32.

about George's ability to appreciate the dangerous consequences of the *Fürstenbund*,[57] Carmarthen noted criticism of the king's policy:

By an intercepted letter from Count Kageneck [Austrian envoy] to Prince Kaunitz, I find the Count has had a conversation with Mr. [Charles James] Fox . . . The German League [*Fürstenbund*] as you may easily imagine made a material part of the conversation. Mr. Fox seems to have been infinitely more severe upon the King than upon the ministers in his remarks upon the subject, stating it as a measure which had been planned and completed without any communication whatever with Administration. That he [foreign secretary in 1782 and 1783] as well as his predecessors in office had frequently experienced the King's reserve respecting Hanover in measures and his fixed determination to pursue such plans as he thought proper in his Electoral capacity at the same time affecting to keep his English ministers totally ignorant of the nature and extent of them.[58]

Fox and David Viscount Stormont, a leading opposition politician who had been an envoy in Vienna and Paris and a secretary of state, told the Austrian envoy that George was not only very attached to Hanover but also kept his British ministers in the dark about German affairs, and ministers did indeed criticize the consequences of the league. The leading Austrian minister, Prince Kaunitz, also asked how the British ministry could believe an Austrian alliance possible, given George's views.[59] More than the *Fürstenbund*, however, lay between Britain and an anti-French alliance system. Joseph II and his ally Catherine II were unimpressed by George, while, conscious of Anglo-French antipathy, Joseph and Kaunitz regarded the prospect of a British alliance with disfavour. Although the French alliance was devoid of much positive content, the Austrian government saw no reason to replace it with a British one. Friedrich, Count Kageneck had reported in February 1785 that domestic problems would prevent Britain from taking an active part in a continental war.[60]

The Russian envoy in London, Count Vorontsov, reported that George was greatly influenced by Alvensleben and York, both of whom had Prussian links, and was overriding Pitt. In practice, this *secret du roi* was largely restricted to German politics, rather than dominating the whole of foreign policy. Thus, at a crucial moment in the Dutch crisis in 1787, York

[57] Carmarthen to Pitt, 4 Jan. 1786, PRO. 30/8/151 fol. 35. For criticism from another cabinet member, Richmond to Pitt, 15 Jan. 1786, PRO. 30/8/170 fols 70–1.
[58] Carmarthen to Pitt, 28 Oct. 1785, PRO. 30/8/151 fol. 29.
[59] Kageneck to Kaunitz, 18, 25 Oct. 1785, Kaunitz to Reviczky, 3 Apr., 27 July 1786, HHStA. EK. 124, 129; K. Aretin, *Heiliges Römisches Reich, 1776–1806* (2 vols, Wiesbaden, 1967), I, 178; Fox to Richard Fitzpatrick, – Nov. 1785, BL. Add. 47580 fols 126–7.
[60] Kageneck to Kaunitz, 1 Feb. 1785, HHStA. EK. 124.

saw Frederick II's nephew and successor, Frederick William II, on behalf of
George, but it was to discuss the coadjutorship of Mainz, on which Hanover
and Prussia were co-operating, not Dutch affairs.[61] In 1791 York married
Frederica, princess royal of Prussia, a match satirized in Gillray's salacious
caricature *The Recruiting Officer*, although they swiftly separated. Frederick
William II had been interested in 1786 in a match between Frederica and
George, prince of Wales, but that would probably not have lasted either.

York's marriage, which involved trying issues of etiquette as well as
practicalities, such as Frederick's concern that Frederica's trousseau should
not incur import duties,[62] is a reminder, like the dispatch of the princes to
Göttingen, that the links between the royal family and Germany were
many and varied.[63] As a conscientious Elector, who acted as *Landesvater*,
George encouraged the development of Hanover, particularly its economy
and its educational facilities, although this was largely a matter of
responding to initiatives by the ministerial council in Hanover. New initiatives included improvements in inland navigation and the foundation of a
mining college at Clausthal.[64] As in England, there was a marked interest
on his part in agriculture, shown not least in the establishment of agricultural societies at Harburg (1764) and Celle (1764). The Elector was
impressed by Otto von Münchhausen's *Der Hausvater*, a call for good
husbandry, and was a supporter of the agricultural improver Jobst Anton
von Hinüber, who twice visited George. The creation of a botanical
garden at Hanover in 1774 and the foundation of a veterinary college in
1778 were aspects of agrarian improvements. George also financed the
large-scale mapping of the Electorate, while, as Elector, he was the
recipient of a range of patronage requests.[65]

[61] J.W. Marcum, 'Vorontsov and Pitt: The Russian Assessment of a British Statesman,
1785–1792', *Rocky Mountain Social Science Journal*, 10 (1973), pp. 50–1; J.M. Black, 'Sir Robert
Ainslie: His Majesty's Agent-Provocateur? British Foreign Policy and the International
Crisis of 1787', *European History Quarterly*, 14 (1984), pp. 2709–1; York to George, 1, 8 June
1787, Aspinall, *George III*, I, 370; F.C. Wittichen, *Preussen und England in der europäischen Politik,
1785–1788* (Heidelberg, 1902), p. 117.
[62] Joseph Ewart, envoy in Berlin, to George Aust, senior clerk at the Foreign Office, 14
Oct. 1791, private collection of the author.
[63] See C.C. Orr, 'Dynastic Perspectives 1714–1837', in Simms and Riotte (eds), *The
Hanoverian Dimension in British History*.
[64] George does not emerge as a central figure in C.C.W. Bauermeister, 'Hanover: *Milde
Regierung* or *Ancien Régime*', *German History*, 20 (2002), pp. 287–308.
[65] O. Ulbricht, "Im Ealinger Feld habe ich Turnips gesehen. . .": Landwirtschaftliche
Aufzeichnungen Jobst Anton von Hinübers während seines England-Aufenthaltes 1766–7',
in *19 Jahresheft der Albrecht-Thaer-Gesellschaft* (Hanover, 1979), pp. 67–109; L. Deicke, 'Die
Celler Sozietät und Landwirtschaftsgesellschaft von 1764', in R. Vierhaus (ed.), *Deutsche
patriotische und gemeinnützige Gesellschaften, Wolfenbütteler Forschungen* (Munich, 1980), pp. 161–94;
W. Achilles, 'Georg III als Königlicher Landwirt. Eine Bestätigung als Beitrag zur
Personalunion', *Niedersächsiches Jahrbuch für Landesgeschichte*, 73 (2001), pp. 351–408; Jenkinson
to Bute, – Sept. 1762, MS.

George's personal commitment emerges more clearly in cultural matters, as he wished to ensure a princely effect in his Hanover palaces. Paintings of George and Charlotte were commissioned for the palace in Hanover.[66] Aside from having the palace of Herrenhausen restored, and having two carriages made in London and sent over to Hanover in 1781, George played an active role in creating the largest and best-documented silver service of any made for a German court in the eighteenth century: he was determined on a new service in Hanover, and one in the new neo-Classical style, rather than a rococo one. Most of the inherited silver service, a rococo design, was melted down to pay for the new service. Sample designs were commissioned from the French goldsmith Robert-Joseph Auguste in 1772, and the first pieces were sent to London for George to approve them. The last delivery was made in 1786, by which time a service for seventy-two people was available. This was prepared for George's long-promised visit,[67] and underlined his sense of public magnificence. More mundanely, George had turnips and ham imported from Hanover for the royal table in England, while dishes at court included 'metwurst' and sauerkraut. Although he lacked his predecessors' commitment to the Electorate, he was more interested in Hanover than he was in Ireland or Scotland.

In the Dutch crisis of 1787, the ousting of the pro-French 'Patriot' government was achieved by a Prussian invasion supported by British naval preparations and by the encouragement and funding of anti-Patriot groups. There was an understandable degree of hesitation on George's part over using Hanoverian forces in this crisis. In 1787, as conflict with France over the future of the United Provinces seemed imminent, Charles, third duke of Richmond, the master-general of the ordnance, suggested to Pitt that it would be 'wise to take this opportunity of immediately entering into a treaty with the king as Elector of Hanover and with the Landgrave of Hesse and such other German princes as can be got, for a supply of an army of at least 50,000 men to be ready to march at a day's notice'.[68] An agreement with the Landgrave of Hesse-Cassel to hire 12,000 troops was indeed signed, but George, although pressed by Pitt to prepare a Hanoverian force, was less than helpful. He sought information about how far Britain would pay, and stated that he could not leave Hanover undefended.[69] This remark

[66] C. Lerche, 'Die Herrenhausener Bildnisse von Johann Zoffany – Georg III und die Darstellung des "Patriot King"', *Niederdeutsche Beiträge zur Kunstgeschichte*, 35 (1996), pp. 99–136.

[67] P. Glanvill, *The King's Silver: George III's Service in Hanover and England* (Waddesdon Manor leaflet, 2003).

[68] Richmond to Pitt, 5 July 1787, PRO. 30/8/170 fol. 82.

[69] William Fawcett, negotiator of treaty with Hesse Cassel, to Malmesbury, 28 Sept. 1787, Winchester, Hampshire CRO., Malmesbury papers vol. 152; Pitt to George III, and reply, both 16 Sept. 1787, Aspinall, *George III*, I, 324–5, PRO. 30/8/103 fol. 255, Manchester, John Rylands Library, Eng. Mss. 912 no. 37. For the cost of the Hessian subsidy, BL. Add. 28068 fol. 254.

indicates George's reluctance, as Prussia was a supporter of the assault on the French-backed Dutch Patriots, and Hanover not therefore vulnerable. Indeed, there was no need for Hanover to act, as Prussian intervention, when it came on 13 September, was speedily successful, although there were reports that Hanover was aiding the attempt to recruit German military support.[70] Three years later, when the ministry again approached George for Hanoverian troops, in this case for reinforcing the garrison of Gibraltar at a time when war with Spain seemed imminent, George was sympathetic.[71]

In the aftermath of the Dutch crisis, reports of plans for an army of 50,000 Hanoverians, Hessians and Brunswickers (Brunswick-Wolfenbüttel was now generally known as Brunswick), designed to support Prussia and paid for by a Prussophile, and Austria- and France-hating, George, as Elector of Hanover, were spread.[72] These reports were inaccurate, for, although George sought an alignment of Britain, the United Provinces and Prussia,[73] which was indeed negotiated in 1788,[74] he did not see Hanover as playing an active role. Nevertheless, the linkage with Prussia, which, however fancifully, was attributed to George's supporters in the council being too powerful for a crucial Pitt,[75] was strengthened as a result of George's anger with the unsuccessful attempt by Joseph II to take the regency of Hanover into his own hands in response to George's breakdown in mental health in the winter of 1788–9.

Caution, however, was one of George's watchwords. Although in 1788 there were suggestions that George as Elector took an aggressive stance in the Baltic crisis,[76] in which Denmark was threatened with attack by Britain and Prussia in order to force it to peace with Sweden (then at war with Russia), in fact George was in favour of caution and opposed to war breaking out.[77] Rather than this being a case of king versus British ministers, the latter were divided on the wisdom of a policy that might lead to war.[78] The prospect of a Baltic war was not seen as an opportunity for Electoral gains, a major contrast to the situation under George I.

---

[70] Chalgrin, French envoy in Munich, to Montmorin, French foreign minister, 25 Oct. 1787, AE. CP. Bavière 172 fols 379–81.

[71] Grenville to George, 25 May, reply 26 May 1790, BL. Add. 58855 fols 106–8.

[72] Luzerne, French envoy in London, to Montmorin, 13 May 1788, AE. CP. Ang. 565 fol. 160. See also, re. concern about George's intentions, supposedly arising from his Electoral interests, Barthélemy to Montmorin, 12 Aug., 21 Oct., 4, 18 Nov. 1788, AE. CP. Ang. 566 fols 168–9, 567 fols 41, 104, 139.

[73] George to ———, 8 June 1788, Bod. MS. Eng. Lett. C144 fol. 79; George to prince and princess of Orange, both of 6 June 1788, Aspinall, George III, I, 376–7.

[74] Wittichen, Preussen und England.

[75] Luzerne to Montmorin, 27 June 1788, AE. CP. Ang. 565 fol. 330.

[76] Elliot to Carmarthen, 29 Nov. 1788, PRO. FO. 22/10 fol. 423.

[77] George to Pitt, 19 Oct. 1788, PRO. 30/8/103 fol. 310.

[78] Lord Hawkesbury to duke of Dorset, 28 Oct. 1788, Maidstone KAO., Sackville papers U269 C 182.

Thus, interventionism had been separated from Hanoverianism. This was a process facilitated by the weaker emotional commitment of George to the Electorate compared to that of his two predecessors, but this was not the sole political factor at play. The greater unity of the ministry, which stemmed from the increased practice of cabinet government and from the longevity of the Pitt ministry, was also significant, making it less likely that George could have prevailed, even had he wanted to stress Hanoverian interests.

If, in the 1780s, George's stronger interest in Hanover in part reflected his concern with the pretensions of Joseph II, from 1792 it was French and, from 1795, Prussian expansionism that were causes for concern. In the French Revolutionary and Napoleonic wars, Britain was to learn that maritime and oceanic gains could not prevent the French from dominating Western Europe, with all the strategic and economic dangers that that posed. George was keen on such gains, but concerned about the situation on the continent. His attitude to maritime warfare and the continental commitment depended very much on the military and political situation in Europe. He responded to Nelson's victory at the battle of the Nile in 1798 by suggesting that, because of the international situation, it was more valuable than a victory over the Brest fleet, which threatened Britain and, more particularly, Ireland: 'the beating and destroying the Brest fleet would be highly glorious and advantageous to this kingdom, but the success of this brave admiral is of more utility to the cause we are engaged in. If it electrifies Austria and Naples, it may save Italy.'[79]

Although there was little revolutionary sympathy, still less activity, in Hanover,[80] George was concerned about 'the present unsettled state of all minds'.[81] More seriously, the Electorate was vulnerable to attack. The Hanoverian army numbered only 17,836 in 1789, but in the initial stages of the French Revolutionary Wars, which broke out in 1792 and which Britain took part in from 1793, conflict was restricted to France's borders, and France had no allies elsewhere. As a result, it was possible to deploy Hanoverian and allied-German forces in the Low Countries without apparent risk to the Electorate, the Hanoverians taken into British pay under the command of York, and Pitt assured that care would be taken only to ask for their true expenses.[82] The situation changed, however, when the French overran first the Austrian Netherlands (Belgium) and then the United Provinces, exposing Hanover to attack. This led George

---

[79] George to George, second Earl Spencer, first lord of the admiralty, 3 Oct. 1794, BL. Add. 75817.

[80] G. Schneider (ed.), *Das Kurfürstentum Hannover und die Französische Revolution. Quellen aus den Jahren 1791–1795* (Hildesheim, 1989).

[81] George to William Grenville, 15 Nov. 1794, BL. Add. 58858 fol. 104.

[82] George to Pitt, 17, 20 Feb. 1793, PRO. 30/8/103 fols 480, 484.

to press for British support for Hanover, but the situation was again transformed in April 1795 when Prussia negotiated the Peace of Basle with
France. Aside from French occupation of the left bank of the Rhine, this
included the creation of a Prussian-controlled north German neutrality
zone.

As Elector, George adhered to the neutrality, but did so under protest,
and only because Austria made it clear it could not defend Hanover.
Indeed the fate of Hanover marked a particularly bitter ratchet down in
George's already low view of allies. From Weymouth, he complained,

> I have received this morning Mr. Secretary Dundas's note accompa-
> nying the letter he has received from Baron Steinberg and its inclosure
> from the Prussian chargé d'affaires. It is impossible that the King of
> Prussia can act more unfriendly, and the line of demarcation he has
> formed between my troops and those of the enemy by the corps he has
> formed has in no one instance been disturbed by me; he ought there-
> fore to have insisted on the French remaining quiet and have threatened
> if they did not that he must oppose this advancing; but he having taken
> the unfair line of conduct I am certainly as Elector in no situation to
> hold the language that best suits my feelings; the British cavalry are to
> return home, the Hessians will certainly on the infamous separate peace
> be also recalled, the Duke of Brunswick will assuredly follow that
> example; I can therefore only act a neutral part as Elector; for I cannot
> like my neighbours submit to make a separate peace with France. I do
> not agree with Mr. Secretary Dundas that the King of Prussia is autho-
> rised by any language the Hanoverian Regency may have held to him
> to treat me in the manner he now does.[83]

The breakdown in co-operation between Britain and Hanover was not
simply due to Prussia. George was angered by British disengagement from
the continent: 'I must say Germany is by this measure completely deserted
by England, and it must the more strongly behove me to insist on all corps
for the service of England being instantly removed out of my
Electorate'.[84] The following year, 1796, George, who was already angry
about British subsidy arrears to his Hanoverian troops, was forced to
accept a new British approach to Prussia entailing the unwelcome
prospect of Prussian territorial gains.[85] George preferred the idea of a

[83] George to Dundas, 14 Sept., George to William Grenville, 10 Sept. 1795, BL. Add.
40100 fol. 155, 58859 fol. 31; George to [Pitt], 6 Mar. 1795, *Maggs Catalogue* 1390 (2006) no.
70. For correspondence with Steinberg, PRO. WO. 1–409.

[84] George to Dundas, 19 Nov. 1795, BL. Add. 40100 fol. 161.

[85] George to Pitt, 8 Dec. 1796, PRO. 30/8/104 fol. 123; M. Duffy, 'Pitt, Grenville and the
Control of British Foreign Policy in the 1790s', in J. Black (ed.), *Knights Errant and True
Englishmen: British Foreign Policy, 1660–1800* (Edinburgh, 1989), p. 163.

subsidy for Prussia and was ready to suggest the use of Hanoverian diplomats for the approach.[86] At the same time, he did not wish to see Austria become more powerful in the empire by means of territorial gains, and he retained his commitment to the established constitution and to the political practice that left a part for second-rank rulers such as himself. This led George to argue that British encouragement to Austria and/or Prussia to make gains could be as malign as French violence, and to press, instead, the need to not oppress weak powers.[87] Such an approach clashed with British determination to win the support of Austria and Prussia.

Nevertheless, Hanover did not have much significance in British politics. The habit of associating Hanover with secret influences was still seen with the fall of the Pitt ministry in 1801, the *Courier* of 2 February claiming that one of the reasons given was 'a difference of opinion in the Cabinet, relative to the conduct which His Majesty should hold as Elector of Hanover; and some persons presumed to add that Mr. Pitt had recommended the admission of Prussian troops into the Electorate'. Catholic emancipation, instead, was the key issue. Two years earlier, Liverpool had commented that George 'never talks with his ministers, or with anyone else, except His Electoral Minister', about Hanover.[88]

The Electorate was still menaced after 1795. The creation of the neutrality zone ended the immediate threat of French attack but was to prove a stage in the conquest and absorption of Hanover into the French system. Furthermore, neutrality contributed greatly to the growing dissociation of Britain and Hanover; instead, Prussian influence rose. Hopes that the accession of Frederick William III in 1797 would bring about a change in Prussian policy proved abortive.[89] In April 1801, Prussia, which had long wished to seize Hanover, did so, with the encouragement of Paul I of Russia and Napoleon, using the excuse not of Hanoverian conduct but of British actions against the armed neutrality of Baltic powers.[90] Prussia restored control to George, however, that October when Alexander I of Russia reversed his assassinated father's policies, encouraged by the entry of a British fleet into the Baltic. The entire

[86] George to William Grenville, 11 Jan., 10, 23, 24 Dec. 1797, BL. Add. 58859 fol. 114, 58860 fols 34, 39, 42.
[87] George to William Grenville, 30 July 1796, 10 Apr. 1797, BL. Add. 58859 fols 69, 129.
[88] Liverpool to earl of Bristol, 27 Nov. 1799, BL. Add. 38311 fol. 35.
[89] George to William Grenville, 23, 30 Dec. 1797, 7 Mar. 1798, BL. Add. 58860 fols 39–40, 45, 61.
[90] George to Hawkesbury, 10, 23 Sept. 1801, BL. Loan 72/1 fol. 87, 89; G.S. Ford, *Hanover and Prussia, 1795–1803. A Study in Neutrality* (New York, 1903); G. Sieske, *Preussen im Urteil Hannovers 1795–1806. Ein Beitrag zur Geschichte der politischen Publizistik in Niedersachsen* (Hildesheim, 1959); P.G. Dwyer, 'Prussia and the Armed Neutrality: The Invasion of Hanover in 1801', *International History Review*, 15 (1993), pp. 661–87.

episode, nevertheless, revealed Hanover's vulnerability. George, who had pressed for British diplomatic support for Hanoverian independence (which initially in 1801 had been limited), was also keen that any secularization of ecclesiastical principalities should lead to the expansion of the Electorate to include Münster and Osnabrück, although the British government offered only limited support in negotiations.[91] Indeed, the negotiations in Germany in 1802–3 over territorial changes, 'shameful usurpations' in George's eyes,[92] which resulted in the *Rezes* of Regensburg (the final Decision of the imperial Deputation) of 25 February 1803, saw Hanover fulfil its long-held goal of acquiring Osnabrück, although Prussia and Bavaria gained more, the former acquiring Hildesheim and much of the bishopric of Münster, which increased its power around Hanover.

In 1803, however, when war resumed between Britain and France, the French rapidly occupied the entire Electorate, although it, and north Germany as a whole, were supposedly neutral. This was 'the most unheard of act of injustice' to an outraged George,[93] whose attitude to Napoleon was not warmed by this act. Hanover fell in June after scant resistance, but George refused to ratify the Convention of Suhlingen by which the civilian government capitulated on 3 June. As a result of the convention, the French pressed the Hanoverian commander, Field Marshal Johann Ludwig von Wallmoden Gimborn, to capitulate, and he did so by the Convention of the Elbe, the second of George II's sons to do so: the seventy-seven-year-old Wallmoden Gimborn was the illegitimate half-brother of William, duke of Cumberland, who had accepted the 1757 neutrality convention.[94] The royal linen, the silver furniture and plate, and the white horses of the Hanover stud, were hastily evacuated; the silver, amounting to seventy crates, arriving in London in December 1803. Melville noted, 'The events in Hanover are a severe blow to the King; but he bears with it with his usual fortitude on the ground that it is brought upon him by no fault of his own but by a conscientious discharge of the

[91] George to Hawkesbury, foreign secretary, 1 Oct., George to Cornwallis, 1 Nov., Hawkesbury to Cornwallis, 1 Nov. 1801, BL. Loan 72/1; C. Ross (ed.), *The Correspondence of Charles, First Marquis Cornwallis* (3 vols, London, 1859), III, 384–5, 388–9. For George's interest in Hildesheim, George to Grenville, 30 July 1796, BL. Add. 58859 fol. 69.

[92] George to Hawkesbury, 16 Aug. 1802, BL. Loan 72/1 fol. 105.

[93] George to Hawkesbury, 17 June 1803, BL. Loan 72/1 fol. 108.

[94] C. Haase, 'Graf Münster, von Lenthe und die Katastrophe von 1803', *Niedersächsisches Jahrbuch für Landesgeschichte*, 53 (1981), pp. 279–88; D.S. Gray, 'The French Invasion of Hanover in 1803 and the Origins of the King's German Legion', *Proceedings of the Consortium on Revolutionary Europe* (1980), pp. 198–211; P.G. Dwyer, 'Two Definitions of Neutrality: Prussia, the European States-system, and the French Invasion of Hanover in 1803', *International History Review*, 19 (1997), pp. 522–40.

duty he owes to his British subjects'.[95] The latter were made aware of the sufferings of the Hanoverians by atrocity literature.[96]

The vulnerability of Hanover was fully displayed in 1803, but this was the product of an international system different to that which had prevailed in Europe, not least the empire, prior to the Revolution. The new system also accentuated differences between British and Hanoverian policy, Grenville, the foreign secretary, writing in 1798 that George was 'well aware that the instructions sent from the Hanoverian Chancery do not always exactly correspond with the sentiments or interests of the English government'.[97] The years 1795–1802 represented the longest period in which Hanover was neutral while Britain fought France: unlike in 1757–8, there was no rapid reversal of Hanoverian policy.

Frederick William III of Prussia was himself still keen to acquire Hanover and in 1803 decided to occupy it once French troops withdrew. The outbreak of the War of the Third Coalition in 1805 did free Hanover from French occupation, but Napoleon's victory over the Austrians and Russians at Austerlitz on 2 December 1805 changed the situation, making Frederick William's possession of Hanover dependent on the French. Accordingly, in a treaty signed at Schönbrunn on 15 December 1805, Prussia got Hanover, fulfilling Napoleon's goal of harming the chances of an Anglo-Prussian reconciliation, but Frederick William had to accept support for French objectives in Europe, and to cede territory to France and its ally Bavaria. Frederick William occupied Hanover, although he did not annex it because that might have entailed war with Britain.

In 1805, the British had sent troops to north Germany to act against France and to restore Electoral authority in Hanover, but Prussia's decision to back Napoleon made the expedition redundant and the force was evacuated. The Ministry of All the Talents, which succeeded the Pitt government in 1806, was reduced to seeking the return of Hanover as part of a peace treaty with France that Napoleon was unwilling, despite negotiations in 1806, to concede. Instead, the fate of the former Electorate was settled by Napoleon's victory over Prussia at Jena/Auerstadt on 14 October 1806, a battle in which George's brother-in-law, Charles of Brunswick, a Prussian field marshal, was killed. Hanover was then

---

[95] Melville to Pitt, 15 June 1803, BL. Add. 40102 fol. 123.

[96] Anon., *A Peep into Hanover, or, A faint description of the Atrocities committed by the French in that City* (London, 1803); Anon., *Horrors upon Horrors; What are the Hellish Deeds that can surprise us, when committed by the Blood-Hounds of that Arch-Fiend of Wickedness, the Corsican Bonaparte? Being a true and faithful narrative of a Hanoverian blacksmith, who died raving mad, in consequence of the dreadful scenes of barbarity, of which he had been late an eye-witness, in his own country* (London, 1803).

[97] William Grenville to Sir Morton Eden, envoy in Vienna, 9 Sept. 1798, BL. Add. 73765.

transferred to become part of a shifting world of French client states and territorial arrangements.[98]

George was unprepared to accept changes, even if they did not involve Hanover. In 1806, in a rejection of the widespread process of constitutional change within the empire, he was unwilling to accept the French-approved promotion of Württemberg from Electorate to kingdom, although the newly created king, Frederick William Charles, was his son-in-law.[99] The Hanoverians themselves were among the less keen of the subjects of the new kingdom of Westphalia created in 1807 for Napoleon's brother Jérôme Bonaparte: in 1810 the Electorate was totally incorporated into the new kingdom. Many fought on in exile for George, serving from 1803 in the King's German Legion, mostly in Portugal, Spain and Sicily. Although the legion made a poor impression in parts of Britain where it was stationed and led to some local violence, its service against France helped to reduce anti-Hanoverian sentiment in Britain. George accepted British ministerial advice on where to send these troops.[100]

Meanwhile, George had shown his continued concern for the Electorate on a number of occasions. In 1804, he was angry with his son Frederick because of 'the removal of the Hanoverian Infantry from Weymouth' and he took pains to wear Hanoverian uniform part of the time he was there.[101] The following February, George organized a patriotic celebration with a German theme in Windsor Castle. German music was performed and the Hanover silver was used for the meal. In 1806, George declared that the occupation of Hanover affected the honour of his crown, and that he would never cede the Electorate. Adversity had helped create a far stronger commitment than that shown at the outset of his reign.

[98] C. von Ompteda (ed.), *Politischer Nachlass des hannoverschen staats und Cabinettsministers. Ludwig von Ompteda aus den Jahren 1804 bis 1813* (3 vols, Jena, 1869); K.F. von Brandes, *Graf Münster und die Wiederherstellung Hannovers 1809–1815* (Berlin, 1938).

[99] George to Fox, 22 Mar. 1806, BL. Add. 51457 fol. 17.

[100] George to Hawkesbury, 3 Nov. 1807, BL. Loan 72/1 fol. 146; N.L. Beamish, *History of the King's German Legion* (2 vols, London, 1832–7).

[101] Duke of Kent to prince of Wales, 27 July 1804, Aspinall, *Prince of Wales*, V, p. 63.

Chapter 16

THE QUEST FOR EMPIRE

George's parental sway and Albion's laws
Spreading where Ammon's empire never spread,
To Thames' blest stream her stores while Commerce draws
From Ganges' Bramin groves and Indus' bed:
From a poem by Henry Pye, the Poet Laureate,
on Strelitzia Reginae from Robert Thornton's
Temple of Flora (1799–1807)

In 1779, firmly stating his resolution never to grant American independence, George claimed that such a measure 'must entirely fix the fall of this empire'.[1] Instead, on the global scale, the reach of British power provided one of the most lasting legacies of George's reign, and one that, in the shape of political culture, survived the end of the British empire. As a result of this reach, this chapter is necessarily eclectic, but it reflects the range of activities and topics in which George was engaged as a result of the spread of empire, and the very different ways in which he was of real or symbolic importance. One of the most enduring aspects was naming, which marked British imperial expansion with the royal presence. The process of naming is still readily apparent, especially in areas where the end of imperial control was not accompanied by a determination to reject the legacy of the past. The royal nomenclature of place indeed is most persistent for the Hanoverian period, when empire was largely a case of North America and the West Indies: Georgetowns and Charlottes testify to the reach of British power and the determination to identify colonies with the crown and royal family. In contrast, there has been a rejection of imperial names across much of the Victorian and Edwardian empire, especially in parts of Africa: Salisbury, for example, becoming Harare.

Imperial expansion led to the spattering of royal names across the face of the map. This was especially pronounced in North America. In modern Canada, Île Saint-Jean, captured from the French in 1758, was called St John's Island, before being renamed Prince Edward Island in 1779. It soon had three counties, Kings, Queens and Prince, a capital at Charlottetown and another major settlement at Princetown. On the Canadian mainland,

---

[1] George to Robinson, 31 Oct. 1779, BL. Add. 37834 fol. 175.

the colony of New Brunswick, created in 1784, had, among its counties, Kings, Queens and Charlotte, and its capital at Fredericton. Nova Scotia's counties included Kings, Queens, Cumberland and Lunenburg, and towns including Lunenburg and Windsor. In the St Lawrence Valley in Quebec after the War of American Independence, loyalists settled in newly surveyed townships that included Charlottesburg, Osnabruck, Williamsburg, Edwardsburg, Augusta, Kingston, Fredericksburg and Adolphustown. Guelph was a land grant to the west of Lake Ontario, and York was the settlement on that lake subsequently renamed Toronto. There was a Fort George opposite the American Fort Niagara. Posts in the fur-trading Canadian interior that stretched north and west of the Great Lakes included Frederick House, Fort Charlotte, Fort William, Cumberland House, Fort George, and Fort Augustus I, II, III in the distant North Saskatchewan Valley. Fort George in the Rockies was joined in 1814 by New Fort George on the estuary of the Columbia river. Earlier, the British presence in Malaysia had begun with the establishment of a British base on the island of Penang by Francis Light in 1786: George Town was the name given to the settlement.

In addition, warships were exploring what for Britain was the 'dark side' of the earth: the Pacific, with George providing more financial support, and showing more interest, than his predecessor had done. Sailing across the Pacific in 1767, Philip Carteret 'discovered' Osnaburg, Duke of Gloucester, and Queen Charlotte islands, each named after a member of the royal family, as well as New Hanover. When territories were not named after the royal family, they were still claimed in the name of George. In August 1770, on what became Possession Island, James Cook claimed the east coast of Australia for the British crown, although his orders in 1768 made such a claim conditional on 'the consent of the natives . . . or, if you find the country uninhabited, take possession . . . as first discoverers and possessors'.[2] Not all of these claimings and namings, however, became permanent settlements. In October 1793, Captain John Hayes hoisted the British flag on the north-west coast of New Guinea and, on behalf of George, took possession of what he called 'New Albion', the first European presence on New Guinea. In this case, the royal imprimatur was designed to cover a privately funded expedition in search of valuable nutmeg. The governor-general in India, Sir John Shore, and his council, however, sceptical about the economic prospects, refused to support the new settlement at Fort Coronation, and in 1795 it was abandoned.[3]

---

[2] G. Williams, '"As befits our age, there are no more heroes": Reassessing Captain Cook', in Williams (ed.), *Captain Cook. Explorations and Reassessments* (Woodbridge, 2004), p. 244.

[3] A. Griffin, 'London, Bengal, the China Trade and the Unfrequented Extremities of Asia: The East India Company's Settlement in New Guinea, 1793–95', *British Library Journal*, 16 (1990), pp. 151–73.

George made a large personal contribution of £4,000 to the Royal Society in 1768 towards the costs of Cook's first voyage,[4] and in August 1771 granted him an hour-long audience on his return. Dr Richard Kaye, the sub-almoner, supplied Cook with George III Maundy coins for burial in newly discovered lands in the name of the king, and Cook presented George with a *heitiki*, or Maori stone embodying the spirits of ancestors, that he had been given in New Zealand in 1769. Omai, the first Polynesian visitor to England, who arrived there in 1774 following Cook's second voyage, was presented by Joseph Banks to George, who treated him courteously, gave him an allowance and ensured that he was inoculated against smallpox. At Covent Garden, George subsequently attended numerous performances of John O'Keeffe's pantomime *Omai, or A Trip Around the World* (1785), being moved to tears by the fate of the protagonist.[5] The previous year, he had been given a copy of the account of Cook's last voyage.[6]

The material George retained for his private working library indicates the king's interest in the transoceanic world. It includes Cook's original drawings for the survey of St Pierre and Miquelon, islands off Newfoundland, as well as a set of topographical drawings of the new Australian colony by Fernando Brambila.[7] The world outside Europe provided George with an opportunity to pursue knowledge in fields that interested him, and, in so doing, to establish his credentials as a patron of Europe's civilizing mission in the shape of scientific knowledge. The botanical garden at Kew offered an important example of this as it could compete directly with continental counterparts, not least the Jardin du Roi in Paris. The location at Kew closely associated George with this project. He founded it, and the collection of rare plants drew on the resources of empire, especially the native plants of the Americas.[8] George's interest was

[4] H.B. Carter, 'The Royal Society and the Voyage of HMS *Endeavour* 1768–71', *Notes and Records of the Royal Society of London*, 49 (1995), pp. 245–6.

[5] *Gentleman's Magazine*, 44 (1774), p. 330; M. Alexander, *Omai. Noble Savage* (London, 1977), pp. 72–5, 132–5; K. Wilson, 'The Island Race: Captain Cook, Protestant Evangelicalism and the Construction of English National Identity, 1760–1800', in T. Claydon and I. McBride (eds), *Protestantism and National Identity. Britain and Ireland, c. 1650–c. 1850* (Cambridge, 1998), pp. 273, 277.

[6] Viscount Howe to George, 31 May 1784, Aspinall, *George III*, I, 66.

[7] P. Barber, 'King George III's Topographical Collection: A Georgian View of Britain and the World', in K. Sloan and A. Burnett (eds), *Enlightenment. Discovering the World in the Eighteenth Century* (London, 2003), p. 161. See also Barber, 'George III and his geographical Collection', in J. Marsden (ed.), *The Wisdom of George the Third* (London, 2005), pp. 263–89, and 'Royal Geography. The Development and Destiny of King George III's Geographical Collections', unpublished paper. I am grateful to Peter Barber for providing me with copies and discussing the subject with me. See also R.A. Skelton, 'King George III's Maritime Collection', *British Museum Quarterly*, 18 (1953), pp. 62–3, and 'The Hydrographic Collections of the British Museum', *Journal of the Institute of Navigation*, 9 (1956), pp. 323–34.

[8] R. Drayton, *Nature's Government. Science, Imperial Britain, and the 'Improvement' of the World* (New Haven and London, 2000), pp. 42–3.

shown when, in 1768, he purchased a unique three-volume set of Mark Catesby's *Natural History of Carolina, Florida and the Bahama Islands*. Four years later, George sent Francis Masson to Cape Town to acquire plants for Kew. One genus, the *Strelitzia*, was named after the queen.[9]

In George's vision of profitable knowledge, not all voyages led to Britain. In 1785 he revived the botanic garden of St Vincent in the West Indies and by 1787 it was seen as a means to introduce Pacific plants to the region. That year, Joseph Banks referred to George's support for the establishment in 1786 of a botanic garden at Calcutta, adding that his 'paternal eye' was 'accustomed to appreciate the value of benefits applicable to the different parts of his extensive Empire'. Furthermore, George extended his concern to improve British wool, by means of secretly imported merino sheep, into a policy of developing new colonies; seven rams and three ewes were sent to New South Wales in 1804.[10]

George himself was happy to approve transportation of felons for life to Botany Bay as a way to build up the new colony,[11] where the British first established a base in 1788. In 1789, he was concerned when three convicted felons chose death instead of transportation: 'It is shocking that men can be so lost to every sentiment of gratitude not to feel the mercy shown them in sparing their lives.' George agreed to a proposal made by the home secretary, William Grenville, to execute one in order to encourage the other two to choose Australia. To this end, the felons were offered an opportunity to reconsider, and, when a judge cast doubt on the legality of a week's respite, George was dubious about this view which, anyway, tended 'to render it highly difficult to continue the plan of transportation'. The convicts in the end decided they preferred Australia to execution, but George then agreed with Grenville that they should make their submission publicly at the next session of the Old Bailey, the king adding that this was 'the best method of preventing similar difficulties with future convicts'.[12] The cost of both transportation and keeping convicts on prison ships led George to press in 1802 for 'a regular plan of sending the convicts' to Australia.[13]

Imperial expansion unsurprisingly provided George with an opportunity to reveal the attitudes to social order he displayed in Britain. Other

[9] Drayton, *Nature's Government*, p. 78.
[10] D. Mackay, *In the Wake of Cook: Exploration, Science and Empire, 1780–1801* (London, 1985), p. 129; Drayton, *Nature's Government*, p. 87; Banks to Dundas, 15 June 1787, Aspinall, *George III*, I, 302. H. Carter, *His Majesty's Spanish Flock: Sir Joseph Banks and the Merinos of George III of England* (London, 1964).
[11] George to Spencer, 12 July 1800, BL. Add. 75839. See also George to William Grenville, 1, 3 Apr. 1790, BL. Add. 58855 fols 76, 80.
[12] William Grenville to George, 20 Sept., George to William Grenville, 20, 21, 24, 25 Sept. 1789, BL. Add. 58855 fols 19, 23, 27, 29, 31.
[13] George to Pelham, 7 Mar. 1802, BL. Add. 33115 fol. 56.

issues, however, also played a role, not only relations with non-European powers but also more general questions of ethnicity. Johann Friedrich Blumenbach, a leading scholar at the university in which George was most interested, Göttingen, classified human types in his *De generis humani varietate* (1776). His theory of monogenesis – the descent of all races from a single original group – assumed the original ancestral group to be white, and that climate, diet, disease and mode of life were responsible for the developments of different races. This was a rejection of polygenism – the different creation of types of humans – which had led to suggestions that blacks were not only a different species, but also related to great apes, such as orang-utans, a theory used to justify slavery.

George was not a supporter of the abolition of the slave trade. He accepted Sir William Dolben's 1788 Bill to lessen crowding on slavers, a measure vociferously opposed by Thurlow and Hawkesbury, ministers close to the king,[14] but abolition was different, and the king's opposition helped ensure that, like parliamentary reform in 1785, it could not become a ministerial measure that benefited from the weight of government support.[15] For George, however, abolition did not become an issue comparable to Catholic emancipation, and he accepted the legislation of 1806–7 that banned the trade: the Foreign Slave Trade Act of 1806, ending the supply of slaves to conquered territories and foreign colonies, and the Abolition Act of 1807 that banned slave trading by British subjects and the import of slaves into the other colonies. George's sympathies, nevertheless, were certainly not engaged by a cause that convinced many of his subjects. In modern eyes, that serves as a stain on his reputation, leading indeed to his description as 'that great slave trader'.[16] George, however, was not alone among convinced Christians in defending slavery and the slave trade, and, for him, issues of property rights and prudence came first. This highlights the degree to which George was disengaged from sentimental issues, while it is a reminder that, if Enlightened is to be employed as a term to describe George, it has to be employed with a full understanding of the diversity of the Enlightenment. The slave trade, like the transportation of convicts and the treatment of aboriginal peoples, explains why George's reign has an ambiguous, not to say contentious, memory across part of the world. The anniversaries of claims of territory for the king are particularly controversial in Australia.[17]

---

[14] La Luzerne to Montmorin, 27 June, 1 July 1788, AE. CP. Ang. 565 fol. 330, 566 fol. 6; Hawkesbury to Dorset, 4 July 1788, KAO. U269 C182.

[15] R. Anstey, *The Atlantic Slave Trade and British Abolition 1760–1810* (London, 1975), pp. 304–6.

[16] J. Sack, 'Britain in Transition: The Age of George III: A Commentary', *Consortium on Revolutionary Europe: Selected Papers, 1997* (Tallahassee, Florida, 1997), p. 61.

[17] L. Ryan, 'Risdon Cove and the Massacre of 3 May 1804: Their Place in Tasmanian History', *Tasmanian Historical Studies*, 9 (2004), pp. 107–23.

Faced by the rapid worldwide expansion of British interests during his reign, George made an *ad hoc* response to individual problems, one that, in his terms, was characterized by a practical attitude. There was no guidance, or encumbrance, affecting policy comparable to the established position of the crown in such questions as Catholic rights within Britain. Thus, in October 1790, at a time when war with Spain seemed imminent and attacks were planned on the Spanish West Indies, George responded to the need to increase troop numbers by addressing practicalities:

the measure of raising Blacks is much improved by attaching ten men to each company rather than forming a company of coloured men to be attached to each regiment, and I trust this will prove of the utmost utility to the preservation of the actual troops, and by preventing much illness enable them to be more complete.[18]

George took a close interest in British campaigning in India, and, far from taking the view that British power was already too extensive, was delighted by success there. In 1791 he noted, 'I feel infinite satisfaction at the splendid success of Lord Cornwallis in taking Bangalore and have not the smallest doubt but Seringapatam must soon have had a similar fate'.[19] The latter comment reflects a misleading over-confidence, though one that was widely shared. Tipu Sultan's capital was not to fall until the next Anglo-Mysore war, in 1799. George was not simply interested in glory. His concern with costs made him appreciate the logistics of the British campaign. 'It is pleasing to find by the private letters from Sir George Oakley, that the troops under the command of Lord Cornwallis have been supplied by the enemy's country whilst in a state of inaction; consequently that the resources of the [East India] Company have been retained for the purposes of the ensuing campaign.'[20]

George admired Cornwallis's conduct of the Third Mysore War, was delighted by the 1792 peace treaty with Tipu Sultan, and was keen to see the map that depicted the company's gains.[21] The royal collections were the beneficiaries of the eventual victory over Tipu Sultan in 1799. The *huma*, or bird of paradise, over his throne was salvaged from the sack of Seringapatam on 4 May and presented to George by the East India Company in 1800. He gave it to Charlotte. Weapons were also presented to the king, Marquess Wellesley giving a flintlock blunderbuss with Tipu's

[18] George to William Grenville, 25 Oct. 1790, BL. Add. 58855 fol. 155.
[19] George to Dundas, 5 Sept. 1791, BL. Add. 40100 fol. 17, cf. 28 Aug. 1791, 23, 25 June 1792, fols 15, 37, 41.
[20] George to Dundas, 29 Jan. 1792, BL. Add. 40100 fol. 27.
[21] George to Dundas, 22, 26 Jan. 1793, BL. Add. 40100 fols 55–6; Dundas to Cornwallis, 17 Sept. 1792, C. Ross (ed.), *The Correspondence of Charles, First Marquis Cornwallis* (3 vols, London, 1859), II, 214.

emblem in 1800, while, in 1811, Sir John Cradock presented a sword that had belonged to Tipu. The transfer to the victor of the ceremonial and fighting belongings of the defeated monarch, who had died defending his capital, was deeply symbolic.

Greater governmental concern with the affairs of the Company meant that George was provided with far more information about India than his predecessor, and had far more drafts to approve.[22] Although George had shown concern about the government of India in the 1770s,[23] and had read reports from India,[24] India was of greater importance as a political and governmental issue in Britain in the latter half of the reign. In large part, this was a result of the legacy of the political crisis of 1783–4. New-found controversy over the character of British rule was also significant. This focused on the impeachment, on charges of corruption, of Warren Hastings, the former governor-general of Bengal,[25] a step George privately deplored, although he had been keen to see him resign.[26] Concerns about the security of the British position in India, in particular in face of Tipu Sultan of Mysore, were also an issue. George did not have a notable role in policy towards India. Although he was interested in legal arrangements in Calcutta and kept an eye on the passage of the legislation through parliament,[27] the establishment, as a result of Pitt's India Act of 1784, of the Board of Control as a government department responsible for many of the functions hitherto resting with the East India Company, was not followed by any increase in royal oversight or intervention. The contrary, instead, was the case. George was indeed interested in attempts to reform the Company's army,[28] and was a supporter of Cornwallis, who became governor-general in 1786, but there was nothing to compare with his concern over Ireland; while Cornwallis was not employed in order to increase royal influence. To George, good government in India was linked to security, and this lent a prudential dimension to the proper use of authority. He had hoped that Pitt's Act might 'lay a foundation for by degrees correcting those shocking enormities in India that disgrace human nature and if not put a stop to threaten the expulsion of the Company out of that wealthy region'.[29]

[22] George to Robinson, 14 Sept. 1776, Robinson to George, 12 Nov. 1777, George to William Grenville, 12 May 1790, BL. Add. 37833 fols 28, 211, 58855 fol. 100.

[23] George to Robinson, 22, 29, 31 Mar., 9 May 1777, BL. Add. 37833 fols 182, 189, 191, 198.

[24] E.g. George to Robinson, 23 May, 8, 27 Oct. 1779, BL. Add. 37834 fols 85, 155, 169.

[25] G. Carnall and C. Nicholson (eds), *The Impeachment of Warren Hastings* (Edinburgh, 1989).

[26] George to Robinson, 3 Oct. 1776, BL. Add. 37833 fol. 71.

[27] George to Robinson, 25 Oct. 1776, BL. Add. 37833 fol. 97; George to Sydney, 3 Aug. 1784, Aspinall, *George III*, I, 77.

[28] George to Jenkinson, 17 Apr. 1781, BL. Loan 72/1 fol. 47.

[29] George to Pitt, 17 July 1784, PRO. 30/8/103, fol. 115. For background, H.V. Bowen, *The Business of Empire. The East India Company and Imperial Britain, 1756–1833* (Cambridge, 2005).

George responded to the sense of opportunity provided by British expansion. When the Andaman Islands in the Bay of Bengal were seized in 1789, George wrote, 'Captain Blair's report of the islands of Andaman which I received this morning . . . gives every reason to suppose that these may prove of great utility'.[30] The king's interest extended to China, and he commented on the drafts of letters sent there.[31]

George's growing commitment to imperial expansion led him to express anxiety that it might be jeopardized by the results of campaigning in Europe, although he preferred to gain compensation for the House of Orange from future British conquests in the Dutch East Indies rather than from the secularization of bishoprics in Germany, a measure he was keen to oppose as Elector of Hanover.[32] George's concern about compensation for the prince of Orange was an aspect of his care for the cause of rulers.[33] In 1800, the king made clear his anxiety about the strength of Austrian determination in the war with France, and his fear that dearly bought transoceanic conquests might be given up in a peace in order to help Britain's allies, 'and contrary to the watchword in the Seven Years War, that America was conquered in Germany, that our conquests will be lost by our allies in Germany'.[34] That July, he claimed that no peace would be reasonable unless it secured 'the greatest part of our acquisitions, particularly the Cape of Good Hope and the West India islands',[35] and, in 1801, he expressed concern that more benefits had not been derived from the former.[36] Captured in 1795, the Dutch Cape Colony was restored under the treaty of Amiens of 1802, as were all Britain's gains from France, Spain and the Dutch, bar Trinidad (captured from Spain) and the Dutch bases in Sri Lanka.

George's position was different to that of 1761–2 when he and Bute had feared that transoceanic conquests, particularly Havana from Spain, would compromise prospects of peace with the Bourbons. This reflected not only the sense that Napoleon, unlike Louis XV, could not be trusted – a constant theme in ministerial speeches, for example by Dundas and Hawkesbury – but also an increased British imperial ambition. George was not in the forefront of this process, but, after Britain in 1793 began a war that he thought necessary, he was more committed to such gains than he had been at the time of the Falklands (1770) and Nootka Sound (1790)

---

[30] George to William Grenville, 20 Dec. 1789, BL. Add. 58855.

[31] George to Dundas, 19 June 1795, BL. Add. 40100 fol. 153.

[32] George to William Grenville, 13 Sept. 1797, BL. Add. 58860 fol. 24.

[33] George to William Grenville, 14, 15 Apr. 1798, BL. Add. 58860 fols 72–3.

[34] George to Dundas, 25 Sept. 1800, BL. Add. 40100 fol. 282, cf. 5 Oct. fol. 293, and to William Grenville, 31 July 1796, BL. Add. 58859 fol. 73.

[35] George to William Grenville, 17 July 1800, BL. 58861 fol. 116; George to Pitt, 17 July 1800, Aspinall, *George III*, III, 376.

[36] F. Bickley (ed.), *The Diaries of Sylvester Douglas, Lord Glenbervie*, (2 vols, London, 1928), I, 151.

crises. Although the case was very different, there was a parallel with George's North American policy of the 1770s: not initially a hardliner, he subsequently became much more determined. His awareness of the opportunities for imperial strategy stemming from Britain's far-flung presence was demonstrated in 1800 when, worried about manpower for an expedition to 'free Egypt from that pest of society', the French army, George urged consideration of the feasibility of moving troops from India.[37] This was indeed done, and was to be a key capability in British strategy until Indian independence in 1947. George was not a rash proponent of imperial expeditions. With a characteristic measure of self-righteousness and concern to defend the record, in 1800 he wrote to Dundas,

> it is with the greatest reluctance I consent to the proposed disposal of the troops in the Mediterranean by sending 15,000 of them under the command of Sir Ralph Abercrombie to Egypt; as that service must probably prove a burial ground for them to as great an extent as St. Domingo; for unless the army be supplied from hence as amply and as regularly as that in America was by the Treasury in the time of Lord North, nothing but famine can attend it; as to any part of it being after-wards fit for other service that cannot be expected; I am therefore not surprised that Lord Grenville and Mr. Windham have dissented from the measure.[38]

He later admitted he had been wrong, and became more committed to the relationship between Britain's Mediterranean position and the security of India. In January 1803, as relations with France deteriorated, George advised delay in the promised evacuation of Malta because of 'the mani-fest views France nourishes of fresh expeditions to the East'.[39] In 1804, George supported the idea of an expedition to take the Dutch Cape Colony which he 'ever looked upon . . . as the key to our possessions in the East Indies'.[40] It was easily captured in January 1806. George was also keen to increase British trade in the Mediterranean, and hoped that Corsica in Russian hands would achieve that end.[41]

In the empire, however, George was exercising his role at a remove. In part, this was a matter of distance, but that was not the key factor, as George no more visited Scotland than Australia. There was a more profound issue in that the royal patronage system that George inherited

---

[37] George to Dundas, 29 Sept. 1800, BL. Add. 40100 fol. 289.
[38] George to Dundas, 5 Oct. 1800, BL. Add. 40100 fol. 293.
[39] George to Hawkesbury, 28 Jan. 1803, BL. Loan 72/1 fol. 107.
[40] George to Dundas, 16 July 1804, BL. Add. 40100 fol. 321.
[41] George to Grenville, 20 Oct. 1796, BL. Add. 58859 fol. 90.

worked reasonably well as far as directing the British élite was concerned and, through them, much of the politics of the metropolis. This was, however, less the case with the expanding empire. Indeed, it was one of the causes of the American Revolution. Most of the empire did not experience revolution against British control, although a serious Patriot opposition developed in Ireland;[42] but the novel administrative issues empire posed ensured that George could exercise authority only through ministerial structures. Even then, distance meant that it was governors who had to exercise royal powers, such as that to pardon transported convicts in Australia.[43] The possibility of the crown overseeing delegated authority in nearby Ireland,[44] a possibility frequently thwarted by the practice of the government there failing to 'communicate business till the hour before undertaken',[45] was not matched at a distance.

The extent to which empire and its expansion offered opportunities for a British warrior aristocracy has been emphasized,[46] and militarization of imperial authority was, indeed, accentuated as a consequence of the combination of the loss of the Thirteen Colonies with the new gains of the following three decades. George understood this character of authority, which provided his fourth son, Edward, duke of Kent, with command positions in Canada and Gibraltar. He also saw the quality of power as different, writing to Pitt in 1786 that, as far as India was concerned, government could not be conducted 'with the same moderation that is suitable to a European civilized Nation'.[47] The context, however, was very different from medieval conquest. In 1169–71 Anglo-Norman baronial forces had overrun much of Ireland, including Dublin, Waterford and Wexford, but in 1171 Henry II arrived in order to establish his rights by imposing his authority on his barons. George did not need to act in such a fashion, because royal authority had to a considerable extent been systematized and shared in the governmental system.

This left him with the symbolic powers expressed by the rhythms of ceremony, for example the singing of 'God Save the King' across the face of the world. At Botany Bay in 1789, the convicts staged George Farquhar's classic comedy *The Recruiting Officer* in celebration of the king's birthday.[48] George Street, the main street of Sydney, was laid out during his reign. Similar themes echoed in Britain. For 22 August 1791, the audi-

---

[42] V. Morley, *Irish Opinion and the American Revolution, 1760–1783* (Cambridge, 2002).

[43] A. Atkinson, 'The Free-Born Englishman Transported: Convict Rights as a Measure of Eighteenth-Century Empire', *Past and Present*, 144 (Aug. 1994), p. 109.

[44] Sydney to George, 13 May and reply, 14 May 1784, Aspinall, *George III*, I, 61.

[45] George to Robinson, 1, 2 Nov. 1779, BL. Add. 37835 fols 1, 5.

[46] C.A. Bayly, *Imperial Meridian. The British Empire and the World 1780–1830* (Harlow, 1989).

[47] George to Pitt, 14 June 1786, PRO. 30/8/103/1 fols 197–8.

[48] G. Mackaness, *Admiral Arthur Phillip, Founder of New South Wales 1738–1814* (Sydney, 1957), p. 204.

ence at Birmingham's New Street Theatre was offered

> A pantomime exhibition called Botany Bay; or, A Trip to Port Jackson, with entire new scenery, painted for the occasion . . . in which will be introduced a picturesque view of the coast of New South Wales . . . arrival of the Grand Fleet, landing, reception, and employment of the convicts. To conclude with the ceremony of planting the British flag, on taking possession of a new discovered island, with a dance by the convicts, and the grand chorus of 'God Save the King'.

Similarly, events in the king's life, such as his marriage, were celebrated across the empire. In 1789, the recovery of George's health was celebrated in Calcutta, with a prominent Armenian paying the money owed by 130 people imprisoned for debt, while the army's cannon sounded across the city. Cornwallis, the governor-general, recorded,

> I gave a concert and supper to the whole settlement, but unluckily, after we had made all our preparations, and flattered ourselves that we should rival the most brilliant part of London, just about sunset there came on a most violent torrent of rain, which lasted the greatest part of the night, and put out our lamps almost as fast as we could light them . . . the supper, which could not be put out by the rain, was a very good one; some of the gentlemen who stayed late however were nearly extinguished by the claret; seven of the finest ladies of the place and twelve gentlemen sang the Coronation Anthem.[49]

Public celebration across the empire focused on the crown, providing memories and examples that were to be sustained for decades. Calcutta was also to be one of the sites of the celebrations of George's Jubilee on 25 October 1809.

The naming referred to at the beginning of the chapter was a more lasting product of the same process of associating state and king. It was driven not only by British action but also by native response. On the northwest coast of North America, the king was so often mentioned by British subjects that in the native mind his name became synonymous with power.[50] When territories were claimed or treaties signed, the name of the king was the key element. In January 1773, the Caribs of St Vincent swore

---

[49] Cornwallis to Viscount Broome, 14 Aug. 1789, Ross (ed.), *Cornwallis*, I, 422–3.

[50] J. Walbran, *British Columbia Coast Names, 1592–1906* (Ottawa, 1909), p. 205, cited in D. Clayton, 'Georgian Geographies "from and for the margins": "King George men" on the Northwest Coast of North America', in M. Ogborn and C.W.J. Withers (eds), *Georgian Geographies. Essays on Space, Place and Landscape in the Eighteenth Century* (Manchester, 2004), p. 31.

allegiance to George in the treaty that ended their war against British control.

Royal symbolism was also important because of the role of monarchy across the world. To foreign rulers, George symbolized Britain. Captain George Vancouver reported that in 1792 Kamehameha I of Hawaii gave him two feather cloaks and several capes for George, writing of one that Kamehameha

> very carefully folded it up, and desired, that on my arrival in England, I would present it in his name to His Majesty, King George, saying, that it was the most valuable thing in the island of Owhyhee, and for that reason he had sent it to so great a monarch, and so good a friend, as he considered the King of England.[51]

Kamehameha thought in terms of confirming his status by asserting a link between two reigning families, with George as crucial a figure as he was. Indeed, the king's totemic significance ensured that he became the recipient of the accoutrements of power. In 1771, on his return with Cook, Joseph Banks presented George with a golden coronet decorated with feathers, a gift from a ruler on the Chilean coast.[52] There were also gorgeous presents from Indian rulers, including two Arabian horses for the king and a young elephant for the queen in 1793,[53] as well as a lavish gift of jewels from Muhammad Ali Khan, the nawab of the Carnatic, in 1767. In 1799, the nawab of Oudh presented six splendid oriental manuscripts to George through the governor-general of India. The king was also the recipient of letters from Indian rulers including, from 1760, the nawab of the Carnatic – and he replied to them:[54] George was the 'dignified' body with whom it was appropriate for them to correspond.

Totemic significance might seem to match the emphasis on the symbolic nature of George's position in Britain in his later years, but, as with the latter, that suggestion, while accurate, is less than a full account of the king's role. Just as the interpretation of the domestic situation in this way leaves out George's considerable role in politics, particularly in the 1800s, so an account of the king and empire needs to note the place of his personal opinion. Until 1783, this centred on the American colonies and involved the defence of authority in the face of challenges from settler

---

[51] W.K. Lamb (ed.), *George Vancouver, 'A Voyage of Discovery ... 1791–5'* (London, 1984), pp. 839–40.

[52] Drayton, *Nature's Government*, p. 94.

[53] Ross (ed.), *Cornwallis*, II, 553.

[54] P.J. Marshall, *The Making and Unmaking of Empires. Britain, India, and America c. 1750–1783* (Oxford, 2005), p. 145; George to Robinson, 12 Apr. 1778, BL. Add. 37833 fol. 218; William Grenville to George, 24 Apr. 1790, Aspinall, *George III*, I, 474.

colonists who, in many respects, were like subjects in Britain, but, thereafter, the focus shifted.

This was most apparent in the case of relations with the now-independent United States. Despite the peace treaty, a range of issues were in dispute, and in the United States, political practice and a national culture different from, and often in opposition to, that of the former mother country was developing.[55] George had been pleased to be away from London when the peace that acknowledged American independence was proclaimed in 1783, but he struck an appropriate note of wise and honest courtesy when he received John Adams on 1 June 1785 as the first American minister to the court of St James. Although he found George's 'pronunciation . . . as distinct as I ever heard', Adams, 'much affected' by the occasion, was not certain about the king's precise words, but recorded George as saying,

> I have done nothing in the late contest but what I thought myself indispensably bound to do, by the duty which I owed to my people . . . I was the last to consent to the separation; but the separation having been made, and having become inevitable, I have always said, as I say now, that I would be the first to meet the friendship of the United States as an independent power . . . let the circumstances of language, religion, and blood have their natural and full effect.

George, who, Adams noted, was 'much affected, and answered me with more tremor than I had spoken with', was revealed as informed, relaxed and quick-witted. With 'an air of familiarity, and smiling, or rather laughing', he astutely teased Adams by saying 'there is an opinion among some people that you are not the most attached of all your countrymen to the manners of France'. It was Adams, not George, who was wrongfooted and stood more on his dignity. 'Surprised' and 'embarrassed', he responded that he had 'no attachment but to my own country', which George, 'as quick as lightning', courteously trumped saying 'an honest man will never have any other', a reflection that joined two of the king's key values.[56]

The following March, Thomas Jefferson on a visit from his embassy in Paris was received by George. There are no detailed contemporary

[55] R.A. Burchell, *The End of Anglo-America. Historical Essays in the Study of Cultural Divergence* (Manchester, 1991). There has also been emphasis on continuities, see e.g. debate in *Historically Speaking* 6, 4 (Mar.–Apr. 2005), pp. 19–22.

[56] Adams to Secretary John Jay, 2 June 1785, C.F. Adams (ed.), *The Works of John Adams* (10 vols, Boston, Massachusetts, 1853), VIII, 255–7; Adams to Thomas Jefferson, 3 June 1785, L.J. Cappon (ed.), *The Adams–Jefferson Letters: The Complete Correspondence between Thomas Jefferson and Abigail and John Adams* (Chapel Hill, North Carolina, 1988), p. 27.

accounts of the meeting, although in his autobiography, written thirty-five years later, Jefferson was very critical. Claiming that he had been ungraciously received at the levee on 17 March, Jefferson added 'I saw, at once, that the ulcerations in the narrow mind of that mulish being left nothing to be expected on the subject of my attendance', although it is likely that his account was over-dramatized, if not totally misleading. Jefferson appears to have blamed on George the failure of his official business in London which included negotiations with Portuguese and Tripolitanian envoys. The British government did not depart from its position that pre-war debts owed to British merchants had to be part of any trade treaty, a position unacceptable to the Americans, and Jefferson certainly blamed the failure to negotiate such a treaty on George. Aside from arguing that his hostility to the Americans had been exacerbated by failure, Jefferson exaggerated George's role in commercial negotiations.[57] Ironically, the two men had much in common, from an interest in architecture and applied science to a disdain for luxury.

Relations with America, from which Edward Thornton reported in 1794 'the malignity against England though less violent, is not less fixed',[58] did not, however, bulk large in governmental concern,[59] and George devoted little attention to them. When war broke out anew in 1812, he was, anyway, in no position to reflect on the situation.

Given his commitment to honour, it is unsurprising that George's prime concern was with the situation of the loyalists whose claims to compensation were largely ignored in America. He was benevolent to those who fled to Britain.[60] Nevertheless one, Mrs Wright, claimed that, although George pitied them, 'he wished the Nation rid of their importunities'.[61] The rebel poet, Philip Freneau, writing in 1783, satirized a loyalist's complaint as he is about to depart from Nova Scotia:

> Nor trusted George, whate'er he chose to say;
> Thrice happy thou who wore a double face,
> And as the balance turn'd could each embrace;
> Too happy Janus! Had I shar'd thy art,
> To speak a language foreign to my heart,

[57] P.L. Ford (ed.), *The Autobiography of Thomas Jefferson 1743–1790* (New York, 1914), p. 94; C.R. Ritcheson, 'The Fragile Memory: Thomas Jefferson at the Court of George III', *Eighteenth-Century Life*, 6, pts. 2–3 (1981), pp. 1–16.

[58] Thornton to Burges, 11 July 1794, PRO. FO. 5/6 fol. 342.

[59] Ritcheson, *Aftermath of Revolution: British Policy toward the United States, 1783–1795* (Dallas, Texas, 1969).

[60] George to Sydney, 18 June 1785, Aspinall, *George III*, I, 166; W. Brown, *The Good Americans: The Loyalists in the American Revolution* (New York, 1969), p. 164; M.B. Norton, *The British-Americans: The Loyalist Exile in England, 1774–1789* (Boston, 1972).

[61] Ibid., pp. 157–8.

And stoop'd from pomp and dreams of regal state,
To court the friendship of the men I hate,
These strains of woe had not been pen'd today,
Nor I for foreign climes been forc'd away;
Ah! George – that name provokes my keenest rage,
Did he not swear, and promise, and engage
His Loyal sons to nurture and defend,
To be their God, their father and their friend –
Yet basely quits us on a hostile coast,
And leaves us wretched where we need him most:
His is the part to promise and deceive,
By him we wander and by him we grieve;
Since the first day that these dissentions grew,
When Gage to Boston brought this blackguard crew,
From place to place we urge our vagrant flight
To follow still this vapor of the night,
From town to town have run our various race,
And acted all that's mean and all that's base –
Yes – from that day until this hour we roam,
Vagrants forever from our native home.[62]

Many loyalists had fled to Canada and George supported schemes to provide them with land there.[63] Royal encouragement accorded with government policy in creating within non-French Canada an Anglican ascendancy. This cannot be seen as indicative of George's earlier intentions toward the Thirteen Colonies, where circumstances were very different, while the king's respect for established rights ensured that his intentions were also very different to those of James II in the 1680s. In Quebec prior to the war there had been an appreciation of the need to recognize the position of the Catholic Church in order to secure the loyalty of the population, and, with the Quebec Act of 1774, this had taken precedence over the creation of any narrowly based Protestant ascendancy.[64] Nevertheless, George's inclinations were glanced at in the Act of 1791 which gave the Church of England a considerable amount of land in Upper Canada in order to provide for its clergy, and also the colleges that would sustain its local position. A hereditary aristocracy was also seen as a way to safeguard loyalty.

[62] M. and P. Borden (eds), *The American Tory* (Englewood Cliffs, New Jersey,1972), pp. 93–4.
[63] A.G. Condon, *The Envy of the American States: The Loyalist Dream for New Brunswick* (Frederickton, New Brunswick, 1984); N. MacKinnon, *This Unfriendly Soil: The Loyalist Experience in Nova Scotia, 1783–1791* (Kingston, 1986).
[64] P. Lawson, *The Imperial Challenge: Quebec and Britain in the Age of the American Revolution* (Montréal, 1989).

Security was a key aspect in imperial expansion under George. It was seen not only across the oceans but also closer to home. The Isle of Man was a sovereign territory under John, third duke of Atholl, that served, in fact, as the base for smugglers. To end this threat to fiscal control, George Grenville decided in 1765 to purchase the sovereignty. As Atholl was not accommodating, Grenville resorted to parliamentary action, and the sovereignty was thereby purchased compulsorily for £70,000 and an annuity of £2,000, although the Atholl family retained manorial and mineral rights and the right to appoint the bishop and clergy. As a result, Claudius Crigan became bishop of Sodor and Man in 1784, a corrupt choice that George would not have been a party to had he had the right of appointment.[65] George, however, supported blocking the appointment in 1805 of a brother of the duke of Atholl as lieutenant-governor of the Isle of Man.[66] In 1781, 1790 and 1805 the duke presented bills to parliament to reverse the sale, but they were unsuccessful and the island was to be a more lasting gain to the crown than many that attracted greater attention.

Ireland was a far more serious issue. George was concerned that Ireland should be fairly treated, being pleased on that head that the Address on the Irish Commercial Regulations passed the Westminster House of Commons in 1785,[67] but Ireland also made him uneasy. Indeed, the problems the measure encountered in Ireland struck George as 'absurd if not presumptuous'.[68] Concerned with the security risk of Irish disaffection, George was a supporter of the firm suppression of the 1798 rising and, thereafter, a keen backer of parliamentary union between Britain and Ireland. This serves as a reminder that the emphasis on the king as a conservative, unenthusiastic about change, has to be tempered by an appreciation not only of his willingness to use force to resist change he regarded as inappropriate, but also of his readiness to accept some change. In 1798, George revealed in his firm opposition to rebellion a note that is too often overlooked when the stress is placed on his symbolic role in later years: 'I trust . . . that as the sword is drawn it [will] not be returned into the sheath until the whole country has submitted without condition; the making any compromise would be perfect destruction'.[69]

Five years later, George was concerned by the news of Robert Emmet's rising in Dublin. Emmet, a United Irishman who had been in France during the 1798 uprising, visited Napoleon in 1802 and received a promise

---

[65] W. Gibson, '"Sully and Lawn Sleeves": The Appointment of Claudius Crigan as Bishop of Sodor and Man, 1784', *Archives*, 23 (1998), pp. 41–50.

[66] George to Hawkesbury, 8 June 1805, BL. Loan 72/1 fol. 142.

[67] George to Pitt, 26 July 1785, Aspinall, *George III*, I, 173.

[68] Ibid., 1 Aug.

[69] George to Dundas, 3 June 1798, Aspinall, *George III*, III, 71.

of support, but his preparations for a rising were made with no anticipation of French backing. With a force of about a hundred men, Emmet marched on Dublin castle on 23 July 1803, but his poorly organized men were dispersed by the garrison and the rising collapsed. George saw this as a prompt for better policing in Dublin, where, in 1795, the opposition had been able to end the commissioner-run, centralized police established in 1786;[70] and also for 'unremitting attention to these deep laid conspiracies'.[71] George, however, saw a greater context and purpose: 'every man that reflects must feel the interposition of Divine Providence which has hurried on this daring insurrection before enough consolidated to effect the mischief intended'.[72] Apocalyptic discussion in Ireland, in contrast, frequently culminated in the toast, 'May The skin of old Geordy [George III] be a drum-head to beat the republicans to arms!'[73]

George's last years as an active monarch were a period of global assertiveness on the part of Britain.[74] In Europe, the failures of the third and fourth coalitions left Britain exposed and Napoleon ascendant as never before. In 1807 at Tilsit, Napoleon reached an agreement with Alexander I of Russia that left France dominant in western and central Europe; in 1808 he invaded Spain and in 1810 married Archduchess Marie Louise of Austria, a union that threatened to lead to a Napoleonic dynasty far more powerful than that of Hanover. Diplomatic hegemony put pressure on the isolated British and affected the flow of conflict. In 1810, the British forces in Portugal were pushed back on to Lisbon. If the French evacuated Portugal the following spring, Wellington was unable to capture the key Spanish border fortresses until early 1812. Yet, on the global scale, the British exploited their clear naval superiority, maintaining naval superiority in European and transoceanic waters and seizing for George an impressive range of positions. These included, from the French, St Lucia, Tobago, St Pierre and Miquelon, Cayenne, Martinique, Fort Louis (Senegal), Guadeloupe, St Martins, and Réunion; and, from the Dutch, Surinam, Cape Town, St Croix, St Thomas, St Johns, the Moluccas, Sulawesi and Aceh.

George was not in a position to know it but, alongside defeats, such as at New Orleans on 8 January 1815, the process of victory continued after he finally became ill. British sway in the East Indies extended further, with

---

[70] George to Pelham, 28, 29 July 1803, BL. Add. 33115 fols 151–2; J. Starr, 'The Dublin Police in the Late Eighteenth Century: or, the Mob Unsubdued, Corruption Enthroned, and Pascal's Dictum Overturned', *Consortium on Revolutionary Europe. Proceedings 1973* (Gainesville, Florida, 1975), pp. 153–60.

[71] George to Pelham, 9 Aug. 1803, BL. Add. 33115 fol. 161.

[72] George to Pelham, 31 July 1803, BL. Add. 33115 fol. 153.

[73] M. Colgan, 'Prophecy against Reason: Ireland and the Apocalypse', *British Journal for Eighteenth-Century Studies*, 8 (1985), p. 209.

[74] Bayly, *Imperial Meridian*.

Mauritius captured from France at the close of 1810, and the Dutch bases on Timor and Bali being captured in 1811 and 1814, respectively, while Batavia on Java fell in 1811. Gains were also made at the expense of non-European powers: the kingdom of Kandy in Sri Lanka was conquered in 1815, the Gurkhas of Nepal were defeated in 1815–16, and the Marathas in India followed in 1817–18. This range of conquests astonished and awed contemporaries, and it helped surround the crown with an aura of success. A reign that had seen, in its early stages, the capture of Havana, Manila, Martinique and St Lucia witnessed Britain triumphant over European and Indian foes at the close. The absence of success in the war of 1812 with America made far less impact in Britain. The defeats of the American Independence War and the travails of the French Revolutionary War had been cast into the shadows. It was not surprising that George's reign would be looked back on as a period of outstanding glory.

Chapter 17

WAR WITH FRANCE, 1793–1801

I am rejoiced at Mr. Secretary Dundas's information of the taking of the island of Tobago, which I trust will at a proper time be followed by that of valuable islands; now is the hour to humble France, for nothing but her being disabled from disturbing other countries whatever government may be established there will keep her quiet.

George, 1793[1]

George was not an ultra and did not press for the restoration of the Bourbons as a crucial war goal. Indeed, he wanted Louis XVI's younger brother, the count of Artois, the future Charles X of France, who was seen as a reactionary, to spend as little time as possible in Britain if he came there to recruit *émigrés* for service against the Revolution. This led to an expression by George of a francophobia that owed something to the conduct of the *émigrés*: 'my own inclination would tend to oblige every one of that perfidious nation here, either to go on that service or by the Alien Act be removed from this country'.[2] Unenthusiastic about fighting on for the Bourbons, although he came to agree that Jacobinism could not be destroyed 'unless Royalty is reestablished',[3] George still wanted France defeated. To a certain extent, although he presented the conflict as 'the cause of withstanding the principles and conduct of those who tyrannise France',[4] there was an opportunity, even need, for revenge for defeat in the War of American Independence. Whether Britain experienced victory or defeat in the war with Revolutionary France George alike pressed for resolve in the struggle.

He was initially very optimistic about the war, both in the Low Countries[5] and overseas, where French colonies were swiftly captured.[6] George also derived personal pleasure from the conduct of Frederick,

---

[1] George to Dundas, 1 June 1793, BL. Add. 40100 fol. 79.
[2] George to William Grenville, 2 Aug. 1794, BL. Add. 58858 fol. 63, cf. re. Artois, 23 Aug. 1799, 58861 fol. 51.
[3] George to Hawkesbury, 1 May 1801, BL. Loan 72/1 fol. 76.
[4] George to William Grenville, 19 Nov. 1794, BL. Add. 58858 fol. 107.
[5] George to Dundas, 7 Apr., 29 June 1793, BL. Add. 40100 fols 75, 83.
[6] George to Dundas, 30 June 1793, BL. Add. 40100 fol. 84.

duke of York, in command,[7] and from the bravery of another son, Ernest, in the Low Countries. In 1793, Ernest displayed 'very gallant behaviour . . . coolness as well as spirit . . . He saved his life by killing a French chasseur and fairly cutting his way through the enemy.'[8] The anticipated defeat of France, however, involved a choice of where to focus efforts. Far from supporting a concentration on operations in France itself, the policy advocated by those who stressed the cause of counter-revolution, George urged both a focus elsewhere and the need to avoid spreading efforts too widely, which ensured a lack of interest in operations in France. George kept a close eye on military policy and was able to discuss and propose plans[9] and make informed comments. Unlike the leading ministers of the period, the king had had experience in directing a war, that of American Independence. This included the allocation of forces, a key issue in both wars. He was correctly wary of claims about royalist support in France,[10] and was subsequently to draw a similar conclusion about the nature of possible support for liberation by the British in Holland, which had been conquered by the French.[11] In November 1793, responding to an expert report that the fortifications of Toulon, the French Mediterranean naval base then under British occupation, were weaker than had been anticipated, George wrote,

> The sentiment of not liking to change a plan that has been formed on mature deliberation is very congenial with my general opinion; but there are circumstances which must make a deviation not only reasonable but necessary . . . The feeding Toulon with troops and at the same time attempting large operations in the West Indies is quite impossible.

George correctly argued that 'all attacks on France if postponed must be more difficult of execution', as the republic consolidated its power, but he still favoured a focus on the West Indies.[12] This accorded with the view of the cabinet. As far as operations in Europe were concerned, George was no longer a supporter of concentration on the 'blue water' coastal attacks advocated by Patriots in the 1750s. If there was to be an attack on St Malo, he wanted an 'active' commander, but, as far as Toulon was concerned,

---

[7] George to Pitt, 29 Mar. 1793, PRO. 30/8/103 fol. 488.

[8] George to Dundas, 13 Aug. 1793, BL. Add. 40100 fol. 88.

[9] George to William Grenville, 29 Mar. 1793, BL. Add. 58857 fol. 105.

[10] The dubious nature of royalist claims emerges repeatedly in M. Hutt, *Chouannerie and Counter-Revolution. Puisaye, the Princes and the British Government in the 1790s* (2 vols, Cambridge, 1983).

[11] George to Dundas, 14 Oct. 1799, BL. Add. 40100 fol. 237.

[12] George to Dundas, 16 Nov. 1793, 9.12 a.m., George to William Grenville, 1 Dec. 1794, BL. Add. 40100 fol. 103, 58858 fol. 114; M. Duffy, *Soldiers, Sugar and Seapower. The British Expeditions to the West Indies and the War against Revolutionary France* (Oxford, 1987).

I entirely agree with Major General Abercromby that the keeping possession of that port and any others on the coast is all that ought to be attempted, no one can conceive to what an expence any inland motion will arise. Lord Balcarreas's letter gives good hopes of some material advantage at Dinan. At all events we must not have so many irons in the fire – Flanders must be our real attack on France in Europe.[13]

In 1794, George only favoured an invasion of France to aid the royalists if it could be achieved without reducing the forces in Flanders,[14] and he became more enthusiastic only as a consequence of failure in the Low Countries.[15] Dissatisfaction with Britain's allies became more pronounced from 1794.[16] George readily contrasted them with the British troops, and was clear in his views. In July, he wrote,

The Marquess Cornwallis views the state of Flanders in the same light every man of common spirit must; I own I am much tempted to encourage my son whose conduct is above all praise when he has collected the troops in the pay of Great Britain together at Gramont to consult the generals under his command whether some stroke cannot be struck to save Flanders; if they can suggest any to make the proposal to the irresolute Prince of Coburg, and then take the part of saving that fine country which would forever redound to the honour of the British name,[17]

– the last an issue that meant much to George. A contrast between the integrity of the duke of York and the cravenness of the allies was readily apparent to the king,[18] but more than integrity was at stake. Furthermore, although George sought to maintain York's command,[19] he was obliged under ministerial pressure to accept his son's recall. In 1799, George explained Austrian failure by contrasting bravery in the field with inappropriate micro-management from the centre, the latter an instance of his habitual emphasis on leadership.[20] Concern about the allies in 1794 led

---

[13] George to Dundas, 16 Nov. 1793, 11.26 p.m., BL. Add. 40100 fol. 105.

[14] George to William Grenville, 13 Sept. 1794, BL. Add. 58858 fol. 83.

[15] Memorandum by George of 30 Nov. enclosed with George to William Grenville, 1 Dec. 1794, BL. Add. 58858 fol. 113.

[16] George to Dundas, 1 July, George to William Grenville, 11, 19 Nov. 1794, 27 July, 22 Sept. 1795, 1794, BL. Add. 40100 fol. 131, 58858 fols 100, 107, 58859 fols 24, 35.

[17] George to Dundas, 7 July 1794, BL. Add. 40100 fol. 133.

[18] George to Dundas, 13 Sept., 6 Oct. 1794, BL. Add. 40100 fols 137, 141.

[19] George to William Grenville, 17 Feb. 1794, BL. Add. 58858 fol. 16.

[20] George to Dundas, 9 Oct. 1799, BL. Add. 40100 fol. 235.

George to stress the need for resolve.[21] It also accentuated the issue of where best to deploy forces. In October 1794, he wrote,

> The minute of Cabinet which Mr. Secretary Dundas has sent to me, meets with my thorough approbation, as the certainty of a large French force going to the West Indies can alone justify the sending the second detachment of the fleet lately proposed, which will be an useful increase to the fleet employed in the Mediterranean.[22]

The collapse of the Allied position on the continent in 1795, with military defeat exacerbated by Prussia's 'disgraceful'[23] abandonment of the struggle, left George, nevertheless, still resolute and also convinced that peace negotiations would be foolish:

> I am neither an advocate for entering into negotiation with the enemy till the West Indies are secured, nor for great exertions on the coast of France; but for a steady attention to obtaining our own advantages that we may be gainers by the stand we have made though betrayed by the European powers who ought to have cooperated with us, and if they had the horrid French fabric must before this time have been destroyed, now I believe its own unnatural formation will effect this if we will but be quiet and not by making peace save the [National] Convention.[24]

He had already argued that, once war had begun and an effort had been made, France must be weakened before Britain could negotiate with what he saw as a 'dangerous and faithless nation'.[25] Failure on land meant George had to consider other means to victory, including 'stopping all provisions and naval stores' by blockade and diplomatic pressure,[26] the policy of the British government against Germany in the early months of World War II. His strategic imagination combined direct and indirect pressure: Austrian successes in November 1795 led George to offer a mathematical certainty: 'I think no problem in Euclid more true than that if the French are well pressed in the next year, their want of resources and other internal evils must make the present shocking chaos crumble to pieces'.[27]

---

[21] George to William Grenville, 1 July, 21 Aug. 1794, BL. Add. 58858 fols 46, 72, cf. re. Austria to Hawkesbury, 21 May 1804, BL. Loan 72/1 fol. 121.

[22] George to Dundas, 25 Oct. 1794, BL. Add. 40100 fol. 145.

[23] George to William Grenville, 17 Apr. 1795, BL. Add. 58859 fol. 11. For similar anger later with Austria, same to same, 5 May 1797, fol. 141.

[24] George to Dundas, 11 Oct. 1795, BL. Add. 40100 fol. 157.

[25] George to William Grenville, 27 Apr. 1793, BL. Add. 58857 fol. 110.

[26] George to William Grenville, 7 June 1795, BL. Add. 58859 fol. 18.

[27] George to William Grenville, 30 Nov. 1795, BL. Add. 58859 fol. 42.

Despite setbacks, George was still certain that the war must continue in order to obtain victories that would provide a better basis for negotiations.[28] In January 1796 he returned to the charge, writing to ministers about the folly of such negotiations.[29] George was convinced that they would discourage allies. He also believed it necessary to fight on in order to make gains in the West Indies, especially the major French sugar colony of St Domingue, so as to safeguard the British position there.[30] George hoped for a peace that would sufficiently humble France to prevent her from giving Britain trouble for several years,[31] and the capture of Dutch and French colonies that year brought the king much pleasure, and the hope that they would help gain an honourable peace for Britain.[32]

The concept of honour linked George's response to the French Revolutionary War with that to the War of American Independence. George was clear that if Britain hurried to make a peace it would be 'disgraceful', and similar to that gained or sought by other powers, such as Spain and Sardinia, with which the country should not be compared.[33] Nevertheless, despite his strong opposition to peace approaches,[34] which included a rejection of the claim that they were necessary in order to confirm public support, George still had to accept them. In this, he acted in a characteristic fashion, accepting the politics of the situation while maintaining his antagonistic and self-righteous moral stance, and doing so in a way that in some circumstances threatened ministerial cohesion:

I certainly have not expressed myself clearly if what I wrote to Lord Grenville carries an idea of postponing the dispatching the messenger with the instructions that have been drawn up with the concurrence of the Cabinet; I therefore consent to his proceeding according to their advice; but I should not have acted either openly or honestly had I not expressed my own sentiments on the subject, and no reasoning of Lord Grenville on this subject could move me from that I think the line of morality though perhaps not of politics; I always chose to act on simple principles, Italian politics are too complicated paths for my understanding,[35]

[28] George to William Grenville, 27 Oct. 1795, BL. Add. 58859 fol. 38.
[29] George to Dundas, 26, 27 Jan., George to William Grenville 31 Jan. 1796, BL. Add. 40100 fols 165, 167, 58859 fols. 47.
[30] George to Dundas, 27 Jan., 17 Nov. 1796, BL. Add. 40100 fols 175, 183.
[31] George to Dundas, 2 Mar. 1796, BL. Add. 40100 fol. 177.
[32] George to Dundas, 3, 26 July 1796, BL. Add. 40100 fols 179, 181.
[33] George to Dundas, 3 July 1796, BL. Add. 40100 fol. 179.
[34] George to Pitt, 27, 31 Jan. 1796, PRO. 30/8/104 fols 88–92; Aspinall, *George III*, II, 455; J.H. Rose, *Pitt and Napoleon* (London, 1911), pp. 288–9; Stanhope, II, appendix, pp. xxxi–xxxii, George to William Grenville, 10 Apr., 23, 24 Sept. 1796, BL. Add. 58859 fols 61, 81, 84.
[35] George to William Grenville, 9 Feb. 1796, BL. Add. 58859 fol. 52.

– the last a reference to Machiavelli. The subsequent negotiations for which James, Lord Malmesbury travelled to Paris, where he arrived on 22 October 1796, did not fail because of George, but he was pleased by their failure.[36]

George again showed his concern about negotiations in 1797, characteristically adopting a moral tone in juxtaposing being 'true to ourselves' with seeking 'a momentary ease'. He feared that seeking peace would merely invite French contempt, while destroying any remaining sign of vigour among the British nation, and that negotiating a peace would leave France stronger than under Louis XIV and with the balance of power destroyed. Calculations of national interest made George argue that if peace was to be obtained it was best for Austria to make a separate peace, so that Britain would not have to surrender colonial gains in order to help Austria to better terms. On this occasion, Grenville shared his opposition. Faced with cabinet approval for negotiations, and with Pitt's argument that it was necessary to persist in a policy already begun, as well as to probe the possibility of peace, George yielded,[37] but also wanted Grenville to stay in the cabinet in order 'to starve off many further humiliations that might be attempted'.[38] Conviction that stemmed from integrity, not factiousness, a distinction to be defined by the king, was acceptable to George, as he had shown when condoning Grenville's holding a minority opinion in 1795:

> I must ever look on a difference of opinion between my ministers on a material question with sorrow; but far be it from me to wish that any of them should ever for unanimity concur in appearance when not dictated by conviction. Lord Grenville may therefore rest assured that his dissent on the present occasion will not in the least diminish my opinion of him.[39]

For George, the issue of negotiations was one in which honour and integrity were aspects of prudence, not distractions from it, and he was opposed to 'any secret treaty with the French'.[40] George saw moral factors as crucial, and to him, policy highlighted character. Dundas was praised for being 'steady', like the king, and contrasted with the 'timid', while Pitt

[36] George to William Grenville, 31 Oct., 26 Nov., 11 Dec. 1796, BL. Add. 58859 fols 92, 101–2.

[37] George to Pitt, 28 Feb., 9, 10 Apr. 1797, PRO. 30/8/104 fols 139, 157–9; George to William Grenville, 10 Apr., 1 June 1797, BL. Add. 58859 fol. 129, 58860 fol. 1.

[38] George to William Grenville, 17 June 1797, BL. Add. 58860 fol. 6; M. Duffy, 'Pitt, Grenville and the Control of British Foreign Policy in the 1790s', in J. Black (ed.), *Knights Errant and True Englishmen. British Foreign Policy 1600–1800* (Edinburgh, 1989), pp. 165–6.

[39] George to William Grenville, 9 Apr. 1795, BL. Add. 58859 fol. 4.

[40] George to William Grenville, 24 July 1798, BL. Add. 58860 fol. 97.

was seen as overly influenced by others. This was generally George's response to his first minister when he did not meet expectations, 'who I am certain has all along at bottom sided with us in opinion, for his arguments have not been of his own sterling growth but as on the Slave Trade a display of those hatched by others'.[41] Concern about ministerial character interacted with George's sensitivity to his own role, leading him to write in February 1796,

> I am much pleased at receiving Mr. Secretary Dundas's sentiments on the fate and temper that appeared in the House of Commons yesterday; but he will be surprised when I communicate to him but in the most perfect confidence that I have not received a line from Mr. Pitt on this material occasion. If the House of Commons showed the becoming spirit Mr. Dundas relates which I truly believe, that may be the reason of the silence that has occurred.[42]

With his concern for order and legitimacy, and his hostility to 'the wanton cruelty of the enemy',[43] the king was unhappy about the idea of negotiating with the French republicans, being persuaded to accept such negotiations in 1796, 1797 and 1800 only with great reluctance. He felt that victory or at least a reasonable degree of success should come first. The failure of those at Lille in September 1797 left George still hopeful that if Britain acted firmly it could win an honourable and lasting peace, helped by factional struggles in Paris and the exhaustion of French resources.[44]

George's part in encouraging ministerial resolve was shown in a letter to Pitt, characteristically dated precisely by the king to the minute. Writing at 11.10 p.m. on 8 May 1798, George noted his pleasure that George Tierney's motion in the Commons for a separate peace with France, which would have split the international coalition, had been defeated. He then expressed his support for throwing Fox out of the Privy Council for giving the toast 'Our Sovereign, the People' at a dinner of the Whig Club. Again, characteristically, George was concerned about correct form:

> I am glad to find by Mr Pitt's note that Mr Tierney's motion has been rejected by so handsome a majority. I entirely coincide in the opinion of the propriety of my striking Mr Fox's name out of the list of the Privy Counsellors; but prior notice should be given to the Lord President [of the council, Pitt's elder brother] that the book may be brought to

---

[41] George to Dundas, 6 Feb. 1796, BL. Add. 40100 fol. 169.
[42] George to Dundas, 16 Feb. 1796, BL. Add. 40100 fol. 173.
[43] George to Pitt, 4 Mar. 1797, PRO. 30/8/104 fol. 145.
[44] George to William Grenville, 2, 10 Aug. 1797, BL. Add. 58860 fols 15, 18; George to Pitt, 11 Nov. 1797, PRO. 30/8/104 fol. 197.

St James's for that purpose, which intimation I desire Mr Pitt will give to his brother.[45]

The previous year, George had shown his hard side when he insisted that the death sentences decreed for the naval mutineers who had threatened British naval capability should be enforced. This mutiny was a mass protest about conditions, particularly a failure to raise wages and the operation of the bounty system, and there was no violence. In responding to the crisis, George had encouraged George, second Earl Spencer, first lord of the admiralty, in his decision to go in person to Portsmouth to deal with the mutiny of the Channel Fleet at Spithead. While the king wanted 'any neglect that may have given reason' for discontent remedied, he was also keen on the enforcement of 'due subordination'.[46] As with the Gordon Riots in 1780, George did not minimize the crisis, and his comments were perceptive:

> The spirit seems to be of a most dangerous kind, as at the same time that the mutiny is conducted with a degree of coolness it is not void of method; how this could break out at once without any suspicion before arising seems unaccountable . . . it must require a cruise and much time before any reliance can be placed on a restoration of discipline.[47]

The original mutiny ended when many of the demands were accepted and a royal pardon was granted, but renewed disturbances on 7 May reflected the failure to fulfil governmental promises. George pointed out the unfortunate consequences of parliamentary delay in increasing naval pay, but was ready to play his governmental role. Having written at 7.50 a.m. on 9 May that he would be at home 'to receive the opinion that may come from the Cabinet by four [p.m.] that no minute may be lost in putting any measure that may be thought necessary into execution', he wrote again at 5.30 p.m., having just received the cabinet's advice that Admiral Howe go to Portsmouth, that he was ready to receive Spencer as soon as convenient to him so that 'not an instant may be lost'.[48] Once again the mutiny ended when the mutineers' complaints were met. Faced, however, by another mutiny on the ships at the Nore, which broke out on 12 May, and later by more extensive demands, George supported the Board of Admiralty in its opposition to further concessions,[49] writing on 30 May,

[45] *Maggs Catalogue* 1345, item no. 86.
[46] George to Spencer, 17 Apr. 1797, BL. Add. 75805.
[47] George to Dundas, 21 Apr. 1797, BL. Add. 40100 fol. 190.
[48] George to Spencer, 9 May 1797, BL. Add. 75805; C. Gill, *The Naval Mutinies of 1797* (Manchester, 1913).
[49] George to Dundas, 27 May 1797, BL. Add. 40100 fol. 192.

I highly approve that no concessions have been made to the mutinous ships; I trust all must now see that vigour with temper can alone restore discipline in the fleet, and the steps now taken will I trust in a little time bring the men to a sense of their duty, and that the preventing their getting fresh water will soon oblige them to submit.[50]

Erosion of support as the mutiny became more extreme ended in its collapse in early June.

George's correspondence with Spencer reveals him as a methodical dispenser of justice, ready to support his officials and keen to see order maintained. Thus, at 8.13 a.m. on 3 December 1799, he wrote to Spencer,

There cannot be a more atrocious offence than the prisoner now brought before me, namely his exciting the Dutch prisoners on board of the Pylades to rise and take possession of that sloop for the enemy. As the fact is clearly proved there cannot be a doubt of the propriety of ordering the law to take its course. I therefore desire Earl Spencer will give the necessary orders for that purpose.[51]

George similarly approved the execution of the mutineers of the frigate *Hermione*.[52] The unpopularity of the brutal and unpredictable captain Hugh Pigot led to the killing of him and nine other officers in September 1797 and the navy then devoted much effort to trying to hunt down the mutineers.[53] The key issue was 'the discipline of the navy',[54] which ensured that executions were 'melancholy though necessary'.[55] At the same time, George praised the 'humanity' of naval officers.[56]

He also publicly associated himself with the war effort. In war George took martial poses, as shown in William Beechey's massive painting of *George III Reviewing the Troops* (1793), which was destroyed in the fire at Windsor Castle on 19 November 1992. The painting depicted George, and his sons the prince of Wales and Frederick, duke of York, reviewing the 10th Hussars and the 3rd Dragoons. A print was made of the picture. A fashionable portraitist, though not the most subtle of painters, Beechey enjoyed royal favour in the 1790s, becoming portrait painter to the queen and being knighted in 1798.

[50] George to Spencer, 23, 27, 30 May 1797, BL. Add. 75805.
[51] George to Spencer, 3 Dec. 1799, BL. Add. 75829.
[52] George to Spencer, 6 July, 3 Aug. 1800, BL. Add. 75839. See also e.g. 19 Feb. 1801, BL. Add. 75848.
[53] D. Pope, *The Black Ship* (London, 1963).
[54] George to Spencer, 12 July 1800, BL. Add. 75839.
[55] George to Spencer, 5 Sept. 1800, BL. Add. 75839.
[56] George to Spencer, 8 Jan. 1795, BL. Add. 75779.

George also continued his reviews of troops. This included the volunteers who came forward in large numbers, and George's reviews helped associate him with the war effort, as well as creating personal links, transient but remembered, with large numbers; links frequently by word and, at least, by sight. On his holiday in Weymouth in 1794, George saw the Dorset Yeomanry exercise and he reviewed the Buckinghamshire Militia. Once returned to Windsor, he inspected the Surrey Yeomanry at Epsom on 24 October and the Prince of Wales's Regiment of Light Dragoons on Ashford Common on 7 November.[57]

Such opportunities satisfied George's desire to do something active. His visits to Weymouth ensured the presence of troops and warships and thus enabled George to review both. In 1804, the presence of the heavy cavalry meant that George could wear his Horse Guards uniform. That year and the next, there were also Hanoverian cavalry to review. Local lore presumably lay behind an account of George published in 1859 by William Barnes:

> He was generally up and about by 5 o'clock in the morning, and in the summer time was fond of riding a pet horse into the rooms of the Light German Legion's temporary barracks at Radipole, and would be delighted if he could catch any of them asleep, and gain over them the early riser's laugh against sluggards.[58]

Alongside the humanizing aspect of this account, there was a bleaker reality: in place of the traditional reliance in England on billeting troops in inns so that they would live 'among the people' rather than in what was seen as the militaristic practice of barracks, the government began in July 1792 a policy of purchasing or erecting barracks.[59] George's habit of early rising was commented on on other occasions in his travels, for example in Cheltenham in 1788.

The domestic radicalism that accompanied the French Revolution led to an upsurge in republicanism, with publications such as Richard Lee's pamphlet *The Death of Despotism, and the Doom of Tyrants* (1795) and his flysheet *King Killing* (1795). George's life was threatened, a background to the reconsideration of the law of treason.[60] Queen Charlotte recorded in her diary for 29 September 1794, '. . . news of a plot being discovered against the life which was to be effected by a poisoned arrow'. There was

---

[57] Queen Charlotte's diary, 5, 16, 26 Sept., 24 Oct., 7 Nov. 1794, RA. GEO/Add. 43/3; George to Dundas, 5 July 1799, BL. Add. 40100 fol. 225.

[58] 'Old Table Tales of Dorset', *Southern Times*, July 1859.

[59] J.R. Breihan, 'Barracks in Dorset during the French Revolutionary and Napoleonic Wars', *Proceedings of the Dorset Natural History and Archaeological Society*, 111 (1989), pp. 9–14.

[60] J. Barrell, *Imagining the King's Death. Figurative Treason, Fantasies of Regicide, 1793–1796* (Oxford, 2000).

indeed an alleged plot by the radical London Corresponding Society to shoot the king with a poisoned arrow fired from an airgun.[61] More seriously, although he kept his customary aplomb, George was actually affected by a mob attack on his carriage *en route* to the opening of parliament on 29 October 1795, and was also fired on by James Hadfield at Drury Lane Theatre on 15 May 1800. The king's display of composure on both occasions won him considerable praise, was widely reported, and led to a burst of loyalist sentiment, not least in Ireland where it helped ease the passage of the Act of Union.[62] Severely wounded at the battle of Roubaix in 1794, Hadfield was a millenarian who believed that his own death would ensure the Second Coming, so he set out to kill George to achieve this end. Unhurt, George resolved to speak to Hadfield who, in a vivid reminder of the unpredictability of his subjects, said 'God bless your royal highness; I like you very well; you are a good fellow.' Tried for high treason, Hadfield was shown to be at least partially deranged, and was imprisoned until he died in 1841.[63] Millenarians prophesied and desired the overthrow of the monarchy as a prelude to the creation of the New Jerusalem. Richard Brothers, for example, who wrote to George in 1792, identified the Beast of Revelations with the British monarchy. Arrested in 1795, he was declared insane and sent to an asylum.[64]

This was not the last of the attempts on George. In 1802, Edward Despard, former army officer and disappointed petitioner, plotted to seize the Tower and the Bank of England and to kill George on his way to open parliament. Betrayed by informants, the conspirators were arrested, tried and hanged. George had requested a précis of Despard's examination, had suggested that the trial be held in Surrey to avoid the independence of 'a Middlesex Jury', a lesson he had learned in the Wilkes controversy, and was glad that the Grand Jury chosen was 'composed of the principal gentlemen of the county of Surrey'.[65] Discussion of attacks and conspiracies,

[61] M. Thale (ed.), *Selections from the Papers of the London Corresponding Society 1792–1799* (Cambridge, 1983), p. 220.

[62] Lady Mary Grantham to Catherine Robinson, 11 Nov. 1795, Plymouth 1259/2/267; J. Kelly, 'Popular Politics in Ireland and the Act of Union', *Transactions of the Royal Historical Society*, 6th series, 10 (2000), p. 285.

[63] J.M. Quen, 'James Hadfield and Medical Jurisprudence of Insanity', *New York State Journal of Medicine*, 69 (1969), pp. 1221–6; R. Moran, 'The Origin of Insanity as a Special Verdict: The Trial for Treason for James Hadfield, 1800', *Law and Society Review*, 19 (1985), pp. 487–519.

[64] T. Prasch, 'Remembering the Prophets of Revolution', *Consortium on Revolutionary Europe: Selected Papers, 1997* (Tallahassee, Florida, 1997), pp. 614–15; C. Garrett, *Respectable Folly: Millenarians and the French Revolution in France and England* (Baltimore, Maryland, 1975); S. Juster, *Doomsayers: Anglo-American Prophecy in the Age of Revolution* (Philadelphia, Pennsylvania, 2003).

[65] George to Lord Pelham, Home Secretary, 20 Nov., 2 Dec. 1802, 21 Jan. 1803, BL. Add. 33115 fols 103, 108, 114.

however, should not detract from the extent to which they were unusual. If George was attacked on his way to parliament in October 1795, his journey there the following May was less tumultuous, 'There was an amazing crowd but all very quiet and orderly except some shouting which was quite proper.'[66]

George was firmly opposed to radicalism, and keen to be kept informed about its progress. At the same time as the king supported his ministry in pursuing vigorous steps abroad, he expected the same in domestic policy at home. George was aware that government was becoming more author-itarian, albeit within an established legal context,[67] and welcomed this as necessary. The king approved a legislative programme aimed at the radi-cals. Political opposition did not put him off: when the suspension of Habeas Corpus – the requirement to produce a person before a court, which prevented imprisonment without trial – was proposed in 1794, George wrote, 'I thought Mr. Dundas much too sanguine when he expected that the measure would not be opposed for though it is highly right and necessary yet being a strong measure it is open to cavil'.[68] Habeas Corpus was indeed suspended that year, a measure George defended in 1800 as 'most salutary' and 'exercised with the greatest moderation'.[69] In September 1794 he thanked Dundas

for his communication of the two letters he has received from the Advocate of Scotland on the two convictions of treason, of which I had no official account. The business seems to have been zealously and ably managed; I perfectly agree with the Advocate that the recommendation of mercy to the second must be attended to but it ought well to be weighed that it does not extend too far.[70]

The proposal in May 1794 that the London Corresponding Society remonstrate to George, outlining their grievances in the hope that he might dismiss the ministry,[71] was naïve, although the Society illustrated the difficulties facing radicals as they sought to advance a new system, while mostly remaining committed to constitutionalism. In 1795, the Treasonable Practices Act made serious criticism of the king, the govern-ment or the constitution a treasonable practice, while the Seditious Meetings Act sought to block the recourse to mass meetings, which had

[66] Theresa Parker to Catherine Robinson, 19 May 1796, Plymouth 1259/2/283.

[67] C. Emsley, 'Pitt's "Terror". Prosecutions for Sedition during the 1790s', Social History, 6 (1981), pp. 155–84.

[68] George to Dundas, 17 May 1794, BL. Add. 40100 fol. 123.

[69] George to Pitt, 20 Feb. 1800, PRO. 30/8/104 fol. 265.

[70] George to Dundas, 10 Sept. 1794, BL. Add. 40100 fol. 135.

[71] Thale (ed.), London Corresponding Society, p. 166.

been used with some effect by the radicals. These measures definitely hindered the radical societies. Furthermore, as most of the élite lined up behind the ministry, many abandoned the Whig party, which, under Fox, became an ineffective rump for the remainder of the decade. After the failure of Charles Grey's motion for parliamentary reform on 26 May 1797, Fox and his followers seceded from the Commons, and most remained away until Pitt fell in 1801.

Nevertheless, clandestine radical activity continued. Disaffection was encouraged by the strains of war, which were greatly accentuated by military failure. Pitt discovered that leadership in wartime was considerably more difficult than in the period of peacetime regeneration he had earlier helped to orchestrate. The 1796 general election was a triumph for the government,[72] with Fox's opposition to the war leading to a marked increase in the government's majority, but the cost and economic disruption of the conflict pressed hard throughout society, providing a key background to this part of the reign. Harvest failures caused serious food rioting in 1795–6 and 1800–1.[73] As well as inflation, the collapse of the gold standard, under which paper currency was met by the Bank of England in 1797, and the introduction of income tax in 1799, much of the working population was hit hard by the problems of the economy and harvest failures, with a stagnation of average real wages and widespread hardship, especially in the famine years of 1795–6 and 1799–1801. In Lancashire, the real wages of cotton weavers fell by more than half in 1792–9. Difficulties encouraged the development of trade unions. These, however, were hindered, although not disbanded, by the Combination Acts of 1799 and 1800, which made it illegal for employees to combine in seeking for improved pay or conditions. There was a nationalist dimension to radicalism in Ireland, where there was a major, though unsuccessful, rebellion in 1798, and also, to a lesser extent, in Scotland.

The year of Trafalgar, 1805, bulks large as the year of most serious threat to Britain, but the crisis of the late 1790s was more savage. If, in 1805, invasion was feared, in 1797 the same was true, and, in addition, part of the navy mutinied, Austria left the war (as it again did in December 1805), and the government's financial demands seriously reduced public confidence. Furthermore, in 1798 rebellion in Ireland was followed by French invasion there. These challenges involved a certain amount of direct criticism of the king. Irish nationalist ballads of 1798 included a parody of 'God Save the King',

---

[72] R.G. Thorne (ed.), *The House of Commons 1790–1820* (5 vols, London, 1986), I, 147–50.
[73] J. Bohstedt, *Riots and Community Politics in England and Wales, 1790–1810* (Cambridge, Massachusetts, 1983); R. Wells, *Insurrection: The British Experience, 1795–1803* (Gloucester, 1986), and *Wretched Faces: Famine in Wartime England, 1793–1801* (Gloucester, 1988).

Long live our gracious king,
To him our treasure bring,
Generous and free!
His feelings are so tough
You ne'er can bring enough;
Why keep you back the stuff,
Rebels you be.

Another added,

May we but live to see the day
The crown from George's head shall fall,
The people's voice will then bear sway
We'll humble tyrants one and all.[74]

Disaffection helped engender a sense of crisis, but was countered by a widespread loyalism that focused on the crown and that drew on a popular patriotism, although radicals also sought to appear as patriots.[75] The focus on the crown was seen in the celebration of George's birthday (4 June), which had been impressive and popular since his recovery in 1789 but was increasingly associated with the struggle with France, with George reviewing volunteers in Hyde Park on his birthday in 1799 and 1800. The birthday was also celebrated effusively outside London, for example in Nottingham in 1793.[76] The public celebration of St George's Day was also a sign of the importance of the monarchy in marking the passage of the year. George was delighted by the enthusiasm of the volunteers, commenting after an inspection in 1799 that it was 'the most loyal scene any sovereign can boast of'.[77]

George was keen to use the honours system to reward merit and success in the pursuit of victory, and his correspondence shows that he took an

[74] N.J. Curtin, The United Irishmen. Popular Politics in Ulster and Dublin, 1791–1798 (Oxford, 1994), pp. 197–8.

[75] R. Dozier, For King, Constitution and Country. The English Loyalists and the French Revolution (Lexington, Kentucky, 1983); T.P. Schofield, 'Conservative Political Thought in Britain in Response to the French Revolution', Historical Journal, 29 (1986), pp. 601–22; D. Eastwood, 'Patriotism and the English State in the 1790s', in M. Philp (ed.), The French Revolution and British Popular Politics (Cambridge, 1991), pp. 146–68; J.J. Sack, From Jacobite to Conservative: Reaction and Orthodoxy in Britain, c. 1760–1832 (Cambridge, 1993); J. Mori, 'Languages of Loyalism: Patriotism, Nationhood and the State in the 1790s', English Historical Review, 118 (2003), pp. 33–58.

[76] J.V. Beckett, 'Nottinghamshire in the 1790s', Transactions of the Thoroton Society of Nottinghamshire, 44 (1990), p. 57.

[77] George to William Grenville, 21 June 1799, BL. Add. 58861 fol. 42. See, more generally, J.E. Cookson, The British Armed Nation, 1793–1815 (Oxford, 1997).

informed interest in the process, while also underlining his belief in the significance of the prestige he controlled and conferred. To George, it was important that he should play a key role in the award of honours. This was seen in 1796 when, although the exigencies of service ensured that the naval officers who were to be distinguished with medals could not be assembled together, George was keen to add a personal touch. He approved the dispatch of the medals with a letter, but sought a change in the latter,

> to mention the cause of his being directed to forward them is the impossibility of their being distributed had I followed the inclination of giving them personally to each person, and therefore to obviate all delay had directed this method of sending them to be adopted.

George subsequently added,

> I entirely coincide with Earl Spencer in the propriety of the officers who have received the medal . . . being presented the first time they appear at St. James's with this decoration; and therefore desire he will have notice of this given to these respective officers.[78]

The sensitivity of rewards for naval officers was shown on 3 March 1797 when the proposal for a parliamentary address to George for royal favour to Admiral Jervis, after his victory over the Spanish fleet in the battle of Cape St Vincent, was withdrawn after government opposition, Pitt declaring that the Commons should not infringe the functions belonging to other branches of government, in this case the crown.[79] In January 1800, George showed his knowledge of military actions and his concern with points of status when he wrote to Spencer,

> I am truly happy at the well planned and executed enterprise of Captain Hamilton of the surprise by which the Hermione has been regained to the British list of ships; I perfectly approve of his being a knight by patent but think his conduct so deserving of record that he ought to be allowed to add to his arms some memorial of this gallant action.

Edward Hamilton had been badly wounded in recapturing the *Hermione*, which the mutineers had handed over to the Spaniards. His wound may have affected his judgement, leading to the ill-treatment of his

[78] George to Spencer, 29 Nov., 5 Dec. 1796, BL. Add. 75792.
[79] Cobbett, XXXIII, cols 2–4.

crew which resulted in his court-martial in 1802. Reinstated in 1803, he
was subsequently to be appointed to command the royal yacht *Mary*. The
use of honours was shown in April 1800, when George agreed to
Spencer's suggestion that the best way to ease Bridport from his command
was for George to mark his approval with a viscountcy. Alexander Hood
had become Lord Bridport in 1794, and in 1801 was advanced to viscount:
he had been replaced in command of the Channel Fleet by St Vincent the
previous year.[80] The combination of merit rewarded and appropriate
precedents was also important to George.[81] He kept a careful eye on
promotions in command, as he also did in the army.[82] George was insistent on proper procedures. In 1794, he complained that, unless Howe criticized Rear Admiral Benjamin Caldwell for his action in the battle of the
First of June, George could not avoid giving him the battle honours
awarded to others, as the king felt that he could not make distinction 'on
private report'.[83] Howe duly left Caldwell unmentioned in the official
dispatches, and the admiral did not receive the gold medal. Although
promoted vice-admiral that July, Caldwell was superseded in command in
the Leeward Islands in 1795 and received no further appointment.

Leadership was important to George because he believed in the place
of moral qualities in war. To him, it was not simply a matter of the
resource-based arithmetic of strength. Indeed, in 1797 he greeted news of
victory at sea with the hope that it would lead to placing 'some confidence
in naval skill and British valour to supply want of numbers. I own I am too
true an Englishman to have ever adopted the more modern and ignoble
mode of expecting equal numbers on all occasions'.[84] Resolve in his admirals was much valued by George, and he had the same view of his
generals, writing in 1793, 'I am pleased with the language of Sir Charles
Grey on being proposed for the command in the West Indies'.[85] In turn,
George himself displayed determination, arguing that failure was an
aspect of the varied fortunes of war.[86]

George's close interest in naval issues was a matter not only of correspondence with the first lord of the admiralty but also of corresponding
with, and meeting, individual admirals, for example Howe in 1795.[87] The
previous year, George had hastened to Portsmouth to congratulate his

[80] George to Spencer, 19 Jan. 1800, BL. Add. 75839.
[81] Spencer to George, 15 Apr., George to Spencer, 16 Apr., 10 Aug. 1800, BL. Add. 75839.
[82] George to Spencer, 4, 17 May, 1795, 5 Sept. 1800, BL. Add. 75779, 75839, cf. George to
Melville, 21 May 1804, BL. Add. 40100 fol. 302; George to Pitt, 26 Aug. 1804, PRO.
30/8/104 fol. 380.
[83] George to Dundas, 22 June 1794, BL. Add. 40100 fol. 127.
[84] George to Pitt, 4 Mar. 1797, PRO. 30/8/104 fol. 145.
[85] George to Dundas, 19 Aug. 1793, BL. Add. 40100 fol. 88.
[86] George to William Grenville, 20 Oct. 1793, BL. Add. 58857 fol. 166.
[87] George to Spencer, 6, 8 Jan. 1795, BL. Add. 75779.

commanders on the victory on 1 June. On 26 June, he presented Howe with a diamond-hilted sword on the deck of the *Queen Charlotte* and presented the admirals who had participated in the action with gold medals. George promised Howe the first vacant Garter, but had to yield when Pitt wanted it for political reasons to be given to Portland, an important sign of the alignment of the Portland Whigs with the government. Howe did not get the Garter until 1797. That December, George took the leading role in the Naval Thanksgiving held in St Paul's Cathedral, after he had processed in state through the thronged streets of London, a celebration for the victories of the First of June, St Vincent, and, most recently, Camperdown (over the French, Spaniards and Dutch, respectively),[88] not held after the even more dramatic victories in 1759. Captured flags were paraded through the streets by sailors and then deposited in the cathedral. The king's reception was better than that of Pitt, whose carriage was pelted. These victories deserved celebration as they lessened the chances of the repetition of a French invasion, such as that of Ireland, thwarted by bad weather in December 1796, or the small-scale landing in Pembrokeshire in February 1797. The French, however, were able to land a force in Ireland in August 1798, although it was forced to surrender the following month by a far larger British army backed by a superior fleet. George had argued in 1796 that 'whilst we are masters of the sea' any French invasion would fail.[89]

George saw personality as a key to command skills, and frequently intervened in order to offer advice on that head. In 1794, when Major-General Charles Stuart was sent to the Mediterranean, George informed Dundas that he needed to hint at the necessity of staying on good terms with the head of the fleet, 'I know Stuart is a zealous and active officer, but not wanting of high feelings therefore a little caution recommended may avoid future trouble'.[90] Stuart, Bute's favourite son, had a reputation for being tricky, but was also to be a successful commander in the Mediterranean, capturing Minorca in 1798. George rewarded Stuart by investing him with the Order of the Bath.

The king also commented on naval operations, and in 1798 Henry Pye, the mediocre poet laureate, dedicated his *Naucratia: or Naval Dominion* to George. In April 1795, the king observed 'as the Ca ira and Censeur are taken I think even Lord Hood cannot complain at the want of force in the Mediterranean' and, subsequently, after the capture of two frigates by a British squadron, that it was 'a proof of the necessity of keeping constantly detached squadrons to keep the Channel, the Bay [of Biscay],

[88] G. Russell, *The Theatres of War: Performance, Politics and Society, 1793–1815* (Oxford, 1995), p. 88; R.J.W. Knight, *The Pursuit of Victory. The Life and Achievement of Horatio Nelson* (London, 2005), pp. 260–2.

[89] George to William Grenville, 18 June 1796, BL. Add. 58859 fol. 62.

[90] George to Dundas, 24 Apr. 1794, BL. Add. 40100 fol. 119.

and [the] North Sea clear of the enemy's ships; had that measure been uniformly adopted by the Admiralty I am certain by this time the trade of France would have been totally annihilated'.[91] Samuel, Lord Hood, had demanded reinforcement to match the strengthening of the Toulon fleet, but his complaint, followed by his appeal to Pitt and Dundas to overrule Spencer, led to his dismissal. The direction of George's comments was consistently in favour of zeal, activity and taking the war to the French, as in 1795, when he wanted a naval squadron off Lorient to prevent the French from leaving the port; to George this close blockade was a necessary adjunct to the Quiberon expedition,[92] but the latter failed as a result of the lack of sufficient royalist support and the swiftness of the response by French troops. In 1798, George pressed for an effort to stop the French fleet sailing from Toulon, and in 1799 he argued for a concentration on Brest.[93]

George took an interest in naval administration, a crucial, but not the most fascinating, aspect of the war effort, writing in 1801,

> I have read over with attention the proposed plan for arranging the dockyards, one part in particular appears to me highly commendable, namely the Admiralty having advanced the salaries of the officers of the yards, which according to the establishment laid down by the Commissioners for examining the Public Affairs, certainly were not adequate to their responsibility. I therefore shall most willingly sanction the report when brought for that purpose to the Privy Council.[94]

No longer the zealous young 'Patriot King', George was not temperamentally a reformer. He was willing to support improvement, but was able to discuss anachronistic established practices without pressing for their replacement, as in 1793 when he noted 'It has ever been the custom for the Ordnance to furnish their own transports not for the Navy Board to provide them.'[95] George, nevertheless, was also interested in institutional processes and effectiveness. A supporter of incremental improvements, he was concerned at signs of inefficiency. In 1798, when invasion seemed a prospect, he approved of a proposal for improved communication between generals in charge of districts of Britain and the admiralty, arguing that 'without previous communication it is impossible that in the moment of action ideas can be so judiciously formed as at a cooler

---

[91] George to Spencer, 6, 17 Apr. 1795, BL. Add. 75779.

[92] George to Spencer, 6 July 1795, BL. Add. 75779.

[93] George to William Grenville, 29 Apr. 1798, 16 Aug. 1799, BL. Add. 58860 fol. 84, 58861 fol. 50.

[94] George to Spencer, 9 Feb. 1801, BL. Add. 75848.

[95] George to Dundas, 29 Apr. 1793, BL. Add. 40100 fol. 77.

period'.[96] Also that year, the delay in the amphibious raid on Ostend, mounted in order to destroy the lock gates of the Bruges canal and to make it harder for the French to use the canal system for invasion preparations, moved George to complain about the naval preparations. In light of the habitual modern praise of the navy, it is instructive to note George's view 'that no Board of Admiralty I ever remember seem to attend that the orders given be punctually obeyed'.[97] Six years later, George complained that 'the Public Offices . . . unfortunately instead of being in full vigour at nine in the morning they now seldom are attended even by the Clerks until Noon'.[98] Over-frequent changes in military plans raised the royal wrath.[99] Reflecting the prudence of long experience, and a caution about coastal expeditions that went back to the 1750s, George warned in 1800,

> as I have [observed] on many former occasions . . . I trust attention will be had to the real state of our forces not to fallacious states on paper which always make a greater appearance than can be depended upon when the troops are collected, and consequently that we may not trust on having a larger force than can be effected.[100]

In addition to pressing for due preparations and cautious goals,[101] George expressed a concern not generally found among the rulers of the period when he wrote about the desirability of success 'and not a wanton loss of lives'.[102]

George kept himself well informed of developments on the continent, not least through correspondence with his son, York, and through regular discussions with his Hanoverian minister, Baron Alvensleben. Queen Charlotte noted in her diary that these discussions were frequent. In late 1794, there were meetings on 28 September, 5, 12, 19 October and 7 December. This was not the sole source of news arising from the Hanoverian connection. On 16 December, Charlotte recorded, 'Today arrived Captain Bock of the Hanoverian Horse Guards with dispatches from General Wallmoden.' Charlotte also noted that George saw William Windham, the secretary at war, on 8 October on his return from the continent.

Military matters were of particular concern to George, and were evidently discussed with Charlotte. She noted on 17 October 1794 that

[96] George to Dundas, 13 Apr. 1798, BL. Add. 40100 fol. 201.

[97] George to Dundas, 14 May 1798, BL. Add. 40100 fol. 206, cf. 21 May 1804, fol. 302.

[98] George to Earl Harrowby, foreign secretary, 27 May 1804, Maggs to author, 7 Mar. 2005.

[99] George to Dundas, 25 July 1800, BL. Add. 40100 fol. 257.

[100] George to Dundas, 22 Feb. 1800, BL. Add. 40100 fol. 245; cf. 25 July fol. 257.

[101] George to Dundas, 28 July 1800, BL. Add. 40100 fol. 274.

[102] George to Dundas, 28 July 1800, BL. Add. 40100 fol. 272.

George had written to York about his anxiety over the troops' lack of discipline. On 24 November, she recorded that George understood the government's pressure for York's recall, but that he had insisted that the Hanoverian troops could only be under the control of their commander, Wallmoden Gimborn, and should never be sent to France. Lines of command were a key issue for George. In the opening British campaign of the war, George had insisted that the forces under York's command should not be made part of the Austrian-commanded Combined Army.[103] He returned to the theme in 1794:

> the troops in the pay of Great Britain must be again formed in one corps and allowed to combine operations with the Austrians but not continue acting a subordinate part; my son has strongly wrote on the subject to me, I have forwarded it to Lord Grenville . . . if this is not adopted I find a degree of ill humour arising in all these troops from the contempt and ill usage they meet with from the Imperialists that will be highly detrimental, but that can by this change be instantly removed and probably will add more activity in the exploits of the campaign.[104]

Correspondence with his 'dear son'[105] York provided a way for George to influence developments,[106] and he retained confidence in his judgement. When, in November 1794, George accepted York's recall, York was made commander-in-chief in order to save face.[107] Furthermore, York's failure in Holland in 1799 did not lead George to doubt his conduct.[108] George was keen to defend his prerogatives, including military appointments, even on distant operations. In the West Indies, disease meant that vacancies were frequent, but in 1793 George insisted that Sir Charles Grey only fill up commissions to the rank of captain and that high ranks remain vacant until he approved such recommendations as Grey might make.[109] Earlier in his career, Grey had been George's aide-de-camp before playing a major role in the American War of Independence, for which he was invested with the Order of the Bath. He was to be raised to the peerage in 1801.

Like George II, the king also took a considerable interest in army administration. In September 1794, it was this that most concerned him. He wrote from Weymouth,

[103] George to Pitt, 29 Mar. 1793, PRO. 30/8/103 fol. 488; George to Dundas, 7 Apr. 1793, BL. Add. 40100 fol. 75.

[104] George to Dundas, 25 May 1794, BL. Add. 40100 fol. 125.

[105] George to Dundas, 15 Aug. 1797, BL. Add. 40100 fol. 196.

[106] George to Dundas, 9 Dec. 1793, BL. Add. 40100 fol. 109.

[107] J. Ehrman, *The Younger Pitt: The Reluctant Transition* (London, 1983), pp. 374–5.

[108] George to Dundas, 14 Oct. 1799, BL. Add. 40100 fol. 237.

[109] George to Dundas, 10 Nov. 1793, BL. Add. 40100 fol. 101.

I object to none of the drafts but that to Lord Amherst in which a demand is made which I know to be unjust because impracticable namely that the regiments just formed must in a month be complete in officers. The measure of so rapidly forming new corps I have uniformly given my opinion against knowing that the service must suffer by it and that every regiment must be in want of officers . . . I have therefore written to Lord Amherst that when he receives that letter he is to understand I wish the officers may be fixed to the regiments without delay, but that I am confident the colonels cannot effect it in one month.[110]

In 1800, the king approved the augmentation of the Marines by five men per company, and four new companies.[111] His concern for detail had extended in 1793 to the dispatch of twenty-five troops to Walmer castle and the stockading of its ditch so that, if Pitt visited it as warden of the Cinque Ports, he should be safe against surprise.[112]

The monarchy had become a more potent symbol of national identity and continuity in response to the French Revolution. George benefited from the strength not only of loyalism, in the sense of an active opposition to democratic and republican societies, but also of loyal adherence to non-partisan principles of constitutional propriety and support for the established order.[113] In 1763, Elizabeth Montagu had expressed the hope that George would be able 'to hold the rod and the balance, and keep licentious and seditious spirits in awe'.[114] To a considerable extent, this was achieved, although awe was supported by the authority and power of the state, and the relationship between the king's personal reputation and other factors was uneasy. Nevertheless, the distancing of George from the daily processes of government that increasingly characterized the Pitt years also contributed to his growing popularity. Long-term trends reduced the active role of the monarch. Royal influence and patronage declined with the abolition of sinecures, the diminishing influence of court favourites, and the growing accountability of parliament. The political and social role of the court became less prominent.[115] The paranoid Fox, who never freed himself from ideas of royal conspiracies, nevertheless felt able to tell his nephew Holland in 1804, 'There is not a power in Europe, no not even Bonaparte that is so unlimited' as that in Britain,[116]

---

[110] George to Dundas, 13 Sept. 1794, BL. Add. 40100 fol. 137.
[111] George to Spencer, 2 Jan. 1800, Maggs to author, 7 Mar. 2005.
[112] George to Pitt, 13 July 1793, PRO. 30/8/103 fol. 502.
[113] A. Gee, *The British Volunteer Movement 1794-1814* (Oxford, 2003).
[114] Montagu to Bath, *c.* Nov. 1763, HL. MO. 4605.
[115] H. Smith, 'The Court in England, 1714-1760: A Declining Political Institution?', *History*, 90 (2005), p. 40.
[116] L.G. Mitchell, *Charles James Fox* (Oxford, 1992), p. 194.

but in practice the power was that of the government, not the monarch. The growth of business and the wider scope of government lessened the ability of one man, whether monarch or minister, to master the situation, although the king still read 'voluminous dispatches',[117] and complained when sent dispatches in boxes that he could not open.[118] With the pace of diplomacy and military business much faster as Britain sought to create and sustain coalitions against France and to wage a major war, George noted the strain: 'I have read the dispatches from Lord Malmesbury but having a little headache and consequently not my head quite so clear as necessary to possess the contents of Mylord Cornwallis's dispatches I have kept them till returned from my ride'. There was no let-up when he went to Weymouth.[119]

The scale of government encouraged the development of the cabinet, and, in turn, this increasingly served as a forum for, and focus of, differences within the ministry, replacing the king's closet. A sense of the government as his allowed George to rely upon it. Ministers were rewarded with royal favour, Pitt being appointed warden of the Cinque Ports in 1792 by a king determined not to allow him to decline the profitable post.[120] Pitt had already declined the reversion to the lucrative tellership of the exchequer and, in December 1790, the offer of the Garter. When Pitt died, George had the wardenship given to Hawkesbury, another trusted minister. George's attitude to patronage was clear: 'I never love throwing favours on enemies and love rewarding steady friends.'[121]

The longevity of the Pitt ministry was crucial in the development of the cabinet, prefiguring the extent to which that of Lord Liverpool from 1812 to 1827 helped shape George IV's kingship. From the 1790s, the discussions and decisions of the inner core of ministers, the cabinet council, became more formal. Collective responsibility and loyalty to the leading minister grew, and this strengthened the cabinet's ties with that minister and increased his power with reference to the monarch.[122] Indeed, George, who appreciated the degree to which 'the initiative in policy-making had passed to the Cabinet',[123] became concerned that the cabinet would not

[117] George to William Grenville, 23 Mar. 1794, BL. Add. 58858 fol. 24.

[118] E.g. George to William Grenville, 9 Nov. 1794, 12 Mar., 8 May, 14 Sept. 1799, BL. Add. 58858 fol. 97, 58861 fols 22, 27, 57.

[119] George to Dundas, 1 July 1794, BL. Add. 40100 fol. 131, cf. to William Grenville, 5 Apr. 1796, 1 Aug. 1800, BL. Add. 58859 fol. 60, 58861 fol. 119.

[120] George to Dundas, 6 Aug. 1792, BL. Add. 40100 fol. 49.

[121] George to Dundas, 9 Sept. 1792, BL. Add. 40100 fol. 59.

[122] A. Aspinall, *The Cabinet Council 1783–1835* (London, 1952); J. Mori, *William Pitt and the French Revolution 1785–1795* (Basingstoke, 1997), p. 270.

[123] C.R. Middleton, 'The Impact of the American and French Revolutions on the British Constitution: A Case Study of the British Cabinet', *Consortium on Revolutionary Europe. Selected Papers 1986* (Athens, Georgia, 1987), p. 321.

be informed of his views before deciding their final opinion on important issues.[124] Anxiety over this influenced George's response when Catholic emancipation was raised in 1801.

Anger with what he saw as the opposition's lack of public spirit,[125] however, restricted George's options in complaining about the Pitt ministry so long as the latter was united. Conversely, a lack of ministerial unity could strengthen the king's position with respect to the cabinet, as with the clash between George and Pitt over emancipation in 1801. By then, cabinet cohesion among the weary and stressed ministers was lacking, and emancipation was a fresh cause of uncertainty and division. In so far as this made a change of government necessary,[126] it threw the role of the monarch into prominence.

Personal factors were central to the shift towards a habitually smaller role for the monarch. The impact of the regency crisis and George's later illnesses interacted with that of Pitt's longevity in office. As a consequence, greater cabinet cohesion and influence, and a consistent united cabinet control of policy-making were more a feature from the 1790s onwards than they had been in the 1780s; this was not to be reversed when George IV or William IV came to the throne in 1820 and 1830 respectively. In 1796, when George gave way over peace approaches to France, he appears to have been affected by the difficulty of retaining a grip on the range and complexity of international relations. His age probably accentuated the situation, but agreement between Pitt and Grenville on pressing the king was also a factor.[127] Pitt gained from his accumulated experience in managing George, not least a preference for doing so in letters rather than meetings, while the position of the king was affected by ministerial shifts, especially the fall of Thurlow in 1792 and the incorporation of the Portland Whigs into the cabinet in 1794. When, in 1799, Dundas informed George that he wanted to give up the War Department in order to concentrate on the East Indies, George replied that he could not comment until Pitt approved the step.[128] As well as his lesser role in government, George also reduced the number of court days after the regency crisis. Partly as a result, but also reflecting social shifts, especially the broadening of the establishment, the centrality of the court in public life declined before his final illness.

George's health – not only his illness but also the fear that it might recur – shaped responses to the king, as did his lengthy absences in Weymouth. George did not necessarily see this as a disadvantage. In 1794 he

[124] George to Pitt, 9 Apr. 1797, PRO. 30/8/104 fol. 157.

[125] George to Pitt, 11 May 1797, PRO. 30/8/104 fol. 173.

[126] C.J. Fedorak, *Henry Addington, Prime Minister, 1801–1804* (Akron, Ohio, 2002), p. 29.

[127] M. Duffy, *The Younger Pitt* (Harlow, 2000), pp. 36–7.

[128] George to Dundas, 9 Dec. 1799, BL. Add. 40100 fol. 243.

responded to a report that the sickly Grenville would join him in Weymouth by remarking, 'I cannot see any reason why the foreign correspondence may not be as well prepared here as in London', and by recommending the bathing for Grenville's health.[129] However much George may have intended to reassure Grenville with his first remark, it was not credible. Apart from distance from the centre of administration when in Weymouth, the need for speed in responding to international crises was also a factor affecting George's role. In 1790, the speech which George had agreed for the prorogation of parliament was changed by Pitt and Grenville, while Grenville did not wait to notify George before issuing news of the Spanish Declaration signed on 24 July as that would have provided an opportunity for stockjobbing, and the king approved this course:

> Mr. Grenville would not have followed that judicious line of conduct I ever expect from him, had he not felt I must approve of his not an instant delaying sending the usual notices of the signature of the Spanish Declaration, that the effects of stockjobbing may be prevented.[130]

Two years later, in response to the loyalism engendered by the crisis caused by rising radicalism and the outbreak of war on the continent, George was happy to use ministers and the publication of messages, rather than act himself, although this decision was seen in terms of the convenience of others:

> It must be infinitely more pleasant to the gentlemen whose zeal may incline them to forward addresses on the present occasion to transmit them to the Secretary of State than take the trouble of coming back to town to deliver them personally to me. I therefore think Mr. Dundas should inform them that the transmitting them to him to lay them before me is the mode that will be looked on as the most proper, and he need not send them but let them be printed in the Gazette.[131]

George's correspondence with Dundas, Spencer and York ensured that he was able to express views on the key topic of the war.[132] Nevertheless, George continued his usual position of leaving matters to ministers, not least because he was at a distance, in Windsor let alone Weymouth, yet remonstrating when he did not like what they did. This was a character-

---

[129] George to William Grenville, 17, 21 Aug. 1794, BL. Add. 58858 fols 69, 72.

[130] George to William Grenville, 10 June, 5 Aug. 1790, BL. Add. 58855 fols 110, 135, cf. George to Dundas, 1 July 1792, BL. Add. 40100 fol. 43.

[131] George to Dundas, 5 June 1792, BL. Add. 40100 fol. 33.

[132] George to Dundas, 28 Oct. 1799, BL. Add. 40100 fol. 239.

istic feature of his kingship, stemming from George's sense of the nature of the constitution, yet a practice that could also be seriously disruptive. At times, George's remonstrations could be very bitter, for example in 1800 when the king firmly opposed the cabinet proposal to send an expedition to Ferrol and Cadiz in order to cripple Spanish naval power. Pitt was furious. George was also very opposed to the expedition to Egypt, although, landing in March 1801, it became the most successful British land operation in the Revolutionary War, leading that August to the capitulation of the French army in Egypt.

In the case of Catholic emancipation, George also complained that he was not informed about discussions,[133] an aspect of his dissatisfaction with increasing inattention on the part of Pitt, who did not attend sufficiently often at the royal levees, and also seemed to write insufficiently frequently.[134] In 1797, in his caricature *Their New Majesties* Newton had shown the throne as occupied by Dundas and a crowned Pitt. In the case of emancipation, indeed, the exhausted Pitt did not really try to overcome the king's opposition.[135] Conversely, Pitt felt that George was listening to others and breaching the correct pattern of constitutional advice, a revival of the long-held concern about secret advisers destabilizing government, and also a product of Pitt's detachment from the court.[136] This interacted with the long-standing difference between the two men over political theory. In relation to the issue of parliamentary reform, this had been contained, but in the 1790s further opportunities arose for uneasiness. Pitt had no time for ultra-Tory positions extolling monarchy, such as *Thoughts on the English Government* (1795) by John Reeves. This presentation of the monarchy as the only essential feature of government was attacked by the opposition and repudiated by Pitt.[137]

Foreign policy was also an issue. George confided to Addington in January 1801 that he had been unhappy with British foreign policy for over two decades, at least in so far as relations with Russia were concerned. This would include the response to the Russian-led armed neutrality during the War of American Independence, 'the most inimical measure adopted by any nation',[138] as well as the Ochakov crisis of 1791; indeed, in 1785 the king had expressed a critical view of Catherine the

---

[133] George to Addington, 7 Feb. 1801, Exeter, 152M/C1801/OR 61, cf. to William Grenville, 6 Feb., and to Dundas, 7 Feb., BL. Add. 58862 fol. 76, 40100 fol. 300.

[134] J. Ehrman, *The Younger Pitt: The Consuming Struggle* (London, 1996), p. 522.

[135] P. Mackesy, *War without Victory: The Downfall of Pit 1799–1802* (Oxford, 1984), p. 199.

[136] Ehrman, *Pitt . . . Consuming Struggle*, pp. 520–1.

[137] A.V. Beedell, 'John Reeves's Prosecution for a Seditious Libel, 1795–6: A Study in Political Cynicism', *Historical Journal*, 36 (1993), pp. 799–824, esp. 820–3. See also D. Eastwood, 'John Reeves and the Contested Idea of the Constitution', *British Journal for Eighteenth-Century Studies*, 16 (1993), pp. 197–212.

[138] George to William Grenville, 19 Mar. 1793, BL. Add. 58857 fol. 104.

Great's policy then and over the previous twenty years.[139] In 1801, George characteristically wanted vigour:

> The present situation of this kingdom with the Northern Powers requires every degree of exertion . . . I have long wished to bring it to an issue, and have not admired the constant attempt for above twenty years to avoid it, which has only on the present occasion, brought it forward with more force: but if properly understood, we must get the better . . . if this will not rouse men, we are fallen low indeed.[140]

However much he might feel neglected, George had an impact across the range of government, and he was kept informed of secret plans.[141] Richard, earl of Mornington, who became governor-general in India in 1797 (where, thanks in part to the generalship of his brother, the future duke of Wellington, in 1803, he was to expand British power greatly), was made aware of George's interest:

> from the King, I have received the most gracious declaration of approbation, and especially of the manner in which I had withstood the temptation of carrying out a train of followers, and filling my hands with engagements from Europe.[142]

George saw his ministers when in London. On 11 February 1801, for example, he held a levee at St James's, attended the Privy Council, where the sheriffs were picked for the following year, and gave an audience to his cabinet ministers. Nevertheless, although the forms remained, the king's role in the nuances of politics was not as pronounced as it had been prior to the Pitt ministry. In 1801 he played a greater part in response to the political crisis he had helped cause, but not as an aspect of the normal conduct of monarchy in recent years.

George's obduracy created problems for his ministers, not only over peace negotiations, but also when, in the 1790s and 1800s, he opposed the extension of rights to Catholics in Ireland and Britain, although in Ireland, under the Catholic Relief Act, they had been given the vote in

[139] George to Pitt, 7 Aug. 1785, PRO. 30/8/103 fol. 172, Manchester, John Rylands Library, Eng. Mss. 912 no. 32. For belief that George was responsible for anti-Russian moves, La Luzerne to Montmorin, 3 June 1788, AE. CP. Ang. 565 fol. 235, Barthélemy to Montmorin, 29 July 1788, AE. CP. Ang. 566 fol. 115.

[140] George to Addington, 15 Jan. 1801, Exeter, 152M/C1801/OR 4, cf. to Dundas, 15 Jan., BL. Add. 40100 fol. 297, to William Grenville, 26 Aug. 1800, BL. Add. 58861 fol. 133, and to Hawkesbury, 9 May 1801, BL. Loan 72/1 fol. 77.

[141] Dundas to George, 23 Jan. 1797, RA. GEO/8315, George to Dundas, 24 Jan. 1797, BL. Add. 40100 fol. 186.

[142] Mornington to William Pole, 31 Oct. 1797, BL. Add. 37924 fol. 10.

1793 and the right to hold certain lower-level public appointments. Pitt's cabinet backed the measure in 1793 and there is no sign that the king opposed it. The legislation did not include the right to sit in parliament, which was seen as crucial to full emancipation, but it was considered by the government to have settled the Irish question. There was no fear of rebellion and the political atmosphere was such that all of the regular battalions and half of the regiments of cavalry serving in Ireland in 1793 had gone abroad by mid-1795. Catholic militia forces were now seen as a valuable resource.[143]

In 1795, William, second Earl Fitzwilliam, the new lord-lieutenant, sought to remove the remaining legal disabilities affecting Irish Catholics, but was disavowed and recalled by the cabinet. This ensured that there was no clash between ministry and king: George had expressed his firm opposition to Fitzwilliam's proposals, presenting them as a threat to the Protestant settlement rashly advanced by an inexperienced lord-lieutenant.[144] Fitzwilliam, Rockingham's nephew and heir and a Portland Whig, had believed that concessions were necessary in order to block the spread of Jacobinism in Ireland, and his failure, accompanied by a pro-active policy on possible internal discontent, strengthened the alienation of Irish Catholic opinion, contributing to the rebellion in 1798. The unsuccessful rebellion demonstrated that the ascendancy could not keep Ireland stable, and encouraged the British government to support union. Like the 1707 Union with Scotland, union with Ireland was a wartime response by politicians in London to the danger of divergence, specifically a fear that Britain would be weakened in her conflict with France by an unstable Ireland.[145] The Act of Union of 1800, which came into effect on 1 January 1801, dissolving the separate Irish parliament in return for Irish representation at Westminster, however, made the rights of Catholics a central issue in Britain.

The king strongly supported union as 'one of the most useful measures that has been effected during my reign',[146] but, criticizing past 'indulgence' to Irish Catholics,[147] did not accept the extension of Catholic rights some

---

[143] T. Bartlett, ' "A weapon of war as yet untried": Irish Catholics and the Armed Forces of the Crown, 1760–1830', in T.G. Fraser and K. Jeffery (eds), *Men, Women and War* (Dublin, 1993), pp. 66–85.

[144] George to Pitt, 10 Mar. 1795, PRO. 30/8/104 fol. 7. E.G. Tenbus, 'Crisis in Ireland: The Tenure of Lord Fitzwilliam, 1794–1795', *Consortium on Revolutionary Europe: Selected Papers, 1998* (Tallahassee, Florida, 1998), pp. 149–57.

[145] G.C. Bolton, *The Passing of the Irish Act of Union* (London, 1966); T. Bartlett, *The Fall and Rise of the Irish Nation: The Catholic Question, 1690–1830* (Dublin, 1992); J.E. Cookson *The British Armed Nation 1793–1815* (Oxford, 1997); conference proceedings, 'The British–Irish Union of 1801', *Transactions of the Royal Historical Society*, 6th ser., 10 (2000), pp. 165–408.

[146] George to Pitt, 6 May 1800, PRO. 30/8/104 fol. 277.

[147] George to Pitt, 11 June 1798, PRO. 30/8/104 fol. 237.

of his ministers, particularly Dundas and, less consistently, Pitt, believed necessary if it was to work.[148] George had been opposed to Catholic emancipation in Ireland in 1795, and was even more so when it was a case of Britain as a whole. The argument that Catholic MPs would be a minority in the new parliament was unacceptable to the king, who had informed Pitt in January 1799 that he would oppose emancipation.[149] Arguing that the move would breach his coronation oath to protect the position of the established Church, a moral qualm that reflected religious concerns, and that it would also produce fresh demands from Ireland and eventually lead to a separation of Britain and Ireland,[150] George stated that he would not give royal assent to such legislation, evidence that the royal veto on legislation was still active. He wrote: 'it is a principle of the strongest nature, that of religious and political duty that has alone guided the King through the present most unpleasant scene'.[151] In January 1799, George also responded angrily to the offer to the Catholic hierarchy in Ireland from Cornwallis, the viceroy, of financial support in return for a veto on episcopal appointments.[152] In contrast, he was concerned about the state of the (Protestant) established Church in Ireland, which he hoped would be able to draw in Catholic support.[153]

George argued that the position of the Church of England rested on fundamental parliamentary legislation, and therefore that any change would challenge the constitutional safeguards that were similarly founded and secured. George claimed that emancipation would destroy the established Church, but felt it necessary not only to refer to his coronation oath, the subject of a supportive pamphlet by John Reeves, *Considerations on the Coronation Oath* (1791), but also to what he saw as prudential arguments: 'This idea of giving equal rights to all Christian Churches is contrary to the law of every form of government in Europe for it is well known that no quiet could subsist in any country where there is not a Church Establishment.' In 1801, George indicated that if the measure was not withdrawn he would publicly oppose it, not least by summoning Henry Addington, the Speaker of the Commons, to see him.[154] This opposition helped to precipitate Pitt's resignation in 1801 and, later, the fall of the Grenville ministry (the Ministry of All the Talents) in 1807, although the

[148] F. Bickley (ed.), *The Diaries of Sylvester Douglas, Lord Glenbervie* (2 vols, London, 1928), I, 152.

[149] Aspinall, *George III*, III, 186.

[150] George to Pitt, 6 Feb. 1795, PRO. 30/8/103 fols 597–8.

[151] George to Spencer, 9 Feb. 1801, BL. Add. 75848.

[152] P.M. Geoghegan, 'The Catholics and the Union', *Transactions*, 10 (2000), p. 251.

[153] George to Pitt, 19 July 1800, PRO. 30/8/104 fol. 293; George to Philip, third earl of Hardwicke, 10 May 1801, BL. Add. 35349 fol. 75.

[154] George to Pitt, 13 June 1798, PRO. 30/8/104 fol. 239; George to Addington, 29 Jan. 1801, Exeter, 152M/C1801/OR 39.

Pitt ministry was already very divided both on military strategy and on foreign policy.

In the event, Catholics could not become MPs in the new parliament created by the Anglo-Irish Union until 1829, an event that allowed carica-turists, such as William Heath in *Finis* and Charles Williams in *My Father's Ghost, or, A Voice from the Grave*, to contrast the stance of George III with the reluctant willingness of George IV to accept the measure. This delay may have undermined the union by strengthening and focusing Catholic resentment; although a fair share of informed British political opinion thought it could go forward on that narrow basis, and there was no mass petitioning for a change in government policy akin to that seen in the early stages of the War of American Independence. When George was born, most European countries still refused to tolerate religious minorities. If, as is sometimes claimed, George was recruited by the Enlightenment, his conservative stance should have been modified in the light of ideological developments from the 1760s (as occurred in 1780s France *vis-à-vis* the Protestant minority, the Huguenots). But it seems clear that a majority of the House of Lords shared his unprogressive attitudes, and, once again, he may have been keen not to get too far ahead of public opinion, in this case the opinion brutally displayed in the Gordon Riots but over the cause of emancipation not acting outside the law. Enlightened causes were not on the whole popular in eighteenth-century Europe, a view strengthened by the response to the French Revolution. The politician most associated with such causes, Shelburne, was possibly the most distrusted. Part of the problem is the overly coherent customary definition of the Enlightenment, and the tendency to assume a level of consistency and homogeneity. In practice, there was a series of overlapping, but not coterminous, enlight-enments, with attitudes to religion being a particular source of variety. A penchant for telescopes and barometers scarcely made George a supporter of the full range of enlightened views on religious matters. He was an enlightened figure in some resects but not in others.

The crown's patronage network already embraced Ireland, and George had taken considerable pains to use it to ensure good government and to bind the social élite there to the monarchy. Irish representation under the union was to be based largely on land, and George's role in élite social politics was valuable in this sphere. Due to his position on emancipation, the king is often seen as a negative force, but he sought to make union work. George himself supported a redrawing of ministerial responsibilities intended to underline the importance of the union. Appointed home secretary, Thomas, Lord Pelham, later second earl of Chichester, was informed by the king that the colonies had been transferred from his to the War Department, in part because of 'the additional business which ought hourly to increase in the Home Department from the Union with Ireland', which, contrary to later nationalist perceptions, was not treated as a colony. George added the next day, the King is convinced that every step that can in the arranging public business blend Ireland into a part of this kingdom is the only means of really consolidating the Union now in *words* effected, and on that principle highly approves of the revocation of the article in the Lord Lieutenant of Ireland's instructions that clash with the Master General of the Ordnance's powers.[155]

At the same time, George was opposed to emancipation as well as the proposed state support for the Catholic and Presbyterian Churches, and this issue led to, or at least precipitated, the fall of the ministry. George did not want Pitt to leave office, but was unwilling to give 'way where conscience and every duty to the country point out the culpability that must attend the King's departing from what he feels to be his religious and civil duty'.[156] Other influential figures thought George mistaken. William Grenville wrote of the ministry's resignation in 1801,

[There is] a firm conviction in our mind that the removal of the remaining disqualifications which still affect the Catholics was necessary in order to complete the measure of the Union and was a just return for the support which that body had afforded us in carrying through the Union itself: and further that whatever difficulties any man thinks he sees in the present situation of the country . . . the propriety of endeavouring to attach the mass of the population of Ireland to the new united Government was increased by them: and therefore that the measure was no less pressing in point of time than expedient and wise in itself. To all these was opposed an invincible repugnance in the King's mind, grounded in a mistaken but respectable principle of adherence to what he conceives to be the sense of his coronation oath. The question was one which admitted of no compromise, and the time was of the essence of the question itself. Under these circumstances men of honour and public principle could do no otherwise than we have done.[157]

Other factors, however, also played a major role in the crisis of the ministry. Serious disagreements over strategy between Dundas, who favoured amphibious operations, and Grenville, the supporter of continental interventionism, ended in a division that Pitt could not resolve and that he found demoralizing. Against this background, likely governmental divisions over peace may have made Pitt readier to resign, while opposition to him may have stemmed from concern on the part of both minis-

[155] George to Pelham, 7, 8 Aug. 1801, BL. Add. 33115 fols 7, 11.
[156] George to Addington, 1 Feb. 1801, Exeter. 152M/C1801/OR 27.
[157] William Grenville to Wellesley, 20 Feb. 1801, BL. Add. 70927 fol. 80.

terial colleagues and the king about the nature of policy-making.[158] By 1800–1, despite George's confidence in Divine Providence,[159] the second coalition against France, formed in 1799, was failing. This helped cause a weakening of government cohesion, or at least an uncertainty of purpose. There had never been complete agreement within ministerial ranks as how best to deal with France and domestic radicals, but differences became more serious, and fresh occasions for disputes arose, as peace with France became again a pressing issue. The approach for peace from Napoleon at the close of 1799 was rejected, but decisive French victories over the Austrians at Marengo (14 June) and Hohenlinden (3 December) in 1800 made it clear that the war could not be waged successfully in Europe.[160]

Serious divisions over the possibility of a genuine peace, and over the terms that should be agreed, made it harder to conceal or contain long-standing differences. Initially confident that Napoleon, who had seized power in a 'shameless revolution' on 9–10 November 1799,[161] could not 'hold long',[162] George was against peace while 'French principles' continued and until there was a stable government on which reliance could be placed,[163] criticized the proposal for a naval armistice and distrusted 'the Corsican tyrant', believing that negotiations with him would discourage allies and that peace would be only an armed neutrality.[164] Indeed, in August 1800 George appears to have considered a ministerial change, with William Windham, the talented secretary at war, replacing Pitt, who wanted peace.[165] Characteristically, George saw his view as uniquely principled, not least because he emphasized his consistency: 'My opinion is formed on principle not on events and therefore is not open to change.'[166]

Yet the Catholic question was the crucial precipitant of a tension between closet and cabinet, king and first minister, focusing on the nature of power. George chose to see its supporters as enemies,[167] and told Dundas this in a loud voice at his levee on 28 January 1801. George had

---

[158] R. Willis, 'William Pitt's Resignation in 1801', *Bulletin of the Institute of Historical Research*, 44 (1971), pp. 239–57; Mackesy, *War without Victory*.

[159] George to William Grenville, 26 May 1799, BL. Add. 58811 fol. 38.

[160] P.W. Schroeder, 'The Collapse of the Second Coalition', *Journal of Modern History*, 59 (1987), pp. 271–82.

[161] George to William Grenville, 24 Nov. 1799, BL. Add. 58861 fol. 64.

[162] George to William Grenville, 20 Nov. 1799, BL. Add. 58861 fol. 61.

[163] George to Pitt, 28 June 1800, PRO. 30/8/104 fol. 287; Pitt to Dundas, 28 July 1800, BL. Add. 40100 fol. 272.

[164] George to William Grenville, 1 Jan., 27 June, 26 Aug., George to Dundas, 16 Sept. 1800, BL. Add. 58861 fols 81, 108, 133, 40100 fol. 278.

[165] Mackesy, *War without Victory*, p. 139.

[166] George to Pitt, 28 June 1800, PRO. 30/8/104 fol. 287.

[167] Bickley (ed.), *Diaries of . . . Glenbervie*, I, 147.

responded angrily to the presence of Robert, Viscount Castlereagh, an
active supporter of emancipation, declaring to Dundas,

> What is this catholic emancipation which *this young lord, this Irish secretary*
> has brought over, that you are going to throw at my head? I will tell, that
> I shall look on every man as my personal enemy who proposes that
> question to me.[168]

This was a reprise of the method against the government employed in
December 1783, but now George took a more direct role. On 31 January
1801, Pitt, whose qualities George had praised three days earlier,[169] told
the king that he would resign unless he could introduce a Catholic Relief
Bill into parliament 'with the whole weight of Government'. Five days
later, George accepted his resignation. Certain that his opposition to
emancipation was correct,[170] the king, nevertheless, was saddened by the
crisis. He blamed Pitt, but wrote to him with regret and without reserve,
beginning 'My Dear Pitt, as you are closing much to my sorrow your
political career'.[171] The new century had already brought yet another
constitutional challenge and ministerial revolution.

[168] Willis, 'Pitt's Resignation', p. 252.
[169] Bickley (ed.), *Diaries of . . . Glenbervie*, I, 148.
[170] George to Pitt, 1 Feb. 1801, PRO. 30/8/104 fols 320–1.
[171] George to Pitt, 18 Feb. 1801, PRO. 30/8/104 fol. 330.

Chapter 18

LAST YEARS, 1801–20

At sixty-six we may still give seasonable advice but the activity of
execution is better done by the vigour of youth.

George, December 1804[1]

The new century brought new titles, in part as a consequence of the Act
of Union with Ireland. Having turned down the idea of becoming
'Emperor of the British Isles', George became king of 'the United
Kingdom of Great Britain and Ireland'. In return, George was the last
ruler of Britain ever to use the title of 'King of France'. This claim, first
advanced by Edward III in 1340, was finally dropped from the royal style
in 1801. The *Courier* of 2 January 1801 noted, 'The arms on the royal
carriages are all altered. The fleur de lis [for France] is left out, in lieu of
which the Electoral cap [for Hanover] is introduced; the shamrock [for
Ireland] is also introduced in the different orders.' As a sign of a marked
shift in the direction of challenge to the Hanoverian dynasty, and the
dominance of the republican threat, George's sympathy for the Stuarts led
to financial support for the Jacobite claimant from 1788, 'Henry IX', the
second son of 'James III and VIII'. Although referred to by Henry as the
Elector of Hanover, George helped 'that unfortunate man'[2] with a
pension from 1800 until his death in 1807, and also purchased the Stuart
papers. As Henry was a Catholic cleric who did not renounce the cloth
and marry, he posed no dynastic threat.

Government and politics continued without Pitt. In his sixties, George
was still playing a central role. The establishment of a new ministry in
1801 gave George the opportunity to take a more active part in government, but this was also necessary if a stable ministry was to be created. It
was as if the political world had not changed from the outset of the North
ministry in early 1770, or that of Pitt at the close of 1783, but, as already
indicated (pp. 368–9), there had been important developments in the
meanwhile, and, alongside the particular circumstances of the moment,
they were to help ensure that the Addington ministry would be short-lived.
George himself remained convinced that politics was a struggle of good

---

[1] George to Hawkesbury, 19 Dec. 1804, BL. Loan 72/1 fol. 130.
[2] George to William Grenville, 24 Nov. 1799, BL. Add. 58861 fol. 64.

versus evil, one in which Providence played a key role. In 1801, he wrote about the victory in Egypt to Charles Jenkinson, since 1796 first earl of Liverpool,

> I feel most fully the honour that must accrue to the British army, but give me credit for saying that I more weigh on the manifest interposition of Divine Providence in a just cause, and for the destruction of the enemies of His Holy Word and of all civil and domestic happiness.[3]

Good versus evil, however, did not provide an easy basis for policy and politics. Concerned to do the proper thing, and interested in proper precedents for titles and arms,[4] George sought to accommodate change to accustomed order. This was not only a matter of lineage and social order. George was also opposed to unnecessary governmental change, writing to Thomas, Lord Pelham, the new home secretary, in 1801,

> The papers the King now returns to Lord Pelham fully explain the propriety of the line of conduct proposed to be adopted on their contents. It seems but too probable that the inclination of Mr. Abbot to innovations in the modes of conducting business in this country has accompanied him to Ireland, and renders his being decidedly prevented from continuing that career before it becomes more detrimental to the public service.[5]

Charles Abbot had been active as an MP in Westminster, introducing much legislation, including the first Census Act in 1800, before being appointed chief secretary for Ireland. He was similarly active in Ireland, but was recalled to become Speaker of the Commons in February 1802, a post he held until 1816. George's suspicion is instructive as they shared an opposition to Catholic emancipation. At the same time, the episode reflected George's industry. He was ready, as he told Pelham, to read 'voluminous' papers,[6] while his oversight of government enabled him to make qualitative statements about the conduct of business: 'The King cannot help remarking that since the very judicious appointment of Mr. [Charles] Yorke to be Secretary at War that there is an appearance of regularity in the War Office which was much wanted.'[7]

An awareness of the role of personalities and a feeling for how best to manage them can be seen in the king's correspondence, as when he suggested to Pelham, whom he had earlier thought an impressive chief

---

[3] George to Liverpool, 30 Apr. 1801, BL. Add. 38564 fol. 41.
[4] George to Pelham, 29 Sept., 10 Oct. 1801, BL. Add. 33115 fols. 16, 18.
[5] George to Pelham, 20 Oct. 1801, BL. Add. 33115 fol. 24.
[6] George to Pelham, 19 Oct. 1801, BL. Add. 33115 fol. 22.
[7] George to Charles Yorke, 1 May 1801, BL. Add. 35644 fol. 77.

secretary in Ireland,[8] that he prevent a possible dispute with Philip, third earl of Hardwicke, the newly appointed lord-lieutenant of Ireland, over the status of the latter:

I desire Lord Pelham will in a private letter to the Earl of Hardwicke acquaint him fully with the cause, for he is a little subject to feel strongly when not fully master of a subject; and perhaps a friendly intercourse of letters may greatly forward the business of Ireland and by degrees bring it into the desirable state which it is unfortunate was not from the first hour of the Union established.[9]

In offering advice, George also displayed his conviction of the importance of moral factors in appointments:

Mr. Addington must not think the King will necessarily take up his time with letters, but at the outset of our business it would be highly wrong to have anything omitted that occurs. The more the King reflects on the conversation of last night and the proposed arrangements the more he approves of them; but he blames himself in having omitted to mention the natural nay necessary return of the Marquess of Cornwallis from Ireland; he well knows many have thought the office of Lord Lieutenant should altogether cease on such an event; the King's opinion is clearly that perhaps hereafter that may be proper but that at present it is necessary to fill up that office with a person that shall clearly understand that the Union has closed the reign of Irish jobs, that he is a kind of President of the Council there and that the civil patronage may be open to his recommendation but must entirely be decided in England. Earl Chatham if he can be persuaded is the man whose honour, rectitude of mind, and firmness is best calculated for that station, particularly from his love for the military profession.[10]

In Francis Bartolozzi's engraving of 1800, *King George III*, a serene George rests in the clouds above Britannia and the British lion. George's recovery after his 1788 attack of porphyria seems to have been only partial, but he was generally seen as having good health in the 1790s. When unable to go to St James's in October 1792, it was only 'a cold with a little complaint in my bowels'.[11] A suggestion that all had not been well was offered on 3 February 1801 when, at the opening of parliament, 'the King looked

[8] George to Pitt, 13 June 1798, PRO. 30/8/104 fol. 239.
[9] George to Pelham, 8 Aug. 1801, BL. Add. 33115 fol. 11.
[10] George to Addington, 11 Feb. 1801, Exeter, 152M/C1801/OR 38; George to Philip, third earl of Hardwicke, 8, 10 May 1801, BL. Add. 35349 fols 73–5.
[11] George to William Grenville, 4 Oct. 1792, BL. Add. 58857 fol. 49.

particularly well, and read his speech with particular energy and clearness, much beyond what has been usual with him for the last ten or fifteen years'.[12] However, in 1797, John, second Lord Boringdon, reported that George delivered his answer to a joint address of the houses of parliament 'in a remarkably firm, impressive and even animated manner'.[13] Nevertheless, George's vigour was less apparent than it had been prior to 1788,[14] although he was of course older. George still exercised; in 1790, Viscount Sydney reported,

> His Majesty's health continues as good as possible, and from the diminution, though not very considerable, which he has made in his exercise, and the reasonable improvement he has made in his diet, he is really much better than he has been for many years.[15]

George had certainly learned from his own experiences and revealed sympathy for mental illness, writing of General William Medows, whose unsuccessful leadership had initially compromised Cornwallis's attack on Seringapatam and caused Medows to attempt suicide in 1792, 'Happy, very happy am I indeed at the communication of Major General Medows's two letters to Mr. Dundas. They show a mind of a most delicate frame but completely restored to its wonted good sense and cheerfulness.'[16] Medows indeed was made a knight of the Bath, and, in 1793, a lieutenant-general. At a more junior level, George wrote to Spencer in 1796,

> I have received this morning the box containing the proceedings of a court martial on a midshipman of the Sandwich for an attempt to stab the first Lieutenant of that ship; but as it appears so clearly that the unhappy man is at times afflicted with fits of insanity I approve of his being pardoned provided his friends will properly confine him, that he may not do mischief to others.[17]

The king also argued that a bout of a dangerous illness might in the end prove advantageous to general health.[18]

---

[12] F. Bickley (ed.), *The Diaries of Sylvester Douglas, Lord Glenbervie* (2 vols, London, 1928), I, 153.

[13] Boringdon to Catherine Robinson, 16 Nov. 1797, Plymouth 1259/2/350.

[14] J. Mori, *William Pitt and the French Revolution 1785–1795* (Basingstoke, 1997), p. 270.

[15] Sydney to Cornwallis, 27 Jan. 1790, C. Ross (ed.), *The Correspondence of Charles, First Marquis Cornwallis* (3 vols, London, 1859), II, 29.

[16] George to Dundas, 27 July 1792, BL. Add. 40100 fol. 46.

[17] George to Spencer, 12 Sept. 1796, BL. Add. 75792.

[18] George to Charles Yorke, 7 May 1801, BL. Add. 35644 fol. 84.

In February 1801, however, at a time of government crisis, which was to be blamed for precipitating his illness,[19] George suddenly became very ill. This was described as a severe cold,[20] but there were disturbing signs of a recurrence of the illness of 1788. That had not been during a political crisis, but in 1801 the succession to the Pitt ministry was a key issue and possibly the precipitant of the illness. At his levee on 28 January, the king, angry about emancipation, had been agitated, and by mid-February he was ill and over-excited. George on one day seemed near to death, but he recovered and the illness lasted less than a month.[21] Furthermore, in 1801 there was nothing to match the political crisis caused by George's ill health in 1788, not least because the 1801 bout of ill health was shorter,[22] while the potential repercussions were contained because the prince of Wales agreed to Pitt's proposal that, if George failed to recover, there would be a restricted regency. George was given more problems by the determination of Dr Robert Willis and his brother John, sons of Francis Willis, to force the king to health by detention and restraint, a regime that required his being placed tied to a chair in front of a fire or, as George put it, 'roasted alive for six hours', as well as being knocked down at least once and his shins being kicked.[23] As he recovered, George was confined until he finally refused to sign any documents unless he was permitted to join the queen. Far from being mad, George was more sane than the Willises suggested, and his distaste for John Willis was understandable.[24] Nevertheless, the crisis left George weaker and under stress. 'He has a great thirst upon him ... His body, mind, and tongue, are all upon the stretch every minute.'[25] Furthermore, his relationship with Charlotte had faltered badly: understandably she was not equal to George's moods and apparently imminent violence.

The trip to Weymouth in the summer of 1801 brought the king much-needed relief. Staying, *en route*, for four days at George Rose's relatively modest seat at Cuffnells Park near Lyndhurst,[26] George reported that 'the gentle exercise, new objects of admiration which this country affords and the real comfort and hospitality of this place have been beneficial to the healths of all the party'.[27] Characteristically, he reviewed the troops

---

[19] Lady Mary Grantham to Catherine Robinson, 4 Mar. 1801, Plymouth 1259/2/569.

[20] George to Addington, 16 Feb. 1801, Exeter, 152M/C1801/OR 26, 28; *Courier*, 23 Feb. 1801.

[21] Theresa Villiers to Catherine Robinson, 25 Feb., 3 Mar., 19 Apr. 1801, Plymouth 1259/2/567-8, 574; J. Ehrman, *The Younger Pitt: The Consuming Struggle* (London, 1996), pp. 525-6.

[22] For a lucid letter from April, see e.g. George to Hawkesbury, 24 Apr. 1801, BL. Add. 38910 fol. 1.

[23] Minutes by Addington of questioning of George's doctors, of Dundas and of George's attendants, 17, 18 Feb., no date 1804, Exeter, 152M/C1804/OR 19-21, 24.

[24] Queen Charlotte to prince of Wales, 1 Aug. 1801, Aspinall, *Prince of Wales*, VIII, p. 74.

[25] Twiss, I, 381.

[26] Illustration of Cuffnells in 1805, Southampton City Archives D/NC 1.

[27] George to Addington, 3 July 1801, Exeter, 152M/C1801/OR 5.

encamped at Lyndhurst. George was 'delighted' with his reception at Southampton when he visited it on 1 July.[28] This visit was to be followed by the erection of a statue of the king wearing Roman garb. At Weymouth, George again found the bathing agreeable and his sleep 'perfect, but that it is necessary to avoid any hurry . . . the nerves certainly are regaining their proper tone, though not so quickly as wished'. Recovery was not rapid, and in September he observed that although 'he certainly is much recovered in point of health, his mind is not equal to much exertion . . . depression of spirits when engaged in business and still more so on what so nearly concerns him'.[29] Hopes of a tour on to Saltram were dashed by concern about French invasion preparations.[30]

The following year, George again benefited from his time at Weymouth, although it was less interesting to him because there were fewer visitors.[31] George's recovery provided a background to the plot of Maria Edgeworth's novel *Belinda* (1804), an instance of the way in which his mental health influenced the depiction of madness in the arts.[32]

The recurrence of the illness in 1801, however, aroused concern that it would recur yet again. This led George to insist that he should not be entrusted to the Willis brothers,[33] and encouraged an attempt to keep him from news that might disturb him, and thereby protect his ministers from the strain of the king's nervous irritability. This attempt was particularly apparent after George was ill again in the second week of February 1804. The cabinet was advised that George should not be presented with issues that required 'long argument or fatiguing discussion'.[34] When North had been ill in 1777, George then had recommended that by 'gentle manner his nerves must be treated in the enabling them by very moderate degrees to bear the weight of public business'.[35]

Recovery in 1804 took time.[36] George did not sign his warrants again until 19 March,[37] and in April Dundas, now Viscount Melville, warned

[28] Twiss, I, 386; Corporation Journal, 1 July 1801, Southampton City Archives, SC2/1/12; *Hampshire Chronicle*, 6 July 1801.

[29] George to Addington, 8, 9 July 1801, Exeter, 152M/C801/OR 1, 3; George to Hawkesbury, 23 Sept. 1801, BL. Loan 72/1 fol. 89.

[30] Theresa Villiers to Catherine Robinson, 15 Aug. 1801, Plymouth 1259/2/594.

[31] Bickley (ed.), *Diaries of . . . Glenbervie*, I, 322–3.

[32] D. Thame, 'Madness and Therapy in Maria Edgeworth's *Belinda*: Deceived by Appearances', *British Journal for Eighteenth-Century Studies*, 26 (2003), p. 271.

[33] Edward, duke of Kent to Addington, 15 Feb. 1804, Exeter, 152M/C1804/OR 14.

[34] Minutes of cabinet, 27 Feb. 1804, Exeter 152M/C1804/OR 48.

[35] George to John Robinson, 13 Mar. 1777, BL. Add. 37833 fol. 161; cf. 5, 12, 19 Mar., fols 141, 159, 172.

[36] Princess Elizabeth to Addington, 6 Feb., bulletins on George's health, 14 Feb.–22 Mar., York to Addington, 15 Feb., cabinet minute, 5 Mar. 1804, Exeter, 152M/C1804/OR 8, 11, 13, 35; Ehrman, *Pitt . . . Consuming Struggle*, p. 637.

[37] Sir Lucas Pepys to Addington, 19 Mar. 1804, Exeter 152M/C1804/OR 49.

that George's health threatened not only political stability but also Britain's place in the international system:

> the precarious state of the King's health, in the best expectation you can form of it, renders it almost impossible that any government can be strong and permanent which rests solely on the health and life of the King, and this observation is peculiarly worthy of attention, when you look abroad and take into the scale of consideration, the importance it is, that foreign nations should have a confidence in the strength and unity and permanence of the British government.[38]

George's health was thus attracting attention to a central functional flaw of a hereditary working monarchy, one not hitherto faced under the Hanoverian kings. Melville himself was told that George was erratic and uninhibited, lacking the majesty and measure of kingship,

> is well enough every day to speak perfectly accurately on any subject with any person, but that he never is for a *whole* day . . . a total want of discrimination of the persons and subjects with whom and on which he did talk. In short, that whether it was the Chancellor, Mr. Addington, the Queen, the Physicians, his Valet de Chambre or his cook, his discussions would be the same, and the topics would be the same, and this want of discrimination, more than any want of coherence in the discussion itself, was his situation at present.[39]

Later in April, Queen Charlotte reported that, although George was improving, 'one does not recover so easily at 66 as at 50'.[40] George was reading dispatches and signing warrants in May 1804, and wrote that his 'nature makes him decisive when he thinks the public service or the honour of his friends call for exertion';[41] but concerns about his health the following month led the prince of Wales to press for a formal report. Edward, duke of Kent, noted an improvement:

> there was a wonderful change in the King's manner from anything I have ever seen since the commencement of his confinement, in as much as instead of hurry, violence and ill humour, there was unusual calmness, quiet and good nature, and on the whole his mode of talking and his gestures were far more like his old ways . . . Asperity against no

---

[38] Melville to Pitt, 3 Apr. 1804, BL. Add. 40102 fols 128–9.
[39] Melville to Pitt, 6 Apr. 1804, BL. Add. 40102 fol. 134.
[40] Charlotte to her brother Charles, 20 Apr. 1804, F. Fraser, *Princesses. The Six Daughters of George III* (London, 2004), p. 203.
[41] George to Pitt, 13 May 1804, PRO. 30/8/104 fol. 340.

person whatever was to be remarked . . . To the Q. he was as usual coolly civil, and to myself all my sisters particularly kind, but in a proper not in an outré way. So far for the fair side of the picture; on the *other* hand I have to observe that his appearance in point of health was unusually bad; no ruddiness on his cheek, a livid yellow all over his face and eyes, a tremor in his limbs, and at times a very unpleasant lethargic look, his right leg a good deal swelled, and his tongue furred half an inch thick.[42]

Nevertheless, George was able to prorogue parliament in person at the end of July, writing that he 'felt no fatigue . . . as he was conscious he was acting as he ought'.[43] The doctors felt able to recommend on 18 August that the attendance of the Willises' replacement, Dr Samuel Simmons, be withdrawn, although they urged that George do nothing unfamiliar, as they feared it would cause a relapse. Poor health, and a wish not to be seen by many, however, may have encouraged a rapid journey to Weymouth later in the month. Leaving Windsor at 9.30 a.m. on 24 August, George reached Weymouth at 5 a.m. on the 25th, having dined with General Sir William Augustus Pitt, governor of Portsmouth, at his seat of Highfield Park, and then travelled overnight.

Reports from Weymouth referred to singularities of conduct but also indicated an improvement in George's health. The king informed Pitt that his health was

perfectly good and the quiet of the place and salubrity of the air must daily increase his strength; by the advice of Sir Francis Milman . . . the king will bathe in the tepid bath in lieu of going into the open sea. His Majesty feels this a sacrifice but will religiously stick to this advice; but does not admire the reasoning as it is grounded on sixty six being too far advanced in life for that remedy proving efficacious.[44]

Milman had become physician extraordinary to the king's household in 1785 and in 1806 became physician in ordinary to the king; created a baronet in 1800, Milman was to be elected president of the College of Physicians in 1811, but, although he acted the part, he was not the most perceptive of doctors.

A sympathetic observer who reported on George to Addington in September 1804 wrote, 'The day would have been a day of no common fatigue to almost any man – he was on horseback before breakfast at the camp, after breakfast at a review and the weather very hot.' Two days later, the day was spent on board the yacht

---

[42] Kent to prince of Wales, 3 June 1804, Aspinall, *Prince of Wales*, V, p. 29.
[43] George to Pitt, 2 Aug. 1804, PRO. 30/8/104 fol. 378.
[44] George to Pitt, 15 May 1805, PRO. 30/8/104 fol. 445.

very pleasantly, the weather very fine and nothing could be calmer and more cheerful than his Majesty – I am quite satisfied that it is impossible for him to spend his time more advantageously to his state of health than on board the yacht – most unfortunately the whole of the Royal Family are prejudicial against it . . . the greatest misfortune attending the King at present is that the Royal Family think worse of him than he is.

Bond's reports indicated that George was still mentally acute:

He at first stared me in the face, and did not know me – asked Lord Hawkesbury who was standing next to me, who I was (this is one of the consequences of illness, a defect of sight, which he often complains of) as soon as he heard my name he recollected me and everything about me – said he was now become a Dorsetshire gentleman – liked nothing better than Dorsetshire though he would never give up Berkshire – had purchased the Lodge at Weymouth – it was the only house to which he had given a name – he called it the King's Lodge . . . he said he should not have been ill, if he had been at Weymouth last summer – said this with great earnestness, and repeatedly . . . that he was always glad to see me – that no one ever did their business better at the Treasury . . . he is gaining ground – the first striking alteration is, a more upright carriage – he is much less in a hurry than when he came to Weymouth – returns to that which in his best days was at Weymouth his custom ever in the afternoon . . . sleep in the rooms, and sleep at the play – he appears to be very much amused with the things that are about him, and is certainly looking better in his countenance.[45]

By December 1804, George's health was regarded as good,[46] but his sight – which had given him trouble for years, making it difficult to read government papers at night in 1792[47] – went in his right eye, from 1804–5. An operation for a cataract was suggested but not attempted as the condition of the eye was judged unsuitable.[48] *The Times* noted on 7 November 1805: 'His Majesty wears a green shade constantly over his eyes, after candle-light; and, we are sorry to say, he cannot distinguish any person except he be very near, and with the assistance of a glass.'[49] The deterioration in his

[45] Bond to Addington, 12, 17 Sept. 1804, Exeter, 152M/C1804/OR 43–4. See also H.G. Mundy (ed.), *The Journal of Mary Frampton, 1779–1846* (London, 1885).

[46] Theresa Villiers to Catherine Robinson, 4, 27 Dec. 1804, Plymouth 1259/2/717, 720.

[47] George to William Grenville, 4 Dec. 1792, BL. Add. 58857 fol. 74.

[48] Theresa Villiers to Catherine Robinson, 28 July, 12 Aug. 1805, Plymouth 1259/2/740, 742.

[49] Cf. re. Weymouth, 14, 21 July 1805, A. Henstock (ed.), 'The Diary of Abigail Gawthorn, 1751–1810', *Transactions of the Thoroton Society of Nottinghamshire*, 33 (1980), pp. 117–18.

sight greatly affected the legibility of George's writing,[50] so that he could 'neither read what is written him or what he writes'.[51] As a result, a secretary, General Herbert Taylor, was appointed, much to George's pleasure.[52] The deterioration ensured that his speech from the throne at the start of the 1805 session was the last he ever delivered personally to parliament. A sense of mortality was driven home in August 1805, when William, duke of Gloucester, George's last surviving brother, died. The problem with his sight also forced George in 1805 to cancel a projected visit to Richard Hurd, bishop of Worcester, and in 1808 affected his reception of an address from the City of London.[53] Nevertheless, there were also reports that George was 'remarkably well'.[54]

Christian fortitude, 'that just sense of religion',[55] continued to offer George solace, and he remained politically important, although there were serious challenges to his views because it proved impossible to recreate a political and governmental force as impressive as the Pitt ministry. That under Henry Addington, formerly a successful Speaker of the Commons, was weaker and less effective. The Peace of Amiens, signed in March 1802, lessened the significance of this weakness, however. The peace had not been regarded in Britain as really satisfactory, but it was just acceptable enough to maintain the government in power. William Grenville, angered by the terms of the peace preliminaries with France, signed in London on 1 October 1801, had gone into opposition that November. George, who had made clear in 1800 his opposition to such a restoration of colonial gains and had pressed for firmness in the negotiations,[56] accepted the restoration as an aspect of a peace of 'mere necessity'.[57] Distrustful of France, George urged the maintenance of an appropriate military establishment.[58] The legacy of Anglo-French mistrust arising from the negotiations was such that in Britain it was regarded as unlikely to last, and this mistrust affected the reputation, then and subsequently, of those who advocated peace with France.

Political divisions within the Pittite 'party' of the 1790s left the political situation unstable. Pitt's resignation had splintered his 'party', or the Tories (if such a term is to be used of politicians who disliked the label), for, instead of being replaced by an opposition party, the different policies

[50] George to Hawkesbury, 8, 9, 26 July 1805, BL. Add. 38190 fol. 10, 38564, Loan 72/1 fol. 143.
[51] George to Pitt, 15 Sept. 1805, PRO. 30/8/104 fol. 457.
[52] Theresa Villiers to Catherine Robinson, 9 July 1805, Plymouth 1259/2/734.
[53] George to Hawkesbury, 27 Mar. 1808, BL. Loan 72/1 fol. 147.
[54] Anne to Catherine Robinson, 3 Sept. 1805, Plymouth, 1259/2/746.
[55] George to his sister, Augusta, duchess of Brunswick, 6 Oct. 1806, RA. GEO/12452.
[56] George to Hawkesbury, 14 Mar. 1802, BL. Loan 72/1 fol. 96.
[57] George to Hawkesbury, 18 Apr. 1802, BL. Loan 72/1 fol. 102.
[58] George to Hawkesbury, 30 Sept., 2 Oct. 1801, BL. Add. 38190 fols 2–3.

of which would maintain Tory unity – in other words a government in which the Foxite Whigs were prominent – Pitt had been succeeded by Addington at the head of a weak ministry. While Pitt, until 1804, maintained a position of theoretically benevolent neutrality, because he did not wish to oppose the king's choice of minister, George was concerned about Pitt's attitude to the opposition and feared that he wanted to create a broad-based ministry including Grenville, which was unacceptable to the king. Such a ministry might seek to reintroduce Catholic emancipation. Pitt's willingness, instead, to back Addington on policy was important to George: 'He made no reserve of expressing the high satisfaction he felt on learning the honorable part you was taking with respect to the budget and the measures for the security of the country.'[59] A slackened drive, stemming from depression and poor health, was possibly as important as any wish not to challenge or be seen to challenge the king's prerogative in choosing ministers, in explaining why Pitt delayed his attack on Addington until April 1804. He was certainly pressed by his political friends to mount such an attack earlier.

Although in 1801 Addington's position in parliament was weak, especially among the capable men of business, while he also lacked landed wealth and the support of those who had a great deal of it, he was strengthened by the trade revival that peace brought, the success of the 1802 election, and divisions among the other political groups. Addington was no Pitt, but he was a capable policy-maker and demonstrated some strong leadership qualities. During the period 1801–4, having started with no followers to speak of, he acquired a large and cohesive personal parliamentary following. This attests to an ability to inspire loyalty among MPs, especially given that he did not possess the traditional assets that created and consolidated political ties: wealth, connections, or control of parliamentary seats. It was this cohesive and loyal band of supporters that, even more than his favour with George, made Addington attractive to future ministries. His deficiencies were his mediocre public-speaking abilities and his neglect of parliamentary and electoral management. Royal backing was crucial to Addington, which made doubts about George's health a threat. The king found Addington's views on Catholic emancipation 'truly sound',[60] and in 1803, writing to Lord Pelham, made his own views clear, 'which can never tend but to Administration holding a strong and firm language and resisting any cabals that may arise'.[61] Indeed, George outlined what he felt was a clear line for ministerial and royal conduct:

[59] Melville to Pitt, 15 June 1803, BL. Add. 40102 fol. 123.
[60] George to Addington, 8 Oct. 1804, Exeter, 152M/C1804/OR 45.
[61] George to Pelham, 27 May 1803, BL. Add. 33115 fol. 143.

He trusts at the same time that ministry will act cordially together and show no encouragement to any of the parties of opposition. That is the line he means steadily to pursue, and trusts he shall have the support of the nation at large.[62]

If this was not a description of George's conduct throughout his reign, he could plead the excuse of the factiousness of ministries, but should not have been surprised that others took a different view both of his position and of the particular one they found themselves in. Possibly, Addington would have been able to consolidate his position. He was a favourite with the king, who remained pleased that he had been willing to offer support in 1801,[63] and who saw him as an ordinary man after his own heart and not, like Pitt, a formidable figure. George claimed only to value those who 'view him as a man and not those who reflect alone on the king'.[64] 'Highly gratified at the repeated marks of the sensibility of Mr. Addington's heart,'[65] George was friendly towards 'his truly beloved friend',[66] liked his family, including his 'lively and engaging youngest daughter',[67] and felt and found that he could trust him.[68] George also found that Addington was accommodating to his patronage requests. George respected Pitt, but never really liked him, and he resented his attitude to Catholic emancipation in 1801. The reasons why Addington kept cropping up in cabinets after 1804 were probably the knowledge of George's favour, the extent of Addington's support, and the degree to which he was seen as having sensible and safe views: he reassured the backbenchers that the government was safe.

French policy ensured that the British government declared war on 18 May 1803 with a relatively united country at its back (to George's pleasure),[69] whereas there had been considerable division at the time of the negotiation of the peace. Distrustful of Napoleon, in part in response to secret information from Paris,[70] and inherently pessimistic, George had supported a firm stance on France,

as the uniform conduct of the French government since the conclusion of the Peace of Amiens fully warrants the contents of it. If any curb can

---

[62] George to Pelham, 21 May 1803, BL. Add. 33115 fol. 135.
[63] George to Pitt, 5 May 1804, PRO. 30/8/103 fol. 334.
[64] George to Addington, 14 May 1804, Exeter, 152M/C1804/OR 38; C.J. Fedorak, *Henry Addington, Prime Minister, 1801–1804: Peace, War, and Parliamentary Politics* (Akron, Ohio, 2002).
[65] George to Addington, 14 June 1801, Exeter, 152M/C1801/OR 35.
[66] George to Addington, 14 May 1804, Exeter, 152M/C1804/OR 38.
[67] George to Addington, 13 June 1801, Exeter, 152M/C1801/OR 63.
[68] George to Hawkesbury, 30 Dec. 1804, BL. Add. 38190 fol. 8.
[69] George to Pelham, 24 May 1803, BL. Add. 33115 fol. 141.
[70] George to Pelham, 15 Oct. 1802, BL. Add. 33115 fol. 99.

be placed to the views of the First Consul it must be by a firm though temperate language from hence which has been well attended to in the formation of the above dispatch. The King shall see with pleasure its occasioning any moderation in the councils of the Tuileries, though he does not expect it.[71]

A firm stance abroad was to be matched by opposition to radicalism at home. Reflecting his customary knowledge of the character of individuals, George was very pleased that Sir James Eamer had been proposed as lord mayor of London,

> that alderman having uniformly conducted himself as a loyal subject and diligent magistrate. Such men are peculiarly suited for the present year, when, by the embarrassed situation from the trial of peace with a turbulent and revolutionary republic, every attention of the police must be exerted to avoid the dangers and difficulties that may otherwise ensue; but the King trusts, if a most respectable peace establishment be kept up, and the act against seditious meetings, and the Alien Bill be continued, that the experiment may not be attended with all the evils that sane persons might expect.[72]

Relative unity behind the decision to declare war did not, however, end political pressure on the government. The 1802 general election had been largely placid and had brought about no significant changes. The Foxite opposition remained in a clear minority. Under the Septennial Act, no other election was necessary until 1809. By 1804, indeed, the Addingtonians were a group large enough to form a useful element in any government, whether broadly or narrowly based. In the absence of clear party identity, however, it was difficult to bridge the policy divides that did exist among those who had been members of the Pittite group and to provide the leadership that might further unity. While not without ability, Addington himself did not prove up to the task of giving an impression of control. He was a political manager, able to reform the finances in 1802 (albeit at the cost of taking out heavy loans), and was backed by most of parliament when he chose for security reasons to declare war in 1803, but the ministry lacked talented debaters to convince parliament of the reasonableness of their management of the war, in the face of the criticism of more eloquent speakers, who themselves preferred no more viable options. As a result, Addington was seen, even by George, to lack leadership for war; he was perceived as a support to the government, not its

---

[71] George to Hawkesbury, 9 Feb. 1803, Maggs to author, 7 Mar. 2005.
[72] George to Eldon, 15 Oct. 1801, Twiss, I, 398.

head. His handling of the armed forces was harshly criticized: army numbers were too low, in part because Addington concentrated on militia and volunteers, raising formidable numbers, while the navy was not kept in a state of preparedness. The renewal of war with France led to pressure for the return of Pitt and for a more broadly based government.

Opposition to the government mounted in 1803, once war had resumed, as it failed to win the crucial appearance of success. Concerned about the value of existing preparations against French invasion,[73] George, not his ministers, played the major public role in symbolizing opposition to the prospect of attack. On 26 and 28 October, he reviewed 27,000 volunteers in Hyde Park, in each case in front of an estimated half a million people. To George's pleasure, the parliamentary session began well,[74] but in the winter of 1803–4 Fox and Grenville came to an agreement, greatly lessening Addington's room for political manoeuvre: the 'New Opposition' of Grenville joined the 'Old Opposition' of Fox. In April 1804, furthermore, Pitt went into opposition to the Addington ministry in order to force himself into office. Although George still supported Addington, the latter resigned, thus protecting the royal prerogative of choosing ministers, rather than being forced out by parliamentary action, which would have left George with fewer options. After defeat in the Lords and a fall in his Commons majority, Addington had seen George on 26 April in order to discuss the ministry's political vulnerability and offer his resignation. An angry George did not want him to resign, but, possibly influenced by Pitt's position, Addington resolved to go. His failure in parliamentary management, and a lack of speaking ability that made a strong impression on observers, helped ensure that Addington's parliamentary majorities, which had been large for his first three years in office, dwindled in the spring of 1804 to the point where he felt it necessary to resign. Nevertheless, Grenville, Fox, Pitt and Dundas had to work very hard, deploying all the resources at their disposal, to drive him from office.

Pitt became first minister again, but George, who on 5 May 1804 resumed a correspondence broken in February 1801, vetoed Pitt's proposal for the inclusion of Fox in the government, and, therefore, the chance of forming a ministry of 'All the Talents', although, as Melville pointed out,[75] this seemed the best way to create a political system that would survive the reign, a key issue in light of George's age and health. The king, whom Pitt found calm and astute, played a crucial part in keeping Fox out of office in 1804: distrusting his views, George saw Fox as an opponent of necessary measures against France and as unsound over the position of the Church.

[73] George to Hawkesbury, 1 July, George to Pelham, 7 July 1803, BL. Add. 38190 fol. 4, 33115 fol. 149.
[74] George to Hawkesbury, 23 Nov. 1803, BL. Loan 72/1 fol. 118.
[75] Melville to Pitt, 3 Apr. 1804, BL. Add. 40102 fol. 129.

George made it clear that he would not appoint Pitt if he insisted on Fox.[76] Furthermore, in response to sharply worded royal concerns ('would be a death warrant to the British constitution'),[77] Pitt promised that he would not raise the issue of Catholic emancipation during the king's reign. This, indeed, was a solution he had offered George in March 1801, but only after Addington had replaced him. The promise meant that the new ministry could not win the support of Grenville, who wanted the issue raised anew and was unwilling to serve without Fox. Although Fox was prepared to stand aside, Grenville accordingly rejected Pitt's approach:

> we rest our determination solely on our strong sense of the impropriety of our becoming parties to a system of government, which is to be formed, at such a moment as the present on a principle of Exclusion . . . An opportunity now offers such as this country has seldom seen for giving to its government, in a moment of peculiar difficulty, the full benefit of the services of those who by the public voice and sentiment are judged most capable of contributing to its prosperity and safety.

Grenville hoped that Pitt would be able to persuade the king to this end,[78] but he was disappointed.

George's role indicated the particular importance of the royal prerogative, and of deference to royal wishes at times of ministerial discontinuity. This refusal to accept Fox led to worse relations between George and the prince of Wales, who decided to support Fox. In addition, in August 1804 an attempt to arrange a meeting between father and son failed, because George remained resolutely against attempts to resolve differences in relation to his hostility to the prince's wish for a command. George was very angry that the prince had published their correspondence when, in 1803, he had again turned down the prince's offer to serve in the military.[79] There was also disagreement over the role of the estranged princess of Wales in the education of her daughter, Charlotte. George regarded the princess's conduct as becoming and irreproachable,[80] which was not the view of his ministers, and certainly not that of the prince, who was angry that his father had met the princess before him. The king was satisfied with her conduct and language when he received her at Kew. The two men did not meet until 12 November 1804, and, despite the use of the return of the Prodigal Son as a model in James Gillray's caricature *The Reconciliation*,

[76] George to Pitt, 5 May 1804, PRO. 30/8/104 fol. 344; Ehrman, *Pitt . . . Consuming Struggle*, pp. 654–60.
[77] George to Pitt, 5 May 1804, PRO. 30/8/104 fol. 334.
[78] William Grenville to Pitt, 8 May 1804, BL. Add. 58909 fols 97, 95.
[79] Addington to prince of Wales, 27 July, 1 Aug. 1803, Exeter, 152M/C1803/OZ 113–14.
[80] George to Hawkesbury, 30 Dec. 1804, BL. Add. 38190 fol. 8.

George's treatment of his son then struck the latter as cold and discouraging. They only discussed commonplace matters. As a result of the failure of the two to agree, the prince refused to allow Charlotte to be brought up at Windsor, depriving George of contact with the generation after next in the royal family.[81]

The background to the formation of the Pitt ministry ensured that it faced difficulties. Pitt's treatment of Addington had made many of the latter's supporters hostile, although others joined the new ministry. On 18 June 1804, the government won a key vote in a full Commons by a majority of only forty-two, a reflection of the consequences of the splintering of the Pittite 'party' of the 1790s. Like the North ministry, the Pittite system had depended on royal backing, the support of a number of political groupings, and the assent of the bulk of the independent parliamentarians. The inherent instability of this system was shown when political groupings within the ministry defined themselves, separated out, and each attracted the backing of some of the independents. The system had divided into groups linked to Addington, Grenville and Pitt (and later to Castlereagh, Perceval and Canning), and it then proved impossible to create the government of national unity that Pitt sought, and that Spencer Perceval was again to attempt, without success, in 1809.

George, who gave Pitt advice on strengthening the position of the ministry as well as lobbying on its behalf,[82] was not only pleased by Pitt's ability to defeat 'the motley opposition',[83] but also delighted that Pitt sought to broaden his support by bringing in Addington, promoted to the peerage as Viscount Sidmouth, as lord president of the council in January 1805.[84] The new session initially went well[85] and George was optimistic that the failure of the parliamentary opposition would make it less troublesome.[86] The new alliance, however, was not a close one, and, although Sidmouth did not attack Pitt over the alleged corruption of his ally and friend Melville, when formerly treasurer of the navy, many of his supporters voted against Melville, in part because they resented his role in engineering Addington's defeat in 1804 and in part because the charges arose out of the Commission of Naval Inquiry that St Vincent had set up while serving under Addington. The Commons decision for the impeachment of Melville led to his being driven from office as first lord of the admiralty, and

[81] Theresa Villiers to Catherine Robinson, 27 Dec. 1804, Plymouth 1259/2/720; Ehrman, *Pitt . . . Consuming Struggle*, pp. 719–21.

[82] George to Pitt, 16, 19 June 1804, PRO. 30/8/104 fols 350, 352.

[83] George to Eldon, 30 June 1804, Twiss, I, 459; cf. George to Pitt, 12 June, 3 July 1804, PRO. 30/8/104 fols 346, 370; George to Hawkesbury, 25 June 1804, BL. Loan 72/1 fol. 123.

[84] George to Pitt, 18, 25 Dec. 1804, PRO. 30/8/104 fols 398, 400; George to Hawkesbury, 24, 25 Dec. 1804, BL. Add. 38190 fols 6–7.

[85] George to Pitt, 13, 22 Feb., 7 Mar. 1805, PRO. 30/8/104 fols 421–5.

[86] George to Hawkesbury, 9 Mar. 1805, BL. Add. 38564 fol. 81.

he was forced to resign from the Privy Council in May. George had a characteristically even-handed ethical response, writing that he was 'much hurt at the virulence against Lord Melville which is unbecoming the character of Englishmen who naturally when a man is fallen are too noble to pursue their blows'.[87] Once the government had lost the vote, Addington pressed Pitt to distance himself from Melville for the sake of the ministry's reputation. The impeachment bitterly divided the ministry. It failed, much to George's pleasure. However, Sidmouth's motion for a criminal prosecution won the support of the Foxites and the Grenvillites, and Pitt was defeated by 238 to 229. George was troubled by the prosecution which he felt to be an unnecessary severity, and was glad when proceedings ended.[88]

The public breach resulted in Sidmouth's resignation from the ministry (to George's concern),[89] and, soon after, Sidmouth was cautiously responsive to an approach from Fox. Pitt, meanwhile, was under great strain, which affected his ability to lead. His judgement can be questioned, for example his willingness to desert Melville and his subsequent refusal to advance Sidmouth's supporters once Melville had fallen. Melville himself had been seen by George as an effective minister.[90] Their correspondence indicates the king's readiness to read and consider papers[91] and his commitment to the navy: 'the bulwark of the nation, the wooden walls of Great Britain'.[92]

In the summer of 1805, Pitt again tried for the inclusion of the Foxites, visiting Weymouth to press George, only to meet with a total refusal: the king had been pleased that the attempt by Fox and Grenville to raise the Catholic question in parliament had recently been defeated. As Pitt had presciently pointed out, an active opposition was not the way to win the sympathy of the king:

> Whatever unfavourable impression may at any time have existed in the highest quarter towards any of the parties engaged in such a system, will of course be strengthened and confirmed; and the natural consequence will be a determination even in case of a change being found necessary, to put if possible a negative on them, in forming a new government.[93]

---

[87] George to Pitt, 5 May 1805, PRO. 30/8/104 fol. 441.

[88] George to Pitt, 12, 13, 15, 27 June 1805, PRO. 30/8/104 fols 447–55; M. Fry, *The Dundas Despotism* (Edinburgh, 1992), pp. 262–71.

[89] J.H. Jesse, *Memoirs of the Life and Reign of King George the Third* (5 vols, London, 1901), V, 259–61.

[90] George to Melville, 30 May, 14 June, 3 July 1804, 18 Mar., 10 Apr. 1805, BL. Add. 40100 fols 306–7, 317, 333, 337.

[91] George to Melville, 14 June, 12 July, 22 Sept. 1804, 7 Feb. 1805, BL. Add. 40100 fols 307, 319, 325, 331.

[92] George to Melville, 12 July 1804, BL. Add. 40100 fol. 319.

[93] Pitt to William Grenville, 4 Feb. 1804, BL. Add. 58909 fols 81–2.

In the winter of 1805–6, the ministry was still in a weak state, facing an assertive, if far from united, opposition in parliament. Nelson's victory at Trafalgar on 21 October 1805, which effectively ended fears that France had the naval capacity to protect a major invasion force, gave a tremendous boost to national confidence and was greeted by George as a brilliant victory that called for Nelson's burial in St Paul's.[94] However, British foreign policy was ruined by Napoleon's sweeping victory over Austria and Russia at Austerlitz on 2 December. Four days later, Austria signed an armistice and, on 26 December, the treaty of Pressburg, accepting French hegemony in Germany. George Canning wrote of Pitt on 9 January 1806, 'He is very ill and the Continent worse.'[95]

Political groupings organized around an individual politician tend to lack mechanisms for finding a new leader, and this is a particular problem if the grouping, or party, is essentially a vehicle for the leader, or becomes such. In the case of a party in office, it was up to the monarch to control, or at least influence, the leadership by his choice of ministers, and also to think about the succession if the first minister became seriously ill. George, however, had no wish to part with Pitt in 1805–6, and this played a part in ensuring that the Pittites had no adequate alternative leader.

Pitt died on 23 January 1806, and George then tried to take a key role in forming a new ministry out of the remains of that of Pitt. He wanted to appoint the home secretary, Robert, Lord Hawkesbury, as Pitt's successor as first lord of the treasury and head of the ministry. Hawkesbury (1770–1828), the son of Charles Jenkinson, first earl of Liverpool, long a minister close to the king, had the necessary experience for high office and policies that commended him to George. An MP from 1790, until raised to the peerage by Addington in 1803, Hawkesbury was an able parliamentary speaker who had supported Pitt until they differed over Catholic emancipation. He had served as foreign secretary under Addington, before being transferred to the Home Office and made leader of the Lords in 1804. Hawkesbury had been highly influential in bringing Addington into the Pitt ministry. Had he enjoyed the support of leading politicians and the backing of parliament in 1806, Hawkesbury would have been a good choice as prime minister and, as second earl of Liverpool, was subsequently to be a long standing one, from 1812 to 1827.

George asked his ministers for their individual opinions, but when it met late on the evening of 24 January 1806 the cabinet decided that it could not undertake the government, and George was advised accordingly on the 25th.[96] Their unwillingness to do so, and to face parliament, obliged

---

[94] George to Pitt, 11 Nov. 1805, PRO. 30/8/104 fol. 461.

[95] Canning to John Hookham Frere, 9 Jan. 1806, BL. Add. 38833 fol. 197.

[96] C.D. Yonge, *The Life and Administration of Robert Banks, Second Earl of Liverpool, K.G., Late First Lord of the Treasury: compiled from original documents* (3 vols, London, 1868), I, 207.

George to turn to the opposition. The majority of the cabinet saw little prospect of holding off opposition attacks, and the lord president of the council, the duke of Portland, advised the king to turn to Grenville. George indeed asked Grenville to form a ministry and yielded to the latter's stipulations of the inclusion of Fox and the dismissal of Lord Eldon, the lord chancellor, who had been George's agent in the cabinet and in relations with his heir, and to whom George felt close: the king wanted a chancellor who was reliable on emancipation. Indeed, when Eldon delivered up the Great Seal on 7 February, George told him to lay it down on a sofa as he was unwilling to take it from him, adding, 'Yet I admit you can't stay when all the rest have run away.'[97] The prince of Wales sought to capitalize on the situation by gaining as much patronage as possible and George's dislike for Grenville owed something to his support for the prince.

The negotiation that resulted in the Ministry of All the Talents represented a failure for George, repeating that of the creation of the Fox–North coalition in 1783. George also displayed an enforced flexibility that he was not to show frequently. Whereas he had refused to yield to Pitt's pressure to take Fox into office, he was willing to accept Grenville's demand that he do so. In policy terms, there was no requirement that Catholic emancipation never be raised by the ministry. This again was a prudent response on the part of George to the political situation, as Grenville would not have accepted such a demand, although, after Grenville had been heavily defeated when 'the Catholic question' was debated in parliament in May 1805, George had hoped that it would 'lie dormant'.[98]

More generally, George insisted that he should have more than simply nominal powers of approval, writing to Grenville in a comment on the development of government practice in the 1790s,

the King must be understood as reserving to himself at all times the undoubted right of *deciding* on the measures which may be proposed to him respecting the military service and the administration of it, both with reference to the prerogatives of the Crown, and the nature and expediency of the measures themselves.[99]

The inclusion of the Addington (or Sidmouth) party in the new ministry, with Sidmouth as lord privy seal and later lord president, lessened the dominance of Fox and Grenville. When Grenville suggested the new cabinet to George, he added, 'the arrangements for the Board and

[97] Twiss, I, 512.
[98] George to Hawkesbury, 11, 14, 15 (quote) May 1805, BL. Loan 72/1 fol. 141, Add. 38190 fol. 9, 38564 fol. 85.
[99] George to William Grenville, 3 Feb. 1806, BL. Add. 58863 fol. 19.

other offices of less importance, would be formed on a similar principle of comprehending as much as possible those persons of different descriptions who might appear likely to be most useful to the carrying on your Majesty's service'.[100]

Nevertheless, Pitt's friends, Canning, Castlereagh, Hawkesbury (from 1808, second earl of Liverpool) and Perceval, did not join the ministry. This was a political challenge to it, and to the idea that a Ministry of All the Talents had been created, but they were disunited,[101] without clear leadership, and also disheartened and constrained by the king's tolerance of the new ministry. George, in turn, was affected by the weakness of those not in the government. In opposition, the Pittites continued to place considerable weight on royal wishes. Canning told Richard, Marquess Wellesley that, if they were approached by the government,

> their first inquiry would be whether it came from the King without whose direct authority none of them would be disposed to enter into any discussions relative to the acceptance of office. Upon the whole it appeared to me that Canning's opinion is that it would be difficult to obtain any considerable aid from the opposition without a previous dissolution of the present government.[102]

George, meanwhile, increasingly focused his life on Windsor, and he moved his effects there from St James's. Convenience and health more and more kept him there. George last visited Kew in January 1806, and never lived in the castellated palace he was having built there at great expense. He last visited Weymouth in 1805. In 1804, the royal family had moved from the Queen's Lodge in Windsor to the new royal apartments there. The King's Apartments were to be his home thereafter. On the ground floor of the upper ward overlooking the North Terrace, they comprised twelve rooms, including much provision for books. Within the Gothic splendour of the castle, George lived in comfort, his rooms containing thick pile rugs and Grecian couches. Royal life at Windsor was not simply about domestic comfort. In 1805, on St George's Day, the king held a spectacular and expensive installation of the Knights of the Order of the Garter in Windsor. George's irritability, however, made him a difficult companion and particularly tried his relations with the queen. The possibility of a separation was mentioned.

[100] William Grenville to George, 31 Jan. 1806, BL. Add. 58863 fols 9–10; J. Sack, *The Grenvillites, 1801–1829: Party Politics and Factionalism in the Age of Pitt and Liverpool* (Urbana, Illinois, 1979).

[101] D. Gray, *Spencer Perceval: The Evangelical Prime Minister 1762–1812* (Manchester, 1963), p. 61.

[102] Wellesley to William Grenville, 2 July 1806, BL. Add. 58913 fol. 1.

To George, Grenville had the unwelcome obstinacy of his father, George Grenville, and, while highly intelligent, he was indeed a man lacking ease of manner and flexibility as a politician, which contributed to his failure in this position.[103] In contrast to their correspondence in the 1790s, George sent essentially formal and short notes to Grenville. The king also abhorred his ministerial colleagues, although there were fewer disputes than might have been anticipated from the Whigs' long-standing critique of the court.[104] More surprisingly, George's attitude to Fox, the foreign secretary, changed for the better. This was in stark contrast to their stormy relationship of earlier years, when they were not just opponents on the political stage, but also personal adversaries. Eldon recorded George's concern with propriety:

> Some time after the dissolution of the Whig Ministry, the King said it was but just to acknowledge, that Mr. Fox, though certainly forced upon him, had never presumed upon that circumstance to treat his sovereign like a person in his power, but had always conducted himself frankly and yet respectfully, as it became a subject to behave. 'His manner,' the King was wont to say, 'contrasted remarkably with that of another of the Whig Ministers, who, when he came into office, walked up to me in the way I should have expected from Bonaparte after the battle of Austerlitz'.[105]

Policies, however, were also at stake. Unlike Fox, the king was reluctant to negotiate with France,[106] and suspicious that French approaches were designed to exclude Britain from the continent and, more specifically, to separate her interests from those of Alexander I of Russia, who continued to fight France until 1807. George urged that negotiations should not begin unless the Russians agreed,[107] and that Britain's commitment to the continent be affirmed. For George, characteristically, principles were involved: it was necessary 'to prove to Europe in general that the government of this country is resolved to assert its dignity and its established rights, and upon no account to submit to restrictions upon its political relations which France in its arrogance may wish to impose'.[108]

---

[103] P. Jupp, *Lord Grenville, 1759–1834* (Oxford, 1985).

[104] For a generally positive view of relations, A.D. Harvey, 'The Ministry of All the Talents. The Whigs in Office, February 1806 to March 1807', *Historical Journal*, 15 (1972), pp. 624–6.

[105] Twiss, I, 510.

[106] George to Fox, 22 Mar. 1806, BL. Add. 51457 fol. 17.

[107] George to Fox, 9 Apr. 1806, BL. Add. 51457 fol. 30.

[108] George to Fox, 20 Apr. 1806, BL. Add. 51457 fol. 34; George to William Grenville, 5 July, 2, 3 Aug. 1806, BL. Add. 58863 fols 72, 86, 88.

George's role was to the fore in Gillray's caricature *Pacific Overtures*, published on 5 April 1806. In this, George, not his ministers, takes centre stage in rejecting Napoleon's terms. Standing firmly next to a statue of Pitt that rests on a pillar marked Integrity, and with the warship *The Royal Sovereign* in the background, George declares, 'Very amusing terms indeed! and might do vastly well with some of the new-made little gingerbread kings, but we are not in the habits of giving up either ships or commerce or colonies merely because little Boney is in a pet to have them.' The reference to Napoleon's client kings was intended to suggest that true kingship, like national interest, entailed a vigorous rebuttal of Napoleon.

Although it was not at the centre of public discussion, the future of Hanover was also a political issue. George could act more freely than under the stronger cabinets of the 1790s. The question whether the Electorate should be left under Prussian occupation, seized by Napoleon, or returned to George, became an important issue in negotiations involving the three, leading to concern that British goals might be affected by Electoral interests, as was indeed the case with Anglo-Prussian relations in 1806; and vice versa. More generally, George was still active in foreign policy, reading instructions and dispatches and discussing negotiations with ministers and foreign diplomats.[109]

George's willingness to consider action against the ministry was evident from June 1806 when he agreed to secret communications with the opposition. The king, however, felt constrained by the need for secrecy, and this accentuated, and was accentuated by, his personality, with its elements of anxiety and paranoia. Fox's death in September weakened the ministry, and it was also hit by the failure of the peace negotiations in Paris. George's position became crucial as the ministry pressed for a dissolution of parliament, in order to be able to hold elections while they controlled government patronage, and thus to prevent the opposition from being given the chance to do the same. George, who had been to see the Pittite leader, Portland, at his seat of Bulstrode on 11 November, and who was being pressed by Eldon and his own son, Ernest, duke of Cumberland, not to give a dissolution, was unenthusiastic about the ministry's request. As so often, his excuse was constitutional propriety: the last election had been in 1802 and another did not need to be held until 1809, but George felt obliged to accept the government's argument that such a step was necessary in order to affirm public support for government policy.[110] As yet, his dislike of the ministry had not been converted into a determination to

[109] George to Fox, 22, 29 Apr., 9 May, 25 June 1806, BL. Add. 51457 fols 37, 40, 42, 52; H. Butterfield, *Charles James Fox and Napoleon. The Peace Negotiation of 1806* (London, 1962); B. Simms, '"An odd question enough". Charles James Fox, the Crown and British Policy during the Hanoverian Crisis of 1806', *Historical Journal*, 38 (1995), pp. 567–96.
[110] George to William Grenville, 13 Oct. 1806, BL. Add. 58863 fol. 111.

overthrow it, not least because the death of Fox and the failure of the peace negotiations had removed potential causes of division, while the Catholic question had not yet provided another. Nevertheless, George's views were shown when he held back from the ministers the £12,000 from the privy purse that he generally provided to help with election expenses. In the event, the elections only strengthened the ministry marginally, perhaps for lack of preparation – the decision to dissolve was very much a snap one.

In response to pressure from Catholics, and to demonstrate its Whig credentials, the Ministry of All the Talents now resolved to extend to Britain the privileges granted to the Irish Catholics in 1793, and also to comprehend Protestant Nonconformists. George was opposed to the Bill, but needed to know that he would be able to rely on parliamentary support for any action he took. Sidmouth, however, persuaded him to accept the measure. The Whig ministers then went further than the concession George had already accepted, the extension of the 1793 Act to Britain,[111] and instead proposed that the military staff appointments then denied Catholics should be open to them, a challenge to the Test Act. Opposed to this extension, Sidmouth rejected Grenville's claim that George had consented to it. The measure had certainly not been explained to George, whose sight, and therefore ability to read documents, was poor. Sidmouth did so instead, on 4 March, and George made clear his opposition to the proposal. On the 5th, nevertheless, Charles, Lord Howick (later the second Earl Grey of the 1832 Reform Act), introduced the measure into the Commons. Fortunately for the king, Sidmouth's opposition to it helped weaken the divided ministry. Sidmouth offered to resign, but George told him to stay and fight and made it clear he was willing to veto the Bill, a course he was urged to by Portland.[112] The ministry's effort to recruit Canning failed.

In the face of royal opposition, the cabinet on 15 March 1807 decided to abandon the Bill, but Grenville wanted the cabinet still to be able to express its views on the Catholic issue. With ministers ready to resign, an unyielding George, however, pushed them further. 'With a view to the prevention of all future mistakes', he demanded from them a written pledge not to raise anew the issue of Catholic emancipation.[113] This was a humiliating step, but one appropriate for George with his desire to have everything under control and to banish his own anxiety. Indeed, it was not a new expedient. In 1780 he had resolved not to admit any of the opposition into his 'service without a written and signed recantation'.[114] The

[111] George to William Grenville, 12 Feb. 1807, BL. Add. 58863 fol. 134.
[112] Portland to George, 12 Mar. 1807, RA. GEO/12706; E.A. Smith, *Lord Grey, 1764–1845* (Oxford, 1990), pp. 120–5.
[113] George to William Grenville, 17 Mar. 1807, BL. Add. 58863 fol. 146, 58864 fols 56–8.
[114] George to Jenkinson, 14 Apr. 1780, BL. Loan 72/1 fol. 39.

ministers' unwillingness to comply in 1807 – they regarded such a humiliating promise as opposed to their duty of advice as privy councillors and
MPs[115] – encouraged George, with his 'principles and his feelings . . . at
stake',[116] to seek replacements.

The fall of the ministry – the ministers surrendered their seals on 24
March – made the role of the crown a contentious issue anew and was to
loom large in the Whig myth about George, being seen as crucial evidence
of his lack of liberal sentiment, and of his bad faith.[117] In fact, the Whigs
had proposed the change in a way designed to mislead the king. It had not
worked: he was still more a master of government business than many
ministers.[118] George distrusted his ministers in 1807, but they had failed to
try to bring him round to the legislation, and trying to mislead him was
foolish, and only encouraged his self-righteousness. Furthermore, the lack
of unity in what was a coalition ministry, and the extent to which MPs
were willing to back the king on the Catholic question, ensured that the
government was weak.[119] Gillray presented the fall of the ministry in his
caricature *The Pigs Possessed or the Broad bottom'd Litter running headlong into the
Sea of Perdition*, showing George as a robust farmer upbraiding the porcine
ministers as they leapt over a cliff, 'O you cursed ungrateful brutes!'

Portland was chosen as first lord of the treasury, and therefore prime
minister, not Hawkesbury as George had intended. The Pittites were
ready to recommend Portland, a mark of the major realignment of politics from the time when he had been first lord of the treasury in the
Fox–North coalition, and of the long-term impact of the Portland Whigs
joining Pitt after the outbreak of the French Revolutionary War. As home
secretary from 1794 to 1801, Portland had taken a firm line against radicalism, being ready to use armed force to that end, and he had developed
a clear support for government and the royal prerogative, as well as
showing hostility to parliamentary reform and Catholic emancipation.[120]
To George, he was reliable, and the lacklustre, indecisive and sickly duke
was not unduly constrained by the king in forming the new government.
With his characteristic loyalty to former servants, George requested the
reinstatement of the members of his household removed by the Grenville
ministry in February 1806, but he was not concerned to dictate ministerial

[115] Cabinet minute, BL. Add. 58864 fols 60–1.
[116] George to Sidmouth, 25 Mar. 1807, Exeter, 152M/OZ/1807.
[117] H. Brougham, 'The State of Parties', *Edinburgh Review*, 30 (1818), p. 196.
[118] M. Roberts, *The Whig Party 1807–12* (London, 1939), p. 32.
[119] W.B. Hamilton, 'Constitutional and Political Reflections on the Dismissal of Lord
Grenville's Ministry', *Report on the Annual Meeting of the Canadian Historical Association*, 49
(1964), pp. 89–104.
[120] D. Wilkinson, *The Duke of Portland. Politics and Party in the Age of George III* (Basingstoke,
2003), pp. 108–56.

choices. George, however, was keen that Eldon again become lord chancellor, and he did so.[121]

The new government decided to strengthen itself by holding a general election, and succeeded in doing so, as was the pattern in an age in which elections rewarded incumbent ministers. In many respects, this was a second version of the 1784 election, with the ministry benefiting from the popularity of the king's cause. The address of thanks to George from the Corporation of London set the tone (and was publicized in the press): the king was congratulated for the 'decided support and protection given by him to the Protestant reformed religion as by law established'. Opposition to Catholic emancipation was to the fore in the election; if it played a role only in nine or so of the eleven county contests and fifteen of their fifty-eight borough counterparts, this was against a background in which national issues were not usually prominent.

The Portland administration (1807–9) was properly mindful that it was the king's ministry. Its dependence on George was underlined in March 1808 when he refused to comply with the ministerial wish that he make known his support for an Offices in Reversion Bill designed to increase parliament's power and to cut expenditure on sinecures. Without this support, the ministry could not count on the backing of the household peers or the bishops, and the Bill had to be abandoned. Although the crown was affected by the attack on corruption and sinecures, the revival of the policy and rhetoric of economic reform hit ministers harder, in part a product of the extent to which crown patronage was under ministerial control. Thus, a motion of censure was launched against Castlereagh, while Perceval was accused of corruption in the use of treasury influence in elections.

The major criticism of the royal family was directed against the duke of York, not George. York was falsely accused as commander-in-chief of selling promotions by a former mistress, Mary Anne Clarke. The Commons rejected the charge of corruption, but he had clearly failed to keep Clarke at a sufficient remove. In another demonstration of his importance, George managed York's resignation early in 1809. Rather than waiting to ascertain ministerial views, George at once chose General Sir David Dundas, intending him as a stop-gap until York could be reappointed, as he was in 1811, holding the post until he died in 1827.[122] More generally, the diligent and experienced king was respected by his ministers, although he had to accept measures he did not like, such as a bold and supportive response to the Spanish rising against Napoleonic rule in 1808, and the appointment of generals, such as Sir John Moore and Sir Arthur

[121] R.A. Melikan, *John Scott, Lord Eldon* (Cambridge, 1999).
[122] Aspinall, *George III*, V, 237–8.

Wellesley, who George, and York, thought too junior for a large command.[123]

George kept himself informed politically, not least on parliamentary debates,[124] and he intervened during the disputes within the ministry in 1809 centred on the bitter rivalry between Canning and Castlereagh. George and Portland wished to keep both in office, and undated notes by Earl Bathurst, the president of the board of trade, indicate the importance of the former. He recounted how when Portland explained the issue,

> The King promised to consider seriously on the subject, and the next Wednesday Mr. Canning had a full explanation with the King on his difficulties in acting with Lord Castlereagh, but confined himself to that subject. The Duke of Portland afterwards proposed to Mr. Canning at the King's suggestion, that instead of Lord Castlereagh's removal, to which the King thought there were many objections there might be a new division of the business in the two departments. That the conduct of the War in Europe should be placed in the hands of the Foreign Secretary of State, and that India should be included in Lord Castlereagh's department. To this arrangement, Mr. Canning consented.[125]

Portland's seizure supervened, but the episode indicated the extent to which, whatever the theory of cabinet cohesion, ministerial divisions left a continued role for the crown. Furthermore, there was a major problem with weak leadership under Portland. During both of his terms (1783, 1807–9), Portland was largely a figurehead, selected only because he had a talented team of cabinet colleagues who would not agree to serve under each other. This weakness affected both the political role of the crown and George's political activity.

The government was also gravely weakened by the unsuccessful expedition sent against the port of Antwerp in 1809, the Walcheren expedition, named after the island where many of the troops died of disease. Ministers were discredited, as was the land commander, Chatham, a royal favourite. The Whigs, however, were unable to take advantage of the unpopularity, divisions and demoralization of the Portland government. George, instead, played a major role in securing the reconstitution of the ministry that October when Spencer Perceval replaced Portland, who was close to death (he died on 30 October 1809). An able debater and effective

---

[123] R.J.B. Muir and C.J. Esdaile, 'Strategic Planning in a Time of Small Government: The Wars against Revolutionary and Napoleonic France, 1793–1815', *Wellington Studies*, I (1996), p. 41.

[124] George to Liverpool, 22 Apr. 1809, 9 June 1810, BL. Add. 38190 fols 17, 20.

[125] Undated notes by Bathurst, BL. Loan 57/4.

minister, Perceval had merit, but George wanted him because he trusted Perceval: both as an individual whom he thought straightforward, and as an evangelical Protestant who had no truck with Catholic emancipation.[126] As a result, George did not try to have Canning, Castlereagh or Liverpool, other potential choices, as head of the ministry, although, alongside the king's role, it is significant that Perceval was recommended by his ministerial colleagues. Furthermore, Liverpool was in the Lords, while relations between Canning and Castlereagh had collapsed, and the latter called Canning out to a duel.

In the negotiations surrounding the formation of the new government, George's views had to be heeded. Perceval had to reassure George in September that his approach for Whig support would not entail raising the Catholic question. Howick, now Grey, and Grenville, however, rejected the approach. Distrustful of George after his treatment of the Talents, they were willing to accept office only if the government was pledged to Catholic emancipation. George would have preferred to abdicate. As a result of the failure of his approach, when Perceval became first lord of the treasury, on 4 October 1809, it was as the head of a narrowly based ministry that many did not expect to last. The political world was far more divided at the time of the celebration of George's Jubilee than it had been when he came to the throne.

In the politics of this period there was a complex intermingling of personal attachments and rivalries with political beliefs. Both government and opposition were mixed in their composition, and individual attitudes varied greatly, an important aspect of the extent to which the 'unreformed' political system, that which preceded the First Reform Act of 1832, was far from static or characterized by simple divides. Although usually seen as politically opposed, there is a real sense in which both Grenville and Grey were as conservative (Grey hated the radicals) as Liverpool and Canning, especially after 1806 when Fox was no longer there to influence Grey; while Liverpool was as firm in opposing royal interference in policy and patronage as any Whig would have been. The limited radicalism of many of the Whigs was partly due to the privileged social context and character of the political system, but also to the extent to which a generally conservative political ideology had become more cautious in response to the challenge of radicalism. Conversely, the division in the ministries after 1806 between those pro- and anti-Catholic emancipation was such that after 1812 it had to be an 'open' question in the cabinet. The crisis over parliamentary reform in 1830–2 was to accentuate and clarify the extent of a two-party division based on ideas rather

---

[126] For George's earlier warmth, George to Perceval, 10 Apr. 1807, Aspinall, *George III*, IV, 560.

than personalities, although the origins of these party divisions clearly existed before 1806. Indeed, in the 1800s a political division was emerging between conservative Tories, such as Eldon, Portland and Sidmouth, the individuals with whom George was most comfortable, and the Pittite-Grenvillites, including Dundas and Grey. Issues such as Catholic emancipation were important, but it was also necessary to construct a ministry which could encompass four or five ministers with a significant following in the Commons, to add to the 'natural' Tories. Perceval's offer of a place in the cabinet to Grenville in 1809 was clearly motivated by this.[127]

Although his eyesight continued very poor, George's health did not otherwise markedly deteriorate in the late 1800s. There were, however, many rumours about him. Some opposition MPs claimed in December 1807 that he must be mad because he rarely left Windsor, while in early 1809 a report on his death led to a rise in the price of black cloth.[128] Furthermore, after his attack in February 1804, George's health did not return to its previous equilibrium, and he remained easily agitated, leading Pitt in March 1804 to avoid meetings likely to upset him.[129] Due to his increasing blindness and to poor health, George was unable to attend the spectacular Jubilee fête held in 1809 at Frogmore only a mile from Windsor. Instead, a portrait of the king was displayed in the temporary temple erected for the occasion. The Jubilee provided a major opportunity for the display of respect and affection for the king as a central part of patriotism, and celebrations were held across the empire, although there were criticisms of the occasion from radicals. In Weymouth, where the Jubilee left a permanent mark in the form of a life-sized statue of George, unveiled in October 1810, the mixed popularity of the king was shown in the refusal of some prominent citizens to subscribe, including Samuel Weston, the mayor, and Thomas Morris, a former mayor. They had earlier displayed a reluctance to oblige George both in building the harbour steps he requested and in responding to his request for a walled esplanade and a roadway from his residence to the harbour.[130]

George's health permanently broke down towards the close of 1810. As late as 18 October he was able to write to Charles Yorke, the first lord of the admiralty, approving a promotion 'in the subordinate ranks of the fleet', but adding 'The King is truly sensible of the affectionate manner in which Mr. Yorke has noticed the distress under which His Majesty suffers from the precarious state of his dear daughter.'[131] The shock of the fatal

[127] W. Hay, *The Whig Revival, 1808–1830* (Basingstoke, 2004).

[128] Gray, *Spencer Perceval*, pp. 399–400. This biography can be supplemented by the Perceval papers in CUL. Add. MS. 8713.

[129] Stanhope, IV, appendix, p. xv.

[130] G.J. Davies, 'Weymouth's Choice: Pulteney or Bankruptcy?', *Proceedings of the Dorset Natural History and Archaeological Society*, 119 (1997), pp. 33–40.

[131] George to Yorke, 18 Oct. 1810, BL. Add. 45035 fol. 7.

illness of his last-born, his favourite daughter Amelia, proved crucial to George's deterioration. It was initially thought that he would be all right despite her illness, but the fact that she did not die quickly helped cause the crisis, and both declined together. George frequently questioned her doctors on her progress, and was popularly supposed to have been pushed over the edge when Amelia gave him a mourning ring containing a lock of her hair. Symptoms of insanity were obvious by 25 October, the day of his last public appearance, when he seemed excited, on 31 October George was described as 'silly', and on 1 November 'a state of debility and vacancy of mind' was reported. Amelia herself died on 2 November. Two days later, coercion was used to administer medicine to the king. Bulletins issued on 11 and 14 November claimed that he was getting better, but he was very seriously ill on 23–26 November. The Privy Council was informed by his doctors on 28–29 November that George's constitution was sound,[132] but this did not answer the problem of how best to ensure that the functions of monarchy were discharged.

On 10 December 1810, Perceval introduced a regency bill, based on Pitt's Bill of 1788. The Regency Act passed on 5 February 1811, with royal assent signified by a commission, and George, prince of Wales, was sworn in as regent on 6 February. The Act and the resulting oaths emphasized the possibility of recovery: *An Act to provide for the Administration of the Royal Authority, and for the Care of His Majesty's Royal Person, during the Continuance of His Majesty's Illness; and for the Resumption of the Exercise of the Royal Authority by His Majesty* gave the prince 'full Power and Authority, in the name and on the behalf of his Majesty'. The first oath obliged him to be 'faithful and bear true allegiance to his Majesty King George', the second to 'consult and maintain the safety, honour, and dignity of his Majesty and the welfare of his people', and the third to protect the settlement of the Protestant religion, a cause dear to George III.

For the first year, at the insistence of Perceval and against the wishes of the Whigs, the prince's powers were limited, in case his father recovered. George's care was entrusted to Queen Charlotte under the Regency Act, but it was a trying responsibility. Calm, quiet and composure on the part of George were the goals sought by his doctors and family, and in the early summer of 1811 they seemed attainable.[133] His situation, however, deteriorated in July: he slept just ten minutes one night, and was 'so violent that correction has been necessary and he is confined', in other words physically restrained. Sir Henry Halford, the oleaginous and formal physician extraordinary to the king, much liked by George, who created him a baronet in 1810, told Cumberland that George was 'totally lost as to mind,

---

[132] Gray, *Spencer Perceval*, pp. 400–3.
[133] Queen Charlotte to prince regent, 5 June, Princess Mary to prince regent, 11 June, 3 July 1811, Aspinall, *Prince of Wales*, VIII, pp. 21, 25, 37.

conversing with imaginary persons, as he is constantly addressing himself to Eliza [Lady Pembroke]. His countenance is much flushed and pulse 84.'[134] Despite the opiates he was given in the form of laudanum, sleep proved difficult, while he ate little.[135] Expectations of a speedy death proved unfounded, and George recovered from his fever, but his mental awareness of the world around him remained limited. In 1812, after the council had been told by George's doctors on 4 February that their patient was insane, the prince regent gained the full prerogative powers of the crown including the right to award pensions and places for life and to grant peerages; in 1811 he had only been allowed to award the latter for military services.

In his youth, the prince had been closely linked both politically and socially to the Whigs, but he had shifted his position from 1807. In part, this reflected changes in British politics, including the character of the Whigs after Fox's death in 1806, but the prince's changing attitudes as he got older were also important. He became more conservative, having a greater concern about the position of the Church of England, and also sought closer relations with his father. Prince George's support for the war led him to oppose what he saw as the Whigs' appeasement of Napoleon: they pressed for negotiations. As prince regent, George followed his father in stressing his patriotism, duty and wish for an inclusive ministry. In his first message to the cabinet after he assumed his full powers in 1812, the regent stated his wish to pursue goals 'common to the whole nation'.

The continuation of the ministry led the Whigs to accuse the regent of being a turncoat. Convinced that he could be swayed, they emphasized the Tory influence of his associates, not least Isabella, marchioness of Hertford, with whom he was very close; but this underestimated his capacity to make his own decisions. In 1812, the regent tried to bring the Whigs into what he hoped would be a widely inclusive ministry, but he refused to accept their liberal views on Catholic emancipation and the war. He had also, with familiarity, become satisfied with the ministers he had inherited: the regent was much older than his father had been when he came to the throne. Furthermore, the regent did not appreciate the criticisms directed at him by Charles Grey and other Whigs. The assassination of the prime minister, Perceval, on 11 May 1812, by a merchant with a private grudge against the government, led to a renewed attempt to create an all-party ministry, but the existing ministers were opposed to the plan and the Whigs demanded too many places. The scheme failed, and the Whigs remained in the political wilderness.

---

[134] Princess Charlotte to Mercer Elphinstone, 16 July, Cumberland to prince regent, 16 July 1811, Aspinall, *Prince of Wales*, VIII, p. 48.

[135] Colonel McMahon to Prince Regent, 29 July 1811, Aspinall, *Prince of Wales*, VIII, pp. 64–5.

George III held his titles until the very end of his life, by which time he had ruled longer than any previous British sovereign, exceeding the record of Henry III (r. 1216–72) by reigning for fifty-nine years. He had become a symbol of longevity. Furthermore, Hanover was raised to the status of a separate kingdom in October 1814, although the title was never included in the royal style as exercised in the British Isles. George, however, was not in a position to enjoy this new status, and was not crowned king of Hanover. Nor was he able to take part in the fête held in Hyde Park in August 1814 to celebrate the centenary of the Hanoverian succession, nor to pre-empt his successor in founding the Guelphic Order to mark the officers of the German Legion who fought at Waterloo, as well as exemplary civilian service to the Electorate. It was to be George IV who benefited from the resulting popularity in the new kingdom when he visited it in 1821, the first visit by its legitimate ruler since the last by George II, in 1755. Hanover also gained territory at the Congress of Vienna, so that, in 1815, it was the fourth largest state in Germany after Austria, Prussia and Bavaria, and the fifth largest in population. Although this was impressive, it has to be set in context. Bavaria, Prussia, Saxony and Württemberg were also kingdoms, while Hanover's territorial gains were modest: East Friesland, Hildesheim, and Osnabrück at last, as well as part of the former prince-bishopric of Münster. These gains were far less than those of Prussia, and were also less impressive than those made by Bavaria and Württemberg over the French Revolutionary and Napoleonic periods. Unlike Prussia, which gained much of the Rhineland as a result of the Vienna settlement, Hanover remained no more than a regional presence in Germany.[136]

On 1 June 1811, Dr Robert Willis took over the total management of George's health, and this change extended to the king's personal circumstances. His pages were replaced by Willis's keepers. Shortly before, Taylor resigned as George's secretary and the king's correspondence was locked away. George was exposed to the 1788 system of seclusion and restraint, a policy that, by cutting him off, made him increasingly isolated. There were similarities with the treatment of Christian VII of Denmark in his last two decades. Elderly, blind and deaf, George was far less fit than he had been in 1788–9. Kept in his apartments in Windsor, where he was out of touch with the world of London, George no longer recognized his family and took solace in imaginary conversations, for example with North. Disconcerted by his state, most of his relatives showed scant interest in him, Princess Augusta preferring to remember him rather than to see him in his current state.[137] Charlotte was in effect a widow.

---

[136] H.G. Aschoff, 'Der Wiener Kongress und die Norddeutschen Staaten', *Niedersächsisches Jahrbuch für Landesgeschichte*, 71 (1999), pp. 111–28.

[137] Augusta to Mrs Williams, 15 Aug. 1811, Aspinall, *Prince of Wales*, VIII, 68.

The situation remained largely unchanged for the last nine years of George's life, although on Charlotte's death on 17 November 1818 Frederick, duke of York, was appointed George's guardian, while it has been argued that senile dementia took hold.[138] His health was such that he was unaware of the passing of those who had been close to him, not only Queen Charlotte, who died holding the prince regent's hand, but also, on 6 November 1817, his granddaughter, Princess Charlotte, who had offered hopes for the future. One of the last images of the king, *George III during his last illness*, attributed to Joseph Lee, was a portrait of a man far removed from grandeur, let alone power.[139] George's treatment was understandably very different from that of the majority of the elderly poor, who were increasingly institutionalized in workhouses.[140] Soon after recovering in 1789, George indeed had visited the Richmond workhouse and shared the inmates' frugal lunch. Institutionalism was a policy opposed by critics who argued that such institutions removed the elderly from their natural place in community and family.[141] Although not institutionalized, George was in this position.

The king died in his room overlooking the North Terrace at Windsor, of pneumonia, in seclusion, if not obscurity, on the evening of 29 January 1820, being succeeded by the prince of Wales. Sidmouth remarked, 'How much better is it to weep over departed excellence in the nearest and dearest of all connections than to be harassed by living profligacy.'[142] The king's death followed speedily on that of his fourth son, Edward, the first of George's adult sons to die. Edward had died suddenly on 23 January 1820, and was buried in St George's Chapel, Windsor on 11 February. Having lain in state for two days, George, in turn, was buried in St George's Chapel on the 16th, returning to a building on which he had lavished so much attention. As George IV was ill with pleurisy, York was the chief mourner. Large numbers attended the funeral of a man who had seen so much history and who had been the king of the vast majority for their entire lives.

---

[138] J.C.G. Röhl, M. Warren and D. Hunt, *Purple Secret. Genes, 'Madness' and the Royal House of Europe* (London, 1998), p. 87.

[139] For a copy of a similar picture kept hidden by George's daughter Charlotte, R.M. Hatton, 'England and Hanover 1714–1837', in A.M. Birke and K. Kluxen (eds), *England und Hannover* (Munich, 1986), p. 21.

[140] S.R. Ottaway, *The Decline of Life: Old Age in Eighteenth-Century England* (Cambridge, 2004), pp. 252–3.

[141] Ibid., p. 275.

[142] Sidmouth to Earl Talbot, 13 Feb. 1820, Exeter, 152 M/C 1820/OH 67.

Chapter 19

REPUTATION AND COMPARISONS

REPUTATION

I have no other view in life than to the best of my judgement to fulfil
my duty.

George, 1800[1]

The British monarchy, or rather the *image* of the monarchy, was recon-
structed during the later years of George's reign. The strong patriotism
of the long war with France, and the king's less conspicuous role in day-
to-day politics, combined fruitfully to facilitate the celebration less of the
reality and more of the symbol of monarchy. In this, the precondition of
the creation of a popular monarchy was (ironically but significantly) the
perceived decline in the crown's political authority in a partisan sense, at
least its use thus in a clear and frequent fashion. Authority was still,
however, retained, for example the crown's usefulness as a guardian of the
Protestant constitution, but unpopular decisions were now more often
blamed on the ministers. George himself contributed to this positive
image, not by making a special effort to change, but by being himself. His
steadfastness and probity helped make him attractive, not irrespective of
differences over policy but taking precedence over them, although there
were always some who rejected that formulation. A series of gestures
underlined his commitment to the country. These included the payment
of £20,000 from his privy purse to the Voluntary Contribution of 1798,
and the extension of taxation to the private income to the crown resulting
from the passage of the Crown Private Estates Act of 1800.

Convinced of the widespread propensity of fallen man, of élite and
populace alike, to corruption and factionalism, George appreciated that
public politics could be unwelcome. In the aftermath of the Gordon Riots,
he had been cautious about large-scale signs of public support: 'it is by no
means either advisable or proper at this hour that persons should be encouraged to bring Addresses attended with numbers, it is the number that sign

---

[1] George to William Grenville, 28 June 1800, BL. Add. 58861.

them only that may make them respectable'.[2] However, in the person of
George, the monarchy was to serve as a popular and potent symbol of
national identity and continuity, a patriotism that was enhanced by the
experience of a difficult war with France from 1793 to 1815 and by the
contrast with the ministerial changes of the 1800s. Although there were
serious differences of opinion, the war with France was less politically
contentious than the War of American Independence had been, and, in so
far as it was unpopular, blame attached largely to the ministers, a marked
contrast with the earlier conflict. The Golden Jubilee of the reign celebrated
on 25 October 1809 was a cause of much celebration and is commemorated
by lasting monuments in Lincoln, Liverpool and Weymouth.

Nevertheless, the customary stress on loyalism has to be matched by an
awareness of criticism. This was not only from self-avowed radicals, such
as Thomas Spence, who joined kings to traitors in a parody of 'God Save
the King', which included the passage,

> Tell Ribbands, Crowns and Stars,
> Kings, Traitors, Troops and Wars,
> Plans, Councils, Plots and Jars,
> FRENCHMEN are FREE![3]

Criticism was also more widely diffused. Readers of the *Courier*, a major
London newspaper, on 22 January 1801 would have noted not only the
ritual of loyalty, with an account of the singing of 'God Save the King'
when George arrived at, and left, the performance of a play at Covent
Garden, but also proceedings at Stafford Sessions stemming from a blunt
remark in a pub. When drunk, the twenty-two-year-old John Adams
declared, 'D——n the King, and his peace, and his peace officers.' He was
sentenced to six months' hard labour, and told,

> 'you have ——d the King; the best, the most virtuous, and most reli-
> gious King in the world; nay, I will say, the best that ever sat on this or
> any other throne; whose whole life has been a pattern of every virtue,
> and has been always employed in defending the property, and securing
> in every way the liberties of his people'.

---

[2] George to Wills, first earl of Hillsborough, secretary of state for the Southern
Department, 13 June 1780, I.R. Christie (ed.), 'George and the Southern Department:
Some Unprinted Royal Correspondence', *Camden Miscellany* XXX (London, 1990), p. 424.

[3] T. Spence, *Pig's Meat; or Lessons for the Swinish Multitude* (3 vols, London, 1793–4), II, 91–3,
cited in C. Pedley, 'Blake's "Tyger" and Contemporary Journalism', *British Journal for
Eighteenth-Century Studies*, 14 (1991), p. 47.

In 1817, the magistrate William Chippendale's offer of five shillings to the band at an outdoor meeting at Oldham if they played 'God Save the King' was refused.[4]

All major figures of the period suffered criticism, but to a certain extent George's reputation was shadowed by that of ministers and commanders, in part because he lived for so long. Although his Jubilee was widely celebrated, much larger sums were raised for the monumental tributes to Pitt and Fox, both of whom died in 1806, than for that to George. A statue in London to be funded by public subscription was proposed soon after George's death, but the funds needed for Mathew Cotes Wyatt's ambitious design of a laurel-crowned George standing in a chariot flanked by figures representing Fame and Victory, and drawn by horses trampling down a monster representing Faction, were not forthcoming. Instead, after the expedient of modifying the St George from an unfinished St George and the Dragon was found impracticable, a more modest equestrian statue was eventually made. Even then, it was not unveiled until 1836, in part because of an injunction against its erection at the junction of Pall Mall and Cockspur Street, on the grounds that it would be a 'nuisance'.[5]

The emphasis was rather on Nelson and Wellington as heroes of the struggle against France. The sense of greatness passing seen with Wellington's funeral in 1851 contrasted markedly with the funerals of George III, George IV and William IV. Similarly, Admiral Hawke and General Wolfe had been the heroes of the Seven Years War. In part, George III suffered because he died at the close of a long period in the shadows while, even had he been fitter, as George I and George II had been in their last years, he was not able to act as a war leader. Nevertheless, his earlier contentious political steps were shadowed by time, and there was much celebration of the king's life when he died.[6] The crowds who turned out for the funeral of George III were not celebrating individual achievement in the way that those who turned out for Wellington did, but they commemorated the passing of a monarch widely seen as a symbol of the greatness of the British constitution.

George's reputation was subsequently to be greatly moulded by contemporaries of the king with their own personal and partisan reasons for likes and dislikes.[7] In part, this was a matter of the search for profit as John Wolcot ('Peter Pindar') admitted when explaining why he had satirized

---

[4] M. Philp, 'Vulgar Conservatism, 1792–3', *English Historical Review*, 110 (1995), p. 59; J. Epstein, 'Radical Dining, Toasting and Symbolic Expression in Early Nineteenth-Century Lancashire. Rituals of Solidarity', *Albion*, 20 (1988), p. 276.

[5] N. Smith, *The Royal Image and the English People* (Aldershot, 2001), p. 170.

[6] E. Holt, *The Public and Domestic Life of His Most Gracious Majesty George the Third* (2 vols, London, 1820).

[7] For an excellent treatment of the king's reputation, G. M. Ditchfield, *George III. An Essay in Monarchy* (Basingstoke, 2002), pp. 4–21. For the first German biography, F. von Bibra, *Georg der Dritte* (Leipzig, 1820).

George, whom he actually thought 'an excellently good man' as well as a clever one,[8] the last the opposite of the depiction in Pindar's accounts. More seriously, criticism was not only more quotable, but also drew on a concern about, or even anger with, George that in part dated from before his accession. James, second Earl Waldegrave, George's governor from 1753 to 1756, was angry that, when George came of age in 1756, and ceased to need a governor, he appointed Bute, and not Waldegrave, as groom of the stool. Waldegrave had not been a popular governor with George, and became positively bitter about his former charge from 1756. His *Memoirs* presented the prince as lazy, poorly educated, and under the thumb of his mother, Augusta, an unimpressive background for kingship. They were not published until 1821,[9] but the unpublished version was consulted by Horace Walpole, whose niece Waldegrave married in 1759.

In turn, Walpole, who very much accepted the interpretation of Augusta and Bute as pernicious influences, also left memoirs. Initially, although those of the last decade of George II's reign were published in 1822, the memoirs of the first decade of George III's were not published, because Henry, third Lord Holland (Charles James Fox's nephew), whose advice the sixth Earl Waldegrave sought, advised that they included questionable claims. His executor, Henry, earl of Euston, the third duke of Grafton's grandson, had fewer qualms, and Walpole's *Memoirs of the Reign of King George the Third* were published in 1845. These proved very influential, as a contemporary source apparently combining the ably written observations of a well-connected commentator with an awareness of the secret springs of politics. This added private spice to the long-standing critique of George's politics expressed by Whig writers and appeared to vindicate them by revealing George as a man brought up with autocratic tendencies that, in their Jacobite background, represented the wrong turn in British history. This was also a theme of the gossip around George from some Whigs at the start of his reign.

The Whigs received further authentication from the *Historical Sketches of Statesmen Who Flourished in the Time of George III* (1839) by Henry, Lord Brougham (1778–1868). A Whig lawyer, who had played a major role in Whig journalism in 1805–7 before becoming an MP in 1810, a prominent popular politician in the 1820s and lord chancellor in 1830, Brougham's first sketch was of the king, and the impact of his work was strengthened when an American edition was published in Philadelphia in 1842. The root cause of George's failure was traced to personality:

> his capacity, whether to appreciate his position, or to aid in the progress of his people and his species, if he should have the wisdom to choose the

---

[8] W. Craig (ed.), *Memoirs of Her Majesty Queen Charlotte of Great Britain* (Liverpool, 1818), p. 555.
[9] For a modern edition, J.C.D. Clark (ed.), *The Memoirs and Speeches of James, 2nd Earl Waldegrave* (Cambridge, 1988).

right path, or to obstruct it, should he erroneously deem resistance the better course, was a matter of the greatest importance both to himself personally, to the order in which his lot was cast, and to the rest of mankind. Unhappily he took the wrong direction; and, having once taken, persevered in it with the pertinacity that marks little minds of all ranks, but which in royal understandings often amounts to a mental disease.

Of a narrow understanding, which no culture had enlarged; of an obstinate disposition, which no education, perhaps, could have humanized; of strong feelings in ordinary things, and a resolute attachment to all his own opinions and predilections, George III possessed much of the firmness of purpose, which, being exhibited by men of contracted mind without any discrimination, and as pertinaciously when they are in the wrong as when they are in the right, lends to their characters an appearance of inflexible consistency which is often mistaken for greatness of mind, and not seldom received as a substitute for honesty. In all that related to his kingly office he was the slave of deep-rooted selfishness; and no feeling of a kindly nature ever was allowed access to his bosom, whenever his power was concerned, either in its maintenance, or in the manner of exercising it.[10]

Brougham's description was much quoted, not least because his political career made his remarks seem authoritative. Those who pressed the cause of reform in the 1820s and 1830s, especially Catholic emancipation and the extension of the parliamentary franchise, saw George's earlier opposition to both as a root of current problems, and as a legacy that, in 'a deliberate intellectual project',[11] had to be both denigrated and overcome, the first appearing crucial to the second. Furthermore, as both issues became key to the Whig myth about the perfectibility of the British constitution, so George's attitude aparently placed him on the side of anachronism. To Whigs, this was underlined by Tory praise for George as the supporter of Protestant constitutionalism. Such High Church views, however, were not fashionable. The strength of the monarchy under Victoria also made it less necessary to praise George, while her positive reputation overshadowed his. The key Whig writer, Thomas Macaulay, was in no doubt that, however privately virtuous, George had been educated into dangerous notions that led him to depart from his predecessor's acceptance of constitutional restraints and instead to pursue 'a vigorous use of the prerogative'.[12] Walpole's *Memoirs* appeared to offer support to this interpretation, and also an explanation in terms of personal foibles, rather than an inherent threat to the constitution stemming

---

[10] H. Brougham, *Historical Sketches of Statesmen Who Flourished in the Time of George III* (2 vols, Philadelphia, Pennsylvania, 1842), I, 13–14.

[11] J.C.D. Clark, *English Society 1660–1832* (2nd edn, Cambridge, 2000), p. 554.

[12] T.B. Macaulay, *Critical and Historical Essays* (2 vols, London, 1907), I, 413–18.

from monarchy. Thus condemning George did not imply criticizing his granddaughter, Victoria.

In his influential *English Constitution* (1867), Walter Bagehot distinguished the 'efficient' parts of the constitution from what he termed the 'dignified' parts, namely the monarchy and the House of Lords. This was a misleading account of the situation in his lifetime, and a teleological presentation of British history, not least in its presentation of George as 'always resisting what ought to be, and prolonging what ought not to be', specifically moves towards democracy.[13] This interpretation drew on Edmund Burke's *Thoughts on the Cause of the Present Discontents* (1770), a work that enjoyed considerable posthumous attention, being, in part, abstracted from its partisan context and presented as an objective account of developments.

Eighteenth-century obloquy was combined with the results of scholarship (or at least the publication of correspondence from the period) to present George not only as reactionary and corrupted – by the influence of Augusta and Bute – but also as a corrupter, keen to use secret advisers and large-scale electoral bribery in order to achieve his goals. This became the orthodoxy, seen in William Hunt's entry in the *Dictionary of National Biography* on a king who 'renounced the proper sphere of a constitutional monarch', and in W.E.H. Lecky's attack on a damaging king who had set out 'to restore the royal power'.[14] At the same time, Lecky noted George's great popularity following the regency crisis, reporting that even 'the poorest cottages', unprompted, lit candles to commemorate his recovery, and claiming that no other member of the dynasty even approached his 'genuine, unforced popularity'.[15] The Whig theme was repeated in other prominent works, such as G.O. Trevelyan's *American Revolution* (1909), C. Grant Robertson's *England under the Hanoverians* (1911), and G.M. Trevelyan's *History of England* (1926), which again opposed a quest for royal power to the democratic and reform movements of a new era. School pupils were assured that George, influenced by Bolingbroke, Bute and Augusta, wished to resume 'all the former royal authority' and to be his own prime minister, and that, due to patronage and the 'King's Friends', he appointed or dismissed ministers as he chose until 1782.[16]

The same theme was taken up in America, where denunciations of the tyrant of the Declaration of Independence served to affirm the foundation myth of the American people. Jefferson's questionable complaint in

[13] W. Bagehot, *The English Constitution* (Oxford, 1928), p. 39.

[14] *Dictionary of National Biography*, VII, 1053; W.E.H. Lecky, *History of England in the Eighteenth Century* (8 vols, London, 1878–90), III, 14, 16, V, 283. See also H. Jephson, *The Platform: Its Rise and Progress* (London, 1892), I, 25–41.

[15] Lecky, *England in the Eighteenth Century*, V, 451–2.

[16] M.W. Keatinge and D.G. Perry, *Britain in the Eighteenth Century* (London, 1935, reprinted 1938, 1941), pp. 323–4.

his autobiography that George had been rude to him at the levee in 1786 (see p. 342) was embellished to demonstrate the king's boorishness. Charles Francis Adams, the editor of the works of his grandfather John Adams, claimed that George had turned his back on Adams and Jefferson, and that this had a lasting impact on American attitudes to Britain.[17]

Yet there were some less critical, even more positive, accounts. In Britain, W.B. Donne offered an important collection of documents when, in 1867, he published correspondence between George and North which, he claimed, showed 'a blunt, busy, positive, shrewd, but not very sagacious man … a restless inquisitive man'.[18] The same year, the prolific John Heneage Jesse, who had already tried to improve the reputation of Richard III, produced a positive account in the *Memoirs of the Life and Reign of King George the Third*. This directly engaged with what Jesse saw as prejudiced Whig views, for example Lord Holland's inaccurate claim that George exulted at the death of Fox in 1806.[19] In 1882, London audiences could listen to praise of the successes of George's reign that brilliantly distinguished constitutional position from national achievement. W.S. Gilbert's lyrics in *Iolanthe* made fun of the House of Lords. The same argument could have been employed about the monarchy, but, instead, the sentiments expressly linked the crown with success:

> The House of Peers, throughout the war,
> Did nothing in particular
> And did it very well:
> Yet Britain set the world ablaze
> In good King George's glorious days!

George's reputation, nevertheless, was long affected by the 'Whig myth'. In this, it paralleled that of the early Stuarts. The loss of America seemed to confirm the critical views of George's rule in Britain, and, as Anglo-Americanism was presented in the twentieth century as based on a shared constitutionalism and love of liberty, there was little admiration for a king who had caused a violent breach in the relationship. The success, in at least the cases of Canada, Australia and New Zealand, of transforming imperial into Dominion relations in the early twentieth century also made George's policies seem maladroit: the USA and, later, Ireland were exceptions to this process and he could be blamed in each case. The

---

[17] C.F. Adams (ed.), *The Works of John Adams* (10 vols, Boston, Massachusetts, 1850–6) I, 420.

[18] W.B. Donne, *The Correspondence of King George the Third with Lord North from 1768 to 1783* (2 vols, London, 1867), I, xiii. In 'Latest from Spirit–Land' (*Punch*, 10 Jan. 1863), in response to the American Civil War, George asked George Washington what he thought of 'your fine republic now!'

[19] J.H. Jesse, *Memoirs of the Life and Reign of King George the Third* (3 vols, London, 1867), V, 334.

resulting impression was summarized by Edmund Clerihew Bentley, an
Oxford-educated journalist, in one of his light verses or 'clerihews',
published in *More Biographies* (1929),

> George the Third
> Ought never to have occurred.
> One can only wonder
> At so grotesque a blunder.

The Unitarian historian Alexander Gordon called him 'George the
Third-rate'.[20] The dominant view, in turn, was caricatured in the popular
skit of received historical wisdom, W.C. Sellar and R.J. Yeatman's *1066 and
All That* (1930):

> George III, An Obstinate King. George III was a Bad King. He was,
> however, to a great extent insane and a Good Man ... One day when
> George III was insane he heard that the Americans never had after-
> noon tea. This made him very obstinate and he invited them all to a
> compulsory tea-party at Boston.

Paradoxically, the previous year Sir Lewis Namier had published a
scholarly work, *The Structure of Politics at the Accession of George III*, that
offered a major re-evaluation of the nature of politics, and thus a reconsideration of the context within which George could be judged. Namier's
stress on the self-interest of parliamentarians, and on the calculations of
electoral interest, undercut the previous emphasis on the probity of the
opposition critique of George's policies. He also demonstrated that, in the
general election of 1761, George had not increased the use of royal influence. This was an important step in the questioning of the hitherto dominant Whig interpretation. Namier, however, neither wrote in an accessible
style, nor sought to popularize his scholarship. The immediate impact of
his work was negligible, certainly when compared to the continued publication of Whig accounts, with G.M. Trevelyan's history in particular
appearing in fresh editions. Brougham, Horace Walpole and G.O.
Trevelyan, for example, were cited by Colwyn Edward Vulliamy in *Royal
George* (1937), a popular work that offered a bleak view of personality and
policies:

> He was a man whose intelligence hardly rose to the level of respectful
> mediocrity; his faults were those of a stupid man, not those of a villain
> or hypocrite ... his fatal obstinacy, his control of party competition as

---

[20] A. Gordon, *Addresses Biographical and Historical* (London, 1922), p. 202.

the means of enforcing his own will upon the government, his dogged opposition to progress, his uncouth appearance and odd manners.[21]

Nevertheless, the basis for a better-grounded and more favourable treatment of George had been strengthened by the publication of much of the king's correspondence. Though poorly edited, Sir John Fortescue's six-volume edition of the correspondence of George as king up to 1783 appeared in 1927–8, and was followed, in 1939, by Romney Sedgwick's edition of George's letters to Bute. These indicated that, far from planning to subvert a clearly established constitution, both men, motivated by Patriotism, were joined in a wish to strengthen a country they saw as weakened by oligarchy. Access to the king's correspondence led Bonamy Dobrée to offer a generous account in 1935 of

a far better King than most have been willing to concede . . . he was not a die-hard, except on the question of Catholic emancipation . . . deeply patriotic . . . but no chauvinist . . . he was an admirable, devoted, indefatigable civil servant, who expected the holder of any post to do the work demanded of him: he was at once too single-hearted and too simple-minded for the complicated world of politics.[22]

At a more popular level, J.D. Griffith Davies offered in 1936 what he presented as a 'protest against a school lesson, which I find still being taught'. Arguing that the king had had a bad deal, he presented George as clever, with a shrewd appreciation of affairs and a fine grasp of the details of government, making few mistakes, not panicking, and having 'the Englishman's amiability and bigotry, courage and obstinacy'.[23]

Yet just as the Whig intellectual ascendancy of the nineteenth century had also witnessed the publication of critical works, so the Namierite position was itself criticized. First, there were differences of opinion among those sympathetic to Namier, with Richard Pares in particular regarding George as more prone to intervene in politics than Namier had done.[24] More searching criticism came from scholars who rejected Namier's 'five men and the Duke of Newcastle' perspective of, and on, the role of the crown and political élite in the politics of the nation. The influential Cambridge historian Herbert Butterfield pressed for more attention to public opinion, and also correctly noted that, in his early years as king, George had himself set the goal of reversing what he saw as the decline of royal power as a result of ministerial dominance. This was a vindication

[21] C.E. Vulliamy, *Royal George* (London, 1937), p. 309.
[22] B. Dobrée, *The Letters of King George III* (London, 1935), p. xii.
[23] J.D.G. Davies, *George the Third* (London, 1936), quotes pp. viii, vi.
[24] R. Pares, *King George III and the Politicians* (Oxford, 1953).

of at least an important aspect of the traditional criticism of George.[25] G.M. Trevelyan was the dedicatee of Butterfield's *George III, Lord North and the People, 1779–1780* (1949). While willing to offer some grudging praise – 'even George III will be seen to have had his impressive qualities' – this was an account of failure that was antithetical to the king, 'Never was a youthful dream so turned to ashes' was the verdict on the 1760s, while the crisis of 1779–80 was largely attributed to 'George III's general system'. Character flaws were also detected: 'those who are obstinately well-intentioned – the men like George III – are too prone to overlook the fact that other individuals, equally valid . . . have their own view'. Butterfield's interest in public opinion was subsequently taken up by another Cambridge historian, John Brewer, whose account of the 1760s focused on Wilkesite agitation, acting as a prelude to work on the 1790s centred on radicals.[26] From both perspectives, George was the enemy and scant effort was made to understand the king's viewpoint.

The immediate impact of Namierite work outside academic circles was limited; instead, a decline in the obloquy heaped on George largely stemmed from a distancing from the constitutional and political struggles of his reign. Furthermore, the 'Whig myth' became less central because progress, after World War II, came to be seen more in terms of egalitarianism and social welfare than in limitations on royal authority. However unconvincing Rockingham and Charles James Fox may have been as stalwart defenders of liberty, they could scarcely be seen as proto-socialists. Liberty was now largely defined in terms of the welfare state. Nevertheless, Whiggish criticisms were still printed and reprinted, John Cuthbert Long's *George III* (1962) presenting the king as 'fatally inflexible', and closing, 'George III made a contribution to history by showing that the stubborn assertion of royal power was forever out of date and his would-be autocratic rule never has been re-attempted in the British realm'.[27]

If George could therefore be displaced from his position in the established narrative of British history, this opened up a distinction between the American coverage of George and its British counterpart. For Americans, George remained a key figure as an unwitting enabler in the fight for independence. In 1971, an American edition appeared of *The King Who Lost America* by the English popular writer Alan Lloyd, who wrote 'George had crippled both his strength and reputation trying to swim against the tides

[25] H. Butterfield, *George III, Lord North and the People, 1779–1780* (London, 1949), *George III and the Historians* (London, 1957), 'George III and the Constitution', *History*, 43 (1958), and 'Some Reflections on the Early Years of George III's Reign', *Journal of British Studies*, 4 (1965).

[26] J. Brewer, *Party Ideology and Popular Politics at the Accession of George III* (Cambridge, 1976).

[27] J.C. Long, *George III* (London, 1962), pp. 304–5.

of the moment',[28] while, in 1982, Robert Middlekauff offered a conventional criticism of George and British policy in *The Glorious Cause: The American Revolution 1763–1789*. Virtue, in this work, was essentially an American prerogative. American views of the king were dominated by the Revolution and this conditioned accounts of his conduct in other spheres. George was seen as a bad loser, and the questionable story of his turning his back on Jefferson was repeated without qualification.[29] In 1968, the academic Merrill Jensen rejected the Whig myth about George subverting the British constitution,[30] but the portrayal of George in conventional oppressive terms endures to this day.

For the British, as George largely ceased to be a major locator in the Whiggish account of progress towards liberty, this gave more space for academic accounts of George and, in particular, for a less critical and often more favourable perception. John Brooke, his most successful modern biographer, was a colleague of Namier and was very much influenced by him, as he acknowledges in the introduction to his *King George III* (1972), which presents his subject in favourable terms. The establishment pedigree of the work is indicated by its foreword by Prince Charles. Brooke's major source, the Royal Archives, clearly influenced the content and tone of the work. Also building on Namier's perspective and scholarship, Ian Christie and Peter Thomas produced scholarly books and articles rebutting important criticisms of George's political position and policies, and offering accounts of aspects of the reign that were favourable to the king.[31] Thomas subsequently published a study that put on record a Namierite account of the entire 1760s as distinct from books and theses covering only a year or two.[32] Other scholars also applauded George and criticized the Whig account. Writing of the fall of the Talents and the Portland ministry's success in the election of 1807, John Derry observed, 'Once again George III had spoken for the nation in voicing disquiet about a scheme which would have given Catholics partial relief from longstanding disabilities.'[33]

---

[28] A. Lloyd, *The King Who Lost America* (New York, 1971), p. 349.

[29] D. Malone, *Jefferson and His Time. II. Jefferson and the Rights of Man* (Boston, Massachusetts, 1951), pp. 54–5; P. Smith, *John Adams* (2 vols, Garden City, New York, 1962), II, 671; F.M. Brodie, *Thomas Jefferson: An Intimate History* (New York, 1974), p. 95; Ritcheson, 'The Fragile Memory', *Eighteenth-Century Life*, 6 (1981), p. 7.

[30] M. Jensen, *The Founding of a Nation. A History of the American Revolution 1763–1776* (New York, 1968), p. 40.

[31] I.R. Christie, 'George III and the Historians – Thirty Years On', *History*, 71 (1986), pp. 205–21; P.D.G. Thomas, 'George III and the American Revolution', *History*, 70 (1985), pp. 16–31.

[32] P.D.G. Thomas, *George III. King and Politicians 1760–1770* (Manchester, 2002); Thomas to Black, 12 Feb. 2004, Black papers.

[33] J.W. Derry, *Politics in the Age of Fox, Pitt and Liverpool* (2nd edn, Basingstoke, 2001), p. 106.

The favourable presentation of George was countered by J.H. Plumb who, in a published lecture, argued that, although George was no tyrant, he was certainly not the 'cynosure of monarchy'. Instead, the king was presented as a blinkered enthusiast for diligence and the rules, unaware of larger issues and processes of political change, with an obsessive personality that required order and regularity.[34] This view, however, was not developed into a full-length study, and it could not have been entirely sustained.

At the same time, George rather dropped from attention in the 1970s and 1980s. This was unsurprising, despite first-rate research by specialists, as academic interest in the royals receded in favour of a concern with social topics and popular politics, while public interest in individuals became more democratic. In so far as the royals enjoyed attention, it was the Tudors and, to a lesser extent, the Stuarts who commanded pages and screens, and not the Hanoverians. There was no story line to win attention akin to the six wives of Henry VIII. By the early 1990s George was a largely forgotten figure, other than in the USA.

This changed when interest in his health was turned into media success. Furthermore, the prominence of Alan Bennett's play *The Madness of George III* (1991) and then film *The Madness of King George* (1994), which offered at once a lurid way to approach royal history but also a corrective of the view of George as mad, made George a recognizable figure in terms of a modern emphasis on a shared humanity. Bennett's intention was not to approach George as a political figure. Instead, George emerged as somewhat absurd as well as human. This was also the case in Kenneth Baker's *The Kings and Queens. An Irreverent Cartoon History of the British Monarchy* (1996), in which royal inexperience moves to incompetence and then to 'his simple old way'. In a review published in 2005, Baker presented George as 'a control-freak' in both political and personal matters.[35] A more sympathetic account was provided by Christopher Hibbert in his popular *George III. A Personal History* (1998). In accordance with Brooke's portrayal, George was presented by Hibbert as a conscientious ruler and a cultured individual. That year, Ohio State University had a search for its new George III chair in British history: a donor wished to establish a chair in British history and felt that the king had had a bad press. Hibbert's theme was taken up in another accessible study, Christopher Wright's *George III* (2005).

The major public attempt to offer a more rounded portrayal has come from Prince Charles who, as a television interview in 2004 made clear, sees his ancestor as not only sympathetic but also impressive. There are major

[34] J.H. Plumb, *New Light on the Tyrant George III* (Washington, D.C., 1978). See also his *The First Four Georges* (London, 1956).

[35] K. Baker, reviews of C. Wright, *George III* and S. Weintraub, *Iron Tears*, in *History Today*, 55, 8 (2005), p. 58.

contrasts between the two men, but they have a sense of duty and obligation in common. Prince Charles amplified his views in his foreword to the
catalogue for the prominent 2004 exhibition in the Queen's Gallery of
works linked to George from the Royal Collection. Culture, indeed,
helped make George seem more impressive. Prince Charles writes:

> In the sixty years of his reign he immersed himself in a tremendous
> range of practical, scientific and artistic interests including agriculture,
> astronomy, architecture, horology and the collecting of books, medals,
> paintings and drawings. His absorption with architecture and his skill as
> an architectural draughtsman I found particularly stimulating and
> appealing, while his creation of the King's Library and his wish to give
> encouragement to artists by founding the Royal Academy have been of
> lasting benefit to the cultural life of this country.[36]

At a rather different level of memorialization, Longleat still has one of
the pair of oak trees planted by George and Charlotte during their
popular visit in September 1789. The other, however, made way for a
tennis court in 1925.

COMPARISONS

> There can scarcely be a greater contrast than between the ease, the
> power, the triumph enjoyed by our monarch, and the confusion in the
> affairs of his brother of France.
>
> *Felix Farley's Bristol Journal*, 26 January 1788

Reputation emerges most clearly through comparison. The contrast
between the fates of the British and French monarchies was due to many
things, but the differences between the personalities and attitudes of
George and Louis XVI were important. These differences should not be
pushed too far, as neither man was grand in his manner, Louis shared
George's marital fidelity, and George's attitude to Catholic emancipation
was an echo, albeit a pale one, of Louis's refusal to accept the need to work
with the Revolutionary government. Yet, in 1791, Louis fled the capital as
part of a scheme to force a change, before being captured at Varennes. In
contrast, although he threatened to abdicate and to leave for Hanover,
George's opposition to ministers and policies he disliked was expressed

---

[36] Foreword to J. Roberts (ed.), *George III and Queen Charlotte. Patronage, Collecting and Court Taste* (London, 2004), p. 7. See also, D. Watkin, *The Architect King: George III and the Culture of the Enlightenment* (London, 2004) and J. Marsden (ed.), *The Wisdom of George the Third* (London, 2005).

within the political system, although in 1783 he pushed his prerogative powers very hard. George, however, was not put under pressure comparable to Louis: there were risings in North America and Ireland, not England, and the Gordon Riots lacked a serious and sustained political dimension.

In September 1789 George praised Louis to the French envoy, La Luzerne, claiming that no prince had ever merited more the respect and attachment of his people and that he had no doubt that the eyes of his subjects would be opened and his authority restored.[37] Louis indeed shared some of George's qualities. Like George he was diligent, fairly (although not outstandingly) intelligent, competent as a monarch, particularly in foreign affairs and economics, and essentially upright, certainly in comparison with Louis XV, and, like George, he never led his forces into battle. Both men were interested in hunting, and in the workings of clocks and watches, as an aspect of their joint interest in technology, manufacture and agriculture. Louis headhunted personnel from British industry and pored over reports of its excellence. Moreover, although Louis's health did not deteriorate as seriously as George's, from 1787 his ability to govern was seriously impaired by acute intermittent depression. Furthermore, just as George appeared to many (but by no means all) more sympathetic in his later years, and was seen as in some way tested by his ill health in 1788–9, so Louis's character was presented as refined by suffering in his last years.

For both men, their political symbolism and value came to be removed from their power. Just as George in his later years read Shakespeare and was associated with King Lear, so history was the favourite reading of Louis, and he showed a close interest in the fate of Charles I of England: the life of the martyr-king played a central role in Louis's sense of impending doom.[38] George also had a sense of historical consciousness. When his brother Henry married a commoner in 1771, the outraged and overwrought George was concerned that such a step might threaten civil war, as he claimed that the fifteenth-century Wars of the Roses owed much to the intermarriage of crown and nobility,[39] an instructive example of the dynastic element in the mid-century political imagination.

At the same time, Louis, like George, failed to manage peaceful reform and avoid revolution. How far the two men were at fault is subject to debate. If they had scant idea of how to unite and lead by exciting the passions or firing the imagination, that recourse of the demagogue was to

---

[37] La Luzerne to Montmorin, 22 Sept. 1789, AE. CP. Ang. 571 fols 10–11. For earlier support for French domestic policy, La Luzerne to Montmorin, 20 May 1788, AE. CP. Ang. 565 fols 183–4.

[38] J. Hardman, *Louis XVI* (New Haven, Connecticut, 1992).

[39] George to duke of Gloucester, 9 Nov. 1771, RA. GEO/15938.

lead France to disaster under Napoleon. In contrast, if solid, but undistinguished, upright leadership is not itself at fault, it gave rise, in the case of both George and Louis, to legalistic, negative and unimaginative responses to challenges. In France, North America and Ireland, the transition from administrative to representative monarchy was a difficult task. It may well be that the chance of managing the transition without violence was impossible, not least due to social, economic and institutional problems,[40] but the monarchs, it can be argued, did not understand the challenge.

Alongside this Whiggish thesis comes the view of the monarchs as able to understand the challenge yet determined to resist what they saw as unwelcome demands for change. George responded to pressure for Catholic emancipation in Ireland in 1784 by urging rapid repression: 'So many evils have arisen from not crushing evils whilst in the bud.' That clearly was the lesson learned from America, and it was an inappropriate one.[41] Louis as well as George can be located accordingly, as it is possible to see the former as beginning a dual policy towards the Revolution from October 1789. On the surface, he appeared to accept the reduced role that the Assembly allotted him, up to, and including, endorsing the constitution. His real aims, however, became escape and the reimposition of royal authority. George was sympathetic to Louis's attempt at escape in 1791 – 'the situation at Paris was so hard that no one can justly be surprised that any attempt was made to get out of it'[42] – but, once free, Louis definitely had no intention of compromising with the Revolution. The flight to Varennes and his repudiation of his oath to uphold the Revolution had a traumatic and destabilizing effect on the country,[43] and sowed further suspicion about Louis's secret policies, but did not prevent the king from renewed efforts to plot against the new government. At the same time, Louis was subject to competing advice, and his wife, Marie Antoinette, in particular, challenged his hesitation, not least in the summer of 1792 when an approach by Lafayette that would have entailed accepting a constitutional monarchy was rejected.[44] George was not exposed to analogous circumstances, but his willingness to act against ministers he distrusted can be seen as evidence of a similar trait.

In April 1791, George told La Luzerne that he supported the reestablishment of order in France. The failure to do this in a legitimist

[40] P. Jones, *Reform and Revolution in France. The Politics of Transition, 1774–1791* (Cambridge, 1995).
[41] George to Sydney, 26 July 1784, Aspinall, *George III*, I, 75.
[42] George to William Grenville, 27 June 1791, BL. Add. 58856 fols 54–5.
[43] T. Tackett, *When the King Took Flight* (Cambridge, Massachusetts, 2003), esp. pp. 221–2.
[44] M. Price, *The Fall of the French Monarchy. Louis XVI, Marie Antoinette and the Baron de Breteuil* (London, 2002).

fashion, however, opened up a major gap between the two countries. The execution of Louis in January 1793 led to a powerful reiteration of monarchical ideology in Britain, becoming part of the process by which the British were differentiated from the French. George took the comforting view that the Revolutionary system could not last. In his eyes, it was more illegal and violent than the American counterpart, and, in common with most commentators, he predicted its demise:

> The account of the fresh tumult at Paris is what must have been expected from the total want of a legal government, and more of the like will arise till the successes of various insurrections in the interior of the kingdom make the majority feel the necessity of returning to a form of government resembling the old one though perhaps ameliorated in many particulars.[45]

The Bourbons, however, were not restored until 1814. In the meanwhile, from 1799, George was favourably contrasted by most British commentators with the tyrannical and bellicose Napoleon. The nature of Napoleonic rule, at once authoritarian and radical, provided a ready contrast to government in Britain, although not always to the process of British territorial expansion.

Lumping George with Louis XVI, as well as the rulers of Naples, Portugal and Spain, Frederick the Great, in 1782, had expressed amazement at the calibre of crowned heads.[46] There was a degree of complacency about such comments on the part of Frederick, but they capture a sense of hereditary monarchy as risking anachronism if the monarchs were not up to their *métier*, or indeed job as it increasingly seemed. The trial and execution of Louis XVI in 1792–3 clearly expressed this, as, in a very different context, did the conspiracies leading to the assassinations of Tsar Peter III in 1762, Gustavus III of Sweden in 1792, and Tsar Paul I in 1801, and the deposition of Gustavus Adolphus IV of Sweden in 1809.[47]

More than personalities were at issue in the political position of monarchs. There was also a more general shift in political culture within the West, with the rise of the public sphere linked to a more utilitarian image of monarchy, seen in the scaling down of the relative role of royal courts. Furthermore, an entire generation of monarchs was bored by ceremony and preferred a simpler lifestyle. Across Europe, the notion of honour and *gloire*, generally presented in the seventeenth and early decades of the eighteenth century in personal and dynastic terms, was now increasingly seen in terms of the nation and country, George being

[45] George to William Grenville, 13 June 1793, BL. Add. 58857 fol. 124.

[46] Frederick to duke of Brunswick, 14 Jan. 1782, *Politische Correspondenz Friedrichs der Grossen* (46 vols, Berlin, 1879–1939), 46 (1939), p. 428.

[47] R.E. McGrew, *Paul I of Russia 1754–1801* (Oxford, 1992).

eventually identified with John Bull. This limited the relevance of dynasties as focuses of identity and as units, instead encouraging royal families to seek a stronger identification with nation and country. There were other related important changes. After mid-century, European monarchs were more prepared to risk abandoning traditional norms, a shift due to a different ideology of kingship, and a response to the particular need to improve governmental capability after the War of the Austrian Succession (1740–8), a lesson underlined by the Seven Years War. A reduced emphasis on the sacral aspect of kingship encouraged a stress on the monarch as first servant of the state. This was an aspect of the social and cultural transformation of established hierarchies, and, partly, of the spread of a reform Catholicism owing much to Jansenism, as well as of ideas grouped subsequently as Enlightened, and of the cultural tropes of neo-classicism. This stress was related to the downgrading of dynasties in favour of the monarchs themselves, although George had a sense of dynastic continuity. In 1786 he wrote to his son Augustus:

> I am pleased with your expressing satisfaction at having seen the coat of mail of King George I, whose descendants cannot enough venerate him, for he was as honest, brave and just a man as ever was born; these are solid ingredients without which no character can be either respectable or amiable,[48]

the admonitory tone being all too characteristic. He sought to maintain the dynastic outlook while tacitly assuming the utilitarian.

George acknowledged the sense of royal service in his draft abdication message of 1782 in which he wrote that he had found he could 'be of no further utility to his native country'.[49] Service was seen by George as both *métier* and means to further his goals; and, to execute the business of kingship effectively, he saw the need not only for diligence and integrity but also for reason. Their absence in his heir distressed George. His emphasis on reason as opposed to the passions, a traditional inheritance from Cicero and the Classical philosophers, is arresting in this context: 'sense, not every frivolous and irregular passion . . . I am certain if the Prince of Wales will consult the different gentlemen of his establishment on their particular branches, that they can form a plan, and that he, like a rational being, will conform to it, he will find things much easier arranged than he may imagine'.[50]

Another aspect of the changing position of monarchs was a shift in their appearance: less as staged figures amidst splendid iconography, and,

---

[48] George to Augustus, 21 July 1786, Aspinall, *George III*, I, 240.
[49] Draft message from the king, – Mar. 1782, Fortescue, V, 425.
[50] George to prince of Wales, 27 Aug. 1784, Aspinall, *George III*, I, 82.

instead, increasingly as working rulers. The wearing of military uniform further demonstrated their role as servants of the state, and George introduced a Windsor Uniform into court dress, being portrayed wearing it by Gainsborough in 1781.[51] In France, monarchy, up to a point, was seen less and less as rooted in the Divine Right of Kings, an ideology that precluded much criticism of the crown, and increasingly in secular contractual terms, which left it much more exposed to criticism. In Britain, although there was a revival of divine right ideas in reaction to the French atheism of the 1790s, an emphasis on the king as servant of the state led to a stress on the other servants too, which diminished the practical and symbolic role of the monarch. In an instructive exchange in 1796, Spencer explained that he could not see George as he had to be at St Albans for the election of the mayor, the king replying 'I am sensible of Earl Spencer's attention in explaining the cause of his being prevented from appearing at St. James's on Wednesday; I know boroughs are apt to feel any supposed neglect on their annual days of municipal election.'[52]

To George and many of his contemporaries, there was also a moral quality in rulership, and thus comparisons were in part a matter of focusing on personalities. In 1793, he wrote of William IX, Landgrave of Hesse-Cassel (r. 1785–1806), a first cousin with whom he had earlier been in a 'friendly state of intercourse'[53] (awarding him the Order of the Garter in 1786),

> the remark of Sir James Murray in his private letter concerning the little pay the Hessians receive is a serious grievance but I do not know any means of remedying it; the Landgrave's real passion is avarice and it is by starving his officers and soldiers that he enriches himself; if we made any representation he would not attend to it, and if we could compel him, he would not furnish any further troops.[54]

In 1793, George was also fairly critical of Frederick William II of Prussia, a second cousin: 'The sudden retreat of the King of Prussia completes the very ill-advised line of conduct that has attended every step he has taken for these four or five years.'[55] Indeed, the conduct of other rulers during the French Revolutionary Wars was to lead to George making frequent

---

[51] P. Mansel, 'Monarchy, Uniform and the Rise of the Frac', *Past and Present*, 96 (1982), pp. 112–17.

[52] Spencer to George, 18 Sept., reply, 19 Sept. 1796, BL. Add. 75792.

[53] George to Carmarthen, 12 Nov. 1785, Aspinall, *George III*, I, 192.

[54] George to Dundas, 23 Aug. 1793, BL. Add. 40100 fol. 93.

[55] George to William Grenville, 10 Oct. 1793, BL. Add. 58857 fol. 165. For comparisons of British and German developments E. Hellmuth (ed.), *The Transformation of Political Culture: England and Germany in the Late Eighteenth Century* (Oxford, 1990), and 'Reform in Great Britain and Germany 1750–1850', *Proceedings of the British Academy*, 100 (1999).

comments on the moral failings as leaders of his counterparts, just as in 1784 he had in part blamed the crisis in Dutch politics on 'the timidity and irresolution' of William V of Orange.[56] Propriety, integrity and good government were all linked in George's view of kingship, and, from this perspective, he received much praise. William Fraser, an experienced official, linked the state of international relations in 1785 to the personal ambitions of monarchs, before absolving George of blame:

these strange disjointed times. Where there is no system, but that of striving to overreach. Surely things must mend, and we shall again see a right understanding in those who ought to form a balance for the preservation of mankind and not for the destruction of those they are born to protect and render happy, merely for the purpose of gratifying their own ambition. We may here say we live under a sovereign who really has no other wish but the laudable one of fulfilling the purpose for which he is placed at the head of a free people.[57]

George himself thought measures to avoid bringing on a war sensible both for Britain and for others,[58] and his support for peace led him to refer to himself as 'a friend to mankind',[59] the sort of remark associated with those described as Enlightened. The Enlightenment should not be rigidly defined, and, once attention shifts from the French *philosophes* to the movement more generally, the extent to which it could be coterminous with elements of Christian reformism emerges clearly. This was true in Britain.[60] One element of overlap, and of continuity with past practice, was provided by the concern to regulate or end popular practices seen as conducive to immorality and waste. George was at one with this, conspicuously so in his concern with the reform of manners in the 1780s. This brought him in line with a powerful current in polite society, one newly strengthened by the crisis of the early 1780s. At the same time, the social politics of the policies associated with George could be harsh, as noted in an unsympathetic caricature published on 17 September 1787, *Reformation, or Their Worships grubbing up a Skittle Ground*. This showed three men grubbing up a skittle ground, one with a spade marked Morality, while a

---

[56] George to Hawkesbury, 16 July 1801, BL. Loan 72/1 fol. 80; George to Philip, second earl of Hardwicke, 18 Mar. 1784, BL. Add. 35349 fol. 70.

[57] Fraser to Keith, 7 June 1785, BL. Add. 35534 fol. 208.

[58] George to Carmarthen, 4 Oct. 1785, BL. Add. 27914 fol. 9.

[59] George to Carmarthen, 26 Aug. 1786, BL. Add. 27914 fol. 17.

[60] R. Porter, *Enlightenment. Britain and the Creation of the Modern World* (London, 2000); D. Beales, 'Christians and "Philosophes": The Case of the Austrian Enlightenment', in Beales and G. Best (eds), *History, Society and the Churches: Essays in Honour of Owen Chadwick* (Cambridge, 1985), pp. 169–94.

pickaxe marked 'Proclamation' lay on the ground, an ass stood in the background, and a publican watched and scratched his head.

A notion of service did not have to entail weak monarchy. There was also the argument that an active, diligent monarch should serve both people and dynasty by reforming the state. This could give rise to the criticism of other political agencies presented as self-serving and unable to engender reform. This was the background of the group of monarchs termed the 'Enlightened Despots', for example the Emperor Joseph II, and it provided a context within which George could be considered, because his assaults on the Whig establishment could be seen to parallel the attack on the French *parlements* by Louis XV in 1771 and Gustavus III's overthrow of the Swedish Age of Liberty the following year.[61] However, the increasingly positive connotation of firm monarchical leadership on parts of the continent had no resonance in Britain and indeed such a notion remained unacceptable.[62]

By temperament and conviction, nevertheless, George had little interest in, or commitment to, the adversarial character and popular aspect of the British political system, although he was a reader of the press, and of American and Irish newspapers.[63] George was also eager for news of elections, interested in ensuring that good candidates came forward,[64] and happy to receive loyal addresses, but, unprepared to accept the value of opposition to government,[65] he was inclined to doubt its legitimacy. In 1777, George wrote, with reference to a dispute over the government of Madras, 'I have seen too much of ballots to have any opinion, whatever favourable appearances may be shown, that any dependence can be had on that mode of decision'. The following year, he referred to the 'opinion I have long had that men who have been active in opposition rarely make useful servants of the Crown', and to his preference for short sessions and not submitting too much business to parliament.[66]

In 1802, Sir Francis Burdett, a radical MP, stood in the general election for the prominent seat of Middlesex against William Mainwaring, the

[61] D. Jarrett, *The Begetters of Revolution: England's Involvement with France, 1759–1789* (London, 1973).

[62] D. Beales, *Enlightenment and Reform in Eighteenth-Century Europe* (Cambridge, 2005).

[63] Remarks on the press in George's handwriting, 31 Oct., 4 Nov. 1760, BL. Add. 36796 fol. 56; Robinson to George, 23 June, 10 Aug., 3, 20, 26, 28 Oct., 9 Dec. 1779, George to Robinson, 28 June, 13 Aug., 3 Oct. 1779, Robinson to George, 23 June 1779, BL. Add. 37834 fols 98–9, 128–9, 148, 150, 161, 168, 172, 37835 fol. 59; George to Robinson, 22 Jan., 8 Feb., 2 Mar., 20 May 1780, BL. Add. 37835 fols 93, 95, 101, 114; George to Pitt, 30 Jan. 1784, 9 May 1804, PRO. 30/8/103 fol. 44, 104 fol. 336.

[64] George to Robinson, 27 Sept., 3 Oct. 1779, BL. Add. 37834 fols 144, 150.

[65] E.g. George to Pitt, 18, 21 Feb. 1792, 18 June 1793, 20 Feb. 1800, 13 Feb., 1 May 1805, PRO. 30/8/103 fols 436–8, 498, 104 fols 265, 421, 439.

[66] George to Robinson, 31 Mar. 1777, 7 Feb., 12 Sept. 1778, BL. Add. 37833 fols 191, 216, 37834 fol. 15.

chairman of the Middlesex and Westminster Quarter Sessions. Burdett had criticized the war and complained about what he presented as the autocratic aspects of government, making a particular impact with his criticism of the treatment in the Coldbath Fields Prison of suspects denied the protection of Habeas Corpus.[67] Mainwaring, who had resisted Burdett's inquiry into prison abuses, had held the seat since 1784, and received a secret service annuity. George clearly did not feel that the seat should have been contested, writing to the home secretary,

> Lord Pelham has acted very properly in having taken steps to prevent the peace of London being disturbed at the close of the Middlesex election, as the contest can have been made for no other object but to try whether mischief could not be effected[68] ... It is much to be wished that the Poll at Brentford should be closed, but as Sir Francis Burdett is not guided by any rules of propriety it must be difficult to ascertain when that will take place[69] ... the Middlesex election ... the conduct that has of late been held too clearly gives reason to expect some riot, and though the magistrates have as yet kept off any outrage without the assistance of the military yet no one can be assured that it may not be necessary.[70]

In the event, Burdett won handsomely, only for his election to be declared void in 1804. A contested election then led to the return of Mainwaring's son, but the result was amended to return Burdett (1805) and then his rival (1806). In 1807 Burdett won again, sitting for Westminster until 1837, but was sent to the Tower in 1810 for breaching the privilege of the House by publishing a contentious speech. George's response to Burdett suggests that his instinctual hostility to populist politics remained. The episode also reveals the king's social views: George described Mainwaring as the son of 'some tradesman',[71] whereas Boulton Mainwaring was in fact a successful architect. In 1803, William Grenville was criticized by George for offering in the Lords 'more an invective than an argumentative statement ... the result of cool reflection',[72] a comment characteristic of his lack of understanding of opposition parliamentary politicians. Two years later, the king complained about an address from London that 'outstrips its true line of duty', and argued that no response

---

[67] See, for generally, P. Spence, *The Birth of Romantic Radicalism: War, Popular Politics and English Radical Reformism, 1800–1815* (Aldershot, 1996).
[68] George to Pelham, 16 July 1802, BL. Add. 33115 fol. 86.
[69] George to Pelham, 19 July 1802, BL. Add. 33115 fol. 91.
[70] George to Pelham, 28 July 1802, BL. Add. 33115 fol. 94.
[71] F. Bickley (ed.), *The Diaries of Sylvester Douglas, Lord Glenbervie*, (2 vols, London, 1928), I, 394.
[72] George to Pelham, 14 May 1803, BL. Add. 33115 fol. 134.

should be made as he did not want to encourage 'haranguers on subjects not properly coming under their cognizance'.[73] Nor was George interested in most areas of reform, for example of prisons. He was happy to give poor debtors a second chance. However, his habit of blaming individuals, rather than considering institutional and social contexts, an aspect of his belief in an active moral universe, was indicated by his response to a report on fever in Newgate Prison in 1803: 'considering the sort of inhabitants it is wonderful that contagious distempers do not more frequently appear there'.[74]

Yet, although George's views on public liberty might be questioned by contemporaries, he was not associated (and did not seek to associate himself), at least, as far as Britain was concerned, with an allegedly Enlightened programme of wide-ranging modernization and centralization akin to that rashly attempted, and maladroitly pushed, by Joseph.[75] In contrast to the emperor, whom George indeed disliked,[76] George sought to put 'this country in as good a state by attention, and not by trying new schemes which mislead, and thus perhaps yet preserve a constitution which has been the admiration of ages'.[77] The king thought Joseph's policies inappropriate, although, in addition, he was sensibly worried about the reaction within the Austrian dominions, and about the possible consequences for Britain. In 1789, George responded with approval to a cabinet minute about the insurrection in the Austrian Netherlands (modern Belgium), arguing that

[British] interest can never be either that the Emperor should become absolute, or that a democracy should be established there, as either must probably unite that country more with France; the keeping the constitution on its old footing is agreeable to treaties as well as the solid rules of policy which have ever best suited the system of this country.[78]

George maintained this position once the French Revolutionary War had broken out, writing in 1794 of Joseph's nephew, Francis II, 'Lord Grenville cannot too strongly express disapprobation of . . . the supposed intention of the Emperor to destroy the constitutions of the different provinces in the Netherlands in case of his recovering the possession of them'.[79]

---

[73] George to Pitt, 26 Apr. 1805, PRO. 30/8/104 fol. 435.
[74] George to Pelham, 13 Feb. 1803, BL. Add. 33115 fol. 119.
[75] T.C.W. Blanning, *Joseph II* (London, 1994).
[76] Barthélemy to Montmorin, 29 May 1787, AE. CP. Ang. 563 fol. 9.
[77] George to Pitt, 10 Apr. 1797, PRO. 30/8/104 fol. 159.
[78] George to Carmarthen, 1 Dec. 1789, BL. Add. 27914 fol. 25.
[79] George to William Grenville, 13 Sept. 1794, BL. Add. 58858 fol. 83.

George's conservatism was well displayed in his response to developments abroad. Integrity and national interest were joined in George's concerns, both being seen as necessary to the appropriate conduct of foreign policy and international relations. In 1796, the prospect of a redrawing of borders to suit the interests of Francis II and Frederick William II of Prussia led George to protest in a manner that reflected both the traditional desire of weaker German rulers to maintain the imperial constitution in order to restrain the more powerful,[80] and a clear sense of the need for morality and restraint in international relations, a lesson that was eventually to be more generally learned from the conflicts of the period:[81]

I cannot approve of any hint though ever so indefinite that bears any allusion to the Court of Vienna giving up the Low Countries and obtaining Bavaria; this would destroy every real utility of Austria to Britain, but what is much worse by disposing of the country of a Prince because less able to defend himself this is so immoral and unjustifiable a proceeding that I cannot but in the outset protest against it and in the same manner against the King of Prussia acquiring any territory from the bishoprics in Westphalia.[82]

Despite his instinctual conservatism, charges of supporting inappropriate governmental change could be made against George, or at least his ministers, with respect to North America, while the imposition of a resident lord-lieutenant in Ireland in 1767 helped encourage a critical Protestant patriotism.[83] He was accurately associated, however, with conservatism, as in his appearance as a ghost in the 1829 caricature *My Father's Ghost, or Surrender of Right and Title*, which was produced when George IV yielded over Catholic emancipation: 'Stay! and *hear* me!!' demands George III of his fleeing son.

Events elsewhere in George's reign made the importance of monarchy as a political system clear. In most cases, monarchs who were overthrown were replaced by others and not by republics: this was true of Peter III (1762) and Paul I (1801) in Russia, and of Gustavus III (1792) and Gustavus IV (1809) in Sweden. In addition, in the Thirteen Colonies, France, Haiti, and, after George died, in Latin America, violent political changes ended in monarchies of some type or another, most dramatically the imperial monarchy of Napoleon, and most lastingly the elected quasi-monarchy of the USA. This serves as a reminder of the difficulty of creating new

[80] P.H. Wilson, *German Armies. War and German Politics 1648–1806* (London, 1998).
[81] P.W. Schroeder, *The Transformation of European Politics, 1763–1848* (Oxford, 1994).
[82] George to William Grenville, 9 Feb. 1796, BL. Add. 58859 fol. 50.
[83] M.J. Powell, *Britain and Ireland in the Eighteenth-Century Crisis of Empire* (Basingstoke, 2003).

political systems that did not revert to monarchy, which appeared the obvious form of government to most commentators, certainly for large states.

The major new political departure in the English-speaking world was not union with Ireland or the spread of the British empire, but rather American independence. There, it was initially difficult to establish political conventions. George Washington's willingness to give up power and not to seek a presidency for life was important to the creation of the particular American combination of elected legitimacy and responsible stability. There was to be no military dictatorship, and thus no equivalent to the Cromwellian Protectorate or to Bonapartism, in the USA. European courtly traditions were rejected, although there was also the argument that the new country required a 'republican court' that could help ensure the coherence of a national political élite.[84] The role of established assumptions in the English-speaking world was important. Oliver Cromwell was an example that was rejected, just as, for monarchs, was that of James II and VII. Given these assumptions, it was unlikely that Washington would have put himself at the head of the officers at Newburgh who, in the winter of 1782–3, considered intimidating Congress into granting concessions over pensions, nor at the head of the troops in June 1783 who briefly held Congress hostage.

Similarly, George was not going to use the troops sent into London in 1780 to suppress the Gordon Riots in order to expand royal power. Henry Fox had warned in the early 1760s that factious opposition might lead to continental-style despotism, but George's care for those under him, including his troops, was not intended as a prelude to any seizure of power. After an audience with the king in 1787, Sir John Sinclair quoted his remark about Gustavus III's suppression of the Swedish Age of Liberty in 1772, 'I never will acknowledge that the King of a limited monarchy can on any principle endeavour to change the constitution and increase his own power. No honest man will attempt it.'[85]

The two Georges, George III and George Washington, shared a commitment to public virtue based on duty, integrity and steadfastness. George III sought to match Washington's self-control and, at the outset of his period in power, shared his desire to new-mould the body politic. The king also retained his conviction that public service was a duty, not a spoils system. In 1804, he wrote to Melville about the new Board of Admiralty, pressing the case against any 'Member of Parliament whom the appointment may suit, but who is unfit for that degree of assiduity which in time of war is required in point of signing protections, commissions and other

---

[84] Report by M. Smuts on 2000 Boston conference 'Courts without kings', *Court Historian*, 5 (2000), p. 267.

[85] Sinclair to Hawkesbury, 2 July 1787, BL. Add. 38222 fol. 91.

commonplace duties'.[86] Washington's republican ideals, however, created a more inclusive, sustained and ostentatious image of civic duty than George's more traditional monarchy.

As president, Washington, who initially favoured as a title 'His High Mightiness, the President of the United States and Protector of Their Liberties', acted like an elected Patriot King,[87] referring to himself in the third person, accepting royal-style iconography, appearing in state in a highly ornamented coach attended by four servants in livery, establishing very formal levees and going on progresses that were akin to those of monarchs. This helped create a Republican opposition headed by Jefferson and Madison that was similar to that of the British Whigs.[88] Though the first national hero, Washington was not to be president for life. The presidency, indeed, provided a way to manage the transition of power, one that Napoleon rejected when he created the imperial system. For monarchs, as George III showed, there were also the problems of transition caused by poor health. Yet that was also a difficulty with ministers. Chatham's mental collapse in 1767 and Pitt's state on the eve of his death in 1806 underline a major problem with the political system in this (and other) ages: the difficulty of parting with a leader who is no longer capable of providing the necessary leadership and success, a situation seen earlier with Walpole in the winter of 1741–2.

Outside the English-speaking world, in the absence of its political assumptions and of a benign international context, it was very difficult to establish a new effective monarchy. In Poland, the attempt in the early 1790s to create a limited monarchy that owed much to the British model[89] was cut short by Russian intervention, while in France a revolution that began as an attempt to centre legitimate limited monarchy on a representative element, failed. This did not mean that limited monarchy was unviable; simply that, as was also to be shown in the newly independent Latin American states which were *de jure* or *de facto* monarchies, it was difficult to operate successfully. The two most conspicuous examples of the success of this system were those in the English-speaking world: the legitimist monarchy of Britain, and the elected, non-hereditary monarchy represented by the American presidency. The former adjusted in the later Hanoverian period, in response not only to the changing political culture

[86] George to Melville, 28 May 1804, BL. Add. 40100 fol. 304.

[87] R. Ketcham, *Presidents above Party: The First American Presidency, 1789–1829* (Chapel Hill, North Carolina, 1984), p. 89.

[88] J.R. Alden, *George Washington: A Biography* (Baton Rouge, Louisiana, 1984); J.J. Ellis, *His Excellency George Washington* (New York, 2004); G.S. Wood, 'The Man Who Would Not Be King', *New Republic*, 20 Dec. 2004, p. 37.

[89] R. Butterwick, *Poland's Last King and English Culture: Stanislaw August Poniatowski, 1732–1798* (Oxford, 1998), pp. 317–18.

but also to the classic problem of hereditary monarchy: its ability to solve the problem of the succession only at the cost of abandoning the option of merit offered by elective monarchy. Poor mental health, however, tested this solution of the problem of the succession, as the regency crisis in Britain and the fate of Christian VII in Denmark indicated. Furthermore, Gustavus IV Adolphus of Sweden (1792–1809) was by 1809 displaying signs of instability, and on 13 March he was deposed in an aristocratic conspiracy in favour of his uncle, Charles XIII. The difficulty caused by illness and madness underlines the extent to which none of these monarchs was a figurehead.

In Britain, constitutional ambiguity could have developed into constant acrimony, whether or not there was a coherent party system. Instead, by exercising restraint, George in the 1780s and 1790s created a businesslike monarchy intent on security and the constitution, not on the accumulation of power and absolute control. In 1763, Elizabeth Montagu had voiced a widespread view when she remarked that she feared that the king would be 'subdued by a faction', but nor did she want him to 'rule by one'.[90] The latter appeared a risk in the winter of 1783–4, but the working out of the crisis ensured that George was able to avoid this impression even if, to critics, George had subverted the political system.

George's 'enmity to novelty'[91] might be inappropriate in governmental or, on occasion, political terms, but his interpretation of the place of the monarch accorded with the social conservatism of much of the élite, and not only the élite. The caricature *Political Mathematics* criticized ideas of novelty, linking 'Scheme for a New Patriotic Administration' with 'New Planetary System', and 'New Scale of Justice'. Although there was an element of such a choice in the 1784 election, George did not try to rally support to the monarch by appealing for backing against portions of the élite, as Gustavus III had done in Sweden in 1772. Instead, he emphasized the social hierarchy as an integral aspect of political rank, welcoming the election of 'more gentlemen of landed property', in the general election of 1774, as likely to be 'ready for the battle' with the American Patriots; while the French Revolutionary crisis caused him to write to Dundas,

> I have carefully perused the draft of the instrument for appointing Lord Lieutenants and Sheriffs Principal in Scotland, the merit of the measure entirely depends on the attention given to appointing the persons of most rank and weight in the respective countries, and that no one may have reason to complain of having been omitted on the occasion, from the

[90] Montagu to Bath, 19 Oct. 1763, HL. MO. 4590.
[91] George to Melville, 21 May 1804, BL. Add. 40100 fol. 302; George to Melville, 6 Mar. 1794, BL. Add. 40100 fol. 117.

preference shown to those of less natural weight, unless their political principles are such as would render their nomination impossible.[92]

Social conservatism was challenged by a measure of democratization in the practice of political discussion, particularly due to the growth of the press, and this created issues for all governments. To critics, there was an unwelcome appeal to the 'Mob'.[93] In late 1792, as French successes engendered a sense of crisis, republican sentiments were increasingly expressed in London. 'No King', however, was not a political programme that was feasible in Britain, nor in the British empire unless authority was overthrown, as in America, and, as was tried unsuccessfully, in Ireland. Far from assuming any necessary opposition between the crown and the growing role of the public, a situation in which 'every tailor . . . is become a politician',[94] it is important to note the degree to which the frequent assumption that the latter was necessarily in favour of change and reform is flawed. More generally, it is possible to emphasize the extent to which, especially from 1793, conservatism was widespread and rested on popular support, in Britain and abroad,[95] although the role of monarchs in responding to, and arbitrating between, conservative and reforming pressures varied.[96] Nevertheless, there was opposition as well as widespread support for George in the second half of his reign, not least as a symbol of national identity. If, for example, in his *Inquiry into the supposed Increase of the Influence of the Crown* (1811), John Ranby denied that the influence was increasing, that was in response to the hostile opposition claim that it was.

The changes in the position of monarchs and the character of monarchy on the continent contributed greatly to a sense of flux that challenged the position of the British crown yet also added to a sense of its importance as a definition and defence of national values. In 1792, a caricature, possibly by William Dent, *Royal Masquerade, or, the European Plotters Discovered and Defeated and the Ex-Princes Crossed in their Masked Design against Liberty*, showed Gustavus III of Sweden, his belt marked Tyranny, and Leopold II, his marked Despotism, being killed (Leopold was not in fact stabbed to death, or, despite rumours, murdered), both attacked by a smiling skeleton while Liberty presided in the character of Death. This was a potent warning, but the theme of tyranny generally played to the advantage of the British crown, not least because George was widely

---

[92] George to North, 24 Aug. 1774, Fortescue, III, 125–6; George to Dundas, 6 Mar. 1794, BL. Add. 40100 fol. 117.

[93] Daniel Wray to Hardwicke, 17 Sept. 1763, BL. Add. 35401 fol. 279.

[94] *St. James's Chronicle*, 28 Sept. 1762.

[95] D. Laven, *Venice and Venetia under the Habsburgs 1815–1835* (Oxford, 2002).

[96] C.C. Noel, 'Opposition to Enlightened Reform in Spain: Campomanes and the Clergy, 1765–1775', *Societas*, 3 (1973), pp. 21–43, e.g. p. 41 on role of Charles III of Spain.

presented in broadsides and caricatures as Farmer George, and the choice offered repeatedly was a simple one of George or Napoleon. Napoleon, not the rulers of Britain's allies, was usually seen as the tyrant,[97] and his claim to be equal to other rulers was mocked, as in James Gillray's 1800 caricature *The Apples and the Horse Turds; or Bonaparte among the Golden Pippins*, which presented Bonaparte as a horse turd pretending to be an apple, and his *Grand Coronation Procession*, which mocked Napoleon's self-aggrandizing imperial coronation of 1804. George referred to Napoleon as 'the French usurper'.[98]

A sense of monarchy, instead, as a calling, characterized by appropriate conduct, not a gift, was indicated by George Woodward's caricature for New Year's Day 1808, his *Royal Amusement or Nature will Prevail*. This showed a peasant woman reading a paper in her kitchen to a smoking farm labourer and saying, 'Why this Bonny-part be making kings every day – I should not wonder if thee wast in France, if he made a King of thee John – What wouldst thee do if thee wast a King', the reply being 'Do–! Why I'd swing on a gate and eat fat bacon all day long'. The creation of new monarchs was also criticized in Gillray's 1806 cartoon *Tiddy-Doll, the great French-Gingerbread-Baker, drawing out a new Batch of Kings*.

The continuity represented by the British monarchy was a significant aspect not only of the maintenance of traditional assumptions and practices but also of the interaction with a range of developments, especially those stemming from economic growth. This continuity supported the political stability that made the processes of compromise, through which different interests reconciled their views, work. A less benign view would suggest that the crown was unable to reach out to new social forces, particularly in the expanding north of England (although George's recovery was welcomed in the north in 1789), and that this was to affect its position in the reform crises of the late 1820s and early 1830s, making any lasting rejection of reform demands difficult. These assessments overlap in that the moral politics, patriotism and reaction against radicalism that helped create a wide-ranging backing for crown and stability from 1784, no longer operated so successfully, or to that effect, in the 1820s.

[97] S. Semmel, *Napoleon and the British* (New Haven, Connecticut, 2004), p. 45.
[98] George to Pitt, 9 Jan., 7 Mar. 1805, PRO. 30/8/104 fols 407, 425.

Chapter 20

GEORGE III AND THE MAKING OF THE
MODERN BRITISH MONARCHY

... if he and his brother will act with a little less lenity (which I really
think cruelty, as it keeps up the contest) the next campaign will bring the
Americans in a temper to accept of such terms as may enable the
Mother Country to keep them in order; for we must never come into
such as may patch for a year or two, and then bring on new broils; the
regaining their affection is an idle idea. It must be the convincing them
that it is their interest to submit, and they will dread farther broils.

George about his commanders in North America, 1777[1]

... indecision is the most painful of all situations to a firm mind ... we
must be men ... half measures are ever puerile and often destructive.

George on the political crisis, 1784[2]

George came to understand compromise and limits, albeit reluctantly and
less than totally. This may not sound much of a triumph, but it was fundamental to the successful operation of the political system. Where restraint
failed was in North America, but the failure to manage the aspirations of
the colonists, or even to respond successfully to the difficult problem of
imperial management, was as much a failure of ministry and parliament
as of George. This was not, however, the case with Catholic emancipation,
and the earlier failure to introduce this measure, which owed much to
George, helped compromise the appeal of parliamentary union in
Ireland. George was also unenthusiastic about the banning of the slave
trade.

Mention of failure, however, draws attention to success, particularly the
avoidance of revolution in Britain. There was no comparison between
George's visit to Worcester in 1788 and the previous royal visit, that by
James II and VII in 1687, when there had been a fuss because the mayor
and aldermen had refused to follow the king into a Catholic chapel to
attend divine service, while the bishop was angry because, while visiting

[1] George to Robinson, 5 Mar. 1777, BL. Add. 37833 fol. 137.
[2] George to Pitt, 25 Jan. 1784, PRO. 30/8/103 fol. 41.

his palace, the king had asked a Catholic priest to give the mealtime blessing. Against such a background, the opposition James encountered in 1688 was scarcely a surprise. Even when he disagreed with his ministers, George was more courteous and emollient than James, let alone Edward II whose tomb in Gloucester Cathedral left him meditative in 1788. However contentious some found them, George's policies were far more in keeping with widespread public assumptions than those of James had been. Furthermore, George's espousal of Patriotism and distancing from Hanoverianism at the outset of his reign served him well in the latter half of his reign when his image was made more attractive in part because its Englishness was stressed.[3]

Comparison with James II and VII is instructive because George was mindful of what the Glorious Revolution meant in terms of the rejection of unacceptable monarchy and the basis of his own claim to the throne. Interested in history, George had no time for the false report that 'James III and VIII', 'the warming pan baby', was a changeling. Instead, he saw his position and that of future British monarchs as resting not on dynastic right but on duty. In 1799, an approach on behalf of 'Henry IX' led George to reflect that he had 'ever thought that' the 'true solid basis' of Hanoverian rule was that 'it came to preserve the free Constitution of this Empire, both in Church and State, which compact I trust none of my successors will ever dare to depart from'.[4]

The avoidance of revolution in Britain (as opposed to North America and Ireland) during George's reign was more prominent as an achievement because of the extent to which there were revolutions elsewhere in Europe. A valuable legacy was also left George's successors. As family man, 'Farmer George', and a head of civil society active in philanthropy and support for national institutions, George did much for the image of the British monarchy and greatly increased the popularity of the crown amongst the middling sort of people. Neither George IV nor William IV was faced by scenes similar to those in Paris in 1830 or 1848. Part of this achievement was a result both of successful adaptation to change, and of responding to the independent institutional and political growth of the country. The Hanoverians managed it, both individually and as a group, more successfully than their Prussian relations or Bourbon contemporaries; although the extent to which new governmental initiatives were responsible for revolution in North America, and in the Austrian Netherlands and Hungary against Joseph II, is a reminder of the complexity of the situation and the danger of providing any simple explanation for revolution or its absence.

---

[3] J. Cannon, 'The Survival of the British Monarchy', *Transactions of the Royal Historical Society*, 5th series, 36 (1986), pp. 149–50.
[4] George to William Grenville, 24 Nov. 1799, BL. Add. 58861 fol. 64.

At times, as with George II's anger, George III's threats about abdication, and George IV's despair about having to yield to Catholic emancipation, the process of adaptation to change was far from comfortable. George III's instinctual conservatism remained strong until the close of his period as an active ruler, and this entailed a deliberate defiance of metropolitan radicalism. In April 1810, George wrote to Perceval,

> The King is glad to learn from Mr. Perceval that Mr. Yorke will take upon himself the Office of First Lord of the Admiralty, and he duly appreciates the principle of zeal and attachment which has influenced this determination. His Majesty cannot also but consider it very desirable that his government should give a proof of its firmness and the conviction of its stability by bringing forward a meritorious individual whose proceedings have ever been upright, in contempt of a clamour which has been excited upon grounds which are not maintainable.[5]

The latter was a reference to Charles Yorke's prominent role in opposing the establishment of an inquiry into the disastrous Walcheren expedition, and the subsequent controversy over his enforcement of the standing order for the exclusion of strangers from the Commons. This led Yorke to complain to the Commons about John Gale Jones, president of the British Forum Debating Society, who was committed to Newgate. In turn, Sir Francis Burdett was sent to the Tower for querying the legality of the proceedings, leading, on 6 April, to riots in which Yorke's windows were smashed. George's support for Yorke was long-standing and reflected shared values. In 1801, the king had written to Yorke,

> He has ever had a most sincere regard for the family of Yorke ... certain Mr. Yorke's talents are such as will be of advantage to the service in any sort of business for with most considerable abilities and a very honorable mind he has the advantage of having had a grandfather and father whose memory must be ever revered by those who value the laws and constitution of this enviable country.[6]

In one respect, this was ironic as Yorke's grandfather, Philip, first earl of Hardwicke, had been a close ally of Newcastle and a key member of the 'Old Corps' Whigs whom George had rejected in 1762. George's favour for Yorke in the 1800s reflected the king's sympathy for continuity and experience of Yorke's activity and zeal as a minister,[7] but also support for Yorke's politics. Addington's secretary at war and then home secretary,

[5] George to Perceval, 29 Apr. 1810, BL. Add. 45035 fol. 6.
[6] George to Yorke, 2 May 1801, BL. Add. 35644 fol. 78.
[7] George to Yorke, 18 Oct. 1810, BL. Add. 45035 fol. 7.

Yorke was a firm opponent of Catholic emancipation. George was not responsible for Yorke's policies, but it is indicative of his preferences that Yorke not only suffered lasting unpopularity, due to his position on the Walcheren inquiry and the clearing of the Commons galleries, but also, in 1814, opposed the abolition of the customary penalties for treason, specifically mutilation after execution and the fixing of 'corruption of blood'.[8] Similarly, in 1804, George approved the conferring of the treasurership of Greenwich Hospital on Admiral Sir John Colpoys. 'A better Admiral or better man does not exist,' wrote the king of a man described thus:

> The murdering Colpoys, Vice-Admiral of the Blue,
> Gave order to fire on the *London*'s crew;
> While the enemy of Britain was ploughing the sea . . .
> He, like a base coward, let them get away
> When the French and their transports sailed for Bantry Bay.

During the 1797 naval mutinies, Colpoys had ordered the officers of his flagship *London* to fire on the mutineers. As far as the verses were concerned, however, Colpoys did not block the French due to cowardice, but in large part as a result of bad weather.[9]

George was certainly no trimmer,[10] and in 1785 made clear his opposition to the parliamentary reform that was to be deemed necessary in 1832. Nevertheless, in the end, the necessary adaptation was achieved, and the monarchy in 1837 was in a more secure state than it had been in 1714. After the dismal story of the last years of George III, and the unpopular and largely purposeless reign of George IV (1820–30), William IV's reign (1830–7) can be seen as beginning the process of revival that was to culminate in the development of imperial splendour under Victoria (r. 1837–1901) and Edward VII (r. 1901–10).[11] The unpopularity of George IV had already helped make George III appear more acceptable, Canning writing in 1825 that 'all parties now agree in taking [George III] as the model of an English King',[12] and William's reign in some senses represented a culmination of that of George III. William, however, came to the throne as a much older man than his father, and also lacked George's initial determination to transform the political system and his subsequent

---

[8] Corruption of the blood was a clause of treason legislation that ensured that those who were judged treasonable lost their noble status. This affected inheritance rights. Attempts to abolish the clause failed in 1813 but succeeded in 1814.

[9] N.A.M. Rodger, *The Command of the Ocean. A Naval History of Britain 1649–1815* (London, 2004), pp. 437–8.

[10] George to Pitt, 15 Dec. 1797, PRO. 30/8/104.

[11] W. Kuhn, *Democratic Royalism: The Transformation of the British Monarchy, 1861–1914* (London, 1996).

[12] A.G. Stapleton, *Canning and His Times* (London, 1859), p. 433.

hostility to change. There were parallels, nevertheless, between George's determination to overthrow ministries in which he lacked confidence and William's dismissal of Viscount Melbourne's Whig ministry in 1834, which was 'the last time a British monarch dismissed his ministers and called on others to take their place';[13] although there were later instances in Canada, South Africa and Australia.

As with George III, and underlining the extent to which the concerns of that monarch were not unusual, the state of the Church was a key issue. Melbourne wished to make Lord John Russell leader of the House of Commons, but William would not accept this. Russell's support for the use of church revenues for secular purposes was seen by William as a threat to the rights of the Church that was a breach of his coronation oath, an echo of George III's and George IV's concerns over Catholic emancipation. Using the excuse that the government was divided on the issue, William dismissed it on 14 November 1834, the dismissal reflecting his conviction that he had the right to choose the government and that, while that government needed to command parliamentary support, it also needed to be his government and to back him. George IV, however, had not acted in this way, and it struck many contemporaries as a disturbing step.

This was a comment on political developments over the previous half-century. Contemporaries saw parallels with the actions of George III in 1783–4. These had been controversial at the time, although validated for many by the election of 1784, just as that of 1807 validated the fall of the Talents, but the parameters of what was acceptable had changed, at least in so far as was suggested by the aftermath. Crucially, indeed, the sequel was different: Pitt won the 1784 election and Portland that in 1807, but the Tories, under Sir Robert Peel, lost the 1835 election, although they gained many seats and only lost because of the results of the election in Ireland (which had not been at issue in 1784). Defeats in the Commons had caused Peel to resign, having been in office for one hundred days. Despite this contrast, and the disturbances that accompanied the popular pressure for the Reform Act of 1832, there was a sense of stabilization that matched that of the aftermath of the crisis of the early 1780s, let alone the far less serious crisis in 1807. This was helped by the extent to which both crises were primarily political, and did not involve fundamental social tensions.

As a monarch, William also continued some of the themes seen with George III, and there was a major contrast on the part of both with George IV. The theatre of majesty was less on display in the case of George III and William IV: while George III enjoyed walking round Windsor and his land, William liked doing so round London without show

---

[13] N. Gash, *Pillars of Government and Other Essays on State and Policy, c. 1770–c.1880* (London, 1986), p. 106.

or ceremony. Both men were less grand than George IV, and were regarded as lacking pretentiousness. This accorded with an emphasis on gentlemanliness rather than grandeur in British public culture, one that George III was seen to satisfy, especially from the 1780s. This stress on appropriate conduct and earned respect had been seen in Burke's Commons speech on the Middlesex election in 1769, 'An English gentleman ... has no rank above his fellow citizens – but what his manners, his affability, his knowledge, his justice, the popular use of his fortune give him'.[14] Although William's personal life was less exemplary than that of his father, it caused less offence than that of George IV. Furthermore, there was a parallel between the large family (ten children) and domesticity of William and the actress Dorothy Jordan between 1790 and 1811, and the family life of George III and Queen Charlotte.

William, however, was more flexible in political matters than his father had been, although whether personality or circumstances played the key role is unclear. It is difficult to see George agreeing to peerage creations if the Lords rejected the Reform Bill, as William did in 1832. Indeed, in 1800, he had referred to parliamentary reform as 'that fallacious subject'.[15] The situation might have been different had William's brother Ernest, duke of Cumberland, instead, become king, and Ernest's position is a reminder of George III's varied legacy. Ernest actively opposed the repeal of the Test and Corporation Acts and condemned Catholic emancipation in the House of Lords, presenting himself as continuing the policies of George III. He also opposed the Reform Act of 1832, the Poor Law Amendment Act of 1834, and the Municipal Corporations Act of 1835. Ernest, a keen admirer of Prussia, who lived much of the 1820s in Berlin, had considerable influence over George IV, bolstering him in his opposition to reform, but lost this influence when William became king in 1830. When he became king of Hanover in 1837, Ernest, however, was able to follow reactionary policies, revoking the 1833 constitution granted by William. Ernest was convinced that his policies brought both popularity and stability, but his attitudes made him a *bête noire* for British liberals, while the revocation of the constitution embarrassed the British Tories.

This underlines the extent to which chance played a role. Because Victoria survived and had children, Cumberland did not also become king in Britain. Indeed, William helped bequeath a secure monarchy to his neophyte niece in 1837, in part because, although he had a diligent commitment to what he saw as effective government, he was willing to be a bystander in the era of reform. The process of reform, which in due course opened the way for considerable further constitutional, political

---

[14] P. Langford (ed.), *The Writings and Speeches of Edmund Burke*, II (Cambridge, 1981), p. 230.
[15] George to Pitt, 26 Apr. 1800, PRO. 30/8/104 fol. 271.

and social change in the nineteenth and early twentieth centuries, was carried through with the active support or passive consent of successive monarchs, creating a sense that the monarchy was on the side of progress. This enduring belief contributed in a very real sense to the survival, and further prospering, of monarchy in Britain.

In this matter George's legacy is ambiguous, and his attitude even more so. To George, pressure for reform and focusing on grievances were almost aspects of the fallen nature of man, unsurprisingly so as he thought the constitution 'the glory of human invention'.[16] More reasonably, George was inclined to argue the need to look to the long term, and to imply that politicians lacked this perspective. Nor did he always imply that the answers to political problems were easy, writing in 1782,

> Undoubtedly the affairs of Ireland are so embroiled that it is most diffi-cult to suggest what can satisfactorily be done; I trust Lord Shelburne sees the magnitude of the question, and that to obviate future evils is as material as to remove those of the present hour.[17]

It is difficult to see George's policies on North America, on parliamentary reform, or with regard to the position of the Church, as successful adaptations to change. Over America, George was in accord with established conventions of kingship in defending legal authority, but he also displayed inappropriate, because unsuccessful, firmness, made concessions too late, and became overly committed to the struggle, believing it necessary to persist with the war, even after defeat at Yorktown. Indeed, it is over America that the most obvious contrast in the recent literature emerges. Criticism of the king's role, including an (undeveloped) riposte against the 'Tory interpretation' by Francis Jennings,[18] culminated in a thoughtful piece by Andrew O'Shaughnessy. In this, the focus is on George's part, not in causing the American crisis, but in undermining the possibility of any last-minute compromise and damagingly sustaining an unsuccessful war against the wishes of his leading minister, North, for a *rapprochement* with the opposition that would have led to compromise in America.[19] In marked contrast, John Cannon's entry on George in the recent *Oxford Dictionary of National Biography* (2004) notes:

---

[16] George to Robinson, 30 Aug. 1778, BL. Add. 37833 fol. 240.

[17] George to Shelburne, 14 May 1782, Fortescue, VI, 23.

[18] R.L. Bushman, *King and People in Provincial Massachusetts* (Chapel Hill, North Carolina, 1985), pp. 218–19; F. Jennings, *The Creation of America: Through Revolution to Empire* (Cambridge, 2000), pp. 109, 212.

[19] A.J. O'Shaughnessy, '"If others will not be active, I must drive". George III and the American Revolution', *Early American Studies*, 2, 1 (spring 2004), pp. 1–46.

It has often been suggested that by his obstinacy George III protracted the American war. But no eighteenth-century ruler would contemplate tamely surrendering the greater part of his empire, nor is it clear why Frederick the Great's resistance in the Seven Years' War should be regarded as heroic, yet George's resistance in America foolhardy.

Given parliament's opposition at the close of the war to the possibility of ceding Gibraltar, Cannon's first point is well taken, while his second is a reminder of the very fine balance in historical interpretation between praise and criticism, and the role of counterfactuals in making such judgements. Equally, the O'Shaughnessy piece is an important critique of the king. It serves as a reminder of his central role in a major disaster, and, more specifically, of how the role of personality, for which the nature of the constitution and the workings of the political system left a significant part, helped set the dynamic of policy. In this case, George's determination was crucial. The balance in interpretation can be seen throughout the reign. George's expulsion of William, fourth duke of Devonshire, from office in 1762, and his defiance of the support the duke received, can be presented as appropriate firmness, George treating the issue 'with scorn and indignation with a mind so determined that no event will shake' in Bute's words;[20] or, on the contrary, as a foolish unwillingness to accept opposition from a senior office-holder.

For George, the defence of legal authority was not solely a matter of doing so to the benefit of Britain. While at peace, he also disclaimed 'in the strongest manner all idea of interfering in the discontents of the inhabitants of the Spanish settlements in South America'. The 'faithless' example of France in North America[21] was not one George wished to copy.

As far as Catholic emancipation was concerned, Pitt's failure to prepare George in 1800–1 for the measure was a serious flaw, as the issue of peace approaches to France in 1796–7 had shown that the king could be brought round to what he instinctively and intellectually opposed. Yet, as George pointed out, his opposition to emancipation was not new, and he displayed to the full his self-proclaimed determination to stick to 'the principles by which he has been guided through life'.[22] More generally, the king's handling of ministerial matters can also be criticized. He was willing to express support for a practice of limited intervention: in February 1784, for example, being careful in his encouragement of Lords opposition to the Commons' Address for the removal of the vulnerable Pitt ministry:

---

[20] Bute to Rigby, 30 Oct. 1762, BL. Add. 36797 fol. 18; Bath to Elizabeth Montagu, 30 Oct. 1762, HL. MO. 4283.
[21] George to Pitt, 3 July 1786, PRO. 30/8/103 fol. 200.
[22] George to Spencer, 10 Feb. 1807, BL. Add. 58864 fol. 17.

I can have no objection to Lord Sydney's saying that he knows that if the ministers think such a measure right it will be pleasing to me, but I should not wish him to communicate my letter before they have taken their determination, from not wishing to guide their opinion, where the part they are to take is in their legislative capacity, and where their own sentiments ought to actuate them.[23]

In practice, George found it difficult to rely on others having satisfactory sentiments, and was often stubbornly unwilling to accept alternative points of view. Convinced of his own integrity, he was grudging in his willingness to extend this to those of contrary views, a position that prefigured that of Margaret Thatcher.[24] Any comparison, however, needs to note the extent to which Margaret Thatcher faced frequent contradiction, something George conspicuously lacked from those he met, while George's powerful religious conviction was also distinctive.

George did not adopt an approach to the politics of kingship akin to that of the deism in religion he abhorred: the king would no more decline to intervene when he deemed it necessary in a ministry he had helped create, than God would eschew concern with Mankind after he had created it. George indeed supported the divine scheme by defending the constitution, writing in 1793, 'I most devoutly pray to Heaven that this constitution may remain unimpaired to the latest posterity as a proof of the wisdom of the nation and its knowledge of the superior blessings it enjoys.'[25]

Demanding loyalty from ministers, George was not loyal in return, but went behind their backs. Furthermore, even in terms of his own goals, royal intervention could be disruptive. George put his personal views on individuals above the interest of ministerial strength and/or coherence. In 1804, when a Ministry of All the Talents could, and should, have come in, he put his private feud with Fox before the public good at a time when invasion threatened. For this and other reasons, it is apparent that the existing consensus on the king is overly favourable.

In other respects, it is possible to point to effective rulership and to George's flexibility. The conscientious diligence of the king bore fruits as he acquired knowledge and experience, including in areas about which initially he knew little, such as Irish government finances[26] or the crucial one of naval power. George gained a very knowledgeable understanding of naval matters, in that he worked hard to make, and keep, himself

[23] George to Sydney, 3 Feb. 1784, Aspinall, *George III*, I, 30.
[24] David Cannadine suggested this comparison to me in a conversation on 13 October 2005.
[25] George to Pitt, 8 May 1793, PRO. 30/8/103 fol. 494.
[26] George to Robinson, 25 Oct. 1776, BL. Add. 37883 fol. 97.

informed, and certainly understood much more about the technology and logistics of sea power than most civilians. His opinions on these matters, as expressed in correspondence, almost always echoed those of his ministers, as constitutional propriety required, and on only a limited number of occasions can the royal voice be clearly heard – the question of whether Admiral Sir Charles Hardy should fight the Bourbon fleet threatening invasion in the summer of 1779 being one of them. George was a shrewd judge of individual merit, and reasonably well informed about his senior sea officers, though undoubtedly he knew more about the generals, whom he saw far more often at court.[27] Hard-working, conscientious and well-briefed did not, however, amount to very clever: George was a good judge of men, but he did not see far below the surface of affairs. It was not just a matter of personality that led him to dislike 'intriguers'.[28]

Flexibility on the part of George can be seen in some ecclesiastical issues, most obviously Catholic Relief legislation and the Quebec Act, but, even more, with the major changes in government in the 1780s, 1790s and 1800s. Already, in 1771, he had proposed the reorganization of the business of the secretaries of state, so that one handled foreign affairs and the other domestic business,[29] the course that was to be successfully adopted in 1782. By the time of the ministry of Pitt the Younger, the concern with public finance and imperial regulation that had played such a prominent role in government from 1763 had broadened out into a more general conscious acceptance of their importance. This was designed to produce effective administration, and to support and foster a system capable of peaceful change and economic growth. George accepted this, but not the political corollary of parliamentary reform, nor the moral one of the end to the slave trade.

In the 1790s and 1800s, major changes introduced in Britain included union with Ireland, the establishment of income tax, and the first British national census. Yet, all of these were really government initiatives, and it is difficult to use them in order to portray George as an innovative figure, although he certainly tried to be an informed one. For example, having sought, and received, returns, George was happy to support changes in the policing in London.[30] The position in which George found himself of responding to ministers was summed up by an episode in 1790 when William Grenville asked for a respite for a woman convicted of coining, so that she could be hanged, after the penalty for women committing treason was changed from burning, because of the 'great inconvenience and disorder which arise . . . such sentences being now executed almost in the

---

[27] I have benefited from the advice of Nicholas Rodger.
[28] George to William Grenville, 11 Dec. 1798, BL. Add. 58860 fol. 135.
[29] George to North, 13 Jan. 1771, Fortescue, II, 206.
[30] George to Hawkesbury, 8, 22 Nov. 1804, 3 Feb. 1805, BL. Loan 72/1 fols 128–9, 135.

center of the town'. George agreed to the respite.[31] At the same time, the king's general position was an aspect of the ability of the British state to respond to the Revolutionary-Napoleonic crisis within existing forms. The very conservatism of the response to revolution, and the stress on continuity, precedent, privilege, law and religion as the ideological focus of nationhood and counter-revolution, ensured that the development of new practices, institutions, ideas and notions took place within a context in which their implications for change were not probed, while their novelty was understated.

Nevertheless, the position of the monarchy altered. For example, the treason trials and legislation of the 1790s placed the emphasis on the combined sovereignty of king, Lords and Commons, and thus on the state, rather than on a personal bond with the king. A similar emphasis on king-in-parliament played a role in government arguments in the debates over the regency legislation of 1789 and 1811.[32] The downplaying of the alternative view, of separate and unique rights of the crown, can be linked to the pressure for Catholic emancipation, which George was not alone in feeling challenged his constitutional position and his semi-sacral symbolic role.

George's instinctive attitude, a caution about change, was revealed in 1789 when he wrote,

> I have read the paper Mr. Grenville has drawn up concerning the new modelling the constitution of the province of Quebec, and trust that as the Lord Chancellor and Mr. Pitt agree with him on the leading points that it has been drawn up with as much attention to the interest of the old inhabitants who by the Capitulation have every degree of right to be first attended to, as its ever having been started in Parliament will permit. I own I am sorry any change is necessary, for I am aware to please all concerned is impossible and that if things could have gone on in its present state for some years it would have been very desirable.[33]

When Eldon as lord chancellor asked George for permission not to wear a wig when not engaged in performing official functions, George replied, 'I will have no innovations in my time', but he lightened the

---

[31] William Grenville to George, and reply, both 18 May 1790, BL. Add. 58855 fol. 103.

[32] L. Steffen, *Defining a British State. Treason and National Identity, 1608–1820* (Basingstoke, 2001), pp. 141–3, 159.

[33] George to William Grenville, 13 Oct. 1789, BL. Add. 58855 fol. 35. For his surprise at the public diplomacy of the French Revolution, George to William Grenville, 16 Nov. 1796, BL. Add. 58859 fol. 97.

atmosphere by being good-humoured:[34] the king was happy to joke with Eldon.[35] He also clearly outlined his views, 'novelties . . . seldom succeed in the transaction of public business, and ought to be reprobated unless the old mode has been proved faulty', and 'I wish to inculcate in his mind, that it is wise to keep to precedents, if no material inconvenience from a change of circumstances shows it to be inapplicable to the occasion'. Using an architectural image that came naturally to him, and referring to Catholic emancipation, George in 1801 told Charles, eleventh duke of Norfolk, a lord of the treasury during the Fox–North ministry, who was altering his seat at Arundel, 'Take care not to meddle with the founda-tions.'[36] Rather than seeing George, however, as a reactionary drag, it is important to consider the degree to which such 'dislike of novelty' was widely shared, as, indeed, Portland argued it was in 1792.[37]

George's sense of humour is not usually discussed, but it reflected an often wry mastery of irony that delighted in the punning popular in the period. His character indeed was varied. Enthusiasm for science, arts and letters can be placed in the context of George's less intellectual passion for hunting, but it is necessary to emphasize his overriding sense of duty, which was inspired by a strong faith that falls outside some definitions of enlightened Christianity.

George's responses to American problems and to Catholic emancipa-tion claim most attention. These responses are understandable in terms of his beliefs as well as those of many of his subjects, and raise the ques-tion of how far George deserves credit for reflecting the commonplace opinions of the time or whether the Whiggish view that he should have been more 'progressive', and thus far less representative of his subjects and inheritance, is appropriate. Whichever the view, it is difficult to see his responses other than as unfortunate in both course and consequences. His responses also challenged George's achievements in other fields, in particular his role in fostering political stability. As a result, a positive assessment of George must be qualified, both as far as his own reign is concerned and with regard to the long-term development of the British state. John Bullion, a perceptive expert on the king's early years, has described George's personal history as 'a testimony to the determination and cunning of the strong and stupid'.[38] George was a nicer man than his two predecessors and he meant well, but his obstinacy helped create

[34] Twiss, I, 339–40.

[35] Twiss, II, 201–2.

[36] Twiss, I, 402; George to Hawkesbury, 14 May 1801, BL. Loan 72/1 fol. 78; F. Bickley (ed.), *The Diaries of Sylvester Douglas, Lord Glenbervie* (2 vols, London, 1928), I, 153. For the perfection of the constitution, George to Pitt, 30 Jan. 1784, PRO. 30/8/103 fol. 44.

[37] Portland to William Windham, 13 Oct. 1792, BL. Add. 37845 fol. 5.

[38] Bullion, review in *Albion*, 36 (2004), p. 530.

serious political difficulties. Not a tyrant, and not mad, and with, in many respects, an attractive personality, George was more impressive, and certainly more successful, than many of his monarchical contemporaries, but in certain key issues he was not a wise ruler. That he was America's last king was both a comment on this and a key aspect of his legacy.

ABBREVIATIONS

Add.	Additional Manuscripts
AE.	Paris, Ministère des Relations Extérieures
Ang.	Angleterre
Aspinall, *George III*	A. Aspinall (ed.), *The Later Correspondence of George III, 1783–1810* (5 vols, Cambridge, 1962–70)
Aspinall, *Prince of Wales*	A. Aspinall (ed.), *The Correspondence of George, Prince of Wales, 1770–1812* (8 vols, London, 1963–71)
AST. LM. Ing.	Turin, Archivio di Stato, Lettere Ministri, Inghilterra
Bayr. Ges.	Bayerischer Gesandtschaft
Beinecke	New Haven, Connecticut, Beinecke Library
BL.	London, British Library, Department of Manuscripts
Bod.	Oxford, Bodleian Library, Department of Western Manuscripts
Cobbett	W. Cobbett (ed.), *Cobbett's Parliamentary History of England . . . 1066 to . . . 1803* (36 vols, London, 1806–20)
CP.	Correspondance politique
CRO.	County Record Office
CUL.	Cambridge, University Library, Department of Manuscripts
Eg.	Egerton Manuscripts
EK.	Englische Korrespondenz
Exeter, 152M	Exeter, Devon Record Office, Addington (Sidmouth) papers
FO.	Foreign Office papers
Fortescue	Sir John Fortescue (ed.), *The Correspondence of King George the Third* (6 vols, London, 1927–8)
HHStA.	Vienna, Haus-, Hof-, und Staatsarchiv, Staatskanzlei
HL.	San Marino, California, Huntington Library
HMC	Historical Manuscripts Commission
HP.	London, History of Parliament, Transcripts

KAO.	Kent Archives Office
MD.	Mémoires et Documents
MO.	Montagu papers
MS	Mount Stuart, papers of John, third earl of Bute
Munich	Munich, Hauptstaatsarchiv
Plymouth	Plymouth, City Archive
PRO.	London, Public Record Office
RA.	Windsor Castle, Royal Archives
Rigs.	Copenhagen, Danske Rigsarkivet, Department of Foreign Affairs
SP.	State Papers
ST.	Stowe papers
Stanhope	Earl Stanhope, *Life of the Right Honourable William Pitt* (3rd edn, 4 vols, London, 1867)
STG.	Stowe papers, general correspondence
Twiss	H. Twiss (ed.), *The Public and Private Life of Lord Chancellor Eldon* (3 vols, London, 1844). (His papers are now at the Georgetown Law Center in Washington, D.C.)
UL	University Library
WW.	Sheffield, Archives, Wentworth Woodhouse muniments

BIBLIOGRAPHY

I. MANUSCRIPT SOURCES

Aberdeen, University Library: Duff of Braco, Tayler papers
Aberystwyth, National Library of Wales: Chirk Castle papers
Alnwick: Northumberland papers
Aylesbury, Buckinghamshire County Record Office: Drake, Grenville, Trevor papers
Bedford, Bedfordshire County Record Office: Lucas papers
Belfast, Public Record Office of Northern Ireland: Keith, Macartney, Tyrawly, Wilson papers
Berlin, Geheimes Staatsarchiv Preussischer Kulturbesitz: correspondence with London
Bloomington, Lilly Library: Chesterfield papers
Bradford, Public Library: Spencer Stanhope papers
Broomhall, Fife: Elgin papers
Bury St Edmunds, West Suffolk County Record Office: Grafton, Hervey papers
Cambridge, University Library: Bute papers
Carlisle, Cumbria Record Office: Lonsdale papers
Carmarthen, Dyfed Record Office: Cawdor papers
Cheltenham, Library: material on George III's visit
Chester, Cheshire Record Office: Wilbraham papers
Chewton House, Chewton Mendip: Waldegrave papers
Copenhagen, Danske Rigsarkivet: Department of Foreign Affairs, reports from London
Durham, University Library: Grey, Wharton papers
Edinburgh, National Library of Scotland: Crawford, Elliot, Liston papers
Edinburgh, Scottish Record Office: Stair papers
Exeter, Devon County Record Office: Drake, Quicke, Sidmouth papers
Farmington, Lewis Walpole Library: Hanbury Williams, Weston papers
Gateshead, Public Library: Ellison papers
Gloucester, Gloucestershire County Record Office: Dickens, Mitford papers
Halifax, Calderdale Archives Department: Fawcett papers
Hanover, Niedersächsisches Hauptstaatsarchiv: Münchhausen papers
Hawarden, Clwyd Record Office: Yorke papers
Hertford, Hertfordshire Record Office: Panshanger papers
Hockworthy House: Oswald papers
Hull, University Library: Hotham, Sykes papers
Huntingdon, Huntingdonshire County Record Office: Manchester papers
Iden Green, John Weston-Underwood: Weston papers

Ipswich, East Suffolk County Record Office: Pretyman, Straton papers
Leicester, Leicestershire Record Office: Finch papers
London, Bedford Estate Office: Russell Manuscript Letters
London, British Library, Additional Manuscripts: Althorp, Auckland, Blenheim, Bowood, Brogden, Conway, Crewe, Drake, Dropmore, Egmont, Fox, Francis, Grantham, Grenville, Hardwicke, Holland House, Keith, Leeds, Liverpool, Melville, Mitchell, Mountstuart, Newcastle, North, Pelham, Pitt, Robinson, Sheffield, Spencer Perceval, Swinburne, Weston, Whitworth, Yorke papers
    Egerton Manuscripts: Holdernesse papers
    Stowe Manuscripts: Phelps papers
    Bathurst, Liverpool loans, also in BL.
London, Guildhall Library: Boddington papers
London, Lambeth Palace Library: Transactions at Court, 1747–66
London, London Metropolitan Archives: Villiers papers
London, National Maritime Museum: Sandwich papers
London, Public Record Office: State Papers Domestic, Confidential, Foreign, Regencies; War Office papers; Chatham, Colchester, Cornwallis, Gower, Pitt, papers
Maidstone, Kent Archives Office: Sackville, Stanhope papers
Manchester, John Rylands Library: Legge, Mountstuart, Poyntz papers
Matlock, Derbyshire County Record Office: Fitzherbert papers, Catton Collection
Mount Stuart: Bute papers
Munich, Haupstaatsarchiv: Bayrischer Gesandtschaft, London
New Haven, Beinecke Library: Osborn Files, Dorset, Hutton, Osborn papers, Townshend
New York, Public Library: Montague papers
Newcastle, Northumberland County Record Office: Blackett, St Paul papers
Norwich, Norfolk Record Office: Buckinghamshire, Townshend, Walsingham papers
Nottingham, University Library: Clumber, Mellish, Newcastle papers.
Oxford, Bodleian Library: Buckinghamshire, Bland Burges, Dashwood, Goodricke, North, Townshend, Tucker, Wilberforce papers, MS. Eng Letters
Oxford, Merton College Library: Nares papers
Paris, Ministère des Relations Extérieures: Correspondance Politique Angleterre, Autriche, Bavière, Espagne, Etats Unis
    Archives Nationales: Archives de la Marine, B^7, reports from Britain
Plymouth, City Archive: Plympton St Maurice Borough records, Morley papers, Saltram Archival Documents
Preston, Lancashire Record Office: Cavendish of Holker papers
San Marino, California, Huntington Library: Hastings, Keith, Loudoun, Montagu, Pulteney, Stowe papers
Severn Stoke, Croome Estate archive: Coventry papers
Sheffield, City Library: Spencer Stanhope, Wentworth Woodhouse papers
Shrewsbury, Shropshire County Record Office: Torrington papers
Southampton, Archives: Corporation Journal
Southampton, University Library: Palmerston, Wellington papers
Stafford, Staffordshire County Record Office: Anson, Congreve papers
Swansea, University Library: Mackworth papers

Trowbridge, Wiltshire Record Office: Wilton House archives
Turin, Archivio di Stato: Lettere Ministri Inghilterra
Vienna, Haus, Hof, und Staatsarchiv: Staatsklanzlei, Englische Korrespondenz
Warwick, Warwickshire County Record Office: Newdigate papers
Washington, Library of Congress: Papers of the Continental Congress
Williamwood: Ewart papers
Winchester, Hampshire Record Office: Malmesbury, Stanley papers
Windsor, Royal Archives: Cumberland, George III, Queen Charlotte, Stuart papers

II. PRINTED PRIMARY SOURCES

Anson, E. and F. (eds), *Mary Hamilton, afterwards Mrs John Dickenson, at court and at home: from letters and diaries, 1756 to 1816* (London, 1925).

Anson, Sir W.R. (ed.), *Autobiography and Political Correspondence of Augustus Henry, Third Duke of Grafton* (London, 1898).

Aspinall, A. (ed.), *The Later Correspondence of George III, 1783–1810* (5 vols, Cambridge, 1962–70).

Aspinall, A. (ed.), *The Correspondence of George, Prince of Wales 1770–1812* (8 vols, London, 1963–71).

Brown, P.D. and Schweizer, K.W. (eds), *The Devonshire Diary. William Cavendish, Fourth Duke of Devonshire. Memoranda on State of Affairs 1759–1762* (London, 1982).

Buckingham and Chandos, Richard, second duke of, *Memoirs of the Court and Cabinets of George the Third* (4 vols, London, 1853–55).

Cannon, J. (ed.), *The Letters of Junius* (Oxford, 1978).

Clark, J.C.D. (ed.), *The Memoirs and Speeches of James, 2nd Earl Waldegrave, 1742–1763* (Cambridge, 1988).

Corbett, J.S., *The Spencer Papers* (London, 1914).

Donne, W.B. (ed.), *The Correspondence of King George the Third with Lord North from 1768 to 1783* (2 vols, London, 1867).

Fortescue, Sir J. (ed.), *The Correspondence of King George the Third* (6 vols, London, 1927–28).

Gibbs, L. (ed.), *The Diary of Fanny Burney* (London, 1940).

Greig, J. (ed.), *The Diaries of a Duchess. Extracts from the Diaries of the First Duchess of Northumberland* (London, 1926).

Harcourt, E.W. (ed.), *The Harcourt Papers* (14 vols, London, 1880–1905).

Laprade, W.T. (ed.), *Parliamentary Papers of John Robinson 1774–1784* (London, 1922).

Namier, L., *Additions and Corrections to Sir John Fortescue's Edition of the Correspondence of George III* (Manchester, 1937).

Pellew, G. (ed.), *Life and Correspondence of the Right Hon. Henry Addington, 1st Viscount Sidmouth* (3 vols, London, 1897).

Russell, Lord J. (ed.), *Correspondence of John, Fourth Duke of Bedford* (3 vols, London, 1853–57).

Russell, Lord J. (ed.), *Memorials and Correspondence of Charles James Fox* (4 vols, London, 1853–57).

Sedgwick, R.R. (ed.), *Letters from George III to Lord Bute, 1756–1766* (London, 1939).

Thomas, P.D.G. (ed.), '"Thoughts on the British Constitution" by George III in 1760', *Bulletin of the Institute of Historical Research*, 60 (1987).
Tomlinson, J.R.G. (ed.), *Additional Grenville Papers, 1763–65* (Manchester, 1962).
Walpole, H. *Memoirs of the Reign of King George III by Horace Walpole* (4 vols, New Haven and London, 1999), ed. D. Jarrett.

III. SECONDARY SOURCES

Aikin, J., *Annals of the Reign of King George the Third* (2 vols, London, 1820).
Alexander, D., *Richard Newton and English Caricature in the 1790s* (Manchester, 1998).
Anderson, R.G.W., Caygill, M.L., MacGregor, A.G. and Syson, L. (eds), *Enlightening the British. Knowledge, Discovery and the Museum in the Eighteenth Century* (London, 2003).
Ayling, S., *George the Third* (London, 1972).
Baldwin, D., *The Chapel Royal. Ancient and Modern* (London, 1990).
Barrell, J., *Imagining the King's Death: Figurative Treason, Fantasies of Regicide 1793–1796* (Oxford, 2000).
Blanning, T.C.W., '"That Horrid Electorate" or "Ma Patrie Germanique"? George III, Hanover and the *Fürstenbund* of 1785', *Historical Journal*, 20 (1977).
Blanning, T.C.W., *The Culture of Power and the Power of Culture: Old Regime Europe 1660–1789* (Oxford, 2002).
Bradley, J.E., *Popular Politics and the American Revolution in England. Petitions, the Crown and Public Opinion* (Macon, Georgia, 1986).
Brewer, J., *Party Ideology and Popular Politics at the Accession of George III* (Cambridge, 1976).
Brooke, J., *The Chatham Administration* (London, 1956).
Brooke, J., *King George III* (London, 1972).
Brooke, J., 'The Library of King George III', *Yale University Library Gazette*, 52 (1977).
Bullion, J., 'The Prince's Mentor: A New Perspective on the Friendship between George III and Lord Bute during the 1760s', *Albion*, 21 (1989).
Bullion, J., 'The Origins and Significance of Gossip about Princess Augusta and Lord Bute, 1755–1756', in Craddock, P.B. and Hay, C.H. (eds), *Studies in Eighteenth-Century Culture*, 21 (1991).
Bullion, J., 'George III on Empire, 1783', *William and Mary Quarterly*, 51 (1994).
Bullion, J., '"George, Be a King!": The Relationship between Princess Augusta and George III', in Taylor, S., Connors, R. and Jones, C. (eds), *Hanoverian Britain and Empire. Essays in Memory of Philip Lawson* (Woodbridge, 1998).
Butterfield, Sir H., *George III, Lord North and the People, 1779–1780* (London, 1949).
Butterfield, Sir H., *George III and the Historians* (London, 1957).
Butterfield, Sir H., 'George III and the Constitution', *History*, 43 (1958).
Butterfield, Sir H., 'Some Reflections on the Early Years of George III's Reign', *Journal of British Studies*, 4 (1965).
Bynum, W., 'Rationales for Therapy in British Psychiatry, 1780–1835', *Medical History*, 18 (1974).

Cannon, J., *The Fox–North Coalition: Crisis of the Constitution, 1782–1784* (Cambridge, 1969).

Cannon, J., *Aristocratic Century. The Peerage of Eighteenth-Century England* (Cambridge, 1984).

Cannon, J., 'The Survival of the British Monarchy', *Transactions of the Royal Historical Society*, 5th series, 36 (1986).

Carretta, V., *George III and the Satirists from Hogarth to Byron* (Athens, Georgia, 1990).

Chapman, H.W., *Caroline Matilda, Queen of Denmark 1751–1775* (London, 1971).

Christie, I.R., *The End of North's Ministry 1780–1782* (London, 1958).

Christie, I.R., *Stress and Stability in Late Eighteenth-Century Britain. Reflections on the British Avoidance of Revolution* (Oxford, 1984).

Christie, I.R., 'George III and the Historians – Thirty Years On', *History*, 71 (1986).

Cobbett, W. (ed.), *Cobbett's Parliamentary History of England . . . 1066 to . . . 1803* (36 vols, London, 1806–20).

Colley, L., 'The Apotheosis of George III: Loyalty, Royalty and the British Nation 1760–1820', *Past and Present*, 102 (Feb. 1984).

Colvin, H.M., et al., *The History of the King's Works: V, 1660–1782* (London, 1976).

Conway, S., *The British Isles and the War of American Independence* (Oxford, 2000).

Cookson, J., *The British Armed Nation* (Oxford, 1997).

Crook, J.M. and Port, M.H., *The History of the King's Works: VI, 1782–1851* (London, 1973).

De-la-Noy, M., *The King Who Never Was: The Story of Frederick, Prince of Wales* (London, 1996).

Derry, J.W., *The Regency Crisis and the Whigs 1788–9* (Cambridge, 1963).

Dickinson, H.T., *The English Satirical Print: Caricatures and the Constitution 1760–1832* (Cambridge, 1986).

Dickinson, H.T. (ed.), *Britain and the French Revolution 1789–1815* (Basingstoke, 1989).

Dickinson, H.T. (ed.), *Britain and the American Revolution* (London, 1998).

Ditchfield, G.M., *George III. An Essay in Monarchy* (Basingstoke, 2002).

Donald, D., *The Age of Caricature. Satirical Prints in the Reign of George III* (New Haven, 1996).

Dozier, R.R., *For King, Constitution and Country. The English Loyalists and the French Revolution* (Lexington, Mass., 1983).

Duffy, M. (ed.), *The English Satirical Print 1600–1832* (7 vols, London, 1986).

Duffy, M., *The Younger Pitt* (Harlow, 2000).

Ehrman, J., *The Younger Pitt* (3 vols, London, 1969–96).

Fedorak, C.J., *Henry Addington, Prime Minister, 1801–1804* (Akron, Ohio, 2002).

Fraser, F., *Princesses. The Six Daughters of George III* (London, 2004).

Fry, M., *The Dundas Despotism* (Edinburgh, 1992).

Fryer, W.R., 'King George III, his Political Character and Conduct, 1760–1784: A New Whig Interpretation', *Renaissance and Modern Studies*, 6 (1962).

Gascoigne, J., *Joseph Banks and the English Enlightenment* (Cambridge, 1998).

Gore-Brown, R., *Chancellor Thurlow* (London, 1953).

Graham, J., *The Nation, the Law and the King, Reform Politics in England, 1789–1799* (2 vols, Lanham, 2000).

Gray, D., *Spencer Perceval. The Evangelical Prime Minister 1762–1812* (Manchester, 1963).

Harris, J. and Snodin, M., *Sir William Chambers, Architect to George III* (New Haven, 1996).

Hatton, R., *George I* (London, 1978).

Hedley, O., *Queen Charlotte* (London, 1975).

Hibbert, C., *George III. A Personal History* (London, 1998).

Hole, R., *Pulpits, Politics and Public Order in England 1760–1832* (Cambridge, 1989).

Holt, E., *The Public and Domestic Life of His Late Most Gracious Majesty George the Third* (2 vols, London, 1820).

Jarrett, D., 'The Regency Crisis of 1765', *English Historical Review*, 85 (1970).

Jesse, J.H., *Memoirs of the Life and Reign of King George the Third* (3 vols, London, 1867).

Jupp, P., *Lord Grenville 1759–1854* (Oxford, 1985).

Königs, P., *The Hanoverian Kings and their Homeland* (Lewes, 1993).

Langford, P., *The First Rockingham Administration 1765–1766* (Oxford, 1973).

Lawson, P., *George Grenville. A Political Life* (Oxford, 1984).

Levey, M., *The Later Italian Pictures in the Collection of Her Majesty the Queen* (2nd edn, Cambridge, 1991).

Lloyd, C., *The Quest for Albion: Monarchy and the Patronage of British Painting* (London, 1998).

Macalpine, I. and Hunter, R., *George III and the Mad-Business* (London, 1969).

McCahill, M.W., *Order and Equipoise. The Peerage and the House of Lords 1783–1806* (London, 1978).

McCahill, M.W., 'Peerage Creations and the Changing Character of the British Nobility 1750–1850', *English Historical Review*, 96 (1981).

McKelvey, J.L., *George III and Bute. The Leicester House Years* (Durham, North Carolina, 1973).

Mackesy, P., *War without Victory. The Downfall of Pitt, 1799–1802* (Oxford, 1984).

Marsden, J. (ed.), *The Wisdom of George the Third* (London, 2005).

Millar, O., *The Later Georgian Pictures in the Collection of Her Majesty the Queen* (2 vols, London, 1969).

Mitchell, L.G., *Charles James Fox* (Oxford, 1992).

Moremen, G.E., *Adolphus Frederick, Duke of Cambridge – Steadfast Son of King George III, 1774–1850* (Lewiston, 2002).

Mori, J., *William Pitt and the French Revolution 1785–1795* (Edinburgh, 1997).

Morris, M., *The British Monarchy and the French Revolution* (New Haven, 1998).

Morton, A.Q. and Wess, A., *Public and Private Science: The King George III Collection* (Oxford, 1993).

Namier, Sir Lewis, *England in the Age of the American Revolution* (London, 1930).

Namier, Sir Lewis, *Personalities and Powers* (London, 1955).

Norris, J., *Shelburne and Reform* (London, 1963).

Orr, C.C. (ed.), *Queenship in Britain 1660–1837. Royal Patronage, Court Culture and Dynastic Politics* (Manchester, 2002).

Ottaway, S.R., *The Decline of Life. Old Age in Eighteenth-Century England* (Cambridge, 2004).

Pain, N., *George III at Home* (London, 1975).

Pares, R., *King George III and the Politicians* (Oxford, 1953).

Parissien, S., *George IV. The Grand Entertainment* (London, 2001).

Philp, M. (ed.), *The French Revolution and British Popular Politics* (Cambridge, 1991).

Plumb, J.H., *The First Four Georges* (London, 1956).

Plumb, J.H., *New Light on the Tyrant George III* (Washington, D.C., 1978).

Prochaska, F., *Royal Bounty. The Making of a Welfare Monarchy* (New Haven, 1995).

Reitan, E.A., *George III: Tyrant or Constitutional Monarch?* (Boston, 1964).

Roberts, J., *Royal Landscapes. The Gardens and Parks of Windsor* (New Haven, 1997).

Roberts, J. (ed.), *George III and Queen Charlotte. Patronage, Collecting and Court Taste* (London, 2004).

Röhl, J.C.G., Warren, M. and Hunt, D., *Purple Secret. Genes, 'Madness' and the Royal House of Europe* (London, 1998).

Sack, J.J., *From Jacobite to Conservative: Reaction and Orthodoxy in Britain c. 1760–1832* (Cambridge, 1993).

Schweizer, K.W. (ed.), *Lord Bute: Essays in Re-interpretation* (Leicester, 1988).

Sedgwick, R., 'The Marriage of George III', *History Today*, 10, 6 (June 1960).

Shefrin, J., *Such Constant Affectionate Care. Lady Charlotte Finch, Royal Governess, and the Children of George III* (Los Angeles, 2003).

Sloan, K., *Enlightenment. Discovering the World in the Eighteenth Century* (London, 2003).

Stanhope, Philip, fifth Earl, *Life of the Right Honourable William Pitt* (3rd edn, 4 vols, London, 1867).

Thomas, P.D.G., *British Politics and the Stamp Act Crisis: The First Phase of the American Revolution 1763–1767* (Oxford, 1975).

Thomas, P.D.G., *Lord North* (London, 1976).

Thomas, P.D.G., 'George III and the American Revolution', *History*, 70 (1985).

Tighe, R.R. and Davis, J.E., *Annals of Windsor* (2 vols, London, 1858).

Tillyard, S., *A Royal Affair. George III and his Troublesome Siblings* (London, 2006).

Twiss, H. (ed.), *The Public and Private Life of Lord Chancellor Eldon* (3 vols, London, 1844).

Weber, W., 'The 1784 Handel Commemoration as Political Ritual', *Journal of British Studies*, 28 (1981).

Wells, R., *Insurrection. The British Experience 1795–1803* (Gloucester, 1983).

Wright, C., *George III* (London, 2005).

Ziegler, P., *Addington: A Life of Henry Addington, First Viscount Sidmouth* (London, 1965).

INDEX